LINCOLN'S
AMERICAN
DREAM

D1414342

LINCOLN'S
AMERICAN
DREAM

Clashing Political Perspectives

Edited and with an
Introduction by
KENNETH L. DEUTSCH
and
JOSEPH R. FORNIERI

Potomac Books, Inc.
Washington, D.C.

Library of Congress Cataloging-in-Publication Data

Lincoln's American dream : clashing political perspectives / edited by Kenneth L. Deutsch and Joseph R. Fornieri.—1st ed.
    p.   cm.
  Includes bibliographical references and index.
  ISBN 1-57488-588-X (acid-free paper)—ISBN 1-57488-589-8 (pbk. : acid-free paper)
  1. Lincoln, Abraham, 1809–1865—Political and social views.   2. United States—Politics and government—1861–1865.   3. United States—Politics and government—Philosophy.   4. Political leadership—United States—Case studies.   I. Deutsch, Kenneth L.   II. Fornieri, Joseph R.

E457.2.L839   2005
973.7′092—dc22   2005001489

Printed in Canada on acid-free paper that meets the American National Standards Institute Z39-48 Standard.

Potomac Books, Inc.
22841 Quicksilver Drive
Dulles, Virginia 20166

First Edition

10   9   8   7   6   5   4   3   2   1

CONTENTS

FOREWORD

Jean Bethke Elshtain

IT IS SAID OF LINCOLN that there were more books written of him than any other person in world history—save Jesus Christ, who is not a person in the ordinary sense of the word. Whether this is true or not, it fits. Lincoln so dominates not only the popular and political consciousness of the United States—with both parties claiming him as their rightful heir—but that of any portion of our troubled globe that yearns for political liberty, that one can scarcely exaggerate his influence. This has been said so often, and in so many ways, that it no doubt sounds banal. And this, too, tells an important tale. It is almost impossible to say anything fresh about Lincoln, we are told.

This volume suggests otherwise, for it contains much that is fresh, bold, and controversial. The reader will no doubt find illumination, confirmation, and vexation in equal measure. And that is as it should be. Lincoln should never become for us a figure fixed forever like a fly in amber. His story has great constancy and extraordinary fluidity. Depending upon the context and the issue, Lincoln takes on different hues and aspects. Through it all, however, his stature and his greatness come through. Although a certain fashionable cynicism about Lincoln is rife in some scholarly circles—he was just another "racist," say some—such views do not and cannot stick because Lincoln's complexity defies any such crude charge or attack.

Lincoln believed in the great political virtues, including prudence. One needs to try to do what is right—that goes without saying. But one must also do what is, well, doable. Given the configuration of forces at play, given the repertoire of political and moral concepts available, given where the public is and where it might be led to go, the political leader can either barrel ahead and do what is right, damn the consequences, or, more cautiously, try to do what is right with a keen eye on the possible consequences. The John Browns of this world can rampage and not worry about taking innocent lives; moral radicals and revolutionists, like Brown and some of the radical abolitionists who were quite prepared to see the country drenched in a flowing river of blood and the constitution overthrown entirely, ignore consequences. Responsible political leaders do not and cannot. They may not get it right, of course, for every political decision is made in a kind of twilight with the understanding that perfect knowledge eludes the decision makers and figuring out what might happen is not, and cannot be, a perfect science.

Lincoln understood this. It makes him no less great and no less a moral hero to acknowledge imperfection; indeed, it only magnifies his greatness to my mind. To have as keen an eye as he did on political necessities, yet to frame everything he did as a statesman with an eye to posterity and to the great judge of the nations, is an extraordinary thing. Also unusual, for an American president, is his articulated awareness of life's shortfalls and tragedies. Many have commented on Lincoln's unusual sensibility, especially for an ambitious politician—and he was certainly that. As Kenneth L. Deutsch and Joseph R. Fornieri point out in their introduction, Lincoln's faith was one grounded on the notion of a moral covenant between a biblically shaped people and their God. Knowing that defenders of slavery used passages from the Bible to legitimate their views, Lincoln pointed to other passages and challenged their interpretations, concluding that the Bible, in fact, offers a story of the injustice of slavery and the dire consequences that befall those who hold slaves and revel in it.

I have visited the Lincoln Memorial on many occasions, and I have observed something interesting there. One can go to the various war memorials, to the Jefferson Memorial, to the new Franklin Roosevelt memorial, and there are always visitors in decent numbers. But go to Mr. Lincoln's memorial and the numbers are magnified many-fold. I suppose statistics exist that can empirically bear out or challenge my personal observation. But the number and the range of visitors standing at the base of that magnificent statue, looking upward at Lincoln's imposing yet benevolent gaze, is impressive. Equally impressive is the Lincoln burial site in Springfield, Illinois, where Mr. Lincoln's nose is rubbed raw, if an inanimate thing can be said to be rubbed raw, by all the hands touching it over the years. At the newly refurbished and reopened Ford's Theater Museum in Washington, D.C., one exhibit features Mr. Lincoln's beautiful greatcoat, handcrafted for him by Brooks Brothers in New York. It features a beautifully embossed design of "The Republic Forever." One is impressed by its length—and that of Lincoln's bootsize over which you can place your pathetically small foot and see that you by no means measure up. The coat, the one he wore the night he was assassinated, always glues me to the spot. The inside lining is stained with his blood. It appears forlorn without its occupant— the only man who could comfortably wear something of that size.

As I stood quietly before the greatcoat exhibit, I thought of the words of Rosemary and Stephen Vincent Benet's poem on Lincoln in their *Book of Americans*, published by Rinehart and Company in 1933. The poem concludes with the lines, "Lincoln was the green pine. Lincoln kept on growing." Even as the massive literature on Lincoln grows, we realize that there is a way in which he stretches all those who study him seriously and in a manner marked by charitable as well as critical habits of interpretation. This volume is testimony to that fact.

PREFACE

THIS BOOK WAS DESIGNED for students, Lincoln aficionados, and scholars who would like to explore Lincoln from the perspective of political science and political philosophy.

The book is structured thematically to provide a discussion of core aspects of Lincoln's political thought and legacy on such issues as equality, slavery, race, the Union, leadership, ambition, and religion. It explores the role of each in understanding the sixteenth president's view of American realities and aspirations. And it is comprised of three basic elements—an introduction, previously published articles from specialized journals, and a number of new pieces that greatly expand our understanding of Lincoln's legacy.

Our introduction provides the reader with an extended overview and framework of the major controversies concerning Lincoln's political thought and leadership. Although we take a stand on many of these controversies, we fully integrate a number of different points of view, enabling the reader to come to his or her own conclusion about Lincoln's contribution to the American regime. The remainder of the book provides key questions and clashing interpretations of the issues listed above.

We would like to thank Don McKeon, our publisher at Potomac Books, for his professionalism, flexibility, support, and guidance; Harry V. Jaffa for his inspiration and generosity; John Murley; Dean Andrew Moore; Allen C. Guelzo; Thomas Schwartz; Gabor Boritt; Alec Mittiga for his indispensable help; Eric Bonus; Sara Gabbard; Joe Garrera; Virginia Fehrenbacher; Debbie Steene; and Elizabeth G. Matthews.

Thanks to Presidents Chris Dahl of SUNY Geneseo and Al Simone of The Rochester Institute of Technology for creating the kind of academic environment which permits us to pursue our scholarly work.

We would both like to thank Joe Fornieri's wife Pam for her patience, her interest, spiritedness, and great culinary skills over the many years.

Finally, we would like to recognize and honor three good families—the Fornieris, the Silvios, and the Hawkins.

INTRODUCTION

"It is for us the living, rather, to be dedicated here to the unfinished work which they who fought here have thus far so nobly advanced."

Gettysburg Address, November 19, 1863

ABRAHAM LINCOLN is of enduring interest to those seeking political wisdom because of his vision of constitutional democracy and his grand statesmanship in saving the Union and ending slavery. The dilemmas of federalism and slavery, left unresolved by the Founders, precipitated a sectional crisis that culminated in civil war. Ironically, the North and South fought to uphold radically different versions of the American Dream and American Republicanism. For the South, the American Dream was one in which sovereign states would be free to defend, extend, and perpetuate the culture of slavery. For Lincoln and the Republican Party, the American Dream promised an equal opportunity for all under a national Union dedicated to the principles of the Declaration of Independence. If the Civil War is the defining event of American history, which shaped and continues to shape our national self-understanding, then Lincoln is the defining figure, who played a pivotal role in that national ordeal. As a leader who both shaped and was moved by events, Lincoln sought to clarify the true meaning of republican government and its elusive yet fundamental principles of equality, liberty, and consent. His quest to provide a sound interpretation of the Union and the principles upon which the Union was established has made him the most articulate spokesman of the American regime. Each generation of Americans who reflect upon the origin, meaning, and development of their regime would do well to reconsider the following perennial questions that he raised about popular governance and political leadership:

- Was the Civil War primarily about states' rights and the Union, or was it about slavery as well?
- Was America's democracy bound to higher standards of moral right, or was the will of the majority sovereign in all cases?
- Was the Union a national entity or a compact of free and sovereign states?
- Did the Declaration of Independence apply to individuals or to collective entities like states and nations?

- Was the affirmation "all men are created equal" a mere statement of fact applying only to white males at the time or a normative standard, an aspiration, that should be applied to all people at all times?
- What does "liberty" mean in American republicanism? Does it embrace the freedom to hold property in a slave, or does it mean that each person should enjoy the God-given right to the fruits of his or her own labor?
- Was the Constitution a proslavery document? Was "the right to property in a slave . . . distinctly and expressly affirmed in the Constitution," as Chief Justice Roger B. Taney claimed in *Dred Scott v. Sanford* in 1857?
- Does the Constitution permit the president to exercise broad discretionary powers in times of crisis, thereby allowing him to suspend the writ of habeas corpus, raise troops without congressional authorization, institute a naval blockade of the South, and emancipate the slaves?
- Can Lincoln's expansionary view of national power be reconciled with constitutionalism, or is republican governance doomed to vibrate perpetually between the extremes of tyranny and anarchy?
- Does the survival of republican government require the support of a civil religion? If so, how may religion and politics be joined in a manner that sustains rather than harms the American republic?

Lincoln posed the enduring problem of republican government (one that must be faced by each generation) in his special message to Congress on July 4, 1861:

> And this issue embraces more than the fate of these United States. It also presents to the whole family of man, the question, whether a constitutional republic, or a democracy—a government of the people, by the same people—can, or cannot maintain its territorial integrity, against its own domestic foes. It presents the question, whether discontented individuals, too few in number to control administration, according to organic law, in any case, can always, upon pretences made in this case, or on any other pretences, or arbitrarily, without any pretence, break up their Government, and thus practically put an end to free government upon the earth. It forces us to ask: "Is there, in all republics, this inherent, and fatal weakness?" "Must a government, of necessity, be too *strong* for the liberties of its own people, or too *weak* to maintain its own existence?"[1]

It was no accident that Lincoln's reflection on the destiny of republican government was delivered on the Fourth of July. By so doing, he not only appealed to the patriotism of his fellow citizens to preserve their sacred Union but also recurred to the regime's first principles of equality, liberty, and consent contained in the Declaration of Independence. By invoking the spirit of the revolution, Lincoln established continuity between himself and the Founders. He saw himself as carrying on the Founders' mission to serve as a standard bearer of democracy and self-government to the world. The success or failure of the American experiment in republican government would reverberate throughout the globe, determining the fate of democracy everywhere and at all times. Like the epic political philosophers of the past, Lincoln probed the moral and ontological foundations of his regime, emphasizing that the will of the majority was bound to a higher standard of moral and religious right. Indeed, Lincoln may be considered a teacher of democracy in view of his ability to provide cogent answers to the enduring problems raised by self-government. The fact that so many other nations and leaders have turned to Lincoln to instruct them about the nature of self-government further confirms his role as a philosopher of democracy to be included in the company of Aristotle, Madison, Rousseau, and Tocqueville.

In his famous essay, "The Hedgehog and the Fox," Sir Isaiah Berlin distinguished two types of thinkers or leaders—the hedgehog who "related everything to a single central vision, a single, universal, organizing principle, and the fox who pursue(s) many ends, often unrelated and even contradictory."[2] As James M. McPherson has put it, "Abraham Lincoln can be considered one of the foremost hedgehogs in American history."[3] Was Lincoln truly a hedgehog, or did he possess the qualities of both a hedgehog and a fox? Lincoln's central vision, to be sure, is found in the Gettysburg Address in which he stated that this "nation, conceived in liberty, and dedicated to the proposition that all men are created equal . . . shall not perish from the earth." Yet he also exhibited qualities of the clever fox, such as his capacity both to respond to and to modify public opinion when necessary.

Abraham Lincoln is arguably our greatest president. He challenged his own generation and future generations to uphold faith in the principles of fraternal democracy. He also influenced subsequent presidents to effectively use the power of that office. He has inspired Americans and all of humanity to find good answers to the great questions of political power, consent of the governed, nationalism, pluralism, multiculturalism, racial harmony, and civil religion. Indeed, Lincoln is at the center of our national story—the "sustaining narrative"—that both orders and challenges us as a people.[4] Such a legacy is truly unique in American history; it is at the same time monumental and highly controversial. Lincoln's teaching on democracy has by no means been universally accepted as the definitive interpretation of American public life. Many important currents in American political thought have objected to his vision of the Union and his actions as chief executive during the Civil War. As in his own time, today, critics from both sides of the political spectrum raise serious objections to Lincoln's political thought and leadership.

Contemporary views of Abraham Lincoln's legacy span a wide range. Walter Berns sees him as the great patriot poet and protector of the Founders' teachings in the Declaration of Independence who recognized that a price must be paid for freedom including "a new birth of freedom." For Thomas J. DiLorenzo, "the real Lincoln" was a "great centralizer" who created the highly activist state by subverting the Constitution and states' rights.[5] For Berns, Lincoln created an honorable patriotism towards the federal union.[6] For DiLorenzo, Lincoln triggered the growth of big government, diminishing personal freedom. The question has also been raised as to whether Lincoln was the "great emancipator" or the reluctant emancipator? Should he be viewed as a calculating politician who waged an unnecessary war between the states, opposed racial equality, and sought ultimately to create an empire?

The editors of this book seek to examine fairly one of the great political controversies in American history—namely, who was the "real" Lincoln? How are we to understand his complex legacy as a political thinker and leader? While the debate continues over whether Lincoln's legacy is salutary or harmful, defenders and critics of the sixteenth president alike agree that for better or worse, he vastly influenced the egalitarian development of the United States. This volume seeks to represent both critical engagements and appreciations of Lincoln's legacy.

1. Lincoln, the Declaration, and Equality

The Civil War has been described as a second American Revolution, but in what sense was it similar to the fight for independence? In what respect, if any, were Lincoln's actions revolutionary? Did he overturn the Constitution to recreate the nation on an entirely different foundation than the one intended by its Framers? In his struggle against slavery, Lincoln viewed the principle of equality in the Declaration of Independence as indispensable to his political thought and leadership: "Public opinion, on any subject, always has a '*central idea*,' from which all its minor thoughts radiate. That 'central idea' in our political public opinion, at the beginning was, and until recently has continued to be, 'the equality of all men.'"[7] He regarded, "The principles of Jefferson" as "the definitions and axioms of free society."[8] Indeed, Lincoln maintained that the viability of American democracy presumed a moral consensus on the meaning of such fundamental norms as equality and consent of the governed. Did the principle of consent therefore justify the South's secession?

Lincoln turned to the Declaration of Independence as a political Decalogue, or Ten Commandments, that promulgated the nation's republican creed. He interpreted the Declaration as more than a statement of fact proclaiming independence from Britain. It also served as a declaration of moral precepts binding the nation, and guarding against future tyranny. The Declaration, in his mind, possessed a constitutional status. It represented the nation's moral compass, precisely calibrated by its Founders in accordance with the laws of God and nature to point the ship of state in the right direction. Just as the original Decalogue provided a code of behavior that included commandments against killing, lying, or stealing, so the Declaration enshrined a code of conduct that included commandments against tyranny, arbitrary government, and despotism. It provided a universal measure whereby to judge the legitimacy of governments. For this reason, the Declaration was quintessential to Lincoln's political thought and leadership:

[All] the political sentiments I entertain have been drawn . . . from the sentiments which originated, and were given to the world from this hall in which we stand [Independence Hall]. I have never had a feeling politically that did not spring from the sentiments embodied in the Declaration of Independence. . . . I have often inquired of myself, what great principle or idea it was that kept this Confederacy so long together. It was not the mere matter of separation of the colonies from the mother land; but something in that Declaration giving liberty, not alone to the people of this country, but hope to the world for all future time. It was that which gave promise that in due time the weights should be lifted from the shoulders of all men, and that *all* should have an equal chance. This is the sentiment embodied in that Declaration of Independence.[9]

Among the principles of the Declaration, Lincoln assigned axiomatic status to equality, which he viewed as the "father of all moral principle."[10] By this he meant that equality represented a principle of fairness and justice governing the relations between persons and their government. As a principle of fairness, it mandated that each person should have an equal chance to compete in the race of life. Most notably, Lincoln interpreted equality as a moral aspiration, "a standard maxim for free society, which should be familiar to all, and revered by all; constantly looked to, constantly labored for, and even though never perfectly attained, constantly approximated, and thereby constantly spreading and deepening its influence, and augmenting the happiness and value of life to all people of all colors everywhere."[11]

Lincoln taught that consent of the governed could only be understood in connection with equality. Politically speaking, the two principles were, in fact, reciprocal. He concisely articulated the relationship between equality and consent in these terms: "No man is good enough to govern another man, *without that other's consent. I say this is the leading principle—the sheet anchor of American republicanism.*"[12] Thus, according to Lincoln, government by consent assumes the equality of all persons based on their inviolable dignity as rational and free beings created in the image of God. Given each person's equal dignity, no class of people in society was so superior that it was entitled to a mastery over others, and no class of people was so degraded that it was to be governed without consent by those who were considered superior in some respect. Because all human beings shared a common humanity, all were entitled to consent in some rudimentary sense. In Lincoln's words, no man was "good enough" to rule over another from a superior vantage point. To deprive a fellow human of consent was to govern him or her despotically, as one would an animal, thereby exalting oneself above the ordinary herd of human beings. In effect, the denial of equal consent in the name of a superior class of people putatively favored by the grace of God was indistinguishable from the retrograde doctrine of the divine right of kings. This doctrine was the very antithesis of republican government.

Lincoln referred to equality in a number of related senses. The common denominator among these related views involved a relation of fairness, equity, and justice between human beings. For example, depending on what was being judged as equal, the term equality could apply to an equality of rights, an equal treatment before the law, and an equal opportunity to advance in the race of life. Equality of rights meant that all human beings were entitled to the God-given, natural rights of life, liberty, and the pursuit of happiness. Equality before the law meant that all were entitled to a fair legal proceeding. Equality as a principle of justice meant that all, regardless of race, creed, or color, should bear public burdens and enjoy public privileges equally. This would prohibit the state from imposing greater burdens on groups of individuals or from conferring greater rewards upon them simply because of the accidents of birth. Equality of opportunity meant that all individuals should be allowed to compete for status and resources in improving their lives. This implies that there must be no permanent class of laborers who are denied an opportunity to improve their material and moral condition.

In sum, Lincoln viewed the Declaration as the very cornerstone of the American Dream, promising all human beings a fair chance to pursue happiness by improving their lives both morally and materially. He believed that the moral imperatives of the Declaration both enjoined and prohibited political actions on the part of government. For example, in a negative sense, the Declaration's affirmation of equality prohibited government from granting titles of nobility or establishing a divine right monarchy. In a positive sense, the same principle also committed the government to policies that would augment the pursuit of happiness. However, if equality is viewed as a moral imperative, to what extent does it positively obligate the government to take active measures to promote opportunities of disadvantaged citizens? A key controversy concerning Lincoln's teachings on these matters raises the question: is he the father of the modern, regulatory "nanny" state?

Critics of Lincoln, both yesterday and today, have repudiated his interpretation of the equality clause in the Declaration as both dangerous to the regime and contrary to limited government. In Lincoln's own time, John C. Calhoun and Jefferson Davis propounded alternative views of both equality and the Declaration. They believed that the Founders never intended to apply the precept of equality to individuals; rather, they claimed that it applied collectively to states and countries. In effect, "all men are created equal" meant "all citizens of South Carolina" are created equal to all British citizens. According to this interpretation, the Declaration did not establish a nation, but "a baker's dozen" of free and independent states similar to the loose confederacy that existed between the ancient Greek city-states.[13] While Calhoun and Davis interpreted equality collectively, Stephen A. Douglas interpreted it narrowly, as applying exclusively to members of the white race. Douglas claimed that the Founders could not have intended to apply equality as an inclusive principle to all human beings of every color because that would have necessitated the immediate abolition of slavery.

Reaffirming the teachings of Davis and Calhoun on state sovereignty, contemporary scholars like Willmoore Kendall, George Carey, and M. E. Bradford contend that Lincoln "derailed" the American regime by committing it to an equality of conditions, paving the way for the welfare or "nanny" state.[14] These conservative critics maintain that Lincoln "refounded" and transformed the fundamental principles of America, imposing a radical egalitarianism that the Framers of the Constitution putatively rejected. They point out that the word "equality" is nowhere to be found in the original Constitution of 1787. The Founders established a republican government that restrained the popular or plebiscitarian excesses of a pure democracy precisely to avoid the leveling impulses that Lincoln would unleash through his "heretical" devotion to equality. Lincoln's conservative critics further argue that once equality is exalted as a political commitment, it inevitably slides down a slippery slope towards an equality of results—a condition in which all outcomes or social relations are to be leveled and real differences in abilities, property, and ownership are disregarded by the state. Lincoln's radical egalitarianism, it is argued, has fostered radical forms of affirmative action, feminism, and multiculturalism. Indeed, Lincoln's critics claim that he inspired a "utopian" demand for equality in American culture, which, in turn, has debased all higher intellectual and spiritual pursuits to "the least common denominator." Respect for established authority, the rule of law, and moral tradition have all been undermined in the name of this utopian ideal.

In his bestseller, *Lincoln at Gettysburg*, Garry Wills concurs with the interpretation of the aforementioned critics that Lincoln was indeed a revolutionary who refounded the nation by making radical equality the cornerstone of the Republic. However, Wills reaches a far different conclusion: what the conservative critics condemn as tyrannical, he praises as a great example of transforming leadership based on the "will to power." Describing Lincoln's creative coup d'état at Gettysburg, Wills states:

> [Lincoln] would cleanse the Constitution—not, as William Lloyd Garrison had, by burning an instrument that countenanced slavery. He altered the document from within, by appeal from its letter to the spirit, subtly changing the recalcitrant stuff of that legal compromise, bringing it to its own indictment. By implicitly doing this, he performed one of the most daring acts of open-air sleight-of-hand ever witnessed by the unsuspecting. Everyone in that vast throng of thousands was having his or her intellectual pocket picked. The crowd departed with a new thing in its ideological luggage, that new constitution Lincoln had substituted for the one they brought there with them. They walked off, from those curving graves on the hillside, under a changed sky, into a different America. Lincoln had revolutionized the Revolution, giving people a new past to live with that would change their future indefinitely.
>
> Some people, looking on from a distance, saw that a giant (if benign) swindle had been performed.[15]

Wills emphasizes Lincoln's creative prowess in redefining the egalitarian ethos of America. Through a poetic "sleight of hand," a noble lie, Lincoln imposed a revolutionary conception of equality upon the Declaration. Wills celebrates Lincoln's linguistic prowess as the shaper of a new horizon, as a noble genius who devised a salutary myth for the nation, thereby remedying the defects of the Founders' narrow view of equality. Wills thus proclaims that "Lincoln does not argue law or history, as Daniel Webster did. He *makes* history. He does not come to present a theory, but to impose a symbol, one tested in experience and appealing to national values, with an emotional urgency entirely expressed in calm abstractions (fire in ice). He came to change the world, to effect an intellectual revolution."[16]

In response to "the refounding thesis" propounded by Wills and some conservative critics, Harry V. Jaffa contends that Lincoln's view of equality is compatible with moral excellence and the "ancient faith" of the Founders. According to Jaffa, Lincoln was traditionally conservative in his efforts to preserve the Founders' understanding of equality against the real heresy of slavery. Jaffa argues that Lincoln's view of equal rights and opportunity are best understood as conservative principles. They serve as a precondition of both merit and excellence in society. The ascertainment of excellence in society presumes that no one be prejudged on the basis of race, creed, or color. Jaffa further argues that Lincoln's critics have confounded equality of results with equality of opportunity. He sees Lincoln not as endorsing equality of conditions, but as inveighing against the inequalities of feudal societies and hereditary monarchies, which granted privileges to certain classes of people by mere accident of birth rather than ability. This prevented potentially talented individuals from social betterment. For Jaffa, Lincoln taught that it is unjust for government to overburden those born of a certain skin color by consigning them to slavery or by preventing them from competing fairly with others. All artificial impediments and barriers bias competition and may result in rewarding those who are less talented. In sum, Jaffa maintains that Lincoln's view of equality paves the way for a natural aristocracy based on ability rather than on an artificial or conventional aristocracy based on privilege. Each person must be given a fair chance to compete for status, property, and social advancement. Legitimate government should promote an equality of opportunity that clears the way for the truly talented to compete fairly. Lincoln's interpretation of equality, says Jaffa, does not guarantee that the outcome of people's efforts will be equal!

2. Lincoln and Political Ambition

The pursuit of glory is one of the defining features of the epic rulers of history—Pericles, Alexander, Caesar, and Washington. Is the desire for fame a necessary condition of great leadership? If it is an inherent trait of statesmen, can it be contained within moral boundaries? Is political ambition always malignant, or can it be benign? Does it inevitably degenerate into the *libido dominandi*—the lust for power? Or can it be the driving force of great statesmanship?

These questions are raised by Lincoln's candid and frequent admissions that he was ambitious. The theme of ambition recurs throughout Lincoln's life from his first campaign statement in 1832 to his election as President in 1860. At twenty-three, in his first run for public office, he revealed: "Every man is said to have his peculiar ambition. Whether it be true or not, I can say for one that I have no other so great as that of being truly esteemed of my fellow men, by rendering myself worthy of their esteem."[17]

Indeed, William Herndon, Lincoln's law partner, once described his colleague's ambition as a "little engine that knew no rest." Perhaps Lincoln's ambition stemmed, in part, from his desire to escape his humble origins. Contrary to popular myth, Lincoln was somewhat ashamed about his rustic background. He rarely mentioned any details of his early life on the frontier. Lincoln's autobiographical account to Jesse Fell on December 20, 1859, which was to be used to promote his candidacy for the Republican Party in 1860, paints a disdainful picture of his youthful upbringing:

> My father . . . grew up, litterally [sic] without education. He removed to Kentucky to what is now Spencer county, Indiana, in my eighth year. . . . It was a wild region, with many bears and other wild animals still in the woods. There I grew up. There were some schools, so called; but no qualification was ever required of a teacher beyond "*reading, writin, and cipherin,*" to the Rule of Three. If a straggler supposed to understand latin, happened to sojourn in the neighborhood, he was looked upon as a wizzard [sic]. There was absolutely nothing to excite ambition for education. Of course when I came of age I did not know much.[18]

Lincoln seems to have resented his father's indifference to education and social advancement. In spite of this lack of support, Lincoln nevertheless taught himself to read and write. Remarkably, his formal education amounted to less than one year. Through his own strength of will, he embodied the American dream of opportunity, advancement, and self-improvement. Lincoln is the quintessential "self-made man." Politics was the avenue through which he would rise, and it would also provide an outlet for his burning ambition.

In 1838 the young Lincoln delivered a speech on the perpetuation of the nation's free political institutions, the Lyceum Address, which warned against the designs of an ambitious demagogue who would pander to the passions of the people. The Lyceum Address has generated a great deal of controversy amongst scholars who regard it as the key that unlocks Lincoln's underlying political and psychological motivations. Allegedly, it provides a window to understanding Lincoln's ambition. In particular, scholars point to the following key passage where Lincoln warns of a tyrant who will rise upon the ruins of the nation's republican institutions, exploiting sectional animosity to advance his own unquenchable lust for glory:

> This field of glory is harvested, and the crop is already appropriated. But new reapers will arise, and *they*, too, will seek a field. It is to deny, what the history of the world

tells us is true, to suppose that men of ambition and talents will not continue to spring up against us. And, when they do, they will as naturally seek the gratification of their ruling passion, as others have *so* done before them. The question, then, is, can that gratification be found in supporting and maintaining an edifice that has been erected by others? Most certainly it cannot. Many great and good men, sufficiently qualified for any task they should undertake, may ever be found, whose ambition would aspire to nothing beyond a seat in Congress, a gubernatorial or a presidential chair; *but such belong not to the family of the lion, or the tribe of the eagle*,[.] What! think you these places would satisfy an Alexander, a Caesar, or a Napoleon? Never! Towering genius disdains a beaten path. It seeks regions hitherto unexplored. It sees *no distinction* in adding story to story, upon the monuments of fame, erected to the memory of others. It *denies* that it is glory enough to serve under any chief. It *scorns* to tread in the footsteps of *any* predecessor, however illustrious. It thirsts and burns for distinction; and, if possible, it will have it, whether at the expense of emancipating slaves, or enslaving freemen. Is it unreasonable then to expect, that some man possessed of the loftiest genius, coupled with ambition sufficient to push it to its utmost stretch, will at some time, spring up among us?[19]

The literary critic, Edmund Wilson, was among the first to interpret this passage of the Lyceum Address as a psychological confession.[20] Wilson speculated that Lincoln had "projected" himself into the role of the Caesarian destroyer he was warning against: "some man possessed of the loftiest genius" who "thirsts and burns for distinction; and, if possible . . . will have it, whether at the expense of emancipating slaves, or enslaving freemen." Did Lincoln have this concern in mind when he wrote the speech? Does this represent a crucial choice in his political career? Would he become a destroyer, or a protector of the American regime?

Wilson holds that Lincoln was driven by an insatiable lust for fame and power that could only be satisfied by surpassing the heights of the Founders. Other scholars concur that Lincoln's own political impotence nurtured an envy toward the Founders. Did Lincoln consider the glorious task of founding a regime already completed, providing no outlet for a self-described "towering genius"? According to Lincoln, this individual would never be satisfied with a mere "seat in Congress, a gubernatorial or a presidential chair" since he belongs "to the family of the lion or the tribe of the eagle"—a metaphor for noble statesmen with a natural instinct to dominate and lord over others. Lincoln's metaphor may even suggest that the towering genius is beyond good and evil. Does he resemble Nietzsche's *übermensch* (superman) who discharges his will to power, imposing his desires over others, very much as an eagle and a lion are driven to hunt without lamenting the kill?

In the Lyceum Address, Lincoln further notes that the glory of founding a regime can only be matched and, perhaps, surpassed, by preserving a regime. Does Lincoln thus seek the kind of immortal fame that Machiavelli argues accrues to those men of extraordinary leadership skills who either founded or preserved states? Many have claimed that Lincoln in his crusade against the states' rights position would fulfill his prophecy as the nation's self-appointed savior of the Union.

After he had lost a senatorial bid in 1855, Lincoln returned to the matter of ambition when comparing his own failing political career to that of his successful rival Stephen A. Douglas:

> Twenty-two years ago Judge Douglas and I first became acquainted. We were both young then; he a trifle younger than I. Even then, we were both ambitious; I, perhaps, quite as much so as he. With *me*, the race of ambition has been a failure—a flat failure; with *him* it has been one of splendid success. His name fills the nation; and is not unknown, even, in foreign lands. I affect no contempt for the high eminence he has reached. So reached, that the oppressed of my species, might have shared with me in the elevation, I would rather stand on that eminence, than wear the richest crown that ever pressed a monarch's brow.[21]

Though never published, the above fragment betrays Lincoln's frustrated ambition. Lincoln's words also betray more than a hint of envy toward his political rival Stephen A. Douglas.

Does Lincoln's reading of Shakespeare, whose works often provided him with a guide to study human nature and to master the English language, confirm critics' interpretation of him as the tyrant described in the Lyceum Address? In a private letter to James Hackett, a Shakespearean actor, Lincoln listed those plays that he read deeply, "Lear, Richard Third, Henry Eighth, Hamlet, and especially Macbeth. I think nothing equals Macbeth. It is wonderful."[22] Was it a mere coincidence that Lincoln reserved his highest praise for *Macbeth*, a work that vividly depicts overweening ambition and political violence? To what extent did Lincoln identify with notoriously ambitious and tyrannical characters, such as Macbeth in Shakespeare's tragedy? The influence of Plutarch's *Lives* can also be found in the Lyceum Address where Lincoln points to Alexander and Caesar as towering geniuses of unquenchable ambition. Did he view these biographies and dramas as mirrors that reflected his own darker impulses? Or did he view them as cautionary tales about what to avoid?

If Lincoln's description in the Lyceum Address is taken to be self-referential, does it follow that he was an opportunist who would subordinate moral principle to his own passion for glory? To be sure, many critics have applied this particular interpretation to Lincoln's leadership with regard to the Emancipation Proclamation. They claim that, in effect, the Emancipation Proclamation was a purely pragmatic act to restore the Union and to advance Lincoln's political ambitions, rather than to free the slaves. This interpretation portrays Lincoln as a "Machiavellian" figure who ruthlessly calculated his own political advantage at the expense of moral principle.

Other scholars have argued that far too much emphasis has been placed on the Lyceum Address as a psychological key that unlocks Lincoln's subconscious motivations. On the contrary, they emphasize that the Lyceum Address should be understood in its proper historical context as a Whig denunciation of Jacksonian democracy; that the towering genius may, in fact, simply be an allusion to Andrew Jackson and the plebiscitarian excesses of Jacksonian democracy that led to a breakdown of the rule of law during this time period. Furthermore, they argue that Lincoln's rhetorical flights were actually tailored to the purpose of the Lyceums as public forums designed to improve the oratory of aspiring statesmen.

Whatever conclusion one draws about the Lyceum Address, it does raise significant questions about the relationship between Lincoln's ambition and his career in politics. There is no doubt that Lincoln was ambitious, and that he was conscious of his superiority over other men. But was his ambition necessarily malignant? Perhaps the desire for recognition is a necessary stimulus to political greatness.[23] Was Lincoln's ambition bounded by standards of moral right and biblical magnanamity, which he ascribed to a higher power?

A careful reading of Lincoln's first political speech reveals that he sought to be "worthy of [the people's] esteem." Significantly, the aspiration to be worthy implies a moral limit and a course of action in conformity with a higher standard. Though Lincoln candidly acknowledged his ambition, he also consistently qualified it by recognizing a nobler calling as well: "While pretending no indifference to earthly honors, I *do claim* to be actuated in this contest by something higher than anxiety for office."[24] Later, during the Lincoln-Douglas debates in 1858, Lincoln reiterated the twin motives of ambition and principle:

> Ambition has been ascribed to me. God knows how sincerely I prayed from the first that this field of ambition might not be opened. I claim no insensibility to political honors; but today could the Missouri restriction be restored, and the whole slavery question replaced on the old ground of "toleration["] by *necessity* where it exists, with unyielding hostility to the spread of it, on principle, I would, in consideration, gladly agree, that Judge Douglas should never be *out*, and I never *in*, an office, so long as we both or either, live.[25]

And in another fragment, during August 1858, Lincoln emphasized that he stood for a cause greater than himself:

> I claim no extraordinary exemption from personal ambition. That I like preferment as well as the average of men may be admitted. But I protest I have not entered upon this hard contest solely, or even chiefly, for a mere personal object. I clearly see, as I think, a powerful plot to make slavery universal and perpetual in this nation.

3. Lincoln, Race, and Slavery

No matter how glorious, the American Founding was tainted by the original sin of slavery, which Lincoln viewed as the very antithesis of self-government. The institution soiled the nation's republican robe and undermined its moral credibility abroad. To Lincoln it was base hypocrisy to enslave another race of human beings in a nation dedicated to the self-evident truth that all men are created equal. Slavery had been "an apple of discord" in the Union—a source of conflict between the sections—

from the time of the Constitutional Convention onward.[26] Leaders failed to come to terms with the slavery issue for the sake of maintaining short-term national unity. Consequently, the canker of slavery continued to fester in the body politic. After the passing of the Founding generation, however, a notable shift in the Southern public mind over slavery took place. Whereas Southerners of the Founding generation like Thomas Jefferson and George Mason condemned slavery in principle, a new generation of Southern clergy, leaders, and thinkers began to defend the institution as a "positive good." The South's tenacious defense of its "peculiar institution" in the early part of the nineteenth century was perhaps a response to a growing sense of slavery's vulnerability at home and abroad. Taken together, the abolition of slavery in the British Empire, the scathing attacks by Northern abolitionists, and Nat Turner's slave revolt seemed to conspire against the very institution upon which the entire Southern culture and economy was based. Southerners viewed abolitionists as lawless fanatics whose inflammatory rhetoric encouraged slave revolts without providing any realistic solutions to resolving the issue of slavery, and the presence of African Americans on the North American continent. What would race relations be like after the slaves were freed? Could former masters and slaves ever live together on equal terms? Because slavery was deeply interwoven into the fabric of Southern society, it could not be removed overnight without shredding and tearing apart that society, particularly the Southern economy. The escalation of sectional tensions began to reach a watershed in the late 1840s with the acquisition of new territories after the Mexican War. The South was bent upon extending its institution into these territories while the North sought to contain its spread to the Southern states. Both sides seemed to recognize that what was at stake was not only the balance of power between slave and free states in Congress, but also the future of slavery as an American institution and the very moral character of the Union.

Lincoln's earliest public opposition to slavery occurred on March 3, 1837 in the Illinois Legislature when he was only twenty-eight years old. Lincoln and his colleague Dan Stone protested a Southern gag resolution that would suppress inflammatory abolitionist doctrines. Lincoln was only one of six in the entire assembly who opposed the gag resolution. He and the five other dissenters explained their protest in these terms:

> They believe that the institution of slavery is founded on both injustice and bad policy; but that the promulgation of abolition doctrines tends rather to increase than to abate its evils.
>
> They believe that the Congress of the United States has no power, under the constitution, to interfere with the institution of slavery in the different States.
>
> They believe that the Congress of the United States has the power, under the constitution, to abolish slavery in the District of Columbia; but that that power ought not to be exercised unless at the request of the people of said District.[27]

Lincoln's early views on slavery in this protest remained fairly consistent throughout his life. He would later explain that he "was naturally anti-slavery. If slavery is not wrong, nothing is wrong."[28] Prior to the exigencies of war, he believed that the national government had no authority to touch slavery where it existed in the South- ern states. Lincoln the statesman applied the "Golden Rule" by emphasizing that slavery must be viewed as an evil: "As I would not be a *slave*, so I would not be a *master*. This expresses my idea of democracy. Whatever differs from this, to the extent of the difference, is no democracy."[29]

Although he opposed slavery in principle prior to the Civil War, Lincoln was not an abolitionist who advocated immediate and uncompensated emancipation at any price. As seen in his 1837 protest in the Illinois Senate, Lincoln believed that the inflammatory rhetoric of the abolitionists was self-defeating and imprudent. It alien- ated the South and endangered the Union by pursuing unrealistic goals. By reck- lessly seeking to transform Southern society overnight without their consent, the abolitionists oversimplified the many legal and practical difficulties of ridding the nation of its moral blight. In his Peoria Address of 1854, Lincoln eschewed the self- righteousness of the abolitionists by acknowledging the North's culpability in slavery and the considerable difficulties of dealing with the existing institution:

> When Southern people tell us they are no more responsible for the origin of slavery, than we; I acknowledge the fact. When it is said that the institution exists; and that it is very difficult to get rid of it, in any satisfactory way, I can understand and appreciate the saying. I surely will not blame them for not doing what I should not know how to do myself. If all earthly power were given me, I should not know what to do, as to the existing institution. My first impulse would be to free all the slaves, and send them to Liberia,—to their own native land. But a moment's reflection would convince me, that whatever of high hope, (as I think there is) there may be in this, in the long run, its sudden execution is impossible. If they were all landed there in a day, they would all perish in the next ten days; and there are not surplus shipping and surplus money enough in the world to carry them there in many times ten days. What then? Free them all, and keep them among us as underlings? Is it quite certain that this betters their condition? I think I would not hold one in slavery, at any rate; yet the point is not clear enough for me to denounce people upon. What next? Free them, and make them politically and socially, our equals? My own feelings will not admit of this; and if mine would, we well know that those of the great mass of white people will not. Whether this feeling accords with justice and sound judgment, is not the sole question, if indeed, it is any part of it. A universal feeling, whether well or ill-founded, can not be safely disregarded.[30]

Were these remarks by Lincoln at Peoria a realistic and prudent concession to the limits of politics and the prejudices of his time? Or, do they betray the underlying racism of a "Great Equivocator" who carefully tailored mixed messages to his audi- ence, thereby providing ample room for political cover, while, at the same time, capitalizing upon the momentary crests of public opinion?

Lincoln's legal distinction between the existence of slavery in the Southern states and its extension into the territories is crucial to understanding his statesmanship before the Civil War. Unlike the radical abolitionists, Lincoln was bound by his fidelity to the Constitution and rule of law. While Lincoln believed that slavery was morally wrong in the abstract, he also believed that the federal division of powers legally prohibited the national government from interfering with the institution where it already existed in the Southern states. Moreover, he acknowledged that the rule of law demanded that fugitive slaves be returned to their masters. Though odious, he conceded that the Fugitive Slave Act of 1850 was legally binding upon the Northern states since it was based upon Article IV, Section 2 of the Constitution. In Lincoln's view, the forcible abolition of slavery in the Southern states would constitute an egregious violation of the Constitution, which could precipitate the dissolution of the Union, the death knell of the American experiment, and the triumph of slavery over freedom. Freed from the moral embrace of the Union, the South's effort to perpetuate its "peculiar institution" would be unimpeded. Perhaps beginning with the oft-stated goal of annexing Cuba, the South could realize its wider dream of a Caribbean slave empire. Provided that the Union was dedicated to the principles of the Declaration, which pledged the nation to the promise of equal freedom for all, Lincoln maintained that slavery in the states had to be tolerated as a "necessary evil": evil because it was wrong, and necessary because its forcible abolition could result in an even greater evil.

What, then, was Lincoln's policy in regard to the existing institution of slavery? Though Lincoln conceded the importance of the national government's legal obligation to the states and to slaveholders, he nonetheless maintained that the overall moral status of slavery as something inherently good or evil had to be resolved ultimately in the public mind. The resolution of this vexing moral question served as a pre-condition for resolving further sectional antagonism. He saw the root cause of the conflict as moral: the South believed that slavery was right and should be extended; the North believed that it was wrong and should be restricted. In Lincoln's view, the agitation would not cease until the nation as a whole recognized the antipathy between slavery and the fundamental principles of the American regime. Though legally prohibited from using coercion against the Southern states, Lincoln could still use the power of moral suasion to nudge them in the right direction. Government incentives and even financial support could be further employed as lawful means to assist Southerners in placing slavery upon an ultimate course of extinction. But all these means required that Southerners first recognize the evil of slavery.

Specifically, then, in regard to the existing institution of slavery, Lincoln proposed the twin policies of gradual, compensated emancipation and the colonization or repatriation of slaves back to Africa. These policies would necessarily depend upon the consent of the Southern states. Lincoln's colonization plan was likely influenced by the example of Henry Clay, his "beau-ideal of a statesman" who also happened to be the leader of the American Colonization Society. During his single term in the Thirtieth Congress in the United States House of Representatives from

1847–1849, Lincoln proposed a compensated emancipation plan for the District of Columbia. The fate of this proposal is quite revealing for what it says about the prospects for a moderate resolution to the existing institution. While Southerners opposed Lincoln's compensated emancipation plan because it interfered with their right to own, trade in, and transport slaves, Northerners did so because they resented having to pay a tax that would reward slaveholders for their odious, human property. In all, Lincoln's policies of gradual, compensated emancipation, his colonization plan, and his acknowledgment of the constitutional obligations owed to slaveholders defined him as a moderate opponent of slavery. In this respect, Lincoln may be contrasted to the radical abolitionists like William Lloyd Garrison who demanded the immediate, uncompensated emancipation of slavery in defiance of the Constitution and the rule of law.

Though Lincoln admitted that the federal government could not touch slavery where it already existed in the Southern states (the existing institution as mentioned above), he believed that the federal territories were quite a different matter. In his view, the federal government had compelling legal and moral reasons to contain the spread of slavery. Unlike the existing institution, he contended that slavery in the territories fell under federal jurisdiction by pointing to Article IV, Section 3 of the Constitution, which states: "The Congress shall have Power to dispose of and make all needful Rules and Regulations respecting the Territory or other property belonging to the United States. . . ." Moreover, Lincoln cited the Northwest Ordinance of 1787 as a significant legal precedent enacted by the Founders, which authorized the federal restriction of slavery in the territories.

John C. Calhoun, the states' rights Senator from South Carolina, provided an alternative view of slavery and the Constitution. He argued that because the national government was the agent of sovereign states, all territories were held for the common benefit of the states. Calhoun's views were adopted by Chief Justice Roger B. Taney in the case of *Dred Scott v. Sanford*, which prohibited the national government from restricting the institution altogether and transformed chattel slavery—the characterization of slaves as merchandise and movable property—into a nationally protected right.

Traditionally, Lincoln has been celebrated in American history as the "Great Emancipator" who freed the slaves. However, in a recent provocative book, *Forced into Glory: Abraham Lincoln's White Dream*, Lerone Bennett, Jr. alleges that almost all "common knowledge" of Abraham Lincoln is a lie. Bennett seeks to deconstruct the myth of Lincoln as the "Great Emancipator" and to reveal him for what he "really" was: an unrepentant racist and white supremacist who sought the "deportation . . . of Blacks and racial cleansing of the United States of America." Lincoln's American dream was merely a "white dream" of a racially pure nation. While Bennett correctly recognizes the Civil War as the defining event in American history and Lincoln as the regime's pivotal figure, he contends that the mythmakers have "white-washed" Lincoln's image, unjustifiably proclaiming him to be a symbol of racial harmony and brotherhood. Bennett boldly declares his intention to shatter the Lincoln myth:

> This is a political study of the uses and abuses of biography and myth, and it suggests, among other things that your identity, whatever your color, is based, at least in part, on what you think about Lincoln, the Civil War, and slavery. Abraham Lincoln or somebody said once that you can't fool all the people all the time. By turning a racist who wanted to deport all Blacks into a national symbol of integration and brotherhood, the Lincoln mythmakers have managed to prove Lincoln or whoever said it wrong. This is the story of how they fooled all the people all the time, and why?[31]

In confirmation of his thesis that the sixteenth president was a racist, Bennett points out that as a young lawyer, Lincoln defended a fugitive slave owner named Robert Matson in 1847. Attempting to expose Lincoln as a fraud, Bennett unfavorably compares him to the future luminaries of the Republican Party who were sincerely committed to extirpating slavery. While men like Salmon Chase and Thaddeus Stevens "earned the title of attorney-general of the slaves" for using their legal skills to defend runaways, Lincoln not only failed to represent a single fugitive, but he also represented a slaveholder instead.[32] Similarly, the abolitionist Wendell Phillips would later deride presidential candidate Lincoln in the 1860 election as the "slave hound from Illinois" for his efforts in the Matson case.

In further support of his view, Bennett adduces the following remarks made by Lincoln during his debate with Douglas at Charleston:

> I am not, nor ever have been in favor of bringing about in any way the social and political equality of the white and black races,—that I am not nor ever have been in favor of making voters or jurors of negroes, nor of qualifying them to hold office, nor to intermarry with white people; and I will say that in addition to this that there is a physical difference between the white and black races which I suppose will for ever forbid the two races living together on terms of social and political equality. And inasmuch, as they cannot so live, that while they do remain together, there must be the position of superior and inferior, and I as much as any other man am in favor of having the superior position assigned to the white race.[33]

Finally, Bennett contends that the Emancipation Proclamation was itself a hoax, a ruse to keep blacks in slavery until they could be deported back to Africa, thereby "racially cleansing" the United States. Bennett explains:

> In what some critics call a hoax and others call a ploy not to free African-Americans but to keep them in slavery, Lincoln deliberately drafted the Proclamation so that it wouldn't free a single slave immediately. . . . A growing body of evidence suggests that Lincoln's Proclamation was a tactical move designed not to emancipate the slaves but to keep as many slaves as possible in slavery until Lincoln could mobilize support for his conservative plan to free Blacks gradually and to ship them out of the country.[34]

Bennett contends that the Emancipation Proclamation "did not free a single slave" since it only applied to rebel controlled areas where it could not be enforced. Moreover, he points out that the Emancipation Proclamation exempted the border states and Union held territory in the South. Bennett thus denigrates the Emancipation as, "The most famous act in American political history [that] never happened." He concludes that, "Lincoln didn't free the slaves. If it had been left up to him, Blacks would have remained in slavery to 1900 or even longer. . . . If Lincoln had his way, Oprah Winfrey, Martin Luther King, Jr., Jesse Jackson, Sr., Lena Horne, Booker T. Washington, Thurgood Marshall, Duke Ellington, Jesse Owens, Louis Armstrong, W. C. Handy, Hank Aaron, Maya Angelou . . . and even Clarence Thomas would have been born in slavery."[35] In sum, Bennett maintains that the true heroes of the Civil War were the radical abolitionists like Wendell Phillips who never wavered in their principled stance against slavery. Lincoln was "forced into glory" by these men in spite of his efforts to thwart racial equality.

In response to the deconstructionist critique of Lincoln by Bennett and others, Don E. Fehrenbacher claims that Lincoln was indeed a principled opponent of slavery and a champion of human equality. Fehrenbacher places Lincoln's remarks at Charleston (above) in context as an accommodation to the racial prejudices of his audience. The racism of the Northern "free state" of Illinois was testified by the fact that 70 percent of its citizens had passed a Negro Exclusion Act ten years earlier, which prohibited free African Americans from even entering the state. And it should be noted that Charleston was located in "Little Egypt"—the southern part of Illinois, which had strong Southern sympathies. In placing Lincoln's remarks in context, it should also be kept in mind that Stephen A. Douglas played the "race card" against him during the debates, pandering to the racial prejudices of the Illinois audience. Throughout the debates, Douglas attempted to paint Lincoln as a radical abolitionist who endorsed full social and political equality between the races, and even miscegenation—racial mixing, an idea particularly repugnant to nineteenth century Americans. Indeed, it would have amounted to political suicide for Lincoln to endorse full social and political equality in the 1858 Illinois campaign. Moreover, Lincoln's tentative use of the conditional—"which I suppose," "and inasmuch, as they cannot so live"—seem to qualify his statement on race. Finally, Lincoln's remarks may be further contextualized by his affirmation of our common humanity at the beginning of the debates: "My friends . . . I have only to say, let us discard all this quibbling about this man and the other man—this race and that race and the other race being inferior, and therefore they must be placed in an inferior position—discarding our standard that we have left us. Let us discard all these things, and unite as one people throughout this land, until we shall once more stand up declaring that all men are created equal."[36] Does this statement, or the remarks at Charleston, represent "the real" Lincoln on race?

In response to those disappointed with Lincoln's failure to endorse full social and political equality in 1858, Fehrenbacher reminds us that slavery, not racial equality, was the major issue confronting Lincoln and his generation at the time. It is important to note that in the Great Debates, Lincoln distinguished between natural and civil and political rights. He suggested that while blacks were justly entitled to their natural rights of life, liberty, and the pursuit of happiness in the Declaration, they were not necessarily entitled to civil and political rights. The former came from the hand of God; the latter were conferred by government and were to be balanced against the public interest. The deeply entrenched institution of slavery had to be ended before proceeding on to the higher aspiration of full social and political equality. This would be the work of another generation and of another leader—namely, Martin Luther King, Jr. Perhaps Lincoln's equivocations on race and slavery can be attributed to the realistic constraints of public opinion. As seen at Peoria, he admitted, "A universal [public] feeling, whether well or ill-founded, can not be safely disregarded."

What does it mean to say that Lincoln ended slavery? Skeptics cite Lincoln's letter to Horace Greeley as proof that the president was a political pragmatist who simply sought to preserve the Union at the expense of black freedom. Greeley was the editor of the influential *New York Tribune* who had written an article entitled "The Prayer of Twenty Millions," criticizing the president for his reluctance to free the slaves. Knowing full well that his response to Greeley would be scrutinized by the public, Lincoln carefully articulated his position on emancipation in these terms:

> My paramount object in this struggle *is* to save the Union, and is *not* either to save or to destroy slavery. If I could save the Union without freeing *any* slave I would do it, and if I could save it by freeing *all* the slaves I would do it; and if I could save it by freeing some and leaving others alone I would also do that. What I do about slavery, and the colored race, I do because I believe it helps to save the Union; and what I forebear, I forebear because I do *not* believe it would help to save the Union. . . .
>
> I have here stated my purpose according to my view of official *duty*; and I intend no modification of my oft-expressed *personal* wish that all men every where could be free.[37]

In the last sentence, Lincoln distinguishes between his personal wish that "all men every where could be free" and his "official duty" to preserve the Union. In judging whether or not Lincoln's motives were sincere in ending slavery, it should be noted that he had already written a draft of the Emancipation Proclamation as early as July, a month before his reply to Greeley. Does this deed suggest that his commitment to black freedom was truly genuine and that he was merely waiting for the appropriate circumstances to act—a union military victory, the necessary support of public opinion, support of the border states—all of which would bolster the Emancipation's survival as well as credibility? For an extensive discussion on these points the reader is directed to the seminal work of Allen C. Guelzo, *Lincoln's Emancipation: The End of Slavery in America*.[38] As David Donald explains, Lincoln carefully selected his words by using the term "paramount" to describe his goal.

Paramount does not mean "sole" or "only;" it means "priority." For Lincoln, the twin goals of preserving the Union and ending slavery were actually linked: preserving the Union meant preserving the fundamental principles for which it stood—namely, the promise of equality in the Declaration. The preservation of the Union was therefore the *sine qua non* (cause without which) of ending slavery. Indeed, one may argue that the question of black freedom would be moot if the Union were dissolved. And, arguably, Lincoln exempted the border states from the Emancipation Proclamation not because he was a racist, but because it was legally justified as a "war measure;" and, as such, it could not possibly apply to non-belligerent states that remained loyal to the Union. Also, Lincoln's many efforts at compensated emancipation—his proposal for having the national government pay the border states to free the slaves—loudly speaks to his sincere commitment to end slavery legally throughout the American regime. Finally, Lincoln's indispensable and politically determined support of the Thirteenth Amendment, which abolished slavery throughout the entire Union, his support for limited black suffrage in Louisiana, his insistence that the end of slavery serve as a pre-condition to the Southern states' readmission to the Union, and his unwillingness to revoke the Emancipation Proclamation during the election of 1864 when it might have been politically expedient to do so are crucial deeds that must be seriously considered when judging whether or not he should be given credit for ending slavery and advancing equality.

4. Lincoln's Democratic Political Leadership: Utopian, Pragmatic, or Prudent?

Never above the fray of political conflicts, the mature Lincoln was a prodigious political manipulator. David Donald has amply demonstrated that despite Lincoln's many failures with the press, the politicians, and even the public, "he was nevertheless a successful politician." Adroitly exercising political skills, Lincoln "gained the opportunity of becoming a superb statesman."[39] Rejecting dogmatic positions, using self-deprecating humor and ribald storytelling, making friends of potential adversaries, and showing his capacity to suffer for the entire nation all contributed to his distinctive political leadership. But far more important to the emergence of that leadership were his great ambition and native intelligence. Norman Graebner put it well when he stated that, "Lincoln's essential greatness lay in the recesses of his mind and being, not in his techniques of group manipulation."[40] For what purpose was he using his keen intelligence concerning the American union, his poetic qualities of speech, or his keen political judgment in finding "the middle ground in hold(ing) the ship of state level and steady"?[41]

Lincoln was dedicated to leading Americans to what is best during his time as well as to what is always just for all times.[42] As a democratic leader, he realized that nothing could be done without public support. He made it quite clear that in this nation, "public sentiment is every thing. With it, nothing can fail; against it nothing can succeed. Whoever moulds public sentiment, goes deeper than he who enacts statutes, or pronounces judicial decisions. He makes possible the inforcement [*sic*] of these. . . ."

Lincoln was also a consummate party leader who was instrumental in the creation of the Republican Party in Illinois and the success of this same party in winning the crucial election of 1860. He possessed the rare ability to balance and integrate the various factions of his party into a unified whole dedicated to a common moral purpose—the containment of slavery as an evil. The same political skills made him an ideal candidate for the Republican Party in 1860. After his party had fairly carried the election, Lincoln refused to be blackmailed by compromises to save the Union that would have undermined the core principles of his party. He was determined to uphold the moral obligation and legal right of the federal government to restrict slavery in the territories even if it risked war. To submit to these demands of "peace at any price," in his view, would have reduced the moral loftiness of the Republican Party to "a mere sucked egg, all shell and no principle in it."[43] As a Republican president, Lincoln gathered together two major elements, among others: (1) conservative republicans who opposed the spread of slavery and sought to preserve the Union, but who were more or less indifferent to the plight of African Americans; and (2) radical republicans who demanded the immediate abolition of slavery. In addition, as a war president, Lincoln had to maintain a broad war coalition to defeat the Confederacy, including the opposition party of Northern Democrats and border state men. In sum, Lincoln's policies were inevitably advanced through the vehicle of the Republican Party, which he navigated prudently between the dangers of "Scylla"—conservative Unionism—and "Charybdis"—radical abolitionism, at times, accommodating various factions, while at others, prodding the party forward, never losing sight of the common purpose of preserving both liberty and Union for all.

The leader as statesman must reawaken when necessary the nation's sense of justice grounded in the Declaration. He must denounce the corruption of public sentiment exemplified by Senator Stephen A. Douglas's doctrine of popular sovereignty on the extension of slavery. Finally, he must gradually mould public sentiment in the direction of fundamental principle, which recognizes that slavery is always wrong while prudently keeping in mind that political "conditions impose necessities upon us."[44] For Lincoln, the valid measure of a statesman is not only his commitment to fundamental principles, but also his ability to effectively put these principles into practice as political conditions and public sentiment will allow. One of the best examples of Lincoln's prudent statesmanship can be found in one of his remarks during the Lincoln-Douglas Debates of 1858:

> [The Republican Party looks] upon [slavery] as being a moral, social and political wrong; and while they contemplate it as such, they nevertheless have due regard for its

actual existence among us, and the difficulties of getting rid of it in any satisfactory
way and to all constitutional obligations thrown about it. Yet having due regard for
these, they desire a policy in regard to it that looks to its not creating any more danger.
They insist it should as far as may be, *be treated* as a wrong, and one of the methods
of treating it as a wrong is to *make provisions that it shall grow no larger.*[45]

Unlike Douglas, Lincoln does not intend to flatter the public. His praise of
America, as Ralph Lerner puts it, looks to the future: "Americans will have reason
to think well of themselves only after learning to think critically of themselves."[46]
Lerner claims that Lincoln's statesmanship represents a form of political *Kalam*,
which he defines as an art of political leadership, which has been defended by the
great medieval Arabic political philosopher, Alfarabi. The *Kalam* is an art that
enables one "to argue in the defense of the specific opinions and actions stated
explicitly by the founder of the religion, and against everything that opposes these
opinions and actions." The *Kalam* is defensive and protective whether religious or
political; its point of reference is some "original intent," says Lerner.[47] What it is
opposing or checking "is prevented as being at odds with, or subversive of, that
earlier understanding. The threat to the old may come as readily from those who
expect too much from reason in politics as from those who behave as though they
expect too little. In neither case, however, can there be any recovery of that earlier,
purportedly sounder arrangement without recollection."[48] The leader provides all of
the arguments in defense of the religious or political founding; the arguments of the
Kalam use a defensive and protective rhetoric of the founding and a criticism of its
opponents. A political *Kalam* uses arguments before the public in order to provide
"a place for reflexion and meditation, and hence for reason, in the elucidation and
defense of the content of the faith." The wise political figure understands "necessity." As Lerner summarizes this teaching, he states, "Their response to necessity
will be to present their own reformation as correction of some intervening distortion
or corruption and certainly not as a case of overruling the founding legislator.
Indeed, regardless of the reach of their corrections, the successors's speech is less of
reformation than of restoration."[49] Is Lincoln's statesmanship concerning the Declaration as founding, his criticism of Stephen A. Douglas as opposition to that founding, and his public speech on equality, slavery, and the Union a restoration and a
serious example of political *Kalam*? Ralph Lerner cogently makes the case for a positive answer to this question in the chapter "Lincoln's Revolution."[50]

Lincoln was passionately committed to the fundamental principles of the Declaration of Independence and the Constitution. For him, the sacred covenant between
the government and the people must be protected and advanced. Such protection
and advancement required the preservation of the Union, the eventual elimination
of slavery, and "an open field and a fair chance" for men of enterprise and industry.
He believed in a society without a permanent class of hired laborers. Society should
be fluid, allowing laborers to become men of enterprise. This means that, according

to Lincoln, "free labor insists on universal education." The spread of literacy would abolish another form of slavery—"slavery of the mind." Government's legitimate role "is to do for a community of people, whatever they need to have done, but cannot do, at all, or cannot so well do for themselves—in their separate and individual capacities."

What is the role of the politician or leader in putting into practice this proper role of government? As a man of strong political principles with "hedgehog" qualities, Lincoln was also a politician. He viewed politicians as "a set of men who have interests aside from the interests of the people, and who, to say the most of them, are, taken as a mass, at least one long step removed from honest men."[51] He claimed that he too was a "politician." Some claim that Lincoln certainly was quite capable of contradicting himself on such questions as "all men are created equal," that sometimes he drifted with the shifts in the currents of public opinion on emancipation and sentiment in the North, and that at times would not speak out decisively against anti-Catholic and anti-foreigner views of the Know-Nothings. Clearly Lincoln could be a sly, crafty and practical politician. The question guiding our search for the "real" Lincoln is the following: was he more than a mere "politician"? If so, what is the basic character of that leadership? Was he a revolutionary utopian leader trying to use activist government to create a radical "society of equals"? Was he a pragmatic politician seeking primarily to pursue his ambitions in the context of democratic public opinion? Or was Lincoln a prudent statesman who balanced his view that "public sentiment is everything" with his passion for the moral Union and its sacred covenant?

5. Lincoln and Executive Power

When Lincoln was inaugurated on March 4, 1861, though facing a severe political crisis, he tried to reassure the South that he would be following a policy of forebearance, not coercion. The "only substantial dispute" facing the nation was over the extension of slavery. Slavery would ultimately be settled in the court of public opinion and national elections.

By the inauguration, seven states had seceded, claiming it was their constitutional right to do so and declaring themselves restored to a "separate and independent place among nations." Lincoln, as chief executive, used his First Inaugural Address to declare the secessionist acts as treasonous: "I hold, that in contemplation of universal law, and of the Constitution, the Union of these States is perpetual. . . . that no State, upon its own mere motion, can lawfully get out of the Union."[52] The new president promised that he would defend and maintain the Union and enforce federal laws in all the states which the Constitution required him to do. As Lincoln would state later in his presidency in 1864, the Southern rebellion imposed upon him as president the obligation to use "every dispensable means" to preserve "the nation, of which the Constitution was the organic law." Lincoln considered it imprudent and senseless to obey certain niceties while the foundation of the law itself—the preservation of the Union—was threatened:

> Was it possible to lose the nation, and yet preserve the Constitution? By general law life *and* limb must be protected; yet often a limb must be amputated to save a life; but a life is never wisely given to save a limb. I felt that measure otherwise unconstitutional, might become lawful, by becoming indispensable to the preservation of the constitution, through the preservation of the nation.[53]

Facing a dire political and legal crisis, Lincoln did not hesitate to make use of "otherwise unconstitutional" measures in dealing with insurrection against the Union. Just moments after Confederate forces fired on Fort Sumter, he called forth state militias to suppress the rebellion, ordered a blockade of southern ports, and suspended the writ of habeas corpus. One month later, he authorized millions of dollars in federal expenditures on behalf of the war, increased the size of the Union's armed and naval forces, and amassed a debt of $250 million. All of this was done by Lincoln's use of the executive power while Congress was in recess.

The suspension of the writ of habeas corpus (literally, "you may have the body") is considered to be especially odious to those who claim that Lincoln acted as a "constitutional dictator." This writ is one of the great guarantors of personal liberty in Anglo-American law; it requires jailors to show reason to hold a prisoner, thereby preventing a person from being held without charges. The Framers of the Constitution provided for this great writ in Article I, which states that it may not be suspended except in times of "rebellion or invasion." Lincoln initially suspended the writ without Congressional approval. And when a case was later brought in *ex parte Merryman*, Lincoln ignored the ruling of Roger B. Taney, Chief Justice of the Supreme Court, against the suspension. Ultimately, Congress ratified his suspension of the writ. Lincoln's broad and bold use of executive power has recast the debate over presidential prerogative during times of political and legal crisis. Before Lincoln, no president had stretched the boundaries of executive power as commander-in-chief. Lincoln would argue that no previous president had been faced with an internal crisis that was remotely comparable to the Civil War.

Americans are presently living in an age of political and legal crisis caused by international terrorism. Lincoln was fighting the first modern war with profound effects on domestic life. Though perhaps less extreme, our own views of civil liberties and executive power during times of crisis can be molded by Lincoln's actions.[54] Do such severe crises justify what James G. Randall referred to as Lincoln's "presidential war?"[55]

From the very beginning of his career in the 1830s, Lincoln was concerned about the "perpetuity of our free institutions"—the survival of the Constitution and the threats by other leaders of great ambition who would subvert the "ancient faith" of the founding generation. What is needed, claims Lincoln, is a reverence for the Constitution and laws. Bad laws must be repealed, but let the political religion of the nation be affirmed by reason—"cold, calculating, unimpassioned reason." Such Lincolnian "reason" was to be exercised in the context of emergency powers, which could be ratified by Congress and be consistent with his oath of office. Most of his "every dispensable means" to preserve the nation were indeed eventually ratified by Congress. Unfortunately, there were examples of the suspension of the writ of habeas corpus in areas removed from any hint of insurrection. To be consistent, Lincoln's "reason" must also consistently criticize his own actions in this regard, making every prudent effort to prevent such actions from taking place in the future. Though reverence for and obligation to the law must be strong, particularly in periods of crisis, Lincoln's own logic dictates that it cannot be uncontestable. Especially during periods of severe crisis, Lincoln warns that demagogy *"thirsts and burns for distinction."* What is needed, therefore, is a rationally grounded "reverence for the Constitution and law," one that acknowledges the importance of legal obedience and the need, at times, to contest rationally the proper application of the law. Such balance of reason and reverence is basic to those who seek to practice political *Kalam.*

6. Lincoln's Religion and Politics

Lincoln's sustaining narrative of the American Dream combined democratic and religious commitments to provide an ultimate moral justification of American public life. According to Lincoln, both nations and individuals were ruled by Providence. He envisioned himself and the American people as playing a unique role in upholding the principles of self-government. Lincoln emphasized that the legitimacy of American democracy was derived from an ultimate source of order, which the Declaration affirmed as "the laws of nature and of nature's God." The moral precepts of the American regime were sacred and therefore worthy of reverence not simply because they were ancestral, but insofar as they participated in God's rational order, which governed the universe.

Even a cursory reading of Lincoln's speeches and writings will reveal that his interpretation of American democracy was thoroughly imbued with the moral and religious teachings of the Bible. His "proneness for quoting Scripture" was even observed by his political rival Stephen A. Douglas.[56] For Lincoln, "the good old maxims of the Bible are applicable and truly applicable to human affairs." Noteworthy in this regard was Lincoln's penchant for describing the fundamental principles of American republicanism in terms of a sacred creed, which he referred to in the comparable terms of a "political religion," a "political faith," an "Ancient faith," the "Old Faith," "the early faith of the republic," the "political religion" of the nation, "the national faith," and the "sacred principles enunciated" by the Found-

ers. All of these expressions used by Lincoln denote a union of religion and politics—a participation of the secular in the sacred. He displayed a prophetic realism,
which condemned the nation's sins, called the country back to its "ancient faith,"
and placed it before the throne of Divine judgment. As a result, Lincoln has been
characterized as "the foremost theologian of the American experiment" and "the
high priest of American civic piety." His blending of religion and politics has been
described in related, though not identical, terms as a "civil religion," a "political
religion," and a "civil theology."

However, critics contend that Lincoln's political faith dangerously confounds
religion and politics, thereby undermining the integrity of both the spiritual and
temporal realms. Does not the fusion of the two inevitably lead to either the divinization of the state or the politicization of religion? Did not the Founders separate
church and state to prevent the dangerous commingling of religion and politics?
Indeed, history is full of nation states drenched in the blood of those who killed in
the name of a religious cause. Is it therefore safer, as Bruce Frohnen contends (see
below), for the national government to leave matters of religion to the local and
state levels? Does Lincoln's "political religion" constitute a dangerous, ersatz secular
ideology, which seeks to attain utopian goals? Was Lincoln's political religion purely
secular, leading to the divinization of the state? Or, finally, did it recognize the ultimate sovereignty of God, thereby enabling Lincoln to "foster the better angels of
our nature"?

Lincoln's biblical view of the Declaration of Independence as a moral covenant
is essential to his political faith. As stated above, Lincoln saw the Declaration as an
American Decalogue, or Ten Commandments, that enshrined the articles of the
nation's political creed—rights that came from the hand of the Creator, binding
the nation to God's eternal justice. In effect, Lincoln interpreted the Declaration of
Independence as a declaration of the precepts of natural law. That is to say, he maintained that the moral legitimacy of human laws must be measured in terms of their
conformity to a universal, transcendent, moral standard. This standard was promulgated by God, and known to man through the cooperation of human reason and
divine revelation in the Bible.

Contrary to some interpretations, Lincoln's political faith was not formulated as
an abstract, philosophical, or theological treatise. Rather, it developed over time as
a concrete, historical response to rival interpretations of American public life vying
for the nation's soul. The struggle over slavery in the mid-nineteenth century raised
ultimate questions about the meaning and moral destiny of the Union. The Civil
War took on the character of a religious conflict fought over competing interpretations of the Bible and Christianity. Both sides invoked the same God, the same Bible
and the same Constitution to vindicate their policies. Lincoln pointed to this irony
in his Second Inaugural Address: "Both read the same Bible, and pray to the same
God; and each invokes his aid against the other."

To be sure, Southern clergymen like Frederick Ross invoked the Bible in support of their claim that "slavery was ordained of God"—an allusion to Romans 13:1. In the North, abolitionists like William Lloyd Garrison declared that there could be "no Union with slaveholders," reviling the Constitution as "a covenant with death, and an agreement with hell." And even Stephen Douglas—certainly no abolitionist and one who decried the mixing of religion and politics—exploited the Bible in defense of popular sovereignty, the policy that territorial settlers should decide democratically for themselves whether or not to have slaves. Whereas Douglas defended popular sovereignty as consistent with the Founders' beliefs, Lincoln repudiated it as a betrayal of their legacy. It is in this context that Lincoln's political faith emerged as a response to rival versions of the American Dream.

The fact that the Bible was exploited by proslavery theologians did not lead Lincoln to repudiate its moral authority. Rather, Lincoln observed that Scripture itself warns against the twisting of the Bible for evil purposes. In a letter to a Baptist group dated May 30, 1864, Lincoln compared the Southern clergy's manipulation of the Bible to Satan's temptation of Jesus Christ, as related in Matthew 4. He explained: "When a year or two ago, those professedly holy men of the South, met in semblance of prayer and devotion, and . . . appealed to the Christian world to aid them in doing to a whole race of men, as they would have no man do unto themselves [Matthew 7:12], to my thinking, they contemned and insulted God and His church, far more than did Satan when he tempted the Savior with the kingdoms of the earth."

Lincoln's audience would have recognized his reference to Matthew 4:1–11, which relates how Satan exploited the letter of the Torah. Jesus responded to Satan's manipulation by providing an alternative interpretation of Scripture that was true in both letter and spirit. Indeed, all of the great teachers of Israel—the prophets, Jesus, St. Paul—warned against manipulating God's word for merely human purposes. By placing himself within this tradition of biblical exegesis, Lincoln upheld the moral authority of Scripture while at the same time warning against its abuse. In a word, Lincoln provides a cogent teaching on the use and the abuse of the Bible in politics.

Lincoln's letter to the Baptist congregation also provides us with a rare glimpse of his righteous indignation. His scornful reference to those "professedly holy men of the South" was likely a jab at the Southern Presbyterian Church, which had recently proclaimed, "it is the peculiar mission of the Southern Church to conserve the institution of slavery, and make it a blessing to master and slave."

A summary of Lincoln's biblical opposition to slavery shows that he relied primarily upon the following precepts: "man created in the image of God" (Genesis 1: 27); "The Great Commandment" to "love one's neighbor as oneself" (Matthew 22: 37–40); "The Golden Rule" to "do unto others" (Matthew 7:12); and God's command that "In the sweat of thy face thou shalt eat bread" (Genesis 3:19).

Specifically, Lincoln affirmed the teaching of Genesis 1:27 that man is created in the image of God when he declared that, "nothing stamped with the Divine image and likeness was sent into the world to be trodden on, and degraded, and imbruted by its fellows." Lincoln appealed to "The Great Commandment" in Matthew 22: 37–40, when he stated, "'Give to him that is needy' is the Christian rule of charity; but 'Take from him that is needy' is the rule of slavery." Lincoln applied the "The Golden Rule" in Matthew 7:12, when he remarked, "As I would not be a slave, so I would not be a master. This expresses my idea of democracy." And Lincoln invoked Genesis 3:19, when he explained: "As Labor is the common burthen of our race so the effort of some to shift their share of the burthen on to the shoulders of others, is the great, durable, curse of the race."

Based upon the teaching of Genesis 3:19, Lincoln developed a theology of labor, whereby God ordained "the burden of work, the individual's duty to engage in it, and the moral right to enjoy the fruits of his labor."[57] In response to the Southern clergy's interpretation of Genesis 9, which claimed that God had willed the servitude of an entire race, Lincoln cited Genesis 3 to reveal that labor was the equal predicament of all human beings—no exceptions. Taking the fruits of another person's labor was stealing. Here we clearly see the context of Lincoln's political faith in which two interpretations of the Book of Genesis were invoked to defend and condemn slavery, respectively. Lincoln further pointed out that the Bible revealed the injustice of slavery through the example of God's chosen people—the Jews, who were once slaves themselves. He poignantly reminded his fellow citizens that, "Pharaoh's country was cursed with plagues, and his hosts were drowned in the Red Sea for striving to retain a captive people who had already served them more than four hundred years. May like disasters never befall us."[58]

Notwithstanding Lincoln's diverse appeals to Scripture, his opposition to slavery did not rely solely upon the Bible. Lincoln's political faith was constituted by the mutual influence and the philosophic harmony between the republican teachings of the Founders, the worldview of the Bible, and unaided human reason. According to Lincoln, the moral precepts of God's revelation in the Bible were confirmed by natural reason: "I think that if anything can be proved by natural theology, it is that slavery is morally wrong. God gave man a mouth to receive bread, and hands to feed it, and his hand has a right to carry bread to his mouth without controversy." Lincoln's playful appeal to natural theology shows that he saw the moral precepts of the Bible not simply as abstractions to be accepted *a priori*, but as truths that were confirmed by concrete experience.[59] Because the teachings of the Bible were made publicly authoritative through the common language of reason, one may speak of the "Three Rs" of Lincoln's political faith: reason, revelation, and republicanism. The complementary insights of these sources of political order reinforced one another in vindicating American democracy.[60]

Granted that Lincoln's speeches and writings contain numerous allusions to the Bible, was he actually a man of faith? Perhaps Lincoln exploited the language of the Bible because it was part of the common currency of the day, and because it was an indispensable tool in maintaining social order or in garnering support for the Union cause. If Lincoln was indeed a religious skeptic, then it follows that "honest Abe" must have been quite dishonest to invoke the God of Israel so much and yet not believe in Him.

Scholars like Michael Zuckert claim that Lincoln was covertly a secular political rationalist—one who was privately skeptical about the claims of revealed religion in the Bible, but who publicly invoked its sanctioning power and rhetoric to induce his fellow countrymen to uphold the rule of law and to sacrifice themselves for the Union. As proof that Lincoln was a skeptic, Zuckert and others point to the partial testimony of William Herndon who claimed that his law partner was an "infidel," the fact that Lincoln never officially joined a church, and charges of infidelity made against him in an election campaign. Replying to these charges, Lincoln acknowledged that he did not belong to a particular Christian denomination; and he admitted that "in early life," he was "inclined to believe in" the "Doctrine of Necessity."[61] He described this doctrine as a belief "that the human mind is impelled to action, or held in rest by some power, over which the mind itself has no control." Yet Lincoln also claimed that he had "never denied the truth of Scriptures," further noting that the very same "Doctrine of Necessity" was "held by several of the Christian denominations." Did Lincoln's youthful interest in the "Doctrine of Necessity" make him an infidel, or was it another way of exploring his predestinarian belief— that is to say, the view that all events are predetermined by God's providence? And if Lincoln was indeed skeptical as a youth, did he remain so throughout his entire life?

Richard J. Carwardine correctly suggests that, "Lincoln's use of the Bible in the struggle over slavery was driven by conviction, not expediency."[62] Even William Herndon, whose partial testimony has been adduced to prove that Lincoln was a skeptic, admitted that Lincoln believed in God and that he "accepted the practical precepts of that great book [the Bible] as binding alike upon his head and his conscience."[63] As David Donald has noted, Herndon was driven to "overstatement" by sectarians who claimed that the martyred president was a member of their congregation.[64] For example, in the same breath that Herndon described Lincoln as an "infidel," he also described him as a "Universalist," a "Unitarian" and a "Theist"—all of which presume a belief in God. Though Lincoln may never have been an Orthodox Christian, and though he may have indeed gone through a skeptical phase in his early adult life, he never fully abandoned theism. In an early, private letter to his friend Joshua Speed in 1842, Lincoln conveyed his belief in God's providence: "I believe God made me one of the instruments in bringing you and your [fiancée] together, which union, I had no doubt He had foreordained. Whatever he designs, he will do for me yet. Stand still and see the salvation of the Lord is my text just now." The final passage of Lincoln's letter is a verbatim quote from Exodus 14:13 where Moses assures the Hebrew people in the face of certain destruction from Pharaoh's approaching army that God is still overseeing events. Indeed, Lincoln applied this teaching from Exodus to his own life. This letter, which was written during

Lincoln's youthful questioning of religion, shows that despite his interest in the "Doctrine of Necessity," he never fully abandoned the robust predestinarian beliefs of his youth. Though Lincoln's faith seemed to deepen with maturity, and though it may have been unorthodox in certain respects, the primary sources reveal that his articulation of this faith in his own private letters and public speeches remained fairly consistent.

Indeed, Lincoln's own speeches and writings reveal the living faith of a man who relied upon a higher power, who bore witness to God's benevolence, who described himself as an "instrument of God," who believed in the efficacy of prayer, and who humbly affirmed the inscrutability of the divine will, trusting that God would ultimately bring good out of suffering.[65] Most notably, Wayne Temple has painstakingly documented Lincoln's personal piety, demonstrating the consistency of the mature Lincoln's church attendance in Springfield, Illinois, prior to the war and also during the war in Washington, D.C. Temple explains that it was not uncommon at the time for religious individuals to eschew church membership, particularly because such membership involved an inquisitional probing into one's private life. In many cases, dancing and bawdy jokes—two activities Lincoln was known for—would have excluded conscientious participation from membership in a congregation. Even though he was not a member, Lincoln consistently attended private prayer sessions during the war each Thursday night at Reverend Gurley's New York Avenue Presbyterian Church. Indeed, Lincoln's reliance upon a higher power to help him through the trials of the war and his belief in the efficacy of prayer are consistently expressed in both his private and public speeches, and corroborated by eyewitnesses. For example, several credible, firsthand sources including members of Lincoln's cabinet testified to hearing him say that his decision to issue the Emancipation Proclamation involved a "solemn vow" to God.[66] And Union Generals James F. Rusling and D. E. Sickles both testified under oath that Lincoln explained to them that he had prayed during the battle of Gettysburg and experienced an inner peace and reassurance that all would go well.[67]

Lincoln manifested biblical faith in different ways throughout his life by humbly seeking to know God's will, by refraining from self-righteousness, by avoiding malice towards his enemies, and by trusting in a higher power to guide him and the nation through its fiery trial. In particular, Lincoln's personal faith was guided by his fervent belief that he was an "instrument of God"—a term he consistently used to describe his mission in life. What did Lincoln mean by this? We know that the fanatic John Brown believed that he was an instrument of God commissioned to kill slaveholders, and John Wilkes Booth likewise described himself as an "instrument of God" called to punish Abraham Lincoln. However, unlike these fanatics, Lincoln's faith was balanced by moderation, moral prudence, and magnanimity. It should be emphasized that Lincoln never claimed a direct revelation from God. On the contrary, he often pointed out the vast gulf between human pretence and the divine will. As an instrument of God, Lincoln envisioned himself not as a crusading fanatic, but as a suffering servant bearing witness to God's providence, whatever that may be and however vaguely discerned. Avoiding the extremes of self-righteousness and despair, he affirmed and embodied the paradox of faith: humbly acknowledging the inscrutability of God's will, yet nevertheless trusting in God's goodness as well. Lincoln had faith in "the purpose driven life" to serve God and sacrifice himself for others. Ultimately, Lincoln's claim to be "an instrument of God" must be judged by his fruits; for as Scripture states, "by the fruits you will know them."

After four years of carnage that claimed the lives of six hundred thousand Americans (more deaths than all other American wars combined), Abraham Lincoln pondered the ultimate meaning of the Civil War in his Second Inaugural Address on March 4, 1865. The Second Inaugural Address may be viewed as a public expression of Lincoln's living faith, and the mature culmination of his political faith. In this speech, which is best described as a national sermon, he pointed to the tragic irony of each side invoking the Bible to sanctify its politics: "Both read the same Bible, and pray to the same God; and each invokes his aid against the other. . . . The prayers of both could not be answered; that of neither has been answered fully. The Almighty has his own purposes."

To the dismay of self-righteous abolitionists who expected a strong vindication of their moral crusade against the soon to be defeated South, Lincoln suggested that neither side was pure in its policies. Both sides were, to some extent, culpable before God. And, if the war was a chastisement for the nation as whole, it was thus merited. To express the collective guilt of both parties, Lincoln characterized slavery in general terms as an American institution, blaming the nation as a whole rather than the South alone.

In the Second Inaugural Address, Lincoln affirmed the inscrutability of the divine will, which was ultimately mysterious and could not be neatly captured and controlled by human measures. He inveighed against a perverse tribal God who could be bribed through burnt offerings, and he affirmed the righteousness of a living God whose providence guided the destinies of both individuals and nations. As a faithful servant bearing witness to providence, he asked his fellow citizens to trust that God would bring some ultimate good out of the ordeal of the Union. Indeed, the very motto, "In God We Trust," stamped upon our nation's coins, was signed by Lincoln into law during his second term of office.

Prefiguring the theological outlook of the Second Inaugural Address, at Gettysburg, Lincoln resolved that this nation "under God" would not perish from the earth. By "under God" Lincoln affirmed his personal belief that the nation was under God's Providence. His Gettysburg Address poetically distilled the essence of the American creed, portraying the Civil War in allegorical terms as a test or trial to remain faithful to the sacred principle of equality in the Declaration. The resounding "four score and seven years" evoked the passage of time in the same manner as the King James Bible (Esther 1:4/Psalm 90). The religious imagery of "dedicate," "consecrate," and "hallow" reinforced the supreme sacrifice made by those who gave their lives so that the nation might live. Soldiers on the battlefield had not died in vain; the national suffering would lead to a "new birth of freedom," which symbolically represented the redemption of the Union from the original sin of slavery. Indeed, Lincoln's political faith at Gettysburg may be viewed as an allegorical application of the New Testament's cycle of consecration, trial, suffering, death, and rebirth to the Union.

7. Lincoln, the Union, and the Role of the State

Lincoln claimed that without strong support for the Union, the American nation could not have achieved equal opportunity for diverse groups. Without the "mystic chords of memory" of the nation's Founding, we would have insufficient faith in fostering "government of the people, by the people, for the people." Lincoln fully agreed with Frederick Douglass, the former slave, who was hopeful that "the white and colored people of this country [could] be blended into a common nationality and enjoy together . . . under the same flag, the inestimable blessings of life, liberty, and the pursuit of happiness of neighborly citizens of a common country."[69] Lincoln's own position on the possibilities of a multiracial democratic nation evolved and matured over time to express politically and poetically a shared dream of peace between descendants of oppressors and the oppressed.[70]

In his First Inaugural Address, Lincoln held that "the Union of these States is perpetual. Perpetuity is implied, if not expressed in the fundamental law of all national governments." He certainly understood that the United States was a nation in the sense that the Supreme Court as a national court could bind the states. In 1793, the Supreme Court stated that, "The sovereignty of the nation is in the people of the nation, and the residuary sovereignty of each state in the people of each state."[71] The people of the United States are sovereign and may prevail over the States. Consequently, Lincoln categorically rejected South Carolina's claim to be a "separate and independent state" with all the powers attending that status, including right of secession. The federal government had done no harm to the South as they were "seceding" from the Union, claimed Lincoln. From a contemporary perspective, we certainly share Lincoln's view that the South cannot claim a legitimate or "unalienable right" to own slaves as a legitimate basis for revolution or secession. Lincoln boldly associated equality and Union. This "moral union" is founded upon mutuality of diverse groups and the elimination of feudal hierarchies of authority. It is not any Union that is to be supported, but a moral and inclusive union that initially must oppose the extension of slavery. Additionally, this meant that Lincoln would open the door to Jewish army chaplains and oppose Ulysses S. Grant's ban on "Jew Peddlers," because it would prohibit "an entire religious class, some of whom are fighting in our ranks."[72] As Lincoln put it quite dramatically two months before the Civil War began, he "would rather be assassinated" than preserve a Union open to the expansion of slavery.[73]

8. Lincoln for Our Time

Lincoln's American Dream views government as having a positive role in society. To preserve the Union guided by the Constitution is to "preserve the Government that it be administered for all as it was administered by the men who made it." Government's proper role is one "whose leading object is, to elevate the condition of men—to lift artificial weights from all shoulders—to clear the paths of laudable pursuit for all—to afford all, an unfettered start, and a fair chance, in the race of life."[74] Lincoln's ultimate goal was to save American liberty by expanding it, and by so doing to advance the Founders' noble but unfinished work. Lincoln's own reverence for the Declaration gradually evolved over the arc of his political career to include "a standard maxim for free society, which should be familiar to all, and revered by all; constantly looked to, constantly labored for, and even though never perfectly attained, constantly approximated, and thereby constantly spreading and deepening its influence and augmenting the happiness and value of life to all people of all colors everywhere."[75] For Lincoln this is exactly what he meant when he stated at Gettysburg on November 19, 1863 that the nation was "conceived in liberty, and dedicated to the proposition that all men are created equal" and "that this nation shall have a new birth of freedom. . . ."

Lincoln's American Dream means providing equal opportunity or a fair chance for each person starting out as a "penniless beginner in the world" who works hard and "saves a surplus with which to buy tools and land for himself . . . and . . . at length hires another new beginner to help him." What clearly distinguished Lincoln from other free labor and "rags to riches" advocates was his insistence that the "new birth of freedom" was to include all: "I want every man to have [this] chance—and I believe a black man is entitled to it, too."[76] Andrew Delbanco summarizes the political and personal significance of Lincoln when he states, "The lesson of Lincoln's life—the life he lived, and that endures in our national memory—is that the quest for prosperity is no remedy for melancholy, but that a passion to secure justice by erasing the line that divides those with hope from those without hope can be."[77] This book explores whether Lincoln's patriotism and politics of hope can truly nurture "the better angels of our nature."

ॐ

Notes

1. Roy P. Basler, ed., *The Collected Works of Abraham Lincoln*, vol. 4 (New Brunswick, NJ: Rutgers University Press, 1953–1955), 426.

2. Isaiah Berlin, *The Hedgehog and the Fox: An Essay on Tolstoy's View of History* (New York: Simon & Schuster, 1966), 1.

3. James M. McPherson, "The Hedgehog and the Foxes," in *For a Vast Future Also,* ed. Thomas F. Schwartz (New York: Gordham University Press, 1999), 106.

4. Andrew Delbanco, *The Real American Dream: A Meditation on Hope* (Cambridge: Harvard University Press, 1999), 1.

5. Thomas J. DiLorenzo, *The Real Lincoln: A New Look at Abraham Lincoln, His Agenda, and an Unnecessary War* (New York: Forum, 2002).

6. Walter Berns, *Making Patriots* (Chicago: University of Chicago Press, 2002).

7. Basler, *Collected Works*, vol. 2, 385.

8. Basler, *Collected Works*, vol. 3, 375.

9. Basler, *Collected Works*, vol. 4, 240.

10. Basler, *Collected Works*, vol. 2, 499.

11. Basler, *Collected Works*, vol. 2, 406.

12. Basler, *Collected Works*, vol. 2, 266.

13. Willmoore Kendall and George Carey, *The Basic Symbols of the American Political Tradition* (Washington, DC: Catholic University Press, 1995), 75–95.

14. Kendall and Carey, *Basic Symbols*, 75–95.

15. Garry Wills, *Lincoln at Gettysburg: The Words That Remade America* (New York: Simon & Schuster, 1992), 38.

16. Wills, *Lincoln at Gettysburg*, 174–175.

17. Basler, *Collected Works*, vol. 1, 8.

18. Basler, *Collected Works*, vol. 3, 511.

19. Basler, *Collected Works*, vol. 1, 113–114.

20. Edmund Wilson, *Patriotic Gore: Studies in the Literature of the American Civil War* (New York: Oxford University Press, 1962), 108.

21. Basler, *Collected Works*, vol. 2, 383.

22. Basler, *Collected Works*, vol. 6, 392–393.

23. Kenneth L. Deutsch, "Thomas Aquinas on Magnanimous and Prudent Statesmanship," in *Tempered Strength: Studies in the Nature and Scope of Prudential Leadership*, ed. Ethan Fishman (Lanham, MD: Lexington Books, 2002), 33–52.

24. Basler, *Collected Works*, vol. 2, 547.

25. Basler, *Collected Works*, vol. 3, 334.

26. See Don E. Fehrenbacher, *The Dred Scott Case: Its Significance in American Law and Politics* (New York: Oxford University Press, 1978).

27. Basler, *Collected Works*, vol. 1, 75.

28. Basler, *Collected Works*, vol. 7, 281.

29. Basler, *Collected Works*, vol. 2, 532.

30. Basler, *Collected Works*, vol. 2, 256.

31. Lerone Bennett, Jr., Preface to *Forced into Glory: Abraham Lincoln's White Dream* (Chicago: Johnson Publishing Co., 2000).

32. Bennett, *Forced into Glory*, 277.

33. Basler, *Collected Works*, vol. 3, 145–146.

34. Bennett, *Forced into Glory*, 7–10.

35. Bennett, *Forced into Glory*, 20.

36. Basler, *Collected Works*, vol. 2, 501.

37. Basler, *Collected Works*, vol. 5, 388–389.

38. Allen C. Guelzo, *Lincoln's Emancipation: The End of Slavery in America* (New York: Simon & Schuster, 2004).

39. David Herbert Donald, *Lincoln Reconsidered: Essays on the Civil War Era* (New York: Vintage Books, 1961), 57–81, 128–143.

40. Norman Graebner, ed. *The Enduring Lincoln* (Urbana: University of Illinois Press, 1959), vi.

41. Graebner, *Enduring Lincoln*, 28.

42. Harry V. Jaffa, *Crisis of the House Divided: An Interpretation of the Issues in the Lincoln-Douglas Debates* (Garden City, NY: Doubleday, 1959), 1.

43. Richard J. Carwardine, *Lincoln: Profiles in Power* (London: Pearson Education, 2003), 143.

44. Basler, *Collected Works*, vol. 2, 504–520.

45. Basler, *Collected Works*, vol. 3, 313.

46. Ralph Lerner, *Revolutions Revisited* (Chapel Hill: University of North Carolina Press, 1994), 61.

47. Lerner, *Revolutions Revisited*, 61.

48. Lerner, *Revolutions Revisited*, 62.

49. Lerner, *Revolutions Revisited*, 62.

50. Lerner, *Revolutions Revisited*, 62.

51. Basler, *Collected Works*, vol. 1, 65.

52. Basler, *Collected Works*, vol. 4, 264–265.

53. Basler, *Collected Works*, vol. 7, 281.

54. James G. Randall, *Constitutional Problems under Lincoln*, rev. ed. (Urbana: University of Illinois Press, 1951), 51.

55. Randall, *Constitutional Problems*, 51.

56. Basler, *Collected Works*, vol. 2, 510.

57. Carwardine, *Lincoln*, 38.

58. Basler, *Collected Works*, vol. 2, 132.

59. Delbanco, *Real American Dream*, 35.

60. See Joseph R. Fornieri, *Abraham Lincoln's Political Faith* (De Kalb: Northern Illinois University Presss, 2003).

61. See Allen C. Guelzo, "Abraham Lincoln and the Doctrine of Necessity," *Journal of the Abraham Lincoln Association* 18, no. 1 (1997): 57–81.

62. Carwardine, *Lincoln*, 37.

63. Carwardine, *Lincoln*, 37.

64. David Herbert Donald, *Lincoln's Herndon* (New York: Da Capo, 1989), 214 and 359.

65. For books on Lincoln's religious views, see Wayne C. Temple, *Abraham Lincoln: From Skeptic to Prophet* (Mahomet, IL: Mayhaven, 1995). Also see the following: David Hein, "Lincoln's Theology and Political Ethics" in *Essays on Lincoln's Faith and Politics*, ed. Kenneth W. Thompson (Lanham, MD: University Press of America, 1983); William E. Barton, *The Soul of Abraham Lincoln* (New York: George H. Doran, 1920); Allen C. Guelzo, *Abraham Lincoln: Redeemer President* (Grand Rapids, MI: William B. Eerdmans, 1999); Fornieri, *Abraham Lincoln's Political Faith*.

66. Fornieri, *Abraham Lincoln's Political Faith*, 50–69.

67. Fornieri, *Abraham Lincoln's Political Faith*, 50–59.

68. Basler, *Collected Works*, vol. 7, 535.

69. Cited in George P. Fletcher, *Our Secret Constitution: How Lincoln Redefined American Democracy* (New York: Oxford University Press, 2001), 62.

70. Fletcher, *Our Secret Constitution*, 63.

71. Fletcher, *Our Secret Constitution*, 61.

72. Carwardine, *Lincoln*, 270.

73. Basler, *Collected Works*, vol. 4, 240; For Lincoln's view of an inclusive Union, see Rogan Kersh, *Dreams of a More Perfect Union* (Ithaca, NY: Cornell University Press, 2001), 177.

74. Basler, *Collected Works*, vol. 4, 438.

75. Basler, *Collected Works*, vol. 2, 406.

76. Cited in Delbanco, *Real American Dream*, 74.

77. Delbanco, *Real American Dream*, 74.

Chapter 1

LINCOLN, THE DECLARATION, AND EQUALITY

Is Lincoln's interpretation of equality in the Declaration a "derailment" of the American political tradition?

I can say in return, sir, that all the political sentiments I entertain have been drawn, so far as I have been able to draw them, from the sentiments which originated, and were given to the world from this hall in which we stand. I have never had a feeling politically that did not spring from the sentiments embodied in the Declaration of Independence. I have often pondered over the dangers which were incurred by the men who assembled here and adopted that Declaration of Independence—I have pondered over the toils that were endured by the officers and soldiers of the army, who achieved that Independence. I have often inquired of myself, what great principle or idea it was that kept this Confederacy so long together. It was not the mere matter of the separation of the colonies from the mother land; but something in that Declaration giving liberty, not alone to the people of this country, but hope to the world for all future time. It was that which gave promise that in due time the weights should be lifted from the shoulders of all men, and that *all* should have an equal chance. This is the sentiment embodied in that Declaration of Independence.

Now, my friends, can this country be saved upon that basis? If it can, I will consider myself one of the happiest men in the world if I can help to save it. If it can't be saved upon that principle, it will be truly awful. But, if this country cannot be saved without giving up that principle—I was about to say I would rather be assassinated on this spot than to surrender it.

Abraham Lincoln, Speech in Independence Hall, Philadelphia, PA, February 22, 1861

★ James G. Randall, "Lincoln the Liberal Statesman"
★ Willmoore Kendall, "Equality: Commitment or Ideal"
★ Harry V. Jaffa, "Equality as a Conservative Principle"
★ M. E. Bradford, "The Heresy of Equality"
★ Harry V. Jaffa, "Equality, Justice, and the American Revolution: In Reply to Bradford's 'The Heresy of Equality'"

‿Ↄ

LINCOLN THE LIBERAL STATESMAN
James G. Randall

I

To WRITE OF Lincoln's fundamental views requires a good deal of caution. It is the commonest thing to see the mind of Lincoln fitted into a preconceived pattern. Sometimes this is done by an elastic or strained interpretation of what he actually said, sometimes by pure conjecture as to what he "would have" said or done on some matter far beyond his time. Writers look into the body of Lincoln's utterances, or skim the surface, for the most diverse purposes. Obviously, not all the Lincolns we have presented to us can be genuine.

Lincoln has been presented to us as a conservative. In an able and eloquent paper his political philosophy has been analyzed in terms of expediency with more than a touch of opportunism.[1] There is validity in thinking of him as conservative if one does not leave it there, but conservatism in the usual sense did not by any means encompass the horizon of his thought. There was, of course, moderation in his preference for orderly progress, his distrust of dangerous agitation, and his reluctance toward ill digested schemes of reform. More especially, he was conservative in his complete avoidance of that type of so-called "radicalism" which involved abuse of the South, hatred for the slaveholder, thirst for vengeance, partisan plotting, and ungenerous demands that Southern institutions be transformed overnight by outsiders. One of the tragic mistakes that Southerners made in an era of incredible blundering was to suppose that this type of intolerant radicalism was typical of the North. Antislavery ideals had their noble aspects. Only the best leadership could have adequately promoted them; but, historically speaking, abolitionist excess was not the sentiment of any substantial Northern element. That was shown even in wartime by the congressional election of 1862.

It was because of Lincoln's more tolerant attitude toward the South that he was nominated by the Republican Party in 1860 at a time when even the conservative Seward was rejected under the mistaken impression that he was too radical. It needs to be understood, however, that the word "radical" in the days of the Civil War and reconstruction was not a generic term. It had a meaning not discernible in the word itself. It was a specific designation of a particular group—Stevens, Chandler, Wade, et al.—whose dominance in the Federal government set the stage for one of the most abusive periods of American history. These men, considered realistically and

*This article originally appeared in J. G. Randall, *Lincoln the Liberal Statesman* (N.Y.: Dodd, Mead, 1947), 175–206.

taken as a group, were the opposite of liberal. As indicated in an earlier essay, they were in fact reactionary. This was evident from their opposition to civil rights, their denunciation of the Milligan decision of the Supreme Court, their denial of autonomy to Southerners, their extreme partisanship, and their friendliness toward exploitive capitalism.

One can ignore this, or deny it. A fabricated, rose-colored portrait of these radicals can be presented, but only if one distorts history. Thaddeus Stevens of Pennsylvania, for example, had, and still has, a reputation for egalitarianism and sympathy for the common man. He has been called the "Commoner" and has superficially been accepted as such. It is a different matter if, in studying this complex personality, one looks at the record instead of the stereotyped portrait. Stevens's dominance over the House of Representatives in Lincoln's day was arrogant, factional, and dictatorial. As Richard Nelson Current has pointed out, he "was not only the embodiment of Pennsylvania capitalism himself but also a go-between for others of that ilk, one whose function it was to convert the votes of the many into the policies of the few." Treating his rise to political power in prewar times, Mr. Current writes: "Lacking the humanitarian impulse, he stood stubbornly for 'vested rights' as against what he called 'the wild visions of idle dreamers,' 'the revolutionary and agrarian folly of modern reformers.'"[2] His "Commoner" label was a handy thing. The reputation of the alleged friend of the people served perfectly to rake in thousands of votes, while maneuvers behind the scenes made use of these votes for special interests that were exclusive and predatory.

It is clear from convincing masses of contemporary evidence—including voluminous unpublished sources known to specialists—that these men who opposed Lincoln were "radical" in the sense of being drastic or violent, not in the sense of being liberal. To combat such men was in truth a mark of liberalism. In Lincoln's case particularly it should be so understood, from earlier stages of rampant sectionalism, on through the wartime days of radical intrigue, and down to the ugly and menacing deadlock by which the vindictives wrecked Lincoln's program for the postwar years.

In all such matters Lincoln emerges as a moderate, but that made him none the less a liberal. Liberalism is associated with democracy and democracy requires moderation. It is among enemies of democracy, as we know by bitter experience in our day, that we find violence, unbridled extravagance of statement, torture, terrorism, fanaticism, and criminal atrocities. Lincoln believed in planting, cultivating, and harvesting, not in uprooting and destroying. He believed in evolutionary democratic progress.

It is possible to take his economic views and, by a superficial showing, argue Lincoln's "conservatism" with reference to such matters as the national bank or the protective tariff. His favoring of the bank—the famous "Bank of the United States" so productive of discord in the Jackson era—was due largely to his attachment to the Whig party. As to the tariff, nearly everything he said on that subject could be classified under the head of tiresome or labored economics. Some of Lincoln's writings or speeches show that he either missed the point as to the working of the tariff or permitted himself to indulge in those meaningless verbalisms or homely illustrations which were characteristic of protectionist politicians; in Lincoln's case, however, there seem to have been twinges of conscience which coarser men lacked. Speaking at Pittsburgh on his presidential journey in February 1861 he related the tariff question to the lack of "direct taxation" and remarked that it "is to the government what replenishing the meal-tub is to the family."[3] These phrases would apply to a tariff for revenue rather than for the protection of manufacturers. Yet his remarks on that occasion were supposed to be an endorsement of the Republican protectionist position.

After reading Lincoln's papers and speeches generally, with their clarity and pithy effectiveness, one turns to this Pittsburgh speech with a sense of let-down or disappointment. Trying to fit himself into the Republican tariff pattern, the more so because of his Pennsylvania audience (where among dominant party men the tariff was a specialty and questions concerning slavery unimportant), he fell into a lameness of statement and a confession of ignorance that were quite uncharacteristic. Republican protectionism was not his forte. Indeed his private correspondence shows that he had doubts on this subject which he did not wish to become public.[4] The party was making a strong appeal to manufacturers, but Lincoln did not want to repel men who believed in freedom of trade or who disliked excessive favors to special groups. One suspects, not without reason, that Lincoln had an un-Republican fondness for freer trade himself.

The subject of the tariff is an example to show the manner in which Lincoln's "conservatism" can be overstated or superficially presented. What is needed is something deeper than superficial indications. It is partly a matter of the use of terms. What does "conservatism" mean? If it means caution, prudent adherence to tested values, avoidance of rashness, and reliance upon unhurried, peaceable evolution, Lincoln was a conservative. If, however, the dignified word "conservative" comes to us with an alloy as with the word "politics," if it has a reactionary connotation, if it casts an aura of respectability over tendencies that are exploitive and unprogressive, or if it signifies indifferent apathy toward human problems, then one can say with complete confidence that Lincoln was no conservative.

To think of Lincoln's conservatism is to think of selected facets of his policy. But the deeply searching mind of Lincoln had more in it than static acquiescence. It had motivating sympathy, awareness of social needs, enthusiasm for effective democracy—qualities appropriately denoted by the word liberal. If in procedure he wanted to be sure of his ground, in the content and purpose of his program he wanted liberal causes to succeed. If his conservatism was a kind of brake or saving common sense, liberalism was his vital spark.

The surest way to judge him is by those statements in which he appeared at his unhampered best. In expounding the protective tariff for the special benefit of manufacturers he fumbled and limped; but, as William H. Herndon said, it was far different when he dealt with fundamental human rights. In one of Herndon's manuscripts we have this description: "If he was defending the right—if he was defending liberty—eulogizing the Declaration of Independence, then he extended out his arms . . . as if appealing to some superior power for assistance and support; or that he might embrace the spirit of that which he so dearly loved. It was at such moments that he seemed inspired, fresh from the hands of his creator. Lincoln's gray eyes would flash fire when speaking against slavery or spoke volumes of hope and love when speaking of Liberty—justice and the progress of mankind."[5]

II

It would not be going far wrong to say that the liberal credo was the key to Lincoln's views of man and the state. His basic ideas were those of Thomas Jefferson. He owed little to Hamilton who wanted a government to please the moneyed interests. Human rights meant more to him than profits. He was not content with lip service to the Declaration of Independence. He took its doctrines seriously in their stress upon equality of men. He cherished Anglo-Saxon muniments of civil justice. On one occasion he spoke out for woman suffrage far ahead of his time. Believing as he did in the broadening of political rights, he did not stop there but urged that such "rights" be carried forward in governmental achievement and human betterment. His thought went out to the less privileged, to the "prudent, penniless beginner."[1] The grasping rich who gained by the misfortunes of their fellow men, or who thought of war as an opportunity for profiteering, had his contempt, but repeatedly he expressed the wish that every poor man should have a chance.

Just how far Lincoln "would have" gone in extending the functions of government, and in using the government to promote the welfare of the country, is difficult to say; but there is ample evidence that his philosophy of man and the state did not begin and end with laissez faire. He vigorously favored what were called "internal improvements"—that being the term used in his day for large appropriations by the Federal government for various kinds of public works all over the country. He also favored such expenditures by the states. In the late 1830s when Illinois was launching upon a grandiose program for improvements in every county Lincoln was one of the most active legislative promoters of the plan. In Congress ten years later he argued elaborately in favor of such governmental expenditures. In this argument he took up, point by point, the objections of those who urged that such a system would "overwhelm the treasury," would provide merely local benefits with the use of general funds, and would be unconstitutional. He summed up the position of his opponents in the phrase "Do nothing at all, lest you do something wrong." This, he said, applied "as forcibly to . . . making improvements by State authority as by the national authority; so that we must abandon the improvements of the country altogether, by any and every authority, or we must resist and repudiate the doctrines of this message [the anti-internal-improvement veto message by President Polk]." Lincoln plainly stated that he favored the latter alternative.

Warming to his theme, Lincoln showed that improvements in the 1820s had by no means overwhelmed the treasury, even in "the period of greatest enormity." He showed that "no commercial object of government patronage can be so exclusively general as to not be of some peculiar local advantage." Then he added: ". . . if the nation refuse to make improvements of the more general kind because their benefits may be somewhat local, a State may for the same reason refuse to make an improvement of a local kind because its benefits may be somewhat general." Such an argument "puts an end to improvements altogether." In this we have a typical Lincolnian argument. We recall the circuit lawyer in Illinois, analyzing the position of the opposing side and exposing the weakness of that position. He dealt with the constitutional objection at some length by quoting Kent and Story, clinching it with the following conclusion: ". . . no one who is satisfied of the expediency of making improvements need be much uneasy in his conscience about its constitutionality." Summarizing his whole position, he said: ". . . let the nation take hold of the larger works, and the States the smaller ones; and thus, what is . . . unequal in one place may be equalized in another, extravagance avoided, and the whole country put on that career of prosperity which shall correspond with its extent of territory, its natural resources, and the intelligence and enterprise of its people."[2]

On other matters Lincoln showed how far he was from the concept of a do-nothing government. He favored government help for the promotion of education. He earnestly advocated an elaborate scheme of state-enacted emancipation with federal sponsorship and compensation. It was under him that the department of agriculture, destined to become one of the most active of government agencies, had its beginnings. As president he signed the Homestead Act of 1862, a measure of far-reaching government aid to the rural homemaker. By that measure Uncle Sam gave away a vast amount of land in order to encourage a democratic system of individual land tenure. The act did not accomplish all that was hoped, because of exploitive tendencies in the post-Lincoln decades, but it assuredly did not proceed on the fundamental assumption that government should forever let the nation's economy alone. Lincoln's disapproval of that do-nothing theory was expressed in a fragment on government attributed to the year 1854. "Government [he said] is a combination of the people of a country to effect certain objects by joint effort. . . . The legitimate object of government is 'to do for the people what needs to be done, but which they can not, by individual effort, do at all, or do so well, for themselves.' There are many such things. . . ."[3]

III

In any survey of Lincoln's beliefs and thought patterns it is important to emphasize the supreme quality of tolerance. Innocent of that holier-than-thou attitude which made extremists of his day particularly irritating, he realized that slavery was a moral question—an institution which he hated—yet at the same time he recognized the moral sense of the Southern people.[1] In personal matters he would deftly put in the tolerant touch. Writing in 1840 to a man who imagined he had been attacked and insulted, he was careful to assure the gentleman: "I entertain no unkind feelings to you. . . ."[2] Any personal altercation he considered regrettable. Often in his correspondence one finds the conscious effort to avoid wounded feelings. I summed up the matter as follows:

> When the conduct of men is designed to be influenced, persuasion, kind, unassuming persuasion, should ever be adopted. It is an old and a true maxim "that a drop of honey catches more flies than a gallon of gall." So with men. If you would win a man to your cause, first convince him that you are his sincere friend. Therein is a drop of honey that catches his heart, which, say what he will, is the great highroad to his reason, and which, when once gained, you will find but little trouble in convincing his judgment of the justice of your cause, if indeed that cause really be a just one. On the contrary, assume to dictate to his judgment, or to command his action, or to mark him as one to be shunned and despised, and he will retreat within himself, close all the avenues to his head and his heart; and though your cause be naked truth itself, transformed to the heaviest lance, harder than steel, and sharper than steel can be made, and though you throw it with more than herculean force and precision, you shall be no more able to pierce him than to penetrate the hard shell of a tortoise with a rye straw. Such is man, and so must he be understood by those who would lead him, even to his own best interests.[3]

It is worthwhile to linger a moment on this passage if one would understand Lincoln. In large part it is a key to his public and private relations. The emphasis is upon friendly approach, upon showing a man that you are his friend. You do not win a man by showing that he is wrong and you are right, by seeking to "command his action" or by setting him down as one to be despised. Your effort should not be to dictate his thought or coerce his judgment. The heart is "the great high road to reason." Gain access to a man's heart first; after that you may convince his judgment. Make sure that your own cause is just, but remember that if a man retreats "within himself" he will not be won over even by the purest truth. Your success does not depend only on the hardness of your lance, the precision or force of your throwing. You might wish it otherwise. You might prefer that naked truth and rightness of clear reasoning should come first and emotions be disregarded, but such is man. You must know what manner of animal he is. You must deal with human nature. If you are to lead you must understand those you are seeking to lead.

Lincoln was not justifying the idea that emotion rather than reason should take command in the formation of a man's attitudes. On other occasions he stressed the importance of clear thinking. In the passage before us he was not hedging on the bedrock value of solid judgment. He did not say that reason was of secondary importance, but that the heart was the "high road to reason." To get acceptance of a position based on tested thinking was his purpose, but he did not want the accomplishment of that purpose prejudiced by the wrong approach. He wanted truth to prevail, but he was thinking in terms of human relations, in which tact and winsome understanding were, by his observation, trump cards.

This attitude is the opposite of the fanatic. Such a man may be righteous, but his righteousness tends in the direction of the witch burner. Those who oppose him are evil; they must be destroyed, or at least suppressed. In that suppressive crusade one's language becomes extravagant; zeal overreaches itself; the lance of argument is thrown as if the Almighty himself were hurling a thunderbolt to strike down the evildoer. One's own motives are pure; the opponent must therefore be a sinister person; there must be no compromise with him. You withdraw from him. You spurn his friendship. Your speeches and articles are presented not so much to your opponent; he is hopeless; they are presented to your own audience; your opponent is treated as a third person. The more you can put him in the wrong the better you are pleased. You stand at Armageddon and you battle for the Lord, but you are the recruiting officer who enlists the Lord services. Public affairs must be viewed in terms of clash, struggle, and crisis, rather than adjustment. To state these contrasting attitudes is to show that Lincoln stood not with the fanatic but with the friendly persuasive statesman.

Lincoln's liberal minded tolerance was evident in his friendly attitude toward foreigners. One must recall the factors working against such tolerance in his day. Men who came from other lands—they came in immense streams in the 1850s—were confronted with difficult conditions.[4] America beckoned but Americans often repelled.

It is not sufficient to say that hostility to foreigners was prevalent in that period. It was rampant. The nativism of that time was characterized by an assumption of racial superiority and a policy of exclusiveness in favor of old-stock Americans. It is amazing how far this movement extended, particularly within the Whig party, in which Lincoln was a vigorous leader. On the political front the evasive nickname for these nativists was "Know-Nothing"; as of 1856 theirs was the "American" party; before that party was formed they had gone so far in organization on the state level as to control some of the key commonwealths. When the Whig caucus of the New York legislature met in February 1855 it was stated by the *Evening Post* that of the eighty senators and assemblymen present "sixty at least" of these Whigs had taken the Know-Nothing oath and joined the order.[5] The mysterious secrecy of the order and the unblushing casuistry of their reasoning enabled them to pay as much or little attention to these oaths as they chose. If it became necessary for political purposes to evade their pledges they could absolve themselves with the greatest of ease. Lines of retreat were prepared in their rear. They could even deny membership. Their "principles," which "smell mouldy and unwholesome in the dark and damp,"[6] were not often ventilated.

In Massachusetts, by the election of 1854, the Know-Nothing party elected the governor (Henry Joseph Gardner), all the state officials, "all but two members of the legislature and every member of Congress from Massachusetts."[7] According to George F. Hoar, Gardner played the game of flattery and demagoguery, using men "who were odious or ridiculous among their own neighbors, but who united might be a very formidable force." He rose to power by organizing "the knave-power and the donkey-power of the Commonwealth."[8] Two names will illustrate the powerful hold which this anti-foreign group had upon leading men of that period—Samuel F. B. Morse, one of the most outstanding nativist propagandists of his time, and Millard Fillmore, ex-president of the United States, who became the candidate of the American party in 1856.

Lincoln was like Fillmore in Whig allegiance; he was like both Fillmore and Morse in ancestral American background; he was, however, firm and outspoken in his opposition to nativism. Writing to his friend Joshua F. Speed in 1855 he said, "I am not a Know-nothing; that is certain. How could I be? How can anyone who abhors the oppression of negroes be in favor of degrading classes of white people? . . . When the Know-nothings get control . . . I shall prefer emigrating to some country where they make no pretense of loving liberty. . . ."[9]

He vigorously opposed anti-alien tendencies in Massachusetts. He was careful to say that he had never been in an American or Know-Nothing lodge.[10] In 1858, in a slightly known message to a committee of Chicago Germans, he offered the following sentiment: "Our German Fellow-Citizens:—Ever true to Liberty, the Union, and the Constitution—true to Liberty, not selfishly, but upon principle—not for special classes of men, but for *all* men. . . ."[11] He made a contract with Theodore Canisius for the control of a German-American newspaper at Springfield. In a letter to Canisius in 1859 he wrote: "Understanding the spirit of our institutions to aim at the elevation of men, I am opposed to whatever tends to degrade them. I have some little notoriety for commiserating the oppressed negro; and I should be strangely inconsistent if I could favor . . . curtailing the . . . rights of white men, even though born in different lands, and speaking different languages from myself."[12]

As president he showed the same tolerance. When General Grant issued an order expelling "all Jews" from the lines of his military department early in 1863 (the purpose being to exclude peddlers), Lincoln revoked the order. It was explained to Grant that he did this because the order "proscribed an entire religious class, some of whom are fighting in our ranks."[13] These are but a few examples; others could be added. Lincoln's Americanism was not a matter of prejudice, of witch hunting, or hatred directed against particular groups or classes of men.

It is instructive to compare Lincoln's record as to Know-Nothingism with that of the alleged *equalitarian* and "Commoner," Thaddeus Stevens. Lincoln was clear cut against the Know-Nothings and against anti-foreign intolerance. Stevens courted the nativists; the roping in of their votes appealed to his politician mind. When the

Republican national convention in 1856 indirectly condemned nativism by a declaration in favor of "liberty of conscience and equality of rights," Stevens tried unsuccessfully to have these words withdrawn. Realizing that the Know-Nothings were politically powerful in Pennsylvania, he did not want to alienate their support and for this reason he favored the colorless McLean of Ohio for presidential candidate instead of Frémont, who was not a Catholic, but against whom the cry of Catholicism had been raised. After the presidential nomination of 1856 had been made, including Fillmore for the "Americans," Stevens (as we learn from reading the biography by Richard Nelson Current) worked hard to enlist the support of Know-Nothing editors for the Republican ticket. In this he succeeded, not without a brazen use of money. He himself stated that he "expended $4,000 in securing presses." One "American editor," he said, "was to change his course and have $350." Mr. Current remarks: "Old Thad was the sort who believed an honest man to be one who, once bought, would stay bought. . . ."[14] All this was in 1856, but the day was to come when Lincoln as President, in his unhappy relations with Congress, would have to deal with the domineering and intriguing Stevens as Republican leader (or boss) in the House of Representatives.

Lincoln's broad tolerance was shown in his speech on temperance. He had nothing of the self-righteous unction so common among temperance reformers. Far from denouncing the drunkard he showed that in his own growing years intoxicating liquor was "a respectable article of manufacture and merchandise." "From the sideboard of the parson [he said] down to the ragged pocket of the houseless loafer, it was constantly found."[15] To berate habitual drunkards as utterly incorrigible was repugnant to his sense of human decency. He considered such an attitude "fiendishly selfish." It was "like throwing fathers and brothers overboard." He himself was not a drinker, but taking drunkards as a class he believed that "their heads and their hearts will bear an advantageous comparison with those of any other class." Proneness to this vice he believed characteristic of generous people. As to those who had not fallen victims to drink, he thought they might have been spared "more by the absence of appetite than from any mental or moral superiority."[16] It should be added that Lincoln spoke vigorously for temperance. The point emphasized here is his manner of doing so. Temperance in his judgment was not promoted by any type of intolerance, nor by unfriendliness toward "a large, erring, and unfortunate class of . . . fellow-creatures."[17]

IV

Lincoln repeatedly spoke in terms of friendliness to labor. Hard work had been his portion in pioneer days. While very young, as he states in his autobiography he "had an ax put into his hands . . . and from that till . . . his twenty-third year he was almost constantly handling that . . . useful instrument."[1] More than once he identified himself with workingmen. He referred to himself as a "penniless boy, working on a flatboat at ten dollars per month."[2] At New Haven, Connecticut, on March 6, 1860, he said: "I am not ashamed to confess that twenty-five years ago I was a hired laborer. . . ."[3] With no thought of denying legitimate profits, he disliked the concept of labor being in a dependent position with reference to capital. One can quote several passages on this point. The following is typical:

> The world is agreed that labor is the source from which human wants are mainly supplied. . . . By some it is assumed that labor is available only in connection with capital—that nobody labors, unless somebody else owning capital . . . induces him to do it. . . . They further assume that whoever is once a hired laborer, is fatally fixed in that condition for life; . . . . That is the "mud-sill" theory. But another class of reasoners [Lincoln associated himself with this group] hold . . . that . . . these assumptions are false, and all inferences from them groundless. They hold that labor is prior to, and independent of, capital; that . . . capital is the fruit of labor, and could never have existed if labor had not first existed; that labor can exist without capital, but that capital could never have existed without labor. Hence they hold that labor is the superior— greatly the superior—of capital.[4]

These words having been uttered in 1859, Lincoln returned to the theme in the same words in his first annual message to Congress in December of 1861, where he spoke unfavorably of "the effort to place capital on an equal footing with, if not above, labor." Speaking now from the presidential chair, he said: "Labor is prior to, and independent of, capital. . . . Labor is the superior of capital, and deserves much the higher consideration." Fairness toward both labor and capital was his aim. He said: "Capital has its rights, which are as worthy of protection as any other rights. Nor is it denied that there is, and probably always will be, a relation between labor and capital producing mutual benefits. . . . No men living are more worthy to be trusted than those who toil up from poverty. . . . Let them beware of surrendering a political power . . . which, if surrendered, will surely be used to close the door of advancement against such as they, and to fix new disabilities and burdens upon them, till all of liberty shall be lost.[5] He did not want laborers "tied down" or "obliged to work under all circumstances." He wanted labor peace, but he favored the right to strike.[6]

It is not to be supposed that Lincoln had any antagonism toward capital. That was not the point. "[W]hile we do not propose any war upon capital [he said], we do wish to allow the humblest man an equal chance . . . with everybody else."[7] Often he recurred to this idea of equality of opportunity. Remarking that his own lot was "what might happen to any poor man's son," he said: "I want every man to have a chance—and I believe a black man is entitled to it—in which he can better his condition. . . ."[8] It was to produce such a result that he favored the cause of the Union. Describing it as "a people's contest" he declared: "On the side of the Union it is a struggle for maintaining in the world that form and substance of government whose leading object is to elevate the condition of men—to lift artificial weights from all shoulders; to clear the paths of laudable pursuit for all. . . ."⁹

In the dark days of the war it gave Lincoln heart for his task to believe that labor's welfare would be promoted by the cause for which he struggled. One of his finest presidential papers was his letter to the workingmen of Manchester, England, in response to a laudatory address which had been sent to him at the time of the New Year, 1863.¹⁰ When honorary membership in the Workingmen's Association of New York was tendered to him in 1864 he indicated his grateful acceptance in a speech especially directed to the cause of labor. Repeating his comments as to labor and capital already given in his message to Congress of December 1861, he showed the breadth and international application of his principle in these words: "The strongest bond of human sympathy, outside of the family relation, should be one uniting all working people, of all nations, and tongues, and kindreds. Nor should this lead to a war upon property, or the owners of property. Property is the fruit of labor; property is desirable; is a positive good in the world. That some should be rich shows that others may become rich, and hence is just encouragement to industry and enterprise. Let not him who is houseless pull down the house of another, but let him work diligently and build one for himself, thus by example assuring that his own shall be safe from violence when built."¹¹

V

Lincoln is known, as much as anything else, for a basic Americanism. At the outset of his presidency he showed the utmost fervor in emotionally underlining "our national fabric, with all its benefits, its memories, and its hopes."¹ Here was national pride historically buttressed, reason enlivened by feeling, present loyalty linked with folk memory. He once said: "I love the sentiments of those old-time men. . . ."²

Yet these thoughts were qualified. They were not naively simple. He did not forget national shortcomings. They brought a sense of humility, though he believed that the United States had the best government in the world. He said as a young man: "We find our selves in the peaceful possession of the fairest portion of the earth . . . under . . . a system of political institutions conducing more essentially to the ends of civil and religious liberty than any of which the history of former times tells us."³ That this was not thoughtless boasting was shown by other statements in which he warned against lawless and antisocial tendencies into which his countrymen were prone to fall.

Not oratorical exaggeration, but clear-headed logic, characterized his thinking on American institutions. The pillars of the national temple, he thought, should be "hewn from the solid quarry of sober reason." Passion would be our enemy. "Reason—cold, calculating, unimpassioned reason—must furnish all the materials for our future support and defense."⁴ Lincoln's head and heart were in balance. His emotions might glow, but his well considered judgment would take command. In reading his writings one finds a constant blend of stirring inspiration with steady reflection.

There is, perhaps, a kind of earth-bound quality in the philosophy of most Americans. Ready pragmatism is more to their liking than the unballasted flights of the mystics. America is of the West, not the East. This attitude of hard practicality—of impatience for "success" and "results"—is impressively evident in scientific achievement, industrial organization, managerial talent, and technological accomplishment. Sometimes, however, the same quality—or a coexisting quality—is expressed in a careless and unambitious acceptance of things as they are so far as governmental and social institutions are concerned, sometimes in impatience toward those who sincerely labor to improve social conditions. Faults of American democracy as imperfectly practiced—rampant partisanship, interracial maladjustment, uninspired "politics," pressure lobbying, congressional inefficiency, and deadlocked government—are too often endured with indifference. The public conscience is never dead, but it is often dormant, inarticulate, or frustrated. The active electorate may be only a fraction of the people. Appeals to prejudice, sometimes on a shockingly low level, may carry an election. The "anti-" agitator (anti-labor, anti-Negro, anti-British, etc.) may win by a kind of default—that is, by the absence of an outstanding candidate to represent the more intelligent element. American democracy has not been in danger from those who would "subvert" it nearly so much as from those who give it superficial adherence and lip service while ignoring its pressing problems.

Lincoln had given thought to certain aspects of this problem, or related problems, as they arose in his time. His Americanism was no mere badge or slogan. He was never the professional patrioteer. Our democracy, he urged, is in danger from within; its threat is a kind of "suicide." In addressing the Young Men's Lyceum at Springfield in 1838, he specified contemporary factors that caused him great distress: "the increasing disregard for law which pervades the country," the breakdown of that "strongest bulwark of any government"—namely, "the attachment of the people," and the tendency of the "best citizens" to become alienated from a government that permits abuses to exist.[5]

In Lincoln's attitude toward these matters of law and order one finds the kind of liberalism that is deeply thoughtful rather than superficially optimistic. He faced unpleasant facts. Speaking of mob rule he said that the process went on "from gamblers to Negroes, from Negroes to white citizens, and from these to strangers, till dead men were seen literally dangling from . . . trees upon every roadside."[6] The thought that men should be impatient of government disturbed him. Bad laws, he thought, ought to be repealed, but while on the books they "should be religiously observed."[7] To give up enforcement of laws because people resisted, disobeyed, or disregarded them he considered highly unfortunate.

He pleaded for eternal vigilance in this matter. "There is no grievance [he said] that is a fit object of redress by mob law." Government in former days had "many props"; in his day he feared that the fruits of government achievement, having been appropriated, were less appreciated. Democracy was an experiment. The very impulse to make the experiment succeed was a stay, a prop, and a chance for death-less distinction. The game having been caught and the crop harvested (at least in the attainment of independence), he hoped that the constant, day-by-day preservation of democratic standards would be as much of an object as their early establishment. To this end he said:

> Let reverence for the laws be breathed by every American mother to the lisping babe that prattles on her lap; let it be taught in schools, in seminaries, and in colleges; let it be written in primers, spelling-books, and in almanacs; let it be preached from the pulpit, proclaimed in legislative halls, and enforced in courts of justice. And, in short, let it become the political religion of the nation; and let the old and the young, the rich and the poor, the grave and the gay of all sexes and tongues and colors and condi-tions, sacrifice unceasingly upon its altars.[8]

In such warnings and pleadings there was sternness in Lincoln's tone. He did not burble about democracy. To describe him briefly, he could be called a tough-minded, liberal realist. He was, of course, a man of ideals. His leadership would not have been worth much otherwise. But it is in fact our liberals who have been the tough-minded men. It is only a misconception to suppose that liberals have been soft minded, nor is it true that they have been removed from practical reality. Some-times we call the wrong ones "realists." Foolish and uncritical acceptance of stereo-typed ideas or slogans is not unknown among "conservatives." Sometimes those who oppose liberal views, or who have appeased reactionaries, have fallen prey to argu-ments or blandishments which are shockingly unreal and flimsy.

VI

In the matter of Negro rights Lincoln's position must be viewed in relation to the background of his time. He opposed intermarriage of the races, resenting the very suggestion. Such intermarriage, however, was not an issue. It was only a bogey or scarecrow intended to mislead and becloud the less intelligent popular mind. Lin-coln was cautious as to political and social equality, though he vigorously objected when the Supreme Court issued its opinion in the *Dred Scott* case to the effect that a Negro, even though a citizen of a state, could not be a citizen of the United States. In the debate with Douglas (1858) he did not favor Negro voting, but that is not to say that he was opposing any actual movement to establish Negro suffrage; there was no such movement. It is more to the point to note that as the nation's leader he became increasingly liberal and that in the latter part of his presidency he took a more advanced position as to the franchise. Writing on March 13, 1864, to Michael

Hahn, governor of Federally occupied Louisiana, he asked "whether some of the colored people may not be let in—as, for instance, the very intelligent, and especially those who have fought gallantly in our ranks. They would probably help, in some trying time to come, to keep the jewel of liberty within the family of freedom."[1]

Often he praised the colored soldiers and emphasized their vitally important contribution to the Union cause. He showed friendliness to the Negro. He wanted him treated as a man. He confessed a sensitiveness on this subject. He could not bear to see Negroes sold at auction, nor strung together "like so many fish upon a trot-line." He argued: "If the Negro is a man, why then my ancient faith teaches me that 'all men are created equal,' and that there can be no moral right in connection with one man's making a slave of another." He added: ". . . no man is good enough to govern another man without that other's consent."[2]

The following passage, which seems to have been but slightly quoted, illustrates Lincoln's sympathy for human beings held in bondage:

> In those days [i.e., earlier days of the republic] our Declaration of Independence was held sacred by all, and thought to include all; but now, to aid in making the bondage of the Negro universal and eternal, it is assailed and sneered at and construed, and hawked at and torn, till, if its framers could rise from their graves, they could not at all recognize it. All the powers of earth seem rapidly combining against him. Mammon is after him, ambition follows, philosophy follows, and the theology of the day is fast joining the cry. They have him in his prison-house; they have searched his person, and left no prying instrument with him. One after another they have closed the heavy iron doors upon him; and now they have him, as it were, bolted in with a lock of a hundred keys, which can never be unlocked without the concurrence of every key—the keys in the hands of a hundred different men, and they scattered to a hundred different and distant places; and they stand musing as to what invention, in all the dominions of mind and matter, can be produced to make the impossibility of his escape more complete than it is.[3]

To make Lincoln out as a practical contender for full equality would be unhistorical, however strong might be the impulse of liberals so to represent him. Very few in his day, in any part of the country, were contenders for complete equality to be applied in their own localities. Even Kansas, famous for antislavery emphasis, proved in many of its laws and social attitudes to be an anti-Negro state. The Negro suffrage amendment did not come until five years after Lincoln's death; the full observance and implementing of that amendment has never come. There were things Lincoln could do and things he could not. There was, as he said, the "argument of necessity."[4] On moral grounds, he favored the ideal of equal rights. He believed that an ideal, though unrealized at the time, could point the way toward future reality. He would not deny the humanity of the Negro. He spoke eloquently of a "sense of justice and human sympathy continually telling you that the poor Negro has some natural right to himself." He spoke in stinging denunciation of "those who deny it and make mere merchandise of him."[5]

Racial bigotry did not control Lincoln's mind. Slavery was legal in his day, till by the hand of war and constitutional amendment it was abolished. Bad laws, he felt, ought to be observed till repealed. Despite many difficulties presented in a slave-holding nation, and in a Northern society that fell far short in interracial relations, he did what he could in his own day to elevate the status of the Negro, to present his case at the bar of humanity, and to urge his claim for sympathy and fair treatment. Lincoln was no Don Quixote. He had to deal in practical terms. Gradualism was essential in his method. He had elements of conservatism as well as liberalism. Steps to elevate the race could not all be taken at one jump. The country had far to go on that road; it still has far to go. No man of genuine feeling can contemplate without painful emotion the long story of the Negro's ordeal, nor deny to him the credit that attaches to his record as faithful servant and loyal soldier. It is in the Lincoln tradition to give the Negro his just place in American social history and to recognize his values in American folklore and culture. These values appear in a hundred varied forms, from strutting cake walk and hilarious minstrelsy to those deeply melodious spirituals through which, rather than through degrading self pity, the age-long memories of a submerged people find undying expression.

VII

Elsewhere the author has treated Lincoln and slavery, and that treatment will not be repeated here. Before the presidency his approach was quite different from that of the abolitionist. During the presidency the working of his policy was, or seemed, slow. It did not always seem like kingdom come. It was hedged in by circumstances, by the paramount urgency of the Union, by political factors, constitutional restrictions, congressional noncooperation, border state reluctance, regard for Southern property rights, the need for proper timing, military considerations, and attention to the realities of Southern home economy.[1] To some his emancipation proclamation had a ringing, messianic fervor; to others it seemed a terroristic invitation to a war of races (a mistaken concept); to still others it appeared utterly futile.

It is essential for the present purpose to note elements of Lincoln's liberalism in his attitude toward human bondage. He kept saying that slavery was an evil, however much its eradication might be impeded by the Constitution, by state rights, or by the existing state of society. His humane sympathy for the slave was combined with that readiness to understand Southern conditions which was ever his characteristic.[2] Though he confessed that he found no easy answer to the problem of doing away with slavery,[3] he looked forward to such an answer in the future and in the meantime he wanted to resist its spread. He wanted no slavery in the territories and he wanted Illinois kept free. Recalling that we once considered it "a self-evident truth" that all men are created equal, he deplored the degradation of the public conscience to the point where, having "grown fat," we called "the same maxim 'a self-evident lie'" and made the "Fourth of July . . . a great day—for burning fire-crackers."[4]

Frequently he showed that he did not want sectional strife because of slavery—that was not the intention of his "house divided" speech[5]—but with equal frequency he showed that in his concept slavery was morally wrong. Tolerant though he was, he wanted no apathetic indifference where moral wrong existed. Though not a hater of men, he said:

> This declared indifference . . . for the spread of slavery, I cannot but hate. I hate it because of the monstrous injustice of slavery itself. I hate it because it deprives our republican example of its just influence in the world; enables the enemies of free institutions with plausibility to taunt us as hypocrites; causes the real friends of freedom to doubt our sincerity; and especially because it forces so many good men among ourselves into an open war with the very fundamental principles of civil liberty, criticizing the Declaration of Independence, and insisting that there is no right principle of action but self-interest.[6]

In the same vein, in the year of his nomination for the presidency, he said: "We think slavery a great moral wrong, and while we do not claim the right to touch it where it exists, we wish to treat it as a wrong in the Territories, where our votes will reach it. We think that a respect for ourselves, a regard for future generations and for the God that made us, require that we put down this wrong where our votes will properly reach it. We think that species of labor an injury to free white men—in short, we think slavery a great moral, social, and political evil, tolerable only because, and so far as, its actual existence makes it necessary to tolerate it. . . ."[7]

If he envisaged "irrepressible conflict," it was not that he preached the need of war between North and South, but rather that ideas were in conflict. "Now these two ideas—the property idea that slavery is right and the idea that it is wrong—come into collision, and . . . produce that irrepressible conflict which Mr. Seward has been so roundly abused for mentioning." He added: "Now I don't want to be misunderstood. . . . I don't mean that we ought to attack it where it exists." If he saw a snake in the road he would seize the nearest stick and kill it; but if it were in bed with his children or his neighbor's children, he would be cautious. "If there was a bed newly made up, to which the children were to be taken, and it was proposed to take a batch of snakes and put them there with them, . . . no man would say there was a question how I ought to decide!"[8]

He deplored as fallacious the assumption that "'In the struggle between the white man and the Negro' . . . either the white man must enslave the Negro or the Negro must enslave the white." This sort of contention he regarded as a misleading catch phrase. "There is no such struggle [he said]. It is merely an ingenious falsehood to degrade and brutalize the Negro. . . . This good earth is plenty broad enough for white man and Negro both, and there is no need of either pushing the other off."[9]

In the phraseology of the Constitution he noted that references to slavery were "ambiguous, roundabout, and mystical"; never was the institution mentioned directly by the word "slavery" or "slave." Why didn't they use the word? "They expected and desired that the system would come to an end, and meant that when it did the Constitution should not show that there had ever been a slave in this good free country of ours."[10] Historically, the name of Lincoln is the one most prominently associated with the abolition of slavery in the United States. Contemporary limitations and legal complexities of his policy are not commonly understood in the popular mind, but it is with valid and well earned distinction that he remains the Emancipator.

VIII

No problem of modern civilization is more urgent than reorientation of outlook and of policy in the matter of war making. The pledges that have been made in establishing the United Nations, and the principles that have been implemented in the Nuremberg trial, have placed war makers in the category of criminals. In terms of international commitments as they now exist, there is no honorable way by which one nation, by its own unilateral action, may begin a war. By principles now solemnly declared there are only two conditions in which one of the United Nations can be honorably at war—by defense against attack, or by action envisaged by the United Nations charter. Such action could legitimately be taken only to check an aggressor. Perhaps the full implications of existing commitments are yet to be realized, but aggressive war, as shown at Nuremberg, is a recognized crime—indeed the highest of crimes.

For this reorientation, and for the revulsion toward war which it involves, one may rightly invoke the spirit and also the words of Lincoln. Nothing was more foreign to his nature than the character of the warlord. He dared to speak out against President Polk for the conduct of his administration at the beginning of the Mexican War. In his Mexican speech he said that "a nation should not, and the Almighty will not, be evaded." As to Polk he said: "he feels the blood of this war, like the blood of Abel, is crying to Heaven against him."

Though many historians would be less severe on Polk, these words of Lincoln may now be seen to have a timeless importance as a denunciation of war itself. It is in this sense that one may now read in this same speech Lincoln's stinging reference to "the exceeding brightness of military glory,—that attractive rainbow that rises in showers of blood—that serpent's eye that charms to destroy."[1] In the *Trent* affair, by reasonable international adjustment instead of warlike truculence, he produced tremendous international as well as American gain. Earlier in that year, 1861, in the July 4 message to Congress, he wrote eloquently that "ballots are the rightful and peaceful successors of bullets." He added, in a context which showed that he was thinking of a world-wide principle, that success in the appeal to ballots instead of bullets would "be a great lesson of peace: teaching men that what they cannot take by an election, neither can they take it by a war; teaching all the folly of being the beginners of a war."[2]

IX

Though primarily interested in popular rights on these shores, Lincoln showed a vigorous sympathy for democracy in other lands. He declared that when he saw a people borne down by tyranny he would do all in his power to raise the yoke. He showed both his lack of isolationism and his sympathy with movements for free institutions in Europe in connection with the Kossuth affair. Here was a question of liberalism abroad which was too hot for the American state department, but it was a subject on which Lincoln did not hesitate to express himself.

Louis Kossuth was a revolutionary leader in Hungary, a defiant opponent of the conservative Metternich, and a spearhead of the movement which culminated in the anti-Hapsburg declaration of Hungarian independence in April of 1849. In September of that year a meeting was held in Springfield, Illinois, to express sympathy for the cause of Hungarian freedom. Lincoln was the spokesman of a committee of four to voice the sentiments of the meeting. The resolutions which he reported extended to the revolting Hungarians "our highest admiration . . . our warmest sympathy . . . [and] our most ardent prayers for their speedy triumph and final success."[1] Success did not come. In that mid-century period liberal revolutionary aims were aflame in many parts of Europe, but they were quenched and reaction lived on. Had these aims succeeded as Lincoln hoped—had Austria-Hungary and the German states (to mention examples) been able to use and encourage, instead of ruthlessly suppressing, their democratic-minded elements—a colossal amount of future grief would have been avoided. Lincoln was no specialist on European matters, but there was more than localism and nationalism in the wide reach of his democratic thought.

In writing a eulogy a man may give a key to his own sentiments. If one is studying Lincoln's thought and faith he cannot ignore the elaborate eulogy of Henry Clay which he delivered in the Illinois state house in 1852. There is much of Lincoln's own ideal in the following statement:

> Mr. Clay's predominant sentiment, from first to last, was a deep devotion to the cause of human liberty—a strong sympathy for the oppressed everywhere, and an ardent wish for their elevation. With him this was a primary and all-controlling passion. Subsidiary to this was the conduct of his whole life. He loved his country partly because it was his own country, and mostly because it was a free country; . . . he burned with a zeal for its advancement . . . because he saw in such the advancement, prosperity, and glory of human liberty, human right, and human nature. He desired the prosperity of his countrymen . . . chiefly to show to the world that free men could be prosperous.

Mr. Clay's efforts in behalf of the South Americans, and afterward in behalf of the Greeks, in the times of their respective struggles for civil liberty, are among the finest on record, upon the noblest of all themes, and bear ample corroboration of what I have said was his ruling passion—a love of liberty and right, unselfishly, and for their own sakes.[2]

It is obvious that no man could have uttered those words with such a glow of enthusiasm and with such genuine appreciation unless he himself had been a man of liberal views. If in that period Lincoln had been conservatively apathetic toward human liberty in other lands, his eulogy of Henry Clay would either have omitted such a passage entirely or he would have presented it without enlisting his own ardor and with less emotional emphasis.

When Lincoln thought of self-government he thought not alone of America, but of the human race. In a passage of unusual literary embellishment he referred to "our political revolution of '76" as having "given us a degree of political freedom far exceeding that of any other nation of the earth." "In it," he said, "the world has found a solution of the long-mooted problem as to the capability of man to govern himself. In it was the germ which has vegetated, and still is to grow . . . into the universal liberty of mankind."[3] In speaking of temperance he hailed it as "a noble ally . . . to the cause of political freedom; with such an aid its march cannot fail to be on and on, till every son of earth shall drink in rich fruition the sorrow-quenching draughts of perfect liberty." He linked the factor of moral self-control with governmental self-rule. "How nobly distinguished that people who shall have planted and nurtured to maturity both the political and moral freedom of their species." In eulogizing Washington he spoke of the might of his name "in the cause of civil liberty, . . . [and] in moral reformation."[4] His bond of sympathy for John Bright, treated in another essay, shows that his view of democracy was international, not nationalistic; cosmopolitan, not provincial.

This world view as to democracy was so strongly underlined by Lincoln that it is fair to regard it as the pivotal factor in his political philosophy. At Gettysburg, with the ghastliness of the war before his eyes and with the butchery still in progress, he spoke not of immediate issues or war problems; nor did he show even a trace of bitterness. The Gettysburg occasion as he viewed it was a high challenge. To meet this challenge, nothing less would serve than a concept so fundamental that it offered a key to the age in which he lived, or rather to the whole sweep of American history in a setting of world history. It was the exaltation of the theme—democracy as a world factor—that gave serenity and timeless significance to this dedicatory vignette. In phrases that were unforgettable he paid tribute to the dead. Then he associated the deepest of patriotic emotions with his dominant political idea—that is, the imperative obligation to make democracy succeed and thus prove to other nations that the American experiment of government by the people is no failure.

Early in the war he said to John Hay that he considered that to be the central idea in the struggle—"the necessity that is upon us, of proving that popular government is not an absurdity."[5] Addressing Congress on July 4, 1861, he pointed out that the issue "embraces more than the fate of these United States." It was, he said, a question of concern "to the whole family of man."[6] With an eye to that larger meaning he wrote to Congress, December 1, 1862: ". . . we cannot escape history. We . . . will be remembered in spite of ourselves. . . . In giving freedom to the slave, we assure freedom to the free. . . . We shall nobly save or meanly lose the last, best hope of earth."[7]

X

Lincoln had rough sailing in his administration. He had a war to wage on a tremendous scale, with inadequate equipment and faulty organization. More than that, he had a mission to perform—not only to lead a nation to victory at arms, not only to save the Union cause, but to shape that cause in terms of adequate ideals and human values. He did not end with ingrowing thoughts of America. He looked to far horizons. Substantially to advance the cause of free government in the world was his fundamental goal.

In struggling toward this goal he had to endure inefficiency, factional bickering, repeated Union defeat, shameful greed and profiteering, defection behind the lines, and alarming division within his own party. There were times when the military machine, because of the inefficiency of central army control at Washington, almost broke down. His cabinet was an ill-assorted group of men who distrusted each other and were targets of constant attack by Congress or the newspapers.

We think of Lincoln rising to meet the fearful responsibilities of state, and that he did; but a typical picture of the time would show him trying unsuccessfully to dodge a horde of office seekers crowding through his door or waylaying him on the street. It is hard to see how he found time for his larger duties, considering the unending pressure of those who wanted a high judicial office, but who might be willing to serve their country as deputy collector or second assistant paymaster. Military men brought him not merely their problems, but also their petty jealousies. If he told Secretary Stanton to do a thing, it might be that the secretary would do the opposite, or perhaps nothing at all. Lincoln is said to have remarked that he had "not much influence with this administration,"[1] meaning his own. Whether or not he said it, the statement had significance. He had to endure the intrigues of cabinet members, and the interference of congressmen whose committee on the conduct of the war was a factor in Union failure and an instrument of inquisitorial abuse.[2]

In meeting these conditions Lincoln became a practitioner of government as a human art. He somehow held his cabinet together. He had a way with governors. In 1862 it might almost have been said that the governors "ganged up" on him. There was a conclave of state executives whose purpose was to criticize and perhaps to do something worse. Some of the papers referred to it as a conspiracy to force the president to resign. The governors met at Altoona, then in Washington; but they found it was Lincoln who held the trumps.[3] They came to assail him, but the interview was so managed that it left Lincoln in command. He had a way with senators. He did not have their cooperation, but he avoided an explosion. A group of Republican senators descended upon him in December 1862 breathing threats; but by shrewdness and tact he turned this senatorial upheaval into a triumph of presidential prestige.[4] He had a way with visiting delegations. He would listen, or perhaps he himself would do the talking, he would tell an amusing story, would bow them out, and act on his own larger judgment. In an age of confusion he kept a clear head. He took the broader view. He saw enduring values, was impatient of unenlightened politics, and refused to surrender to cynicism.

Undoubtedly an important element in Lincoln's statesmanship was mastery of language. Somewhere back in early self-training there was a study of the forms and substance of speech not for their own sake, not just to win applause, but because Lincoln had an object to accomplish, a message to convey, and he realized the effectiveness of the written and spoken word in reaching and controlling men's minds. With Lincoln, as with Woodrow Wilson, the art of language was a means to an end. In stating a law case, Lincoln had a knack of brushing away technicalities and getting at the core of the subject. Few men could match him in the prairie years as a stump speaker. The people delighted to hear him. Most of the speeches common in his day were rhetorical and florid after the manner of Sumner; they were one with the fashion plates which showed elaborately dressed women and grandiloquently attired men. But Lincoln's speech was not like the Godey fashion plate; it had little in common with Sumner's rhetoric. There was in his diction something suggestive of the King James version of the Bible, something also of Shakespeare, and much that was just Lincoln. What made him a master of words was fitness to the occasion, a readiness of epigram, a cogency of speech that served well in place of adornment, a sense as to how adornment itself should be used, and the ability to take the simplest words and give them the greatness of inspired dignity.

At his Second Inaugural he made no effort to review the events of his administration, but delivered a brief address which ranks among his greatest papers. He refused to blame the South for the war, and counseled his countrymen to judge not that we be not judged. "With malice toward none"; he said, "with charity for all; . . . let us strive on to finish the work we are in; to bind up the nation's wounds; . . . to do all which may achieve and cherish a just and lasting peace." In the cacophony of war the note he struck was that of conciliation, of friendliness, of peace and charity. He avoided the language of contemporary preachers, but in his life and utterance he gave sincere expression and devotion to the Christian faith.

He could turn a trick by a good humored story. Your self-important soul, or your strutting dictator, does not often smile. In Lincoln the priceless element of humor was an index to the shape and quality of his mind. To his overburdened spirit,—

amid strain and fatigue so overwhelming that, as he said, the remedy "seemed never to reach the tired spot"[5]—laughter was a saving blend of play, restorative relaxation, and mental hygiene. It supplied a sense of proportion. At times it was a refreshing pause. On a very solemn occasion in cabinet meeting when the Emancipation Proclamation was coming up, he got a big laugh out of Artemus Ward, much to the disgust of his humorless secretaries.[6] He liked Petroleum V. Nasby (David Locke). His humor was down to earth, yet in point and originality it was above the level of his time. His stories, verbal sallies, and quips of expression are a rich part of the American tradition. In treating Lincoln's laughter alongside his religion, Carl Sandburg shows that, in enjoying fun, he was no mere joker or buffoon. The man of backwoods pioneer origin must have courage, and humor is part of that courage. "This side of him [writes Sandburg] was momentous in one respect at least. It had brought him to folk masses as a reality, a living man. . . . Did he truly have something of the cartooned figure of Uncle Sam, benign, sagacious, practical, simple, at times not quite beyond taking a real laugh for himself and the country? Whatever the elements of this trait, it rested on American material, connected with an immense variety of American circumstances and incidents, and had become inevitably associated with Lincoln's name and personality."[7]

Lincoln's greatness arose from a combination of qualities in a balanced personality. One could never define his conduct as springing from mere automatic reaction. It came rather from informed study and mature reflection. Mere slogans and stereotypes did not impress him. He was a simple man—he was unpretentious in manner and straightforward in expression—but he was never naïve. He could be enthusiastic, but he was never extravagant. He combined humanitarianism with practical common sense. He attained a position of lofty eminence and moved among the great without making other men feel small. He was a sturdy individual; this, however, should be understood not as a denial of needful social cooperation, but rather in the Robert Burns sense of emphasis upon human worth. He could assert himself without becoming a dictator. He had ambition, but without selfishness. He had that largeness of soul that we call magnanimity. If a colleague, a subordinate, or a cabinet member were attacked, he would take the blame upon his own shoulders. Sometimes he would write a letter as an outlet for overwrought feeling, think it over, realize that it might wound the recipient, and then withhold it.

He encouraged the North without abusing the South. Though a war leader he wanted no perpetuation of war attitudes in peace time. He opposed the abuses of militarism. It is of present significance that in 1848 he had uttered a crushing denunciation of what would now be called "preventive war."[8] The "war mind" never possessed him. His main feeling toward the war was deep regret that the avoidable tragedy had happened, a sense of mystery as to the ways of Providence, a realization that the scourge was as much a punishment of the North as of the South. He wanted the war to end with the surrenders. As the men after Appomattox went back to their plowing, he wanted healing and restoration. Coarser men took the saddle and

Lincoln's plan of reconstruction was defeated, but Lincoln would have brought the South back if possible without bitterness and without treating Southerners as inferiors.

The Lincoln record is no mere success story of a railsplitter who became president, a prairie lawyer who reached world fame. One might wonder just how he became to the majority of his countrymen the embodiment of the American genius. Perhaps the inner source of his strength has not been fully plumbed. It might be hard to answer where and how he learned statecraft, but statesmen even yet will do well to take him as guide and mentor. In each new recurring crisis—in colossal wars that have shaken the world—men continue to carry the appeal to the spirit of Lincoln. Only in poetry does his ghost stalk at midnight, but his inspired words and the rugged vigor of his ideals seem today to have a greater vitality than during the vexed years of his presidency.

Equality: Commitment or Ideal

Willmoore Kendall

The idea is as old, of course, as that magical first sentence of the Gettysburg Address: "Four score and seven years ago our fathers brought forth on this continent a new nation, conceived in liberty, and"—but here we must begin to underline—*"dedicated to the proposition that all men are created equal."* Nay, older: Lincoln had used the idea, time and again, in his speeches on slavery (which both were and were not "antislavery," both were and were not "egalitarian" in any sense that, say, a present day liberal college professor would recognize as egalitarian); after Gettysburg, the idea rapidly acquired *sensu stricto,* biblical status, which is to say: Like many perplexing sentences in Holy Scripture, it now comes readily to the lips—all too readily, one is tempted to say—as a statement that (a) must be correct, somehow, or one wouldn't hear it so often from such highly authoritative quarters, and (b) need not, cannot, be acted upon, because we are so far from clear as to what they mean. The idea has, so far as I know, never been challenged, directly anyhow—partly, no doubt, for the reason I've just mentioned, namely: No one, over the main part of the long pull, has ever suggested that over, and above freeing the slaves on the one hand, and running free public schools on the other, we have been supposed actually to do anything about it. Today, however, with people making noises to the

*This article originally appeared in the *Intercollegiate Review,* Vol. 24, no. 2, Spring 1989, published by the Intercollegiate Studies Institute, Inc. Reprinted with permission from the Intercollegiate Studies Institute, Inc.

effect that we must do something about it, we can hardly avoid the obligation to take a second (or perhaps a first?) look at it.

Lincoln's statement, we notice at once, breaks down into four distinct—to use his own words—"propositions." First, the United States, as a nation, was born in 1776. Second, the United States was conceived in liberty. Third, the United States, in the very act of being born, was "dedicated" to an overriding purpose—that is, began its life with an understanding of its own meaning that is best expressed in a single supreme symbol. Fourth, that the proposition to which we are dedicated is "all men are created equal," and the supreme symbol that expresses our meaning as a nation is "equality." To which we may add a fifth—add because it is not actually present in Lincoln's formulation, but is, clearly, the conclusion to which the other four propositions are intended to lead. Fifth, that we Americans—in the absence of an express repudiation or modification of the "proposition" of the Declaration of Independence (I suppose no one would deny our capacity to repudiate or modify it)—are committed to equality; collectively committed to equality as a national goal, and, insofar as we are true Americans, individually committed to it as a good that we are called upon to promote even when, on personal grounds, we should prefer not to.

The four propositions are, I think, distinct and separable, in the sense that one of them might be valid and three of them invalid, two valid and two invalid, etc. Put otherwise: we do not need, in order to call one or another of them into question (as I am, evidently, about to do), to call them all into question; and perhaps I had best speak, first, of those of the four—or, if you like, five—that I not only do not call into question, but whole-heartedly adopt as part of my own political creed.

(a) The United States was, indeed, as a new nation—nor could the idea be more nobly expressed than it is in Lincoln's language—"conceived in liberty." So—ever since we Americans have been a nation and have sought to explain to ourselves our meaning as a nation—so, I say, we have always put it; so, I hope, we will continue to put it so, both to ourselves, and to the world. Our roots, as a nation, are struck deep in the soil of liberty, the freedom to govern ourselves, that we had lately wrested from the British, and the high aspiration to infuse—in the act of governing ourselves—the spirit and habits and philosophy of liberty into the minds and hearts of all Americans so soon as that may be done. Liberty—liberty in the peculiar American understanding of the word liberty, liberty that is to say and not, liberty, is of the very essence of American political tradition, and Lincoln did well to remind his, listeners, at Gettysburg, that that is true, and true in part because of the way in which, as a nation, we sprang into being, because of our origins. For it was certainly love of liberty, the determination to govern themselves, that impelled the thirteen colonies to rebel against Britain, and bring about the state of affairs in which the Founding Fathers, our Founding Fathers, could accomplish their great design. No one understands America, and the meaning of America, unless he understands that it was conceived in liberty—nay, born in liberty, nurtured in liberty, and grown to fullness and maturity in liberty. Had Lincoln let it go at that, I should not be taking issue with the first sentence of the Gettysburg address.

(b) The American nation was indeed, in the act of being born, dedicated to an overriding purpose, did indeed declare its subordination to a supreme symbol; and for that is Lincoln's tacit premise—clarity as to the nature of that overriding purpose, penetration of the meaning of that supreme symbol, should indeed be our primary concern, both collectively and individually. If that was true in Lincoln's day, as it certainly was, it is doubly true in our day, when thanks, I think, in large part to Lincoln himself—we not only do not possess such clarity and penetration, but make a public display of our confusion both as to our overriding purpose and as to the meaning of our supreme symbol. For let us not deceive ourselves about that: Today we do make, and make constantly, a public display of our confusion: as to who—what kind of people—we actually are, of our uncertainty as to the task that we have come into history to perform. We hesitate over a great national decision as, for example, we hesitate today in Vietnam? Our hesitation and bumbling is a confession, a confession to ourselves and to the world, that we have lost our sense of identity, and lost it—I borrow the phrase from Courtney Murray—in the way the schizophrenic has lost his sense of identity, so that we have not one but two answers to the question: Who—what manner of being—are you? We have deeply divided counsels over a choice between alternatives bearing deeply upon our destiny as a people, as to the kind of society we are to become. Our counsels are deeply divided—as when, these days, are they not—because, again like the schizophrenic, we cannot answer the posterior question "what shall we do about this?" because there is conflict within us over the prior question (which, once more like the schizophrenic, we are reluctant to haul out into the open), "what are we to do in general?" And again I can say: Had that been the point Lincoln went to Gettysburg to make, I should not be picking a quarrel with him about that magic first sentence; for that too is a major tenet in my own political creed. We do have an overriding purpose, and cannot too often remind ourselves what it is.

So, finally, with the fifth of our five points, the point that follows logically from the other four, namely: That we Americans are committed, collectively and individually, to the overriding purpose that we adopted, and proclaimed to the world, at the moment of our founding; that, if I may put it so, we are mortgaged, collectively and individually, to that overriding purpose; that the obligation to keep up the payments on the relevant obligation runs so to speak, with the land we inhabit; that we inherit that obligation along with our citizenship, our way of life, and the institutions devised for us by our Founding Fathers; and that nothing short of a solemn act of national deliberation—an act of deliberation no less solemn, no less national, than that by which we first became a nation and first embraced our overriding purpose can release us from that obligation (Lincoln, I am saying, certainly believed something very like all that, and I believe it too). There are, as I am aware, great difficulties here—difficulties that, as the students of political theory well know, have

at all times dogged the steps of political philosophers who grounded political obligation, in whole or in part, in consent; and we should, I think, pause for a moment
and remind ourselves what the main difficulty, as old as Locke, actually is: The men
of generation "A"—the generation, say of the American Founding Fathers—
establish a political society, they pose, and answer for themselves, the important
questions (what kind of political society is it to be? How is it to be governed?). They
set the new political society in motion with the consent—most probably, as in our
own case, with the enthusiastic approval—of the men of that generation; and the
latter, in the very act of giving their consent and approval, commit themselves to
that kind of political society, that form of government, that definition of the business which, as a society, they are in. They have, in giving their consent, promised to
obey the laws of the society as, in Rousseau's phrase, commands that they give to
themselves; they have, by a free act of their own wills, embraced as their very own,
the principles upon which, tacitly or explicitly, the society is founded: they have, in
a word, so situated themselves that if, on some later day, one of them is tempted to
say "Look, all this is proving more costly than I had expected it to," or "Look, you
are asking me to go along with things that, in my view, contravene the principles
we have embraced"—if on some later day it comes to that, his fellows can turn to
him and say, say, moreover, with good conscience, "Ah! But you promised—in the
very act of giving your consent you promised—and we call upon you now to keep
your promise, that is, not begrudge the sacrifice that our kind of society, with this
form of government and this purpose, or set of purposes, now demands of you." He
is, if I may put it so, stuck with that earlier act of consent; and if, subsequently, he
refuses to fulfill the relevant obligation, and his fellow citizens—as fellow citizens
are wont to do—take it out of his hide for his refusal, he has no one to blame but
himself. (They are, as Rousseau put it, forcing him to be free; nor, I think, has
America ever viewed the question differently from Rousseau.) The difficulties arise
when we put the question not about the generation of the Founding Fathers, but
about subsequent generations, not about the individual to the principles to which it
was dedicated, who gave his consent to the Founding but about that individual's
son, and grandson, and great-great-grandson, down to the Vietnik at Berkeley who,
at the margin, will ask: Just when and where did I give my consent—to anything;
and if I have not given it, how can anyone say that I am obligated? I will not be
ruled by the dead hand of the past. Now: the consent philosophers, beginning with
Locke and including the Framers of the Philadelphia Constitution, have ended up
answering that question as follows: By remaining within the territorial limits of
America, by accepting the protection of its government, by exercising the rights our
legal system confers upon you and enjoying the benefits of the duties it imposes
upon others, you have given your consent, as your forefathers gave their consent—in
your case, to be sure, tacitly not explicitly, but in a manner that makes it not less
binding upon you than it was upon them; you, too, are stuck with it. Nothing of
the kind, replies the Vietnik: What you call my tacit consent, which you claim I

give by mere physical presence upon American territory, has in fact been forced out of me; I have had no choice but to give it. Ah, replies the philosopher of consent (who knows that Locke's answer is not wholly convincing, and has, therefore, modified and extended it in a couple of ways)—Ah!, but you did have a choice. Ours, like other free countries, leaves people free to migrate, to shake our dust off their feet, any time they like; you know that as well as a grown person. Yet we see no sign of your opting for Australia, where you can herd sheep, or for Central America, where you can grow cotton; your decision—and surely it was yours, not anybody else's—to remain amongst us reenacted the gesture of the men of the Founding Fathers' generation, and we can interpret it only as a tacit acceptance, on your part, of the same commitments that oblige the rest of us. More—so the Framers of the Constitution of the United States to the Vietniks, who may well deny that those commitments oblige even the "rest of us"—more: you must not forget Article V of our Constitution, which leaves us the American people free, as time goes on, to repudiate or revise the commitments we inherit from the past; in the act of not revising the commitments handed down to us by the generation of the Founding Fathers, we have tacitly made them our own; but, if you like, acquiescing in them, we have imposed them on ourselves. More still: we maintain, in these matters, a very considerable degree of freedom of speech—a discussion process, which so to speak invites individual Americans like yourself, who seek revision of our traditional commitments, to get out and persuade other Americans that those commitments should be set aside; you have either accepted that invitation, and failed to win over any significant number of your fellow Americans to your point of view (in which case, (a) their acquiescence, as we have just noted, expresses their tacit acceptance of the traditional commitments, and (b) your very exercise of your right to participate in the discussion process obligates you to accept, from moment to moment, the verdicts at which it arrives) or you have not accepted the invitation, not attempted to win others over to your point of view, in which case, again, you have no business taking exception to the verdict by pretending that no commitment exists. You, personally, nevertheless repudiate the commitment? Well—so the generality of Americans, as I understand them, to the Vietnik—that does indeed create a difficult situation, but one that we see only one way to handle; either you mean that you do in fact wish to emigrate, and live amongst us no longer, in which case you will probably find us reasonable enough; or you don't mean that you wish to emigrate, in which case we shall treat you, and with good conscience believe us, as if your commitments were the same as ours, and will take it out of your hide if you try to behave as if they were not. (We will, for instance, march you off to the war in Vietnam, regardless of your personal opinion as to whether our commitments as a nation warrant our presence in Vietnam, or, if you prefer, we will march you off to jail.)

Let us, at this point, pause to take our bearings: With two of the four explicit propositions set forth in the first sentence of the Gettysburg Address—the United States was conceived in liberty, the United States, in the fact of being born, was dedicated to an overriding purpose—I am in fullest agreement. So too with that fifth proposition, not explicit in the Gettysburg Address but "there" nevertheless as a conclusion intended to flow from the explicit four: The commitment involved in our dedication to an overriding purpose is, so to speak, hereditary. Each generation of Americans hands the commitments along, if I may put it so, to the next generation, which can repudiate or modify it only by the same kind of solemn act—but let me, as I repeat that phrase "solemn act," now emphasize it in a way that I have not done before—by the same kind of solemn act by which the commitment became our commitment to begin with; in the absence of such a solemn act, the commitment, lying as it does at the heart of our political tradition, runs with the American land, as does the obligation, an obligation that is simultaneously collective and individual, to do something about the commitment, to forward the overriding purpose, to make sacrifices for it and, when that becomes necessary, to die for it. The alternative—as Lincoln appears to have seen it—is to say that the meaning of America is that it has no meaning, that those who have shed blood in our wars, or given unselfishly of their time and energies in order to be about the nation's business, shall indeed have done so "in vain." So far, I say, with Lincoln and the Gettysburg Address; but not, I hasten to add, one step further; for the remaining two of our four propositions are, from the standpoint of the American political tradition, heretical, and the moment is long overdue for exposing them as what they are, namely, heresies and, worse still, heresies decked out in precisely the kind of plausible and apparently innocuous rhetoric that enables heresies to pass themselves off as restatements of the truths that they distort, and caricature, and so degrade and deny.

Let us look first at Heresy Number One: "Four score and seven years ago our fathers brought forth on this continent a new nation. . . ." Now: Lincoln speaks in 1863; four score and seven years ago translates from biblical language into plain English into the number eighty-seven. Subtract eighty-seven from 1863—we do not know how many of the audience at Gettysburg could do simple arithmetic in their heads, but we may be sure Lincoln could—subtract eighty-seven from 1863 and what you get, of course, is 1776, that is, the date of the Declaration of Independence, and what you end up with is the proposition: The Founding Fathers did their work in the year 1776; the "new nation" the United States of America was established through the writing and signing of the Declaration of Independence—to which, accordingly, we must look if we would understand the origins and thus the meaning of our political experience as a single people, organized for action in history and capable of defining its appointed role in history, and—for we must, with heads appropriately bowed, follow the logic where it leads us—the Declaration of Independence suddenly acquires (and remember: we do not use this term lightly, we Americans) Constitutional status suddenly becomes a document—the document—to which we properly turn in order to learn what our commitments are. That, if I may put it so without seeming flippant, is what the Man says.

Now, let me not compound Lincoln's acts of heresy with, on my own part, an act of impiety: July 4, 1776 is a sacred moment in the history of the English-speaking people on this side of the Atlantic; let us celebrate it, in the future as in the past, with firecrackers, oratory, and libations. It is, moreover, a sacred moment because it is the day on which the Declaration of Independence was signed; let us continue, in the future as in the past, to quote from the Declaration of Independence, to publish it in our anthologies—or even, though few of us have ever done that, to sit down now and then and actually read it, if only to find out what it says. More: let us not hesitate, if and when that becomes necessary for our self-understanding as a people, to seize upon a delicate and well-threaded needle to embroider it, it and the events surrounding it, with a bit of myth, since nothing is more beneficent in the life of a nation than the myths that drive home the truths and aspirations that it embodies. But that, as a moment's reflection will convince you, is not what Lincoln did in that opening phrase at Gettysburg; what he did, rather, was to falsify the facts of history, and to do so in a way that precisely confuses our self-understanding as a people. The facts, as it happens, are extremely simple and, moreover, well-known to all of us save as we fall under the spell of Lincoln's rhetoric. The Declaration of Independence, as signed at Philadelphia, declared the independence of "the thirteen United States of America"—the independence not of a nation but of a baker's dozen of new sovereignties; "united" to be sure, but not as Oxfordshire and Lincolnshire, or even England and Wales were united, but united rather in a loose confederation that each of the thirteen states was free, and clearly understood to be free, to go along with or not to go along with. (Tom Paine, to be sure, will soon initiate, in *The Crisis*, the falsification that Lincoln will attempt to nail down, once and for all, at Gettysburg, by speaking of the Confederation as if it were a nation; nor is it necessary to my position to deny either (a) that there were men present at Philadelphia who were already thinking in national, not confederational terms, or (b) that the language of the Declaration includes, here and there, a phrase intended to give those men hope and encouragement, or (c) that the Declaration was "conceived in liberty," which indeed it was.) The Declaration was, in short, just what its plain language shows it to be, namely: a notice served on the government of Great Britain that thirteen of the English colonies were dissolving the political bonds that had hitherto connected them with Great Britain, that, as I put it a moment ago, they—not it, but they— were henceforth going to govern themselves, and not be governed, or rather misgoverned, from faraway London. The Declaration is not only a Constitution, that is, a solemn act by which a people, having identified itself as a single people, constitutes itself as a nation; it does not, even by remote implication, pretend to be a Constitution. What it does, if I may repeat myself once again, is to bring into being the state of affairs in which, eleven long years later, our Founding Fathers were to initiate the series of steps by which we were to bring ourselves forth—not, if you please, be brought forth—as a nation. To ask or claim more than that for it is, I contend, an act of political heresy, compounded by an act of impiety toward the nation's true Founding Fathers, who were the men who wrote, and submitted for ratification by the American people, the Philadelphia Constitution. The Gettysburg Address should begin with the words: "Three score and sixteen years ago. . . ."(Nobody, incidentally, knew that better than the Lincoln of the "House Divided," who had spoken repeatedly of the need—mark the words—the need, there in the mid-nineteenth century, for a "new act of founding" which would transcend the work of the actual Founding Fathers and return the nation to its first principles [that is, the principles Lincoln sees in the Declaration]. For Lincoln, that is to say, the Founding Fathers were the heretics, responsible, in Eric Voegelin's phrase, for a derailment of the American experience. Nor does Lincoln leave us in any doubt as to the identity of the Founding Father of the "new act of Founding.")

So much for the first of the two Lincoln propositions with which I am taking issue; and, happily (since my time grows short) we have, in disposing of it, largely disposed of the second one: "[The] new nation . . . [was] dedicated to the proposition that all men are created equal." Here we can rely not primarily on a simple appeal to history but a simple appeal to logic. If the Declaration of Independence did not bring forth a new nation, as it certainly did not, if it was not a solemn act which a single people constituted itself an agent or action in history, then we cannot tear from the Declaration—that is, tear from its proper context—a single proposition, and do with it what Lincoln tries to do with the words "all men are created equal"; and if we cannot, then the whole case for our commitment to equality as a national goal crashes to the ground. We have no such commitment (unless—I do not exclude the possibility—we have acquired it at some later date); we have, collectively and individually, no obligation to promote the overriding purpose; the whole business is a further Lincolnian heresy, accompanied by a further Lincolnian act of impiety toward the Founding Fathers. The relevant considerations, over and above those I have mentioned, would appear to be these:

First, even if the Declaration of Independence did put itself forward as a claimant for Constitutional status, even if it did claim the kind of "rank" that would make of it a proper place to look for our national commitments, we should be obliged (however reluctantly some of us) to refuse that claim—and for this reason: It is not a "solemn act" in the sense I have intended where, in the foregoing, I have used that phrase to describe the kind of act by which we in America acquire, or repudiate, or modify, a commitment, or an overriding purpose, or a supreme symbol. Such a solemn act must, as *The Federalist* puts the point so well, be an expression of the deliberate—deliberate, mind you—the deliberate sense of the American people; and we the American people worked out, in our very infancy as a people, the ground rules for recognizing an expression of the deliberate sense of the American people on matters of major import. Such an expression begins with—as we should expect—deliberation, by one or more duly-accredited representatives. More: just as Newton, according to the old story, when he said "Scat" to his cats, meant "Scat," so we in America, when we say "deliberation," mean—deliberation, that is, cool, crisp, rational, sustained discussion of the alternative courses of action apparently open to us, of the probable consequences of our adopting this course of action instead of that one, of the arguments pro and con. The more important the problem—so the works of our political tradition would seem to suggest—the longer that deliberation is likely to take, and the more the discussion is likely to take place on the floor of the Assembly or Assemblies, not in committees. The Assembly, moreover, does not deem itself, where the matter in hand is a grave matter, as authorized, in and of itself, to perform the entire solemn act; rather it submits its handiwork to us the people for what, since Philadelphia, we have called "ratification" by our local, that is, state representatives. Strictly speaking, therefore—since in its absence the proposal lapses—we the people, and only we the people, perform the solemn acts by which we impose lasting commitments upon ourselves. Now: the contrast, on this showing, between the Declaration of Independence and the Bill of Rights, could not be more obvious. Far from being the work of a representative assembly, the Declaration is the work (and who is more eager to remind us of that than the Declaration's glorifiers?) not merely of a committee, but of a committee that, largely, turned its responsibilities over to a single committee member—on the (for me at least) preposterous grounds that he was the most facile writer of the bunch; the Assembly itself, as the Declaration's chief glorifiers proudly boast, had very little to do with it. The whole affair was hasty—witness the conspicuous solecism, the like of which is to be found in no other great American document, in the first paragraph, a matter of hours not, as at Philadelphia, weeks; and such discussion as occurred was not, as at Philadelphia, over matters of high principle, but over tiny questions of detail. In a word: the Declaration's credentials as a solemn act, an expression of the deliberate sense of the American people, leave much to be desired, and far too much to support the claim that it is a national commitment.

Secondly, even if the Declaration's credentials as an act of deliberation were unexceptionable—even if it had been ratified by the American people as the act by which it constituted itself as a nation—even if it possessed therefore, the Constitutional *status sensu stricto* that Lincoln attributes to it at Gettysburg—even if it were a proper place to look for our commitments as a nation—I say that Lincoln is unwarranted in reading out of it a commitment to equality as a national goal or purpose, to say nothing of an overriding national purpose. Put otherwise: we have only to look at the actual words the Declaration uses in order to see that the only way you can read such a commitment out of it is by first reading it into it—which, I contend, is just what Lincoln did. "We" it says in point of fact, "hold these truths to be self-evident, that all men are created equal, that they are endowed by their Creator with certain unalienable Rights, that among these are Life, Liberty, and the Pursuit of happiness." The proposition "all men are created equal" is—I shan't burden you with further quotation—if we look closely, only one of five propositions that the Declaration's Framers list as a sort of creed, a corpus of basic beliefs, that the people of America put forward as their creed, their corpus of basic beliefs (the less said about those words "self-evident," let me say in passing, the better; as I hope to show in another place the "self-evident" had best be reserved for the fact that the tenets of the creed—perhaps because of the haste with which it was pieced together—are in part self-contradictory, or at least cannot keep house together). None of them is properly speaking what I should call an explicit declaration of purpose, and if purposes are what we are looking for we shall have to settle for an implied purpose, or determination if you like, to maintain, in the new state of affairs that the Declaration brings into being, governments that will (a) secure men's inalienable rights, and (b) derive their powers from the consent of the governed. Finally, the word "dedicated" is conspicuously absent, and unless you want to make something of the fact that it is the first tenet of the creed, not the second or third or fourth or fifth, the proposition "all men are created equal" is given no claim to priority over the other four. Here, just as with "new nation," Lincoln is playing games—that is, taking unwarranted liberties with the text he professes to be construing.

Thirdly—but we must add now to our "even ifs"—even if the Declaration possessed Constitutional status, even if it began with a recitation of goals and purposes, even if we let Lincoln father off onto the Declaration his "dedicated to the proposition that" we should still have to raise the following pretty urgent points:

(a) The proposition "all men are created equal" is so ambiguous as to merit classification as, for all practical purposes, meaningless and therefore useless—especially if, in reading it, we take into account the time at which it was written. The phrase "all men," to begin with, is by no means so simple and unambiguous as (for reasons too complicated to go into on this occasion) it is likely to seem to the unsuspecting undergraduate in 1967. The Declaration's Framers might have written, but chose not to write, "each man is created equal to every other man," and they might have added, but did not add, "and therefore ought to be treated, for governmental purposes, as the equal of every other man." Much has been made, as some of you know, even or perhaps especially by the glorifiers of the Declaration, of the fact that the assembly that approved the Declaration suppressed the passionate denunciation of slavery that Jefferson wrote into the original draft (how could they, critics ask, have been so "inconsistent," or, variously, how could they have been so "hypocritical"—is it not obvious that if you believe that "all men are created equal" you have got to denounce slavery?). Either the one, or the other: they were poor logicians, or they were hypocrites, that is, vicious men paying the vicious man's normal tribute to virtue. Yet, curiously, very little has been made of the fact—one doesn't need to be particularly nimble intellectually to recognize its relevance—that the Declaration of Independence not only does not denounce slavery, it does not denounce the inferior status of women either, for all that it seems obvious to us that if all men are created equal all women are created equal, too. You will, of course, see my point even before I get around to making it; even the Levellers of Cromwell's armies, the truly radical egalitarians, who like the Declaration made free with the expression "all men" and "every man" and with claims for equal rights had left out women (as, also, "servants" and those who had fought against Cromwell) the Levellers, indeed, used as a variant for "all men" the expression "every he" that is in England. There is, in other words, a third possible explanation for the suppression of Jefferson's denunciation of slavery, namely, that the men who approved the Declaration did not mean by "all men" what their critics choose to mean by "all men," but rather, like the Levellers, something more like "all men that count." The claim for equal political rights put forward by the Virginia Declaration, on the eve of the Declaration of Independence, had been confined to those who had demonstrated their permanent attachment to the Commonwealth—which would make them guilty neither of inconsistency, nor of hypocrisy, but simply (a) of using language differently from their intellectual betters, that is, ourselves, and (b) of not entertaining political opinions congruent with those of members of Americans for Democratic Action. There are, I say then, difficulties about "all men." But there are also difficulties about the words "are created equal. " Do they indeed mean that "all men," or "all men who count" ought to be created equally? Do they mean merely—for that is a real possibility—that "all men" or "all men who count" are created equal in the sight of God? Do they mean merely that "all men" or "all men who count" are treated with an equal right to justice? It is, I fear, anybody's guess, for no answer is to be found in the text of the Declaration of Independence. And so we come back to the main point: no proposition that comes so near to being meaningless can possibly do service as an overriding national purpose.

Fourthly, even if we withdraw the objection that the proposition to which we are allegedly "dedicated" is meaningless—keeping, meantime, all our other "even ifs" there remains this point that we have heard curiously little about from our egalitarian political scientists and historians. The Founding Fathers at Philadelphia, who did deliberate, and did produce a document in which we the American people do constitute ourselves a nation, and did dedicate us to an overriding purpose, and did submit their handiwork for ratification by *us* the American people, certainly had in front of them the Declaration of Independence, certainly since the war that had made possible the steps they were about to take had been fought under the Declaration of Independence—certainly I say had at some point to face the question "What are we going to do about the Declaration of Independence?" and seem to have decided—well, two possibilities: either first to ignore it (to make no reference to it or repeat any of its language), or, second, to, if I dare say it, repudiate it—by forestalling any appeal back to it, and to its credo, of the kind that Lincoln was to make in the mid-nineteenth century. "We the people of the United States," they write, so bringing forth a new nation, "do ordain and establish this constitution"—so the nation is constituted, organized, as an agent for action upon the stage of history (I vary the order, but without infidelity to the text)—"in order to"—and so we the American people adopt, by our own free act, an overriding purpose, a supreme symbol, a commitment that is truly ours unless and until we repudiate or modify it "in order to form a more perfect Union, establish justice, ensure domestic tranquility, provide for the common defense, promote the general welfare, and secure the blessings of liberty to ourselves and our posterity." Union, justice, domestic tranquility, the common defense, the blessings of liberty. Never mind that the overriding purpose is a six-fold purpose—nations that get it into their heads that there is one good, other than salvation, that merits absolute priority over all other goods, are sure to come to a bad end—as, happily, we have not. (Well, not yet, anyhow.) Never mind, either, that the six-fold purpose is pretty obviously cribbed from medieval Catholic political philosophy—there are worse wells to carry your jugs to (for example: the John Locke well that the Framers of the Declaration carried their jug to). In short: I find myself unable to read the Preamble of the Constitution (which we have never repudiated, never revised) as other than an express repudiation of the tenet of the Declaration's creed that might seem to commit us somehow to equality.

And I conclude: The Declaration of Independence does not commit us to equality as a national goal—for more reasons than you can shake a stick at.

ॐ

Equality as a Conservative Principle

Harry V. Jaffa

> So whatever you wish that men would do to you, do so to them; for this is the law and the prophets.
>
> —Jesus

> As I would not be a *slave*, so I would not be a master. This expresses my idea of democracy. Whatever differs from this, to the extent of the difference, is no democracy.
>
> —Abraham Lincoln

I.

THAT CONSERVATISM should search for its meaning implies of course that Conservatism does not have the meaning for which it is searching. This might appear paradoxical, since a Conservative is supposed to have something definite to conserve.

*This article originally appeared in Harry V. Jaffa, *How to Think About the American Revolution* (Durham, NC: Carolina Academic Press, 1978). Reprinted with permission from the Claremont Review of Books.

For a differing view of the issues raised by Professor Jaffa, see John A. Murley, "On the 'Calhounism' of Willmoore Kendall," in *Willmoore Kendall: Maverick of American Conservatives*, eds. John A. Murley and John E. Alvis (Lanham, MD: Lexington Books, 2002).

Unfriendly critics sometimes suggest that what we Conservatives conserve, or wish to conserve, is money. But since many of us, like Socrates, live in thousand-fold poverty, this is manifestly untrue. Yet our plight might be said to resemble that of a man with a great hoard of gold or diamonds. Suppose such a man suddenly awoke to find that his treasure was no longer precious, and that it held no more meaning for the rest of the world than sand or pebbles. How strange the world would look to that man! How strange that man would look to the world, vainly clinging to his pile of rubbish.

In today's political vocabulary, Conservatism is contrasted with Liberalism and Radicalism. In this strange world, however, I cannot imagine Liberalism or Radicalism searching for meaning. Liberalism and Radicalism are confident of their meaning, and the world is confident of their confidence. Yet once upon a time, a Liberal was thought to be more diffident. He was someone who recognized the fallibility of human reason and its susceptibility to the power of the passions. He tended therefore to be tolerant of human differences. A liberal regime was one in which such differences were in a sense institutionalized. James Madison's extended republic embracing a multiplicity of factions, in which no faction might become a majority or impose its will upon a majority, is the classic instance in the modern world of such a regime. But the New Liberal is committed to policies which tend not to recognize the propriety of differences. Consider the rigidity of such slogans as "one man, one vote," "racial balance," "affirmative action," "guaranteed income," "war on poverty," "generation of peace." All these imply a degree of certainty as to what is beneficial, which makes those who doubt appear to be obscurantists or obstructionists, standing in the way of welfare either out of stupidity or out of a vested interest in ill fare.

The only significant differences I can see between today's Liberals and today's Radicals concern means rather than ends. How often during the "troubles" of the late 1960s did we hear the Liberals deplore the Radicals' violence, telling them that they should "work within the system"? How often did we hear these same Liberals praise the Radicals for their "idealism," asking only that they learn patience? But the Radicals made a great deal more sense. If their ideals were so praiseworthy, then a system which obstructed their fulfillment was blameworthy. And why work within a blameworthy system for praiseworthy ends?

Liberalism and Radicalism both reject the wisdom of the past as enshrined in the institutions of the past, or in the morality of the past. They deny legitimacy to laws, governments, or ways of life which accept the ancient evils of mankind, such as poverty, inequality, and war, as necessary—and therefore as permanent—attributes of the human condition. Political excellence can no longer be measured by the degree to which it ameliorates such evils. The only acceptable goal is their abolition. Liberalism and Radicalism look forward to a state of things in which the means of life, and of the good life, are available to all. They must be available in such a way that the full development of each individual—which is how the good life is defined—is not merely compatible with, but is necessary to, the full development of all. Competition between individuals, classes, races, and nations must come to an end. Competition itself is seen as the root of the evils mankind must escape. The good society must be characterized only by cooperation and harmony. The Old Liberalism saw life as a race, in which justice demanded for everyone only a fair or equal chance in the competition. But the New Liberalism sees the race itself as wrong. In every race there can be but one winner, and there must be many losers. Thus the Old Liberalism preserved the inequality of the Few over and against the Many. It demanded the removal of artificial or merely conventional inequalities. But it recognized and demanded the fullest scope for natural inequalities. But the New Liberalism denies natural no less than conventional inequalities. In the Heaven of the New Liberalism, as in that of the Old Theology, all will be rewarded equally. The achievement of the good society is itself the only victory. But this victory is not to be one of man over man, but of mankind over the scourges of mankind. No one in it will taste the bitterness of defeat. No one need say, "I am a loser, but I have no right to complain. I had a fair chance." The joys of victory will belong to all. Unlike the treasures of the past, the goods of the future will be possessed by all. They will not be diminished or divided by being common. On the contrary, they will for that very reason increase and intensify. No one will be a miser—or a Conservative.

I have intimated that what is today called Conservatism—the New Conservatism—may in fact be the Old Liberalism. Indeed, it may be the Old Radicalism as well. Leo Strauss used to delight in pointing out that the most conservative or even reactionary organization in the United States was called the Daughters of the American Revolution. Certainly, if American Conservatism has any core of consistency and purpose, it is derived from the American Founding. The uncertainty as to the meaning of American Conservatism is, as we shall see, an uncertainty as to the meaning of the American Founding. But this uncertainty does not arise from any doubt as to the status of the Revolution. So far as I know, there has never been any Benedict Arnold Society of American Patriotism. Nor do American Conservatives meet, either openly or secretly, to toast "the King (or Queen) across the water." The status of feudalism and monarchy are for American Conservatives exactly what they are for American Liberals or Radicals. Perhaps the best description of the ancien régime from the American point of view is still that of Mark Twain in *A Connecticut Yankee in King Arthur's Court*.

American Conservatism is then rooted in a Founding which is, in turn, rooted in revolution. Moreover, the American Revolution represented the most radical break with tradition—with the tradition of Europe's feudal past—that the world had seen. It is true that the American revolutionaries saw some precedent for their actions in the Whig Revolution of 1689. But that revolution at least maintained the fiction of a continued and continuous legality. The British Constitution that resulted from the earlier revolution may have had some republican elements. But the American constitutions—state and federal—that resulted from the later revolution had *no* monarchical or aristocratic elements. They were not merely radically republican, but were radically republican in a democratic sense.[1] The sovereignty of the people has never been challenged within the American regime, by Conservatives any more than by Liberals or Radicals.

The regime of the Founders was wholly devoted to what they understood as civil and religious liberty and was in that sense a liberal regime. But the Founders understood themselves to be revolutionaries, and to celebrate the American Founding is therefore to celebrate revolution. However mild or moderate the American Revolution may now appear, as compared with subsequent revolutions in France, Russia, China, Cuba, or elsewhere, it nonetheless embodied the greatest attempt at innovation that human history had recorded. It remains the most radical attempt to establish a regime of liberty that the world has yet seen.

2.

What were the principles of the American Revolution? What are the roots of the American Founding? One would think that after nearly two hundred years this question could be easily answered. Never did men take more pains to justify what they were doing at every step of the way than did the patriots of the Revolution. Never was the fashioning of a plan of government better documented than that hammered out in Philadelphia in the summer of 1787. Never was such a plan more fully debated before adoption than that which came before the several ratifying conventions. Never was an actual regime, as distinct from a hypothetical one, so enshrined in theoretical reasoning as was the constitution of 1787 in the *Federalist Papers*. And yet the matter is unresolved.

Our perplexity that this should be so is less surprising when we reflect that the course of American history for more than "four score and seven years" was one of deep-seated controversy, culminating in one of the bitterest wars of modern times. Until the resort to arms, these conflicts almost always took the form of debates as to the meaning of the Founding. And the Founding documents, and their principal glosses, were invariably cited on both sides in these debates. In more respects than one, American history and Jewish history resembled each other. Mid-century British liberals, like their American counterparts, were also divided. In 1861 Lord Acton wrote an essay entitled "Political Causes of the American Revolution,"[2] in which he expressed no doubt that the Confederacy was fighting for the same principles of independence for which Washington had fought. But Lord Acton's countryman, John Stuart Mill, in another essay written shortly afterward,[3] was just as sure that Lincoln's government was fighting to preserve these same principles. That the contestants appealed to the same political dogmas—even as they read the same Bible and prayed to the same God—only intensified the struggle. As sectarians of the same faith, they fought each other as only those fight who see their enemies as heretics.

American Conservatism today is still divided, not surprisingly, along lines which have divided Americans since before the Civil War. Sir Winston Churchill once said that the American Civil War was the last great war fought between gentlemen. Certainly Churchill had in mind the patriotism and the gallantry of men like Lee, Jackson, and Davis on the Confederate side, and Lincoln, Grant, and Sherman on the side of the Union. But I think he also had in mind the dignity of the principles that both sides held, and the tragedy inherent in the possibility that these same principles should seem to speak differently to men of equal integrity and devotion.

But gentlemanship, like patriotism, is not enough. Not Jefferson Davis or, for that matter, John C. Calhoun—surely one of the most intelligent men who ever lived—saw as deeply into the meaning of the American principles as Abraham Lincoln. And so—to borrow a phrase from the late Willmoore Kendall—let us have no foolishness about both sides being equally right. That the South lost the war on the battlefield does not in the least mean that it lost the argument. From Alexander Stephens to Willmoore Kendall, its champions have lost none of their fervor. So far are they from admitting defeat, that, on the contrary, they repeatedly proclaim victory.

In a recent book entitled *The Basic Symbols of the American Political Tradition* (Baton Rouge: Louisiana State University Press, 1970, xi, 163), Kendall, together with George Carey, takes the position that the arch-heretic, the man who "derailed" our tradition, was Abraham Lincoln. According to Kendall and Carey, all the Liberal and Radical demands, which would today transform constitutional into totalitarian government, are imperatives of Equality. And the power of this idea, or the power which the Radicals and Liberals have derived from it, stems from a misinterpretation or misapplication of the Declaration of Independence. According to Kendall and Carey, the Declaration is not the central document of our Founding, nor is it the true source of the symbols of the Founding. Nor does the expression of the doctrine of Equality in the Declaration mean what Abraham Lincoln said it meant, nor what the Liberals and Radicals of today wish it to mean. Nothing in our pre-Revolutionary past, or in the constitution-building period of the Revolutionary generation, justified making Equality the end or goal to be secured by the American regime. Equality as an end became the official principle of the regime only by a retrospective interpretation of "four score and seven years," an interpretation enshrined by Abraham Lincoln at Gettysburg. The Gettysburg Address, say Kendall and Carey, was a rhetorical trick. It made the victory of the Union armies the occasion for an official transformation of our constitutional, Conservative revolutionary past, into a sanction for a Radical-Liberal revolutionary future.

3.

Now we maintain that the truth about these matters is almost the exact opposite of what Kendall and Carey say it is. We believe that the Declaration of Independence

is the central document of our political tradition, not because of any trick played by
Abraham Lincoln, but because it is the most eloquent, as well as the most succinct,
statement of the political teaching of all the great documents of the period. The
sentiments of the Declaration are not unique to it. Jefferson was the draftsman of a
representative assembly, and his gift lay in finding memorable phrases that articulated the thoughts that everyone wished expressed. The doctrine of Equality, which
is indeed the key to all the thoughts in the Declaration, is also to be found in at least
seven of the bills of rights accompanying the original state constitutions.[4] It is
implied if not expressed in the Declaration of the First Continental Congress (1774)
and in the *Declaration of the Causes and Necessity of Taking Up Arms (1775)*. Kendall
and Carey believe that the idea of Equality dropped out of sight when the Constitution of 1787 came to be written, and that the constitutional morality of the *Federalist
Papers* has nothing to do with it. They are dead wrong on both counts. The idea of
Equality, as expressed in the Declaration, is the key to the morality of "the laws of
nature and of nature's God." It is this natural law which the Constitution—and
the regime of which the Constitution is a feature—is designed to implement. The
abandonment of the idea of Equality is perforce an abandonment of that morality
and that constitutionalism. It is perforce an abandonment of the "ought" for the
"is." It would be an abandonment of that higher law tradition which is the heart of
that civility—and that Conservatism—which judges men and nations by permanent
standards. As we propose to demonstrate, the commitment to Equality in the American political tradition is synonymous with the commitment to those permanent
standards. Whoever rejects the one, of necessity rejects the other, and in that rejection opens the way to the relativism and historicism that is the theoretical ground
of modern totalitarian regimes.

                                              4.

Basic Symbols is replete with references to the "enormous impact on American scholarship and thinking"[5] of Lincoln's alleged "derailment" of the American political
tradition. Yet Kendall and Carey do not provide a single example of that "derailed
scholarship." The central role of Equality in American life and thought was asserted
long ago by Alexis de Tocqueville in his *Democracy in America*, written in the 1830s.
Lincoln grew up in the Jacksonian America that Tocqueville had observed, and it is
hardly surprising that he responded powerfully to what was already the most powerful force in the world in which he moved. That the Gettysburg Address somehow
transformed the *ethos* of American life—and of American scholarship—would have
required a demonstration that Kendall and Carey nowhere attempt. It would have
required an analysis of Lincoln's reasoning on Equality, in its theoretical and practical bearings, pointing out how and why this was a new way of understanding Equality and how this new way had affected others. That is to say, it would have required

evidence that Equality was now understood differently because of Lincoln and that the way Equality was now understood was not because of an inheritance from pre-Lincolnian egalitarianism, or from that inheritance modified by any of the other countless writers on the subject.

In fact, the only work which has ever attempted a full analysis of the theoretical and practical meaning of Equality in Lincoln's political thought is my *Crisis of the House Divided.*[6] In it I pointed out that American historical scholarship, insofar as it had perceived the impact of Equality upon Lincoln's policies in the 1850s, had thoroughly rejected it. Indeed, in the field of Lincoln scholarship, as distinct from popular writing, *Crisis of the House Divided* was, as far as I know, the first book in the twentieth century to take a distinctly favorable view of Lincoln's policies in the 1850s. Since its publication in 1959, Don E. Fehrenbacher's *Prelude to Greatness: Lincoln in the 1850's* (1962), has made a powerful addition to this point of view.

The seven hundred years' providential march of Equality, of which Tocqueville wrote,[7] has certainly continued, as Tocqueville predicted it would. Many of its effects have been bad, as he also predicted. Tocqueville was much influenced in his view of Jacksonian America by the American Whigs he met—by the party of Adams, Clay, and Webster. He never met a young follower of these men named Abraham Lincoln. Yet Lincoln's articulation of the Whig critique of a demagogic egalitarianism, expressed particularly in his Lyceum (1838)[8] and Temperance (1842)[9] speeches, contains remarkable parallels to Tocqueville. Certainly Lincoln and Tocqueville saw the threat to the nation from slavery and racial difference in very similar ways. To impute an indiscriminate egalitarianism to Lincoln, as Kendall and Carey do, is as absurd as to impute it to Tocqueville.

Vaguely imputing Lincolnian effects to American scholarship, *Basic Symbols* nowhere comes to grips with the character of Lincoln's thought. Nor does it ever allude to the articulation of that thought in *Crisis of the House Divided.* This is all the more remarkable, in that Kendall not only had read *Crisis,* but had published a lengthy review of it in *National Review,*[10] which he reprinted in *The Conservative Affirmation.*[11] Had he thought ill of it, we could understand his passing over it later. But in fact he praised it extravagantly. We believe it to be the most generous review ever written about a book with which the reviewer so thoroughly disagreed. We feel obliged to quote it at some length now, not because of the praise, but because of the disagreement. We do so, moreover, because it seems to us to explain a missing link in *Basic Symbols'* polemic against Lincoln. *Basic Symbols* is silent not only about the actual reasoning in Lincoln's thought about Equality, but also about the great subject that occasioned nearly everything Lincoln said and wrote about Equality: slavery. So far as I can recall, the word "slavery" never occurs in *Basic Symbols.* Yet *Basic Symbols* wrestles with Equality on every page—like Jacob wrestling with the Angel of the Lord, we are tempted to say. To do so, without once mentioning slavery, would be like a critique of *Hamlet* that never mentions the ghost. Fortunately, Kendall does mention slavery in his review of *Crisis of the House Divided* and enables us thereby to form a juster view of what he says about Equality in *Basic Symbols.*

Kendall states, quite correctly, that "The central problem of *Crisis of the House Divided* is the status in the American political tradition of the 'all men are created equal' clause of the Declaration of Independence."[12] He adds that:

> Jaffa's Lincoln (and Jaffa) sees it as the indispensable presupposition of the entire American political experience; either you accept it as *the* standard which that experience necessarily takes as its point of departure, or you deny the meaning of the entire American experience. As for the status of Abraham Lincoln *vis-a-vis* the Signers and Framers, Jaffa's Lincoln sees the great task of the nineteenth century as that of affirming the cherished accomplishment of the Fathers by *transcending* it. Concretely, this means to construe the equality clause as having an allegedly unavoidable meaning with which it was always pregnant, but which the Fathers apprehended only dimly.[13]

According to Kendall, the question which is "tacit, but present on every page of the book,"[14] is the question:

> whether the Civil War was, from the standpoint of natural right and the cause of self-government, the "unnecessary war" of the historians of the past fifty or sixty years, or a war that *had* to be fought in the interest of freedom for all mankind.
>
> Jaffa's answer to the question is that the war did indeed have to be fought—once the South had gone beyond slaveholding . . . to assert the "positive goodness's" of slavery, and so to deny the validity of the equality-clause standard as the basic axiom of our political system. . . . And, *within the limits* to which he for sound reasons of strategy confines himself, Jaffa's case for that answer seems to this reviewer as nearly as possible irrefragable.
>
> His readers will, therefore, be well-advised to keep a sharp lookout *for those limits*, lest Jaffa launch them, and with them the nation, upon a political future the very thought of which is hair-raising—a future made up of an endless series of Abraham Lincolns, each persuaded that he is superior in wisdom and virtue to the Fathers, each prepared to insist that those who oppose this or that new application of the equality standard are denying the possibility of self-government, each ultimately willing to plunge America into Civil War rather than concede his point. . . .
>
> The limits I speak of are set by the alternatives that Jaffa steadfastly—plausibly but steadfastly—refuses to consider, namely: that a negotiated solution might have been worked out in terms of compensating the Southerners for their slaves and attempting some sort of radical confrontation of the Negro problem, and that the Southerners were entitled to secede if the issue was to be drawn in Lincoln's terms.[15]

In his concluding paragraph, Kendall declared:

> The idea of natural right is not so easily reducible to the equality clause, and there are better ways of demonstrating the possibility of self-government than imposing one's own views concerning natural right upon others.[16]

5.

What are those "limits" which Kendall so earnestly warned my readers to beware? We confess to having been completely unaware of them. If they have served any reasons of strategy the reasons are Kendall's, not ours. These limits turn out, upon inspection, to be certain "alternatives" that we are "plausibly but steadfastly" supposed to have refused to consider. But there is a simple explanation why we did not consider them in *Crisis of the House Divided*. That book was an interpretation of the Lincoln-Douglas debates, which we viewed as embracing the principal issues dividing the American people between the Mexican War and the Civil War. The preface to *Crisis* stated plainly that it was intended as the first of two volumes. The topics Kendall said we had avoided belonged plainly to the second volume, to the period after Lincoln's election in 1860. There was then no strategy behind our alleged refusal other than a chronological division within my subject.

Although that second volume has not yet appeared, there is a survey of the great issues of Lincoln's presidency in my essay, "The Emancipation Proclamation."[17] In it I faced squarely enough the issues Kendall said I had avoided in *Crisis*. Kendall knew therefore that if the case for Lincoln was, "as nearly as possible irrefragable" within the hypothetical limits he had assigned to it, it was just as irrefragable despite them. He and Carey simply refused to face that argument in *Basic Symbols* and preferred instead to pretend that it did not exist. We shall see why.

6.

What then were the proposals that Kendall said that Jaffa—he really meant Lincoln—had refused to consider, that might justly have prevented the Civil War? First, "that a negotiated solution might have been worked out in terms of compensating the Southerners for their slaves. . . ."[18] Second, that there might have been "some sort of radical confrontation of the Negro problem."[19] And third, that the South should have been allowed "to secede if the issue was to be drawn in Lincoln's terms."[20]

What in the world did Kendall mean by a "negotiated solution"? Many attempts at compromise were made in the winter of 1860–1861, the most famous of which bore the name of Senator Crittenden of Kentucky. Many long books have been written about these efforts, and we propose to write another one—but not now. Suffice it to say that Lincoln would not consent to any compromise which involved conceding to the South the right to extend slavery into federal territories. However, under existing federal law—i.e., under the Supreme Court's ruling in the case of *Dred Scott*[21]—there was no legal inhibition in 1861 against any slaveowner actually taking slaves into any federal territory open to settlement. Moreover, there was no immediate prospect that that ruling would change. Nor could there be any Republican or antislavery majority in either house of Congress, unless the Southern members absented themselves. It was against fears of the *future* that secession took place, and it is hard to know what compromise Kendall wished Lincoln to endorse that presumably would have made him the statesman of Kendallian consensus. Lincoln himself thought that nothing would satisfy the South at that juncture except a complete reversal on the slavery question by the most moderate and conservative of the antislavery leaders. They must cease saying slavery is wrong and that it should be restricted to those states where it was now lawful and must say instead that it is right and should be extended to wherever slaveowners could carry it. Did Kendall believe that, in a free society, men could be asked to declare against their deepest convictions?

Kendall speaks of "compensating the Southerners for their slaves."[22] By this I presume he intends some scheme of compensated emancipation. But given the state of parties and of political opinion in 1860–1861, such a proposal is wildly anachronistic. It would resemble a proposal today that détente with the Soviet Union be pursued by a plan for buying up the Soviet state industries and returning them to free capitalistic enterprise. Kendall seems not to recognize that the issues which divided Americans on the eve of the Civil War had no direct nor immediate reference to slavery in the states where it existed, but had solely to do with the *extension* of slavery. In his Inaugural Address, Lincoln said—repeating a passage from an earlier speech—"I have no purpose, directly or indirectly, to interfere with the institution of slavery in the States where it exists. I believe I have no lawful right to do so, and I have no inclination to do so."[23] For more than a generation, John C. Calhoun had drilled the South in the lesson that they must never, never, never, never, by the remotest inference, concede the slightest federal jurisdiction over the domestic institution of slavery. For example, they must not concede federal power over slavery even in the District of Columbia, because it had been carved out of slave states. Nor must they admit the right of Congress to receive abolitionist petitions even for the purpose of rejecting them. Nor must they admit the right even of the federal post to deliver abolitionist literature in the states that outlawed it. While Lincoln certainly did not share these extreme views, he was nonetheless sympathetic with the difficulties of the white South in dealing with what he called the "necessities" of the actual presence of slavery amongst them. It was just because he estimated those necessities so justly that Lincoln would not consider any compromise that carried slavery into lands where it was not already rooted. But to have proposed emancipation in 1860 or 1861 would have been regarded as an act of bad faith. Far from being an instrument of negotiation or compromise, as Kendall seems to think, it would have been a firebrand.

7.

We digress briefly here to consider the actual plans of emancipation that Lincoln put forward at different times in his career—although not in the secession crisis of

1860–1861. We do so, among other reasons, because they demonstrate the absurdity of a myth that Kendall and Carey assiduously promote, that Lincoln was somehow the spiritual father of the New Deal, of the expanded presidency of the twentieth century, and of the welfare state. Lincoln took almost no part in the formulation of what we might call the "domestic legislation" of his presidency. The Republican Party over which he presided sponsored a great deal of new legislation, dealing with a national banking system, promoting a national railroad system, providing homestead legislation, providing the land grants that led to the great system of state universities, and providing new tariffs for the growing manufacturing industries of the North, and so on. Lincoln signed these bills into law as a matter of course. Most of them were basically Whig measures which he had long endorsed. They were the foundation of that ebullient capitalism later called the age of the "robber barons." Lincoln himself was almost wholly occupied with the prosecution of the war. Any expansions of federal authority attributable to Lincoln stemmed from his interpretation of his Constitutional duty "that the Laws be faithfully executed" and from his authority, "in Cases of Rebellion or Invasion," as commander in chief. These were crisis powers, they were not expansions of the commerce clause, of the general welfare clause, or of any of those enumerated powers by which *Congress* has in the twentieth century added to the powers of the presidency. Lincoln did very little, if anything, to expand the powers of the federal government *per se.* What he did under the war powers did *not* set precedents for an expanded peace time role of the presidency in particular, or for the federal government in general. In fact, much of Lincoln's long struggle against the Congressional Radicals was a struggle to keep Congress from assuming powers over persons and property that Lincoln did not believe the federal government possessed. As long as the executive exercised them, as incidents of the war powers, they did not become permanent additions to federal jurisdiction.

Ever since Lincoln had been a Whig Congressman during the Mexican War he had supported the idea of emancipation for the District of Columbia. Although he believed that Congress had full sovereignty over all aspects of slavery in the District, he was opposed to outright abolition. The plan that had his support had these three elements. First, the abolition had to be gradual. (The plan that he proposed during the Civil War would have allowed up to thirty-seven years for its accomplishment.) Second, it had to be authorized, not only by Congress, but also by a majority of the qualified voters of the District. (Does this sound like Kendall's Lincoln, "imposing his own view concerning natural right upon others"?) And third, compensation had to be made to the owners of the slaves emancipated.

When Lincoln came to propose a national plan for emancipation in December, 1862, it possessed all these elements of voluntarism. To insure that this was so, Lincoln insisted that the authorizing legislation be incorporated in a series of constitutional amendments. These amendments would provide that the federal government be enabled to indemnify those states which had voluntarily adopted systems of gradual, compensated emancipation. The federal government would not, under Lincoln's plan, require the states to adopt such plans. But it would facilitate their doing so, by assuming all or most of the financial burden of such plans. But true to his inaugural pledge that the Constitution did not authorize *any* federal jurisdiction over slavery in the *states,* Lincoln required an amendment to the Constitution even to pay money to enable the states to do more conveniently what they might wish to do about slavery. It is worth noting that Lincoln's proposal would not have provided any precedent for the innumerable federal grant-in-aid programs of the twentieth century. By requiring a Constitutional amendment to permit the federal government to pay money to the states for one particular specified purpose, Lincoln would not—to repeat—have done anything to expand federal jurisdiction over the domestic institutions or internal commerce of any state.

But why did Lincoln propose any scheme of emancipation during the war? The answer to this is that Lincoln's inaugural pledge could not be maintained in the face of a war it did not contemplate. By September of 1862 Lincoln was convinced that he had to strike at slavery if the war was to be won and the Union preserved. Every slave who deserted his Confederate master weakened the Confederate economy that much. Every white Southerner who had to stay on farm or factory could not take his place in the Confederate firing line. As we have seen, Lincoln did not believe that either he or the Congress possessed any lawful power over slavery in the states, and whatever powers he possessed over enemy contraband did not apply to loyal owners. The terms of the Emancipation Proclamation included a careful enumeration of all those states and parts of states that were in rebellion against the authority of the United States. The Proclamation had no effect in Delaware, Maryland, Kentucky, Missouri, and large parts of Virginia and Louisiana. Lincoln knew, and told the Congress, that slavery was doomed everywhere in the United States, if it was doomed anywhere. The process of war was breaking up the entire social and police system upon which the peculiar institution depended. Lincoln's system of emancipation was the only way he knew to prevent loyal slaveholders from ultimately suffering the same fate as disloyal ones. And there is no doubt in my mind that, had Lincoln's plan been adopted, and had Lincoln survived the war, he would have attempted to secure some indemnification for loyal slaveholders behind the Confederate lines. Lincoln always thought of slavery as a national moral responsibility, even if the legal responsibility was limited by state rights. He did not think that a man who had sold a slave had the right to keep his money, while the man who bought him might rightfully have his purchase confiscated. The confiscation of private property during the war troubled Lincoln deeply, for the same reason that slavery troubled him. For what was slavery itself but a denial of the foundation of all property rights, by the confiscation of the right that a man had in himself and in the fruits of his own labor?

We have told the story of the Emancipation Proclamation in our essay of that name.[24] We mention now only that Lincoln failed to secure the passage of his plan through the Congress. His failure stemmed from his inability to persuade the border slave state Congressmen to support it. Although the border slave states had now sealed their fidelity to the Union with their blood, they were as stubborn as their Confederate brethren in refusing any step that might, in their own minds, and however indirectly, admit the wrongfulness of slavery. There was both a guilt and a pride which seems to have infected all who had been immediately touched by the peculiar institution. They would not take the most obvious measures in their own interest, if by so doing they might seem to cast a reproach upon their own past. Kendall and Carey's inability even to mention slavery in a book dominated by that subject testifies that the power of that reproach has not yet ceased. The Thirteenth Amendment, necessary as it proved to be, ended the legal existence of slavery in the United States in a way which Lincoln never desired. But the failure to achieve a better way cannot be made a matter of reproach to him.

8.

Among the alternatives that Kendall said that Jaffa—and Lincoln—had refused to consider was "some sort of radical confrontation of the Negro problem."[25] But this is just as nebulous as the proposal of a "negotiated solution" to the sectional crisis. If it means anything, it means facing the social and political consequences of eventual and complete emancipation. But of course there had been a great deal of contemplation of this possibility. And the South had concluded, because of it, that emancipation must never come. The North had also concluded, because of it, that slavery must never be extended. The free state settlers in the territories had no wish to meet Negroes there, free or slave. And the slave South believed that unless slavery were to expand, it would eventually contract, and that emancipation would come as an economic, if not as a political, necessity. And so there was a steady hardening of positions on both sides.

In the decade before the Civil War the laws governing slavery had grown steadily harsher. It became impossible in many states for owners to free slaves, even if they wished to do so. Many of the slaves that such owners wished to free were of course their own children. There are countless stories—not all of them invented by Harriet Beecher Stowe—of the deathbed agonies of men whose children were security for their debts and who would be sold "down the river" after their demise. Because of fear of this, some wealthy New Orleans families sent their mulatto children to France. The laws also became stringent in forbidding teaching slaves to read, in forbidding their congregating except under strict supervision, in forbidding association between slaves and free Negroes, and in forbidding free Negroes from crossing state lines. Free states also had laws forbidding free Negroes from entering. But above all, the South had decided, in the wake of the Wilmot proviso controversy, that new slave states must, from time to time, be added to the Union, to balance the growing power of the free states within the federal structure. However impossible such balance might be in the House, it must at least be preserved in the Senate. Ironically enough—from the viewpoint of Kendall and Carey—Southern orators constantly appealed to Equality. They said the South must have Equality with the North, the slave states must have Equality with the free states. To have less than Equality meant degradation and—yes—slavery. And to that they would never submit. But if there were to be new slave states, slaveholders must enter the territories during their formative period and control the drafting of the state constitutions with which the new states would apply to Congress for admission. But as time and experience showed, the legal right of entrance was not enough. Slavery was a fragile institution. Stray slaves were not like stray cattle. They had heads as well as legs, and it required an enormously complicated system of slave patrols, of police regulations integrated into a proslavery society, to keep slaves working in their places and to make slavery economically viable. And so the doctrine developed that came to quintessential expression in Taney's opinion in the case of *Dred Scott*.[26] That opinion held not only that every slaveholder had a constitutional right to migrate with his slaves to any federal territory that was open to settlement, but also that the sole power that Congress had over the subject of slavery was the power *coupled with the duty* to protect the slaveowner in the exercise of his rights. It was this that brought about the sectional crisis in its final form. Whether Kendall was simply ignorant of the history of the period, or only pretended to be so, we do not know. But in no just sense was it "Lincoln's terms" which determined the crisis of 1860. Secession actually began when the Southern radicals walked out of the Democratic Convention. And they walked out when *Stephen A. Douglas,* and *his* supporters *in the Democratic* Party, refused to countenance the demand for a federal slave code. The demand for a federal slave code had exactly the same status in the North that a demand for emancipation would have had in the South. No politician could survive one moment who gave it a moment's countenance.

The Civil War came then not, as Kendall seems to suppose, merely because the Republican Party, a free-soil party, had elected Abraham Lincoln president. Lincoln wished to have federal law forbid slavery in federal territories. In this he differed from Douglas, who wished to permit the settlers to decide for themselves whether they would have freedom or slavery. But by 1860 the South had rejected Douglas as completely as they had rejected Lincoln. In some ways he was more hated, as they regarded him a traitor to their cause. Nothing less than "affirmative action" guaranteeing slavery in the territories would have kept the South in the Charleston Convention; nothing less would have averted secession after Lincoln's election.

We come finally to Kendall's assertion that the South was "entitled to secede if the issue was to be drawn on Lincoln's terms."[27] We have just seen that it was not Lincoln who drew the terms of the issue. Even if one wishes—however extravagantly—to place all responsibility in the North, it was the Northern Democrats no less than the Republicans who shared it. And the overwhelming majority of Democrats, led by Douglas, opposed secession as much as Lincoln. We might argue the case against secession in the familiar terms of national supremacy versus state rights. We might easily demonstrate why the "national" interest of the North made inconceivable the surrender of the navigation of the Mississippi to a foreign power and why the land-locked midwest in particular—the section from which Lincoln came—could never contemplate the alliance of an independent and hostile Confederacy with British Canada. But we think the issue is simpler even than these obvious political considerations.

In his inaugural address, Lincoln pointed out that the two sections could not, physically speaking, separate. Political separation, far from solving any problems, would make them all more acute. The fugitive slave law, now imperfectly enforced, would then not be enforced at all. The foreign slave trade, now imperfectly suppressed, might be openly revived. But above all, what would be done about the territories? The territories belonged to the United States. Would the South surrender its share in them in quitting the Union? If so, why secede? Would the North, recognizing the Confederacy, agree to divide the territories? If so, why not cease to resist the extension of slavery—and in particular the extension below 36 degrees 30 minutes, the Missouri Compromise line, as in the Crittenden Compromise—and keep the seceding states in the Union? In short, it would have been senseless for Lincoln to have resolutely opposed the extension of slavery and then to have agreed to secession—as Kendall proposes. For secession, had it succeeded, would have emancipated the South from nearly all restrictions upon the extension and perpetuation of slavery. Unless the South was willing to fight the North for the territories, it made no sense for them to secede. Unless the North was willing to fight against secession, it made no sense to stand firm against the extension of slavery into the territories. To agree to secession, after not agreeing to slavery extension, would only have made the war much harder to win, without making it any less necessary. Surely Kendall must have seen that. There is not doubt that Lincoln did!

<h1 style="text-align:center">9.</h1>

According to Kendall and Carey, the supreme "symbol" of the American political traditions is the virtuous people, or the representatives of the virtuous people, deliberating under God. We have no quarrel with this formulation, as far as it goes. We prefer, on the whole, to speak of the principles of the tradition, rather than its symbols. We propose to prove by the American political tradition, that a people become a people only by virtue of the principle of Equality. Here we would point out that it was this same American people, deliberating according to the laws laid down in the Constitution, laws to which all equally had consented, that elected Abraham Lincoln president of the United States. No violence was used in this election, unless it was in the South, where there were no electors for Lincoln. No one has ever been entitled to take office according to the canons of consensus laid down by Kendall and Carey, if it was not Lincoln. Did he not appeal to the "basic symbols" precisely in their sense when he spoke these fateful lines on March 4, 1861?

> Why should there not be a patient confidence in the ultimate justice of the people? Is there any better, or equal hope, in the world? . . . If the Almighty Ruler of nations, with his eternal truth and justice, be on your side of the North, or on yours of the South, that truth, and that justice, will surely prevail, by the judgment of this great tribunal, the American People.[28]

Was not the decision of the seceding states, to break up the government, rather than submit to Lincoln's election, a defiance of the virtuous people, deliberating according to the rules of the Constitution, and under God? Was not that election a decision by a constitutional majority, in which all rights of constitutional minorities had been carefully preserved? Had not Lincoln sworn an oath, before God and the people, to "take Care that the Laws be faithfully executed" and to "preserve, protect, and defend the Constitution"? How can Kendall—how can anyone—call Lincoln's fidelity to that oath, incorporating as it does all that is sacred to the American political tradition, "imposing one's own view concerning natural right upon others"?[29]

Kendall thought that Jaffa would "launch [his readers] and with them the nation upon a political future the very thought of which is hair-raising. . . ."[30] This future would be made up

> of an endless series of Abraham Lincolns, each persuaded that he is superior in wisdom and virtue to the Fathers, each prepared to insist that those who oppose this or that new application of the equality standard are denying the possibility of self-government, each ultimately willing to plunge America into Civil War rather than concede his point. . . .[31]

My readers will by now perceive that this is good Confederate caricature suitable for declamation—after playing "Dixie"—at a meeting decorated by the stars and bars. The warning strikes me as somewhat extravagant, given the number of my readers and the magnitude of the intellectual demands that Kendall says my book puts upon them. Kendall's premise seems to be that Lincoln—or anyone—who opposed American slavery thereby favored each and every "application of the equality standard." But this standard, we are also told, leads to "the cooperative commonwealth of men who will be so equal that no one will be able to tell them apart."[32] In short, it will lead to the modern totalitarian slave state. Kendall's case against Lincoln then comes down to this: Lincoln's opposition to slavery leads to slavery.

Now, even if this were not self-contradictory, we would have the right to ask, why is the slavery to which Lincoln leads us worse than that which he helped to end? But of course, we are faced here with a play on words, or a confusion of two meanings of Equality. Lincoln never sought, or believed in, an equality of *condition*.

What he did believe in was an quality of *rights*. Over and over again, he denied that he thought that men were equal in wisdom, virtue, or ability, or that they should all have the same rewards. Lincoln said in 1858:

> Certainly the Negro is not our equal in color—perhaps not in many other respects; still, in the right to put into his mouth the bread that his own hands have earned, he is the equal of every other man. . . . In pointing out that more has been given [to] you, you cannot be justified in taking away the little which has been given [to] him. All I ask for the Negro is that if you do not like him, let him alone. If God gave him little . . . that little let him enjoy.[33]

Surely no simpler nor more eloquent appeal ever was made to the principles of natural justice. Equality here meant nothing more than the equal right of all men to be treated justly. In his message to Congress of July 4, 1861, Lincoln defined the cause of the Union. It was, he said, to maintain in the world

> that form, and substance of government, whose leading object is, to elevate the condition of men—to lift artificial weights from all shoulders—to clear the paths of laudable pursuit for all—to afford all, an unfettered start, and a fair chance, in the race of life.[34]

Kendall and Carey refer repeatedly to Lincoln having "curious" notions of what Equality meant which, they say, "even his worshipers cannot deny."[35] But, curiously enough, they give no explanation whatever of this assertion. One of the speeches which they list as supporting this contention is the one from which we have just quoted. Is giving everyone an *unfettered* start and a fair chance what is "curious"? Is not this the idea behind the Statue of Liberty? Is it curious that we should be proud to call ourselves the land, not of the slave, but of the free? Have we not been the Promised Land for countless millions who have fled from persecution and oppression in the Egypt of the Old World? Was it not always an anomaly for the Promised Land itself to have slavery? And is not Abraham Lincoln himself the very most "basic symbol" within the American political tradition of personal self-reliance, of bootstrap individualism? In this connection we cannot refrain from telling one of our favorite Lincoln stories. A visitor came into his office in the White House one day to find him blacking his boots. "Why, Mr. President," the astonished man exclaimed, "do you black your own boots?" "Whose boots do you think I black?" growled Lincoln.

10.

We observed that Kendall and Carey never, to our knowledge, mention slavery in *Basic Symbols*. But the following passage seems to elevate Inequality to the status we had thought belonged to its opposite.

Is the American political tradition [they ask] the tradition of the textbooks, which indeed situates the "all men are created equal" clause at the center of our political experience, *or is it the tradition of American life as it is actually lived and thus a tradition of inequality?* [36]

Here Kendall and Carey confuse the "is" with the "ought" of a political tradition. "Life as it is actually lived" should refer not only to what people *do,* but also to the ethical norms or imperatives by which they understand the meaning of what they do. Kendall and Carey refer repeatedly to the American people as being a Christian people. Would they identify Christians solely by their observance of the golden rule, i.e., only by their lives as they are "actually" [i.e., selfishly] lived?

Kendall, we noted, thinks that Lincoln (and Jaffa) points us toward a state of society in which men are "so equal that no one will be able to tell them apart." Yet were not all slaves equally denied the privileges of freedom, without regard to age, sex, virtue, or intelligence? Did they not all receive the same "wages," regardless of how much or how little they worked? Kendall and Carey speak—inaccurately—of the Declaration of Independence as referring to a Christian people. Christianity is a revealed religion. But in its references to "self-evident" truths and to "Nature" and "Nature's God," the Declaration certainly has reference to natural, not to revealed theology. Still, the moral commands of the Decalogue are held by many Christians to be knowable by unassisted human reason as well as by biblical revelation. And American slavery was as much an institutionalized denial of the moral claims of the Ten Commandments as Hitler's concentration camps or the Gulag Archipelago. Since slaves were legally chattels, they could make no legal contracts, including marriage. How could children honor their fathers and mothers, when the fathers and mothers were not lawfully married, when they had no lawful power over their children, and when they could not acquire any of the property which is at the foundation of family life? How could the prohibition against adultery be regarded, when there was no lawful distinction between fornication and adultery? How could chastity be a virtue for those who had no lawful power over their own bodies? How could prohibitions against covetousness and theft be addressed to those who could possess no property and all the fruits of whose labor were taken from them? How could slaves regard the injunction against bearing false witness, when their testimony could never be given in court against white men? And did not the example of Moses, who had killed a slave master, justify anyone in striking down another who obstructed his path to freedom?

American slavery treated all men of a certain class as having their worth determined by their membership in that class. This is equally the root of contemporary totalitarianism. To be elevated, or regarded as worthy, because one is white, proletarian, or Aryan, or to be degraded and scorned as a Negro, a capitalist, or a Jew, does not involve any ultimate distinction of principle. Kendall's denunciation of the "cooperative commonwealth" of those whose identities are lost in "equality" is utterly stultified by his refusal to condemn American slavery and by his condemnation of Lincoln for condemning it.

The "real" American political tradition, say Kendall and Carey, is not one of Equality. Except in the form of a rhetorical question, they do not positively assert that it is one of Inequality. Putting together their various formulations, the "basic symbols" of our tradition are—or is—the representative assembly (or assemblies) of the virtuous people deliberating under God. (There is the same difficulty with singular and plural here, as in the case of The United States.) We have no quarrel with the emphasis they place upon deliberation, or upon the need for morality and religion among the institutions of a *free* people. We think there is a fundamental misunderstanding implied in their case for legislative supremacy among the three branches of government. We think they confuse the supremacy of legislation, conceived as an act of the sovereign people in its constitution-making role, and legislation as an exercise of the ordinary powers of government provided by the Constitution. But this difference arises from the far more fundamental difference we have, concerning what it is that makes discrete individuals into a sovereign people, and hence what it is that authorizes any people to institute government, "laying its foundation on such principles and organizing its powers in such form, as to them shall seem most likely to effect their Safety and Happiness." Kendall and Carey assume the existence of the people, and never ask what it is, from the viewpoint of the Founding Fathers, that entitled the American people to consider themselves as sovereign. But the answer to that question, as we propose to demonstrate, is Equality.

The Declaration of Independence, of course, affirms it to be a self-evident truth, "that all men are created equal." Within short intervals during the Revolution, the people of the several states adopted new constitutions. Most of these contained preambles, bills or declarations of rights, which gave the "foundation of principles" upon which they were to erect the "forms" of government they thought most likely to effect their safety and happiness. For example, Virginia stated, "That all men are by nature equally free and independent"; Pennsylvania, "That all men are born equally free and independent"; Vermont, "That all men are born equally free and independent"; Massachusetts, that "All men are born free and equal"; New Hampshire, that "All men are born equally free and independent"; Delaware, "That all government of right originates from the people [and] is founded in compact only. . . ."[37] Maryland also said, "That all government of right originates from the people, [and] is founded in compact only. . . ."[38]

Now we contend that all these statements of principle, where they are not verbally identical, all mean one and the same thing. It will be observed that Virginia, Pennsylvania, Vermont, and New Hampshire say "equally free and independent." Massachusetts says "free and equal." Clearly, "equal" and "independent" mean the same thing. Also, "born" and "by nature" mean the same thing. Delaware and Maryland vary this language slightly by saying that rightful government is "founded in compact only." This expression, we shall see, means simply that government is the result of an agreement by men who were originally, or by nature, or born, equally free and independent. Jefferson's "created equal" is simply the most succinct formulation of this commonly understood doctrine.

Willmoore Kendall devoted the last years of his life to an extraordinary effort to read John Locke out of the American political tradition. That there was a compact theory much older than the American, he knew. That Socrates had appealed to one, he knew from the Crito of Plato. But he didn't trust the Old Pagan, as "The People versus Socrates Revisited" showed. With a great swoop, he lighted finally upon the Mayflower Compact. Here he found at last, if not a compact theory, at least a compact. No matter, if the Pilgrims didn't have a theory, Kendall would supply it to them! The important thing was that there was not a word in the Mayflower Compact about Equality, and there was something—not much, but something—about "advancing the Christian faith." So Kendall labelled his second chapter in *Basic Symbols*, "In the Beginning: The Mayflower Compact," and tried to prove that the Founding Fathers—who were now, in fact, the Founding Great-great-great-great-Grandsons—had always meant substantially what the men of the Mayflower Compact had meant. That is to say, they had meant what they would or could or should have meant if they too had been born before John Locke. But all this effort was in vain. While we would never contend that there are no non-Lockean elements in the Founding, or that the Founding Fathers always interpreted the Lockean elements in a Lockean manner, Locke is nonetheless there. The primary appeals to principles in the Revolution are Lockean. The principle of limited, constitutional government, by which the Fathers rejected despotism and by which they constructed their own governments, were fundamentally Lockean. Without understanding this, no other aspects of the Revolution, or of the American political tradition, are intelligible.

The spirit of Locke's political teaching is conveyed well by the opening sentence of his *First Treatise:* "Slavery is so vile and miserable an estate of man, and so directly opposite to the generous temper and courage of our nation, that it is hardly to be conceived that an Englishman, much less a gentleman, should plead for it."[39] The major part of the treatise is devoted to a refutation of Sir Robert Filmer's *Patriarcha* (1680), a work which attempts to found absolute monarchy upon a title derived from Adam. Locke demonstrates the absurdity of such a title, not to mention the difficulty of finding its rightful possessor! But consider the language of the Continental Congress, in the Declaration of the Causes and Necessity of Taking Up Arms, July 6, 1775:

> If it was possible for men, who exercise their reason to believe, that the divine Author of our existence intended a part of the human race to hold an absolute property in, and an unbounded power over others . . . the inhabitants of these colonies might at least require from the parliament of Great Britain some evidence, that this dreadful authority over them, has been granted to that body.[40]

Did ever a great revolution in human affairs ever begin with such sarcasm? Can one not hear the very accents of Locke's *First Treatise* as he rakes old Filmer over the coals? One thinks, for example, of Sir Robert's derivation of kingly power from paternal power, citing the biblical injunction to honor one's father. To this Locke retorted with evident glee that the Bible speaks of honoring one's father *and mother* and asks why Sir Robert does not find queenly as well as kingly authority in such injunctions. But the Continental Congress, in rejecting the proposition that any part of the *human race* (not merely Englishmen *vis-a-vis* Englishmen) might hold a right of property in any other part, clearly condemned in principle all slavery. And this they might do, only if, in their right to non-despotic rule, *all men are equal.*

In his attack on Filmer, Locke characterizes his "system" in this "little compass." "[I]t is," says Locke, "no more but this":

> That all government is absolute monarchy.[41]

"And the ground he builds on is this":

> That no man is born free.[42]

Robert A. Goldwin observes that "Locke's own political teaching may be stated in opposite terms but with similar brevity. . . ."[43] Goldwin's first Lockean proposition is this:

> All government is limited in its powers and exists only by the consent of the governed.[44]

And, says Goldwin, the ground Locke builds on is this:

> All men are born free.[45]

The argument for absolute monarchy—or despotism, for they are the same—is grounded in Locke in the proposition that no man is born free. The argument for limited government (or constitutional government, for they are the same) is grounded in Locke in the proposition that all men are born free. But we shall see that in Locke—and *in the nature of things*—the proposition that all men are born free is itself an inference from the proposition that all men are born equal. The equality of all men by nature and the freedom of all men by nature differ as the concavity of a curved line differs from its convexity. The two are distinguishable, but inseparable.

Let us now turn to the famous passage in the *Second Treatise,* in which Locke considers "what state all men are naturally in."[46] It is, he says,

> a state of perfect freedom to order their actions and dispose of their possessions and persons as they think fit, within the bounds of the law of nature, without asking leave or depending upon the will of any other man.[47]

But it is also, he continues,

> [a] state . . . of equality, wherein all the power and jurisdiction is reciprocal, no one having more than another; there being nothing more evident than [meaning thereby that it is self-evident] that creatures of the same species and rank . . . should also be equal one amongst another without subordination and subjection. . . .[48]

We would rephrase Locke's argument as follows: there is no difference between man and man as there is between man and, for example, dog, such that one is recognizable as the other's natural superior. And if men are not *naturally* subordinate, one to another—as all the brute creation are *naturally* subordinate to man—then they are *naturally* not in a state of government, or civil society. They are, instead, *naturally* free and independent, or *born* free and independent. But they are born free and independent, *because* they are born—or created—equal.

There can be no question Kendall and Carey do not question—that the just powers of government in the American political tradition are derived from the consent of the governed. Kendall and Carey treat consent, however, as if it were an ultimate and not a derived principle. But that is not the way Locke or the Founders treated it. They derived it from man's natural freedom and equality. It is the recognition of Equality which not only gives rise to consent, but also which provides consent with a positive content of meaning. Kendall and Carey, by allowing consent to stand alone, as if it were an ultimate principle, have no basis for saying what it is to which men might reasonably consent. In 1854, Lincoln quoted his notable antagonist thus:

> Judge Douglas frequently, with bitter irony and sarcasm, paraphrases our argument by saying: "The white people of Nebraska are good enough to govern themselves, *but they are not good enough to govern a few miserable Negroes!!*"
> Well, I doubt not that the people of Nebraska are, and will continue to be as good as the average of people elsewhere. I do not say the contrary. What I do say is, that no man is good enough to govern another man, *without that other's consent.*[49]

Kendall and Carey, like Douglas, do not see that the people's right to give their consent is itself derived from the equality of *all* men and therefore limits and directs what it is to which they may rightfully consent. Their view leads to the conclusion that whatever any particular people may be persuaded by demagogues to agree or consent to, becomes "right." Calling the people "virtuous" and saying that they deliberate "under God" may become a mere cloak for vice and hypocrisy, as our examination of the ethics of slavery showed.

That men are by nature free and equal is the ground simultaneously of political obligation—of consent as the immediate source of the just powers of government—and of a doctrine of limited government and of an ethical code. Because man is by nature a rational being, he may not rule other rational beings as if they were mere brutes. Because man is not all-wise or all-powerful, because his reason is swayed by his passions, he may not be a judge in his own cause, and he may *not* therefore rule other men despotically. Men do not need the consent of brute creation to rule over it. Nor does God need the consent of men rightfully to exercise his Providential rule over them. Man is the in-between being, between beast and God, "a little lower than the angels." Consent is that ground of obligation which corresponds with this "in-betweenness." It is the contemplation of this universe, articulated as it is into the intelligible hierarchy of beast, man, and God, which not only brings consent as a principle into view, but also enlightens it, and brings it thereby into harmony with "the Laws of Nature and of Nature's God." To repeat, the proposition that all men are created equal implies an understanding of man, in the light of the universe, in the light of the distinction between the human and the subhuman on the one hand, and of the human and the superhuman on the other. As we have already observed, it does *not,* for this reason, ignore the very important differences between man and man. On the contrary, it is for the sake of those differences that it denies any man the right to rule others, *as if* those others were beasts. And there are no standing rules, and impartial judges, to govern the differences between slaves and their owners and masters. For the rule of a master to be a matter of right, the master would have to differ from the servant, as God is supposed to differ from man. Whatever one's beliefs as to the *existence* of Divinity, it is evident—or self-evident—that no man possesses that power or wisdom which we suppose that God—if He exists— possesses. While not supposing for a moment that the Founders did not believe in the actual existence of God, their assumptions about Equality—which include assumptions about the subhuman and the superhuman—are independent of the validity of any particular religious beliefs. In the decisive respect, their assumptions are not assumptions at all, but observations of a world in which the difference between men and beasts provides a clear and distinct idea of what the Divine nature, in its politically relevant aspects, must be.

Kendall and Carey suppose that the constitutional morality of *The Federalist* has nothing whatever to do with Equality. That they are wrong becomes clear the moment one understands that the proposition that all men are created equal is not about man alone, but about man, God, and Nature; and that Nature implies the difference between the human and the subhuman, as well as that between the human and the superhuman. Consider the famous passage of Madison's in the fifty-first *Federalist*:

> If men were angels, no government would be necessary. If angels were to govern men, neither external nor internal controls on government would be necessary. In framing a government which is to be administered by men over men, the great difficulty lies in this: you must first enable the government to control the governed; and in the next place oblige it to control itself.[50]

Here the very nature of the problem that constitutionalism is meant to solve is determined by the meaning of Equality.

But does not constitutionalism imply an ethics as well as a politics? Do we not recognize that the equality of all men by nature, leading as it does to civil society, is the justification for the *inequalities* of civil society? Do we not thereby see that officials are but men and must live under the laws that they make and administer? (Abraham Lincoln: "The master not only governs the slave without his consent; but he governs him by a set of rules altogether different from those which he prescribes for himself."[51]) Do we not recognize that *our* consent makes *their* acts lawful, and that in obeying them, we are not deferring to our superiors in nature, but only to the principle of authority that is in ourselves? Is it not this that makes obedience not demeaning (not slavish), but dignified, and sometimes even noble? But still further, does not Equality, which makes *our* consent necessary to the laws *we* obey, oblige us to recognize the *same* rights in *other* men? Does it not also tell us that we may not consider other men mere means to our ends—as we may consider the brute creation—or as we may be considered by a divine providence whose power and wisdom so far transcends our own? (Are we not taught by Revelation that God does *not* consider us as mere means, but that this is not necessary to his being, but represents the miracle of His grace?) Do not all the totalitarian slave states of our time rest upon theoretical propositions in which race or class differences delude some men to consider themselves superhuman? And does not this delusion lie at the root of their bestiality? Is it not this that makes them think that, for the sake of the classless society, or the thousand year Reich, everything is permitted to them? Surely Abraham Lincoln was right when he said that the doctrine of human equality was "the father of all moral principle [amongst] us."[52]

II.

There is a tendency among Conservatives to identify Equality with some species of socialism or—in Kendall's words—with "the cooperative commonwealth of men who will be so equal that no one will be able to tell them apart." But the doctrine of Equality, in particular in its Lockean sense, is essential to the defense of the institution of private property in the modern world. For the doctrine of Equality holds that what men are by nature, that is, prior to civil society, determines what purposes civil society may rightfully serve. It is this that determines what rights are inalienable, and what rights may—or must—reasonably be surrendered to society. It was axiomatic for the Founders that the rights of conscience were never surrendered to civil society, and that therefore civil society might never rightfully enact laws in matters that were wholly and exclusively matters of conscience. It took more than a generation after the Revolution to uproot all the colonial laws which, directly or indirectly, "established religion," by giving one or another religious belief the assistance of law. Moreover, the determined way in which men like Jefferson and Madison acted to get rid, not only of religious establishment in all its forms, but also of such vestiges of feudal law as primogeniture and entail, proves how little regard they had for that colonial past Kendall tried to make the ground of the American political tradition.

Primogeniture and entail were anachronisms on the American scene. They were essentially limitations upon the right of a man to control his own property and to dispose of it at his pleasure. They were props of aristocracy, inimical to the spirit both of democracy and of capitalism. They were, so to speak, elements of a "Tory socialism." But Locke had taught that men were by nature property-acquiring animals. He had taught that both life and liberty became valuable and were themselves natural rights, above all because they culminated in the possession and enjoyment of property. No one in America who heard the Declaration of Independence read out for the first time had any doubt that pursuing happiness meant primarily, as Virginia had already put it, "acquiring and possessing property." It was because the Parliament of Great Britain had appeared to assert a right to tax the colonists without their consent by making laws and statutes "in all cases whatsoever," that they had revolted. But men like George Washington—as vigorous a land speculator as ever lived—were driven into rebellion in part by their inability to get the government at Westminster to grant patents and titles to the land they had surveyed in such places as the Ohio valley. Government, in their view, existed to facilitate the acquisition and enjoyment of private property. Such property might be taxed—with their consent—so that the government might be able to protect that same property. But it might not tax them to render nugatory, in any manner or sense, their efforts *in* acquiring and possessing property. The principle of Equality, far from enfranchising any leveling action of government, is the ground for the recognition of those human differences which arise *naturally*, but in *civil society*, when human industry and acquisitiveness are emancipated. We saw that Madison reflected the doctrine of Equality, when he attributed the need for constitutional government, and constitutional morality, to the difference between men and angels. But he reflected it no less when, in the tenth *Federalist*, he put as the "*first* object of government," the protection "of different and *unequal* faculties of acquiring property. . . ."[53] In his *Second Treatise*, Locke had put the origin of property in human labor. It was the natural right—the equal right—which each man had to his own body, and therefore to the labor of that body, that was the ultimate foundation of the right to private property in civil society. How can Kendall and Carey not have seen, as Lincoln saw, that the denial of Equality was the denial of the principle upon which private property, as well as every other personal freedom, rested? Nothing illustrates better Lincoln's egalitarianism, and his attitude toward property, than the following message, which he sent to a meeting of the Workingmen's Association in New York, during the Civil War:

> Let not him who is houseless [wrote Lincoln] pull down the house of another; but let him labor diligently and build one for himself, thus by example assuring that his own [house] shall be safe from violence when built.[54]

Surely here is the wisdom of Solomon and of a just and generous Conservatism.

12.

We turn finally to two myths propagated by Kendall and Carey which, it seems to us, have been stumbling blocks for American Conservatives—particularly for those who have forgotten their American history. According to *Basic Symbols* it was Lincoln who somehow invented a "*Constitutional status*" for the Declaration and, by his enumeration of "four score and seven years" in the Gettysburg Address, spuriously caused the occasion for Independence to become that of our birth "*as a nation*." What was established on July 4, 1776, they say, was not a nation, but only "a baker's dozen of new sovereignties."[55] In short, what the thirteen colonies did that day was not merely to declare themselves independent of Great Britain, but to declare themselves independent of each other. Here is Lincoln, taking up that claim, in his message to Congress, July 4, 1861:

> Therein [that is, by the Declaration of Independence] the "United Colonies" were declared to be "Free and Independent States"; but, even then, the object plainly was not to declare their independence of *one another*, or of the *Union*; but directly the contrary, as their mutual pledge, and their mutual action, before, at the time, and afterwards, abundantly show.[56]

How can Kendall and Carey revive this old Confederate propaganda without even alluding to the "abundant" evidence with which Lincoln had refuted it?

However indeterminate the character of American federalism may have been at that early date, there can be no question but that the thirteen former colonies, now states, remained united, and always, before the rest of the world, assumed the character of a single person. Passing over the pledge of unity in the Declaration itself, and the further pledge in the Articles of Confederation that the Union shall be perpetual, we would direct attention to Article VI of the Constitution. It declares that "All Debts contracted and Engagements entered into, before the Adoption of this Constitution, shall be as valid against the United States under this Constitution, as under the Confederation." Thus the United States "before the Adoption of this Constitution," the United States "under the Confederation," and the United States "under this Constitution," are all *the same United States*. According to Article VI, the one from which the many were formed—according to *e pluribus unum*, the motto of the United States—did not result from the Constitution. But if the Constitution did not cause the Union, then the Union (that is the Union of the People of the United States) must have caused the Constitution. But if the Union as a sovereign entity had an origin before 1787, when else can it have been except on July 4, 1776? If the Declaration gave birth to the Union which gave birth to the Constitution, it must itself have *constitutional status*.[57] And so it always has had in the statutes of the United States. Lincoln was of course perfectly correct in what he said at Gettysburg, and elsewhere, upon this topic.

But is it proper to refer to the Union which came into being in 1776 as a *nation*?

Certainly neither Union nor nation were fully formed—any more than any other infant at birth. But Thomas Jefferson, writing to James Madison, on August 30, 1823, referred without hesitation to a meeting that had taken place in the previous month, as "an anniversary assemblage of the nation on its birthday."[58] I would venture to doubt whether anyone can find any expression by any American statesman during the first fifty years following independence that contradicts the opinion that July 4, 1776, was the birthday *of the nation*. These were the formative years of Lincoln's life. He grew up, strange to say, believing what Jefferson said about our being a nation, just as he grew up believing Jefferson when he wrote "that all men are created equal."

We come now to Kendall and Carey's contention that Equality, which had admittedly (and unfortunately) loomed so large in the Declaration, had somehow disappeared when the Constitution, and the federal bill of rights, came to be written. Our readers will readily perceive that this alleged omission *is* an omission, only if the Declaration itself lacked *constitutional status*. But we have just proved that it *does* have that *status*. The Declaration authorized each of the thirteen states separately, and all of them collectively, to "institute new Government" such as to them "shall seem most likely to effect their Safety and Happiness." The statement of principles in the Declaration of Independence properly accompanied a revolutionary change in political allegiance. It also properly accompanied a dissolution of one social compact and the formation of another (or others). There was a good deal of contemporaneous discussion as to whether the dissolving of the political allegiance of the colonists to the British crown also constituted a dissolution of the social compact among themselves. According to James Madison, "The question was brought before Congress at its first session by Doctor Ramsay, who contested the election of William Smith; who, though born in South Carolina, had been absent at the date of independence. The decision was, that his birth in the Colony made him a member of society in its new as well as its original state."[59] We can easily imagine some Tories, who were driven out of the country, contesting this decision! In any event, there was no such revolutionary change as occurred in 1776, in the interval between 1776 and 1787. The absence of a new declaration of principles in 1787, far from indicating that the Framers had forgotten the old one, is a sign that they remembered it perfectly. Had they changed their minds about those principles in any way, a new one might have been indicated. But they had not changed their minds, and the country that ratified the Constitution understood perfectly that the principles of 1776, as expressed not only in the national Declaration of Independence, but also in all the state declarations accompanying the state constitutions, governed the new Constitution as well.

The principles of the Declaration are not, however, merely presupposed in the Constitution. They are present in the very first words of the Constitution as those words were understood by those who drafted and adopted it. "We the People of the United States," implies the existence of a *compact* in precisely the sense in which

Delaware and Maryland used that term in their declarations of rights. In the debates on nullification, in the early 1830s, speakers on all sides of that difficult question, prefaced their remarks by saying that compact was the basis of all free government. In one of his last writings, an essay on "Sovereignty," Madison affirmed as a matter of course "that all power in just and free governments is derived from compact."[60] By compact, he said, he meant "the theory which contemplates a certain number of individuals as meeting and agreeing to form one political society, in order that the rights, the safety, and the interest of each may be under the safeguard of the whole."[61] "The first supposition" of such an agreement, said Madison, "is that each individual being previously independent of the others, the compact which is to make them one society must result from the free consent of *every* individual."[62] If then the people of the United States, who ordained the Constitution of the United States, are a free people, they must have been formed into civil society by the free consent of *every* individual. But that would not be possible unless every individual, then and since, forming part of the people of the United States, like all mankind, in the original and originating sense, had been by the laws of nature and of nature's God, "created equal."

᠎ᢁ

THE HERESY OF EQUALITY: A REPLY TO HARRY JAFFA

M. E. Bradford

I

LET US HAVE no foolishness indeed.* Equality as a moral or political imperative, pursued as an end in itself—Equality, with the capital "E"—is the antonym of every legitimate conservative principle. Contrary to most Liberals, new and old, it is nothing less than sophistry to distinguish between equality of opportunity (equal starts in the "race of life") and equality of condition (equal results). For only those who are equal can take equal advantage of a given circumstance. And there is no man equal to any other, except perhaps in the special, and politically untranslatable, understanding of the Deity. *Not intellectually or physically or economically or even*

*This essay is a direct response to Harry Jaffa's "Equality as a Conservative Principle," Loyola of Los Angeles Law Review, VIII (June, 1975), 471–505, which is itself a critique of *The Basic Symbols of the American Political Tradition* by Willmoore Kendall and George W. Carey. Lincoln's reading of the Declaration of Independence is the central subject of this entire exchange. Jaffa's piece invites direct comparison with mine.

Reprinted from *A Better Guide than Reason: Studies in the American Revolution* by M. E. Bradford. Sherwood Sugden & Company, Publishers, 315 Fifth Street, Peru, Illinois 61354. By permission.

morally. Not equal! Such is, of course, the genuinely self-evident proposition.[1] Its truth finds a verification in our bones and is demonstrated in the unselfconscious acts of our everyday lives: vital proof, regardless of our private political persuasion. Incidental equality, engendered by the pursuit of other objectives, is, to be sure, another matter. Inside the general history of the West (and especially within the American experience) it can be credited with a number of healthy consequences: strength in the bonds of community, assent to the authority of honorable regimes, faith in the justice of the gods.

But the equality of Professor Jaffa's essay, even in the ordinary sense of "equal rights," can be expected to work the other way around. For this equality belongs to the post-Renaissance world of ideology—of political magic and the alchemical "science" of politics. Envy is the basis of its broad appeal. And rampant envy, the besetting virus of modern society, is the most predictable result of insistence upon its realization.[2] Furthermore, hue and cry over equality of opportunity and equal rights leads, *a fortiori*, to a final demand for equality of condition. Under its pressure self-respect gives way in the large majority of men who have not reached the level of their expectation, who have no support from an inclusive identity, and who hunger for "revenge" on those who occupy a higher station and will (they expect) continue to enjoy that advantage. The end result is visible in the spiritual proletarians of the "lonely crowd," Bertrand de Jouvenel has described the process which produces such non-persons in his memorable study, *On Power*.[3] They are the natural pawns of an impersonal and omnicompetent Leviathan. And to insure their docility such a state is certain to recruit a large "new class" of men, persons superior in "ability" and authority, both to their ostensible "masters" among the people and to such anachronisms as stand in their progressive way.

Such is the evidence of the recent past—and particularly of American history. Arrant individualism, fracturing and then destroying the hope of amity and confederation, the communal bond and the ancient vision of the good society as an extrapolation from family, is one villain in this tale. Another is rationalized cowardice, shame, and ingratitude hidden behind the disguise of self-sufficiency or the mask of injured merit. Interdependence, which secures dignity and makes of equality a mere irrelevance, is the principal victim. Where fraternity exists to support the official structure of government, it can command assent with no fear of being called despotic or prejudiced in behalf of one component of the society it represents. But behind the cult of equality (the chief if not only tenet in Professor Jaffa's theology, and his link to the pseudoreligious politics of ideology) is an even more sinister power, the uniformitarian hatred of providential distinctions which will stop at nothing less than what Eric Voegelin calls "a reconstitution of being": a nihilistic impulse which is at bottom both frightened and vain in its rejection of a given contingency and in its arrogation of a godlike authority to annul that dependency.[4] As Robert Penn Warren has recently reminded us, distinctions drawn from an encounter with an external reality have been the basis for the intellectual life as we have known it: prudent and tentative distinctions, but seriously intended.[5] With the reign of equality all of that achievement is set at peril.

II

So much in prologue. Concerning equality Professor Jaffa and I disagree profoundly; disagree even though we both denominate ourselves conservative. Yet this distinction does not finally exhaust or explain our differences. For Jaffa's opening remarks indicate that his conservatism is of a relatively recent variety and is, in substance, Old Liberalism hidden under a Union battle flag. To the contrary I maintain that if conservatism has any identity whatsoever beyond mere recalcitrance and rationalized self-interest, that identity must incorporate the "funded wisdom of the ages" as that deposition comes down through a particular national experience. Despite modifications within the prescription of a continuum of political life, only a relativist or historicist could argue that American conservatism should be an utterly unique phenomenon, without antecedents which predate 1776 and unconnected with the mainstream of English and European thought and practice known to our forefathers in colonial times. Jaffa of course nods toward one face of Locke and, by implication, the chiliastic politics of Cromwell's New England heirs.[6] And I have no doubt that he can add to this hagiography a selective (and generally misleading) list of earlier patrons of his view. I cannot in this space encounter the full spectrum of Straussian rationalism. To specify what I believe to be lacking in Jaffa's conservative model (and wrong with the intellectual history he uses in its validation), it will serve better for me to concentrate first on how I read the Declaration of Independence and then append, in abbreviated form, my estimation of Lincoln's lasting and terrible impact on the nation's destiny through his distortions upon that text. This of course involves me incidentally in Jaffa's quarrel with Kendall-Carey and *The Basic Symbols of the American Political Tradition*. But it must be understood that my object is not to defend these worthy gentlemen. To the contrary, my primary interest is in a more largely conservative view of the questions over which they and Professor Jaffa disagree. And therefore, incidentally with the operation and quality of my adversary's mind which lead him to conclusions so very different from mine. With those concerns I propose to organize and conclude my remarks.

III

Professor Jaffa begs a great many questions in his comment on the Declaration. But his greatest mistake is an open error, and supported by considerable precedent in both academic and political circles. In truth, his approach is an orthodox one, at least in our radical times. I refer to his treatment of the second sentence of that document in abstraction from its whole: indeed, of the first part of that sentence in abstraction from its remainder, to say nothing of the larger text. Jaffa filters the rest of the Declaration (and later expressions of the American political faith) back and forth through the measure of that sentence until he has (or so he imagines) achieved its baptism in the pure waters of the higher law. He quotes Lincoln approvingly that "the doctrine of human equality was 'the father of all moral principle [amongst us].'"[7] Jaffa sets up a false dilemma: we must be, as a people, "committed" to Equality or we are "open to the relativism and historicism that is the theoretical ground of modern totalitarian regimes." The Declaration is, of course, the origin of that commitment to "permanent standards." And particularly the second sentence. The trouble here comes from an imperfect grasp of the Burkean calculus. And from the habit of reading legal, poetic, and rhetorical documents as if they were bits of revealed truth or statements of systematic thought. My objections derive principally from those antirationalist realms of discourse. For I assume, with Swift, that man is a creature capable of reason, *capax rationis*, but not a rational animal. Therefore the head and heart must be engaged together where instruction is attempted. The burden of poetry and rhetoric is inherent in the form through which the idea is embodied: its meaning is its way of meaning, not a discursive paraphrase. And it achieves that meaning as it unfolds. According to this procedure we are taught from of old that the soul may be composed, the sensibility reordered. Reason enters into this process with modesty and draws its sanction for whatever new truth it may advance from cooperation with sources and authorities that need produce no credentials nor prove up any title with the audience assumed. For in poetry as in law and rhetoric all matters are not in question. There is a prescription, or something equivalent to what Burke calls by that name. And usually a theology to channel and gloss the prescript. Tropes and figures, terms weighted more or less by usage, norms of value configured and dramatic sequences of associated actions discovered through an unbroken stream of place and blood and history operate in this mode of communication as something logically prior to the matter under examination. And likewise the law, especially where the rule is *stare decisis*. Where myth or precedent or some other part of the "wise prejudice" of a people is presupposed and identity therefore converted into a facet of ontology, a providential thing ("inalienable" in that word's oldest sense, not to be voted, given, or reasoned away), there is nothing for mere philosophy to say. And that *philosophe* abstraction, political Man, who once theoretically existed outside a social bond, nowhere to be seen. As a wise man wrote, "Where the great interests of mankind are concerned through a long succession of generations, that succession ought to be admitted into some share in the councils which are so deeply to affect them."[8] For the "moral essences" that shape a commonwealth are "not often constructed after any theory: theories are rather drawn from them"— the natural law, made partially visible only in the prescription, but made visible nonetheless.[9]

IV

To anyone familiar with English letters and the English mind in the seventeenth and eighteenth centuries, the Declaration of Independence is clearly a document produced out of the *mores majorum*—legal, rhetorical, poetic—and not a piece of reasoning or systematic truth. No sentence of its whole means anything out of context. It unfolds *seriatim* and makes sense only when read through. Furthermore, what it does mean is intelligible only in a matrix of circumstances—political, literary, linguistic, and mundane. Nevertheless, no one trained to move in the rhetorical world of Augustan humanism would take it for a relativistic statement any more than they would describe Dryden's *Religio Laici*, Addison's *Cato*, Johnson's *Rasselas*, or Burke's *Reflections on the Revolution in France* in that fashion.[10] Jaffa revives the error of his master, Leo Strauss, in speaking of the bugbear historicism and of "mere prescriptive rights."[11] For it is in our day the alternatives which carry with them a serious danger of the high-sounding despot. Radicals (to use his term, meaning the Liberals who see in politics a new "Queen of the Sciences" and employ a sequence of private revelations to exalt her condition) believe in a "higher law"—have done so at least since the politics of secularized Puritanism first appeared in European society."[12] Even Marxists finally worship the demiurge of history—and rest the remainder of their argument upon that authority. And the goddess Reason is still with us, available to sanction whatever her hand finds to do in erasing all that survives from what Peter Gay rightly labels the mythopoeic vision.[13] I agree with Professor Jaffa concerning the danger of relativism. A Christian must. And also about behavioristic political science. Such study is description only, or else mere manipulation. But, hunger for the normative aside, we must resist the tendency to thrust familiar contemporary pseudoreligious notions back into texts where they are unlikely to appear. Any Englishman of 1776 (colonial or not) should not be expected to construe natural rights so rigorously as Justice Black—except perhaps for hyperbole in argument. In between our day and that first July 4 stand a number of revolutions, especially the French. And also two hundred years of liberal and radical thought. We are bemused by the spectre of Locke (an authority to some of the revolutionary generation, but read loosely and in the light of Sir Edward Coke and William Petyt, and the 1628 Petition of Right, and the 1689 Declaration of Rights).[14] The legacy of English common law is lost upon us. And in the process we have forgotten, among other things, that Edmund Burke is our best guide to the main-line of Whig thought: *not Locke or Paine, or even Harrington, but Burke*. It is, of course, a truism that all colonial Americans did their political thinking inside the post-1688 Whig legal tradition.[15] Some years ago Professor Jaffa attempted to counter this line of objection to his Lincolnian construction of the Declaration by setting Paine and Locke (plus an irrelevant bit of Blackstone) upon Daniel J. Boorstin's excellent *The American: The Colonial Experience*. But in so doing he only evaded his antagonist and obfuscated the question of what is typically Whig and behind our "revolution."[16] For Locke is not so consistent a source of equal rights as Jaffa would lead us to believe. Indeed, that worthy theorist of liberty was an eager part to the creation of a slavocracy in South Carolina.[17] And on occasion he justified the peculiar institution with nothing more sophisticated than an appeal to race or right of conquest.[18] Blackstone, for his part, was a high Tory and a poor sponsor for equality of any sort. And Paine relates to very little that became American in our Constitution of 1787. Recent scholarship on early American history has, by and large, exhibited an anachronistic tendency to ignore all patriot utterances that do not sound like Locke in his highest flights of freedom or Paine before the Mountain: like the Whig "Left," in other words.[19] They have ignored the problems in logic set up by "all men are created equal" when understood as one of Lincoln's beloved Euclidian propositions and the larger problems for libertarians determined not to call for equality of condition when they start from such a postulate.[20] Along with the political philosophers they have approached the task of explication as if the Declaration existed sui generis, in a Platonic empyrean.[21] A gloss upon what transpired in a real (i.e., intellectually "messy") convention in a real Philadelphia seems not to interest these sages: what with reason could be expected to occur.[22] With a non-Lockean Whig machinery (and as a practicing rhetorician) I will attempt to draw the inquiry down toward such probabilities.

V

Contrary to Professor Jaffa, it is my view that the Declaration of Independence is not very revolutionary at all. Nor the Revolution itself. Nor the Constitution. Only Mr. Lincoln and those who gave him support, both in his day and in the following century. And the moralistic, verbally disguised instrument which Lincoln invented may indeed be the most revolutionary force in the modern world: a pure gnostic force.[23] The Declaration confirms an existing state of affairs, even in its announcement of a break with George III. For the colonies existed as distinctive commonwealths with (and out of) English law. Yet they were English with a difference. It required only a fracturing of spiritual bonds that it be made official. In the spring and summer of 1776 things came to a head. As Jefferson wrote, a British army was descending upon Long Island: an army bent on putting an end to petitions, inquiries, declarations, and all such irritants. The King had declared the members of the Continental Congress rebels, without the law. And likewise those who thought themselves represented by that body. No security from deportation for trial, summary execution, and confiscation were the alternatives to unconditional submission and allegiance outside the law.

Rhetorical criticism begins with a careful description of circumstances antedating composition.[24] For without that information well established, the meaning of language is uncertain; and a piece of literature may be treated as if it had been prepared only for the gods. Connection of a document with a set of writings made and/or exchanged before or after its appearance is certainly such necessary information. There is no Declaration apart from it. Effacing himself, Thomas Jefferson wrote what completed a conversation concerning the law which had gone back and forth across the Atlantic for many years before exhausting its purpose. Everything in this sequence appeals to the *consensus gentium* of sensible men (common reasonableness but not philosophy) and to English law. James II had set himself outside that rule, using the dispensary powers to invent a new equality of rights. This usurpation resulted in a royal "abdication" and a new king who promised to uphold the charters and ancient laws and thus to preserve to Englishmen and their posterity the rights they had inherited through a providentially blessed history. This was the common understanding of that period. It is implicit in the dialogue between Philadelphia and Whitehall and in the antecedent quarrel between the Crown and various colonial assemblies after the Stamp and Declaratory Acts and the Albany Congress. The American "parliament" first convened in September of 1774 and soon issued its "Declaration and Resolves of the First Continental Congress, October 14, 1774." Even there it is unmistakably clear that a composite identity is addressing a related composite identity, that the mode of address is forensic (determining praise or blame between respective parties in dispute over the meaning of a "given" phenomenon), and that the point of reference is not divine revelation or a body of doctrine maintained according to the precepts of philosophy, but rather a wisdom inherited as prescription, to be applied reasonably, but not in *Reason's* name. This particular Declaration makes it plain that Englishmen are in dispute with Englishmen, groups with groups, and on English grounds. The colonial charters set up this situation. At law they connect the colonies to a paternal source, even while they set them apart. They create an ambiguity in relations with the English parliament and the independent reality of other governments. And they leave law and king and common enemies to hold the mix together.[25]

In their first declaration we learn that the remonstrants are entitled to "life, liberty and property"; that these basic rights come from their ancestors (God perhaps acting through them); that removal over the sea can involve no alienation of such inherited rights; that such alienation is now proposed by way of taxation *and by the machinery of enforcing that tax*; and, finally, that kindred offences against "immunities and privileges granted and confirmed" by royal charters and "secured by their several codes of provincial law" are in prospect. Here and in the later (and similarly argued) "Declaration of the Causes and Necessities of Taking up Arms, July 6, 1775," we can recognize the lineaments of a position finally developed in July of 1776. And also a line of thought coming down directly from the great Charter of 1689—or even more remotely from Bracton and Fortescue. The king is the king, the subject the subject, only within the law. The American colonies are by blood and law part of the English *res publica*, set apart from the old Island Kingdom by England's destruction of that organic relationship. To repeat, it is well to remember that the king declared them "rebels" (Prohibitory Acts, August 1775) well before they had accepted that title for themselves. As they insist, it is for no "light or transient causes" that they make his appellation official. Their charters have become mere paper. By virtue of relocation across the seas they have been defined as alienated Englishmen, without security even in such fundamental matters as life, liberty, and the fruits of their labors. And all men recognize these rights as being the precondition of submission to any government. Their fathers had, of course, grown violent over much smaller affronts. But the "authors" of the Declaration are determined to keep within the law and appear as unusually conservative men. Only when the king denies them all representation, asserts his right to bind them *collectively*, to seize their goods *collectively*, to quarter an angry army upon them, and to punish their entreaties that he restrain his servants to observe the Bill of Rights—only then will they close with a last "appeal from reason to arms."

VI

We are now prepared to ask what Mr. Jefferson and his sensible friends meant by "all men" and "created equal." Meant together—*as a group*. In rhetoric it is a rule to ask how the beginning leads through the middle to the end. If end and middle consort well with one another, if they point in one direction, that agreement defines what may be discovered in between.[26] The last three-fourths of the Declaration (minus the conclusion, its original draft) is a bill of particulars.[27] The king, their only acknowledged link with England, has decapitated the body politic and hence is no longer king on these shores. The law/prescription cannot otherwise be preserved. And these men intend such a preservation. Something in existence declares itself in possession of "honor" and "sensible of the regard of decent men," prepared to draw a new charter out of those it possesses, to act as an entity in forming a confederal government. But first these commonwealths must file an official bill of divorcement, designed to the pattern of a countersuit in an action already initiated on the other side. The generation of a new head for this body is not yet, but will, we can assume, present no problem when a necessity for its creation is made explicit.[28]

The *exordium* of the Declaration begins this appeal with an argument from history and with a definition of the voice addressing the "powers of the earth." It is a "people," a "we" that are estranged from another "we." The peroration reads the same: "we," the "free and independent states," are united in our will to separation— and prepared to answer to high and low for that temerity. They act in the name (and with the sanction) of the good people whose several assemblies had authorized their congregation. This much formally. No contemporary liberal, new or old, can make use of that framework or take the customary liberties with what is contained by the construction. Nor coming to it by the path I have marked, may they, in honesty, see in "created equal" what they devoutly wish to find. "We," in that second sentence, signifies the colonials as the citizenry of the distinct colonies, not as individuals, but rather in their corporate capacity. Therefore, the following "all men"—created equal in their right to expect from any government to which they might submit freedom from corporate bondage, genocide, and massive confiscation—are persons prudent together, respectful of the law which makes them one, even though forced to stand henceforth apart: equal as one free state is as free as another.

Nothing is maintained concerning the abilities or situations of individual persons living within the abandoned context of the British Empire or the societies to be formed by its disruption. No new contract is drawn. Rather, one that exists is *preserved by amputation*. All that is said is that no component of a society can be expected to agree, even though it is part of that society by inheritance, that it is to be bereft of those securities that make life tolerable simply by geographical remoteness. And, if even the Turk and infidel would not as a people submit to a government such as George III proposes to impose through Lord Howe's army, how can Englishmen be expected to agree to that arrangement? So much is "obvious" to everyone, in other words, "self-evident." Thus even if the law of nature and of nations is drawn into our construction of "endowed by their Creator," what is left to be called "inalienable" with respect to American colonials and demonstrative of a certain minimal equality of rights in their collectivities is not so much. What happens in the remainder of the Declaration, following sentence two, is even more depressing to the contemporary Jacobin who would see in the new beginning a departure from the previous political history of Western man. Note particularly the remarks concerning the part played by the king's servants in encouraging a "servile insurrection," the xenophobic objections to the use of foreign mercenaries, and the allusion of the employment of savages as instruments of royal policy. Note also Jefferson's ironic reference to "Christian Kings" and anger at offences to the "common blood." These passages draw upon a received identity and are not "reasonable" in character. Certainly they do not suggest the equality of individual men. But (and I am sure that Professor Jaffa will agree with me on this), even though racist, xenophobic, and religious assumptions have no place in the expression of philosophic truth, they can readily operate in an appeal to prescriptive law. And therefore, I say, in our Declaration of Independence.

VII

Though I agree with Kendall and Carey that there is a distance between the Declaration and the Constitution of 1787, and that silence on equality in the latter reflects a conscious choice, I agree also with Professor Jaffa that the two are not in conflict. The Constitution, like the Articles of Confederation before it, built a structure of common government (to handle all difficulties made by being one and thirteen) upon a common legal inheritance, common origins, and an established unity of purpose. It is a limited contract, resting on an external and prior bond of free and independent states, perfecting or improving their union.[29] It *does not* abrogate what it rests upon. The Declaration was a necessary prologue to its adoption. But, in logic, the Declaration is not implicit in the Constitution except as it made possible free ratification by the independent states. In truth, many rights are secured under the Constitution that are not present in the Declaration, however it be construed. Yet not equal voting rights in state or federal elections. Or economic rights in taxation. Or rights for women. Or even equal footing for various religions—or species of irreligion. To say nothing of slaves. All of this is well known. But, if we reasoned as do some gifted scholars, it might be maintained that the Constitution takes us even further away from equality for slaves than does the Declaration.[30] For in Article I, Section 9, provision is made that no law shall be passed by Congress to restrict the slave trade prior to 1808. Slavery exists by acknowledgment of the same document. Yet it encourages that there be more slaves in the Republic than are present in 1787. More in a proportion that twenty-one years can be expected to provide. Hence this provision can be described in logic as presenting Negro slavery as a positive good. For reasons of history I do not insist upon this commentary. The evidence of what lies behind the text suggests another view.[31] And for the same reasons I cannot follow the practical advice of the late Everett McKinley Dirksen and "get right with Lincoln."[32]

VIII

It would be unreasonable for me to attempt to develop in this essay all that I wish to say in objection to the politics of Abraham Lincoln. For it is a great deal and will perhaps involve some years. Therefore I must raise only my primary objections, most of them proceeding from Lincoln's misunderstanding of the Declaration as "deferred promise" of equality. I am of course close to the late Professor Kendall in these matters and have learned much from him and from Professor Carey.[33] For one thing, I agree with those gentlemen that Lincoln's "second founding" is fraught with peril and carries with it the prospect of an endless series of turmoils and revolutions, all dedicated to freshly discovered meanings of equality as a "proposition." I do not, however, look so much as they do to New England. It is not my preference for a colonial precedent to the national identity.[34] The millenarian infection spread and almost institutionalized by Lincoln (and by the manner of his death) has its impetus from that "other Israel" surrounding Boston.[35] And its full potential for mischief is yet to be determined. What Alexander Stephens called Lincoln's "religious mysticism" of Union, when combined in "cold, calculating reason" to the goal of "equal rights" and an authoritarian (that is, irrational) biblical rhetoric, constitutes a juggernaut powerful enough to arm and enthrone any self-made Caesar we might imagine:

even an unprepossessing country lawyer from Illinois. For by means of that mixture and solution a transfer of authority and energy is effected, from the Puritan dream of a New Jerusalem governed by an elect to the manifest destiny of American democracy led by keepers of the popular faith. Both are authorized from on High to reform the world into an imitation of themselves—and to lecture and dragoon all who might object. Both receive regular intimations of the Divine Will through prophets who arise from time to time to recall them to their holy mission. And both operate from that base to paint all prospective opposition in the darkest of colors, the rhetoric of polarity being a fundamental correlative of all genuinely Puritan activity, with no room for shadings in between and no mercy for the wicked.

This is, of course, not to minimize the role played in Lincoln's rise to power by the tireless "engine" of his ambition. Nor his political gifts—for which I have an ever-growing admiration. As is announced obliquely in the "Address Before the Springfield Young Men's Lyceum, 1838," Lincoln was, very early, touched by a Bonapartist sense of destiny. His papers (all nine volumes, plus a recent supplement) reflect a steady purpose, an inexorable will to rise, to put his stamp upon the world.[36] Yet there was always another side to his nature—glum, ironic, pessimistic, self-deprecatory: in a word, inscrutable. It has deceived and puzzled many. Yet, as is ordinary in a Puritan, this meandering reflected private doubt of the wisdom behind personal choices and (perhaps) the status of motives which directed him toward their enactment: self-doubt, but not doubt of the ideals. And he knew how to cure the ailment—by "striving to finish the work." He had his ends in mind, his religion of Union in Equality, but he left it to the "providential" flow of history to carry them to realization. However, after 1854 he condescended to give that flow a little help.

The Kansas-Nebraska Act *made* the political career of Abraham Lincoln, opened the door for the "Reign of Reason," made it possible to put behind the "living history" of the revolutionary generation ("oaks," an organic image), and provided for an opportunity to roll out the big guns of priestly language to give what he meant by "freedom" that "new birth" he came to speak of at Gettysburg. He played with consummate skill the circumstances of free-soil reaction in 1854 and then the tumult surrounding the campaigns of 1858 and 1860. Nor are there many scholars who do not find some mystery or subtle craft in his first months as president, to say nothing of his subsequent conduct. But that story, as I read it, is a large book—larger than Professor Jaffa's. Suffice it to say that Lincoln was indeed a man whose "policy was to have no policy."[37] He loved to quote from *Hamlet* that "there is a divinity that shapes our ends,/Rough-hew them how we will."[38] And from the total pattern of his conduct we can extract the following formula: Wait, set up or encourage pressure, then jump, and call it God. The original behind this procedure could be any one of a dozen historic tyrants, all of whom announced a noble purpose for their acts. But when the pattern is encapsulated by the high idiom of Holy Scripture (the authority of which no man can examine), the Anglo-Saxon prototype emerges as Oliver Cromwell, the Lord Protector. And in searching for what is significant in that analogy, the logical point of departure is the House Divided speech to the Illinois Republican convention of June 1858.

IX

Lincoln's political gnosticism does not come to a head in the House Divided speech, and does not begin there. For even in the Springfield Lyceum address (made when he was twenty-nine), he concludes on a Puritan note: Let us refound the Union, and "the gates of hell shall not prevail against it." The new founder, having propped up the temple of Liberty/Equality on the solid pillars of "calculating reason," will therefore be, in relation to the powers of evil (i.e., those who do not care for the arrangement) as was the faith of Peter to the Christian church after its foundation. And God is thus, by implication, the security for the quasireligion of Equality. In a similar fashion Lincoln finds God as a verification for his rectitude as President in his address to Northern moderates, men who loved the old "divided" house, which we find in his Second Inaugural. Here is the heresy of a "political religion" at the beginning of Lincoln's political career, and also at its end. But one prudent shift is observable. Except for an occasional mention of "propositions" or their equivalent, the debt to European rationalism (the source of Lincoln's puzzling theological heterodoxy), fades into the background once Honest Abe appears on the center of the national stage in Peoria, Illinois (October 1854). And in the opposite direction the biblical element grows to be more and more dominant after 1858. But we should not infer from this that Lincoln's design changed after he got the Republican nomination against Douglas. Only his perception (drawing from the abolitionists) of the proper instrument for its execution.

The House Divided speech was, beyond any question, a Puritan declaration of war. And therefore also Lincoln's election on the basis of its contents as transcribed in the Republican platform of 1860. A Lincoln admirer, Don E. Fehrenbacher, in his *Prelude to Greatness: Lincoln in the 1850's* calls it "Garrisonian."[39] The South saw it that way, as did much of the North. And neither forgot those words:

> A House Divided against itself cannot stand. I believe this government cannot endure, perpetually half *slave* and half *free*. I do not expect the Union to be *dissolved*—I do not expect the house to *fall*—but I *do* expect it will cease to be divided. It will become *all* one thing, or *all* another.

Yet we should not abstract the speech from the intellectual milieu to which it belongs. By means of his political manipulation, Lincoln, in the words of his one-time friend, Alexander Stephens, "put the institution of nearly one-half the states under the ban of public opinion and national condemnation." And, continued Stephens, "this, upon general principle, is quite enough of itself to arouse a spirit not only of general indignation, but of revolt on the part of the proscribed."[40] Other people in these days made noises like Lincoln. After 1854 they got a good hearing. One of them, old John Brown, received beatification from the Northern newspapers which supported Mr. Lincoln in 1860. What this juxtaposition signified, despite certain cluckings of disapproval among Republican stalwarts, no one could mistake.

Of course the central motif of the House Divided speech, as quoted above, echoes the Bible (Mark 3:25): Christ speaking of the undivided hosts of Satan.[41] Lincoln's authority is thus, by association, elevated to the level of the hieratic. But he adds something to the mixture. The myth that slavery will be either set on its way to extinction by an official gesture on the part of the federal government or else all states will eventually become slave-states establishes a false dilemma, describes a set of conditions which, once fixed in the minds of his free-soil audience, was certain to create in them a sense of alarm. Thus he participates in what Richard Hofstadter calls the "paranoid style" in politics.[42] Fear of the slave power (Southern political and economic domination) and racist hostility to the idea of massive Negro influx, free *or* slave, into the North made predictable that one of these alternatives would be perceived as intolerable—and we can guess which one. Thus the size of the Republican Party might be augmented from the ranks of persons who despised Abolition and all its works.

For Lincoln to say after 1858 that the Constitution and the laws were sacred to him, that he would "preserve" the "old Union of the Fathers," is mere window dressing. For to argue that your enemy is evil incarnate (the burden of his rhetoric), in league with Satan, and then add that you respect him and his legal rights is to indulge in pietistic arrogance—as Alexander Stephens specified in the passage I quoted just above. Jaffa confuses matters no end in maintaining that Lincoln addressed a real danger in his imaginary "division." As the South perceived the question, the real issue in Kansas and Nebraska was whether or not there could be a federal policy on the "morality" of its conduct in any connection not covered by the original federal covenant: whether they could stay under the gun.

For houses are always divided, in some fashion or another. And, no doubt, should slavery be gone, some new infamy was bound to be discovered by the stern examiners whose power depends upon a regularity in such "crusades". A law prohibiting slavery in the territories, in that it affected the ability of a new state to grow to maturity as a child of the total Union, would define the South as outside of that communion. Furthermore, it would set in motion a chain of circumstances that could be used against the region where antinomian morality could be read into law—could touch slavery or any other "peculiarity," unless a Constitutional amendment (requiring a three-fourths vote of the states) existed to protect it. A Union of this sort was not the old Union. Nor was its issue, a Union by force—in 1865 or *now*. Whatever the intent of armies in blue, it could not be the same—not the contract ratified by all the states who were party to it. Rather, it involved Lincoln's worship of the law as the Constitution *with the Declaration drafted into (and over) it*—Lincoln's Declaration: and therefore (*vide supra*), no worship of the law whatsoever, but instead devotion to perpetually exciting goals, always just beyond our reach. Thus, under the aegis of a plurality president, the principle of assent is put aside for the sake of an idea (read ideology) which only a small minority of Americans could be expected to approve, either in 1860 or today. And the entire project accomplished by rhetoric—Kendall's "magic." On the record of American history since 1858, Lincoln stands convicted as an enemy of the "founding."[43] Which is to say, as our new Father—even though many of us still refuse to live in the cold uniformitarian temple he designed.

Of course military resistance to radical Union (i.e., statism covered by a patina of law) ended in 1865. Lincoln saluted these developments at the beginning of his second term. And I must conclude my remarks on Lincoln's politics with some observations on that address. His conduct in using the presidential powers has been treated to my satisfaction by Gottfried Dietze.[44] What that amounts to is the creation of an Eastern priest/king—an epideictic personage such as we hear in the voice at Gettysburg. Speech and deeds together did change the country—and in respects more important than the abolition of Negro slavery: together opened the door to portentous changes that finally touch even liberty.[45] The argument of this essay is, in sum, that what Lincoln did to preserve the Union by expanding and enshrining equality left the prescription of the revolution of law in our national beginning and the "unwritten constitution" of our positive pluralism very much in doubt. Such was his purpose. But (and I again repeat) this plan is something which he concealed until he prepared the Second Inaugural—where in victory he became a scripture in himself.

X

There is of course a clear conflict between the Cooper Union speech, the First Inaugural, Lincoln's letters of the time, and the posture Lincoln assumed a few weeks before Lee's surrender. If we would discover in Father Abraham the "crafty Machievel," the conflict between his assent to a constitutional amendment making slavery "perpetual" where established and the House Divided speech is our point of departure. But the Lincoln who kept Kentucky and Missouri from secession is hard to penetrate. It is wise to assume that he followed the times. For it cannot be demonstrated that he ever really attempted to pacify Southern anxieties without reconstituting the Republic. Certainly he wanted no peace on any grounds but unconditional surrender. And in 1865, he looked back on his five years as national leader, "scanned the providences," and "found himself approved."

When seen in the context of his career after 1858 and within the pattern of a lifetime of deliberate utterances, Lincoln's Second Inaugural turns out to be something very different from what most Americans have believed it to be: a completion of a pattern announced in the House Divided speech, unfolded in its fullness at

Gettysburg, and glossed in a letter to Thurlow Weed written just before his death. Historically, the misconception of this performance may be attributed to a disproportionate emphasis upon the final paragraph of the Second Inaugural treated (once again) as if it had an independent existence outside the total document. Furthermore, what Lincoln means by "malice toward none" and "bind up the nation's wounds" is, even within this single paragraph, modified beyond recognition by "as God gives us to see the right." For he means here revelation, not conscience. Americans are so accustomed, since Lincoln's time, to a quasireligious rhetoric in their public men that the combination has passed without notice for a century and more. But to discover its full meaning we must look up into the body of the speech. There it becomes clear what Lincoln is about behind his mild forensic tone.

Said another way, what I here contend is that the attribution of his own opinions to an antinomian revelation of divine will as regards America's political destiny is more completely and intensively visible in this particular Lincoln document than in any other. For what he does in the Second Inaugural is to expand the outreach of his rhetorical Manicheanism beyond the limits made familiar to us in a thousand expressions of piety toward the Union (and most particularly at Gettysburg) to include not only his obviously beaten enemies in the South but also all those who accepted the Union as it had existed from the Founding until 1860. Indeed, the targets of his rhetoric on this occasion are all moderate Unionists who did not aforetimes recognize, as did their prophet for the day, the necessity for a greater perfection in their bonds. The war was long, says Father Abraham, not simply because the rebels were wicked but furthermore because many of their adversaries were reluctant. In the letter to Weed (March 15, 1865) Lincoln observes, in speaking of the unpopularity he expects to be the fate of the remarks in question, that "men are not flattered by being shown that there has been a difference of purpose between the Almighty and them. To deny it, however, in this case, is to deny that there is a God governing the world."[46] Since no Southerners were present to be offended by the Second Inaugural, and since Lincoln's teaching in that address refers chiefly to those who had been patient with the divided house, it is evident that his targets in interpreting long war and heavy judgment are those who did not see *before secession* the necessity for conflict. How this reading of the American teleology could be expected to bind up wounds in any conventional sense is difficult to determine. But the end result is to give Lincoln a rhetorical upper hand he had not sought at any point in his presidency and to prepare him to do whatever he means by "finish the work." It is to leave him, finally, alone as the agent of his master, beyond the most ultra-Republicans as an instrument of providence and with an authority few mortal men have ever aspired to hold in their hands. Death confirmed him (or rather, his design) in that condition. Consider for an illustration Edward M. Stanton's words after reading the Gettysburg Address to an 1868 political audience in Pennsylvania: "That is the voice of God speaking through the lips of Abraham Lincoln . . . You hear the voice of Father Abraham here tonight. Did he die in vain?"[47] Such politics are beyond reason, beyond law, though they may embody a rationalist objective. They are also Jaffa's model—from authority and passion. And with consequences I shall now consider.

XI

"Style," Sir Herbert Read once observed, "is the ultimate morality of mind." By style I would understand him to mean all the elements that go into the composition of a piece of rhetoric, its structural elements as well as its textural; and, in examining the "style" of this particular essay, I find an extraordinary laxity—which suggests that Professor Jaffa is not at his best. Indeed, I can hardly recognize here the consummate and ethical rhetorician of *Crisis of the House Divided*, a work which I obviously admire—though from a certain distance, The argument of this later essay is loose and meandering, like some ancient river that is constantly winding back on itself, Lincoln as a young legislative candidate once advocated (like a good, money-minded Whig) the straightening of such rivers by cutting off the neck of the loops. In closing, I shall attempt to do the same for Mr. Jaffa's argument, if only to indicate the tortuous nature of the "moral" impulse which lay behind its composition.

In the first place, as my metaphor suggests, this is an old river, an ancient argument which need not be developed again in detail since everyone is familiar enough with its tenets (i.e., the equation of the social-contract theory with some theory of equality). What is new in this lengthy diatribe is no more than the ostensible targets of Professor Jaffa's attack, Kendall and Carey. And indeed they could be a valid point of departure for an egalitarian like Professor Jaffa, since Kendall and Carey do define the true American political tradition as both conservative *and* hostile to Equality.

But unfortunately Kendall and Carey do not raise their standard on that spot of polemical ground where Professor Jaffa would like to do battle. They do not become overly preoccupied with slavery; and for obvious reasons Professor Jaffa would rather talk about slavery than the political documents which are the announced topic of *Basic Symbols*. And so he does, curving around obstacles to reach the sacred subject, turning his argument in that direction by charging that Kendall and Carey never mention the word in their study and that such an omission avoids the essential question of the American political experience. He repeats this charge several times during the windings of his thesis, despite the fact that it is unfounded (pp. 479, 486, and 491). For an instance, he ignores the following comment on page 92 of *Basic Symbols*, a passage that raises perhaps a most difficult question for him to consider:

> However, the assembly that approved the Declaration would not subscribe to the denunciation of slavery that Jefferson sought to include, so that we might be led to believe that the signers were talking of equality of men in a sense far short of that which modern egalitarians hold.

Small wonder that Professor Jaffa's rhetorical river veers sharply away from this high ground. Was it forgotten or ignored in order to avoid the issue it raises? Whatever the reasons, it flows off in that direction, attacking Kendall's review of *Crisis of the House Divided*, a Kendall essay in which the issues are relevant to slavery and furthermore a matter of historical interpretation. Soon we are curling and gliding through familiar territory, much of it mythic in nature and therefore simpler and purer than life. In Jaffa's imaginary history of the United States, Jefferson is the drafter of the Declaration, but not the slaveholder who wrote in *Notes on the State of Virginia* of his suspicion that blacks "are inferior to the whites in the endowments both of body and mind" and that this "unfortunate difference of colour, and perhaps of faculty, is a powerful obstacle to the emancipation of these people"; and *certainly not* the Virginian who called "Equality" a "mere abstraction" and its devotees a "Holy Alliance." There, Locke is the philosopher of *The Second Treatise*, but *not* the man responsible for *Fundamental Constitutions for Carolina*. Antebellum slavery is a kind of Buchenwald;[48] and the United States Constitution is drafted with a tacit understanding that "all men are [really] created equal," that this is a proposition with "constitutional status," *in spite of the fact* that the Constitution itself recognized the established legal institution of slavery and discouraged interpolation into its provisions of what is not clearly there. All of these oversimplifications ignore one overriding question, the question that Kendall and Carey raise and which Professor Jaffa is careful not to consider. Some "truths" are more important than the Truth. Even the Truth that we have a political tradition that is conservative and contrary to Lincoln. Thus, though the river of Professor Jaffa's argument seems erratic, its wanderings (like the wanderings of a real river) have a predictable pattern; they follow the course of least resistance. And it is in the pattern—tortuous and circuitous—that one can see the relationship between his "style" and his "ultimate morality of mind."

Yet we cannot entirely blame Professor Jaffa for these aberrations, this great falling away from scholarly rectitude and right reason. His errors are endemic among his kind—such Old Liberals identify their politics with the Lincolnian precedent. As I have tried to indicate, such errors constitute what amounts to a "genetic flaw" within that intellectual tradition, a fracture impossible to heal. Trying to preserve property, secure tranquility, and promote equal rights, all at the same time, insures that none of these purposes will be accomplished. And insures also a terrible, unremitting tension, both among those in power and among those whose hopes are falsely raised. Especially with persistence in thinking of men outside of all history that is not Lincoln, and apart from the durable communions of craft and friendship, faith and blood. It has been, however, a distinctive trait of American political thought to do its worst as it touches upon the Negro: to break down when unable to make it through the aforementioned impasse of objectives. Class struggle has been the result, to say nothing of race conflict. And that failing attaches by definition to the Republican identity, flawing it perhaps forever as a viable conservative instrument. Said another way, the more a people derive their political identity from Lincoln's version of Equality, the more they are going to push against the given and providential frame of things to prove up the magic phrase. And, therefore, the more they will (to repeat one of my favorite images) kick the "tar baby."[49] And we all know how that story ends.

~

EQUALITY, JUSTICE, AND THE AMERICAN REVOLUTION: IN REPLY TO BRADFORD'S "THE HERESY OF EQUALITY"

Harry V. Jaffa

"LET US HAVE no foolishness indeed," writes Professor Bradford, in his reply to "Equality as a Conservative Principle," echoing my echo of Willmoore Kendall:*

> Equality as a moral or political imperative, pursued as an end in itself—Equality, with the capital "E"—is the antonym of every legitimate conservative principle.[1]

In *The Federalist*, No. 51, Madison writes that "Justice is the end of government. It is the end of civil society. It ever has been and ever will be pursued until it be obtained, or until liberty be lost in the pursuit."[2] But what is justice? Let me enter into the record of our differences a passage from the *Nicomachean Ethics* which I would hope Professor Bradford might accept as canonical. In Book V, Chapter 3[3] both the unjust man and the unjust action are said to be unequal. Every action admitting more or less, says Aristotle, admits also of a mean, which is the equal. "If then," he continues, "the unjust is the unequal, the just is the equal."

---

*This article originally appeared in Harry V. Jaffa, *How to Think About the American Revolution* (Durham, NC: Carolina Academic Press, 1978). Reprinted with permission from the Claremont Review of Books.

*"The Heresy of Equality: Bradford Replies to Jaffa," *Modern Age*, Vol. 20, No. 1, Winter, 1976, pp. 62–77. The original title of Professor Bradford's essay, which he was kind enough to send me in typescript, was "Black Republicanism Redivivus: A Reply to Harry Jaffa." I greatly regret the change of title. Professor Bradford and I are carrying on a debate which reached a climax in the 1850s. His original title accurately indicates the political character of our differences. In applying to me the appellation that belonged above all to Abraham Lincoln, he has paid me a compliment that, however undeserved, I cannot forgo. As Professor Bradford explains in a note to his *Modern Age* essay, he is replying to my "Equality as a Conservative Principle," originally published in the *Loyola of Los Angeles Law Review*, VIII, (June 1975), and now Chapter II of the present volume. As Professor Bradford correctly notes, "Lincoln's reading of the Declaration of Independence is the central subject of this entire exchange." But see also "Time on the Cross: Debate," in National Review, March 28, 1975, pp. 340–342, and 359. Here Bradford and I crossed swords for the first time.

Aristotle divides justice into two kinds. The one, the justice that is in exchanges. The other, the justice that is in distributions either of honors or profits. As an example of the first kind, consider an exchange of shoes for grain. Somehow the quantity of shoes exchanged for a quantity of grain must be made equal. A common measure is needed, such as money. The shoes and the grain should then both be valued by the same amount of money. If they are so valued—things equal to the same thing being equal to each other—then the transaction may be said to be just. As an example of the second kind of justice, consider the honors or prizes awarded at the end of a race. The first place prize should go to the first place finisher, and the second place prize to the second place finisher. Or, 1/1 equals 2/2. The first kind of justice—in exchanges—is an equality of number: ten dollars worth of shoes equals ten dollars worth of grain. The second kind of justice—in distributions—is an equality of proportion. In both cases, however, the just is a species of the equal.

Equality is a conservative principle because justice is conservative, and equality is the principle of justice. Where exchanges are just—that is, where one party does not overreach the other—and where distributions are just—that is, where rewards are proportioned to merit—men tend to become friends. Where the opposite is the case, they tend to become enemies. In Book V of the *Politics*[4] Aristotle declares that the most general or universal cause of *stasis* (faction or sedition) is inequality. Inequality—whether numerical or proportional—tends to disrupt and destroy political communities, and equality tends towards their harmony and their preservation. Equality as the ground of justice is then both good in itself and good for its consequences.

In the course of my praise of equality I had referred to a New Conservatism, properly so called, as being identical with the Old Liberalism, which was in my view the Liberalism of the Founding Fathers of the American regime. For the Liberalism of the Founders, in my understanding, was not merely that of locally disaffected British Whigs. Once the separation from the British crown was decided upon, they set out to build a new and more radically just political order than had existed in practice in any antecedent model. It was indeed intended to be the *novus ordo seclorum*, the new order of the ages, announced on the great seal of the United States. It was to decide, as Hamilton announced in the first *Federalist*, whether "societies of men [might be] capable of establishing good government [by] reflection and choice," or whether mankind was forever destined "to depend for their political constitutions on accident and force." From the perspective of the American founding, all previous governments, including that of Great Britain, however excellent some of their features, did not embody that reasonableness implied in the human capacity for "reflection and choice."[5] But the American founding was intended to do just that. The rule of priests and kings, and of priestly kings, and the legal privileges of hereditary orders generally, were regarded by our Founders as elements of unjust inequality in all European constitutions, including the British. The forbidding of the issuance of patents of nobility, either by the States or by the United

States, the prohibition of any religious test for office, the absence of any property qualification for office, in the Constitution of 1787, all attest the revolutionary thrust against inequality. So does the prohibition of slavery in the great Northwest Ordinance, which was adopted by the old Congress, even as the Constitution was being drafted. Professor Bradford plays upon our present familiarity with many of these things, to inform us that "the Declaration of Independence is not very revolutionary at all. Nor the Revolution itself. Nor the Constitution." But this is to read history backward, to pretend that the man was never a child, or that something was never new because it is not longer so!

I have observed many times that the independence of the United States was accomplished by a Declaration that constituted a political act without parallel in the history of the world. Professor Bradford opposes this thesis in writing that

> only a relativist or historicist could argue that American conservatism should be an utterly unique phenomenon, without antecedents which predate 1776, and unconnected with the mainstream of English and European thought and practice known to our forefathers in colonial times.[6]

But I never said or implied that the principles of the American Revolution were "without antecedents." No one would insist more than I that the colonies had enjoyed a learning process, of nearly two centuries, in constitutionalism and the rule of law. Some of the ideas incorporated into the Declaration—including the connection between equality and justice—had a history of more than two thousand years. But the rooting of constitutionalism, and the rule of law in a doctrine of universal human rights, in the political act of a people declaring independence, *is* unique and unprecedented.[7] Professor Bradford denies that the Declaration is revolutionary—or that it is unique—because he denies that it contains a declaration of universal human rights. And, I admit, if there were no such declaration, then the Declaration would cease to be everything I have claimed for it. Our debate turns upon what it is we find in the famous second paragraph. Professor Bradford, like Willmoore Kendall—and indeed like Chief Justice Taney in the case of *Dred Scott*—expends a great deal of ingenuity in pretending that the words do not mean what they plainly do mean.

> We hold these truths to be self-evident, that all men are created equal, that they are endowed by their Creator with certain unalienable rights, that among these are life, liberty, and the pursuit of happiness.

Because of the rights here affirmed—but only because of them—the American people are said to have a right to resist any attempt "to reduce them under absolute despotism." Professor Bradford thinks that white Americans had the right to resist despotism, because somehow such a right had become prescriptive under British tradition. Leaving aside the question of how such a tradition could have originated, we merely insist that that is not what the Declaration says. It says that *all* men have a right to resist despotism, and because all Americans are men, all Americans have this right. The right to resist despotism, that is, the right *not* to be slaves, is possessed equally by every human being on the face of the earth. That some might not have the capacity to make good this right, lacking either the power or the inclination, is nothing to the purpose. The form of the proposition contained in the second paragraph implies by unbreakable necessity, that unless the rights mentioned are possessed by everyone, they are possessed by no one. That is what the Signers said, and that, I am convinced, is what they meant.

The proposition that all men are created equal is, on the most elementary level, a principle of political obligation. It occurs in a context in which men are withdrawing their allegiance from an authority that has lost its legitimacy, and are transferring that allegiance to a new repository of legitimate authority. It is a principle for distinguishing when it is that men are, and when they are not, under a duty to obey. For anyone to argue, as does Professor Bradford, that the Signers of the Declaration did not understand their principles to apply to all men—in particular that they did not apply to Negro slaves—it would be necessary for him to find evidence that they (or anyone of the Revolutionary generation who had deliberately subscribed to the principles of the Declaration) considered that slaves had a *duty* to obey. That slaves may have been under a *necessity* to obey—or that the Signers or anyone else considered it expedient to place them under such a necessity—is nothing to the purpose. Abraham Lincoln, and many others, argued that in some sense American slavery was a necessity, imposed by circumstances, on both masters and slaves. Whether or not such an argument was disingenuous we need not enter into here. What is relevant is that such an argument in no way contradicts the opinion that the rights set forth in the second paragraph of the Declaration are universal rights. To say that white men have such rights, but that black men did not, would indeed have been inconsistent with the language of the Declaration. Professor Bradford is on common ground with the Marxist and Black Power historians of recent years, who have all along maintained that the Declaration was a bourgeois or racist document, never intended to be understood in the universalistic sense in which it is expressed. None of them has produced any such evidence of inconsistency as I have demanded, nor have they tried to show why any other evidence ought to be acceptable. I shall look forward to seeing whether Professor Bradford can supply this defect in his brief.

Professor Bradford's polemic against what he is pleased to call "the heresy of equality" occurs on at least two levels. On the one hand, he denies that there is any politically relevant sense in which it can be said with any truth that all men are created equal. On the other hand, he denies that the Signers of the Declaration meant it in any of the politically relevant senses attributed to it by Jefferson or the arch-heretic, Abraham Lincoln. Professor Bradford launches his attack by denying that there is any difference between what I had called the Old Liberalism—which demands equality of opportunity (which Professor Bradford correctly identifies with equality of rights)—and the New Liberalism, which demands equality of results. "Contrary to most Liberals, new and old," he writes,

> It is nothing less than sophistry to distinguish between equality of opportunity (equal starts in the "race of life") and equality of condition (equal results). For only those who *are* equality can take equal advantage of a given circumstance. And there is no man equal to any other, except perhaps in the special and politically untranslatable, understanding of the Deity. *Not intellectually or politically or economically or even morally. Not equal!* Such is, of course, the genuinely self-evident proposition [Emphasis by Bradford].[8]

We have already seen that Professor Bradford maintains that neither the Declaration, the Revolution itself, or the Constitution are ("contrary to Professor Jaffa") very revolutionary. They became revolutionary, he says, "Only [because of] Mr. Lincoln and those who gave him support, both in his day and in the following century."[9] This is Bradford's expression of Kendall's thesis, that Abraham Lincoln had somehow "derailed" an American political tradition that had not heretofore worshipped the golden calf of equality. Yet Bradford, like Kendall, is doing little more than paraphrase Senator John C. Calhoun, in his great speech on the Oregon Bill, in the Senate, June 27, 1848. All the essentials are there, only with this difference: the arch-heretic is Jefferson instead of Lincoln!

In his speech, Calhoun calls "the most false and dangerous of all political errors" a proposition which, he said, "had become an axiom in the minds of a vast many on both sides of the Atlantic," a proposition which is "repeated daily from tongue to tongue, as an established and incontrovertible truth."[10] This is the proposition that "all men are born free and equal," a proposition which occurs in this precise form, not in the Declaration of Independence, but in the Massachusetts Bill of Rights (1780). But the doctrine it embodies was endemic to political public opinion in the revolutionary generation, as I have demonstrated by citing its variant expressions in seven of the original state constitutions, in "Equality as a Conservative Principle."

Calhoun refutes this dangerous falsehood by declaring that men are not born, that on the contrary only infants are born! And infants are so far from being either free or equal, that they are in a condition of perfectly unfree dependence.[11] He then takes up the proposition in the Declaration of Independence, that "all men are created equal." This form of expression, he says, "though less dangerous, is not less erroneous." Calhoun does not explain why it is less danger Oils, but we may suppose that to call all men by nature free, is more directly subversive of slavery than to call them equal. Calhoun then continues as follows:

> All men are not created. According to the Bible, only two—a man and a woman—ever were—and of these one was pronounced subordinate to the other. All others have

come into the world by being born, and in no sense, as I have shown, either free or equal.[12]

Now Calhoun knew that he was here merely taking words in their wrong sense. He knew that when Jefferson had penned his immortal lines—for the universal approval of his patriot fellow-citizens—he was making assertions, not about particular individuals in any particular state of individual or social development, but about the entire human race, seen in the light of the Creation. He was distinguishing man, as man had been distinguished in philosophic discourse even before Socrates, from the beast on the one hand, and from God or the gods on the other. Indeed, he was distinguishing man, as man had been distinguished in the first chapter of Genesis, when God gave him dominion over all the brute creation, while subject to Himself. Jefferson was laying down a premise by which despotic rule might in certain cases be regarded as natural and legitimate: the case of man ruling beast, or God ruling man. But by this same premise it was seen that man does not differ from man, as man differs from beast, or as man differs from God. As Jefferson rephrased the same thought fifty years later, shortly before his death, some men are not born with saddles on their backs, and others, booted and spurred, to ride them! Legitimate government does not then arise directly from nature; and therefore it does arise from consent. As the citizens of Maiden, Massachusetts declared, in their instructions to their representatives in the Continental Congress, May 27, 1776, "we can never be willingly subject to any other King than he who, being possessed of infinite wisdom, goodness, and rectitude, is alone fit to possess unlimited power."[13] It is in this eminently reasonable sense that the proposition that all men are created equal is to be understood. And so it was understood, until the serpent of slavery, tempted some Americans to understand it differently.

Professor Bradford has declared with strident emphasis, that no man is equal to any other, intellectually, physically, or morally. In his speech on the *Dred Scott* decision,[14] Abraham Lincoln also asserted that the Signers of the Declaration did not intend to say that men were equal in color, size, intellect, moral development, or social capacity. And where Professor Bradford agrees with Abraham Lincoln we have, I suspect, a good practical definition of self-evident truth. But why cannot Professor Bradford understand that equality of *rights* is perfectly consistent with inequality of ability? Indeed, why cannot he understand that equality of rights is the *only* ground upon which inequality of ability can properly manifest itself?

Let us consider again the case of an exchange of shoes for grain. Should such an exchange be governed by the relative I.Q.s, or moral reputation, or color, or the physical strength, of the buyer and the seller? Or should it be governed by the equal money value of the shoes and the grain? At bottom, an exchange of shoes for grain is an exchange between a shoemaker and a grain-grower. But what qualities of the shoemaker and the grain-grower are relevant to a just exchange, except those manifest in the shoes and the grain? Now good shoes should bring more money—and hence more grain—than poorly made shoes. But the good shoemaker can be known only by his shoes. To return less to the shoemaker for his labor, not because of the quality of the shoes, but because he is black (or, for that matter, because she is female), is manifestly unequal and hence unjust.

Professor Bradford has made the extraordinary assertion, that it is sophistry to distinguish equality of opportunity from equality of results. He observes that "only those who *are* equal can take equal advantage of a given circumstance." I confess myself unable to assign any intelligible meaning to this assertion. Does he mean that a fair start in a race is advantageous only to someone who is fast enough to win it? But this is nonsense. The purpose of the race is to find out who *is* the fastest, and this can be done only if the start of the race is fair. I think it useful here to distinguish an open race from a handicap race. Only an open race is a true race—that is, only a race in which every runner has a chance to compete, can reveal who it is who can run the fastest. And a true race is one in which everyone starts from the same line at the same time, and runs the same distance. Moreover, it is one in which none of the runners are hobbled, and none are given packs to carry. Or, alternatively, if hobbles or packs are part of the race, then everyone must be hobbled or burdened in exactly the same way. But it is precisely when everyone starts together in a fair race, that they do *not* end together. According to Professor Bradford, the "hue and cry over equality of opportunity and equal rights leads, *a fortiori*, to a final demand for equality of condition." But is it not evident; indeed, is it not *self-evident*, that the truth is the exact opposite? In a fair race, the natural inequalities of the runners emerge in the results, and these inequalities are expressed in the order of the finish. The only equality which we see—or wish to see—in the result, is the proportional equality of unequal prizes for unequal finishers.

Now what is a handicap race? A handicap race is one designed to overcome the natural inequality of the runners. It is one designed to give the slower runner an *equal* chance with the fastest runner. The handicapper does this by assigning a longer distance (or a later start) to the fast runner, and a shorter distance (or an earlier start) to the slow runner, and in theory, a perfectly handicapped race would be one in which everyone finished together. In practice, a perfectly handicapped race introduces the greatest amount of uncertainty into the outcome. Both theoretically and practically, handicapping overcomes natural ability in favor of equality of results. But Professor Bradford's prescriptive rights, in particular the prescriptive right of a master to own slaves, as against the equal natural rights he opposes, bring about a handicapped society. That they do produce a spurious "equality of results," is the testimony of the supreme spokesman for the old South.

In Calhoun's Oregon speech, speaking in defense of that social order which, Professor Bradford would have us believe, was a partnership in every virtue and all perfection, the Senator declared that

> With us [of the South] the two great divisions of society are not the rich and poor, but white and black; and all tile former, the poor as well as the rich, belong to the upper

class, and are respected and treated as equals, if honest and industrious; and hence have
a position and pride of character of which neither poverty nor misfortune can deprive
them.[15]

What a confession of moral blindness is this! All whites are assigned upper class
status (if honest and industrious!), with pride of position and character assigned to
them, without regard to their inequality of achievement or excellence. And all blacks
are assigned lower class status (however honest or industrious) simply because they
are black (free blacks not being distinguished from slaves.) All distinctions of virtue
or intelligence are, in the decisive respect, assimilated to the single distinction of
color. All intrinsically important human qualities are debased and degraded from
the honors due to them, by the distinction of color alone. And except for the
inequality resulting from color, the antebellum South, according to its most distinguished spokesman, produced the most perfect *equality of results*, in the race of life,
that the world has ever seen!

Professor Bradford's case against the "heresy of equality," rests upon both logical
and historical grounds. That is, he regards it both as false in itself, and false as a
doctrine ascribed to the Founding Fathers. He denies that the doctrine of equal
human rights can properly be found in the Declaration of Independence. To find it
there is, he maintains, to misread the Declaration. Professor Bradford's argument is
a theme with many variations, and it is some times difficult to detect the theme
within the variation. But his case as a historical scholar—as distinct from a political
philosopher—comes down to this. When the Declaration reads "all men are created
equal," we are not to understand "men" to refer to *individual* human beings, but
only to human beings in their *collective* capacity, acting politically within civil society
as members of a "people."

> We are now prepared to ask [writes Professor Bradford] what Mr. Jefferson and his
> sensible friends meant by "all men" and "created equal." Meant together—*as a
> group* . . .[16]

Professor Bradford, be it noted, thought Jefferson's *friends* were sensible. What
they meant *as a group* (the emphasis is Bradford's) must be sensible, because of the
friends. Jefferson's well-known strictures against slavery make it impossible for Professor Bradford ever to regard him as a sensible *individual*. However, one can only
wonder why those sensible friends were so agreeable to having the non-sensible Jefferson draft the Declaration in the first place.

> The *exordium* of the Declaration begins . . . with an argument from history and with
> a definition of the voice addressing "the powers of the earth!" It is a "people," a "we"
> that are estranged from another "we." The peroration reads the same: "we," the "free
> and independent states," are united in our will to separation. . . . No contemporary
> liberal, new or old, can make use of that framework or take the customary liberties

with what is contained by the construction. Nor coming to it by the path I have marked, may they, in honesty, see in "created equal" what they devoutly wish to find. "We," in that second sentence, signifies the colonials as the citizenry of the distinct colonies, not as individuals, but rather in their corporate capacity. Therefore, the following "all men"—created equal in their right to expect from any government to which they might submit freedom from corporate bondage . . . [hence] equal as one free state is as free as another. Nothing is maintained concerning the abilities or situations of individual persons. . . .[17]

We have quoted at length here, because we wished there to be no doubt that any assertions we make concerning Professor Bradford's text, are solidly grounded in that text. We observe, first of all, that Professor Bradford and I do not differ at all, concerning the proposition that when the Signers of the Declaration speak of "one people" or "we" or "these united colonies," they were referring to themselves, and those whom they represented, in a corporate or collective, or political capacity. Indeed, I suspect that I go further than Professor Bradford, since I am convinced that "one people" meant just that, and that the several "peoples" of the several colonies or states, were already formed into one single people. And I hold—with Presidents Jackson and Lincoln—that the several states also were formed into one indissoluble union. But how in the world can the expression "men" be synonymous with "people"? Consider the text: "We hold these truths to be self-evident, that all men are created equal, that they are endowed by their Creator with certain unalienable rights. . . ." The first "We" is indeed the colonials, or the former colonials, citizens of the formerly distinct (but now united) colonies. But why are "we" endowed with "certain unalienable rights"? According to Professor Bradford, it is because they possessed those rights as colonials. But why should they possess those rights when they are no longer colonials? Rights granted by civil society are rights which can be taken away by civil society. But the Declaration here is most explicit. The rights of which it speaks are not civil or political rights, rights resulting from human or positive law. They are rights with which they had been "endowed by their Creator." Unless therefore Professor Bradford believes that the Creator endowed colonial Americans with rights with which he had not endowed other human beings, then the "men" in the phrase "all men are created equal" *must* be a more comprehensive category than the men in the "we" who hold these truths.

It is also a rule of interpretation for archaic documents that the meaning of words or phrases is to be sought in the light of contemporary usage. In Calhoun's Oregon speech, he assumed as a matter of course that "all men are born free and equal," and "all men are created equal" were mere variations of expression for the same fundamental idea. The former was, as we have noted, taken from the Massachusetts Bill of Rights. Article I of that document reads in full as follows.

All men are born free and equal, and have certain natural, essential, and inalienable rights; among which may be reckoned the right of enjoying and defending their lives and liberties that of acquiring, possessing, and protecting property; in fine, that of seeking and obtaining their safety and happiness.[18]

Can anyone doubt that the "men" referred to here are *individuals*, not societies of men in any collective sense? Instead of being "endowed by their Creator" with certain rights, they are born with them. And the rights with which they are born, are said to be "natural, essential, and unalienable," the three terms clearly being synonymous. But Professor Bradford's reading, as we have seen, regards the rights which the collective "we" declares, to be rights held only "in their corporate capacity." Such rights are ineluctably civil or political, they could not possibly be called "natural" or "essential," any more than they could be called "unalienable."

But we may, I think, settle the matter beyond cavil. In the very Preamble of the Massachusetts Bill of Rights, we find the following:

> The body politic is formed by a voluntary association of individuals; it is a social compact by which the whole people covenants with each citizen and each citizen with the whole people that all shall be governed by certain laws for the common good.[19]

Since the Massachusetts Bill of Rights was adopted in 1780, I submit further these lines from the Virginia Bill of Rights, adopted less than a month before the Declaration of Independence:

> That all men are by nature equally free and independent, and have certain inherent rights [inherent being synonymous with natural, essential, and unalienable], of which when they enter into a state of society, they cannot by any compact deprive or divest their posterity.[20]

Can there then be any reasonable doubt, can there indeed be any possible doubt, that for the revolutionary generation, human beings, as human beings, as men, had rights antecedent to, and independent of, civil society? Or that civil society, properly so called (that is, legitimate civil society), resulted from an agreement among men possessed of such rights? Can there then be any doubt that when the Declaration speaks of "all men" being created equal, it does indeed then refer to individuals?

This record is not, contrary to Professor Bradford, an invention of liberals, new or old. Had John C. Calhoun, when he delivered his Oregon speech in 1848, had the slightest suspicion that this interpretation of the Declaration was a perversity of abolitionist propaganda, he would certainly have been as forward as Professor Bradford in pointing it out. Yet in the peroration of that speech he declared that

> We now begin to experience the danger of admitting so great an error to have a place in the declaration of our independence. . . . It had strong hold on the mind of Mr. Jefferson, the author of that document [Calhoun did not see the difference between Jefferson and his sensible friends], which caused him to take an utterly false view of the subordinate relation of the black to the white race in the South; and to hold in

consequence, that the latter, though utterly unqualified to possess liberty, were as fully entitled to both liberty and equality as the former; and that to deprive them of it was unjust and immoral.[21]

Clearly, it never occurred for a moment to Calhoun that the "men" in "all men are created equal" did not refer to Negroes, how ever erroneous he may have believed the proposition to have been. We see then that the American Civil War resulted from a new revolution, a revolution in opinion in the South. That revolution denied the axiomatic premise of the older, better Revolution, which had declared—and meant—that all men are created equal.

Professor Bradford has a great many things to say about Abraham Lincoln, none of them complimentary. His remarks cover a spectrum that ranges all the way from the nonsensical to the absurd. As a specimen, we cite one which even he felt constrained to put into the small print of the end notes. After observing a comparison of Lincoln to Bismarck and Lenin by Edmund Wilson, he adds:

> Another useful analogue (a firm higher law man, and no legalist or historicist) is Adolf Hitler. For he writes in *Mein Kampf* that "human rights break state rights," calls for illegal as well as legal instruments in "wars of rebellion against enslavement within and without," observes that all governments by oppression plead the law, and concludes, "I believe that I am acting in the sense of the Almighty Creator . . . fighting for the Lord's work."[22]

I think that if Professor Bradford had searched long enough he might have found a documented quotation from Hitler, in which he had said that some of his best friends were Jews. Such a quotation would have had exactly the same significance as the one presented above.

Professor Bradford does not like Lincoln's attachment to higher law doctrine. In particular, he does not like the fusion, in Lincoln's rhetoric, of higher law drawn from both the natural law, as expressed in the Declaration of Independence, and from the divine law, as found in the Bible. Let us concede that Lincoln was the greatest master of this rhetorical fusion. But it is utterly misleading to suppose that it was his invention, or that it was more characteristic of him than of any one of a large number of his contemporaries, North or South.

According to Professor Bradford, the House Divided speech—with which Lincoln opened the campaign for Douglas's Senate seat in 1858—"was, beyond any question, a Puritan declaration of war." It was so, says Bradford, because, quoting the words of Lincoln's "one-time friend, Alexander Stephens," it "put the institution of nearly one-half the states under the ban of public opinion and national condemnation." Bradford continues:

> Of course the central motif of the House Divided speech . . . echoes the Bible (Mark 3:25): Christ speaking of the undivided hosts of Satan. Lincoln's authority is thus, by association, elevated to the level of the hieratic. But he added something to that mix-

ture. The myth that slavery will either be set on its way to extinction . . . or else all states will eventually become slave states establishes a false dilemma. . . . Thus he participates in what Richard Hofstadter calls the "paranoid style" in politics.[23]

Later on, Bradford adds, in words which he italicized for emphasis:

For houses are always divided in some fashion or another.[24]

Thus Lincoln, invoking the higher law, natural and divine, against slavery, demanding that the house be undivided, was introducing a revolutionary, gnostic, antinomian morality, as the ground of politics. He was thus assuring that politics would forever after be a crusade against sin, the sin to be defined, not by priests, but by egalitarian, ideological politicians.

Since Bradford has introduced Alexander Stephens as a witness against Lincoln, it would be particularly instructive to see how Stephens's views of the crisis of the divided house compared with Lincoln's. In December, 1860, shortly after South Carolina had adopted its Ordinance of Secession, Lincoln wrote to Stephens, saying that

you think slavery is *right*, and should be extended, and we think it is *wrong*, and should be restricted. That, I suppose, is the rub. It certainly is the only substantial difference between us.[25]

Stephens, it should be remarked, was a Southern moderate. As an old Whig, he was a strong Unionist, and fought against secession in his state of Georgia as long as he could. But he went with his state when it left the Union, and became Vice President of the Confederate States of America. After the adoption of the Confederate Constitution, he propounded a defense of the new regime, which has come down in history as the "Corner Stone" speech. It has its name from precisely the same source as Lincoln's House Divided speech. Both are built around biblical texts. Stephens certainly elevates his doctrine to the level of the hieratic, as Bradford puts it, every bit as much as Lincoln. But Stephens's speech is more than a defense of the new regime. It is the most comprehensive Southern reply to *all* of Lincoln's speeches, from 1854 to 1860, of any that the record of the times shows. What the speech proves, beyond doubt, is that Lincoln was perfectly accurate when he said that Stephens's thinking slavery right, and Lincoln's thinking it wrong, was the *only* substantial difference between them. In every other respect, as we shall see, Stephens was in *agreement* with Lincoln, and in *disagreement* with Professor Bradford.

Lincoln held, in virtually all his speeches between 1854 and 1860—notably in the debates with Douglas, and in the Cooper Union speech—that the Founding Fathers had all regarded slavery as a great moral wrong. They had inherited slavery as part of their colonial legacy, and its presence among them imposed certain "necessities" which they were powerless to change. But they supposed that slavery was nonetheless "in course of ultimate extinction," and although they gave guarantees to slavery while it should last, they did not expect it to last. Its presence was tolerable because, but only because, they expected it gradually to die out. The House was not a Divided House, in Lincoln's sense, if the moral wrong of slavery were acknowledged, and public policy based upon that acknowledgment as a premise. What does Alexander Stephens say about this?

> The prevailing ideas entertained by [Jefferson] and most of the leading statesmen at the time of the formation of the old Constitution, were that the enslavement of the African was in violation of the laws of nature: that it was wrong in principle, socially, morally, and politically. It was an evil they knew not well how to deal with, but the general opinion of the men of that day was, that somehow or other, in the order of Providence, the institution would he evanescent and pass away.[26]

We see now that Jefferson's sensible friends were no more sensible than he! It is axiomatic for Stephens that "most of the leading statesmen" of the time, were anti-slavery. All of them understood "all men are created equal" to include *all* men, and therefore to include Negroes. It was the "general opinion of the men of that day" that slavery was a transient phenomenon. Hence general opinion agreed with Lincoln that at the Founding slavery was in course of ultimate extinction, and that the House of the Founders was not a Divided House.

Stephens does not disagree by one iota with Lincoln's interpretation of the Founding. *But he disagrees with the Founding.* "Those ideas," he writes, viz., of the Founding Fathers,

> were fundamentally wrong. They rested upon the assumption of the equality of the races. This was an error. It was a sandy foundation, and the idea of a government built upon it; when the "storm came and the wind blew, it fell."[27]

The quotation by Stephens is taken from Mark 7:26–27. Jesus is speaking, and says, "And every one who hears these words of mine and does not do them will be like a foolish man who built his house upon sand: and the rain fell, and the floods came, and the winds blew and beat against the house, and it fell; and great was the fall of it." What was the sandy foundation? It was the doctrine that the races were equal. And what is the rock which, asserts Stephens, is the truth upon which a government can stand? What is it for which he claims, by analogy, the hieratic authority of Jesus himself?

> Our new government [declared Stephens] is founded upon exactly the opposite idea; its foundations are laid, its corner stone rests upon the great truth that the Negro is not the equal to the white man. That slavery—the subordination to the superior race, is his natural and normal condition.
> This our new Government [the Confederate States of America] is the first in the

history of the world, based upon this great physical and moral truth. This truth has been slow in the process of its development, like all other truths in the various departments of science.[28]

We have seen Professor Bradford's distaste for political novelty. Time and again, he has defended the cause of the Confederacy as the cause of traditional society attempting to preserve tradition against a radical break with the past, a break enforced by Lincoln's militant, uniformitarian Unionism. But here we find a most eminent apologist for the Confederacy, its supremely articulate Vice President, in March, 1861, declaring the cause of the Confederacy to be the *exact opposite* of what Professor Bradford has declared it to be.

Not only does Stephens say that the Confederacy is the first government of its kind in the history of the world, but he says that it is based upon a truth that has emerged from the progress of science. Although he says that such truths are slow in their process of development, it is also the case that they cause profound upheavals where they make their appearance. The examples which Stephens himself gives span less than two centuries. The fault of the Founding Fathers was not that they were perverse, but that the progress of science had not enlightened them. Stephens's doctrine is then not merely a commitment to novelty, but a commitment to a perpetual revolution of morals and politics, whenever the progress of science shall reveal new truths. It is the most radical denial possible, of that "funded wisdom of the ages" in which Professor Bradford would have us place our faith. It is a denial of such permanent standards as are incorporated in the natural law teaching of the Declaration of Independence.

Stephens compares the new truth about the races, to the discoveries of Galileo, Adam Smith, and Harvey. Harvey's theory of the circulation of the blood, he says, was not admitted by "a single one of the medical profession living at the time," yet now it is "universally acknowledged." "May we not," asks Stephens," therefore

> look forward with confidence to the ultimate universal acknowledgment of the truths upon which our system rests? It is the first government ever instituted upon principles of strict conformity to nature, and the ordination of Providence, in furnishing the materials of human society. Many governments have been founded upon the principle of certain classes; but the classes thus enslaved, were of the same race, and in violation of the laws of nature. Our system commits no such violation of nature's laws. The Negro, by nature, or by the curse of Canaan, is fitted for that condition which he occupies in our system.[29]

Surely, Abraham Lincoln never set forth the case for an undivided house with greater assurance or conviction! Nor did Lincoln appeal to greater authority, either natural or divine, in support of his version of what the undivided house should be. Yet there is something self-contradictory in Stephens's appeal, as there is not in Lincoln's. Why should it have come to be known only so recently, that the Negro is fitted by nature only for slavery? Especially if the "cause" of that nature is the curse of Canaan? Whence could it have arisen, that so enlightened a generation as that of the Founding Fathers should have been so completely wrong about so fundamental a reality? For it is clear that Stephens *does* regard them as enlightened, in all respects except one. The many governments which, he says, were founded upon "the principles of certain classes," is certainly meant to encompass all the unequal regimes of the old world. The founding that began on July 4, 1776, is certainly, albeit indirectly, endorsed by Stephens, in precisely the sense in which we have endorsed it. It too must have been "the first in the history of the world," in just the way in which we have described it above. Stephens has no quarrel—any more than did Calhoun—with a system which is radically egalitarian as far as white men are concerned. But, like Calhoun, he thinks that this egalitarianism can only he properly realized, upon the foundation of Negro slavery. From Stephens's perspective the Revolution accomplished by the Declaration and the Constitution, was perfect in its kind. There is no question but that that Revolution represented a break with everything that went before it. But it needed one further step forward in enlightenment—the step represented by the discovery of the inferiority of the Negro race. (Never mind if this opinion is inconsistent with the idea of unknowable future scientific progress.)

> The architect, in the construction of buildings, lays the foundation with proper materials. . . . The substratum of our society is made of the material fitted by nature for it, and by experience we know that it is best, not only for the superior, but for the inferior race that it should be so. It is indeed in conformity with the ordinance of the Creator. . . . The great objects of humanity are best attained when conformed to His laws and decrees, in the formation of government, as we as in all things else. Our Confederacy is founded upon principles in strict conformity with these laws. This stone which was first rejected by the first builders "is become the chief stone of the corner" in our new edifice.[30]

Thus ends the first and greatest apology for the Confederacy, made in the flush of its confidence in long life and prosperity. Stephens's apology *after* the Civil War, contained in his *Constitutional View of the War Between the States*, is very different. The "cornerstone" sinks from sight, and states' rights, as the ground of constitutionalism, replaces it. But I think the Corner Stone speech is the more authentic, as revealing the character of the Confederacy when it felt full confidence in its principles. The "corner stone" quotation comes from Psalms 118:22. "The stone which the builders refused is become the head stone of the corner." It appears however in both Matthew and Mark, where Jesus quotes it, and quotes it in such a way as to indicate that he, or his teaching, is the stone in question. Certainly Stephens yielded nothing to Lincoln, in his assumption of what Bradford calls "hieratic" authority.

We began this part of our essay by giving Professor Bradford's quotation from Adolf Hitler, in which he shows that Hitler, like Lincoln, was a "firm higher law man." Hitler, we saw, like Lincoln believed that "human rights" take precedence over "state rights"; and that Hitler, like Lincoln believed he was "fighting for the Lord's work." But we see now that Union and Confederate causes did not differ, with respect to being higher law causes. Had Hitler looked back for precedent, it is not likely that he would have looked to Abraham Lincoln. All the precedent he would have needed in the higher law sense was certainly present in Stephens's Corner Stone speech. And in the decisive sense, that speech, like the cause it represented, would have been entirely congenial. Certainly Hitler's doctrines of racial inequality went much beyond that of Stephens. Yet when Hitler spoke of "human rights," he certainly did not do so in the sense of Lincoln or Jefferson. "Human rights" were for him, primarily and essentially the rights of the master race. And the Confederate States of America represented the first time in human history, that a doctrine of a master race was fully and systematically set forth as the ground of a regime. More precisely, it was the first time that such a doctrine was set forth *on the authority of modern science*. It was this authority that made it so persuasive, and so pernicious.

National Socialism and Marxist Communism are, as I have argued elsewhere,[31] alternative versions of the social Darwinism that was so rife in nineteenth century thought. They are alternative foundations of the totalitarian tyrannies that have so blotted and befouled the life of man in our time. That at least one of them never took root in the United States we owe, more than to any other man, to Abraham Lincoln. Let us carry on his work, building upon that rock upon which he built his undivided house, the teaching that, with respect to the rights to life, liberty, and the pursuit of happiness, "*all* men are created equal."

ॐ

Notes to Chapter 1

Lincoln the Liberal Stateman

I

1. Stanley Pargellis, "Lincoln's Political Philosophy," *Abr. Lincoln Quar.*, III, 275–290 (1945).

2. Richard Nelson current, *Old Thad Stevens: A Story of Ambition*, 53, 226.

3. *Works*, VI, 126.

4. *Lincoln the President*, I, 281–282. See also Reinhard H. Luthin, "Abraham Lincoln and the Tariff," *Amer. Hist. Rev.*, XLIX, 609–629 (1944).

5. William H. Herndon to Truman H. Bartlett, July 19, 1887, MS., Mass. Hist. Soc.

II

1. *Works*, V, 249.

2. For Lincoln on internal improvements, see speech in House of Representatives, June 20, 1848, *Works*, II, 28–48. Quoted passages are from this speech.

3. Fragment on government [July 1, 1854?], *Works*, II, 182–183.

III

1. *Works*, VI, 312–313.
2. *Works*, I, 151–152.
3. *Works*, I, 197–198.
4. Ray Allen Billington, *The Protestant Crusade, 1800–1860: A Study of the Origins of American Nativism*.
5. *New York Evening Post*, Feb. 3, 1855, article headed "Albany [Correspondence of the Evening Post]."
6. "Albany."
7. Dic. of Amer. Biog., VII, 142.
8. "George F. Hoar, *Autobiography of Seventy Years*, I, 189.
9. *Works*, II, 287.
10. *Works*, VI, 45.
11. *Lincoln the President*, I, 161 n.
12. *Works*, V, 130.
13. *Works*, VIII, 200. Explanation of the revocation is here given in a letter from Halleck to Grant, Jan. 21, 1863. The quoted words may well have been Lincoln's own. (When the Lincoln papers in the Library of Congress are opened in 1947 we will probably know the reason why this Halleck communication is included in Lincoln's works. At times Lincoln would himself draft an order or communication to be issued in the name of the secretary of war or the general in chief.)
14. Current, *Old Thad Stevens*, 103–104.
15. *Works*, I, 199.
16. *Works*, I, 206.
17. *Works*.

IV

1. *Works*, VI, 26.
2. *Works*, I, 262.
3. *Works*, V, 361.
4. *Works*, V, 247–248.
5. For quoted portions in this paragraph, see *Works*, VII, 56–59.
6. *Works*, V, 360.
7. *Works*, V, 361.
8. *Works*.
9. *Works*, VI, 321.
10. *Works*, VIII, 194–197.
11. *Works*, X, 53–54.

V

1. *Works*, VI, 177.
2. *Works*, II, 229.
3. *Works*, I, 35.
4. *Works*, I, 49–50.

5. In this passage (on Lincoln's warnings as to unfavorable tendencies in American democracy) the quoted portions are from his address before the Young Men's Lyceum of Springfield, Illinois, Jan. 27, 1838 (misdated 1837 by Nicolay and Hay). *Works*, I, 35–50.

6. *Works*, I, 38.

7. *Works*, I, 44.

8. *Works*, I, 43.

VI

1. *Works*, X, 39.

2. *Works*, II, 227–228.

3. *Works*, II, 327–328.

4. *Works*, II, 229.

5. *Works*, II, 226.

VII

1. Lincoln's attention to domestic economy in the South, and his wish that emancipation should proceed by easy transition rather than by serious disruption, appear in his letter to General N. P. Banks, Aug. 5, 1863. Referring to Louisiana he thought "it would not be objectionable for her to adopt some practical system by which the two races could gradually live themselves out of the old relation to each other, and both come out better prepared for the new." (This is but one example; there were others.) *Works*, IX, 56.

2. Various factors which enabled Lincoln to understand Southern viewpoints have been briefly presented by the author in *Lincoln and the South*.

3. "If all earthly power were given me, I should not know what to do as to the existing institution." Speech at Peoria, Oct. 16, 1854, *Works*, II, 206.

4. *Works*, II, 279–280.

5. For Lincoln's explanation of his house divided declaration, and his regret that the famous slogan was misinterpreted, see *Lincoln the President*, I, 117–118.

6. *Works*, II, 205.

7. *Works*, V 345.

8. *Works*, V, 345–348.

9. *Works*, V, 351–352.

10. *Works*, V, 356–357.

VIII

1. For quoted portions of the Mexican War speech, see *Works*, I, 340–341.

2. *Works*, VI, 322.

IX

1. *Works*, II, 127–128.

2. *Works*, II, 164–165, 171.

3. *Works*, I, 207–208.

4. *Works*, I, 208–209.

5. Tyler Dennett, ed., *Lincoln and the Civil War in the Diaries and Letters of John Hay*, 19–20.

6. *Works*, VI, 304.

7. VIII, 131.

X

1. Allen Thorndike Rice, ed., *Reminiscences of Abraham Lincoln by Distinguished Men of His Time*, 7g. The newspaper correspondent Noah Brooks, an intimate friend of the president, doubted that Lincoln made the remark. Brooks, *Washington in Lincoln's Time*, 29.

2. Well treated in T. Harry Williams, *Lincoln and the Radicals*.

3. *Lincoln the President*, II, 229–232. In A. K. McClure, *Abraham Lincoln and Men of War-Times*, 268 ff., the conference is treated with what would now be called window-dressing, or after-the-event publicizing. One needs to go behind the more obvious record to discover the difference between the conference as planned, in which lack of confidence in Lincoln was a prominent motive, and the public understanding of the conference as held, and as managed by the president. For a fuller treatment see William B. Hesseltine, "Lincoln's War Governors," *Abr. Lincoln Quar.*, IV, 153–200 (Dec. 1946).

4. *Lincoln the President*, II, 241–249.

5. F. B. Carpenter, *The Inner Life of Abraham Lincoln: Six Months at the White House*, 217.

6. Diary of Salmon P. Chase, in Annual Report, Amer. Hist. Assoc., 1902, II, 87.

7. Carl Sandburg, *Abraham Lincoln: The War Years*, III, 300.

8. In the month after his Mexican War speech Lincoln sent a notable letter to his partner Herndon, concerning the contention that "if it shall become necessary to repel invasion, the President may . . . invade the territory of another country," the president being the judge as to whether the necessity exists. Vigorously refuting this contention, Lincoln wrote: "Allow the President to invade a neighboring nation whenever he shall deem it necessary to repel an invasion, and you allow him to do so whenever he may choose to say he deems it necessary for such purpose, and you allow him to make war at pleasure. Study to see if you can fix any limit to his power in this respect, after having given him so much as you propose. If to-day he should choose to say he thinks it necessary to invade Canada to prevent the British from invading us, how could you stop him?" Lincoln to Herndon, Washington, D.C., Feb. 15, 1848, *Works*, II, 1–3. See also Herndon's *Lincoln* (Angle ed.), 224–226.

Equality as a Conservative Principle

1. On the difference between the Whiggery of the English and American Revolutins, see H. V. Jaffa, *Equality and Liberty: Theory and Practice in American Politics*, (New York: Oxford University Press, 1965), ch. 6 [hereinafter cited as *Equality and Liberty*]

2. 5 The Rambler (New Series), May 1861, at 17 (reprinted in *Essays on Freedom and Power* 171 [G. Himmelfarb ed. 1955]).

3. The Contest in America (1862). Preprinted from *Fraser's Magazine*, Feb.–May 1862.

4. See text accompanying notes 37–38 infra.

5. *Basic Symbols*, p. 156.

6. H. V. Jaffa, *Crisis of the House Divided: An Interpretation of the Issues in the Lincoln-*

Douglas Debates (Doubleday, 1959; Reissued in paper with a new Introduction, University of Washington Press, 1973). Hereinafter this will be cited as *Crisis*.

7. 2 Alexis de Tocqueville, *Democracy in America*, 34–35, 99–103, 215–221, 226–227, 304–305 (H. Reeve ed., 1945).

8. 1 *The Collected Works of Abraham Lincoln* 108–115 (R. Basler ed. 1953). Hereinafter cited as Lincoln.

9. Id. at 271–79.

10. Kendall, Book Review, 7 *National Review* 461 (159). Hereinafter cited as *Book Review*.

11. W. Kendall, *The Conservative Affirmation*, 249–252 (1963).

12. *Book Review*, supra note 10, at 461.

13. *Book Review*.

14. *Book Review*.

15. *Book Review*. At 461–462.

16. *Book Review*.

17. In *100 Years of Emancipation* 1 (R. Goldwin ed., 1963) Reprinted in *Equality and Liberty*, supra note 1, at 140.

18. *Book Review*, supra note 10, at 462.

19. *Book Review*.

20. *Book Review*.

21. *Dred Scott v. Sanford*, 60 U.S. (19 How.) 393 (1857).

22. *Book Review*, supra note 10, at 462.

23. 4 Lincoln, supra note 8, at 263.

24. See note 17 supra and accompanying text.

25. *Book Review*, supra note 10, at 462.

26. *Dred Scott v. Sanford*, 60 U.S. (19 How.) (1857).

27. *Book Review*, supra note 10, at 461–462.

28. 4 Lincoln, supra note 8, at 270 (footnotes omitted).

29. *Book Review*, supra note 10, at 461–62.

30. *Book Review* at 462.

31. *Book Review*.

32. *Book Review*.

33. 2 Lincoln, supra note 8, at 520.

34. 4 Lincoln, supra note 8, at 438.

35. pp. 14, 156.

36. pp. 14–15 (emphasis added).

37. *Sources of Our Liberties* 311–82 (R. Perry ed. 1964).

38. *Sources of Our Liberties* at 346.

39. J. Locke, *Two Treatises of Government* 7 (T. Cook ed. 1947). Hereinafter cited as *Two Treatises*.

40. *Documents of American History* 92 (H. Commanger ed. 1963). Hereinafter cited as *Documents*.

41. *Two Treatises*, supra note 39, at 8.

42. *Two Treatises*.

43. *History of Political Philosophy* 451 (L. Strauss and J. Cropsey eds. 1972).

44. *History of Political Philosophy*.

45. *History of Political Philosophy*.

46. *Two Treatises*, supra note 39, at 121.

47. *Two Treatises*.

48. *Two Treatises*.

49. 2 Lincoln supra note 8, at 266.

50. *The Federalist*, 337 (Modern Library ed. 1937). Hereinafter cited as *The Federalist*.

51. 2 Lincoln, supra note 8, at 266.

52. 2 Lincoln at 499.

53. *The Federalist*, supra note 50, at 55 (emphasis added).

54. 7 Lincoln, supra note 8, at 259–60.

55. Pp. 88, 90.

56. 4 Lincoln, supra note 8, at 433 (footnotes omitted).

57. *Documents*, supra note 40, at 100 (editor's note).

58. *A Casebook on the Declaration of Independence* 32 (R. Ginsberg ed. 1967).

59. 4 *Letters and Other Writings of James Madison* 392 (R. Worthington ed. 1884).

60. 4 *Letters and Other Writings of James Madison* at 391.

61. *Letters and Other Writings of James Madison*.

62. *Letters and Other Writings of James Madison* at 392.

The Heresy of Equality

1. When pressed in debate by the righteous minions of Equality, an antebellum Northern statesman once called sentence two of the Declaration a "self-evident lie." Consider also *The Federalist*, No. 10.

2. See Helmut Schoek, *Envy: A Theory of Social Behavior* (New York: Harcourt Brace Jovanovich, 1970).

3. *On Power: Its Nature and the History of Its Growth* (Boston: Beacon Press, 1962).

4. See Eric Voegelin, *Science, Politics and Gnosticism* (Chicago: Henry Regnery Co., 1968), 99–100.

5. Robert Penn Warren, "Democracy and Poetry," *Southern Review*, XI (January, 1975), 28.

6. See my "A Writ of Fire and Sword: The Politics of Oliver Cromwell," in No. 3 of *The Occasional Review* (Summer, 1975), 61–80.

7. Doctrine is a loaded word. It is here suggestive of theology, revealed truth, though Lincoln means by it the kind of demonstrable "abstract truth" of the sort Jefferson "embalmed" into a "merely revolutionary document." See Lincoln's letter to Messrs. Henry L. Pierce & Others, April 6, 1859, 374–376 of Vol. III of *The Collected Works of Abraham Lincoln* (New Brunswick, N.J.: Rutgers University Press, 1953). The usage is thus a device for "having it both ways," as does Jaffa when claiming that the commandments of Sinai are knowable by unassisted human reason. For the commandments are explained only in Christ—a scandal to the Greeks.

8. Edmund Burke, *Reflections on the Revolution in France* (Chicago: Henry Regnery Co., 1955), 240.

9. Burke, *Reflections*, 244. See also on this manner of thinking Louis I. Bredvold's *The Intellectual Milieu of John Dryden* (Ann Arbor: University of Michigan Press, 1934) and also *The Brave New World of the Enlightenment* (Ann Arbor: University of Michigan Press, 1961) by the same author. Swift is a major illustration of this intellectual *habitus*. I identify with it.

10. I borrow from the title of Paul Fussell's *The Rhetorical World of Augustan Humanism* (Oxford: The Clarendon Press, 1965). In the same connection see J. T. Bolton's *The Language of Politics in the Age of Wilkes and Burke* (Toronto: University of Toronto Press, 1963).

11. See Jaffa's *Equality & Liberty: Theory and Practice in American Politics* (New York: Oxford University Press, 1965), 122; and Leo Strauss' *Natural Right and History* (Chicago: University of Chicago Press, 1953), 1–9.

12. Jaffa accepts the Puritan typology for the American venture. There are, we should remember, alternative formulations (*Equality & Liberty*, 116–117)—formulations less infected with secularized eschatology. And if Jaffa pursues his analogue, he should remember that there was slavery in Israel and among the ancient Jews a racism so virulent that they considered some neighboring peoples too lowly even for enslavement and fit only for slaughter. Or too wicked (Indians, the Irish at Drogheda, etc.)

13. Peter Gay, *The Enlightenment; An Interpretation* (New York: Alfred A. Knopf, 1966), ix–xiv.

14. See Maurice Ashley, *The Glorious Revolution of 1688* (New York: Scribners, 1966), 97–106.

15. And this of course includes certain established rights, plus a balance between the values of liberty and community. I do not mean to minimize the value of these achievements. Clearly I identify with them.

16. *Equality & Liberty*, 114–139. For correction (in some respects), see Leonard Woods Labaree's *Conservatism in Early America* (Ithaca: Cornell University Press. 1959), 119–122, and Clinton Rossiter's *The Seedtime of the Republic* (New York: Harcout, Brace & World, 1953), especially 345; also Ashley, op. cit., 193–198.

17. David Duncan Wallace, *South Carolina: A Short History*, 1520–1948 (Columbia: University of South Carolina Press, 1966), 25.

18. John Locke, *Two Treatises of Government; A Critical Edition with Introduction and Apparatus Criticus*, by Peter Laslett (Cambridge, England, 1960), 159.

19. For examples consider Bernard Bailyn's, *The Ideological Origins of the American Revolution* (Cambridge, Mass.: Harvard University Press, 1967); and Gordon S. Wood's *The Creation of the American Republic*, 1776–1787 (Chapel Hill, University of North Carolina Press, 1964). Somewhat better are H. Trevor Colbourn's *The Lamp of Experience: Whig History and the Intellectual Origins of the American Revolution* (Chapel Hill: University of North Carolina Press, 1965); and Merrill Jensen's *The Founding of a Nation: A History of The American Revolution*, 1763–1776 (New York: Oxford University Press, 1968). These last two books are especially good on the "reluctant rebels," who were Burkean, not Lockean Whigs, postulating law, not a state of nature (i.e., where a fullscale, new contract can be drawn) See also Wallace (op. cit., 273) for an account of a prescriptive South Carolina patriot—William Henry Drayton. (Or see my essay on him elsewhere in this volume.)

20. In strict logic there is a problem with quantification if the proposition is supposed to be universal, a universal proposition would read "every man is created equal to every other man." Jefferson's phrase is merely a loose generalization, when seen in this light. For the libertarian the trouble goes the other way around: if all men are by nature equal (morally, in will, intellect, etc.), then only circumstances can explain the inequalities which develop. And these circumstances are thus offences against nature and the Divine Will—offences demanding correction. What some libertarians try to get out of "created equal" is "created unequal, but given an equal start." Jefferson's phrase will not submit to this.

21. An exception is Russell Kirk's *The Roots of American Order* (La Salle, Ill.: Open Court, 1974). (See my estimate of that work in the last study in this volume.)

22. One has the temptation to say, as Socrates did of the rhapsode in Plato's *Ion*, that they understand the subject not by art or knowledge but by "inspiration."

23. I began to develop this view in "Lincoln's New Frontier: A Rhetoric for Continuing Revolution," *Triumph*, VI, No. 5 (May, 1971), 11–13 and 21; VI, No. 6 (June, 1971), 15–17. I use the term from Eric Voegelin's New Science of Politics (Chicago: University of Chicago Press, 1952).

24. For a chronicle of these events see Jensen (op. cit.) and Lawrence H. Gipson's *The Coming of the Revolution, 1763–1775* (New York: Harper & Brothers, 1954).

25. Charter and compact are usually synonyms in the language of the Whigs, and usually imply a relation of unequals.

26. There is no room for "secret writing" in public declarations.

27. I cite Volume I of Julian P. Boyd's edition of *The Papers of Thomas Jefferson* (Princeton: Princeton University Press, 1950), 315–319 and 414–433. Carl Becker, in his valuable *The Declaration of Independence: A Study in the History of Politics and Ideas* (New York: Vintage Press, 1958), argues unreasonably that this bill of particulars is not really important to the meaning of the Declaration. He was, however, as we should remember, an admirer of the *philosophes*— and no rhetorician.

28. The image here is drawn from one of the Fathers of English law, from chapter 13 of the *De Laudibus Legum Angliae* (1471) of Sir John Fortescue (Cambridge, England: Cambridge University Press, 1949), the edition and translation by S. B. Chrimes.

29. Jaffa's argument that one national Union was decided upon in 1774–1776 or before is easily refuted by John R. Alden's *The First South* (Baton Rouge: Louisiana State University Press, 1961); in Alden's *The South in the Revolution, 1763–1789* (Baton Rouge: Louisiana State University Press, 1957); and in Donald L. Robinson's *Slavery in the Structure of American Politics, 1765–1820* (New York: Harcourt Brace Jovanovich, 1971), 146 et passim. More than one Union has always been a possibility to be entertained by deliberate men. See Staughton Lynd's "The Abolitionist Critique of the United States Constitution," in *The Antislavery Vanguard: New Essays on the Abolitionists*, ed. Martin Duberman (Princeton: Princeton University Press, 1965), 210–239.

30. For instance, Professor Jaffa in forcing the notion of a Union before the Constitution into the "We the People" of the Preamble. Few scholars deny that the people acted through the states to ratify—as they had to form a Constitutional Convention. To this day they act through the states to amend. They existed at law through the maintenance of their several freedoms in battle. They formed the Confederation. The Declaration was only a negative precondition to a Union and to the firmer connection that followed. Underneath all of this may stand an unwritten Constitution, joining the partners of the Declaration in more ways than are specified in 1787. And perhaps also committing them to other ends: ends which Professor Jaffa would not care to consider. That compact was the prescription which sanctioned the Continental Congress—a creature of the chartered colonies. If the Declaration commits to anything, it is to that prescription—a compact of "the living, dead, and yet unborn." The continued operation of a society united in such a compact constitutes assent, regardless of official legal relations. New members are the only ones who are "sworn in."

31. For instance, the 32 acts passed by Virginia's colonial House of Burgesses which called for a restriction of the trade, all of them negated by the Crown at the behest of Northern

traders. Reports of the Constitutional Convention of 1787 indicate the same sort of pressures, resolved there by reasonable men determined to close out a divisive subject.

32. See "Getting Right with Lincoln," 3–18 of David Donald's *Lincoln Reconsidered* (New York: Vintage Press, 1961).

33. And especially from Kendall's "Equality: Commitment or Ideal?" *Phalanx*, I (Fall, 1967), 95–103, which answers some of Jaffa's complaints about Kendall's silences. I find it curious that Jaffa does not mention this piece.

34. Except for reasons of strategy (guilt by association), I cannot see why Jaffa identifies *Basic Symbols of the American Political Tradition* with the South. For Kendall and Carey begin with Massachusetts and Connecticut.

35. See p. 226 of Jaffa's own *Crisis of the House Divided* (Seattle: University of Washington Press, 1973).

36. See Edmund Wilson's magisterial *Patriotic Gore: Studies in the Literature of the American Civil War* (New York: Oxford University Press, 1962), 99–130. Surely Wilson cannot be mistaken in arguing that Lincoln saw himself in his portrait of the "new founder." For Lincoln clearly knows the animal he describes on a more intimate basis than mere speculation or observation could provide. Wilson compares Lincoln (xvi–xx) to Bismarck and Lenin—the other great founders of our age. Another useful analogue (a firm higher-law man, and no legalist or historicist) is Adolph Hitler. For he writes in *Mein Kampf* that "human rights break state rights," calls for illegal as well as legal instruments in "wars of rebellion against enslavement from within and without," observes that all governments by oppression plead the law, and concludes, "I believe today that I am acting in the sense of the Almighty Creator . . . fighting for the Lord's work." (I cite the edition of 1938, published in New York by Reynal and Hitchcock, 122–123 and 84).

37. Donald, op. cit., 131.

38. Roy P. Basler, *The Touchstone for Greatness: Essays, Addresses and Occasional Pieces about Abraham Lincoln* (Westport, Conn.: Greenwood Press, 1973), 206–227.

39. Jaffa praises Fehrenbacher's work.

40. *A Constitutional View of the Late War Between the States* (Philadelphia: National Publishing Co., 1868), Volume II, 266.

41. Lincoln's use of this passage is curious. For, as the context makes clear, Christ's point in setting up the dichotomy is that the Devil would not help his servants to ruin his own plans.

42. See David Brion Davis's *The Slave Power and the Paranoid Style* (Baton Rouge: Louisiana State University Press, 1969), especially 10–11.

43. I use quotation marks because I deny that they were ever founded, in that term's strict sense.

44. *America's Political Dilemma: From Limited to Unlimited Democracy* (Baltimore: Johns Hopkins Press, 1968), 17–62. He is supported by papers published in *National Review* by the late Frank Meyer (Aug. 24, 1965; Jan. 25, 1966).

45. Liberty is clearly the American value of greatest traditional authority—meaning "liberty to be ourselves," a nation which assumes an established, inherited identity. On the part played by the Gettysburg Address in this process, see my *Triumph* essay cited above and revised for this volume.

46. Lincoln, *Collected Works*, vol. VIII, 356.

47. Donald, op. cit., 8.

48. This analogy smacks of Stanley Elkins's now discredited theory in *Slavery: A Problem in American Institutional Life* (Chicago: University of Chicago Press, 1959). For correction see Eugene D. Genovese's *Roll, Jordan, Roll: The World the Slaves Made* (New York: Pantheon Books, 1974). Also consider the fact that Jews were proscribed under Hitler—all Jews, in the same way—while antebellum Southern blacks could be slaves or freemen or even slaveholders.

49. "A Fire Bell in the Night: The Southern Conservative View," *Modern Age*, XVII (Winter, 1973), 9–15. In those pages I maintain that an expansive view of natural rights" with respect to Negroes has undermined our inherited constitutional system.

Equality, Justice, and the American Revolution

1. "The Heresy of Equality," op. cit., 62.

2. Modern Library Edition, 340.

3. 1131 a 10 to 1131 b 24.

4. 1301 b 27.

5. Modern Library Edition, 3.

6. "The Heresy of Equality," op. cit., 63.

7. "It was not because it was proposed to establish a new nation, but because it was proposed to establish a nation on new principles, that July 4, 1776, has come to be regarded as one of the greatest days in history." And again. "But we should search these charters [of the Dutch and of the British] in vain for an assertion of the doctrine of equality. This principle had not before appeared as an official political declaration of any nation. It was profoundly revolutionary. It is one of the corner stones of American institutions." President Calvin Coolidge, speaking on the one hundred and fiftieth anniversary of the Declaration of Independence. In *Foundations of the Republic: Speeches and Addresses* by Calvin Coolidge (New York and London: Scribner's, 1926), 445, 447.

8. "The Heresy of Equality," op. cit., 62.

9. "The Heresy of Equality," 66.

10. *The Works of John C. Calhoun*, Richard K. Cralle, ed., (New York: Appleton, 1854), Vol. 4, 507.

11. *The Works of John C. Calhoun.*

12. *The Works of John C. Calhoun*, 508.

13. *Documents of American History*, Henry Steele Commager, ed., (New York: Appleton-Century-Crofts, Seventh Edition, 1963), 97, 98.

14. *The Collected Works of Abraham Lincoln*, Roy P. Basler, ed., (New Brunswick, New Jersey: Rutgers University Press, 1953), Vol. 2, 398–410.

15. Calhoun, op. cit., 505, 506.

16. "The Heresy of Equality," op. cit., 67.

17. "The Heresy of Equality," 67, 68.

18. Commager, op. cit., 107.

19. Commanger.

20. Commanger, 103.

21. Calhoun, op. cit., 512

22. Bradford, "The Heresy of Equality," op. cit., 77 (note 36.)

23. "The Heresy of Equality," 70, 71.

24. "The Heresy of Equality," 71.

25. *Collected Works*, Vol. 4, 160.

26. *The Political History of the Great Rebellion*, Edward McPherson, ed., (Washington, D.C. 1865), 103.

27. *The Political History of the Great Rebellion.*

28. *The Political History of the Great Rebellion.*

29. *The Political History of the Great Rebellion*, 104.

30. *The Political History of the Great Rebellion.*

31. E.g., in "On the Nature of Civil and Religious Liberty," *Equality and Liberty* (Oxford, 1965), 169–189.

Chapter 2

LINCOLN AND POLITICAL AMBITION

Was Lincoln an American Caesar? Were there limits to his political ambition?

Every man is said to have his peculiar ambition. Whether it be true or not, I can say for one that I have no other so great as that of being truly esteemed of my fellow men, by rendering myself worthy of their esteem.

Abraham Lincoln, To the People of Sangamo County, March 9, 1832

★ Richard N. Current, "Lincoln after 175 Years: The Myth of the Jealous Son"
★ Richard O. Curry, "Lincoln after 175 Years: Conscious or Unconscious Caesarism: A Critique of Recent Scholarly Attempts to Put Lincoln on the Analyst's Couch"
★ M. E. Bradford, "The Lincoln Legacy: A Long View"
★ Mark E. Neely, Jr., "Lincoln's Lyceum Speech and the Origins of the Modern Myth"

☙

LINCOLN AFTER 175 YEARS:
THE MYTH OF THE JEALOUS SON
Richard N. Current

BELIEVE IT OR NOT, the Civil War came because Abraham Lincoln suffered from an Oedipus complex. He had no use for his father, refused to visit him in his last illness, subconsciously wished him dead. He found a surrogate in George Washington, the father of his country. Still, Lincoln was a jealous as well as a worshipful son, for he was inordinately ambitious, and he had to compete with Washington's incomparable fame. No longer could any American gain immortality as a founder of the republic, but there remained the possibility of making oneself the savior of it. Lincoln indulged in fantasies of saving it from a would-be destroyer and dictator—

*This article originally appeared in Papers of the American Lincoln Association, Vol. 6, 1984, published by the Abraham Lincoln Association. Reprinted with permission from the author and the Abraham Lincoln Association.

fantasies, that is, of saving it from himself. Consciously or unconsciously he aspired to destroy and refound the republic, to slay the Founding Fathers and take their place. "The way that Lincoln cast himself into the center of the political conflict between the sections over slavery transformed that conflict into a civil war that created a modern nation while it destroyed forever the old Republic of the fathers." In the process he won the immortality he sought, and he won it "by becoming the very tyrant against whom Washington had warned in his Farewell Address."

Lincoln the tyrant! Lincoln the father-killer! If he was Oedipus Rex, one wonders who, in this latter-day scenario, was Jocasta, the Mother whom he married. More seriously, one wonders whether all this amounts to anything more than the latest in a long series of base and baseless characterizations of Lincoln. Certainly he has taken Washington's place as first in the hearts of his countrymen. Since 1948, historians have rated the presidents in at least a half dozen polls, and in every one of them Lincoln has emerged as the greatest. Yet, one hundred and seventy-five years after his birth, he continues to be, as he was during his lifetime, the subject of denigrating myth.

A pioneer among the mythmakers and psychologizers was, of course, Lincoln's onetime law partner William H. Herndon. "If there is anything that a poor ignorant Sucker like myself can arrogate to myself," Herndon once wrote, "it is this, namely, an intuitive seeing of human character." He thought he, if anyone, could look right into Lincoln's very "gizzard." From Herndon's remarkable insight came a number of familiar stories, among them the story that Lincoln never loved any woman except Ann Rutledge and that Mary Todd married him not out of love but out of revenge.

Though not adopting those particular themes from Herndon, the recent psychologizers look to him for much of their information and insight, especially in regard to Lincoln's ambition—that "little engine that knew no rest," as Herndon called it. But mainly they draw their inspiration from Sigmund Freud and other psychoanalysts, most notably Erik H. Erikson, author of *Young Man Luther: A Study in Psychoanalysis and History* (1958). The new interpreters of Lincoln also acknowledge a debt to the literary critic Edmund Wilson, who included a Lincoln essay in his study of Civil War literature *Patriotic Gore* (1962). For Wilson and his psychologizing followers, the key document in Lincoln's self-revelation is his address before the Young Men's Lyceum of Springfield on January 27, 1838.

On that occasion, about two weeks before his twenty-ninth birthday, Lincoln took as his topic "The Perpetuation of Our Political Institutions." We the "legal inheritors" of "fundamental blessings" from our Revolutionary forefathers, he proceeded to orate, now face a possible threat to our republican inheritance, not from some enemy abroad but from developments at home.

Recent lynchings in various parts of the country indicate a trend toward "mob law." If this should reach a point where government can no longer protect lives and property, citizens generally may become alienated from government. Then, promising law and order, some extraordinarily ambitious man may take over as dictator.

"Many great and good men sufficiently qualified for any task they should undertake, may ever be found, whose ambition would aspire to nothing beyond a seat in Congress, a gubernatorial or a presidential chair; but such belong best to the family of the lion or the tribe of the eagle. What! Think you these places would satisfy an Alexander, a Caesar, or a Napoleon? Never!" The way to avert this danger, Lincoln concluded, is to cultivate a "political religion" that emphasizes "reverence for the laws" and puts reliance on "reason, cold, calculating, unimpassioned reason."

Reading between the lines, Edmund Wilson says, "It is evident that Lincoln has projected himself into the role against which he is warning" here. According to Wilson, the young Lincoln already was "extremely ambitious" and "saw himself in the heroic role." So he issued an "equivocal warning against the ambitious leader, describing this figure with a fire that seemed to derive as much from admiration as from apprehension." Not only was he revealing his own self perception but he was also being "startlingly prophetic" when he spoke of a "towering genius" who would "burn for distinction" and if possible would "have it, whether at the expense of emancipating slaves or enslaving freemen."

One of the recent psychobiographers, George B. Forgie, in his *Patricide in the House Divided* (1979), concedes that "Wilson was partially correct, for Lincoln's image of danger is on the one hand so precise and on the other so far removed from any plausible threat that it must have appeared first on some inner mirror." But Forgie insists that, to "clarify or amend" Wilson's proposition that Lincoln was identifying with the would-be dictator, it is important to add that "Lincoln was doing so unconsciously. So close is the description to certain traits of the describer that only a man completely unconscious of what he was doing would have presented it." Forgie maintains that, at a "conscious level," Lincoln was "among the most devoted of all sons of the revolutionary fathers. There is no evidence that at this level he ever questioned that it was his duty to preserve"—not to destroy, the republican edifice the fathers had erected.

Another of the new interpreters, Charles B. Strozier, in *Lincoln's Quest for Union* (1982), accepts the Wilson thesis but agrees with Forgie that Lincoln was expressing only his "unacknowledged (or unconscious) wishes." "His desire to be the greatest and most powerful leader of all time, to be the towering genius, appears in the speech as motivating someone else," Strozier explains. "The other figure he feared because it spoke for his forbidden self; the wish, as Freud has observed, is father to the fear." Strozier underscores the "Oedipal implications" of the speech. After quoting Lincoln's metaphor comparing the fathers of the republic to "giant oaks . . . shorn of . . . foliage . . . with mutilated limbs," he comments: "The imagery here suggests emasculation and castration at the hands of the aspiring son."

Strozier freely indicates the influence of Erik H. Erikson. His chapter title "Young Man Lincoln" obviously derives from Erikson's book title *Young Man Luther*. To his own analysis of Lincoln he applies principles that Erikson uses in analyzing his subject—for example, the principle that avoidance of personal commitment and intimacy "may lead to a deep sense of isolation and consequent self-absorption," which, Strozier says, "fits well with what we know about Lincoln." Strozier finds a significant similarity between Luther's and Lincoln's paths to greatness. "After 1854 Lincoln turned outward and attempted, as Erik Erikson might say, to solve for all—what he could not solve for himself." That is to say, after failing to overcome the divisive forces within his own personality, he succeeded in his "quest for union" by overcoming the divisive forces in the nation at large.

A third analyst, Dwight G. Anderson, in *Abraham Lincoln: The Quest for Immortality* (1982), states frankly that his "definition of the subject matter is dependent upon Freud's theory of the origins of monotheism and Erik Erikson's study of Martin Luther." Monotheism is presumably relevant because, according to Anderson, Lincoln wanted to be God. "His project of becoming 'God' worked itself out in both a private and public context, against both his natural father and his political father, with the result that a personal death anxiety became transformed into a symbolic immortality both for himself and for the nation." Anderson adds: "Some assistance in understanding Lincoln's preoccupation with death is offered by Erik Erikson's comments on the 'young great man' in the years before he becomes the 'great young man.' Erikson had Martin Luther in mind, but his words describe Lincoln just as well."

Anderson agrees with Forgie and Strozier in accepting the Edmund Wilson thesis, but disagrees with them by insisting that Lincoln consciously identified himself with the "towering genius," the potential tyrant. To clinch the point, Anderson directs attention to one particular clause in the Lyceum speech. Lincoln is saying that many have sought and achieved fame in pursuit of independence and the new government. "But," he continues, "the game is caught; and I believe it is true that with the catching, end the pleasures of the chase." Anderson provides the following gloss: "Here was Lincoln . . . projecting himself ('and I believe it is true') into the very role against which he warned his audience—a Caesarean role in which the player would have his distinction no matter what the cost—whether by freeing slaves or enslaving free men."

Anderson is not content with disagreeing with Forgie but goes on to denounce him and his views with considerable virulence. "Forgie's work," he declares, "is an illustration of why psychohistory is so widely held in disrepute. He argues that Lincoln treated the tyrant out of 'undesirable wishes he could not recognize in himself,' which 'he expelled and then reified . . . into the image of the bad son.' In a footnote he explains, 'Psychoanalysts call this operation "projection."'" Actually, however, it is Forgie's projection rather than Lincoln's that is the relevant factor in this interpretation. For not only does Forgie ignore Lincoln's explicit statement of identification with those who might become tyrant ('and I believe it is true. . .'), it is hardly bold to assume that he may also have been unconsciously hostile to Lincoln's actual words, because his central thesis is that Stephen A. Douglas is the 'bad son' of the Lyceum Address whom Lincoln symbolically killed in the 1850s. This preposterous conclusion . . . would seem to be a monumental case of intellectual regression in service of the professional ego (to alter slightly a characterization Forgie applies to Lincoln)."

Now, that is surely an instance of the pot calling the kettle black. If Forgie, as charged, reads Lincoln in the light of private preconceptions, Anderson certainly does the same—and with results that are even more far-fetched. Nowhere does Lincoln make, as Anderson claims, an "explicit statement of identification with those who might become tyrant." Lincoln's words "and I believe it is true" lead up to no such statement. Lincoln is not saying, "I believe it is true that I am one of those aspiring dictators." He is merely saying, "I believe it is true that the pleasures of the chase end when the game has been caught." His meaning is perfectly plain to any reader who is neither riding a hobby nor being ridden by one.

Anderson's book lacks the redeeming qualities that both Forgie's and Strozier's possess. Dealing not only with the words of Lincoln but also with those of many of his contemporaries, Forgie has sought out the metaphor of the house and the family in a wide range of antebellum American writing, and he has shown imagination and skill in arranging the quotations to fit a Freudian pattern. Strozier, generally a careful historian as well as a competent psychiatrist, has written what is on the whole a warm, sympathetic, and moving as well as illuminating account, one that adds to our understanding of Lincoln's private motives and their relation to his public stance.

It seems too bad that these two historians should have taken at face value the *ipse dixit* of Edmund Wilson, illustrious though he may have been as a fiction writer and a literary critic. The credulity of Anderson is perhaps more understandable, since he is a political scientist, not a historian. All three authors, in adopting Erik H. Erikson's model, abandon the historian's standards. According to Erikson, "the making of legend is as much part of the scholarly rewriting of history as it is part of the original facts used in the work of scholars. We are thus obliged to accept half legend as half history, provided only that a reported episode does not contradict other well-established facts; persists in having a ring of truth; and yields a meaning consistent with psychological theory.

Well, the assertion that Lincoln aspired to dictatorship, even to godhood, contradicts no known facts—except perhaps for the fact that as president he showed great restraint in the exercise of his powers and great respect for the constitutional limits on them. The assertion has the "ring of truth" for those who think it has, and it yields meanings that appear to be consistent with one psychological theory or another. Thus it may meet the requirements of "half-history," but it does not meet those of whole history. Historians are taught to accept only the testimony that two or more independent and competent witnesses confirm. The hypothesis of Lincoln the would-be patricide and tyrant gets no support whatever from historical evidence. Rather, the record of his career suggests that he himself was one of those "great and good men" he referred to in the Lyceum speech—one of those who would have been satisfied with a presidential chair or even a senatorial seat.

We may reasonably conclude that in this speech Lincoln means exactly what he says. If we are to draw inferences from his remarks, we ought to keep in mind the context of the time. When he speaks of a rising "mobocratic spirit" he gives examples of it, and we could easily add other examples. When he warns against a leader who may seek power and fame "whether at the expense of emancipating slaves, or enslaving freemen," we do not have to jump to the conclusion that he is prophesying his own future, as Edmund Wilson does. We may safely assume that he is thinking of the abolitionist and proslavery feelings of the very moment—feelings that accounted for the recent mob murder of Elijah Lovejoy in nearby Alton, Illinois.

And when Lincoln talks of overweening ambition—of a homegrown Alexander, Caesar, or Napoleon—we do not have to probe his psyche to find out what he really means. He was a Whig, and the Whigs were used to referring to Andrew Jackson as "King Andrew the First," a veritable tyrant or at least an incipient one, as they saw him. Whigs and other Americans—those of them with even a bit of schooling— were familiar with the name of Julius Caesar and with the fate of the Roman republic. They were even better acquainted with the career of Napoleon Bonaparte, who after all was nearly a contemporary, having been dead less than seventeen years when Lincoln addressed the Lyceum. How curious it is that any present-day American historian should think, as Forgie does, that Lincoln's "image of danger" was also far removed from any plausible threat that it must have appeared first on some inner mirror! Whether plausible or not to Forgie, the potential threat was real enough in the view of early nineteenth-century Americans who knew something of the history of republics, ancient, medieval, and modern. Politicians from the generation of George Washington and John Adams to that of Daniel Webster and John C. Calhoun made their constituents aware of the possible danger. To discover it, Lincoln did not have to peer into his inner consciousness or subconsciousness.

Not for any cryptic meanings but for its manifest message the Lyceum speech is a remarkable production to have come from a twenty-eight-year-old man of Lincoln's background. One of its insights, neglected by commentators, qualifies the author as something of a psychologist, a social psychologist, himself. In explaining why it was easier to maintain republican institutions during the Revolutionary period than in his own time, he says that during the Revolution, "the deep rooted principles of hate, and the powerful motive of revenge instead of being turned (by Americans) against each other, were directed exclusively against the British nation." Since then, however, in the absence of a menacing external foe, the "passions of the people" could be expected to divide and weaken the republic rather than to unite and strengthen it. Here Lincoln is adumbrating the sociological law that the degree of solidarity of the in-group is more or less proportional to the intensity of conflict with an out-group. As a practical proposition . . . this had been familiar to politicians from time immemorial. Lincoln as president was to decline to apply the principle when Secretary of State William H. Seward, in his memorandum of April 1, 1861, recommended foreign war as a means of preventing civil war.

Psychologizers of Lincoln today ought to exercise at least as much caution as the first of them, William H. Herndon, advised. "He was the most secretive—reticent—shut-mouthed man that ever existed," Herndon said of Lincoln, "You had to guess at the man after years of acquaintance, and then you must look long and keenly before you guessed or you would make an ass of yourself." And all of us who are eager for the truth ought to heed Lincoln's own request of 1858: "I only ask my friends and all who are eager for the truth, that when they hear me represented as saying or meaning anything strange, they will turn to my own words and examine for themselves."

ॐ

Lincoln after 175 Years: Conscious or Subconscious Caesarism: A Critique of Recent Scholarly Attempts to Put Lincoln on the Analyst's Couch

Richard O. Curry

Historians' fascination with the life and career of Abraham Lincoln—especially his views on slavery and race and, indeed, his astuteness as a political leader—continues unabated, and deservedly so. During the past fifteen years Lincoln has received mixed reviews at best. A number of historians (including Jacque Voegeli, David Donald, T. Harry Williams, Otto H. Olson, Hans Trefousse, and Richard O. Curry, among others) have emphasized Lincoln's fundamental radicalism on slavery and his political brilliance in moving a reluctant nation toward a commitment to emancipation. But, few have concluded that Lincoln was unalterably or unqualifiedly committed to egalitarian ideals. Harold Hyman was perhaps the first modern historian to do so, arguing as early as 1966 that Lincoln, during the war, was moving by his own volition toward egalitarian ideals. Hyman was taken to task by Ludwell H. Johnson, who maintained that it has yet to be demonstrated that Lincoln ever acted for reasons other than political expediency; and in 1970, Bruce Catton admonished historians to "admit once and for all that Lincoln did not believe in racial equality."[1]

But, as Lincoln would phrase it, "the signs of the times are changing." Three years ago LaWanda Cox published *Lincoln and Black Freedom*, a book that Eric Foner admiringly characterized as "a brief for the defense," and a book that has already had an impact in historical circles. For example, a session was devoted to

*This article originally appeared in *Journal of the Illinois State Historical Society*, Vol. 77, Spring 1984. Reprinted with permission from the Journal of the Illinois State Historical Society.

assessing the implications of her book at the meetings of the Southern Historical Association in 1983.[2]

In conceptual terms, Cox's book breaks little new ground in emphasizing Lincoln's radicalism on slavery and emancipation and, in general, his astuteness as a politician. But Cox's chapters on Lincoln's Louisiana policies offer brilliant new insights. In Louisiana, Lincoln attempted—albeit unsuccessfully—to get black citizenship and suffrage into the new state constitution. Unfortunately, General Nathaniel P. Banks was not up to his assigned task, but the important point Cox makes is that Lincoln, despite the political realities he had to face and, indeed, the necessity to compromise and dissemble—was attempting to commit one Southern state to the ideal of legal equality with whites. Although Cox emphasizes that Lincoln cannot be considered apart from his age and concedes that his commitment to equality may have been tentative or qualified by modern standards, the burden of her argument offers a serious challenge to the views of Cation, Johnson, and others who have dismissed this argument entirely.

Only a year after Cox's book was published, David Lightner went even farther than Cox in making a case for Lincoln's commitment to equalitarian ideals. Lightner, whose article was published in this journal in 1982, has provocatively argued that the emergence of "a more benign interpretation of Lincoln's racial attitudes" in recent years may now "be extended to what perhaps is its logical conclusion." "I am convinced," Lightner boldly posits, "that Abraham Lincoln . . . was genuinely devoted to the ideal of human equality—not only in the closing days of his life but throughout his years of prominence in American politics."[3] In my opinion, Lightner has made the most compelling case to date—one that is not only a major contribution to the continuing dialogue on Lincoln's racial views in its own right, but one that adds force to Cox's views on the war years. From now on, Lightner's article and Cox's book undoubtedly will be read in tandem.

Although one of my primary concerns in this review is to call attention to the recent major reassessment of Lincoln's views and policies on slavery and race in a favorable light, my major undertaking here is to analyze the significance and implications of a second major recent approach to the life and career of Abraham Lincoln. I am referring, of course, to the attempt of psychohistorians to put Mr. Lincoln on the "analyst's couch." The books in question are George B. Forgie's *Patricide in the House Divided: A Psychological Interpretation of Lincoln and His Age*; Dwight G. Anderson's *Abraham Lincoln: The Quest for Immortality*; and Charles B. Strozier's *Lincoln's Quest for Union: Public and Private Meanings*.[4]

Since, in my view, most of the conclusions reached by Forgie, Strozier, and Anderson on Lincoln's political motivations are erroneous, let me state quite clearly at the outset that I have nothing against sophisticated psychological interpretations of history. The psychological dimension is one that historians overlook or utilize at their peril. Let me state further: Lawrence B. Goodheart and I have recently completed an extended review essay of works in the psychobiographical and psychosocial realm that, in our view, are important contributions to historical scholarship. I am referring to Perry's *Marriage, Childhood, and Reform*, a biography of Henry Clarke Wright (1980); Peter Walker's *Moral Choices: Memory, Desire, and Imagination in Nineteenth-Century American Abolition* (1978); and Lawrence J. Friedman's *Gregarious Saints: Self and Community in American Abolitionism, 1830–1870* (1982).[5]

The books by Perry and Friedman are on the availability of voluminous archival sources. Wright, for example, left behind over a hundred personal diaries to which he confided his most intimate thoughts; and Friedman's prodigious use of archival material allows him to go beyond psychobiography and provide important psychological insights in the realm of group dynamics. Peter Walker's work is uneven; but his analysis of fundamental differences that characterize each of Frederick Douglass's three autobiographies reveals much of the inner turmoil that Douglass attempted to hide—and that his earlier biographers missed. Walker's work is all the more striking because his insights are similar to those of the psychiatrist Frantz Fanon in *Black Skin, White Masks* (1952, 1967), which deals with the psychopathology of racism in a colonial context. In sum, Douglass's mulatto heritage created inner tensions and turmoil that he was never quite to reconcile in a society that did not permit him to do so.

But returning to present psychoanalytical interpretations of Lincoln, let me deal first with the work of George B. Forgie. Forgie not only writes without fear but without historical evidence to buttress his conclusions and conceptual framework. First, he argues that "any convincing psychological interpretation of Abraham Lincoln must take into consideration his strong filiopiety—not toward his actual father, from whom he was estranged, but toward the 'our fathers' of the Gettysburg Address, the Founders of the Republic." At this point Forgie invents a subconsciously malevolent Lincoln. If he "venerated the fathers," Forgie writes, he also resented them because "their immortality obstructed his extraordinary ambition." Why? Because, Forgie maintains, of the fathers' success," there was no "need for another generation of heroes." Lincoln, however, instead of "renouncing his own desire for historic distinction, devised "a strategy for achieving it." What was that strategy?

According to Forgie, Lincoln decided to destroy the "House" that our forefathers had built. The only "evidence" that Forgie cites is a speech that the young Lincoln gave in 1838 in which he stated that there " 'will at some time spring up among us' a dangerously ambitious genius who, finding 'nothing left to be done in the way of building up' would 'set boldly to the task of pulling down.' " "This prophecy arose," Forgie "suspects," from "Lincoln's own understandable hostility toward the preempting fathers, an attitude filiopiety could disguise, but not destroy. Unable to recognize his antagonism, he expelled and projected it onto an imagined bad son." In Forgie's opinion the bad son was Stephen A. Douglas, leader of the Democratic party and champion of popular sovereignty—a policy designed to take the slavery expansion issue out of national politics and provide theoretical legitimacy to the

South's peculiar institution. "Surely," Forgie writes, "the man whose chance for immortality depends on the appearance of his basest passions embodied in a tyrant is likely to recognize the tyrant when he comes, search for him if he does not appear, and invent him if he cannot be found." Thus, we are asked to believe that the subconscious Lincoln "stalked Douglas as a 'dangerous enemy of liberty' plotting to destroy the Republic and institute despotism in its place." This, Forgie continues, was the "central (and usually misunderstood) point of Lincoln's famous 'House Divided' speech which marked the beginning of Lincoln's campaign for Douglas' Senate seat in 1858." The strategy worked, Forgie declares, isolating Douglas and leading Lincoln to the Presidency and to fame and immortality. In Forgie's words: "The good son defeated the bad one and went on to win immortal fame. The irony, here, of course, is that in attempting to save the father's work from a nonexistent threat, Lincoln set the stage for the calamities of the 1860s."[6]

Such conclusions defy all canons of historical evidence—being based on nothing more than conjecture, faulty logic, and a lack of understanding of the historical setting in which Lincoln lived and operated. Although Forgie attempts to qualify his "discovery" of the subconscious Lincoln by using the phrase "one suspects," it is a lame construction on what follows. Forgie, apparently, is not aware that there is surely a difference between what one knows and what one (for whatever reasons) suspects. Equally important, Forgie characterizes the sectional controversy over slavery expansion as "a nonexistent threat." What is this supposed to mean? Presumably, Forgie is saying that slavery, which had been abolished or was on the road to extinction throughout the Western Hemisphere during the nineteenth century, was not a threat to American ideals of democracy, equality, and republican government. Had it not been for Lincoln's subconscious fanaticism—symbolic patricide of a filiating son gone mad in his desire to achieve fame and immortality—secession and a bloody civil war could have been averted.

Forgie overlooks, among other things, the fact that his "moderate hero" Douglas was nearly as unacceptable a candidate in the South in 1860 as Lincoln. Even if one recognizes that Douglas was morally obtuse on the question of slavery, he was not a "Doughface" (a Northern man with Southern principles) catering blindly to Southern demands for the absolute security for slavery in the territories (and indeed, in the South itself) in his own quest for power, fame, and the Presidency. By the late 1850s it was clear to many politicians in the South that popular sovereignty—although it recognized the theoretical rights of the South in the territories—meant the ultimate triumph of Free Soil by the back door had it been implemented; and, in the end, Douglas was no more willing to tolerate secession than Lincoln.

More important, Forgie's analysis assumes that Lincoln was personally able to manipulate all the major actors and issues of his time in order to fulfill his own subconscious desires. Clearly, this much skill and control over events cannot even be attributed to Hitler, Stalin, or Idi Amin—although Hitler, at least, has been the subject of a provocative if controversial psychoanalytic analysis by the historian Rob-

ert G. L. Waite. Lincoln's racial attitudes are controversial and debatable; and emancipation did not resolve the racial dilemmas that continue to plague American
society. But Forgie's *Patricide in the House Divided* is what Peter Walker calls "mythopoeic history."[7] Even if we admit that Lincoln and the Republicans presented no
immediate threat to the South and its institutions, Forgie does not even come to
grips with the concept of misperception or "perceived threat" by "fanatical abolitionists" and their "Black Republican" allies, which characterized much of the social
and political thinking in the lower South about the North. To do so would stand
Forgie's argument on its head—as the burden of guilt would then fall primarily on
the heads of "irrational" Southern Fire-Eaters. Whether Forgie knows it or not, his
interpretation and those of Anderson and Strozier, despite its psychoanalytic paraphernalia, is little more than a restatement of the "needless thesis that characterized
the writings of historians such as James G. Randall and Avery O. Craven in the 1930s
and 1940s—even though in Forgie's work Lincoln, rather than the abolitionists, is
the chief villain of the piece. As Craven once said, "Garrison, if living today, could
profitably consult a psychiatrist." According to Randall, abolitionism reflected nothing more than the "avenging force of Puritanism in politics" that precipitated a
needless war in a world where slavery was not only becoming unprofitable, but
dying.[8]

Dwight G. Anderson, like Forgie, also focuses attention on "the interrelationship
between Lincoln's psychology and the dominant cultural and political forces of his
time." Like Forgie, Anderson also places greater importance than it can possibly bear
on Lincoln's 1838 Lyceum speech. But there are important differences. Forgie posits
the existence of a subconsciously malevolent Lincoln. Anderson, following the lead
of the literacy critic Edmund Wilson, argues that Lincoln consciously projected
himself into the role of an "evil genius" and became the "very tyrant against whom
Washington had warned in his Farewell Address, a tyrant who would preside over
the destruction of the Constitution to gratify his own ambition." Thus, Lincoln's
filial rebellion, a psychopathic desire to displace what Anderson terms these "collective historical fathers," caused Lincoln to establish a national "political religion."
This "political religion" would not only serve to purify the nation but justify its
"role as lawgiver to the world" and provide Lincoln with the immortality that his
narcissism and thirst for eternal Fame yearned for. Phrased another way, "Anderson's creation of a mythopoeic Lincoln is an astonishing variation on the theme of
'Manifest Destiny and Mission' in American history" has not only been used to
attack or justify American imperialism—but one that identifies Lincoln as its
founder and chief theoretician. Shades of William Appleman Williams, who characterizes the War for Union as an imperialistic venture against the South without uti-
lizing all the psychological paraphernalia found here.[9]

Charles Strozier's work, in contrast to Forgie's and Anderson's, is admirable.
That is to say: when confining his analysis to Lincoln's private life—Lincoln's well-
known fears of sexual inadequacy, his fear of insanity, his morbid preoccupation

with death, his periodic bouts with melancholia and depression, his estrangement from his father, the death of his children, his wife's descent into madness—Strozier has many important and useful things to say. It is also plausible if not necessarily accurate to suggest that Lincoln's search for order and stability in his personal life was related to the stability and cohesion of the political process itself.[10] But once Strozier departs from analyzing the private Lincoln and turns his attention to the public arena (especially in a chapter entitled "The Group Self and the Crisis of the 1850s") his work becomes little more than a speculative, ahistorical treatise in which he posits the existence of a "cohesive group self" in sum, the existence of a Northern psyche. This leads Strozier down a primrose path in which he argues that Lincoln and other antislavery spokesmen, mistaken in their belief that slavery and the slave power represented a major threat to republican institutions, were expressing narcis-sistic—in fact, paranoid—rage toward what Strozier terms the "fragmenting self."[11] Strozier, nevertheless, in contrast to Forgie and Anderson, is basically sympathetic to Lincoln and the achievements of his presidency—although this provides scant comfort to those who take a somewhat more benign view of human nature than do speculative, psychological reductionists.

One final commentary on the work of Forgie and Anderson: both place inordi-nate emphasis on Lincoln's speech in 1838. Both virtually rest their case for Lincoln's "hidden agenda" on this speech (that is, his narcissism and pathological desire for immortality). Both view his warning against "Caesarism" and the emergence of an "evil genius" as a conscious or subconscious revelation that he, Abraham Lincoln, was determined to achieve personal greatness—regardless of cost. Whatever the sig-nificance of that speech, the twenty-eight-year old Lincoln, a devout Whig, was uti-lizing standard Whig rhetoric—which continually employed the imagery of Caesarism in attacking "King Andrew I." It should not be surprising that the young French nobleman Alexis de Tocqueville—who talked more with upper-class Whigs than Democrats in preparing his classic *Democracy in America*—was taken in by Caesaristic rhetoric. His major concern was France, and Tocqueville, after all, did live to see the triumph of Napoleon III. But for Forgie, Anderson, and, indeed, Edmund Wilson, to place such dubious constructions on a standard Whig cliche—is obtuse.[12]

For those wishing to discredit psychohistory as a genre, the books by Forgie and Anderson provide prime targets.[13] But to repeat: In the hands of a Lewis Perry or a Lawrence Friedman, whose conclusions are based not only on theory but the exis-tence of massive empirical evidence, psychobiography and the psychology of group dynamics provide exciting—in fact, indispensable—tools for attempting to recon-struct our meaningful past.

~~

THE LINCOLN LEGACY: A LONG VIEW
M. E. Bradford

WITH THE TIME AND MANNER of his death Abraham Lincoln, as leader of a Puritan people who had just won a great victory over "the forces of evil," was placed beyond the reach of ordinary historical inquiry and assessment. Through Booth's bullet he became the one who had "died to make men free," who had perished that his country's "new birth" might occur: a "second founder" who, in Ford's Theater, had been transformed into an American version of the "dying god." Our common life, according to this construction, owes its continuation to the shedding of the sacred blood. Now after over a century of devotion to the myth of the "political messiah," it is still impossible for most Americans to see through and beyond the magical events of April 1865. However, Lincoln's daily purchase upon the ongoing business of the nation requires that we devise a way of setting aside the martyrdom to look behind it at Lincoln's place in the total context of American history and discover in him a major source of our present confusion, our distance from the republicanism of the Fathers, the models of political conduct which we profess most to admire. The examination of Lincoln's career as divided according to the formula of my study into Whig, artificial Puritan, and serious Cromwellian phases should facilitate that recovery. And provide a proper word to break the silence that will not let us know and judge. Of course, nothing that we can identify as part of Lincoln's legacy belongs to him alone. In some respects the Emancipator was carried along with the tides. Yet a measure of his importance is that he was at the heart of the major political events of his era. Therefore what signifies in a final evaluation of this melancholy man is that many of these changes in the country would never have come to pass had Lincoln not pushed them forward. Or at least not come so quickly, or with such dreadful violence. I will emphasize only the events that he most certainly shaped according to his relentless will, alterations in the character of our country for which he was clearly responsible. For related developments touched by Lincoln's wand, I can have only a passing word. The major charges advanced here, if proved up, are sufficient to impeach the most famous and respected of public men. More would only overdo.

The first and most obvious item in my bill of particulars for indictment concerns Lincoln's dishonesty and obfuscation with respect to the nation's future obligations to the Negro, slave and free. It was of course an essential ingredient of Lincoln's

*This article originally appeared in *Modern Age*, Vol. 24, 1980, published by Intercollegiate Studies Institute, Inc. Reprinted with permission from the Intercollegiate Studies Institute, Inc.

position that he make a success at being anti-Southern or antislavery without at the same time appearing to be significantly impious about the beginnings of the Republic (which was neither anti-Southern nor antislavery)—or significantly pro-Negro. He was the first Northern politician of any rank to combine these attitudes into a viable platform persona, the first to make his moral position on slavery in the South into a part of his national politics. It was a posture that enabled him to unite elements of the Northern electorate not ordinarily willing to cooperate in any political undertaking. And thus enabled him to destroy the old Democratic majority—a coalition necessary to preserving the union of the states. Then came the explosion. But this calculated posturing has had more durable consequences than secession and the federal confiscation of property in slaves. Even after the passage of over a century, with each new day they unfold with additional and ever-deepening iteration and threaten to produce divisions that make those explored on the battlefields of Virginia, Maryland, and Tennessee seem mild indeed: so threaten most especially since it has become impossible to single out the South as the particular locus of "improper" attitudes on the subject of race.

In the nation as a whole what moves toward fruition is a train of events set in motion by the duplicitous rhetoric concerning the Negro that helped make Abraham Lincoln into our first "sectional" president. Central to this appeal is a claim to a kind of moral superiority that costs absolutely nothing in the way of conduct. Lincoln, in insisting that the Negro was included in the promise of the Declaration of Independence and that the Declaration bound his countrymen to fulfill a pledge hidden in that document, seemed clearly to point toward a radical transformation of American society. Carried within his rejection of Negro slavery as a continuing feature of the American regime, his assertion that the equality clause of the Declaration of Independence was "the father of all moral principle among us," were certain muted corollaries. By promising that the peculiar institution would be made to disappear if candidates for national office adopted the proper "moral attitude" on that subject, Lincoln recited as a litany the general terms of his regard for universal human rights. But at the same time he added certain modifications to this high doctrine: modifications required by those of his countrymen to whom he hoped to appeal, by the rigid racism of the Northern electorate, and by "what his own feelings would admit." The most important of these reservations was that none of his doctrine should apply significantly to the Negro in the North. Or, after freedom, to what he could expect in the South. It was a very broad, very general, and very abstract principle to which he made reference. By it he could divide the sheep from the goats, the wheat from the chaff, the patriot from the conspirator. But for the Negro it provided nothing more than a technical freedom, best to be enjoyed far away. Or the valuable opportunity to "root hog or die." For the sake of such vapid distinctions he urged his countrymen to wade through seas of blood.

To be sure, this position does not push the "feelings" of that moralist who was our sixteenth President too far from what was comfortable for him. And it goes without saying that a commitment to "natural rights" which will not challenge the Black Codes of Illinois, which promises something like them for the freedman in the South, or else offers him as alternative the proverbial "one-way ticket to nowhere" is a commitment of empty words. It is only an accident of political history that the final Reconstruction settlement provided a bit more for the former slave—principally, the chance to vote Republican, and even that "right" didn't last, once a better deal was made available to his erstwhile protectors. But the point is that Lincoln's commitment was precisely of the sort that the North was ready to make—while passing legislation to restrict the flow of Negroes into its own territories, elaborating its own system of segregation by race, and exploiting black labor through its representatives in a conquered South. Lincoln's double talk left his part of the country with a durable heritage of pious self-congratulation, what Robert Penn Warren has well described as "The Treasury of Virtue." Left it with the habit of concealing its larger objectives behind a facade of racial generosity, of using the Negro as a reason for policies and laws which make only minimal alterations in his condition, and also with the habit of seeming to offer a great deal more than they are truly willing to give. In the wake of the just concluded "Second Reconstruction" of 1955–1965, the Northern habit has become national, visible every time one of the respected polls examines our ostensible opinions on race relations. There we appear the soul of charity, though our conduct voting "with our feet" belies every statistic that we produce. Where such insubstantial sentiment will lead we cannot say. It is enough to observe that mass hypocrisy is a contagious disease. Or to put matters another way, it would be well if we learned to say no more than we meant. For the alternative is to produce in the targets of our beneficence the kind of anger that comes with the receipt of a promissory note that contains, as one of its terms, the condition that it need never be paid. Better than this would be a little honest dealing, whatever its kind.

The second heading in this "case against Lincoln" involves no complicated pleading. Neither will it confuse any reader who examines his record with care. For it has to do with Lincoln's political economy, his management of the commercial and business life of the part of the Republic under his authority. This material is obvious, even though it is not always connected with the Presidency of Abraham Lincoln. Nevertheless, it must be developed at this point. For it leads directly into the more serious charges upon which this argument depends. It is customary to deplore the Gilded Age, the era of the Great Barbecue. It is true that many of the corruptions of the Republican Era came to a head after Lincoln lay at rest in Springfield. But it is a matter of fact that they began either under his direction or with his sponsorship. Military necessity, the "War for the Union," provided an excuse, an umbrella of sanction, under which the essential nature of the changes being made in the relation of government to commerce could be concealed. Of his total policy the Northern historian Robert Sharkey has written, "Human ingenuity would have had difficulty in contriving a more perfect engine for class and sectional exploration: creditors finally obtaining the upper hand as opposed to debtors, and the developed East holding the whip over the underdeveloped West and South." Until the South left the Union. Until a High Whig sat in the White House, none of this return to the "energetic government" of Hamilton's design was possible. Indeed, even in the heyday of the Federalists it had never been so simple a matter to translate power into wealth. Now Lincoln could try again the internal improvements of the early days in Illinois. The difference was that this time the funding would not be restrained by political reversal or a failure of credit. For if anything fell short, Mr. Salmon P. Chase, "the foreman" of his "green printing office," could be instructed "to give his paper mill another turn." And the inflationary policy of rewarding the friends of the government sustained. The euphemism of our time calls this "income redistribution." But it was theft in 1864, and is theft today.

A great increase in the tariff and the formation of a national banking network were, of course, the cornerstones of this great alteration in the posture of the federal government toward the sponsorship of business. From the beginning of the Republican Party Lincoln warned his associates not to talk about their views on these subjects. Their alliance, he knew, was a negative thing: a league against the Slave Power and its Northern friends. But in private he made it clear that the hidden agenda of the Republicans would have its turn, once the stick was in their hand. In this he promised well. Between 1861 and 1865, the tariff rose from 18.84 percent to 47.56 percent. And it stayed above 40 percent in all but two years of the period concluding with the election of Woodrow Wilson. Writes the Virginia historian Ludwell H. Johnson, it would "facilitate a massive transfer of wealth, satisfying the dreariest predictions of John C. Calhoun." The new Republican system of banking (for which we should note Lincoln was directly accountable) was part of the same large design of "refounding." The National Banking Acts of 1863 and 1864, with the earlier Legal Tender Act, flooded the country with $480,000,000 of fiat money that was soon depreciated by about two thirds in relation to specie. Then all notes but the greenback dollar were taxed out of existence, excepting only U.S. Treasury bonds that all banks were required to purchase if they were to have a share in the war boom. The support for these special bonds was thus the debt itself—Hamilton's old standby. Specie disappeared. Moreover, the bank laws controlled the money supply, credit, and the balance of power. New banks and credit for farms, small businesses, or small town operations were discouraged. And the Federalist model, after "four score and seven years," was finally achieved.

As chief executive, Lincoln naturally supported heavy taxes. Plus a scheme of tax graduation. The war was a legitimate explanation for these measures. Lincoln's participation in huge subsidies or bounties for railroads and in other legislation granting economic favors is not so readily linked to "saving the Union." All of his life Lincoln was a friend of the big corporations. He had no moral problem in signing a bill which gifted the Union Pacific Railway with a huge strip of land running across the West and an almost unsecured loan of $16,000 to $48,000 per mile of track. The final result of this bill was the Credit Mobilier scandal. With other laws favoring land speculation it helped to negate the seemingly noble promise of the Homestead Act of 1862—under which less than 19 percent of the open lands settled between 1860 and 1900 went to legitimate homesteaders. The Northern policy of importing immigrants with the promise of this land, only to force them into the ranks of General Grant's meatgrinder or into near slavery in the cities of the East, requires little comment. Nor need we belabor the rotten army contracts given to politically faithful crooks. Nor the massive thefts by law performed during the war in the South. More significant is Lincoln's openly disgraceful policy of allowing special cronies and favorites of his friends to trade in Southern cotton—even with "the enemy" across the line—and his calculated use of the patronage and the pork barrel. Between 1860 and 1880, the Republicans spent almost $10,000,000 breathing life into state and local Republican organizations. Lincoln pointed them down that road. There can be no doubt of his responsibility for the depressing spectacle of greed and peculation concerning which so many loyal Northern men of the day spoke with sorrow, disappointment, and outrage. Had they known in detail of Lincoln's career in the Illinois legislature, they would have been less surprised by the disparity between the lofty platform language of their leader and his domestic performance.

A large part of the complaint against Lincoln as a political precedent for later declensions from the example of the Fathers has to do with his expansion of the powers of the presidency and his alteration of the basis for the Federal Union. With reference to his role in changing the office of chief magistrate from what it had been under his predecessors, it is important to remember that he defined himself through the war powers that belonged to his post. In this way Lincoln could profess allegiance to the Whig ideal of the modest, self-effacing leader, the antitype of Andrew Jackson, and, in his capacity as commander in chief, do whatever he wished. That is, if he could do it in the name of preserving the Union. As Clinton Rossiter has stated, Lincoln believed there were "no limits" to his powers if he exercised them in that "holy cause." Gottfried Dietze compares Lincoln in this role to the committee of public safety as it operated in the French Revolution. Except for the absence of mass executions, the results were similar. War is, of course, the occasion for concentration of power and the limitation of liberties within any nation. But an internal war, a war between states in a union of states, is not like a war to repel invasion or to acquire territory. For it is an extension into violence of a domestic political difference. And it is thus subject to extraordinary abuses of authority—confusions or conflations of purpose which convert the effort to win the war into an effort to effect even larger, essentially political changes in the structure of government. War, in these terms, is not only an engine for preserving the Union; it is also an instrument for transforming its nature. But without overdeveloping this structure of theory, let us shore it up with specific instances of presidential misconduct by Lincoln: abuses that mark him as our first imperial president. Lincoln began his tenure as a dictator when between April 12 and July 4, 1861, without interference from Congress, he summoned militia, spent millions, suspended law, authorized recruiting, decreed a blockade, defied the Supreme Court, and pledged the nation's credit. In the following months and years he created units of government not known to the Constitution and officers to rule over them in "conquered" sections of the South, seized property throughout both sections, arrested upwards of twenty thousand of his political enemies and confined them without trial in a Northern "Gulag," closed over three hundred newspapers critical of his policy, imported an army of foreign mercenaries (of perhaps five hundred thousand men), interrupted the assembly of duly elected legislatures and employed the Federal hosts to secure his own reelection—in a contest where about eighty-eight thousand votes, if shifted, might have produced an armistice and a negotiated peace under a President McClellan. To the same end he created a state in West Virginia, arguing of this blatant violation of the explicit provisions of the Constitution that it was "expedient." But the worst of this bold and ruthless dealing (and I have given but a very selective list of Lincoln's "high crimes") has to do with his role as military leader per se: as the commander and selector of Northern generals, chief commissary of the federal forces, and head of government in dealing with the leaders of an opposing power. In this role the image of Lincoln grows to be very dark—indeed, almost sinister.

The worst that we may say of Lincoln is that he led the North in war so as to put the domestic political priorities of his political machine ahead of the lives and the well being of his soldiers in the field. The appointment of the venal Simon Cameron of Pennsylvania as his secretary of war, and of lesser hacks and rascals to direct the victualing of Federal armies, was part of this malfeasance. By breaking up their bodies, the locust hoard of contractors even found a profit in the Union dead. And better money still in the living. They made of Lincoln (who winked at their activities) an accessory to lost horses, rotten meat, and worthless guns. But all such mendacity was nothing in comparison to the price in blood paid for Lincoln's attempts to give the nation a genuine Republican hero. He had a problem with this project throughout the entire course of the war. That is, until Grant and Sherman "converted" to radicalism. Prior to their emergence all of Lincoln's "loyal" generals disapproved of either his politics or of his character. These, as with McClellan, he could use and discharge at will. Or demote to minor tasks. One thinks immediately of George G. Meade—who defeated Lee at Gettysburg, and yet made the mistake of defining himself as the defender of a separate Northern nation from whose soil he would drive a foreign Southern "invader." Or of Fitz John Porter, William B. Franklin, and Don Carlos Buell—all scapegoats thrown by Lincoln to the radical wolves. In place of these heterodox professionals, Lincoln assigned such champions of the "new freedom" as Nathaniel P. ("Commissary") Banks, Benjamin F. ("Beast") Butler, John C. Frémont, and John A. McClernand. Speaking in summary despair of these appointments (and adding to my list, Franz Sigel and Lew Wallace), General Henry Halleck, Lincoln's chief of staff, declared that they were "little better than murder." Yet in the East, with the Army of the Potomac, Lincoln made promotion even more difficult to defend, placing not special projects, divisions, and brigades but entire commands under the authority of such "right thinking" incompetents as John Pope (son of an old crony in Illinois) and "Fighting Joe" Hooker. Or with that "tame" Democrat and late favorite of the radicals, Ambrose E. Burnside. Thousands of Northern boys lost their lives in order that the Republican Party might experience rejuvenation, to serve its partisan goals. And those were "party supremacy within a Northern dominated Union." A Democratic "man-on-horseback" could not serve those ends, however faithful to "the Constitution as it is, and the Union as it was" (the motto of the Democrats) they might be. For neither of these commitments promised a Republican hegemony. To provide for his faction both security and continuity in office, Lincoln sounded out his commanders in correspondence (much of which still survives), suborned their military integrity, and employed their focus in purely political operation. Writes Professor Johnson:

> Although extreme measures were most common in the border states, they were often used elsewhere too. By extreme measures is meant the arrest of anti-Republican candidates and voters, driving anti-Republican voters from the polls or forcing them to vote the Republican ticket, preventing opposition parties from holding meetings, removing names from ballots, and so forth. These methods were employed in national, state and local elections. Not only did the army interfere by force, it was used to supply votes. Soldiers whose states did not allow absentee voting were sent home by order of the president to swell the Republican totals. When voting in the field was used, Democratic commissioners carrying ballots to soldiers from their state were . . . unceremoniously thrown into prison, while Republican agents were offered every assistance. Votes of Democratic soldiers were sometimes discarded as defective, replaced by Republican ballots, or simply not counted.

All Lincoln asked of the ordinary Billy Yank was that he be prepared to give himself up to no real purpose—at least until Father Abraham found a general with the proper moral and political credentials to lead him on to Richmond. How this part of Lincoln's career can be reconciled to the myth of the "suffering savior" I cannot imagine.

We might dwell for some time on what injury Lincoln did to the dignity of his office through the methods he employed in prosecuting the war. It was no small thing to disavow the ancient Christian code of "limited war," as did his minions, acting in his name. However, it is enough in this connection to remember his policy of denying medicines to the South, even for the sake of Northern prisoners held behind the lines. We can imagine what a modern "war crimes" tribunal would do with that decision. There may have been practicality in such inhumane decisions. Practicality indeed! As Charles Francis Adams, Lincoln's ambassador to the Court of St. James and the scion of the most notable family in the North, wrote in his diary of his leader, "the . . . President and his chief advisers are not without the spirit of the serpent mixed in with their wisdom." And he knew whereof he spoke.

For practical politics, the necessities of the campaign of 1864 had led Lincoln and Seward to a decision far more serious than unethical practices against prisoners and civilians in the South. I speak of the rejection by the Lincoln administration of peace feelers authorized by the Confederate government in Richmond: feelers that met Lincoln's announced terms for an end to the Federal invasion of the South. The emissary in this negotiation was sponsored by Charles Francis Adams. He was a Tennessean living in France, one Thomas Yeatman. After arriving in the United States, he was swiftly deported by direct order of the government before he could properly explore the possibility of an armistice on the conditions of reunion and an end to slavery. Lincoln sought these goals, but only on his terms. And in his own time. He wanted total victory. And he needed a still resisting, impenitent Confederacy to justify his reelection. We can only speculate as to why President Davis allowed the Yeatman mission. We know that he expected little of such peace feelers. (There were many in the last stages of the conflict.) He knew his enemy too well to expect anything but subjection, however benign the rhetoric used to disguise its rigor. Adams's peace plan was perhaps impossible, even if his superiors in Washington had behaved in good faith. The point is that none of the peace moves of 1864 was given any chance of success. Over one hundred thousand Americans may have died because of the Railsplitter's rejection of an inexpedient peace. Yet we have still not touched upon the most serious of Lincoln's violations of the presidential responsibility. I speak, finally, of his role in bringing on the War Between the States.

There is, we should recall, a great body of scholarly argument concerning Lincoln's intentions in 1860 and early 1861. A respectable portion of this work comes to the conclusion that the first Republican President expected a "tug," a "crisis," to follow his election. And then, once secession had occurred, also expected to put it down swiftly with a combination of persuasion, force, and Southern loyalty to the Union. The last of these, it is agreed, he completely overestimated. In a similar fashion he exaggerated the force of Southern "realism," the region's capacity to act in its own pecuniary interest. The authority on Lincoln's political economy has remarked that the Illinois lawyer/politician and old line Whig always made the mistake of explaining in simple economic terms the South's hostile reaction to antislavery proposals. To that blunder he added the related mistake of attempting to end the "rebellion" with the same sort of simplistic appeals to the prospect of riches. Or with fear of a servile insurrection brought on by his greatest "war measure," the emancipation of slaves behind Southern lines, beyond his control. A fullscale Southern revolution, a revolution of all classes of men against the way he and some of his supporters thought, was beyond his imagination. There was no "policy" in such extravagant behavior, no human nature as he perceived it. Therefore, on the basis of my understanding of his overall career, I am compelled to agree with Charles W. Ramsdell concerning Lincoln and his war. Though he was no sadist and no warmonger, and though he got for his pains much more of a conflict than he had in mind, Lincoln hoped for an "insurrection" of some sort—an "uprising" he could use.

The "rational" transformation of our form of government which he had first predicted in the Springfield Lyceum Speech required some kind of passionate disorder to justify the enforcement of a new Federalism. And needed also for the voting representatives of the South to be out of their seats in the Congress. It is out of keeping with his total performance as a public man and in contradiction of his campaigning after 1854 not to believe that Lincoln hoped for a Southern attack on Fort Sumter. As he told his old friend Senator Orville H. Browning of Illinois: "The plan succeeded. They attacked Sumter—it fell, and thus did more service than it otherwise could." And to others he wrote or spoke to the same effect. If the Confederacy's offer of money for Federal property were made known in the North and business relations of the sections remained unaffected, if the Mississippi remained open to Northern shipping, there would be no support for "restoring" the Union on a basis of force. Americans were in the habit of thinking of the unity of the nation as a reflex of their agreement in the Constitution, of law as limit on government and on the authority of temporary majorities, and of revisions in law as the product of the ordinary course of push and pull within a pluralistic society, not as a response to the extralegal authority of some admirable abstraction like equality. In other words, they thought of the country as being defined by the way in which we conducted our political business, not by where we were trying to go in a body. Though once a disciple of Henry Clay, Lincoln changed the basis of our common bond away from the doctrine of his mentor, away from the patterns of compromise and dialectic of interests and values under a limited, Federal sovereignty with which we as a people began our adventure with the Great Compromise of 1787–1788. The nature of the Union left to us by Lincoln is thus always at stake in every major election, in every refinement in our civil theology; the Constitution is still to be defined by the latest wave of big ideas, the most recent mass emotion. Writes Professor Dietze:

> Concentrations of power in the national and executive branches of government, brought about by Lincoln in the name of the people, were processes that conceivably complemented each other to the detriment of free government. Lincoln's administration thus opened the way for the development of an omnipotent national executive who as a spokesman for the people might consider himself entitled to do whatever he felt was good for the Nation, irrespective of the interests and rights of states, Congress, the judiciary, and the individual.

If a president could behave in this way, so might Congress or the Supreme Court, interpreting something like Rousseau's General Will, as understood by those prophets who know what we need better than we, lacking their afflatus, can expect to understand it. It is a formula which makes of the private morality of men a law. And of Union its instrument. Which is a long way from the government of laws with which we began.

But in my opinion the capstone of this case against Lincoln as an American model, this bill of particulars contra the Lincoln myth, is not the patricide (as one recent historian has called it) of his refounding, his conversion of the national government into the juggernaut with which we are all more familiar than we would like. Rather, his overall worst is what he has done to the language of American political discourse that makes it so difficult for us to reverse the ill effects of trends he set in motion with his executive fiat. When I say that Lincoln was our first Puritan president, I am chiefly referring to a distinction of style, to his habit of wrapping up his policy in the idiom of Holy Scripture, concealing within the Trojan horse of his gasconade and moral superiority an agenda that would never have been approved if presented in any other form. It is this rhetoric in particular, a rhetoric confirmed in its authority by his martyrdom, that is enshrined in the iconography of the Lincoln myth preserved against examination by monuments such as the Lincoln Memorial, where his oversized likeness is elevated above us like that of a deified Roman emperor. Or in the form of a god-king, seated on his throne. The place is obviously a temple, fit for a divinity who suffered death and was transformed on Good Friday. It is both unpatriotic and irreligious to look behind the words of so august a presence. And to imitate Lincoln's epideictic, quasi-liberal rhetoric employing his favorite normative terms is to draw upon the authority generated by Lincoln idolatry and the imagery that surrounds it. In this universe of discourse, this closed linguistic system, all questions are questions of ends, and means are beside the point. And every "good cause" is a reason for increasing the scope of government. All that counts is the telos, the general objective, and bullying is not merely allowed, but required. It would be simple enough to be ruled directly by messages from God. But an imitation of that arrangement most properly leaves us uneasy.

For over one hundred years we have been on the course charted out for us by the captain of the flying ship of Lincoln's recurrent wartime dreams. Though as we recall, even that captain was not sure of his destination, only of the velocity of the voyage, and of the necessity for holding on to the boat. As in Lincoln's dream. we sail in darkness. Under such circumstances the worry is that we are more likely to arrive at the final plain of desolation than to a happy port in the New Zion of the Puritan Vision. Once we have become "all one thing or all another," we may understand better what it means to "loose the fearful lightning of the terrible swift sword."

༄

LINCOLN'S LYCEUM SPEECH AND THE ORIGINS OF A MODERN MYTH

Mark E. Neely, Jr.

ABRAHAM LINCOLN'S ADDRESS before the Young Men's Lyceum of Springfield, delivered January 27, 1838, is fast becoming one of the most famous of his speeches. It has long enjoyed some fame, though historian Albert Beveridge as late as 1928 had

*This article originally appeared in *Lincoln Lore*, No. 1776, February 1987. Reprinted with permission from the Lincoln Museum, Fort Wayne, IN.

to correct the date given the speech by Nicolay and Hay in Lincoln's collected works. Beveridge then called attention to Lincoln's address as "the most notable of his life thus far and, in fact, for many years thereafter."

The address was entitled "The Perpetuation of Our Political Institutions," a worrisome prospect in Lincoln's view because of recent outbreaks of lawless mob violence in unrelated incidents across the United States. In an oft-quoted admonition, the young Illinois legislator said: "Let reverence for the laws, be breathed by every American mother, to the lisping babe, that prattles on her lap—let it be taught in schools, in seminaries, and in colleges;—let it be written in Primmers, spelling books, and in Almanacs;—let it be preached from the pulpit, proclaimed in legislative halls, and enforced in courts of justice. And, in short, let it become the political religion of the nation; and let the old and the young, the rich and the poor, the grave and the gay, of all sexes and tongues, and colors and conditions, sacrifice unceasingly upon its altars."

After this classic law—and warning, Lincoln then delved into the problem of ambition. With the heroic work of the generation of the revolutionary fathers completed, there seemed to be little left for the man of genius to do. Merely perpetuating their works was an unromantically tepid goal, and there was danger, therefore, that some ambitious person of genius might find heroic satisfaction only in destroying the work of the fathers. Lincoln's final warning then invoked "reason, cold, calculating, unimpassioned reason" as a bulwark against the passion that was useful only in revolutionary times. He hoped to see this reason embodied in "*general intelligence, [sound] morality* and, in particular, *a reverence for the constitution and the laws.*"

Although he called dramatic attention to this speech in 1928, Beveridge failed to say specifically why the speech was so "notable." Other historians would attempt to say why later.

James G. Randall, in the first two volumes of his famous Lincoln biography, issued in 1945, found his protagonist "already definitely Lincolnian in epigrammatic force" when he spoke before the Lyceum. He praised Lincoln's address by saying it was "as good a speech against Fascism, or elements characteristic of Fascism, as was ever delivered."

This was high praise in 1945, of course, but not destined to prove very useful for later generations of historians. When Benjamin F. Thomas referred briefly to the speech in his fine 1952 biography of Lincoln, he interpreted it, not as a ringing denunciation of Fascism, but as proof of Lincoln's interest in the slavery question and of his caution in addressing it. Lincoln denounced mob rule before his Lyceum audience but did not specifically dwell on the anti-abolition mob that had murdered Elijah Lovejoy in Alton about eleven weeks before Lincoln spoke.

In 1960 Reinhard Luthin, in his solid biography entitled *The Real Abraham Lincoln*, characterized the Lyceum address as Lincoln's "first speech of distinction." What Luthin liked about the speech was its unusual lack of partisan purpose or party rhetoric (until the publication of Gahor S. Boritt's *Lincoln and the Economics of the*

American Dream in 1978 most historians thought of Lincoln as a narrow partisan in his Whig years).

By 1960, then, modern scholars had agreed at least on the fact that the speech was somehow significant. They disagreed as to what the precise significance was: Beveridge was silent on that point, Randall thought of it as a principled denunciation of mob rule, Thomas admired its politic savvy, and Luthin pointed to its transcendance of the categories of ordinary partisanship. None seems to have found in it profound clues to Lincoln's hidden character. These biographies all stopped to deal with this early speech in a respectful way, but the biographies more or less resumed where they had left off before dealing with the speech. This would not always be so.

Back in 1954 literary critic Edmund Wilson had published an essay destined to have great influence on Lincoln scholarship: it was called "Abraham Lincoln: The Union as Religious Mysticism." In the article Wilson argued that "Lincoln's view of the [civil] war as a crisis in American history and his conception of himself as an American leader" both "emerge[d] very early." This was a remarkable statement and only the first of many to follow in the brief essay. Wilson seemed to challenge the one point on which the biographers agreed, namely, that the Lyceum speech was exceptional, that it somehow stood out among what were then thought to be Lincoln's unexceptional early utterances. Instead of a rather ordinary politician, about thirty years old, Wilson found in the Lincoln who stood before the Young Men's Lyceum audience what other biographers could not at this stage, a self-conscious leader.

The other thing Wilson found, of course, must have been a mirage. How could Lincoln's "view of the war as a crisis in American history" have emerged before 1861? This is a meaningless statement, but Wilson prided himself on being a journalist as well as a literary critic, a serious writer who nevertheless reached a broad audience, and a charitable reader must allow him the sort of anachronistic slip of the pen which occasionally creeps into articles written against magazine deadlines.

Wilson sought to prove Lincoln's self-conscious charisma by lengthy quotations from the Lyceum address stitched together with a little pop psychology. In the speech Lincoln said that the heroes of America's revolutionary beginnings satisfied their ambitions in service to the exciting cause of overthrowing British rule. The generations that followed would have their ambitions too, but with "this field of glory harvested," they would not find satisfaction in the mere maintenance of an edifice erected by older heroes.

> Towering genius [Lincoln continued] disdains a beaten path. . . . It *scorns* to tread in the footsteps of any predecessor, however illustrious. It thirsts and burns for distinction; and, if possible, it will have it, whether at the expense of emancipating slaves, or enslaving freemen. Is it unreasonable then to expect, that some man possessed of the loftiest genius, coupled with ambition sufficient to push it to its utmost stretch, will at

some time, spring up among us? And when such a one does, it will require the people to be united with each other, attached to the government and laws, and generally intelligent, to successfully frustrate his designs.

Immediately after quoting these lines, Wilson concluded: "Now, the effect of this is somewhat ambiguous: it is evident that Lincoln has projected himself into the role against which he is warning them."

Wilson, in fact, explained no ambiguity but instead clinched his assertion that Lincoln thought of himself as the very threat against which he warned by quoting from Lincoln's later speech against the Sub-Treasury (December 26, 1839), which concludes thus:

The probability that we may fall in the struggle *ought not* to deter us from the support of a cause we believe to be just; it *shall not* deter me. If ever I feel the soul within me elevate and expand to those dimensions not wholly unworthy of its Almighty Architect, it is when I contemplate the cause of my country, deserted by all the world beside, and I standing up boldly and alone and hurling defiance at her victorious oppressors.

After this, Wilson concluded: "The young Lincoln, then, was extremely ambitious; he saw himself in a heroic role." In truth, that is not exactly what Lincoln said in the two passages from different speeches. The heroism he allowed himself to aspire to in the second speech was patriotism in standing by his country even when her oppressors were victorious. This is not at all the amoral heroic role warned against in the first speech. Lincoln "projected" himself in the second passage into a role in which, "alone and hurling defiance," he defied the sort of oppressor he warned against in the first. There is no ambiguity in this (and no "projection" in the perverse psychological sense). Lincoln warned against ambitious oppressors in the first and in the second he allowed himself to dream melodramatically of defying oppression to the last.

There are far more serious problems with the rest of Wilson's analysis of Lincoln, and it will delay coming to grips with them if this article quarrels at every step of the way as the previous paragraph did. Still, it seemed worthwhile at least to provide an example of the slippery nature of Wilson's famous essay. At no point can it be held in a tight grasp of logical comprehension, for it is not logical and in some places it is hardly even comprehensible.

After several interesting musings on other aspects of Lincoln's career, Wilson, at the end of the essay, returns to the theme of premonition by discussing Lincoln's famous White House dreams, that is, not his aspirations but the things which passed through Lincoln's head while asleep.

The night before Lincoln was murdered, he dreamed again of the ship approaching its dark destination. He had foreseen and accepted his doom; he knew it was part of the drama. He had in some sense imagined this drama himself—had even prefigured Booth and the aspect he would wear for Booth when the latter would leap down from the Presidential box crying, "*Sic semper tyrannis!*" Had he not once told Herndon that Brutus was created to murder Caesar and Caesar to be murdered by Brutus? And in that speech made so long before to the Young Men's Lyceum in Springfield, he had issued his equivocal warning against the ambitious leader, describing this figure with a fire that seemed to derive as much from admiration as from apprehension—that leader who would certainly arise among them and "seek the gratification of [his] ruling passion," that "towering genius" who would "burn for distinction, and, if possible . . . have it, whether at the expense of emancipating slaves or enslaving freemen."

Once again, the charitable reader will allow some dramatic license to Wilson, though it is hard to imagine the old lawyer of Illinois' Eighth Judicial Circuit having any serious premonitions of his own death without writing a last will and testament (which, of course, Lincoln did not do). Finally, Wilson brings the curtain down with this stunning last line: "He must have suffered far more than he ever expressed from the agonies and griefs of the war, and it was morally and dramatically inevitable that this prophet who had crushed opposition and sent thousands of men to their deaths should finally attest his good faith by laying down his own life with theirs."

Bravo! the reader wants to shout, but as the lights come up and he walks away from this drama, it occurs to the reader once again that something slippery has happened on Wilson's stage. In the end, the "prophet" is the genius "who had crushed opposition and sent thousands of men to their deaths." But in the Lyceum address Lincoln had prophesied that a towering genius might arise who could satisfy ambition only by "emancipating slaves, or enslaving freemen." In fact, these are the only words that caused this passage from Lincoln's speech to catch so much later attention. Had he not, as a twenty-nine-year-old frontier legislator, mentioned emancipation in this speech, twenty-five years before accomplishing it himself as President of the United States, not much notice would have been taken of this part of the Lyceum speech. So, why did Edmund Wilson not bring down the curtain on his essay by saying, "it was morally and dramatically inevitable that this prophet who had emancipated the slaves should finally attest his good faith by laying down his own life with theirs"? What Wilson did was unfair to Lincoln even by the terms of Wilson's own essay, but he did it for a reason—one which has not been called sufficiently to our attention heretofore. One might almost say that Wilson had a "hidden agenda" here. But, before examining Wilson's reasons for so depicting Lincoln, it is necessary to describe and explain the extraordinary fame enjoyed by Wilson's essay.

A landmark of its fame—and a good hunch would say a principal cause of its fame as well—was the prominence given the Lyceum speech and Wilson's interpretation of it in Harry V. Jaffa's *Crisis of the House Divided: An Interpretation of the Issues in the Lincoln-Douglas Debates*, a book first published in 1959. There were more references in Jaffa's index to the Lyceum speech than to any other Lincoln utterance outside the speeches given in the debates themselves (there are, for example, over twice as many index entries for the early speech as for the Gettysburg Address). In fact, Jaffa devoted a full fifty pages of his 409 pages of text—well over ten percent of the book—to the Lyceum speech and the issues suggested by it. Although he disagreed with Wilson in some particulars, he did not in regard to the speech's proof of Lincoln's "conscious dedication to preparation for the crisis with which he one day grappled on so vast a scale." This, Jaffa goes on to say,

> may disturb the image of the folklore Lincoln, the hero who resembles Everyman, fashioned from the clay of the common people, sharing their joys and sorrows, yet able to turn from the concerns of everyday life to discharge, with deeper wisdom, duties heretofore regarded as the province of kings and potentates. This is the Lincoln who is supposed to have written the Gettysburg Address on the back of an envelope as he rode from Washington. Yet a careful reading of the earlier deliverance will show that the ideas crystallized in 1863, in prose not unworthy of the greatest master of our language, had been pondered and matured full twenty-five years before.

The folklore Lincoln described here by Jaffa is precisely the enemy of Wilson's essay: it is Carl Sandburg's *Lincoln*. "There are," Wilson wrote, "moments when one is tempted to feel that the cruellest thing that has happened to Lincoln since he was shot by Booth has been to fall into the hands of Carl Sandburg." Wilson adds in telltale language: "It [Sandburg's biography of Lincoln] would . . . be more easily acceptable as a repository of Lincoln folklore if the compiler had not gone so far in contributing to this folklore himself. . . . Sandburg is incapable of doing justice to the tautness and hard distinction that we find when, disregarding legends, we attack Lincoln's writings in bulk. These writings do not give the impression of a folksy and jocular countryman swapping yarns at the village store or making his way to the White House by uncertain and awkward steps or presiding like a father, with a tear in his eye, over the tragedy of the Civil War."

Whatever his exact conclusions about the nature of Lincoln's political thought, Jaffa has granted Wilson a lot of ground. And he has given the greatest acknowledgment of the force of Wilson's argument by the sheer amount of space devoted in his book to his own analysis of the Lyceum address.

Eventually, others would make the Lyceum speech even more important, for one key ingredient to its future fame was missing in Professor Jaffa: a wide-eyed belief in psychoanalysis and in its usefulness when applied to dead men.

George B. Forgie's well-received *Patricide in the House Divided: A Psychological Interpretation of Lincoln and His Age*, published in 1979, included an entire chapter on "Lincoln at the Lyceum: The Problem of Ambition in the Post-Heroic Age." In it the author attempted to explain the phenomenon of "projection" that Edmund Wilson had identified. Forgie contended that Lincoln's Lyceum address "probably proceeded from an intense self-consciousness about the progress of his own career." Characterizing Lincoln in the 1830s and 1840s as a bright young man whose early success was temporarily stymied, Forgie found illumination of Lincoln's psychological plight in the "Nobel Prize complex." This psychological theory attributes fairly deep depression to those who are conscious of their superior abilities, aim high, but fail in their early middle age to attain the highest rewards. Thus the Lyceum speech "reflected . . . his personal problem with ambition." Lincoln needed the reassurance of a fantasy that he would some day slay the ambitious genius tyrant who would otherwise destroy the work of the Founding Fathers. Then, one day, Lincoln found that enemy—or created him—in Stephen A. Douglas. Lincoln's "charges against Douglas accorded precisely with the dangers predicted in the Lyceum speech." He fit Lincoln's long-nurtured psychological needs so precisely that Lincoln made of Douglas a melodramatic villain.

Dwight G. Anderson followed Wilson's lead in a more literal-minded fashion. In *Abraham Lincoln: The Quest for Immortality*, published in 1982, Anderson also devoted his primary attention to solving the puzzle of the Lyceum speech as interpreted by Wilson. Reduced to its essentials, Anderson's argument went this way. Inspired by reading about George Washington in his early youth, Lincoln, as a member of Congress in the late 1840s, refused to tell a lie about the Mexican War and opposed it out of conscience. His "reward" proved to be political oblivion. Enfuriated by this, Lincoln decided to reject Washington by wrecking the Union the father had created. Lincoln became, in Anderson's words, "demonic," a "Robespierre," a man who "acted from motives of revenge," and "a tyrant who would preside over the destruction of the Constitution in order to gratify his own ambition."

Anderson seems most literally in Wilson's tradition, though all the recent psychohistorians are heavily indebted to Wilson, because Anderson's Lincoln is like the Lincoln pictured at the end of Wilson's essay, crushing opposition and sending men to their deaths. In other words, Anderson depicts a genuine tyrant.

In truth, Wilson did not quite do that in his essay, not fully. He was to do it elsewhere, after 1954 and the publication "Abraham Lincoln: The Union as Religious Mysticism." Wilson's "agenda" was as yet hidden from view at that early date, but, as he was to admit later, Wilson had been evading paying his income taxes for the better part of a decade by the time the Lincoln article appeared in a 1954 book of Wilson's essays. When in 1955, the famous critic told the law that he had filed no income tax returns since 1946, he became aware of the severe penalties for such evasion. The state seemed to reach out to crush this naively impractical scribbler (as Wilson at times depicts himself in *The Cold War and the Income Tax: A Protest*, his 1963 explanation of his fraud). He found "the despotic IRS system" intolerable in a land of once free men, and the humiliation and limitation of freedom he suffered—including house arrest and being fingerprinted—caused him to regard the government in new ways.

By the time he got around to writing the introduction to the book which would make his Lincoln essay famous—*Patriotic Gore: Studies in the Literature of the American Civil War*, published by Oxford University Press in 1962—Wilson was able to see precisely what kind of tyrant Lincoln became. The famous introduction to *Patriotic Gore* compared Lincoln to Bismarck and Lenin.

Each established a strong central government over hitherto loosely coordinated peoples. Lincoln kept the Union together by subordinating the South to the North; Bismarck imposed on the German states the cohesive hegemony of Prussia; Lenin . . . began the work of binding Russia, with its innumerable ethnic groups scattered through immense spaces, in a tight bureaucratic net.

Each of these men, through the pressure of the power which he found himself exercising, became an uncompromising dictator, and each was succeeded by agencies which continued to exercise this power and to manipulate the peoples he had been unifying in a stupid, despotic and unscrupulous fashion, so that all the bad potentialities of the policies he had initiated were realized, after his removal, in the most undesirable way. . . . We Americans have not yet had to suffer from the worst of the calamities that have followed on the dictatorships in Germany and Russia, but we have been going for a long time now quite steadily in the same direction.

It may seem like a heavy-handed piece of reductionism to link Wilson's depiction of Lincoln as a tyrant with the author's discomfort at learning the state's efficiency in punishing income tax evasion, but Wilson made the link himself. In an undated letter sent to Max Eastman, probably in 1962, Wilson spoke of *Patriotic Gore*:

I know my Introduction is inadequate, but I am supplementing it with a kind of pamphlet, which I'll be sending you in due course. The chief reason that we're being soaked for taxes is that we're supposed to need billions for national defense against the Russian bugaboo, in which (the bugaboo) I do not believe. . . . I can't conceive that there is or has ever been any danger of the Russians invading and dominating the U.S. . . .

It seems quite illuminating to look at Wilson's famous introduction to *Patriotic Gore*, with its comparison of Lincoln to Bismarck and Lenin, as an essay which could be logically "supplemented" with a tract on income tax evasion. Wilson did characterize in his little book the rate of taxation as extortionate because the money was to be spent for a ridiculous purpose, the Cold War. But he was candid in the book and nowhere stated that his income tax evasion *began* as a political protest. Instead, he explained his straitened financial circumstances in the mid-1940s, the domestic turmoil of the period in his life when he decided not to file a return, and his ignorance of the rigors of the law regarding failure to pay taxes.

How does all this affect Lincoln? The peculiar political bias of Wilson's introduction to the book containing the Lincoln piece warns the reasonable reader that the author may have unreasonable views on the legitimacy of the power of the state—so unreasonable that any defense of its power in history or extension of its powers in the course of such a defense might seem suspect and dangerous. Abraham Lincoln, after all, imposed the first national income tax in the country's history while attempting to save the national state from disintegration.

The historical writers most influenced by Wilson admired his work primarily for its psychological approach or insight. That is what they sought to imitate. They were not necessarily seeking an argument proving that Abraham Lincoln was a dictator during the Civil War, but they got one, or rather the assumption that Lincoln was. In other words, in the course of adopting Wilson's *approach* to Lincoln through psychoanalysis they also unconsciously adopted part of the substance of Wilson's argument, that is, the view that Lincoln was a dictator.

Most reasonable scholars would think twice before swallowing the assertion that Lincoln was a tyrant if they knew that the champion of such a view was an oddball political thinker who regarded the income tax as tyrannical and refused to pay it! But *The Cold War and the Income Tax* appeared after *Patriotic Gore* was published, and Wilson wrote mostly on non-historical subjects. Most American historians probably read only one of his books. They probably did not realize what a bizarre political odyssey Edmund Wilson had taken from the socialist beliefs of his early life to the income tax evasion of his later years, And this significant change in attitude toward the confiscatory and income distributing powers of the government occurred while Wilson was writing *Patriotic Gore.*

In the end, Wilson embraced an old and familiar attitude toward Abraham Lincoln, which he revealed in a letter written to one Lewis M. Dabney, who had reviewed *Patriotic Gore.* Dabney had attributed New England roots to Wilson, but the author corrected him, saying that his important ancestors came from central New York.

> This is important [Wilson explained] because the New York point of view is quite distinct from the New England one. . . . I purposely left out of *Patriotic Gore* the disaffection of New York toward the Civil War—which I suppose is behind my own attitude—Horatio Seymour, Harold Frederic, the Copperheads, and all that; but I am now going to write about it.

Seymour, a Democrat, was New York's governor at the time of the New York City draft riots in 1863. Frederic, a novelist and journalist, was the author of a novel called *The Copperhead*, about a stubbornly partisan Democratic farmer in upstate New York during the Civil War. Wilson's was a Copperhead view of Abraham Lincoln.

Of course, Copperheads knew no more about Freudian psychology and the so-called Oedipus complex than did Abraham Lincoln. But historians who were interested in psychoanalysis took over from Wilson, unawares, an essentially Copperhead view of Lincoln. More than anything else, the modern study of "The Perpetuation of Our Political Institutions" has perpetuated a Copperhead myth.

Among the less fortunately titled books on Abraham Lincoln is John M. Zane's *Lincoln the Constitutional Lawyer.* As a lawyer, Lincoln was occasionally involved in constitutional cases, and as president, he certainly faced stupendous constitutional problems. Yet it was not a habit of Abraham Lincoln's mind to think first of the constitutional aspects of the problems he faced in his political career. His impulse was almost always toward the practical.

When Lincoln thought about the constitutional aspect of a question, the doctrines of his political party shaped his ideas in important ways. By the standards of his own day, his constitutional heritage was that of broad rather than narrow interpretation, and this was probably a function of his Whiggery. Lincoln was a thorough-going Whig in politics, a member of that party from its beginning to its end, a Whig twice as long as he was a Republican. In general, the Whig party took a broad view of what the Constitution allowed the federal government to do: create a national bank and fund canals, roads, and railroads, for example. As the youthful victim of rural isolation and lack of economic opportunity, Lincoln proved eager in his later career as a politician to provide the country with what had seemed lacking in his own hardscrabble past. That eagerness made him quite impatient with Democratic arguments that internal improvements funded by the federal government were unconstitutional.

As a United States Congressman in the late 1840s, Lincoln thought "the question of improvements" was "verging to a final crisis," in part because the national Democratic platform in 1848 declared "That the Constitution does not confer upon the general government the power to commence, and carry on a general system of internal improvements." Speaking in the House of Representatives on this subject, Lincoln expressed plainly his feeling that "no man, who is clear on the questions of expediency, needs feel his conscience much pricked upon this."

The emphasis on the practical was characteristic of Lincoln, as was his care in the speech to include all the constitutional arguments on his side as well. In context, his statement was not cavalier in tone, for Lincoln had already reiterated the impressive constitutional arguments for his side of the question. In effect, he was saying that the constitutional arguments, though this be admittedly a controversial question, were good enough for the Whig view that one could vote for it without violating one's conscience.

The policies advocated in this 1848 speech on internal improvements were standard for an economic Whig like Lincoln, but the speech was uncharacteristic of the young Illinois politician in one respect: its heavy emphasis on constitutional questions. Despite suggesting that practical demands for internal improvements should outweigh any minor constitutional doubt or controversy, Lincoln seemed nevertheless preoccupied with the constitutional side of the question in the speech, devoting eight of twenty-six paragraphs—almost a third of his time—to that issue. And all of this he prefaced with a modest disclaimer:

> Mr. Chairman, on the . . . constitutional question, I have not much to say. Being the man I am, and speaking when I do, I feel, that in any attempt at an original constitutional argument, I should not be, and ought not to be, listened to patiently. The ablest, and the best of men, have gone over the whole ground long ago.

Lincoln then quoted and summarized at some length arguments from Chancellor Kent's commentaries on the Constitution. Yet the Illinois congressmen proved not to be content with deferring to authority. He went on instead with four paragraphs on the question of amending the Constitution, President James K. Polk having suggested that such an amendment would be necessary to make internal improvements possible. Lincoln did not much like this idea, no doubt in part because of its impracticality, but he attacked it with an invocation of constitutional conservatism:

> I have already said that no one, who is satisfied of the expediency of making improvements, needs be much uneasy in his conscience about its constitutionality. I wish now to submit a few remarks on the general proposition of amending the constitution. As a general rule, I think, we would [do] much better [to] let it alone. No slight occasion should tempt us to touch it. Better not take the first step, which may lead to a habit of altering it. It can scarcely be made better than it is. New provisions, would introduce new difficulties, and thus create, and increase appetite for still further change. No sir, let it stand as it is. New hands have never touched it. The men who made it, have done their work, and have passed away. Who shall improve on what *they* did?

Often quoted by constitutional conservatives, this passage has almost ironic meaning in context: what Lincoln was really saying was that amendment was not needed if a broad interpretation of the existing document were accepted.

To dwell on constitutional issues as Lincoln did in this 1848 speech was unusual. Before that, he had rarely made pronouncements on constitutional questions. Back in 1832, when he spoke at length on internal improvements (mainly for the Sangamon River) in his first political platform, Lincoln had spoken only of practical questions of cost and navigability. Again in 1836, when declaring his candidacy for reelection to the Illinois state legislature, Lincoln went on record in favor of a plan to make internal improvements possible, and he focused only on the financial difficulty: "Whether elected or not, I go for distributing the proceeds of the sales of the public lands to the several states, to enable our state, in common with others, to dig canals and construct rail roads, without borrowing money and paying interest on it." Except for a brief comment in 1837 on the legality of the Illinois State Bank under the state constitution, Lincoln's first statement of some length on a constitutional question came in his speech on the sub-treasury, delivered on December 26, 1839. After a long argument on the practical questions, insisting that the national bank would increase the circulation of the money supply, operate more economically, and provide more security, Lincoln addressed the question of constitutionality. He was satisfied that a national bank had been declared constitutional by the United States Supreme Court and by a majority of the country's founders, but, rather than go over that well-trod path again, he wanted "to take a view of the question which I have not known to be taken by anyone before. It is, that whatever objection ever has or ever can be made to the constitutionality of a bank, will apply with equal force in its whole length, breadth and proportions to the Sub-Treasury." If there were no "express authority" in the Constitution to establish a bank, he quipped, there was none to establish a sub-treasury either.

Of course, Lincoln thought them both constitutional:

> The Constitution enumerates expressly several powers which Congress may exercise, superadded to which is a general authority "to make all laws necessary and proper," for carrying into effect all the powers vested by the Constitution of the Government of the United States. One of the express powers given Congress, is "To lay and collect taxes; duties, imports, and excises; to pay the debts, and provide for the common defence and general welfare of the United States." . . . To carry it into execution, it is indispensably necessary to collect, safely keep, transfer, and disburse a revenue.

In the end, Lincoln sounded almost impatient with his adversaries on this point:

> The rule is too absurd to need further comment. Upon the phrase "*necessary and proper*," in the Constitution, it seems to me more reasonable to say, that *some* fiscal agent is *indispensably necessary*; but, inasmuch as no *particular sort* of agent is thus *indispensable*, because some *other* sort might be adopted, we are left to choose that sort of agent, which may be most "*proper*" on grounds of expediency.

Lincoln had returned to more comfortable ground for this practical legislator from central Illinois; he seemed not much to care for the inflexible high ground of constitutional dictate.

Lincoln appeared to be marching steadily toward a general position of gruff or belittling impatience with arguments against the constitutionality of the beleaguered Whig economic program in the 1840s. A set of resolutions adopted at a Whig meeting in Springfield in 1843, for example, reiterated Lincoln's position on the constitutionality of a national bank and followed that with this brief discussion of the constitutional aspect of Henry Clay's bill for the distribution of revenues from the sale of the national lands: "Much incomprehensible jargon is often urged against the constitutionality of this measure. We forbear, in this place, attempting to answer it, simply because, in our opinion, those who urge it, are, through party zeal, resolved not to see or acknowledge the truth."

But Lincoln's movement away from constitutional modes of thought was halted abruptly by the presidential administration of James K. Polk. When he had spoken against the sub-treasury back in 1839, Lincoln had devoted but three of fifty-one paragraphs to the constitutional issue. When he made his last-ditch defense of internal improvements in 1848, he devoted 8 of 26 paragraphs to the constitutional question. The reason was not so much the greater importance of the constitutional question to the subject of internal improvements rather than the national bank as it was Lincoln's heightened awareness of the importance of constitutional issues altogether. And that awareness was probably a function of the Mexican War.

Like most Whigs, Lincoln hated the Mexican War, which he considered to be "unconstitutional and unnecessary." He was not an internationally-minded man, worried about Mexico and Mexicans. In a lecture on discoveries and inventions which he gave in 1859, Lincoln revealed this when he celebrated what he called the Yankee "habit of observation and reflection": "But for the difference in habit of observation, why did Yankees, almost instantly, discover gold in California, which had been trodden upon, and overlooked by Indians and Mexican greasers, for centuries?" Nor was Lincoln's an abolitionist critique of the Mexican War. He told one Williamson Durley, on October 3, 1845, that "individually I never was much interested in the Texas question. I never could see much good to come of annexation; inasmuch, as they were already free republican people on our own model; on the other hand, I never could very clearly see how the annexation would augment the evil of slavery. It always seemed to me that slaves would be taken there in about equal numbers, with or without annexation." Indeed, Lincoln stated flatly while campaigning for Zachary Taylor in the East in the summer of 1848 that he "did not believe with many of his fellow citizens that this war was originated for the purpose of extending slave territory."

Lincoln claimed, rather, that "it was a war of conquest brought into existence to catch votes," an interpretation which he had further refined by 1860, when, as a presidential candidate, he found himself liable to criticism for his opposition to the war:

> Mr. L. [he wrote in his third-person autobiography for newspaperman John Locke Scripps] thought the act of sending an armed force among the Mexicans, was *unnecessary*, inasmuch as Mexico was in no way molesting, or menacing the U.S. or the people thereof; and that it was *unconstitutional*, because the power of levying war is vested in Congress, and not in the President. He thought the principal motive for the act, was to divert public attention from the surrender of "Fifty-four, forty, or fight" to Great Britain, on the Oregon boundary question.

Thus, even twelve years later as the head of a political party committed to halting the expansion of slave territory, Lincoln did not embrace the antislavery interpretation of the origins of the Mexican War.

When Lincoln's law partner William H. Herndon, disputed his interpretation of the origins of the Mexican War in 1848, Lincoln had indulged himself in a rare exercise: a long letter, lecturing in tone, on a constitutional question. Herndon's letter (now lost) protesting his partner's speech in Congress against the Mexican War probably caused Lincoln to focus more exclusively on the constitutional question, for Lincoln's letter began, "Your letter of the 29th. Jany. was received last night. Being exclusively a constitutional argument, I wish to submit some reflections on it. . . ." Whatever the cause, once focused, Lincoln's scrutiny of the question proved close and intense. He concluded his letter to the junior partner this way:

> The provision of the Constitution giving the war-making power to Congress, was dictated, as I understand it, by the following reasons. Kings had always been involving and impoverishing their people in wars, pretending generally, if not always, that the good of the people was the object. This, our Convention understood to be the most

oppressive of all Kingly oppressions; and they resolved to so frame the Constitution that *no one man* should hold the power of bringing this oppression upon us. But your view destroys the whole matter, and places our President where kings have always stood.

When he thought about the Constitution in the 1850s, and he seems to have done so more than in the previous decades, Lincoln interpreted it as most antislavery men did. Unlike abolitionists, who saw the document as a covenant with death because it protected the institution of slavery in the Southern states, Lincoln saw the Constitution as a reluctant guarantor of the slave interest which existed at the government's foundation.

Antislavery sentiments and Whig tradition explain Abraham Lincoln's views on the Constitution, and not, it should be stressed, his choice of profession. There has been too much emphasis in recent years on the influence of Lincoln's profession as a lawyer upon his political ideas. In part, this has been brought on by biographers and historians interested in psychological interpretation who have, in turn, created a vogue of emphasis on one early speech in Lincoln's corpus, the Lyceum speech of January 27, 1838. This speech contains, not any constitutional thought of real substance, but rather some cheerleading for the constitution and the laws, widely quoted in later years:

> Let reverence for the laws, be breathed by every American mother, to the lisping babe, that prattles on her lap—let it be taught in schools, in seminaries, and in colleges;—let it be preached from the pulpit, proclaimed in legislative halls, and enforced in courts of justice. And, in short, let it become the *political religion* of the nation; and let the old and the young, the rich and the poor, the grave and the gay, of all sexes and tongues, and colors and conditions, sacrifice unceasingly upon its altars.

Later, Lincoln invoked "Reason, cold, calculating, unimpassioned reason" to "furnish all the materials for our future support and defence. Let those [materials] be moulded into *general intelligence*, [sound] *morality* and, in particular, *a reverence for the constitution and laws. . . .*"

Historian George M. Frederickson has relied particularly upon this speech for his judgment that "Abraham Lincoln's early speeches as an aspiring young lawyer and Whig politician were clearly party of . . . [a general] 'conservative' response [from lawyers] to the unruly and aggressive democracy spawned by the age of Jackson." In the Lyceum speech Lincoln was "giving eloquent expression to the developing ideology of his profession."

Frederickson goes on to posit a strong conservative law-and-order strain in Lincoln's political thought, an element that, though gradually modified, remained substantially unshaken until the *Dred Scott* decision in 1857 undermined "Lincoln's faith in the bench and bar as the ultimate arbiters of constitutional issues." The problem with this interpretation lies in its approach, that of "intellectual history," which

Frederickson forthrightly declares to be his method in the first sentence of his article on this subject. Lincoln was not an intellectual, certainly not a systematic political thinker; he was a politician and one slights the instrumental side of Lincoln's statements only at great peril. He was not always or often thinking about the Constitution and the laws. He thought about them only when a particularly pressing political problem arose. It seems less significant to note that Lincoln, at the time of the Lyceum speech in 1838, had recently been admitted to the bar and may have been justifiably proud of his new professional status than to notice what his invocation of the Constitution aimed to accomplish in context. Broadly, it was meant in the Lyceum speech to protect the rights of minorities: Mississippi gamblers, unfortunate black people, and abolitionists. In general, most interpreters of Lincoln's speech in modern times have assumed that the real shadow hanging over the words was that of the martyred Elijah Lovejoy, recently killed by an anti-abolition mob in Lincoln's state. Using this to put Lincoln at odds with the "aggressive democracy spawned by the age of Jackson" seems hardly fair to Lincoln, and it quite misrepresents the way Lincoln thought about the Constitution.

He mostly thought about it when he had to. James K. Polk forced it on Lincoln's attention dramatically in 1846, 1847, and 1848, and Herndon apparently caused Lincoln to spell out his constitutional arguments more explicitly than he had done for his constituents in his speech in Congress on the Mexican War. There was less a profound "search for order and community," to borrow Frederickson's words, than a search for usable arguments.

This is not to say that Lincoln's constitutional thinking was nakedly opportunistic or embarrassingly shallow, only that he certainly changed his mind from time to time, especially during the Civil War. This is not to say, either, that an instrumental responsiveness to political events alone characterized Lincoln's political thought in general. It tended more to characterize his constitutional thinking because thinking in constitutional ways did not come naturally to Lincoln. It seemed always somehow secondary with him, of less importance than other approaches to ordinary political questions.

As for Frederickson's general conclusion, it is difficult to find tough threads of legalistic, procedural, or constitutional conservatism woven in Lincoln's political thought in the 1850s, even before the *Dred Scott* decision. In fact, Lincoln quickly embraced a moralistic antislavery ideology which stressed the Declaration of Independence and the political libertarianism of Thomas Jefferson and which relegated the Constitution and the laws to a rather pale secondary role. Immediately after passage of the Kansas-Nebraska Act in 1854, Lincoln told a Springfield audience that "The theory of our government is Universal Freedom. 'All men are created free and equal,' says the Declaration of Independence. The word "Slavery' is not found in the Constitution." This was a succinct statement of Lincoln's antislavery reading of early American historical documents, and his political message on that subject varied little from 1854 to 1861.

Lincoln began to invoke Jefferson's name frequently, and now to more profound ends than mere embarrassment of those Democrats who claimed Jefferson as the founder of their party. On October 16, 1854, in a speech in Peoria, Lincoln spoke of "Mr. Jefferson, the author of the Declaration of Independence," as "the most distinguished politician of our history." He pointed to Jefferson's prohibition of slavery in the Northwest Ordinance of 1787 as the historic origin of modern Republican policy:

> Thus, with the author of the Declaration of Independence, the policy of prohibiting slavery in a new territory originated. Thus, away back of the constitution, in the pure, free breath of the revolution, the State of Virginia, and the National congress put that policy in practice.

Lincoln did not entirely ignore or abandon the Constitution to the Democrats. Antislavery Republicans, rather, embraced an antislavery interpretation of the document. Lincoln put it this way:

> This same generation of men, and mostly the same individuals of the generation, who declared this principle [self-government]—who declared independence—who fought the war of the revolution through—who afterwards made the Constitution under which we still live—these same men passed the ordinance of '87, declaring that slavery should never go to the north-west territory.

In such passages as these, Lincoln made of the Founders basically a single cohort of heroes who drafted the Declaration of Independence, won the Revolution, and wrote the Constitution. Yet in the passage quoted just above this one, Lincoln had spoken of the revolutionary era as "away back of the constitution," as though the years from 1776 to 1787 spanned generations and made time-tested and ripened traditions.

The fact of the matter is that the Constitution was something of an embarrassment to antislavery men. The Constitution protected slavery in the states, and all politicians, Republican and Democrat alike, knew it. The best antislavery politicians could do was to find antislavery tendencies in the Constitution, to deduce from its language a reluctance on the part of the nation's founders to embrace slavery warmly as an essential part of the national fabric. The word "slavery," as Lincoln often said, was not in the document and "Thus, the thing is hid away, in the Constitution, just as an afflicted man hides away a wen or a cancer, which he dares not cut out at once, lest he bleed to death; with the promise, nevertheless, that the cutting may begin at the end of a given time." Lincoln was never prepared to denounce the Constitution as a whole. No legitimate politician can, for that document defines legitimacy. Lincoln was not prepared even to dwell on certain defective parts of the Constitution. But he found it easier to wax enthusiastic over the Declaration of Independence.

The following passage from a speech in Chicago on July 10, 1858, shows the typical range of tone in speaking of the two documents:

> It may be argued that there are certain conditions that make necessities and impose them upon us, and to the extent that a necessity is imposed upon a man he must submit to it. I think that was the condition in which we found ourselves when we established this government. We had slavery among us, we could not get our constitution unless we permitted them to remain in slavery, we could not secure the good we did secure if we grasped for more, and having by necessity submitted to that much, it does not destroy the principle that is the charter of our libereties. Let that charter stand as our standard.

The spirit of the Constitution, properly and carefully looked at, was antagonistic to the Kansas-Nebraska Bill, Lincoln could say, but it was easier and far more stirring to say that the "spirit of seventy-six" and "the spirit of Nebraska" were utter antagonisms.

In the years following the *Dred Scott* decision and preceding the Civil War, Lincoln's constitutional views changed little from their 1854 antislavery adumbration. He was, perhaps, forced to speak more about the Constitution than had been his custom early in his political life, but he did not change his manner of interpreting it. Nor did *Dred Scott* cause him acute embarrassment over the apparent conflict between Republican doctrine and Supreme Court dictum. He merely pointed out the juristic weaknesses of the *Dred Scott* decision, characteristically avoiding long comment on Latinate distinctions:

> Perhaps you will say the Supreme Court has decided the disputed Constitutional question in your favor. Not quite so. But waiving the lawyer's distinction between dictum and decision, the Court have decided the question for you in a sort of way. The Court have substantially said, it is your constitutional right to take slaves into the federal territories, and to hold them there as property. When I saw the decision was made in a sort of way, I mean it was made in a divided Court, by a bare majority of the Judges, and they not quite agreeing with one another in the reasons for making it; that it is so made as that its avowed supporters disagree with one another about its meaning, and that it was mainly based upon a mistaken statement of fact—the statement in the opinion that "the right of property in a slave is distinctly and expressly affirmed in the Constitution."

Lincoln had said time and time again that the Constitution said nothing distinct or express about "slavery," for it eschewed the very word. Moreover, he kept on saying that the Constitution showed the reluctance of the founders to contemplate the permanence of slavery in the United States. Indeed, he dwelled on that subject, in considerable historical detail, in one of his most famous speeches, the Cooper Institute address of February 27, 1860. And he had reminded Stephen Douglas of it repeatedly in their famous debates in 1858:

It is not true that our fathers, as Judge Douglas assumes, made this government part slave and part free. Understand the sense in which he puts it. He assumes that slavery is a rightful thing within itself,—was introduced by the framers of the Constitution. The exact truth is, that they found the institution existing among us, and they left it as they found it. But in making the government they left this institution with many clear marks of disapprobation upon it.

When Lincoln became president and faced the issues of civil war, he focused on other constitutional questions, many of which he had surely never thought of as an Illinois lawyer and politician. But his manner of approach to constitutional issues was rather well established: the constitutional side of political questions would not usually come first to his mind, he would rely on arguments provided by his party heritage when forced to examine constitutional questions, and his constitutional views would be decidedly shaped by antislavery feeling.

ॐ

Notes to Chapter 2

Lincoln after 175 Years

1. Hyman, "Lincoln and Equal Rights for Negroes: The Irrelevancy of the Wadsworth Letter, *Civil War History*, 12 (1966), 258–66; Johnson, "Lincoln and Equal Rights: The Authenticity of the Wadsworth Letter," *Journal of Southern History*, 32 (1966), 83–87; Johnson, "Lincoln and Equal Rights: A Reply," *Civil War History*, 13 (1967), 67–73; and Catton, *The Inescapable Challenge Lincoln Left Us* (Springfield, Ill.: Abraham Lincoln Association, 1970), 5.

2. Cox, *Lincoln and Black Freedom: A Study in Presidential Leadership* (Columbia: University of South Carolina Press, 1981). Foner's review of Cox's book was published by the History Book Club in May 1983.

3. Lightner, "Abraham Lincoln and the Ideal of Equality," *Journal of the Illinois State Historical Society*, 75 (1982), 291.

4. Forgie (New York: W.W. Norton, 1979); Strozier (New York: Basic Books, 1982); and Anderson (New York: Alfred A. Knopf, 1982).

5. Curry and Goodheart, "Knives in Their Heads: Passionate Self-Analysis and the Search for Identity in American Abolitionism," *Canadian Review of American Studies*, 14 (1983), 401–14; and Goodheart and Curry, "Psychological Approaches to American Abolitionism," in Joseph Dorinson and Jerrold Atlas, ed., *Proceedings, Sixth Annual Meetings of the International Psychological Association* (New York: International Psychological Association, 1983), 61–71.

6. The direct quotations are taken from Forgie's article "A Lincoln Divided," *New York Times*, Feb. 12, 1979. Much of Forgie's book does not focus on Lincoln alone but the entire Civil War generation. The key chapters on Lincoln are "Abraham Lincoln and the Melodrama of the House Divided" (Ch. 7, 243–81) and "the New Birth of Freedom" (Ch. 8, 282–93). But see also pp. 61–84 for important comments on Lincoln's "hidden agenda"—that is, the subconscious sources of his pathological desire to achieve greatness at all costs.

7. Walker, *Moral Choices: Memory, Desire, and Imagination in Nineteenth-Century Aboli-tion* (Baton Rouge: Louisiana State University Press, 1978), 349.

8. Craven, The Coming of the War Between the States: An Interpretation," *Journal of Southern History*, 2 (1936), 136; and Randall, *The Civil War and Reconstruction* (Boston: D.C. Heath, 1937), 146.

9. Anderson, *Abraham Lincoln*, 11, 197; and Wilson, *Patriotic Gore: Studies in the Literature of the American Civil War* (New York: Oxford University Press, 1962), 99–130.

10. Strozier, *Lincoln's Quest for Union*, 123, 181, 232.

11. Ibid., 182–204.

12. For a sophisticated treatment of the implications of the Lyceum speech, see Major L. Wilson, "Lincoln and Van Buren in the Steps of the Fathers: Another Look at the Lyceum Address." *Civil War History*, 29 (1983), 197–211.

13. A qualitative distinction must be made between Strozier's work and that of Forgie and Anderson. Although Strozier also attaches unwarranted significance to Lincoln's Lyceum Speech (59–60), and even though his chapter "The Group Self and the Crisis of the 1850's" is based on theoretical speculation, not evidence, his analyses of Lincoln's private life, which comprise the major part of the book, are rich and rewarding—a few major exceptions to the contrary notwithstanding. See, for example, Strozier's questionable association between a wild turkey Lincoln killed and his dead mother (25–26).

Chapter 3

LINCOLN, RACE, and SLAVERY

Was Lincoln a racist? Did his view on race evolve? Did Lincoln end slavery? Should he be viewed as the "Great Emancipator"?

I am naturally anti-slavery. If slavery is not wrong, nothing is wrong. I can not remember when I did not so think, and feel. And yet I have never understood that the Presidency conferred upon me an unrestricted right to act officially upon this judgment and feeling.

Abraham Lincoln, to Albert G. Hodges, April 4, 1864

★ Don E. Fehrenbacher, "Only His Stepchildren: Lincoln and the Negro"
★ Jason H. Silverman, "In Isles Beyond the Main: Abraham Lincoln's Philosophy on Black Colonization"
★ Lucas E. Morel, "Forced into Gory Lincoln Revisionism: A Review of *Forced into Glory: Abraham Lincoln's White Dream* by Lerone Bennett"
★ Stephen B. Oates, "Towards a New Birth of Freedom: Abraham Lincoln and Reconstruction"

ॐ

ONLY HIS STEPCHILDREN: LINCOLN AND THE NEGRO

Don E. Fehrenbacher

THE TWO MOST SUCCESSFUL biographies of Lincoln published in the second half of the twentieth century have been those by Benjamin P. Thomas (1952) and Stephen B. Oates (1977).[1] One of the notable differences between the two books—a difference reflecting profound changes in American society during the twenty-five-year interval—is the greater attention that Oates gives to the subject of race. "Only His Stepchildren" was written four years before the appearance of the Oates biography, at a time of deepening historical interest in American racial attitudes as already

*Reprinted with permission from Mrs. Don E. Fehrenbacher and The Civil War Institute.

manifested in such works as Winthrop D. Jordan's *White over Black* (1968) and George M. Fredrickson's *The Black Image in the White Mind* (1971). Presented as the annual Robert Fortenbaugh Memorial Lecture at Gettysburg College in November 1973, it was published a year later in Volume 20 of *Civil War History* and subsequently reprinted in George M. Fredrickson, ed., *A Nation Divided: Problems and Issues of the Civil War and Reconstruction* (Minneapolis, Minn., 1975). Much has been written since then about Lincoln and race, but in preparing this essay for republication, I have let the original interpretation stand, making only a few stylistic and bibliographical changes. The newer literature on the subject, such as LaWanda Cox's important book *Lincoln and Black Freedom* (1981), is given some attention in later chapters.[2]

If the United States had a patron saint it would no doubt be Abraham Lincoln; and if one undertook to explain Lincoln's extraordinary hold on the national consciousness, it would be difficult to find a better starting point than these lines from an undistinguished poem written in 1865:

> One of the people! Born to be
> Their curious epitome;
> To share yet rise above
> Their shifting hate and love.[3]

A man of the people and yet something much more, sharing popular passions and yet rising above them—here was the very ideal of a democratic leader, who in his person could somehow mute the natural antagonism between strong leadership and vigorous democracy. Amy Lowell, picking up the same theme half a century later, called Lincoln "an embodiment of the highest form of the typical American."[4] This paradox of the uncommon common man, splendidly heroic and at the same time appealingly representative, was by no means easy to sustain. The Lincoln tradition, as a consequence, came to embrace two distinct and seemingly incompatible leg ends—the awkward, amiable, robust, rail-splitting, storytelling, frontier folklore hero, and the towering figure of the Great Emancipator and Savior of the Union, a man of sorrows, Christlike in his character and fate.

Biographers have struggled earnestly with this conspicuous dualism, but even when the excesses of reminiscence and myth are trimmed away, Lincoln remains a puzzling mixture of often conflicting qualities—drollness and melancholy, warmth and reserve, skepticism and piety, humbleness and self-assurance. Furthermore, he is doubly hard to get at because he did not readily reveal his inner self. He left us no diary or memoirs, and his closest friends called him "secretive" and "shut-mouthed." Billy Herndon in one of his modest moods declared, "Lincoln is unknown and possibly always will be."[5] Plainly, there is good reason for scholarly caution in any effort to take the measure of such a man.

No less plain is the intimate connection between the Lincoln legend and the myth of America. The ambiguities in his popular image and the whisper of enigma in his portraits have probably broadened the appeal of this homespun Westerner, self-made man, essential democrat, and national martyr. Almost anyone can find a way to identify with Lincoln, perhaps because "like Shakespeare . . . he seemed to run through the whole gamut of human nature."[6] What ever the complex of reasons, successive generations of his countrymen have accepted Abraham Lincoln as the consummate American—the representative genius of the nation. One consequence is that he tends to serve as a mirror for Americans, who, when they write about him, frequently divulge a good deal about themselves.

Of course the recurring election of Lincoln as Representative American has never been unanimous. There was vehement dissent at first from many unreconstructed rebels and later from iconoclasts like Edgar Lee Masters and cavaliers of the lost cause like Lyon Gardiner Tyler.[7] In the mainstream of national life, however, it became increasingly fashionable for individuals and organizations to square themselves with Lincoln and enlist him in their enterprises. Often this required misquotation or misrepresentation or outright invention; but however it could be arranged, lobbyists and legislators, industrialists and labor leaders, reformers and bosses, Populists, Progressives, Prohibitionists, and presidents all wanted him on their side. New Deal Democrats tried to steal him from the Republicans, and the American Communist party bracketed him with Lenin. Lincoln, in the words of David Donald, had come to be "everybody's grandfather."[8]

Most remarkable of all was the growing recognition of Lincoln's greatness in the eleven formerly Confederate states, ten of which had never given him a single vote for president. This may have been a necessary symbolic aspect of sectional reconciliation. Returning to the Union meant coming to terms with the man who had saved the Union. No one took the step more unequivocally than Henry W. Grady, prophet of the New South, who told a New York audience in 1866 that Lincoln had been "the first typical American, the first who comprehended within himself all the strength and gentleness, all the majesty and grace of this Republic."[9] When Southerners talked to Southerners about it, they were usually more restrained. Nevertheless, by the early twentieth century, the Lincoln tradition was becoming a blend of blue and gray, as illustrated in *The Perfect Tribute*, a story from the pen of an Alabama woman about a dying Confederate soldier's admiration for the Gettysburg Address.[10]

Bonds of sympathy between Lincoln and the South had not been difficult to find. He was, after all, a native Southerner—implacable as an enemy, but magnanimous in victory and compassionate by nature. In his hands, nearly everyone agreed, the ordeal of Reconstruction would have been less severe. Even Jefferson Davis concluded that his death had been "a great misfortune to the South."[11]

In addition, Lincoln seemed to pass the supreme test. He could be assimilated to the racial doctrines and institutional arrangements associated with the era of segregation. The historical record, though not entirely consistent, indicated that his opposition to slavery had never included advocacy of racial equality. With a little editing here and some extra emphasis there, Lincoln came out "right" on the Negro question. This was a judgment more often understood than elaborated in Southern writing and oratory, but certain self-appointed guardians of white supremacy were sometimes painfully explicit in claiming Lincoln as one of their own. He had been willing, they said, to guarantee slavery forever in the states where it already existed. He had issued the Emancipation Proclamation with great reluctance. He had opposed the extension of slavery only in order to reserve the Western territories exclusively for white men. He had denied favoring political and social equality for Negroes, had endorsed separation of the races, and had persistently recommended colonization of Negroes abroad. This was the Lincoln eulogized by James K. Vardaman of Mississippi, perhaps the most notorious political racist in American history, and by the sensational Negrophobic novelist Thomas Dixon. In his most famous work, *The Clansman*, Dixon had Lincoln as president parody himself during a discussion of colonization: "We can never attain the ideal Union our fathers dreamed, with millions of an alien, inferior race among us, whose assimilation is neither possible nor desirable. The Nation cannot now exist half white and half black, any more than it could exist half slave and half free."[12]

When one remembers that all this time millions of black Americans were still paying homage to the Great Emancipator, dualism seems all the more characteristic of the Lincoln tradition. Racist elements, to be sure, were never very successful in promoting the image of Lincoln as a dedicated white supremacist, but support from an unlikely quarter would eventually give the idea not only new life but respectability in the centers of professional scholarship.

During the first half of the twentieth century, Lincoln studies became a functional part of the literature of the Civil War, in which the problem of race was present but not paramount. Titles of the 1940s indicate the general bent of interest: *Lincoln and His Part in the Secession Crisis*; *Lincoln and the Patronage*; *Lincoln's War Cabinet*; *Lincoln and the Radicals*; *Lincoln and the War Governors*; *Lincoln and the South*. There was, it should be observed, no Lincoln and the Negro. That would come, appropriately, in the 1960s.

The sweep of the modern civil rights movement, beginning with the Supreme Court's antisegregation decision in 1954, inspired a new departure in American historical writing. Never has the psychological need for a usable past been more evident. Black history flourished and so did abolitionist history, but the most prestigious field of endeavor for a time was white-over-black history. Attention shifted, for example, from slavery as a cause of the Civil War to slavery as one major form of racial oppression. With this change of emphasis, the antebellum years began to look different. A number of monographs appearing in the 1960s, such as Leon F. Litwack's *North of Slavery*, demonstrated the nationwide prevalence of white-superiority doctrines and white-supremacy practices. Many Republicans and even some abolitionists, when they talked about the Negro, had sounded curiously like the slaveholders whom they were so fiercely denouncing. In fact, it appeared that the North and the South, while bitterly at odds on the issue of slavery, were relatively close to one another in their attitudes toward race. And Lincoln, according to Litwack, "accurately and consistently reflected the thoughts and prejudices of most Americans."[13]

The racial consensus of the Civil War era made it easy enough to understand why black Americans failed to win the equality implicit in emancipation, but certain other historical problems became more difficult as a consequence. For instance, if most Northerners in 1860 were indeed racists who viewed the Negro with repugnance as an inferior order of creation, then why did so many of them have such strong feelings about slavery? And why did racist Southerners fear and distrust racist Republicans with an intensity sufficient to destroy the Union? And does not the achievement of emancipation by a people so morally crippled with racism seem almost miraculous—like a one-armed man swimming the English Channel? No amount of talk about overwrought emotions or ulterior purposes or unintended consequences will fully account for what appears to be a major historical paradox, with Lincoln as the central figure.

When the civil rights struggle got under way in the 1950s, both sides tried to enlist Lincoln's support, but the primary tendency at first was to regard desegregation as a belated resumption of the good work begun with the Emancipation Proclamation. Many leading historians agreed that during the presidential years there had been a "steady evolution of Lincoln's attitude toward Negro rights."[14] The changes carried him a long way from the narrow environmental influences of his youth and made him, in the words of Richard N. Current, more relevant and inspiring than ever "as a symbol of man's ability to outgrow his prejudices."[15]

This was the liberal interpretation of Lincoln's record on racial matters. It came under attack from several directions, but especially from the ranks of intellectual radicalism and black militancy, both academic and otherwise. New Left historians, many of them activists in the battle for racial justice, could find little to admire in Abraham Lincoln. Compared with abolitionists like William Lloyd Garrison and Wendell Phillips, he seemed unheroic, opportunistic, and somewhat insensitive to the suffering of black people in bondage. He was "the prototype of the political man in power, with views so moderate as to require the pressure of radicals to stimulate action."[16] His prewar opposition to slavery, embracing the Republican policy of nonextension and the hope of ultimate extinction, reflected a "comfortable belief in the benevolence of history." It amounted to a "formula which promised in time to do everything while for the present risking nothing."[17]

Election to the presidency, in the radical view, produced no great transformation of his character. "Lincoln grew during the war—but he didn't grow much," wrote Lerone Bennett, Jr., a senior editor of *Ebony*. "On every issue relating to the black man . . . he was the very essence of the white supremacist with good intentions."[18] He moved but slowly and reluctantly toward abolishing slavery, and his famous

Proclamation not only lacked "moral grandeur," but had been drafted "in such a way that it freed few, if any, slaves."[19] His reputation as the Great Emancipator is therefore "pure myth."[20] Most important of all, Lincoln probably believed in the inferiority of the Negro and certainly favored separation of the races. He was, in Bennett's words, "a tragically flawed figure who shared the racial prejudices of most of his white contemporaries."[21]

This, then, was the radical interpretation of Lincoln's record on racial matters, and what strikes one immediately is its similarity to the views of professional racists like Vardaman and Dixon. The portrait of A. Lincoln, Great White Supremacist, has been the work, it seems, of a strange collaboration.[22]

No less interesting is the amount of animus directed at a man who died more than a hundred years ago. In the case of black militants, hostility to Lincoln was no doubt part of the process of cutting loose from white America. Thus there is little history but much purpose in the statement of Malcolm X: "He probably did more to trick Negroes than any other man in history."[23]

For white radicals too, rejection of Lincoln signified repudiation of the whole American cultural tradition, from the first massacre of Indians to the Vietnam War. In what might be called the "malign consensus" school of United States history, Lincoln remained the Representative American, but the America that he represented was a dark, ugly country, stained with injustice and cruelty. Plainly, there is much more at stake here than the reputation of a single historical figure.

James K. Vardaman, it is said, used to carry with him one particular Lincoln quotation that he would whip out and read at the slightest opportunity. This excerpt from the debate with Douglas in 1858 at Charleston, Illinois, is fast becoming the most quoted passage in all of Lincoln's writings, outstripping even the Gettysburg Address and the Second Inaugural. Pick up any recent historical study of American race relations and somewhere in its pages you are likely to find the following words:

> I will say then that I am not, nor ever have been in favor of bringing about in any way the social and political equality of the white and black races,—that I am not nor ever have been in favor of making voters or jurors of Negroes, nor of qualifying them to hold office, nor to intermarry with white people; and I will say in addition to this that there is a physical difference between the white and black races which I believe will forever forbid the two races living together on terms of social and political equality. And inasmuch as they cannot so live, while they do remain together there must be the position of superior and inferior, and I as much as any other man am in favor of having the superior position assigned to the white race.[24]

The quotation seemed especially relevant in the 1960s and 1970s, when problems that had once preoccupied Lincoln's biographers, such as his part in bringing on the Civil War and the quality of his wartime leadership, were more or less pushed aside by a question of greater urgency. It was well phrased in the preface to a collection of documents titled *Lincoln on Black and White*: "Was Lincoln a racist? More important, how did Lincoln's racial views affect the course of our history?"[25]

Anyone who sets out conscientiously to answer such a query will soon find himself deep in complexity and confronting some of the fundamental problems of historical investigation. In one category are various questions about the historian's relation to the past: Is his task properly one of careful reconstruction, or are there more important purposes to be served? Does his responsibility include rendering moral judgments? If so, using what standards—those of his own time or those of the period under study? Then there are all the complications encountered in any effort to read the mind of a man, especially a politician, from the surviving record of his words and actions. For instance, what he openly affirmed as a youth may have been silently discarded in maturity; what he believed on a certain subject may be less significant than the intensity of his belief; and what he said on a certain occasion may have been largely determined by the immediate historical context, including the composition of his audience.

Terminological difficulties may also arise in the study of history, and such is the case with the word "racist," which serves us badly as a concept because of its denunciatory tone and indiscriminate use.[26] Conducive neither to objectivity nor to precision, the word has been employed so broadly as to invite much subdividing. Thus we have been asked to distinguish between ideological racism and institutional racism,[27] between scientific racism and folk racism,[28] between active racism and inactive racism,[29] between racism and racial prejudice,[30] between racism and racialism,[31] between hierarchical racism and romantic racialism.[32]

In its strictest sense, racism is a doctrine, but by extension it has also come to signify an attitude, a mode of behavior, and a social system. The *doctrine*, a work of intellectuals, is a rationalized theory of inherent racial inferiority. In a given person, however, it can be anything from a casual belief to a philosophy of life. As an *attitude*, racism is virtually synonymous with prejudice—an habitual feeling of repugnance, and perhaps of enmity, toward members of another race. It can be anything from a mild tendency to a fierce obsession. Racism as a *mode of behavior* is prejudice activated in some way—a display of racial hostility that can be anything from mere avoidance of the other race to participation in a lynching. Racism as a *social system* means that law and custom combine to hold one race in subordination to another through institutional arrangements like slavery, segregation, discrimination, and disfranchisement. Individuals can help support such a system with anything from tacit acquiescence to strenuous public service in its defense. These multiple and graduated meanings of the word "racism" are important to remember in exploring the historical convergence of Abraham Lincoln and the American Negro.

"One must see him first," says Bennett, "against the background of his times. Born into a poor white family in the slave state of Kentucky and raised in the anti-black environments of southern Indiana and Illinois, Lincoln was exposed from the very beginning to racism."[33] This is a familiar line of reasoning and credible enough on the surface. Any racial views encountered during his youth were likely to be unfavorable to the Negro. But more important is the question of how often he encountered such views and how thoroughly he absorbed them. Besides, the assumption that his racial attitudes were shaped more or less permanently by his early social environment does not take into account the fact that youth may rebel against established opinion. Lincoln did in a sense reject his father's world, leaving it behind him forever soon after reaching the age of twenty-one. Certainly his personal knowledge of black people was very limited. After catching a few glimpses of slavery as a small boy in Kentucky, he had little contact with Negroes while growing up in backwoods Indiana or as a young man in New Salem, Illinois. Those first twenty-eight years of his life take up just three pages in Benjamin Quarles's book *Lincoln and the Negro*.[34]

If Lincoln entered manhood with strong feelings about race already implanted in his breast, one might expect to find indications of it in his earlier letters and speeches. For instance, on a steamboat carrying him home from a visit to Kentucky in 1841, there were a dozen slaves in chains. They had been sold down the river to a new master, and yet they seemed the most cheerful persons on board. Here was inspiration for some racist remarks in the "Sambo" vein, hut Lincoln, describing the scene to a friend, chose instead to philosophize about the dubious effect of "condition upon human happiness."[35] That is, he pictured blacks behaving, as George M. Fredrickson puts it, "in a way that could be understood in terms of a common humanity and not as the result of peculiar racial characteristics."[36] Although one scholar may insist that Lincoln's racial beliefs were "matters of deep conviction,"[37] and another may talk about "the deeply rooted attitudes and ideas of a lifetime,"[38] there is scarcely any record of his thoughts on race until he was past forty years of age. Long before then, of course, he had taken a stand against slavery, and it was the struggle over slavery that eventually compelled him to consider publicly the problem of race.

There is no escape from the dilemma that "relevance" makes the past worth studying and at the same time distorts it. We tend to see antebellum race and slavery in the wrong perspective. Race itself was not then the critical public issue that it has become for us. Only widespread emancipation could make it so, and until the outbreak of the Civil War, that contingency seemed extremely remote. Our own preoccupation with race probably leads us to overestimate the importance of racial feeling in the antislavery movement.[39] In fact, there is a current disposition to assume that if a Republican did not have strong pro-Negro motives, he must have acted for strong anti-Negro reasons, such as a desire to keep the Western territories lily-white.[40]

Actually, much of the motivation for antislavery agitation was only indirectly connected with the Negro. For example, the prime target often seemed to be not so much slavery as the "slave power," arrogant, belligerent, and overrepresented in all branches of the federal government.[41] In Lincoln's case, no one can doubt his profound, though perhaps intermittent, sympathy for the slave. Yet he also hated slavery in a more abstract way as an evil principle and as a stain on the national honor, incompatible with the mission of America.[42]

It is a mistake to assume that Lincoln's actions in relation to the Negro were determined or even strongly influenced by his racial outlook. He based his antislavery philosophy squarely upon perception of the slave as a person, not as a Negro. According to the Declaration of Independence, he said, all men, including black men, are created equal, at least to the extent that none has a right to enslave another. This became a point at issue in the famous debates with Stephen A. Douglas, who vehemently denied that the Declaration had anything to do with the African race. Lincoln, in turn, accused his rival of trying to "dehumanize" the Negro. But he had constructed an argument against slavery which, carried to its logical conclusion, seemed to spell complete racial equality. So Douglas insisted, at any rate, while Lincoln protested: "I do not understand that because I do not want a Negro woman for a slave I must necessarily want her for a wife."[43]

Opponents of slavery everywhere had to contend with the charge that they advocated Negro equality. In the Democratic press, Republicans became "Black Republicans," and political survival more often than not appeared to depend upon repudiation of the epithet. Thus the race question was most prominent in the antebellum period as a rhetorical and largely spurious feature of the slavery controversy.

Lincoln's first general remarks about racial equality on record were made in 1854, when the repeal of the Missouri Compromise restriction drew him back to the center of Illinois politics. What to do, ideally, with Southern slaves, he pondered in a speech at Peoria. "Free them, and make them politically and socially our equals? My own feelings will not admit of this; and if mine would, we well know that those of the great mass of white people will not."[44] More often that year, however, he talked about the humanity of the Negro in denouncing the extension of slavery. Then came the election of 1856 and Frémont's defeat, which Lincoln analyzed with some bitterness: "We were constantly charged with seeking an amalgamation of the white and black races; and thousands turned from us, not believing the charge . . . but *fearing* to face it themselves."[45] It was at this point, significantly, that he became more aggressive and explicit in disavowing racial equality. He began using census figures to show that miscegenation was a by-product of slavery. He spoke of the "natural disgust" with which most white people viewed "the idea of an indiscriminate amalgamation of the white and black races." And, under heavy pounding from Douglas during the senatorial campaign of 1858, he responded again and again in the manner of the notorious Charleston passage quoted above.[46] Indeed, his strongest feeling about race appears to have been his vexation with those who kept bringing the subject up. "Negro equality! Fudge!!" he scribbled on a piece of paper. "How long, in the government of a God, great enough to make and maintain this Universe, shall there continue knaves to vend, and fools to gulp, so low a piece of demagoguism as this."[47]

Most of Lincoln's recorded generalizations about race were public statements made in the late 1850s as part of his running oratorical battle with Douglas.[48] Furthermore, nearly all of those statements were essentially disclaimers rather than affirmations. They indicated, for political reasons, the maximum that he was willing to deny the Negro and the minimum that he claimed for the Negro. They were concessions on points not at issue, designed to fortify him on the point that was at issue—namely, the extension of slavery. If he had responded differently at Charleston and elsewhere, the Lincoln of history simply would not exist. Words uttered in a context of such pressure may be less than reliable as indications of a man's lifetime attitude.

At least it seems possible that Lincoln's remarks in middle age on the subject of race were shaped more by his political realism than by impressions stamped on his mind in childhood. The principal intellectual influence, as Fredrickson has demonstrated, was Henry Clay, Lincoln's political hero, whom he studied anew for a eulogy delivered in 1852. Clay, in his attitude toward slavery, represented a link with the Founding Fathers. A slaveholder himself who nevertheless believed that the institution was a "curse," he began and ended his career working for a program of gradual emancipation in Kentucky. He helped found and steadily supported the American Colonization Society. In his racial views, moreover, Clay emphasized the Negro's humanity and reserved judgment on the question of innate black inferiority. Lincoln not only adopted Clay's tentative, moderate outlook but extensively paraphrased and sometimes parroted his words.[49]

Considering, then, the peculiar context of his most significant remarks on the subject of race, and considering also his dependence on Clay, it seems unwise to assert flatly, as some scholars do, that Lincoln embraced the doctrine of racism. Not that it would be astonishing to find that he did so. The assumption of inherent white superiority was almost universal and rested upon observation as well as prejudice. Comparison of European civilization and African "savagery" made it extremely difficult to believe in the natural equality of white and black races. Yet Lincoln's strongest statements, even if taken at face value and out of context, prove to be tentative and equivocal. He conceded that the Negro *might not* be his equal, or he said that the Negro *was not* his equal *in certain respects*. As an example, he named *color*, which can be viewed as having a biological implication. But we cannot be certain that he was not merely expressing an aesthetic judgment or noting the social disadvantages of being black. He never used the word "inherent," or any of its equivalents, in discussing the alleged inferiority of the Negro, and it is not unlikely that he regarded such inferiority as resulting primarily from social oppression. In 1862, he compared blacks whose minds had been "clouded by slavery" with free Negroes "capable of thinking as white men." His last recorded disclaimer appears in a letter written as president-elect to a New York editor. He did not, it declared, "hold the black man to be the equal of the white, unqualifiedly." The final word throws away most of the declaration and scarcely suits a true ideological racist. Here there is a doubleness in the man as in the legend. It appears that he may have both absorbed and doubted, both shared and risen above, the racial doctrines of his time.[50]

Lincoln, who had four sons and no other children, was presumably never asked the ultimate racist question: "Would you want your daughter to marry a Negro?" He did indicate a disinclination to take a Negro woman for his wife, thereby agreeing with most of his white contemporaries in their aversion to miscegenation. Otherwise, there is little evidence of racism as an attitude or racism as a mode of behavior in his relations with blacks. Frederick Douglass, sometimes a severe critic of his policies, said emphatically: "In all my interviews with Mr. Lincoln I was impressed with his entire freedom from popular prejudice against the colored race."[51] During the war years in Washington, the social status of Negroes underwent a minor revolution, exemplified in the arrival of a black diplomat from the newly recognized republic of Haiti. Lincoln opened the White House to black visitors in a way that set aside all precedent.[52] Douglass and others appreciated not only his friendliness but his restraint. There was no effusiveness, no condescension. "He treated Negroes," says Quarles, "as they wanted to be treated—as human beings."[53]

On the other hand, Lincoln in the 1850s did plainly endorse the existing system of white supremacy, except for slavery. He defended it, however, on grounds of expediency rather than principle, and on grounds of the incompatibility rather than the inequality of the races. Assuming that one race or the other must be on top, he admitted preferring that the superior position be *assigned* to the white race. There was little association of institutional racism with ideological racism in his thinking. Although he was by no means insensitive to the deprivation suffered by free Negroes,[54] he saw little hope of improving their condition and in any case regarded slavery as a far greater wrong. Moreover, it appeared that any serious attack on institutional racism would raise the cry of "Negro equality," and thereby damage the antislavery cause.

But then, if he hated slavery so much, why did Lincoln not become an abolitionist? There are several obvious reasons: fear for the safety of the Union, political prudence, constitutional scruples, a personal distaste for extremism, and perplexity over what to do with freed slaves.[55] In addition, it must be emphasized that Lincoln, as Lord Charnwood observed, "accepted the institutions to which he was born, and he enjoyed them."[56] Social reformers were a relatively new and not very numerous breed in antebellum America. Lincoln cannot be counted among them. This author of the greatest reform in American history was simply not a reformer by nature. He even acquiesced in the retention of slavery, provided that it should not be allowed to expand. For him, the paramount importance of the Republican anti-extension program lay in its symbolic meaning as a commitment to the principle of ultimate extinction. Some later generation, he thought, would then convert the principle into practice. What this amounted to, in a sense, was antislavery tokenism, but it also proved to be a formula for the achievement of political power, and with it, the opportunity to issue a proclamation of emancipation.

Of course, it has been said that Lincoln deserves little credit for emancipation— that he came to it tardily and reluctantly, under radical duress. "Blacks have no reason to feel grateful to Abraham Lincoln," writes Julius Lester. "How come it took him two whole years to free the slaves? His pen was sitting on his desk the whole time. All he had to do was get up one morning and say, 'Doggonit! I think I'm gon' free the slaves today.'"[57] But *which* morning? That turned out to be the real question.

Lincoln, it should be remembered, was under strong pressure from *both* sides on the issue of emancipation, and so the radical clamor alone will not explain his ultimate decision. Nevertheless, when the war began, many Americans quickly realized that the fate of slavery might be in the balance. Veteran abolitionists rejoiced that history was at last marching to their beat, and Lincoln did not fail to read what he called "the signs of the times." Emancipation itself, as he virtually acknowledged, came out of the logic of events, not his personal volition, but the time and manner of its coming were largely his choice.

There had been enough Republicans to win the presidential election, but there were not enough to win the war. They needed help from Northern Democrats and border-state loyalists, who were willing to fight for the Union, but not for abolition. A premature effort at emancipation might alienate enough support to make victory impossible. It would then be self-defeating, because there could be no emancipation without victory. Lincoln's remarkable achievement, whether he fully intended it or not, was to proclaim emancipation in such a way as to minimize disaffection. He did so by allowing enough time for the prospect to become familiar in the public mind, and by adhering scrupulously to the fiction that this momentous step was strictly a military measure. Much of the confusion about the Emancipation Proclamation results from taking too seriously Lincoln's verbal bowings and scrapings to the conservatives while all the time he was backing steadily away from them.[58]

The best illustration is his famous reply of August 22, 1862, to the harsh criticism of Horace Greeley, in which he said that his "paramount object" was to save the Union. "What I do about slavery, and the colored race," he declared, "I do because I believe it helps to save the Union; and what I forbear, I forbear because I do not believe it would help to save the Union."[59] The most striking thing about the entire document is its dissimulation. Although Lincoln gave the impression that options were still open, he had in fact already made up his mind, had committed himself to a number of persons, had drafted the Proclamation. Why, then, write such a letter? Because it was not a statement of policy but instead a brilliant piece of propaganda in which Lincoln, as Benjamin P. Thomas says, "used Greeley's outburst to prepare the people for what was coming."[60]

There were constitutional as well as political reasons, of course, for casting the Proclamation in military language and also for limiting its scope to those states and parts of states still in rebellion. In a sense, as historians fond of paradox are forever pointing out, it did not immediately liberate any slaves at all. And the Declaration of Independence, it might be added, did not immediately liberate a single colony from British rule. The people of Lincoln's time apparently had little doubt about the significance of the Proclamation. Jefferson Davis did not regard it as a mere scrap of paper, and neither did that most famous of former slaves, Frederick Douglass. He called it "the greatest event of our nation's history."[61]

In the long sweep of that history, emancipation had come on, not sluggishly, but with a rush and a roar—over a period of scarcely eighteen months. Given more time to reflect on its racial implications, white America might have recoiled from the act. Lincoln himself had never been anything but a pessimist about the consequences of emancipation. Knowing full well the prejudices of his countrymen, he doubted that blacks and whites could ever live together amicably and on terms of equality.

With stark realism, Lincoln told a delegation of free Negroes in August 1862: "On this broad continent, not a single man of your race is made the equal of a single man of ours. Go where you are treated the best, and the ban is still upon you." And while blacks suffered from discrimination, whites suffered from the discord caused by the presence of blacks. "It is better for us both, therefore, to be separated," he said.[62] But Lincoln apparently never visualized a segregated America. For him, separation meant colonization, which, as a disciple of Henry Clay, he had been advocating at least since 1852. Perhaps the strangest feature of Lincoln's presidential career was the zeal with which he tried to promote voluntary emigration of free Negroes to Africa or Latin America. He recommended it in his first two annual messages, urged it upon Washington's black leadership, and endorsed it in his preliminary Emancipation Proclamation. He had foreign capitals canvassed in a search for likely places of settlement. Furthermore, with funds supplied by Congress, he launched colonization enterprises in Haiti and Panama, both of which proved abortive.[63]

What surprises one the most about these activities is their petty scale. Lincoln implored the delegation of Washington Negroes to find him a hundred, or fifty, or even twenty-five families willing to emigrate. The Haitian project, if completely successful, would have accommodated just five thousand persons—about the number of Negroes born every two weeks in the United States. Back in 1854, Lincoln had admitted the impracticability of colonization as anything but a long-range program.[64] Why, then, was he in such feverish haste to make a token beginning in 1862?

One interesting answer emerges from the chronology. Most of the colonization flurry took place during the second half of 1862. After that, Lincoln's interest waned, although according to the dubious testimony of Benjamin F. Butler, it revived near the end of the war.[65] After issuing the Emancipation Proclamation on January 1, 1863, Lincoln, by all logic, should have pressed harder than ever for colonization, but he never made another public appeal on the subject. It appears that his spirited activity in the preceding six months may have been part of the process of conditioning the public mind for the day of jubilee. The promise of colonization had always been in part a means of quieting fears about the racial consequences of manumission. Offered as the ultimate solution to the problem of the black population, it could also serve as a psychological safety valve for the problem of white racism. This combination of purposes had inspired a number of Republican leaders to take up the cause of colonization in the late 1850s. As one of them put it, the movement would "ward off the attacks made upon us about Negro equality."[66]

In his second annual message of December 1, 1862, Lincoln said, "I cannot make it better known than it already is, that I strongly favor colonization." Then he continued in a passage that has received far less attention: "And yet I wish to say there is an objection urged against free colored persons remaining in the country, which is largely imaginary, if not sometimes malicious." He went on to discuss and minimize the fear that freedmen would displace white laborers, after which he wrote:

But it is dreaded that the freed people will swarm forth, and cover the whole land? Are they not already in the land? Will liberation make them any more numerous? Equally distributed among the whites of the whole country, and there would be but one colored to seven whites. Could the one, in any way, greatly disturb the seven? There are many communities now, having more than one free colored person, to seven whites; and this, without any apparent consciousness of evil from it.[67]

Here, along with his last public endorsement of colonization, was an eloquent plea for racial accommodation at home. The one might remain his ideal ultimate solution, but the other, he knew, offered the only hope in the immediate future.

Yet, if his plans for reconstruction are an accurate indication, Lincoln at the time of his death had given too little consideration to the problem of racial adjustment and to the needs of four million freed men. How much that would have changed if he had not been killed has been the subject of lively controversy.[68] Certainly his policies by 1865 no longer reflected all the views expressed in 1858 when he had repudiated both Negro citizenship and Negro suffrage. Now, by fiat of his administration in defiance of the *Dred Scott* decision, blacks were citizens of the United States, and he had begun in a gentle way to press for limited black enfranchisement. He had overcome his initial doubts about enlisting Negroes as fighting soldiers, was impressed by their overall performance, and thought they had earned the right to vote.

Lincoln once told Charles Sumner that on the issue of emancipation they were no more than six weeks apart.[69] The relative earliness of his first favorable remarks about Negro enfranchisement suggests that he had again read the "signs of the times." It is not difficult to believe that after the war he would have continued closer to the Sumners than to the conservatives, whom he had placated but never followed for long. And one can scarcely doubt that his postwar administration would have been more responsive to Negro aspirations than Andrew Johnson's proved to be.

But for several reasons Lincoln's role was likely to be more subdued than we might expect from the Great Emancipator. First, during peacetime, with his powers and responsibilities as commander in chief greatly reduced, he probably would have yielded more leadership to Congress in the old Whig tradition. Second, at the time of his death, he still regarded race relations as primarily a local matter, just as he had maintained during the debates with Douglas: "I do not understand there is any place where an alteration of the social and political relations of the Negro and the white man can be made except in the State Legislature."[70] Third, Negroes as Negroes were nearly always connotative in Lincoln's thinking. Their welfare, though by no means a matter of indifference to him, had never been, and was not likely to become, his "paramount object." They were, in the words of Frederick Douglass, "only his step-children."[71]

Finally, in his attitude toward the wrongs of the free Negro, Lincoln had none of the moral conviction that inspired his opposition to slavery. He never seems to have suspected that systematic racial discrimination might be, like slavery, a stain on the national honor and a crime against mankind. Whether that is the measure of his greatness must be left to personal judgment. Of Copernicus we might say: What a genius! He revolutionized our conception of the solar system. Or: What an ignoramus! He did not understand the rest of the universe at all.

⤳

IN ISLES BEYOND THE MAIN: ABRAHAM LINCOLN'S PHILOSOPHY ON BLACK COLONIZATION

Jason H. Silverman

SPEAKING TO Springfield, Illinois in 1857, Abraham Lincoln obliquely referred to the emancipation and colonization of blacks when he remarked: "The plainest print cannot be read through a gold eagle; and it will be ever hard to "find many men who will send a slave to Liberia, and pay his passage, while they can send him to a new country—Kansas, for instance—and sell him for fifteen hundred dollars and the rise."[1] The assumption of the idea of deportation of freed blacks as the test solution for the racial problem of the South and the nation underlies this entire passage. Indeed, such was Lincoln's attitude toward colonization. He advocated that policy from the early 1850s until his death in 1865. Largely because of Lincoln's efforts, colonization gained Congressional sanctions and for a short time appeared to gain momentum as a means to avoid racial conflict. The President even attempted to start black colonies in two foreign counties, although neither plan reached fruition. Despite his personal belief in colonization, though, Lincoln's efforts to effect that plan abruptly halted in 1864 as a result of changing political opinion. Thus, the present study of Lincoln's attitude on colonization of freed blacks will reflect an interesting mixture of political expediency, racial pragmatism, and economic impracticability on the part of the sixteenth president.

*This article originally appeared in *Lincoln Herald*, Vol. 80, Fall 1978, published by Lincoln Memorial University (Harrogate, Tennessee). Reprinted with permission from Lincoln Memorial University.

The idea of colonization of freed blacks had begun years before, in the age of Jefferson. A man whom Lincoln greatly admired, Thomas Jefferson heartily endorsed the principle of colonization. In fact, Jefferson believed that the abolition of slavery could only be accomplished in conjunction with expatriation of freed slaves. The removal of free blacks from this country would ensure racial harmony and prevent further racial miscegenation. Thus, to Jefferson, colonization was *sine qua non* to any proposal for emancipation. He strongly supported the objective of the American Society for Colonizing the Free People of Color of the United States—the Colonization Society—to resettle blacks in Africa; "beyond the reach of mixture."[2]

Another of Lincoln's heroes, Henry Clay, helped found the American Colonization Society in 1816 and served as its president for many years. Clay vehemently espoused the cause, saying "There is a moral fitness in the idea of returning to Africa her children, whose ancestors have been torn from her by the ruthless hand of fraud and violence. Transplanted in a foreign land, they will carry back to their native soil the rich fruits of religion, civilization, law, and liberty. May it not be one of the great designs of the Ruler of the universe . . . thus to transform an original crime, into a signal blessing, to that most unfortunate portion of the globe?"[3]

Lincoln's admiration for Henry Clay and Thomas Jefferson doubtless influenced his opinion on the subject of colonization. Regardless of its inception, though, Lincoln's attitude on colonization became politically manifest in his eulogy of Henry Clay in July, 1852. Commenting on Clay's statement quoted above, Lincoln added his fervent sanction to the goal of colonization, "May it indeed be realized!" he continued at length, concluding that "if as the friends of colonization hope, the present and coming generation of our countrymen shall by any means succeed in freeing our land from the dangerous presence of slavery; and, at the same time, in restoring a captive people to their long-lost fatherland, with bright prospects for the future . . . it will indeed be a glorious consummation."[4] At this stage of his political career then, Lincoln embraced the concurrent abolition of slavery and expatriation of freed blacks.

Yet Lincoln, the astute politician, knew that every speech must be written with a cognizance of the occasion. When delivering his eulogy on Henry Clay, a man firmly committed to colonization, Lincoln appropriately concurred with that principle. The Lincoln-Douglas debates a few years later, however, demanded a more subtle approach. In a speech at Peoria, Illinois on October 16, 1854, Lincoln exhibited caution when broaching the subjects of emancipation and colonization. "If all earthly power were given me, I should not know what to do as to the existing institution. My first impulse," he remarked, "would be to free all the slaves and send them to Liberia—to their own native land, but a moment's reflection would convince me that in the long run its sudden execution is impossible. If they were all landed there in a day, they would all perish in the next ten days; and there are not surplus shipping and surplus money enough in the world to carry them there in many times ten days. What then?"[5] In this situation where public opinion ran against repeal of the Missouri Compromise and in favor of upholding the institution of slavery where it already existed, Lincoln proposed a gradual emancipation program to assuage fears of massive black invasion into the area.

Approximately three years later, Lincoln again enthusiastically endorsed colonization in a speech on more familiar political ground at his home of Springfield, Illinois. He reiterated Jefferson's belief that separation provided the only means of preventing racial amalgamation, and that the only effectual separation would be colonization. Here Lincoln confidently employed both moral and economic sanctions in his case for colonization. He acknowledged,

> The enterprise is a difficult one; but "when there is a will there is a way;" and what colonization needs most is a hearty will. Will springs from the two elements of moral sense and self-interest. Let us be brought to believe it is morally right, and at the same time favorable to, or at least not against, our interest to transfer the African to his native clime, and we shall find a way to do it, however great the task may be.[6]

Undoubtedly, Lincoln or any other political candidate could not have made such bold statements unless in a congenial, favorable atmosphere like that of a hometown audience.

Nevertheless, Lincoln's attitude on colonization remained constant throughout the period prior to his presidency. He vacillated in degree of support according to the situation, but consistently endorsed the principle of colonization as the best solution to America's racial problem. The feasibility of transforming his theory into practice, though, still remained in question.

Lincoln sought to answer that question when he assumed the presidency. As early as May, 1861, land developer Ambrose W. Thompson approached President Lincoln on the subject of colonization at the Isthmus of Chiriqui in Panama. On the recommendation of the commission investigating the Chiriqui Improvement Company, Lincoln sent representatives there "for the purpose of reconnaissance of, and a report upon the lands, and harbors of the Isthmus of Chiriqui, the fitness of the lands to the colonization of the Negro race, and the works which will be necessary . . . to protect the colonists as they may arrive."[7] With this action, Lincoln commenced the implementation of a racial program he hoped would serve as a panacea for the troubled nation.

Meanwhile, Lincoln prepared his annual message to Congress, including a portion on colonization. He firmly recommended that Congress provide funds for colonizing blacks "in a climate congenial to them." Anticipating potential objections, he commented,

> To carry out the plan of colonization may involve the acquiring of territory, and also the appropriation of money beyond that to be expended in the territorial acquisition. . . . If it be said that the only legitimate object of acquiring territory is to

furnish homes for white men, this measure effects that object; for the emigration of colored men leaves additional room for white men remaining or coming here.[8]

Congress responded in part by appointing a nine-member Select Committee on Emancipation and Colonization, whose task it became to scrutinize various proposed deportation plans and to recommend allocations for the most feasible. Congress as well passed the District of Columbia Emancipation Act on April 16, 1882. This law freed the slaves residing in the nation's capital and provided three hundred dollars per slave in compensation to their owners. More significantly, however, it also furnished one hundred thousand dollars "to aid in the colonization and settlement of such free persons of African descent now residing in said District, including those liberated by this act, as may desire to emigrate."[9] Lincoln eagerly welcomed the passage of this bill, as it gave him both the sanction and allocation to proceed with colonization. He warmly responded, "I am gratified that the two principles of compensation and colonization, are both recognized, and practically applied in the act."[10] A second confiscation act was passed in July 1862, giving Lincoln another five hundred thousand dollars to arrange for the transportation, colonization, and settlement of freed blacks who chose to go to "some tropical country beyond the limits of the United States . . . with all the rights and privileges of freemen."[11] In conjunction with their legislative accomplishments, the Committee on Emancipation and Colonization endorsed the racial theory that the United States would flourish best with a totally white population.[12] Lincoln's pet project had now received all the necessary impetus to proceed.

In view of the circumstances, the time appeared appropriate for Lincoln to approach black representatives with his colonization proposal. His newly titled Commissioner of Emigration, the Reverend James Mitchell, arranged an historic interview with a deputation of five blacks.[13] The meeting, however, soon evolved into a soliloquy, with Lincoln educating his guests as to his intentions. He presented racial prejudice as the reality with which all freed blacks would have to contend, commenting frankly "even when you cease to be slaves, you are yet far removed from being placed on an equality with the white race. You are cut off from many of the advantages which the other race enjoy. The aspiration of men is to enjoy equality with the best when free, but on this broad continent, not a single man of your race is made the equal of a single man of ours."[14] He concluded that it would be best for all concerned to separate the two races. Lincoln suggested colonization in Central America as most feasible, in a place with fine harbors, rich coal mines, and apolitical atmosphere in which blacks would be "made equals, and have the best assurance that you should be the equals of the best."[15] He requested that the black delegation consider his proposal, and advise him as to whether he should expect to send twenty-five to one hundred families.

As a result of the events recently transpired, Lincoln was greatly encouraged in 1862 regarding prospects for black colonization. He had received both economic and moral sanctions from Congress while the plan to colonize at the Isthmus of Chiriqui had been progressing smoothly. One member of the investigative task force, Solicitor of the Treasury Edward Jordan, supported the project because in addition to promoting the idea of colonization it would facilitate mail delivery in the Pacific region. In addition, Secretary of the Interior Caleb B. Smith emphasized the importance of the Chiriqui location with its proximity to the United States and its coal resources.[16] Smith further advocated contracting the project to a private company or developer in order to avoid the need for new treaties or time-consuming legislation. Lincoln therefore proceeded in September with a provisional contract with Ambrose Thompson providing for colonization at Chiriqui. Under the provisions of the contract, Thompson would issue land titles to emigrants, lay out town sites, and develop coal and other mines. The United States Government would reimburse Thompson one dollar per acre for allotted plots, and would financially aid in road construction and other internal improvements and developments. Senator Samuel C. Pomeroy of Kansas, Presidential Colonization Agent, launched a publicity campaign concerning the project in hopes of attracting applicants, and consequently some 13,700 applications poured in.[17] Before the colonists could set sail, however, the Chiriqui project was suspended. Secretary of State William Seward feared diplomatic repercussions among the Central American countries who denied the validity of Thompson's land claims, and disputed the land ownership himself. Furthermore, several Central American countries protested the "dreadful deluge of Negro emigration . . . from the United States."[18]

Additional support for the abandonment of the Chiriqui project came from Joseph Henry, secretary of the Smithsonian Institution, who declared Chiriqui coal "as nearly worthless as any fuel can be."[19] Thus, the colonization plan that Lincoln once thought so promising was forsaken and the contract with the Chiriqui company vitiated.

Although the Chiriqui project met a premature end, a disappointed Lincoln continued to lobby for black colonization. In 1862, as part of the text of a preliminary emancipation proclamation, Lincoln warned that "the effort to colonize persons of African descent, with their consent, upon this continent or elsewhere, with the previously obtained consent of the Governments existing there, will be continued."[20] Indeed, Lincoln requested more appropriations for colonization in his second annual message to Congress on December 1, 1862. He anticipated increased response from freed blacks to leave the country for either Liberia or Haiti, "as yet, the only countries to which colonists of African descent from here could go with certainty of being received and adopted as citizens." The president continued his message by stating:

> I cannot make it better known than it already is, that I strongly favor colonization and yet I wish to say there is an objection urged against free colored persons remaining in the country, which is largely imaginary, if not sometimes malicious. It is insisted that

their presence would injure and displace white labor and white laborers. . . . Emancipation even without deportation would probably enhance the wages of white labor and very surely would not reduce them.[21]

For the first time it appears Lincoln had become sensitive to the fact that successful colonization might not be realized. He thenceforth maintained a politically pragmatic position which allowed more than one solution to the problem of freed black labor.

Before 1862 ended, however, Lincoln signed a contract to establish a colony on Vache Island, Haiti. Businessman Bernard Kock had approached the President concerning colonization on this island of the Republic of Haiti, noting how "soil and climate are adapted for all tropical production, particularly sugar, coffee, indigo, and more especially cotton, which is indigenous. Attracted by its beauty, the value of its timber, its extreme fertility and its adaptation for cultivation," continued Kock, "I prevailed on President Ceffrard of Hayti [sic] to concede to me the island." Kock agreed to furnish homes, churches, schools, doctors, and wages to five thousand black colonists at the rate of fifty dollars per person. Most important, he guaranteed their rights as free men. Before the contract could be finalized, though, Kock and the entire project was thoroughly investigated in order to avoid a situation similar to the Chiriqui fiasco. In the process it was discovered that Kock had proposed the same scheme to businessmen in Boston and New York. Evidence also pointed toward duplicity between Kock and "certain confederates to hand over slaves to him as captured runaways on the condition of receiving a price for their return."[22] Discouraged and frustrated, Lincoln promptly cancelled the Kock contract. A similar contract was then signed with New York businessman Paul S. Forbes and Charles K. Tuckerman, who had gained lease of the same island. Ironically with Kock as foreman, approximately four hundred colonists departed for Haiti in 1863 to join other black emigrants there.[23] Rather than a lush tropical garden, the colonists encountered poverty, starvation, and disease. A dismal failure, Lincoln dispatched a ship in February 1864 to "the colored colony . . . at the island of Vache . . . to bring back to this country such of the colonists there as desire to return."[24]

Thus, by 1864 all of Lincoln's attempts at black colonization had proven fruitless. Opposition from foreign countries, lack of enthusiastic support from black leaders, cancellation of contracts, and failure of the Haiti colony all spelled defeat for Lincoln's plans to establish separate black colonies. In July of 1864, Congress repealed its appropriations for colonization, and in so doing killed any future governmental sanctions for the expatriation of freed blacks. Secretary of the Interior John Palmer Usher summarized the official status of colonization after this time by reporting, "No further agreements have since been entered into, and no further efforts made, looking to the colonization of persons of African descent beyond the limits of the United States."[25] As a result, Lincoln turned to other measures to alleviate the racial problem in the war torn country.

Abraham Lincoln had embraced colonization as one means of securing racial harmony in the United States. He first advocated expatriation of freed blacks in conjunction with gradual emancipation, as political expediency dictated this approach. Lincoln realized that a solution to the problem of slave labor had to be effected, and the idea of colonization permitted him to proceed toward denouement backed by broad public support. Regarding Lincoln and colonization, one political observer wondered "whether there is [even] one who will oppose you on that score. On the other hand there are many who have great faith in it, and who if not before friendly would be apt to support you for that reason."[26] Thus, Lincoln utilized colonization as a political vehicle by which he hoped to persuade the public that the Republican Party could solve America's burning racial problem.

Beneath the surface of political expediency, Lincoln's endorsement of black deportation had both an economic and a moral basis. Although he chose to ignore the economic cost factors involved in a massive program of colonization, Lincoln justified the validity of deportation in other economic terms. Specifically, Lincoln and other northern whites feared the economic consequences of competition between a great influx of cheap black labor and white workers. Colonization was therefore an attempt to reassure white labor that their economic interests would be protected. Lincoln emphasized self-interest, then, as the economic motive far black colonization. Yet it also represented a moral answer to the present crisis. It would be to the benefit of both races, according to Lincoln, to prevent further racial assimilation by separating blacks and whites. He pragmatically evaluated racial prejudice as the permanent barrier which all freed blacks would encounter. He could not foresee racial equity for blacks within the United States but rather the reverse—so Lincoln equated racial equality with colonization outside the country. Others did the same as well, as is evidenced in the following contemporary poem:

> Ho! Children of the dusky brow!
>   Why will ye wear the chain?
> A fairer home is waiting you,
>   In isles beyond the main![27]

Lincoln saw colonization as the practical means to ensure black identity and equality while concurrently preserving the white supremacy in which he believed. Hence, Lincoln's stance on colonization was purely pragmatic—politically, economically, and morally.

In the final analysis, however, Lincoln himself contributed to the death of the colonization movement. The sixteenth president had falsely assumed that blacks would prefer to leave the country rather than remain in the United States as second-class citizens. By issuing the Emancipation Proclamation, though, Lincoln provided hope and optimism for the black freedmen in this country. By so doing he alleviated any need, urge, or desire that might have precipitated black emigration, for there now appeared to be the "opening of a new and better future for the black man in America."[28]

⁂

Forced into Gory Lincoln Revisionism: A Review of *Forced into Glory: Abraham Lincoln's White Dream*

Lucas E. Morel

Lerone Bennett, Jr. published an article in the February 1968 issue of *Ebony* magazine that asked, "Was Abe Lincoln a White Supremacist?" He answered in the affirmative. Thirty-two years later, *Ebony*'s executive editor has expanded his six-page critique into a book more than six hundred pages in length. As the new title suggests, Bennett argues that Lincoln was "forced into glory" against his personal and political wishes by "the real emancipators," black and white abolitionists (among others), to whom Bennett dedicates his book. At the heart of his revisionist appraisal of Lincoln's legacy is the claim that the Emancipation Proclamation did not free a single slave, nor was it Lincoln's intention to do so. If the "Great Emancipator" had his way, Bennett adds, he would have instigated "the racial cleansing of the United States of America."

Where to begin? Never has so much been so wrong about so important a subject. The only way to misrepresent Lincoln more would be to misspell his name. Add to this Bennett's denigration of George Washington, Thomas Jefferson, Booker T. Washington, Winston Churchill, Ronald Reagan, and conservatism generally, along with frequent references to Lincoln's endorsement of "ethnic cleansing" and a "final solution" to the race problem, and his diatribe becomes almost impossible to take seriously. The wonder of it all is that Bennett consulted not only Lincoln's own speeches and writings, but also a host of primary and secondary sources that should have cleared up much of his confusion about Lincoln's approach to slavery under the Constitution. Here, more was not better. Bennett allows Lincoln's rivals to second-guess Lincoln's own explanations for what he was attempting to do as president of a republic during a rebellion. Bennett's attempt to understand Lincoln's principles and policies regarding American slavery falters on so many fronts that we will focus on the greatest misunderstandings, especially as they pertain to the American form and practice of self-government. Although Frederick Douglass heads the list of "real emancipators" on his dedication page, Bennett quotes selectively from his

*This article originally appeared in the Fall 2000 edition of the *Claremont Review of Books*, vol. 1, no. 1 (November 2000). Reprinted with permission from the Claremont Review of Books.

"Oration in Memory of Abraham Lincoln" (1876). To portray Douglass as a tepid supporter of Lincoln, Bennett violates his own admonition against "the fallacy of the isolated quote" by highlighting only criticisms of Lincoln by the famous abolitionist speaker. Douglass does say that Lincoln "was preeminently the white man's president, entirely devoted to the welfare of white men." But Bennett omits several passages that show Douglass's more sober and deliberate assessment of Lincoln. Speaking as an escaped slave, Douglass remarks that under Lincoln's "wise and beneficent rule we saw ourselves gradually lifted from the depths of slavery to the heights of liberty and manhood." Unlike Bennett, Douglass praises the Emancipation Proclamation as "the immortal paper, which, though, special in its language, was general in its principles and effect, making slavery forever impossible in the United States."

Douglass goes on to conclude that if Lincoln "put the abolition of slavery before the salvation of the Union, he would have inevitably driven from him a powerful class of the American people and rendered resistance to rebellion impossible." Viewed from the abolitionist ranks, "Mr. Lincoln seemed tardy, cold, dull, and indifferent; but measuring him by the sentiment of his country, a sentiment he was bound as a statesman to consult, he was swift, zealous, radical, and determined."

It's as if Douglass grows in his understanding of Lincoln's statesmanship as the speech progresses. But Bennett sours from the very beginning, unable to appreciate with Douglass the great difficulty of Lincoln's task and the nobility of what he ultimately accomplished.

Bennett also dedicates his book to a couple of "radical humanitarians," John Brown and Wendell Phillips. (Bennett crosses abolitionist extraordinaire William Lloyd Garrison off his list because he became a Lincoln supporter during the 1864 election.) These so-called freedom-lovers sought to free Americans by preaching against the limitations of constitutional self-government and free elections. Bennett admits these and other abolitionists "inflame" public opinion and "create contempt" for the Constitution, but he applauds them for it because of the purity of their motives. Upon finding several of Lincoln's contemporaries complaining of his contempt for abolitionists, Bennett concludes that Lincoln did not, in today's parlance, "feel the slaves' pain." A better indication of Lincoln's personal feelings regarding the plight of American slaves, however, can be found in an 1855 letter he wrote to his best friend, Joshua F. Speed: "I confess I hate to see the poor creatures hunted down, and caught, and carried back to their stripes, and unrewarded toils; but I bite my lip and keep quiet." Lincoln also reminded Speed, a Kentucky slaveholder who professed "the abstract wrong" of slavery, of the shackled slaves they saw onboard a steamboat they rode in 1841: "That sight was a continual torment to me." Lincoln then explained that he and most Northerners "do crucify their feelings, in order to maintain their loyalty to the Constitution and the Union." Lincoln's refusal to join the abolitionist cause, therefore, derived not from callous indifference toward the slave but from principled devotion to the American regime—a form of government that would extend its protection of freedom as far as the governed would allow. As he put it to his long-time friend, "I also acknowledge your rights and my obligations, under the constitution, in regard to your slaves." Lincoln, in short, distinguished his personal sentiments from his political responsibility regarding a subject that had "the power of making me miserable."

Simply put, Lincoln's hesitation to emancipate slaves during the Civil War derived from his recognition that the American experiment in self-government was in danger. "We already have an important principle to rally and unite the people in the fact that constitutional government is at stake," he wrote. "This is a fundamental idea, going down about as deep as any thing." Lincoln was at pains to figure out how to preserve a constitutional regime from the physical force of rebellious southerners as well as the rhetorical force of rebellious abolitionist: the former were unwilling to obey a duly elected Republican administration, while the latter were unwilling to support a constitutional union of freemen and slaveholders. To act simply according to an abstract truth about the natural equality of human beings—by proclaiming the natural injustice of slavery—without acting as well in accordance with the coeval truth that government can act legitimately only by the consent of the governed would be to subvert the very form of government and law-abiding habits that make for a free society.

The Constitution vests limited powers in the three branches of the national government. This was always Lincoln's understanding, and one he reiterated at the outset of his First Inaugural Address as it pertained to slavery in the South. "I have no purpose, directly or indirectly, to interfere with the institution of slavery in the States where it exists," he said. "I believe I have no lawful right to do so." The Constitution restricted what Lincoln as president could do about "the peculiar institution," and as the most deliberate and settled will of the American people, the Constitution stood as the political lodestar for Lincoln.

Upon what authority, then, did he proclaim freedom to slaves in the South almost two years later? As the final Emancipation Proclamation states it: "by virtue of the power in me vested as Commander-in-Chief, of the Army and Navy of the United States in time of actual armed rebellion against authority and government of the United States, and as a fit and necessary war measure for suppressing said rebellion." The nation had moved from peace to war since his inauguration, which legitimated his war-making authority; in addition, Lincoln judged that the uneven progress of the war now called for eliminating the support that slavery gave to the southern war effort.

In his preliminary Emancipation Proclamation, Lincoln emphasized that his war aim had not changed: "hereafter, as heretofore, the war will be prosecuted for the object of practically restoring the constitutional relation between the United States, and each of the states, and the people thereof, in which states that relation is, or may be, suspended, or disturbed." Thus, he wanted the nation to understand his wartime emancipation proclamation not as a mere exercise of will or force on behalf of a moral objective but as a military measure in accord with his constitutional oath to uphold the laws in all the states. Lincoln gave the clearest statement of his intention as president and commander in chief regarding slavery and the war effort in response to a public letter by *New York Tribune* editor Horace Greeley. "My paramount object in this struggle is to save the union, and is not either to save or to destroy slavery," Lincoln wrote. "If I could save the Union without freeing any slave, I would do it; and if I could save it by freeing all the slaves, I would do it; and if I could save it by freeing some and leaving others alone I would also do that." Of course, he led the nation through all three scenarios by the time of his second inauguration, at which point the Thirteenth Amendment had been approved by Congress and was on the way to state ratification by year's end.

Lincoln's devotion to the constitutional union took precedence over the abolition of slavery, but in a way that set the nation back on course to ridding itself of slavery. Miss this, as Bennett does from cover to cover, and you misunderstand the Emancipation Proclamation and its connection to the Union war effort.

This priority reflected Lincoln's concern for finding legitimate ways to put down the rebellion without losing the allegiance of unionist southerners, some of whom included slaveowners who had a constitutional right to own slaves that Lincoln as president was sworn to uphold. As William C. Harris shows in *With Charity for All: Lincoln and the Restoration of the Union* (1997), "wartime reconstruction was designed to initiate the restoration of civil self-government in the South." Harris reminds us that Lincoln's expressed war aim was to quash the rebellion without "depriving Unionists of their constitutional rights" or "making it more difficult for them to cooperate in the restoration of loyal governments in the South." Lincoln's apparent hesitation to free slaves simply cannot be understood without a clear understanding of his constitutional obligations, which Bennett summarily overlooks.

Bennett also claims that Lincoln deliberately undermined the Emancipation Proclamation by its selective application: "What Lincoln did—and it was so clever that we ought to stop calling him honest Abe—was to 'free' slaves in Confederate-held territory where he couldn't free them and to leave them in slavery in Union-held territory where he could have freed them." This argument implies that what Lincoln should have done regarding slavery concerned only military might, and not constitutional right. But Lincoln omitted the so-called "border slave states" of Missouri, Kentucky, Maryland, and Delaware from the Emancipation Proclamation because they were not in rebellion against the federal government and therefore its citizens deserved the full protection of their constitutional rights.

The explicit exceptions Lincoln made of southern, slaveholding areas under Union Army control prior to January 1, 1863 (i.e., the counties constituting West Virginia and portions of Virginia and Louisiana) also fall under this category. When Secretary of the Treasury Salmon P. Chase argued for applying the Emancipation Proclamation to the exempted areas of Virginia and Louisiana, Lincoln replied he could only do so "without the argument of military necessity, and so, without any argument, except the one that I think the measure politically expedient, and morally right." He added, "Would I not give up all footing upon the constitution or law? Would I not thus be in the boundless field of absolutism?"

Lincoln shows that a president, even acting as commander in chief, must exercise authority not as a dictator—benevolent or otherwise—but within the limits set forth by the Constitution. Lincoln wanted to rid the nation of slavery, but not at the price of free government. As for the claim that the Emancipation Proclamation was a dead letter to slaves behind Confederate lines, Lincoln committed "the Executive government of the United States, including the military and naval authorities thereof," to "recognize and maintain the freedom of said persons." Slaves escaping from their rebellious masters would no longer be viewed as fugitives from justice but receive legal protection of their freedom by the national government. For Bennett, this amounts to an empty promise because the slaves were free only on paper and not in practice. But what alternative was there for slaves behind enemy lines?

As Lincoln himself admitted only nine days before his preliminary proclamation: "Would my word free the slaves, when I cannot even enforce the Constitution in the rebel states?" He therefore waited for a Union victory as a sign that as commander in chief he could back ink on paper with swords on the battlefield. (For the definitive exposition of the Emancipation Proclamation, see George Anastaplo's chapter on it in *Abraham Lincoln: A Constitutional Biography* [1999].)

Bennett chides Lincoln for promoting gradual, compensated emancipation and the colonization of freedmen as the means of achieving his dream of a "lily-white America." In this context, the preliminary Emancipation Proclamation, announced one hundred days before its implementation on January 1, 1863, was merely a ruse, Bennett asserts, to delay emancipation until Lincoln could persuade Congress to "deport" all blacks from the United States. To be sure, Lincoln favored gradual emancipation as well as colonization of blacks, but not because he was a white supremacist. Although he recognized the manifest injustice of slavery, he also believed that emancipation was always at best only half the battle. As Anastaplo observes, one then had to devise a way for former masters and former slaves to live with each other as free men.

On this question, Lincoln was neither sanguine nor alone in the recognition that slavery's demise "was piled high with difficulty." That most famous foreign observer of the American republic, Alexis de Tocqueville, wrote in *Democracy in America* (1835) that "it is impossible to foresee a time when blacks and whites will come to mingle and derive the same benefits from society." Moreover, American slavery had so poisoned each race's view of the other that if blacks continued to concentrate in the South, "sooner or later in the southern states white and blacks must come to blows." This conclusion of a disinterested commentator on the American regime makes Lincoln's support of colonization less a reflection of racism than a sober consideration of the social and political reality of his day.

Tocqueville noted, "In antiquity the most difficult thing was to change the law; in the modern world the hard thing is to alter mores, and our difficulty begins where theirs ended." If American mores were such that American democracy could not avoid this coming clash of erstwhile enemies, former white masters versus former black slaves, then Lincoln along with Henry Clay and other colonizationists may not have been the most optimist republicans. But they could hardly be faulted for attempting to prevent a regional race war that might tear the entire nation and its experiment in self-government into pieces. Bennett makes no allowance for sensible and learned men like Lincoln to believe that American blacks and whites en masse simply would not live peaceably with each other at the close of an oppressive history. The racial divide still present in America today confirms the difficulty Lincoln, Tocqueville, and others anticipated when former slave owners and former slaves, and their descendants, continued to reside in the same territory.

Bennett's exercise in exasperation over Lincoln as the Great Emancipator displays his woeful ignorance about the principles and practices of American self-government. Lacking even a rudimentary grasp of how the ideas of human equality and the consent of the governed inform the constitutional operation of the American government, it's no wonder Bennett is unable to grasp Lincoln's political prudence. Bennett concludes, "There is thus nothing we can learn from Abraham Lincoln about race relations, except what not to say or do." By reading *Forced Into Glory*, one learns nothing from Lerone Bennett about the requirements of statesmanship within a constitutional democracy. With Lincoln as his tutor instead of his target, you would think he might have learned something.

ᘐ

Towards a New Birth of Freedom

Stephen B. Oates

TODAY, BOTH IN AND OUT of the academies, it is still popular to equate Lincoln's reconstruction policy with his ten percent plan of 1863. Actually, as William B. Hesseltine demonstrated in his *Lincoln's Plan of Reconstruction* (1960), the ten percent plan was only one of several approaches Lincoln tried in the matter of reconstruction. And all in Hesseltine's judgment were failures, leaving the harried president without a plan in April, 1865.[1] More recently, Herman Belz has shown that both the president and Congress were deeply involved with reconstruction from the very out-

---

*This article originally appeared in *Lincoln Herald*, Spring 1980, published by Lincoln Memorial University (Harrogate, Tennessee). Reprinted with permission from Lincoln Memorial University.

set of the Civil War—that reconstruction was indeed the central political issue from secession to Appomattox.[2] True, reconstruction was a major problem throughout the War. And true, Lincoln embraced various stratagems to restore the rebel states. But I submit that his concern for reconstructing the South really began back in 1854, when Douglas's Kansas-Nebraska Act overturned the Missouri Compromise line, and in Lincoln's view profoundly altered the course and perhaps the structure of the Republic so far as slavery was concerned. From this point, Lincoln's approach to reconstruction evolved through three distinct phases, until in 1865 he was prepared to reform and reshape the South's shattered society.

But before I discuss the phases of Lincoln's program, I should like to examine something that gave his entire approach to reconstruction a remarkable continuity of purpose. That was a core of unshakable convictions that derived from Lincoln's vision of the meaning and mission of the American Republic. From early manhood, Lincoln had idolized the Founding Fathers and extolled them for beginning a noble experiment in popular government on these shores, to convince a skeptical Europe that a free people could govern themselves without hereditary monarchs and aristocracies. And the foundation of the American experiment was the Declaration of Independence, which in Lincoln's view proclaimed the highest political truths in history: that all men are created equal and are entitled to liberty and the pursuit of happiness. This meant that men like him were not chained to the condition of their births, that they could better their station in life and harvest the fruits of their own talents and labor. For Lincoln, the American experiment was the way of the future for nations all over the earth. A product of the Age of Enlightenment, the American system stood as a powerful beacon for "the liberty party throughout the world."[3]

Yet the one retrograde institution that marred the American system was Negro slavery. Indeed, Lincoln thought it the only issue that had ever menaced the Union and its experiment in popular government. Personally, Lincoln hated slavery as much as any abolitionist, and he insisted that it should never have existed in this country. At the same time, Attorney Lincoln had to admit that bondage was a thoroughly entrenched institution in the Southern states and that it was protected by the Constitution and a web of national and state laws. And this created a terrible dilemma for Lincoln: a system he deeply cherished had institutionalized a thing he personally abominated. What, then, could be done? Lincoln conceded that the federal government had no legal authority in peacetime to molest a state institution like slavery. And yet it should not remain in what he considered "the noblest political system the world ever saw." Caught in an impossible predicament, Lincoln convinced himself that the Founding Fathers had also hated slavery. He persuaded himself that they had tolerated bondage as a necessary evil that could not be removed where it already flourished without causing widescale destruction. But, Lincoln contended, the Fathers had intended that slavery in America should disappear someday, and they had adopted measures (had prohibited slavery in the old Northwest Territories, had outlawed the international slave trade) to hem bondage into the narrowest possible limits and so to place the institution on the course of ultimate extinction. And the task of Lincoln's generation was to keep the Republic steadily on the course charted by the Founders, guiding America toward that great and distant day when slavery would finally perish and the nation would be righted at last with her own ideals.[4] It was this vision—this sense of America's historic mission in the progress of human liberty—that shaped Lincoln's approach to reconstruction from 1854 to the end of his life.

Phase one of Lincoln's reconstruction policy, lasting from 1854 to 1862, was a reaction to what he deemed a monstrous Southern plot to nationalize slavery. In his eyes, the conspiracy began when the Kansas-Nebraska Act opened the vast Northern area of the old Louisiana Purchase country to a proslavery invasion. The next step was the *Dred Scott* decision, whose net effect was to legalize bondage in all federal territories from Canada to Mexico. At the same time, proslavery theorists were out to undermine the Declaration of Independence, to discredit its equality doctrine as "a self-evident lie," and to replace the Declaration with the principles of inequality and human servitude. The next stage in the conspiracy, Lincoln feared, would be to nationalize slavery: the pro-Southern Supreme Court would hand down another decision, one declaring that states could not prohibit slavery either. Then the institution would sweep across the free North, until at last slavery would be nationalized and America would end up a slave house. At that, as George Fitzhugh advocated (and Lincoln had been reading Fitzhugh), the conspirators would enslave all American workers—white as well as black. The Northern free-labor system would be vanquished, the Declaration overthrown, self-government abolished. The world's best hope—America's experiment in popular government—would be expunged, and mankind would spin backward into feudalism.[5]

For Lincoln, the Union had reached a monumental crisis in its history. And that crisis shook him to his foundations. Now slavery was not going to perish some day as the Fathers had planned. Now an aggressive slave power and its Northern allies had revolted against the Founders and inaugurated an insidious "new design" that placed slavery on the high road to expansion and perpetuity and that imperiled the very existence of popular government. To block the conspiracy, Lincoln and his Republican colleagues formulated a policy that would restore the old Union as it was—as they thought the Fathers had framed it—and that would again place slavery on the road to its ultimate doom. By excluding slavery from the territories through federal law, the Republicans would contain the peculiar institution in the Southern states and there leave it alone as a necessary evil. Confined to the South, slavery would eventually die out, Lincoln believed, and the Republic would be freed of a monstrous moral wrong that sullied its global image, that cheated the United States of the hope it should hold out to oppressed people everywhere.

In this phase, then, Lincoln envisioned a peaceful reconstruction of Southern society within the Union. He assumed that when slavery was no longer workable, Southern whites would voluntarily free their own Negroes, voluntarily transform their own way of life. And he hoped that it would all occur so gradually "that neither races nor individuals should have suffered by the change." To solve the ensuing problem of racial adjustment, Lincoln would have all black people sent back to Africa. Once the danger of slavery were removed, the future of the Republic ensured, and a lost people returned to their homeland, it would indeed, Lincoln said, "be a glorious consummation."[6]

When the Civil War began, Lincoln strove to be consistent with all he and his party had said about slavery and the South: his purpose in the struggle was to save the Union—and with it America's cherished experiment in popular government. His armies would subdue the rebellion with swift and decisive victories and restore the national authority in the rebel South with slavery intact. Then Lincoln and his party could resume and implement their policy of slave containment, once again placing the peculiar institution on the course of ultimate extinction.

But as the war ground on with no end in sight, Lincoln modified his approach to reconstruction and entered a second phase concerning the slave-based South. This new phase came in no small part from the proddings of Charles Sumner and several of his Republican congressional associates, who called repeatedly at the White House and exhorted Lincoln to emancipate the slaves. After all, they told the President, the Southern people were in rebellion against the national government and no longer enjoyed the protection of its Constitution and its laws. They contended that the federal government could now eradicate slavery by the War Power, and they wanted Lincoln to do it in his capacity as commander in chief in time of war. If he freed the slaves, it would maim and cripple the Confederacy and hasten an end to the rebellion. Most persuasive of all, they argued that slavery had caused the war, was the reason why the Southern states had seceded, and was now the cornerstone of the Confederacy. It was preposterous, they asserted, to fight a war without removing the thing that had brought it about. Should Lincoln restore the South with slavery preserved, Southerners would start another war over the peculiar institution, whenever they thought it threatened, so that the current struggle would have accomplished nothing at all. If Lincoln really wanted to save the Union and its experiment in popular government, he must uproot slavery and annihilate the South's arrogant master class—the very class Sumner and his colleagues believed had orchestrated secession and fomented war. The destruction of slavery, George W. Julian declared, was no longer "a debatable and distant alternative, but a pressing and absolute necessity."[7]

By early 1862, Lincoln agreed that something had to be done about slavery during the war. But still regarding a presidential decree as "too big a lick," Lincoln searched about for an alternative—something short of federally enforced emancipation and all the wreckage that would surely cause.[8] In March, 1862, he proposed a plan to Congress that marked a new approach to reconstruction, one that would reform the slave South through federal-state cooperation. This was the chimerical scheme that called on the loyal slave states to abolish bondage voluntarily over the next thirty years, with the federal government to compensate slaveowners for their loss and to colonize emancipated blacks abroad. If his gradual, voluntary, state-guided plan were adopted, Lincoln contended that a presidential edict—federally enforced emancipation—would never be necessary. With Lincoln acting only in an advisory capacity, abolition would begin on the local level in the loyal border states and then be extended into the rebel states as they were conquered. Thus by a slow and salubrious process would the cause of the war be removed and the future of a free Union guaranteed.[9]

At the same time, Lincoln addressed himself to another reconstruction problem: how to build loyal state regimes in captured rebel territory? Earlier he had relied on pro-Union elements within a state to create loyal governments, only to find that Unionist sentiment in the Confederacy was too impotent for such a policy to work. Now, in the spring and summer of 1862, the president installed military governors in occupied Tennessee, North Carolina, Louisiana, and Arkansas, instructing them to restore those states to their former places in the Union. As in his plan of state-guided emancipation, Lincoln sought merely to advise his military governors and not interfere directly in their efforts to establish loyal state regimes. But even so, as Professor Belz has observed, Lincoln's use of military governors was "a radical extension of federal authority into the internal affairs of the states"—and a harbinger of what was to come in the president's evolving reconstruction policy.[10]

Phase two of that policy proved an unmitigated failure. For one thing, the military governors foundered in their attempts to harmonize conflicting Unionist sentiment and woo back disaffected rebels. For another, the loyal slave states emphatically rejected Lincoln's gradual, compensated emancipation program, forcing on him the painful realization that slaveowners—even loyal slaveowners—were too entrenched in their system ever to free their own Negroes and voluntarily reform their way of life. If abolition must come, it must begin in the rebel South by military action and be extended into the loyal border later on. Which meant that the president must remove slavery himself, that he must take a direct presidential hand in reconstructing the rebel South.[11]

When Lincoln issued his Emancipation Proclamation of January 1, 1863, he embarked on a third phase of reconstruction: now he aimed to smash the very foundation of the rebel South with his armies. His proclamation, in fact, was a declaration of war against slavery as a state institution there. In his capacity as Commander-in-Chief of the armed forces in time of war, Lincoln would use the military to free all slaves in the rebellious states—those of loyalists and rebels alike. Thus he went further than anything Congress had done about slavery, and he justified his action as a military necessity to save the Union—the world's last, best hope for popular government.[12]

Lincoln's proclamation was the most revolutionary measure ever to come from an American President up to that time. As Union armies slashed into Confederate territory, they would destroy slavery as an institution, automatically liberating all slaves in the areas and states they conquered. Until the details of permanent legal freedom could be worked out, Lincoln ordered his armies to guarantee and protect the liberty of emancipated blacks. Thus (as Lincoln said) the war brought on changes more fundamental and profound than either side had expected when the conflict began. Now slavery would perish as the Confederacy perished, would die by degrees with every Union advance, every Union victory. By November 1864, estimated the *Philadelphia North American*, more than 1,300,000 Negroes had been freed by Lincoln's proclamation or "the events of the war."[13]

As Lincoln assumed control of emancipation, he also took direct charge of restoring conquered rebel states to their "proper practical relation with the Union." On December 8, 1863, in his Proclamation of Amnesty and Reconstruction, Lincoln promulgated his celebrated ten percent plan for constructing loyal, slaveless state regimes in occupied Dixie. Far from being a lenient plan as many have claimed, Lincoln's proclamation made emancipation the very basis of reconstruction, thus placing him again on the side of Sumner and the so-called radicals and moderates of his party (conservative Republicans and Democrats wanted to restore the rebel South with slavery preserved). By Lincoln's plan, Southerners who qualified for a pardon must not only swear "henceforth" to support the Union, but vow to obey and support all presidential proclamations and congressional laws against slavery. They must do this before they could even begin the process of reconstruction. Moreover, Lincoln would employ the army to oversee the task of building free-state governments in the occupied South, designating generals there as the "masters" of reconstruction."[14]

Lincoln also offered a solution to one of the most perplexing difficulties of Southern restoration: "how to keep the rebellious populations from overwhelming and outvoting the loyal minority," as he put it, and returning the old Southern ruling class to power. For now, the president's solution was to protect the loyal minority with the army, offer a fair oath that separated "the opposing elements, so as to build only from the sound," and follow a realistic procedure—thus his ten percent equation—that he hoped would expedite reconstruction and weaken the Confederacy.[15] As for the old Southern ruling class, Lincoln agreed with Sumner that it should be eradicated, and his emancipation and reconstruction policy was calculated to do just that. Emancipation, after all, would obliterate the very institution on which the Southern master class depended for its existence. Furthermore, Lincoln's Proclamation of Amnesty and Reconstruction denied political rights to virtually all rebellious Southern leaders, thus excluding them from participating in his reconstruction governments. It is true that the president let disqualified individuals apply to him for clemency. But in his message to Congress in December 1864, Lincoln warned that the time might come—probably would come—when "public duty" would force him to "close the door" on all pardons and adopt "more rigorous measures." At all events, Lincoln had no intention of allowing prewar Southern leaders—a class he had once castigated as slave-dealers in politics—to regain power in postwar Dixie.[16]

Apart from eliminating slavery and the Southern ruling class, Lincoln made it clear that he would be flexible in reconstructing the rebel South, that the ten percent plan was only one formula and that he would gladly consider others. As he set about restoring Louisiana and Arkansas by the ten percent plan, he indicated that his approach as to the mode of reconstruction would be empirical: what plan he adopted for other conquered areas would depend on the circumstances and exigencies of each place and moment. The ten percent plan above all was a war-time measure, designed to create loyal governments in occupied areas brimming with hostile Confederate sympathizers.

As Lincoln's proclamation made clear, he regarded reconstruction as chiefly an executive responsibility. But though he and Congress were to clash over this, Lincoln acknowledged that Capitol Hill had a powerful voice in reconstruction, since both houses would decide whether to accept representatives from the states he restored. Aside from jurisdictional disputes, though, Lincoln and most congressional Republicans—including the so-called radicals agreed on a number of crucial issues. Both agreed that the South must be remade. Both meant to abolish slavery there forever, and they cooperated closely in guiding the present Thirteenth Amendment through Congress. Both were concerned with the welfare of the freedmen; and both intended for Southern Unionists to rule in postwar Dixie. Above all, both wanted to prevent ex-Confederate leaders from taking over the postwar South and forming a coalition with Northern Democrats that might imperil the gains of the war. Lincoln and his congressional associates often differed on how to implement their goals, as evidenced by the Wade-Davis bill. And they disagreed, too, on the issue of Negro political rights, as I shall discuss in a moment. But even so, the president and congressional Republicans retained a close and mutually respectful relationship, so much so that many contemporaries—Julian, Isaac Arnold, and Hugh McCulloch among them—thought they would remain as united in working out reconstruction problems as they had in prosecuting the War.[17]

Inevitably bound up in any program of emancipation and reconstruction was the nagging problem of racial adjustment, of what to do with the Negroes Lincoln liberated. By 1863, with former slaves now fighting in his armies, the president abandoned colonization as a solution to the race problem. His resettlement schemes had all foundered, and in any case black people adamantly refused to join in Lincoln's voluntary program. As a consequence, he concluded that whites and emancipated Negroes must somehow learn to live together in the South. After he issued the Emancipation Proclamation, Lincoln never again urged colonization in public. And there is no reliable evidence that he ever supported it in private either. True, in his 1892 autobiography, Benjamin F. Butler claimed that in April, 1865, Lincoln feared a race war in the South and still wanted to ship the blacks abroad.[18] But historians must beware of Butler's claims. Not only is he a highly dubious witness, but there is not a scintilla of corroborative evidence for the position he attributed to Lincoln, not a single other source that quotes the president, in public or in private, as stating that he still favored colonization. In any case, such a stance would seem glaringly inconsistent with Lincoln's Gettysburg Address, which called for a new birth of freedom in America for blacks and whites alike . . . and inconsistent, too, with Lincoln's appreciation of the indispensable role his black soldiers played in subduing the rebellion. No man of Lincoln's honesty and sense of fair play would enlist some 186,000 black troops to save the Union and then advocate throwing them out of the country.

In place of colonization, the Lincoln administration devised a refugee system, installed by the army in the occupied South, which utilized blacks there in a variety of military and civilian pursuits. For a time in 1863, the president vacillated as to whether the freed people should work for wages by contract, or whether they should first labor for whites as temporary apprentices. On several occasions he said he had no objection if white authorities assumed control of former slaves "as a laboring, landless, and homeless class" and adopted some temporary arrangement by which the two races in Dixie "could gradually live themselves out of their old relation to each other, and both come out better prepared for the new."[19] But with congressional Republicans steadfastly opposed to any such arrangement, Lincoln dropped the apprenticeship idea and ordered those involved in the refugee system to employ contract labor for southern blacks, so that they could become self-supportive. And he happily approved when his ten percent government in Louisiana rejected apprenticeship and granted economic independence to Louisiana Negroes. In this respect, Lincoln doubtlessly expected the Louisiana constitution to serve as a model for other rehabilitated states.[20]

While there were many faults with Lincoln's refugee system, it was based on sound Republican dogma: it kept Southern blacks out of the North, and it secured them jobs as wage earners on captured farms and plantations. The system thus helped Southern Negroes to help themselves and prepared them for life in a free society in postwar Dixie.[21]

When it came to Negro suffrage, Lincoln displayed the same capacity for growth and change that had characterized his approach to emancipation. Before the war, with Douglas race-baiting him all over Illinois, Lincoln had publicly rejected black political rights. It was either that or forget about political office in his white-supremacist state. But by 1864, with emancipation a central war objective and Negroes serving in his armed forces, Lincoln privately endorsed limited suffrage for Louisiana blacks. He wrote Governor Michael Hahn that he wished "the very intelligent" Negroes and especially those "who have fought gallantly in our ranks" could be enfranchised.[22] Yet Lincoln would not force Negro suffrage on Louisiana, certainly not in a presidential election year, because he knew what a combustible issue Negro suffrage was in both the North and the South. What is more, he feared that mandatory Negro suffrage would alienate white Unionists in Louisiana and ruin all his reconstruction efforts there.

Nevertheless, when the Louisiana constitutional convention refused to give black men the vote, Lincoln helped persuade the lawmakers to reconsider their decision and forge a compromise: while the Louisiana constitution did not enfranchise Negroes, it did empower the legislature to do so. At the same time, the constitution not only outlawed slavery (as Lincoln insisted it must), but opened the courts to all persons regardless of color and established free public education for both races.[23] For his part, Lincoln accepted this as the best that could be done in Louisiana, and he commented—with a touch of irony—that Louisiana's new constitution was "better for the poor black man than we have in Illinois." Maybe Louisiana's all-white government was imperfect, but Lincoln thought it better than no government at all. And though he wished it had provided limited Negro suffrage, he believed this could be accomplished faster "by saving the already advanced steps toward it, than by running backward over them." The Louisiana government, in short, was a foundation to build on for the future—for blacks as well as whites.[24]

Contrary to what some scholars have claimed, Lincoln's interest in Negro suffrage was not restricted to Louisiana, with its relatively well-educated and outspoken black community in New Orleans. Over the winter of 1864–1865, in fact, Lincoln approved limited Negro suffrage for all other rebel states as well. This was a part of a compromise he made with Sumner, James Ashley, B. Gratz Brown, and a few other congressional Republicans, who demanded universal male suffrage for Southern blacks so that they could protect their liberty. But the compromise fell apart because most congressional Republicans regarded even limited Negro suffrage as too radical.[25] Thus, in the matter of black political rights, Lincoln was ahead of most members of his party—and far ahead of the vast majority of Northern whites at that time.

So far, Lincoln had supported limited Negro suffrage only in his correspondence and private negotiations. But in his last speech, on April 11, 1865, the president publicly endorsed enfranchising intelligent Southern blacks and especially those who had served in the Union military. In fact, he went farther than that. In a telling line toward the end of his address, Lincoln granted straight out that the black man deserved the elective franchise. Though he was still not ready to make that mandatory, it seems clear in what direction Lincoln was evolving. And that was toward full political rights for the Negro, not away from them. Certainly Secretary of War Edwin M. Stanton and other contemporaries thought the president now appreciated the need for Southern blacks to vote and thus to protect themselves from their former masters. On the last day of Lincoln's life, Attorney General James Speed told Salmon Chase, a champion of universal Negro suffrage, that the President "never seemed so near our views."[26]

By war's end, Lincoln seemed on the verge of a new phase of reconstruction, a tougher phase that would call for some form of Negro suffrage, more stringent voting qualifications for ex-Confederates (as hinted at in his 1864 message to Congress), and perhaps an army of occupation for the postwar South. At his last Cabinet meeting, Lincoln and his Secretaries unanimously agreed that such an army might be necessary, not just to maintain order and stability in a war-torn land, but to safeguard Negro freedom and protect the Unionist minority on whom Lincoln's entire reconstruction program depended.[27] In other words, the president was already considering in 1865 what Congress would later adopt in the days of "Radical Reconstruction." Perhaps a new and tougher program was what Lincoln had in mind in the closing line of his last speech: "It may be my duty to make some new announcement to the people of the South. I am considering, and shall not fail to act, when satisfied that action will be proper."[28]

He never got the chance to make an announcement. But given his position on reconstruction at war's end, it seems absurd to argue (as David Donald has done) that Lincoln was growing increasingly lenient toward conquered ex-Confederates, or to contend (as Carl Sandburg and many others have contended) that the president was ready to restore the defeated South with tender magnanimity.[29] Lincoln would be magnanimous in the sense that he would not resort to mass jailings and executions of Southern insurrectionaries. And he bore them no malice, since he had come to see the war as a divine punishment for the crime of slavery, as a terrible retribution God had visited on a guilty people, in North and South. But there can be no doubt that Lincoln desired to bring the South into the mainstream of American republicanism, to install a free-labor system there for blacks as well as whites, to establish public schools for both races, to look after the welfare of the freedmen, to grant them access to the ballot and the courts—in short, to build a new South dedicated to the ideals of the Declaration of Independence. "Let us strive on to finish the work we are in," Lincoln proclaimed in his Second Inaugural; "to bind up the nation's wounds" and "do all which may achieve and cherish a just, and a lasting peace, among ourselves, and with all nations." In sum, let a reunited America, liberated from the haunting contradiction of slavery in a country based on the Declaration, dedicate itself anew to the dreams of the Founding Fathers. Let Americans North and South strive to fulfill their great and noble mission—to ensure that government of, by, and for all the people would not perish from the earth.

$\sim$

Notes to Chapter 3

Only His Stepchildren

1. Benjamin P. Thomas, *Abraham Lincoln, a Biography* (New York, 1952); Stephen B. Oates, *With Malice Toward None: The Life of Abrahan Lincoln* (New York, 1977).

2. See text, 153–56.

3. Richard Henry Stoddard, *Abraham Lincoln: An Horatian Ode,* cited in Roy P. Basler, *The Lincoln Legend: A Study in Changing Conceptions* (Boston, 1935), 234.

4. Basler, *The Lincoln Legend,* 264–65.

5. David Donald, *Lincoln's Herndon* (New York, 1948), 305; Richard N. Current, *The Lincoln Nobody Knows* (New York, 1963), 11–13.

6. John T. Morse, Jr., *Abraham Lincoln* (2 vols.; Boston, 1893), 2: 356.

7. See Chapter 15 for development of this theme.

8. David Donald, *Lincoln Reconsidered* (2nd ed.; New York, 1969), 16.

9. Michael Davis, *The Image of Lincoln in the South* (Knoxville, Tenn., 1971), 159.

10. Davis, *Image of Lincoln*, 138.

11. Jefferson Davis, *The Rise and Fall of the Confederate Government* (2 vols.; New York, 1881), 2: 683.

12. Thomas Dixon, Jr., *The Clansman: An Historical Romance of the Ku Klux Klan* (New York, 1905), 47; Davis, *Image of Lincoln*, 147–52.

13. Leon F. Litwack, *North of Slavery: The Negro in the Free States, 1790–1860* (Chicago, 1961), 276.

14. Fawn M. Brodie, "Who Defends the Abolitionist?" in Martin Duberman, ed., *The Antislavery Vanguard: New Essays on the Abolitionists* (Princeton, N.J., 1965), 63–64.

15. Current, *Lincoln Nobody Knows*, 236.

16. Howard Zinn, "Abolitionists, Freedom-Riders, and the Tactics of Agitation," in *Duberman, Antislavery Vanguard*, 438–39.

17. Martin Duberman, "The Northern Response to Slavery," in *Anti-slavery Vanguard*, 396, 402.

18. Lerone Bennett, Jr., "Was Abe Lincoln a White Supremacist?" *Ebony*, 23 (February 1968): 37.

19. Bennett, "Lincoln a White Supremacist?" 37–38, 40.

20. Richard Claxton Gregory, *No More Lies: The Myth and the Reality of American History* (New York, 1971), 182.

21. Bennett, "Lincoln a White Supremacist?" 36.

22. Davis, *Image of Lincoln*, p. 156 "There is something sadly ironic in seeing black extremists and Ku Kluxers clasping hands over the grave of the Great Emancipator's reputation."

23. Robert Penn Warren, *Who Speaks for the Negro?* (New York, 1965), 262.

24. Roy P. Basler, Marion Dolores Pratt, and Lloyd A. Dunlap, eds., *The Collected Works of Abraham Lincoln* (9 vols.; New Brunswick, N.J., 1953–55), 3: 145–46.

25. Arthur Zilversmit, ed., *Lincoln on Black and White* (Belmont, Calif., 1971).

26. See Michael Banton, "The Concept of Racism," in Sami Zubaida, ed., *Race and Racialism* (London, 1970), 17–34.

27. David M. Reimers, ed., *Racism in the United States: An American Dilemma?* (New York, 1972), 5.

28. Banton, "Concept of Racism," 18.

29. Forrest G. Wood, *Black Scare: The Racist Response to Emancipation and Reconstruction* (Berkeley, Calif., 1970), 15.

30. George M. Fredrickson, *The Black Image in the White Mind: The Debate on Afro-American Character and Destiny, 1817–1914* (New York, 1971), 2.

31. Margaret Nicholson, *A Dictionary of American-English Usage* (New York, 1958), 469.

32. Fredrickson, *Black Image*, 101.

33. Bennett, "Lincoln a White Supremacist?" 36.

34. Benjamin Quarles, *Lincoln and the Negro* (New York, 1962), 16–18.

35. Basler et al., *Collected Works*, I: 260.

36. George M. Fredrickson, "A Man But Not a Brother: Abraham Lincoln and Racial Equality," *Journal of Southern History*, 41 (1975): 44.

37. George Sinkler, *The Racial Attitudes of American Presidents from Abraham Lincoln to Theodore Roosevelt* (Garden City, N.Y., 1971), 75.

38. Fredrickson, "A Man But Not a Brother," 58.

39. See Banton, "Concept of Racism," 22–24, for the "inductivist explanation of racism," which, he says, "is chiefly found in the writings of American sociologists. They are acquainted with racism in its modern forms and work backwards, viewing earlier statements about race from a modern standpoint instead of setting them in the intellectual context of the time in which they were made."

40. For example, although he carefully qualifies his stated conclusions, this is the effect of Eugene H. Berwanger's *The Frontier Against Slavery: Western Anti-Negro Prejudice and the Slavery Extension Controversy* (Urbana, Ill., 1967).

41. See Larry Gara, "Slavery and the Slave Power: A Crucial Distinction," *Civil War History*, 15 (1969): 5–18.

42. "Our republican robe is soiled, and trailed in the dust," said Lincoln in 1854. In the same speech, he called slavery a "monstrous injustice," and then added, "I hate it because it deprives our republican example of its just influence in the world." Basler et al., *Collected Works*, 2: 255, 276. Ditherman, "Northern Response to Slavery," 399–401, points to nationalism as one reason for opposition to abolitionism; but it should also be emphasized that national pride fortified the antislavery movement.

43. Basler et al., *Collected Works*, 3: 9–10, 29, 80, 95, 112–13, 146, 216, 280, 300–304, 470.

44. Basler et al., *Collected Works*, 2: 255–56.

45. Basler et al., *Collected Works*, 2: 391.

46. Basler et al., *Collected Works*, 2: 405, 408; 3: 16, 88, 249.

47. Basler et al., *Collected Works*, 3: 399.

48. The principal exceptions are the Peoria speech of Oct. 16, 1854, and the statement to the delegation of Negroes on Aug. 4, 1862.

49. Fredrickson, "A Man But Not a Brother," 40–44. But for an argument belittling Clay's influence on Lincoln, see Marvin R. Cain, "Lincoln's Views on Slavery and the Negro: A Suggestion," *Historian*, 26 (1964): 502–20.

50. Basler et al., *Collected Works*, 3: 16; 4: 156; 5: 372–73.

51. Allen Thorndike Rice, ed., *Reminiscences of Abraham Lincoln by Distinguished Men of His Time* (New York, 1886), 193.

52. James G. Randall and Richard N. Current, *Lincoln the President: Last Full Measure* (New York, 1955), 317–18.

53. Quarles, *Lincoln and the Negro*, p. 204.

54. See especially his comment on a statement by Chief Justice Roger B. Taney implying that the Negro's status had improved since the framing of the Constitution, Basler et al., *Collected Works*, 2: 403–4.

55. See the discussion of factors discouraging abolitionism in Duberman, "Northern Response to Slavery," 398–401.

56. Lord Charnwood, *Abraham Lincoln* (New York, 1916), p. 452.

57. Julius Lester, *Look Out, Whitey! Black Power's Gon' Get Your Mama!* (New York, 1968), 8.

58. For a good statement of Lincoln's strategy, see Hans L. Trefousse, *The Radical Republicans, Lincoln's Vanguard for Racial Justice* (New York, 1969), 182.

59. Basler et al., *Collected Works*, 5: 388–89.

60. Thomas, *Abraham Lincoln*, 342. For further discussion of the Greeley letter, see text, 283–84.

61. Speech at Cooper Institute, Feb. 1863, quoted in Zilversmit, *Lincoln on Black and White*, 133.

62. Basler et al., *Collected Works*, 5: 372.

63. Quarles, *Lincoln and the Negro*, 108–23, 191–94.

64. Basler et al., *Collected Works*, 2: 255.

65. Benjamin F. Butler, *Butler's Book* (Boston, 1892), 903–8. The credibility of Butler's statement has been pretty well destroyed by Mark E. Neely, Jr., in his "Abraham Lincoln and Black Colonization: Benjamin Butler's Spurious Testimony," *Civil War History*, 25 (1979): 76–83.

66. Eric Foner, *Free Soil, Free Labor, Free Men: The Ideology of the Republican Party Before the Civil War* (New York, 1970), 271. See also Harry V. Jaffa, *Crisis of the House Divided: An Interpretation of the Issues in the Lincoln-Douglas Debates* (Garden City, N.Y., 1959), 61.

67. Basler et al., *Collected Works*, 534–35. See also Lincoln's letter to John A. Andrew, Feb. 18, 1864, in ibid., 7: 191. Lincoln's argument bears some resemblance to the doctrine of "diffusion," which Southerners had used earlier in the century to justify the expansion of slavery.

68. See William B. Hesseltine, *Lincoln's Plan of Reconstruction* (Tuscaloosa, Ala., 1960); Ludwell H. Johnson, "Lincoln and Equal Rights: The Authenticity of the Wadsworth Letter," *Journal of Southern History*, 32 (1966): 83–87; Harold M. Hyman, "Lincoln and Equal Rights for Negroes: The Irrelevancy of the 'Wadsworth Letter,'" *Civil War History*, 12 (1966): 258–66; Ludwell H. Johnson, "Lincoln and Equal Rights: A Reply," *Civil War History*, 13 (1967): 66–73; Herman Belz, *Reconstructing the Union: Theory and Policy During the Civil War* (Ithaca, N.Y., 1969); Peyton McCrary, *Abraham Lincoln and Reconstruction: The Louisiana Experiment* (Princeton, N.J., 1978); Stephen B. Oates, "Toward a New Birth of Freedom: Abraham Lincoln and Reconstruction, 1854–1865," *Lincoln Herald*, 82 (1980): 287–96; LaWanda Cox, *Lincoln and Black Freedom, a Study in Presidential Leadership* (Columbia, S.C., 1981). See also text, 153–56, 171–72.

69. *The Works of Charles Sumner* (15 vols.; Boston, 1870–83), 6: 152.

70. Basler et al., *Collected Works*, 3: 146.

71. *Life and Times of Frederick Douglass, Written by Himself* (New York, 1962, reprint of 1892 edition), 485.

In Isles Beyond the Main

1. Temple Scott (ed.), *The Wisdom of Abraham Lincoln* (New York, 1918), 52

2. John C. Miller, *The Wolf by the Ears: Thomas Jefferson and Slavery* (New York, 1977), 264–272. For general information of the colonization movement see Early L. Fox, *The American Colonization Society, 1817–1840* (Baltimore, 1919) and P. J. Staudenraus, *The African Colonization Movement, 1816–1865* (New York, 1961).

3. Roy P. Basler, et al. (eds.), *The Collected Works of Abraham Lincoln* (9 vols., New Brunswick, 1953–1955), Volume II, 132. (Hereafter cited as *Collected Works*, II, 132).

4. Basler, *Collected Works*. For a general introduction to Lincoln and black colonization see James G. Randall, *Lincoln the President* (4 vols., New York, 1945–1955), II, 137–141; Benjamin P. Thomas, *Abraham Lincoln* (New York, 1952), 362–363; Stephen B. Oates, *With Malice Toward None: The Life of Abraham Lincoln* (New York, 1977), 325–370. See also the following

articles: Charles H. Wesley, "Lincoln's Plan for Colonizing Emancipated Negroes," *Journal of Negro History* IV (January 1919), 7–21; N. A. N. Cleven, "Some Plans for Colonizing Liberated Negro Slaves in Hispanic America," *Journal of Negro History* XI (January 1926), 35–49; Warren A. Beck, "Lincoln and Negro Colonization," *Abraham Lincoln Quarterly* VI (September 1950), 162–183; Walter A. Payne, "Lincoln's Caribbean Colonization Plan," *Pacific Historian* VII (May 1963), 65–72; George R. Planck, "Abraham Lincoln and Black Colonization: Theory and Practice," *Lincoln Herald* LXXII (Summer 1970), 61–77; and G. S. Boritt, "The Voyage to the Colony of Lincolnia: The Sixteenth President, Black Colonization, and the Defense Mechanism of Avoidance," *The Historian* XXXVII (August 1975), 619–633.

5. *Collected Works*, II, 255–256. See also George Sinkler, *The Racial Attitudes of American Presidents from Abraham Lincoln to Theodore Roosevelt* (Garden City, 1972), 48–56.

6. *Collected Works*, II, 409. See also Benjamin Quarles, *Lincoln and the Negro* (New York, 1962), 108–123.

7. Abraham Lincoln to Simon Cameron, December (?) 1861 as quoted in Beck, "Lincoln and Negro Colonization," 167–169. See also Paul J. Scheips, "Lincoln and the Chiriqui Colonization Project," *Journal of Negro History* XXXVIII (October 1952): 418–453.

8. *Collected Works*, V, 48.

9. 37th Congress, 2nd Session, *Public Laws of the United States* (Boston, 1861–1862), XII, 378. See also Quarles, *Lincoln and the Negro*, 109.

10. *Collected Works*, V, 192. See also Arthur Zilversmit, *Lincoln on Black and White: A Documentary History* (Belmont, 1971), 84.

11. Second Confiscation Act, July 17, 1862 in *Congressional Globe*, 37th Congress, 2nd Session, Appendix (1862), 413.

12. Quarles, *Lincoln and the Negro*, 109–110.

13. One noted historian has described this occasion as the first meeting between a United States president and a group of blacks on a "matter of public interest." See Quarles, *Lincoln and the Negro*, 115.

14. *Collected Works*, V, 370–375. See also Zilversmit, *Lincoln on Black and White*, 95–99; and James M. McPherson, *The Negro's Civil War* (New York, 1965), 91–92.

15. *Collected Works*, V, 370–375. Lincoln was referring to the Isthmus of Chiriqui.

16. Proximity was important for two reasons. First, the majority of freed blacks did not wish to leave the western hemisphere. Second, there would be greater opportunity for the United States to exercise influence over a neighboring country with American colonists.

17. Scheips, "Lincoln and the Chiriqui Colonization Project," 431–438.

18. Beck, "Lincoln and Negro Colonization," 181.

19. Beck, "Lincoln and Negro Colonization," 181.

20. *Collected Works*, V, 434.

21. *Collected Works*, V, 520.

22. Wesley, "Lincoln's Plan for Colonizing Emancipated Negroes," 17–18.

23. Kock has apparently pre-arranged for this position with Forbes and Tuckerman. See Elmo R. Richardson and Alan W. Farley, *John Palmer Usher: Lincoln's Secretary of the Interior* (Lawrence, 1960), 46–47. James Redpath, a "white British born radical," and reporter for the *New York Tribune* had previously organized the emigration of about one thousand free blacks to Haiti in 1861–1862 that resulted in total failure. For more information on that colonization movement see McPherson, *The Negro's Civil War*, 78–89; and Willis D. Boyd, "James Red-

path and American Negro Colonization in Haiti, 1860–1862," *The Americas* XII (October 1955), 169–182.

24. *Collected Works*, VII, 164. See also Frederic Bancroft, "Schemes to Colonize Negroes in Central America," and "The Ile a Vache Experiment in Colonization," in Jacob E. Cooke (ed.), *Frederic Bancroft, Historian* (Norman, 1957), 212, 231.

25. *Collected Works*, VII, 417. See also Robert H. Zoellner, "Negro Colonization: The Climate of Opinion Surrounding Lincoln, 1860–1865," *Mid-America* XLII (July 1960), 141–145; and Brainerd Dyer, "The Persistence of the Ideas of Negro Colonization," *Pacific Historical Review* XII (March 1943), 53–66.

26. V. Jacque Voegeli, *Free But Not Equal: The Midwest and the Negro During the Civil War* (Chicago, 1967), 45.

27. McPherson, *The Negro's Civil War*, 81.

28. McPherson, *The Negro's Civil War*, 97.

Towards a New Birth of Freedom

1. William B. Hesseltine, *Lincoln's Plan of Reconstruction* (Tuscaloosa, Ala., 1960). Though informative, Hesseltine's study is marred, among other things, by the author's unbridled hostility toward the so-called radical Republicans. "Violent and vituperative," he writes, they suffered from a "hate-psychosis" toward the South that paralyzed their powers of reason (11, 92).

2. Herman Belz, *Reconstructing the Union: Theory and Policy During the Civil War* (Ithaca, N.Y., 1969), 1–13 and passim.

3. Abraham Lincoln, *Collected Works* (ed. by Roy G. Basler and others, 9 vols., New Brunswick, N.J., 1953–1955), II, 276.

4. Lincoln, *Collected Works*, 230–283, 288, 390–410, 461–469, 484–501, 537–538, and III, 38ff, 522–550.

5. In numerous speeches and fragments between 1854 and 1860, Lincoln elaborated on what he considered a proslavery plot to expand and nationalize human bondage. But see especially Lincoln, *Collected Works*, II, 247–283, 398–410, 461–469, and III, 53–54, 204–205, 548–549. For a trenchant analysis of Lincoln's "House Divided" speech and the proslavery conspiracy outlined there, see Don E. Fehrenbacher, *Prelude to Greatness: Lincoln in the 1850's* (Stanford, Cal. 1962), 70–95.

6. Lincoln, *Collected Works*, II, 127–132. Of course, other Republicans also expatiated on the Founding Fathers and slavery, on the seeming plot to nationalize the institution, and on the need for slave containment, and Lincoln learned much from them. See Eric Foner, *Free Soil, Free Labor, Free Men: The Ideology of the Republican Party Before the Civil War* (New York, 1970), 73–102, 301–317; and Stephen B. Oates, *With Malice Toward None: The Life of Abraham Lincoln* (New York, 1977), 113ff.

7. George W. Julian, *Political Recollections, 1840–1872* (Chicago, 1884), 240; Hans L. Trefousse, *The Radical Republicans: Lincoln's Vanguard for Racial Justice* (New York, 1969), 203–205, 210, and Trefousse, *Benjamin Franklin Wade, Radical Republican from Ohio* (New York, 1963), 181, 187; David Donald, *Charles Sumner and the Rights of Man* (New York, 1970), 17, 27, 29–30, 46, 48; Horace White, *The Life of Lyman Trumbull* (Boston and New York, 1913), 171; Patrick W. Riddleberger, George W. Julian, *Radical Republican* (Indianapolis, 1966), 153,

165–166; Edward Magdol, *Owen Lovejoy, Abolitionist in Congress* (New Brunswick, N.J., 1967), 299–302; Detroit *Post and Tribune, Zachariah Chandler* (Detroit, 1880), 253.

8. See Lincoln, *Collected Works*, V, 29–31, 489; Orville Browning, *Diary* (ed. by Theodore Calvin Pease and James G. Randall, 2 vols., Springfield, Ill., 1927, 1933), I, 512: Charles Sumner, *Works* (15 vols., Boston, 1870–1883), VI, 152; Edward Everett Hale, *Memories of a Hundred Years* (2 vols., New York, 1902), II, 191; Donald, *Sumner and the Rights of Man*, 50, 60.

9. Lincoln, *Collected Works*, V. 145–146, 153, 317–319, 531, and VII, 282; John G. Nicolay Memorandum, March 9, 1862, John G. Nicolay Papers, Library of Congress.

10. Belz, *Reconstructing the Union*, 291–292; Hesseltine, *Lincoln's Plan of Reconstruction*, 48ff.

11. Lincoln, *Collected Works*, VII, 281–282; Gidoon Welles, "Emancipation," *Galaxy* (December, 1872), 842–843; Welles, *Diary* (ed. by John T. Morse, Jr., 3 vols., Boston, 1911), I, 70–71.

12. Lincoln, *Collected Works*, V, 336–337, 433–436, and VI, 28–30. For a discussion of the differences between Lincoln's proclamation and the second confiscation act, see Oates, *With Malice Toward None*, 309–310. In the final proclamation, Lincoln temporarily exempted occupied Tennessee and certain occupied places in Louisiana and Virginia. But later, in reconstructing those areas, Lincoln withdrew the exemptions and made emancipation a mandatory part of his reconstruction program. See not only Lincoln's Message to Congress and Proclamation of Amnesty and Reconstruction, December 8, 1863, *Collected Works*, VII, 51, 54, but also the president's correspondence with Andrew Johnson, Edward H. East, and Nathaniel Banks in Lincoln, *Collected Works*, VI, 364–365, 440–41, and VII, 1–2, 149–150, and 209. Lincoln also excluded the loyal border states from his emancipation proclamation, because they were not in rebellion and he lacked the legal authority to remove slavery there. But he kept pressing them to abolish slavery (Maryland and Missouri finally did so) and later pushed for a constitutional amendment that permanently outlawed slavery in loyal and rebellious states alike.

13. Lincoln, *Collected Works*, VII, 281–282, and VIII, 332–333; Charles Sumner, *Complete Works* (20 vols., reprint of 1900 ed., New York, 1961), IX, 199–200, 247; *Philadelphia North American* as cited in Carl Sandburg, *Abraham Lincoln, the War Years* (4 vols., New York, 1939), IV, 3. See also Don E. Fehrenbacher, "Only His Stepchildren: Lincoln and the Negro," *Civil War History*, II (December, 1974), 306–307.

14. Lincoln, *Collected Works*, VII, 51, 54, 89–90, VIII, 106–107, also VI, 358; Belz, *Reconstructing the Union*, 147, 162–163, and Herman Belz, *A New Birth of Freedom: The Republican Party and Freedmen's Rights, 1861–1866* (Westport, Conn., 1976) 42; Harold M. Hyman, *A More Perfect Union: The Impact of the Civil War and Reconstruction on the Constitution* (paperback ed., Boston, 1975), 264–266.

15. Tyler Dennett (ed.,), *Lincoln and the Civil War in the Diaries and Letters of John Hay* (reprint ed., Westport, Conn. 1972), 113; Lincoln, *Collected Works*, VII, 51.

16. Lincoln's reference to the Southern ruling class as an "odious and detested" bunch of slavedealers is in Lincoln, *Collected Works*, II, 322.

17. See Trefousse, *Radical Republicans*, 286–304; Belz, *Reconstructing the Union*, 309–310; Donald, *Charles Sumner and the Rights of Man*, 207–208; and Hyman, *A More Perfect Union*, 276–281.

18. Benjamin F. Butler, *Autobiography and Personal Reminiscences of Major-General Benj. F. Butler: Butler's Book* (Boston, 1892), 903. I agree with Trefousse and Fehrenbacher that

Butler's testimony is dubious at best. On the other hand, Belz, George M. Fredrickson, and Ludwell H. Johnson all accept Butler's claims as true. But their arguments based on Butler simply cannot be substantiated by corroborative evidence. In addition, Butler's statements about Lincoln and colonization contradict the president's evolving race and reconstruction policies, as I try to demonstrate in this essay. See Belz, *Reconstructing the Union*, 282; Fredrickson, "A Man But Not A Brother: Abraham Lincoln and Racial Equality," *Journal of Southern History*, XLI (February, 1975), 56–58; and Johnson, "Lincoln and Equal Rights: A Reply," *Civil War History*, XIII (March, 1967), 68.

19. Lincoln, *Collected Works*, VI, 49, 365, and VII, 55. Lincoln warned, however, that he would not tolerate abuses of Southern blacks and that white authorities must recognize their permanent freedom and provide for their education.

20. Lincoln, *Collected Works*, VII, 145, 217–218, VIII, 20, 30–31, 107–402.

21. For a discussion of the system, see V. Jacque Voegeli, *Free But Not Equal: The Midwest and the Negro During the Civil War* (Chicago, 1967), 95–112; Dudley Taylor Cornish, *The Sable Arm: Negro Troops in the Union Army, 1861–1865* (paperback ed., New York, 1966), 112–131; Bill I. Wiley, *Southern Negroes, 1861–1865* (Baton Rouge, 1938), 199–259; Benjamin Quarles, *Lincoln and the Negro* (New York, 1962), 188–190; John D. Winters, *The Civil War in Louisiana* (Baton Rouge, 1963), 394–395.

22. Lincoln, *Collected Works*, VII, 243.

23. Quarles, *Lincoln and the Negro*, 224–230.

24. Lincoln, *Collected Works*, VIII, 107, 404. For a full and trenchant account of reconstruction in Louisiana, see Peyton McCrary, *Abraham Lincoln and Reconstruction: the Louisiana Experiment* (Princeton, N.J., 1978).

25. See Belz, *Reconstructing the Union*, 258–262, 290–291. Donald, *Sumner and the Rights of Man*, 196–197, gives a somewhat different version of the compromise.

26. Lincoln, *Collected Works*, VIII, 403–404; Benjamin P. Thomas and Harold M. Hyman, *Stanton: The Life and Times of Lincoln's Secretary of War* (New York, 1962), 355; Salmon Chase, *Inside Lincoln's Cabinet: The Civil War Diaries of Salmon P. Chase* (ed. by David Donald, New York and London, 1954), 268; McCrary, *Lincoln and Reconstruction*, 304.

27. Thomas and Hyman, *Stanton*, 357–358, 358n; Oates, *With Malice Toward None*, 427–428, 473, Hesseltine, Belz, and others have argued that in April, 1865, Lincoln considered a new approach to reconstruction, that he hoped to work through existing rebel legislatures to effect civil reorganization. There is no convincing evidence to support this. True, on April 6, 1865, Lincoln issued an order tentatively authorizing those who "have acted as the legislature of Virginia" to assemble in Richmond and help disband Virginia troops. And true, Welles in his diary quotes Lincoln as saying vaguely that he wanted influential rebel leaders "to come together" so as "to undo their own work" and help restore civilian rule. But Lincoln himself, in rescinding his order after Lee's surrender, emphatically denied that he had desired any such thing. He had never meant, he said, to let the Virginia legislature convene as a legal body, with the power to settle all differences with the Union. All he had intended was for individuals of that body to gather in Richmond and demobilize Virginia troops. See Welles, *Diary*, II, 279–280, and Lincoln, *Collected Works*, VIII, 389, 406–407.

28. Lincoln, *Collected Works*, VIII, 405.

29. See David Donald, *The Politics of Reconstruction, 1863–1865* (Baton Rouge, 1965), 18.

Chapter 4

LINCOLN'S DEMOCRATIC POLITICAL LEADERSHIP: UTOPIAN, PRAGMATIC, OR PRUDENT?

Was Lincoln a utopian, a secular messiah, a Machiavellian, or a prudent statesman?

Our government rests in public opinion. Whoever can change public opinion, can change the government, practically just so much. Public opinion, on any subject, always has a *"central idea,"* from which all its minor thoughts radiate. That "central idea" in our political public opinion, at the beginning was, and until recently has continued to be, "the equality of men." And although it was always submitted patiently to whatever of inequality there seemed to be as matter of actual necessity, its constant working has been a steady progress towards the practical equality of all men.

Abraham Lincoln, Speech at a Republican Banquet, Chicago, IL, December 10, 1856

★ T. Harry Williams, "Abraham Lincoln: Principle and Pragmatism in Politics"
★ Ethan Fishman, "On Professor Donald's Lincoln"
★ Ralph Lerner, "Lincoln's Revolution"
★ Stephen B. Oates, "Abraham Lincoln: Republican in the White House"
★ Colleen Shogan and Robert Raffety, "A Political Source of Greatness: Lincoln and the Republican Party"

⟨ornament⟩

ABRAHAM LINCOLN: PRINCIPLE AND PRAGMATISM IN POLITICS

T. Harry Williams

LINCOLN WOULD NOT have been able to comprehend the attempts of modern writers to classify his ideas into an ideology. Indeed, he would not have known what an ideology was. Although he believed deeply in certain principles which might be called his philosophy of politics, those principles were at the opposite pole of what is termed ideology today. If Lincoln were confronted by a group like the professional thinkers of the New Deal with their doctrinaire tendencies, he would have been amazed and amused. At the same time he would have considered them dangerous, as he believed the abolitionists of his own time were dangerous, because they had a logical plan based on a preconceived abstract theory about human nature or society and because they proposed to put their plan into effect regardless of consequences. To the "ideologues" of the New Deal or to those of other contemporary groups, Lincoln would have seemed theoretically backward, which is the way the abolitionists considered him. Lincoln distrusted deep theoretical thinkers and their slick assurance that they knew what the world needed. He was too conscious of the realities in every situation to be an ideologue. One of the keys to his thinking is his statement that few things in this world were wholly good or wholly evil. Consequently the position he took on specific political issues was always a pragmatic one. His personal or inner opinions were based on principle; his public or outer opinions were tempered by empiricism. As somebody has remarked, Lincoln was not the kind of man who is ready to do what God would do if God had all the facts.

There were four fundamental principles in Lincoln's thought. These principles were the common beliefs of most Americans in the middle period of our history. Lincoln, who was not a primary thinker, did not originate any of them. He found them already in existence; he thought about them; he extended the interpretation of them; and he spoke of them in words that men could remember and quote. The first principle was a conviction that a guiding providence or some supernatural force largely directed the affairs of men. A corollary to this belief was that God had created a moral law for the government of men and that men should seek to approximate human law to the Divine law. The second principle was a concept of human nature. The men of Lincoln's time believed that man had a higher nature. He possessed a mind and a conscience, and consequently he was capable of governing himself

*This article originally appeared in *Mississippi Valley Historical Review*, Vol. 40, 1953, published by the Organization of American Historians. Reprinted with permission from the Organization of American Historians.

through democratic government. He could also achieve a more and more perfect society. The third principle dealt with the economic activities of man and the relationship of those activities to the general welfare. The economic thought of the men of the middle period was capitalistic. They believed in an economic system in which most people would own property and in which all had equal opportunities to acquire it. The way to property must be open to all; no group should enjoy special privileges which gave it an artificial advantage over others. The fourth principle was an exaltation of the idea of the American Union. In the United States man would create a society that would be the best and the happiest in the world. The United States was the supreme demonstration of democracy. But the Union did not exist just to make men free in America. It had an even greater mission—to make them free everywhere. By the mere force of its example America would bring democracy to an undemocratic world.

Lincoln subscribed to every one of these four articles of belief, and during the course of his political career he gave expression to all of them. They stand out all over the pages of the *Collected Works*, both in his letters and his speeches. The notion that a guiding providence largely directed the activities of men was basic with Lincoln. Even in his early years, when he inclined to be critical of organized religion, he felt that some supernatural force, which he sometimes referred to as history, controlled men. As he grew older, he came to call this force God. There can be no doubt that as Lincoln matured he became increasingly mystic and religious. His sense of fatalism, both personal and public, was at its fullest in the crisis of the Civil War. The great event which history associates with his name, the destruction of slavery, was, he believed, an act of Divine power of which he was but the instrument. In a letter to a Kentucky friend in 1864 he discussed the impact of the war upon slavery. The nation's condition after three years of war, he said, was not what either party or any man "devised or expected" in 1861. No one had then thought that as a result of war slavery would be destroyed; yet now it was approaching the point of extinction. "God alone can claim it," he said. "Whither it is tending seems plain. If God now wills the removal of a great wrong, and wills also that we of the North as well as you of the South, shall pay fairly for our complicity in that wrong, impartial history will find therein new cause to attest and revere the justice and goodness of God." He returned to this theme in the Second Inaugural when he said that the war was God's way of removing the evil of slavery as a punishment to the North and the South for having condoned it. He knew that some people would object to this mechanistic interpretation of history. "Men are not flattered by being shown that there has been a difference between the Almighty and them," he remarked. "To deny it, however, in this case, is to deny that there is a God governing the world."

Lincoln also accepted the corollary to the principle of a guiding providence, the existence of a supernatural law which human law should seek to approximate. His state papers are filled with references to this concept. In the First Inaugural he said: "I hold, that in contemplation of universal law, and of the Constitution, the Union of these States is perpetual." Without being a document worshipper, Lincoln revered the two great documents which the men of his time revered, the Declaration of Independence and the Constitution. He believed they were animated with the spirit of Divine law, and he respected them because they had been proved good by the test of experience. The American federal system, he believed, embodied the best experience of man in government. Lincoln faced up to the central problem of government when he asked, with his own government in mind: "Must a government, of necessity, be too strong for the liberties of its own people, or too weak to maintain its own existence?" He answered the question in his description of the working of the principle of majority rule under the Constitution: "A majority, held in restraint by constitutional checks, and limitations, and always changing easily, with deliberate changes of popular opinions and sentiments, is the only true sovereign of a free people. Whoever rejects it, does of necessity, fly to anarchy or to despotism." Lincoln sensed that the great merit of the American system was in the balance it established between the government and the individual and between the nation and the states. Carl Sandburg has said that Lincoln understood the mystery of democracy because he had a sort of occult sense of the necessary balance in a democracy between freedom and responsibility.

Lincoln's belief in the principle that man possessed a higher nature and was competent to govern himself is implicit in almost everything he wrote. Surprisingly enough he made few specific references to the goodness or the wisdom of the people. Obviously he took this proposition so much for granted that he thought it did not need frequent stating. Nevertheless, on occasion Lincoln did state notably his belief in the ability of the people to exercise the art of government; certainly he acted on this belief in his political activities. Nowhere in the *Collected Works* is there any evidence that Lincoln feared the tyranny of numbers or the reign of the mob. "Why should there not be a patient confidence in the ultimate justice of the people?" he asked in the First Inaugural. "Is there any better, or equal hope, in the world?" Lincoln believed that the American political system so operated as constantly to increase the political wisdom of men because it had been founded on the principle of equal rights for all. Some governments had been based on the denial of equal rights because it was believed some men were too ignorant to share in government; ours began by affirming those rights. The difference was fundamental, Lincoln said. "We proposed to give all a chance, and we expected the weak to grow stronger, the ignorant wiser; and all better, and happier together." The promise of American life had been fulfilled, he thought.

Lincoln's economic views have been labeled by later students as both liberal and conservative. Probably most academic writers have classified him as a liberal, because he said human rights were above property rights and because he spoke friendly words about labor. Apparently one of the assumptions of the academicians is that a conservative puts property above people. Another school, more to the left than the first group and proceeding on another assumption, have concluded that Lincoln was a conservative or, at best, a confused liberal. They have believed that modern industrial capitalism, which developed in and after the Civil War, has been exploitative, illiberal, and possibly antidemocratic. Because Lincoln said that men, given equality of opportunity, could rise in the economic scale by working hard and because he justified economic individualism, they have written him down as a kind of economic simpleton who did not understand the economic trends of his time or as a folksy front for the robber barons of business, who talked liberal and acted, knowingly or not, conservative.

Actually Lincoln's economic thought cannot be called either liberal or conservative in the contemporary sense of the words. He belongs to no party or ideology today and certainly not to the New Deal. His ideas about economics were peculiarly a product of the economic system in which he lived and have little application to the present system. In the system that Lincoln knew, an extraordinarily large number of people owned property, in the form of farms, plantations, factories, shops, and operated their property to make a living. In simple terms, this was a capitalistic system in which most of the people were capitalists. Unlike the present system, relatively few people worked for other people in return for wages or salaries. Big business, in the shape that came after the Civil War, did not exist. This was the preindustrial age in which many owners of property were also laborers.

Lincoln's ideas about economics were those of the average man of his time, which means they were the ideas of a small capitalist. He desired a system in which all men would have an equal opportunity to acquire property; equal opportunity would mean a system in which most men would own property. Lincoln respected and admired labor because labor was necessary to create and secure capital. By labor a man could become an owner, an employer, as Lincoln himself had become one. Lincoln's tributes to labor, often misunderstood and misapplied today, were not delivered to labor as a rival power to capital but to labor as a means of creating capital. He always denied that American society was divided into two classes, employers and workers, or that in America there was a permanent class of hired laborers. The majority of men, he said, neither worked for others nor hired others to work for them. Most men worked for themselves, most were both capitalists and laborers. "What is the true condition of the labored?" he asked in a speech at New Haven in 1860 in which he gave full expression to his economic philosophy. "I take it that it is best for all to leave each man free to acquire property as fast as he can. Some will get wealthy. I don't believe in a law to prevent a man from getting rich; it would do more harm than good. . . . When one starts poor, as most do in the race of life, free society is such that he knows he can better his condition; he knows that there is no fixed condition of labor, for his whole life." It is because of statements like this, apparently glorifying unbridled individualism, and because his economic vision of America was an optimistic one that some writers have concluded Lincoln was a conservative or economically naive. These critics have been oppressed with the predatory quality of capitalism in the period between 1865–1900. Perhaps they would change their opinion if, as Frederick Lewis Allen has recently suggested in *The Big Change*, they would look beyond 1900.

Of all the principles which Lincoln held to, the one that stirred him most deeply was the exaltation of the American Union and the mission of America to bring democracy to the world. This concept provoked his most eloquent passages; to it he made in words and action his most original contribution as a political thinker. Three ideas are apparent in Lincoln's thinking about the Union. One, he believed that the nation was an organic whole, an entity that could never be artificially separated. As he said to the South in the First Inaugural: "Physically speaking, we cannot separate. We cannot remove our respective sections from each other, nor build an impassable wall between them." The "mystic chords of memory" might snap, but the physical realities of the oneness of the nation would still exist. In his message to Congress in December 1862, one of his best but least known state papers, he gave a moving description of the United States as a physical entity dominated by the great interior heartland. Feelingly he referred to the nation as "our national homestead." Our national strife, he said, does not spring from any sectional division of the country or from a natural line between the North and the South, but from ourselves, "the passing generations of men." The national homestead, he said, "in all its adaptations and aptitudes . . . demands union, and abhors separation." Second, Lincoln believed that the strongest bond binding the Union was the idea of equal opportunity for all, embedded in the Declaration of Independence and the structure of the government and permeating the minds of the people. And this made America uniquely different from all other nations, whose bonds of unity were culture, tradition, or race. On his way to Washington in 1861 to become the president of a divided nation, Lincoln made a brief address at Independence Hall in Philadelphia. Deeply moved by the historical associations of his surroundings, he uttered a classic expression of the meaning of America's great idea: "I have often inquired of myself, what great principle or idea it was that kept this Confederacy so long together. It was not the mere matter of separation from the motherland, but that sentiment in the Declaration of Independence which gave liberty not alone to the people of this country, but hope to the world for all future time. It was that which gave promise that in due time the weights would be lifted from the shoulders of all men, and that all should have an equal chance." Third, he regarded the Union with a sacred reverence because it made men free in America and eventually would make them free everywhere. Lincoln's finest and most frequent references to the mission of America were made, of course, in the Civil War, when the world's greatest demonstration in democracy was threatened with division. The "great republic . . . the principles it lives by, and keeps alive" represented "man's vast future." In the concluding paragraph of his message to Congress in December 1862, one of the best things he ever wrote, he said: "We shall nobly save, or meanly lose, the last, best hope of earth." Because the Union was the great guardian of the idea of equal opportunity, Lincoln was always ready to sacrifice anything to preserve it. For if the Union was destroyed the idea it represented was also destroyed. And that idea was too precious to be lost.

The great specific issue to which Lincoln applied the four principles of his philosophy was slavery. All of the principles, in varying degree, influenced his position in regard to the institution. He defined his views at an early date and never modified them in any essential way. He was opposed to slavery. He was opposed to it on moral, democratic, and economic grounds. He believed that slavery and the aristocratic philosophy of its advocates threatened to subvert the idea of equal opportunity. He thought that a vigorous and expanding slavery gave the lie to the American ideal of democracy and weakened the influence of America as the supreme example of successful democracy upon the rest of the world. He shivered to pieces in one sentence the whole pretentious proslavery argument when he said: "although volume upon volume is written to prove slavery a very good thing, we never hear of the man who wishes to take the good of it, by being a slave himself."

Yet Lincoln also opposed the abolitionists, before 1860, and plans of emancipation aimed at the South. His views were eminently practical and pragmatic. To him it was tremendously important that slavery existed and was believed in by millions of people. The presence of slavery, the physical presence, was a fact that must be considered by the opponents of slavery. "Because we think it wrong, we propose a course of policy that shall deal with it as a wrong," he said. It should be dealt with as any other wrong: it should be prevented from growing (by expanding into the territories) and placed in a state of ultimate extinction. But, he added, "We have a due regard to the actual presence of it amongst us and the difficulties of getting rid of it in any satisfactory way and all the constitutional obligations thrown about it." Lincoln voiced no criticism of the southern people for supporting slavery. "They are just what we would be in their situation," he observed in a speech in 1854. "If slavery did not now exist amongst them, they would not introduce it. If it did now exist amongst us, we should not instantly give it up." In this 1854 speech Lincoln admitted, as he did on other occasions, that he did not know any absolutely satisfactory way of dealing with slavery. If all earthly power were given him, he said, he would not know what to do. His first impulse would be to free all the slaves and send them to Liberia, but he realized this was impractical. What of freeing the slaves and making them the equals of the whites? The mass of the white people would not concede this, and hence immediate emancipation was impossible. Whether the feelings of the whites were just or sound was no part of the question, Lincoln said, because "A universal feeling, whether well or ill-founded, can not be safely disregarded."

Lincoln disliked the abolitionists, those nineteenth-century ideologues who were certain they had an absolutely satisfactory way of dealing with slavery and who if they could not have their way, were willing to break up the Union. He disliked their fanatical assumption that they were doing God's work, their readiness to impose their inner opinions upon society, and their eagerness to ram abolition down southern throats. He distrusted their abstract impracticality and their refusal to consider the complex problems involved in sudden emancipation. Above all, he was disturbed by their lack of feeling for the Union, their willingness to destroy it if they could not reform it. To him the preservation of the Union and the idea it stood for was infinitely more precious than the immediate striking down of slavery. "Much as I hate slavery," he said, "I would consent to the extension of it rather than to see the Union dissolved, just as I would consent to any great evil, to avoid a greater one."

Lincoln's opposition to the abolitionists, his entire position on the slavery issue, was in the best American pragmatic tradition. He was opposed to abolition because it would disrupt the Union, because it was not sound in the light of national experience or the realities of the moment. He was convinced that if slavery was penned up in the South and not permitted to expand it would eventually die a natural death. He wanted to make a needed change, right a wrong, but at the right time; while he was waiting he wanted to keep the machine of the Union running. He was against destroying the machine or getting a new one or adding a new part at the wrong time. The coming of the Civil War, the result of many men in the North and the South insisting that they were going to impose their inner opinions on other people, ended Lincoln's hopes for a kind of patient emancipation.

Some writers have criticized Lincoln's qualities as war leader of the North because he opposed the wartime destruction of slavery. According to this view, Lincoln, because he tried to check the antislavery impulses generated by the war, opposed a logical social revolution, the nature of which he did not understand. So many people, from Salmon P. Chase to contemporary authors, have thought that Lincoln was simple! Actually Lincoln understood clearly the dynamics in the war situation. He was well aware that slavery was the provoking cause of the war. It was, he said, "the disturbing element" in the national house; it would always stimulate national strife until it was removed. Lincoln dealt with slavery during the war in the same pragmatic spirit with which he had treated it before. To Lincoln the preservation of the Union was the paramount object of the war. The Union dwarfed all other issues, including slavery. He intended to save the Union at any cost and by whatever methods seemed most likely to succeed. This war was important, he believed. It was for keeps, it went all the way. It was a war to preserve democratic government in America and to preserve the democratic ideal in the world, "a people's contest" to maintain "in the world, that form and substance of government, whose leading object is, to elevate the condition of men." It was also a war "to teach that there can be no successful appeal from a fair election but to the next election."

Lincoln proposed that the restoration of the Union should be the sole objective of the war for two reasons. One was that in the opening days of the struggle he sought to rally all parties and factions in the North to support the war. This necessitated a statement of war aims so broad and national that men of every shade of opinion could unite behind them. Lincoln supplied the formula with his war for the Union alone policy. His second reason was that he did not desire to make emancipation one of the results of the war. He did not want to see slavery destroyed suddenly and angrily in the fury of civil conflict, to see the war become, as he told Congress, "a violent and remorseless revolutionary struggle." To destroy slavery as a part of the war process would, he feared, so derange race relations as to bring more evil than good.

Lincoln finally did adopt an antislavery policy; he did make emancipation a second aim of the war. He changed his position when he decided that the new situation created by the war had altered the status of slavery and that a new policy was demanded. Pragmatic as always, he issued the Emancipation Proclamation in the light of the nation's war experience—but his motive for issuing it was to save a fundamental principle, the American Union. The very facts of the war, the sacrifice and the bloodshed, inevitably made the northern people more and more hostile to slavery. The longer the war continued the more hostile they became. By the middle of 1862 it was abundantly evident that they wanted slavery destroyed as a result of the war. Lincoln then faced this problem: if he opposed the popular will—if he insisted on preserving the Union with slavery intact—he would divide Northern opinion and defeat his larger objective of saving the Union. Now, if he wanted to keep the machine running, he had to make a change, add a new part; if he did not, the machine would break down. Put another way, Lincoln's problem about slavery in the war was reversed from what it had been before. Then he had fought abolition because it would destroy the Union. Now he had to champion it to save the Union. He opposed an unneeded and unwise change and supported a necessary and sound one. In both cases he was completely moral.

It is easy to pick out shortcomings in Lincoln's philosophy, as well as contradictions and errors. The same thing can be done to the other great American political leaders. Jefferson, Jackson, Lincoln, the two Roosevelts were not doctrinaire, systematic thinkers. Sometimes they were governed in their actions by a wise expediency, and often when confronted by demands for change they improvised. For this they have been scorned by the abstract thinkers of their own time and those of later ages. It would also be possible to point out mistakes and faults in the *Collected Works*. But it would be wrong to cavil in either case. What we deal with in both is too vast for malice.

ॐ

On Professor Donald's Lincoln

Ethan Fishman

FOR THE LAST HALF CENTURY, David Herbert Donald has developed a reputation as one of the preeminent Abraham Lincoln scholars.[1] Among Professor Donald's

---

*This article originally appeared in *Tempered Strength*, published by Rowman & Littlefield Publishers, Inc. Reprinted with permission from Rowman & Littlefield Publishers, Inc.

most often quoted observations about Lincoln, contained in the essay "A. Lincoln, Politician," is that his fame as a statesman was "made possible by his accomplishments as a politician. Perhaps it is too cynical to say that a statesman is a politician who succeeds in getting himself elected."[2] To Donald, moreover, Lincoln's political prowess can be traced back to his "extraordinary frank pragmatism—some might call it opportunism."[3] While Donald does not explore these issues in great depth, he thus seems to imply that the ability to be a power broker represents the main attribute of a statesman and that statesmen are above all pragmatists. For a more highly developed and much different perspective on the meaning of statesmanship and its relation to political power and pragmatism, it is necessary to return to the third century B.C. and consult the political philosophy of Aristotle.

Twenty-four hundred years ago Aristotle taught that statesmen are leaders who possess the virtue of *phronesis* or prudence, the unique ability to reconcile universal moral principles with every day practical politics.[4] The model statesman for Aristotle is Pericles, the great Athenian lawgiver.[5] Among the occasions that Pericles demonstrated the prudent quality of his leadership was during the Peloponnesian War in 429 B.C. when Athens was besieged by Sparta. Against the masses who panicked in the face of the siege, Pericles urged solidarity and caution. Against the majority who desired to counterattack against the full strength of the Spartan invaders, Pericles proposed that they rely on their navy and concentrate on defense of the city. Against those Athenians who wished to use the war as a means to expand their empire, Pericles advised restraint.

Pericles, Aristotle observes, displayed the qualities that define prudential leadership: the desire to articulate and support noble standards that serve the public interest by calling upon societies to treat all citizens with fairness, decency, and justice; the competence to delineate a particular society's public interest by envisioning its present needs in light of both its past successes and failures and future hopes and fears; the talent to translate the leaders' vision into reforms capable of dealing effectively with existing social, economic, and political issues; and the skill to devise methods to overcome obstacles to their proposed reforms by convincing others to accept them.

Aristotle explains the rationale for his theory of statesmanship based upon *phronesis* in Book VI of his *Nicomachean Ethics*. There he distinguishes between the theoretical and practical forms of reason and the intellectual and moral virtues or talents that each form of reason employs. Theoretical reason and the intellectual virtues, he argues, apply to such subjects as metaphysics and mathematics that are learned in abstract for their own sake and yield universal truths that humans cannot alter. Practical reason and the moral virtues, on the other hand, apply to subjects such as ethics and politics that yield truths which hold true in only a majority of cases and involve knowledge of the noblest human motives for the sake of noble action. The task of *phronesis,* which Aristotle considers to be the architectonic moral virtue, is to take the first principles discovered by the intellect and integrate them with constantly changing life experiences.

By facilitating the process by which abstract ends are realized through concrete means, Aristotle writes, *phronesis* enables political leaders to do the right thing to the right person at the right time "for the right motive and in the right way."[6] According to Aristotle, political leaders who strive to meet the standards of statesmanship are required to do their very best to create laws and policies that attempt to prevent the subversion of moral principles even under the direst circumstances. They must aim high but accept less when their efforts inevitably fall short of the mark. They must never give up hope for a better world even as they respect the stumbling blocks to such hope. They are required, in other words, to expect neither too much nor too little from the politics they practice.

For these reasons the statesmen Aristotle describes are neither cultural relativists nor ideologues. Since his theory of statesmanship as prudential leadership posits the existence of universal moral principles, it repudiates claims made by relativists that all values are culturally biased. Since the function of prudence is to reconcile transitory political issues with transcendent political standards, moreover, it rejects ideological thinking for advancing one doctrinaire solution such as socialism, capitalism, or feminism to every problem regardless of the circumstances. From the perspective of Aristotelian political theory, indeed, relativists, who discount forever, and ideologues, who neglect today, appear to have engineered simplified, one-dimensional versions of politics based on reductionist views of reality and human nature.

What further differentiates statesmen from cultural relativists and ideologues is their emphasis on the immutable and the transcendent, but not to the exclusion of the imminent and the transitory. Statesmen thus accent forever but still pay close attention to today. They look first to the universal but are not blind to particulars. They stress the forest but do not neglect the trees. They view human behavior with a compassion that does not preclude toughness. And they are not prepared to excuse human pettiness even as they understand that it constitutes an inescapable part of the political process.

The methods statesmen can utilize to best serve the public interest of a given society at any given time are clarified by Aristotle's discussion of plutocratic regimes in Book V of his *Politics*. He is unable to justify rule of the rich because he realizes that the ability to govern well is not directly related to the acquisition of material possessions. He nevertheless recognizes that knowledge of plutocracy's inherent unreasonableness alone is inadequate to reform well-established plutocratic states. He thus develops a strategy, exploiting the greed underlying all plutocracies, to convince plutocrats that the preservation of their rule requires them to share power with those poorer citizens who, unlike themselves, possess genuine leadership capabilities. In this fashion Aristotle combines his theory of good government, that citizens should perform tasks for which they are best suited, with the practice of unjust regimes and mediates the political realities of selfishness and incompetence with his values of justice and reason.

A common misconception about statesmanship as a function of *phronesis* is that it represents a type of cunning. Cunning implies great skill in discovering the most efficient way to achieve an end whose morality is never seriously questioned. Even Nazi SS men can be cunning. Prudent political leaders, however, cannot divorce themselves from moral principles. They must dedicate themselves to serve the public interest and are required to choose means that are commensurate with that goal. On the other hand, Aristotle does not prohibit statesmen from having recourse to cunning schemes and ploys as long as their use abides by scrupulous guidelines. At Aristotle's insistence they must serve just ends, must be a means of last resort, and leaders must never become smug or complacent about employing them.

Nor is statesmanship characterized by an exact middle-of-the-road compromise mentality. It is true that, when political leaders act prudently, they are able to reconcile variable concrete circumstances with immutable abstract principles. Aristotle also teaches that the goal of *phronesis* is to steer a moderate course between unreasonable laws and policies. Nevertheless, the reconciliations for which prudent leaders strive are created for the express purpose of serving a higher end, namely the public interest, not for the sake of compromise itself. Statesmen "are willing to make compromises only because they value some things more than they do the things which they are compromising," John Hallowell reminds us. "When a society no longer values common interests above personal interests the society disintegrates, compromise is no longer possible and politics ceases."[7] Moreover, Aristotle warns that attempts by leaders to compromise by pinpointing the exact location of the mean will always be futile because, as a practical form of reason, politics is incapable of such precision.[8] "We must not think of the mean as being a fixed point between the extremes," Walter Lippmann observes. "The true mean is at the tension of push and pull, of attraction and resistance among the extremes."[9]

Aristotle, furthermore, upholds personal moral character as a *sine qua non* for statesmanship. Human beings, he argues, cannot provide prudent political leadership, that is, virtuous leadership, unless they are virtuous themselves. "Virtuous actions are not done in a virtuous—a just or temperate—way merely because *they* have the appropriate quality," he writes. "The *doer* must be in a certain frame of mind when he does them."[10] Since Aristotle is quite aware of human pride, greed, and selfishness, however, he cannot require statesmen to be wholly without sin— only that they honestly strive to act with as much common decency as possible. The standard of virtue by which he evaluates leaders applies to lifetime behavior patterns, not to isolated acts of human weakness that may have been performed while in or out of office.

On this point, indeed, Aristotle is adamant: it is possible to be personally virtuous and fail as a political leader, he insists, but impossible to succeed at political leadership without the type of personal virtue to which people become habituated over the course of their lives. According to Aristotle:

> If a man possesses the two qualifications of capacity and loyalty to the constitution, is
> there any need for him to have the third qualification of goodness, and will not the

first two, by themselves, secure the public interest? We may answer this question by asking another: May not men who possess these first two qualifications be unable to command their passions? and is it not true that men who have no command of their passions will fail to serve their own interest—even though they possess self-knowledge and self-loyalty—and will equally fail to serve the public interest (even though they possess a knowledge of public affairs and public loyalty)?[11]

In sum, Aristotle teaches that authentic statesmen consider abstract moral principles to be necessary but insufficient for politics. Political leaders informed by the virtue of *phronesis* judge abstract values to be necessary because they provide infallible standards of justice towards which fallible human beings who tend to be unjust can strive. Statesmen judge abstract values to be insufficient because such values are unable to adjust themselves to the constantly changing complex demands and challenges of everyday life. But this is not to say that Aristotle considers statesmanship to be a simplistic mixture of one-half moral principles and one-half material circumstances. Entertaining no illusions about the ability of human beings to undermine even the most basic standards of decency, he makes it clear that moral principles constitute the most important ingredient in his theory of prudential leadership. According to Aristotle, as imperfect creatures we must seek to achieve moral perfection through rational control of our selfish impulses if we hope to gain some measure of justice and fulfillment in our lives. "Rather ought we," he writes, "so far as in us lies, to put on immortality and to live in conformity with the highest thing within us."[12]

Herein lies the crucial distinction between what Professor Donald seems to think statesmanship entails and Aristotle's definition of the term. When Donald writes that "the secret of Lincoln's success is simple: he was an astute and dextrous operator of the political machine,"[13] he creates the image of a "politico" for whom personal ambition and the desire to gain and maintain power are at least as important as moral principles. For Aristotle, however, the desire to serve the public good takes precedence and constitutes the raison d'étre for holding office in the first place. Above all, Aristotle writes, it was Pericles' superior ability to use political power for the good of humanity that distinguished him from other leaders of ancient Greece.[14]

The truth is that the political career of Abraham Lincoln, which Donald has dedicated a lifetime to chronicling, comes much closer to matching Aristotle's meaning. Lincoln clearly was a highly ambitious person. According to his friend and law partner, William Herndon, Lincoln's motivation to succeed was "a little engine that knew no rest."[15] Yet, as another of his friends, Joshua Speed, observed, Lincoln's main ambition was to gain distinction for himself by "serving the interest of his fellow man."[16] This penchant for combining concrete political realities with abstract moral values and for reconciling personal ambition with concern for the public interest, that lie at the heart of Aristotle's theory of statesmanship, can perhaps best be seen in Lincoln's conduct of the Civil War.

Lincoln's chances for relection in 1864 were tied to his ability to win the war and restore the Union. As he told Horace Greeley in 1862: "My paramount object in this struggle *is* to save the Union, and is *not* either to save or destroy slavery. If I could save the Union without freeing *any* slave I would do it, and if I could save it by freeing *all* the slaves I would do it; and if I could save it by freeing some and leaving others alone I would also do that."[17] At the same time, Lincoln's opportunity to serve the public interest of the United States was based on his ability to free the slaves and integrate them into American society. "I am naturally anti-slavery," he wrote Alfred Hodges in 1864. "If slavery is not wrong, nothing is wrong. I can not remember when I did not so think, and feel."[18] Earlier in 1854 he said: "If the Negro *is* a man, is it not to that extent, a total destruction of self-government, to say that he too shall not govern *himself*?"[19] How did Lincoln manage to harmonize two such apparently inconsistent objectives?

During the first years of the hostilities prospects for a Union victory were quite grim. Strategic opportunities and key battles were being lost by incompetent generals. Under these circumstances Lincoln became determined not to lose the support of such border states as Delaware, Maryland, Kentucky, and Missouri where slavery was still practiced. In 1861 he thus countermanded an order by General John C. Frémont to free slaves in Missouri. Two years later, however, when the course of the war started to turn around for the Union, Lincoln considered a new strategy. On January 1, 1863 he issued the Emancipation Proclamation, which had the practical effect of freeing Confederate slaves alone. Lincoln had found a dramatic way to simultaneously remind Americans that slavery is an evil institution, keep the border states on his side, and encourage Confederate slaves to take up arms against their masters.

Once victory was in sight Lincoln began to more directly pursue his humanitarian goals. In his 1865 Inaugural Address he called for a reconstruction program emphasizing "malice toward none . . . charity for all."[20] After Appomatox, indeed, Lincoln extended the spirit of charity to his treatment of the rebels. Jefferson Davis himself was only briefly imprisoned. Against congresssional opposition, moreover, he proposed a "ten percent plan" that would restore any Confederate state to the Union once one-tenth of its citizens who voted in the 1860 presidential election pledged their loyalty to the Constitution. Concerning African Americans specifically, Lincoln worked for the passage of the Thirteenth Amendment, expressed general support for what later became the Fourteenth and Fifteenth Amendments, and encouraged the formation of the Freedmen's Bureau to provide aid to former slaves.

Lincoln also felt compelled to explain why he often used despotic, unconstitutional methods to fight for freedom and the restoration of the Union. Among the dubious powers he exercised were to raise an army without congressional consent, suspend the writ of habeas corpus, permit government tampering with private correspondence, and declare martial law behind the lines. These methods led some Americans to portray him as a "presidential dictator." While admitting the unconstitutionality of these powers, Lincoln claimed that they were necessitated by the noble ends they were meant to serve as well as by the extraordinary challenge that the war posed to the Constitution itself. "I did understand," he argued in 1864:

> that my oath to preserve the constitution to the best of my ability, imposed upon me the duty of preserving, by every indispensable means, that government—that nation—of which the Constitution was the organic law. Was it possible to lose the nation, and yet preserve the constitution? By general law life *and* limb must be protected; yet often a limb must be amputated to save a life; but a life is never wisely given to save a limb. I felt that measures, otherwise unconstitutional, might become lawful, by becoming indispensable to the preservation of the nation. Right or wrong, I assumed that ground, and now avow it.[21]

Another apparent miscalculation on Professor Donald's part is his allusion to a link between statesmanship and pragmatism. Donald informs readers that he considers Lincoln to be a statesman and then describes him repeatedly as a pragmatic leader. In his *Lincoln Reconsidered* Donald locates Lincoln squarely within what he calls "the American pragmatic tradition."[22] In Donald's celebrated biography, *Lincoln*, he refers to his "pragmatic approach to politics,"[23] his "flexibility and pragmatism,"[24] and his "characteristic pragmatism."[25] Actually, pragmatism differs significantly from statesmanship and Lincoln was not primarily a pragmatist. Once again the issue hinges on the significance of moral principles in the political decision-making process.

Pragmatic leaders simply do not place the same emphasis on moral principles that Aristotle observes in statesmen. Pragmatists do not reject values *per se*. They just are more willing than statesmen to bargain them away when, for the sake of accumulating political power, it becomes convenient to do so. It comes down to a question of priorities. If, in their deliberations, leaders consider moral principles to be secondary to personal success in government, they are pragmatists. If, on the other hand, leaders emphasize moral principles without romanticizing them and do their very best to overcome obstacles to the absorption of values into law and public policy, they are statesmen in the Aristotelian sense. The dissimilarity between statesmanship and pragmatic leadership is illustrated by the positions taken by Lincoln and Stephen Douglas on extending slavery to the territories. In their famous debates during the 1858 election to choose an United States senator from Illinois, Lincoln played the role of statesman to Douglas's pragmatist.

Douglas argued that the national government was neither legally nor morally authorized to interfere with slavery in the South and maintained that each territory should be permitted to decide its own fate with regard to slavery through the use of local plebiscites. He offered his position as the least objectionable, most expedient way to preserve the United States by appeasing Americans on both sides of the slavery question. He accused Lincoln of being an enemy of popular sovereignty. Lincoln charged Douglas with neglecting to pay sufficient attention to the immorality of slavery and with trying to buy an election at the expense of this country's most cherished ideal, the essential dignity of all human beings. He agreed that using the national government to attack the South's "peculiar institution" was a bad idea, but for reasons unrelated to those proposed by Douglas.

To compel Southerners to overturn ingrained social, political, and economic practices that had existed among them for two hundred years, Lincoln reasoned, would produce a level of chaos much worse than the status quo for everyone concerned, including the slaves themselves. Since he believed that technological changes, including the mechanization of farming, would render slavery anachronistic in the near future, he recommended that it be left to die a natural death in the South over time. Lincoln could not countenence the spread of slavery to the territories, however, where it had never taken root. The use of plebiscites to decide on its future there, he argued, could only serve to "blow out the moral lights around us."[26]

Having declared his opposition to human bondage in principle, Lincoln, in genuine statesmanlike fashion, found a way to reconcile that antagonism with the distinct histories of the South and the territories, without violating the integrity of his principles. As he said at the Alton, Illinois debate:

> The Republican party . . . looks upon (slavery) as being a moral, social, and political wrong; and while they contemplate it as such, they nevertheless have due regard for its actual existence among us, and the difficulties of getting rid of it in any satisfactory way. . . . Yet having due regard for these, they desire a policy in regard to it that looks to its not creating any more danger. They insist that it should as far as may be, *be treated* as a wrong, and one of the methods of treating it as a wrong is to *make provision that it shall grow no larger.*[27]

On a personal level, Lincoln and Douglas apparently shared many of the commonly held racial prejudices of the nineteenth century. At the Charleston, Illinois, debate, for example, Lincoln admitted that: "I am not, nor ever have been in favor of bringing about in any way the social and political equality of the white and black races. . . . There is a physical difference between the white and black races which I believe will for ever forbid the two races living together on terms of social and political equality. And inasmuch as they cannot so live, while they do remain together there must be the position of superior and inferior, and I as much as any other man am in favor of having the superior position assigned to the white race."[28] For a time Lincoln also supported a plan to deport African Americans to central America and/ or back to Africa.

At Ottawa, Illinois, Douglas asserted: "If you desire Negro citizenship, if you desire to allow them to come into the State and settle with white men, if you desire them to vote on an equality with yourselves, and to make them eligible to office, to serve on juries, and to adjudge your rights, then support Mr. Lincoln and the Black Republican party, who are in favor of the citizenship of the Negro. . . . For one, I am opposed to Negro citizenship in any and every form. . . . I believe this Government was made on the white basis. . . . I believe it was made by white men, for the benefit of white men and their posterity forever, and I am in favor of confining citizenship to white men, men of European birth and descent, instead of conferring it upon Negroes, Indians, and other inferior races."[29]

If Lincoln and Douglas shared such narrow personal prejudices, how can either one of them be considered a statesman according to the Aristotelian definition that posits moral character as one of its basic prerequisites? Unlike Douglas, however, Lincoln was able to transcend his narrow personal prejudices. Unlike Douglas, Lincoln was able to transform his narrow personal prejudices into universal social values. And unlike Douglas, Lincoln was able to translate his universal social values into laws and policies that benefited the public interest of the United States in 1865. As Harry Jaffa explains, Lincoln's leadership "pointed simultaneously in two directions: one, towards the philosopher's understanding of the universal, transpolitical dimension of human experience; the other, towards the political man's understanding of the particular experiences of particular peoples in particular regimes."[30]

Just how much bargaining away of moral principles for self-serving political purposes must occur before statesmanship devolves into pragmatism? Since the distinctions between political leaders and their respective policies can be subtle, this question often is easier to answer in theory than in practice. The effort to set statesmen and pragmatists apart from one another remains worthwhile, however, because their leadership styles are capable of producing such contrary results. Had Lincoln lost the 1860 presidential election to Douglas, for example, it is plausible to conclude that the Civil War would not have been fought, at least not in 1861, and the course of American history would have been altered significantly.

The discrepancies between Lincoln's and Douglas's leadership styles were pronounced, moreover, not subtle. If Lincoln is closer to the American Pericles, Douglas was more like the dyed-in-the-wool turn of the twentieth century American "politico" George Washington Plunkitt of Tammany Hall. Like Pericles, Lincoln defined politics as the art of the preferable. Like Plunkitt, Douglas saw it as the art of the convenient or possible. Perhaps Plunkitt's infamous conceptions of honest and dishonest graft can clarify this distinction. Plunkitt grew rich and powerful at the expense of the people of New York without getting caught and without letting his greed get too far out of control.

Dishonest graft, according to Plunkitt, involves politicians accepting payoffs from "blackmailin' gamblers, saloonkeepers, disorderly people, etc."[31] Honest graft occurs when politicians use insider information to stuff their own pockets. "Supposin' it's a new bridge they're going to build," Plunkitt says. "I get tipped off and buy as much property as I can that has to be taken for approaches. I sell at my own price later on and drop some money in the bank."[32] Plunkitt's behavior was not statesmanlike because he deemphasized morality and the common good. It was pragmatic because his recognition of limits to political graft indicates that he did not completely abandon moral standards.

Since there is no evidence to suggest that Lincoln was a student of Aristotelian political philosophy or the exploits of Pericles, he must have come by his classical leadership skills instinctively. By instinct Lincoln learned that authentic statesmen try to do the very best they can under the circumstances with as much justice and decency as possible. They seek to discover practical solutions to insolvable problems through a form of politics described by Reinhold Niebuhr as a convergence of conscience and power: "where the ethical and coercive factors of human life . . . interpenetrate and work out their tentative and uneasy compromises."[33] They endeavor to strike a balance between what Niebuhr calls "the wisdom of the serpent and the harmlessness of the dove" in order to "beguile, deflect, harness, and restrain self-interest, individual and collective, for the sake of the community."[34] In Aristotle's own words, they aim to "make good shots at some attainable advantage."[35]

Asked to explain his leadership style, Lincoln wrote: "I claim not to have controlled events, but confess plainly that events have controlled me."[36] "I expect the best," he later acknowledged, "but am prepared for the worst."[37] By instinct Lincoln also must have learned that, because it involves the most precarious of political skills, "knowledge of the correct ends or values as well as the calculation of the correct means to these ends,"[38] there is a tremendous amount of uncertainty in Aristotelian statesmanship. As Aristotle well knew, even Pericles ultimately was defeated by conditions and events beyond his control. Having decided to abandon a direct counterattack against the Spartan siege of Athens in favor of a defensive strategy, a deadly plague engulfed the city, killing a third of its inhabitants including Pericles himself. In view of Pericles' own experiences, Aristotle cautions leaders that those who hold public office have a responsibility to serve the public interest that is neither excused nor relieved when their best efforts prove inadequate.

There are thus extensive parallels to be found between the leadership of Abraham Lincoln and Aristotelian statesmanhip, which is primarily an ethical politics based upon Aristotle's concept of *phronesis*. Nevertheless, Professor Donald implies that Lincoln, while allowing moral values to influence his behavior, was above all a disingenuous politician. Despite Lincoln's demonstrated ability to "guide political men, who need to know what is right here and now, but to guide them in the light of what is just everywhere and always,"[39] Donald portrays him as a pragmatist. Endorsement for Donald's interpretation can be found in the scholarship of J. G. Randall and Richard Hofstadter. Randall, author of an authoritative multivolume Lincoln biography, concludes that "it would be a perversion of history" to think that there were any profound differences between the positions taken by Lincoln and Douglas in their debates.[40] In his widely read essay, "Abraham Lincoln and the Self-Made Myth," Hofstadter accuses Lincoln of being a "deliberate and responsible" opportunist, a courtier of "influential and financial friends," a world-class "political propagandist," a "professional politician looking for votes," and a "follower . . . not a leader of public opinion."[41] The Emancipation Proclamation, Hofstadter determines, had "all the moral grandeur of a bill of lading."[42]

Fortunately, a corrective to these views is supplied by another prominent Lincoln scholar, Richard Current. Lincoln "has been described as essentially a politician's politician, as a pragmatist, a man more interested in immediate, practical advantages than in underlying principles." Current writes:

> He has been characterized as a flexible man rather than one of fixed determination. In fact, however, he was flexible and pragmatic only in his choice of means and in his sense of timing. Though no doctrinaire, Lincoln was a man of deep conviction and settled purpose. Only by compromising with the necessities of his time could he hope to gain and hold political power. And only by holding political power could he hope to give reality, even in part, to his concept of the Union and its potentialities.[43]

In his essay, "Abraham Lincoln and the American Pragmatic Tradition," Professor Donald observes that Lincoln "possessed what John Keats called the 'quality (that) went to form a Man of Achievement,' that quality 'which Shakespeare possessed so enormously— . . . *Negative Capability*, that is when a man is capable of being in uncertainties. Mysteries, doubts, without any irritable reaching after fact and reason.'"[44] Donald apparently is unaware that statesmen such as Pericles share with Shakespeare the attributes prized by John Keats. Power hungry politicians and pragmatists are far removed from poetry, however. The former are not uncertain about their motivation. The latter hasten to achieve personal success in government without recourse to mystery.

ᔐ

LINCOLN'S REVOLUTION
Ralph Lerner

BY THE TIME ABRAHAM LINCOLN first finds his way to the public podium, the traditional objects of American political celebration have been much altered. In the beginning, and especially to the east of the Hudson, the Lord had been praised by governors no less than by clerics. Both knew whence all blessings flowed and were intent that the public at large never lose sight of that source. Later, the controversies that lead at last to revolution and independence lay greater stress on English law and institutions, the rightful inheritance of a free people. To laud this legacy is at once to justify the struggle and to condemn the corruption and heartlessness of an unfeeling imperious mother. Next, a free America, with a future as unbounded as the very land, offers itself as a new topic fit for orators and poets. But in congratulating themselves for their land, their institutions, their separate and equal station among the nations of the earth, Americans become great self-flatterers. Full of themselves, they are in no mood to listen to European visitors complain about boorish complacency and absurd puffery.

The European caricature is not entirely unfair. By the time it is Lincoln's turn to begin raising his voice among his fellow citizens, egregious self-celebration is a staple of American oratory. It is astonishing that he makes himself heard in such a congratulatory clamor, for he speaks in a different key. To be sure, Lincoln has no principled objection to praising America to the Americans. But his conception of the praiseworthy in America is singular, and in the future tense: Americans will have reason to think well of themselves only after learning to think critically of themselves. In the meantime, one does not have to be a European observer, just a far-seeing American, to understand that the American people's self-satisfaction is the greatest obstacle to a well-deserved pride in themselves. In a time and place where thousands heap wholesale flattery (and wholesale damnation) upon uncritical millions, Lincoln's is a voice apart.

No aspiring politician needs to be told that there is a public pulse to be taken, and no halfway competent politician needs to grope for long to take it. Lincoln is more than halfway competent. He understands from the outset and with perfect clarity that the realm of politics is the realm of opinion. He sees that any speaker who would induce a people to hold a critical opinion of itself must first induce it to trust and have a good opinion of himself. But it will presumably not trust or have a good opinion of one who criticizes the opinions it holds dear. It would seem, then, that in order to gain a hearing for his critical, nonflattering speech, a speaker must first dissemble his critical opinions and flatter his audience, thus exacerbating the very sickness he wishes to cure.

Lincoln escapes his dilemma in a manner worthy of study. He flatters the people and gains their trust, not by catering to their present noncritical opinions of themselves and their affairs, but by bringing them with him, as equals somehow, into the problem of public opinion as such. He takes them into his confidence and makes them his partners in seeking a solution for the problem of popular government. And in this he succeeds. Not the least of Lincoln's extraordinary political achievements is his success in making general an awareness of the problem of public opinion—his nurturing of an opinion about the signal importance of opinion. A greater achievement, yet impossible without the first, is his persuading many American people to criticize and repudiate the many base opinions about political right and prudence that their base flatterers would have them basely cling to. His *kalam* is directed against the enemy within.

Lincoln's beginning point is the recognition that the basis of any government, "and particularly of those constituted like ours," lies in the attachment of the people to their government's laws and institutions (SW 1:31; CW 1:111).[1] That affection, in

turn, although usually arising out of an untroubled confidence or habit, can nonetheless be alienated. The unspoken attachment of a silent multitude can suddenly
and terribly show itself to be conditional, evanescent. Thus, far from being something to be presumed, the positive engagement of private sentiment and public
structures has rather to be cultivated, nourished, and, in the last analysis, earned.
The first fact is that "our government rests in public opinion. Whoever can change
public opinion, can change the government, practically just so much" (SW 1:385;
CW 2:385). That public opinion might as readily be thought of as "a public sentiment" or as a public will that "springs from the two elements of moral sense and
self-interest" (SW 1:402 CW 2:409). Politicians no less than policies are to be gauged
by public sentiment: "In this age, and this country, public sentiment is everything.
With it, nothing can fail; against it, nothing can succeed" (SW 1:493; CW 2:552–53).
But by the same token, politicians no less than policies are to be gauged by their
effect upon public sentiment. When someone of influence molds public sentiment,
he "goes deeper than he who enacts statutes or pronounces decisions. He makes
statutes and decisions possible or impossible to be executed" (SW 1:525; CW 3:27).

Rather than remain the tacit understanding in a politician's private calculations,
the shaping of public sentiment itself becomes, thanks to Lincoln, a subject of public
reflection and debate. His insistence on addressing the " 'central idea' in our political
public opinion" (SW 1:385; CW 2:385) also enables or rather compels others to perceive how a "mighty, deep seated power . . . somehow operates on the minds of men,
exciting and stirring them up in every avenue of society—in politics, in religion, in
literature, in morals, in all the manifold relations of life" (SW 1:805; CW 3:310).

Lincoln's concern with public opinion differs from the radicalizing summons of
a principled politician. A William Lloyd Garrison, a John C. Calhoun, even an
Alexis de Tocqueville, might single out some central idea as the shaper of social
thoughts and ways. Lincoln goes further and deeper. He offers more than a dissect-
ing tool of analysis or a call to arms. Lincoln contends that "no policy that does not
rest upon some philosophical public opinion can be permanently maintained" (SW
2:136; CW 4:17). In raising this concern at all, he in effect attempts to mold and
create a philosophically grounded public opinion. Where others see a public wanting
in belief, Lincoln sees a public also wanting in understanding. Others would rouse
their people to subscribe to some principle or article of faith. Lincoln does too; but
beyond that, he strives to get as many as possible to pause, to reflect on the place
and importance of true opinion in their collective lives.

Lincoln's analysis of the crisis of his time leads him to understand that it is no less
the crisis of popular government itself. Only a general clarity about the conditions of
popular government and only a greater awareness of the role of public opinion
within it can enable the Americans to recover their balance and find themselves.
Failing that, they will remain victims of their delusions and deluders.

If public opinion is the bedrock on which institutions and policies might be
erected, it is also a formidable and omnipresent constraint on the hopes and dreams

of theoretic politicians. "The universal sense of mankind, on any subject, is an argument, or at least an *influence* not easily overcome" (SW 1:85; CW 1:275). Confronting such opinions demands not only persistence and adroitness—qualities common enough to fanatics as well—but a genuine and cautious respect for limits, both one's own and those of others. In impinging on the deepest feelings of the people, politicians stir matters not to be trifled with. From early on Lincoln has understood and publicly acknowledged (as in his handbill replying to charges of infidelity) that no one "has the right . . . to insult the feelings, and injure the morals, of the community in which he may live" (SW 1:140; CW 1:382). Still less can a "statesman" feign indifference to some "great and durable element of popular action" (SW 1:346; CW 2:282). Indeed, the same may be said of more contentious and problematic popular sentiments. Whether a particular prejudice "accords with justice and sound judgment, is not the sole question, if indeed, it is any part of it. A universal feeling, whether well or ill-founded, can not be safely disregarded" (SW 1:316; CW 2:256).

All this, to repeat, bespeaks a need for caution, not a mindless acceptance. Lincoln is far, very far, from the resigned man of sorrows, controlled by events, that he is sometimes portrayed as being. His reentry into national politics is triggered by the crisis over the Kansas-Nebraska Act of 1854. No small part of his resolve to do battle comes from his perception of the injury that the mere passage of that legislation has already inflicted on a fragile, vulnerable public sentiment. Underlying the entire political system of the United States is a "spirit of mutual concession—that spirit which first gave us the Constitution, and which has thrice saved the Union" (SW 1:335; CW 2:272). Who now, after the effectual repeal of the Missouri Compromise, could ever again put their trust in such mutual accommodations? More immediately, how might one account for so startling a reversal and repudiation? This latter question is the great device with which Lincoln seeks to arouse and redirect public opinion. In the course of doing so he succeeds in reversing the trajectories of both his own and Stephen A. Douglas's fortunes.

Central to Lincoln's purpose is his effort to impress upon the public mind the realization that "on the question of liberty, as a principle, we are not what we have been." The spirit that drove "the political slaves of King George" to wrest freedom for themselves and to desire a peaceful end to the enslavement of others has "itself become extinct, with the *occasion*, and the *men* of the Revolution" (SW 1:359; CW 2:318). Americans are abandoning the equality of men, that original "central idea" of American public opinion "from which all its minor thoughts radiate" (SW 1:385; CW 2:385). What is more, those keenest on overturning and replacing that principle have the audacity to deny publicly that any such reversal has taken place. The untruth buried in Chief Justice Taney's discreetly disingenuous assumption—"that the public estimate of the black man is more favorable now than it was in the days of the Revolution" (SW 1:396; CW 2:403)—is being asserted more brazenly by members of Congress. Thus John Pettit of Indiana, without a word of rebuke from "the forty odd Nebraska Senators who sat present and heard him," could pronounce the Declaration of Independence "a self-evident lie" (SW 1:339; CW 2:2). And Stephen Douglas can maintain in effect "that Negroes are not men—have no part in the declaration of Independence— . . . that liberty and slavery are perfectly consistent—indeed, necessary accompaniments—that for a strong man to declare himself the *superior* of a weak one, and thereupon enslave the weak one, is the very *essence* of liberty—the most sacred right of self-government" (SW 1:493–94; CW 2:553). Here is the "central idea of the Democratic party" under Douglas's leadership (SW 1:741; CW 3:256); under his influence "a vast change in . . . Northern public sentiment" has been effected in but a few years (SW 2:66; CW 3:444). It is a bitter irony that those who might rightly claim political descent from Jefferson have "nearly ceased to breathe his name everywhere" (SW 2:18; CW 3:375).

Lincoln presents Douglas's "Nebraskaism in its abstract purity" as a policy designed "to educate and mold public opinion to 'not care whether slavery is voted up or voted down'" (SW 1:416, 418; CW 2:451, 453). By "*impressing* the 'public heart' to care nothing about it" (SW 1:433; CW 2:467), Douglas is securing the "gradual and steady debauching of public opinion" (SW 2:56–57; CW 3:423). Coming from a man of great influence, Douglas's "bare opinion" goes far to fix that of others. "The susceptable young hear lessons from him, such as their fathers never heard when they were young" (SW 1:493; CW 2:553). The struggles, then, against Nebraskaism, against Douglas's "don't care" policy, against his insidious interpretation of popular sovereignty, are all presented by Lincoln as so many efforts to recover an earlier, authentic public opinion. Should Douglas's new heretical doctrines succeed in "penetrating the human soul" (SW 1:527; CW 3:29), there is little hope that slavery may be contained or that the public mind may once again come to "rest in the belief that it is going to its end" (SW 2:37; CW 3:406). To persuade his contemporaries that such an act of political recollection and recovery is both possible and desirable is the greatest challenge Lincoln faces until the coming of the war.

As with his treatment of public sentiment, Lincoln chooses to make persuasion an explicit theme. To succeed in persuading, a speaker or writer has to come to terms with prevailing modes of thought, especially where these are reinforced by "interest, fixed habits, or burning appetites." These passionate involvements maybe worked for good or for ill, but in no case are they to be ignored or despised. Thus it is futile to expect humankind at large to sacrifice now for the sake of generations yet unborn. "Posterity has done nothing for us; and theorise on it as we may, practically we shall do very little for it, unless we are made to think, we are, at the same time, doing something for ourselves." This understanding, according to Lincoln, informs the "more enlarged philanthropy" of the Washington Temperance Society (SW 1:85–86; CW 1:275–76). Less benign by far is the passion-driven misanthropy that can reduce the black man to a being intermediate to the white man and the crocodile. Here public passion is being worked so as to "still further brutalize the negro, and to bring public opinion to the point of utter indifference whether men so brutalized are enslaved or not" (SW 2:1; CW 4:20). Here too, as elsewhere, the public's passions are being catered to through use of ingenious falsehood and sophism. In this manner the unspeakable is concealed, "sugar-coated," and rendered plausible; the public mind is debauched and drugged (SW 2:138–39, 255; CW 4:19, 433).

For one engrossed in public affairs, the passion-driven preferences of the people must thus remain a matter of continuing concern and interest. However one views those particular passions—as something to be used or deflected, or even as something to be replaced and transcended—it is these passions that the politician must first somehow reach and affect. In this task the preeminent instrument of action is the politician's power of persuasion. Yet it is striking that so great a master of persuasive speech as Lincoln should insist on the limitations of such speech and thus also on the limits of politics. He understands the grip of mere fashion on ordinary behavior, "the strong inclination each of us feels to do as we see all our neighbors do" (SW 1:88; CW 1:277). He knows that "the plainest print cannot be read through a gold eagle" (SW 1:403; CW 2:409). He knows as well that it will not do to ignore a niggling charge, for although "it is no great thing, yet the smallest are often the most difficult things to deal with" (SW 1:624; CW 3:135).

All this bespeaks a kind of modesty or perhaps realism when assessing politicians' effectiveness on their chosen fields of engagement. And yet in seeking to ground public opinion anew, Lincoln's objectives are hardly modest and certainly not timid. With the fading of public memories, with the dying-off of the men of '76—those impassioned embodiments of the revolution and its principles—Lincoln's generation has due warning that the temple of liberty "must fall, unless we, their descendants, supply their places with other pillars, hewn from the solid quarry of sober reason. Passion has helped us; but can do so no more. It will in future be our enemy" (SW 1:35–36; CW 1:115). Henceforth the politics of freedom must rest on the persuasiveness of reason.[2]

There is abundant evidence that Lincoln does indeed act on this estimate of his, and the American people's, situation. He takes it for granted that he will be held to account for positions he has adopted earlier and elsewhere, that "all the reading and intelligent men in the community would see them [in print] and know all about my opinions" (SW 1:703; CW 3:221). Similarly, he holds the opinions of his opponents to public accounting. They will need "a far better argument than a mere sneer to show to the minds of intelligent men" that they are not responsible for the necessary implications of their pronouncements (SW 1:715; CW 3:232). The ultimate political judge will be, has to be, a thinking public: "I never despair of sustaining myself before the people upon any measure that will stand a full investigation" (SW 1:42; CW 1:147).

Yet this confidence, which Lincoln articulates at the very outset of his political career and to which he holds firm till death, dare not be read as the manifesto of a *philosophe*. For although Lincoln loves a demonstrative proof as much as any man in public life, he holds no illusions as to its sufficiency either before the jury box or on the hustings. A widespread public opinion heavily discounts the pronouncements of "Preachers, Lawyers, and hired agents:" "They are supposed to have no sympathy of feeling or interest, with those very persons whom it is their object to convince and persuade" (SW 1:81; CW 1:272). It is commonplace to write these types off as self-servers, especially when they assume high moral ground in denouncing and dictating to their erring fellow-citizens. Is it any surprise that the latter are "slow, *very slow*, . . . to join the ranks of their denouncers, in a hue and cry against themselves"? To expect otherwise is to anticipate what can never be—a reversal of human nature itself. This much at least is given: that "a drop of honey catches more flies than a gallon of gall. So with men." Lincoln insists that "the great high road" to a man's reason has first to be gained, not assumed or commanded or despised. The ethos of the speaker has first to he established as that of a friend. Failing that, "tho' your cause be naked truth itself, transformed to the heaviest lance, harder than steel, and sharper than steel can be made, and tho' you throw it with more than Herculean force and precision, you shall no more be able to pierce him, than to penetrate the hard shell of a tortoise with a rye straw" (SW 1:83; CW 1:273).

Here, then, is a universal truth that informs and undergirds Lincoln's exertions on behalf of a politics of reason. His repeated appeal is of course to thoughtfulness. "I take it that I have to address an intelligent and reading community, who will peruse what I say, weigh it, and then judge . . ." (SW 1:704; CW 3:222). He tells the audience he shares with Douglas at Galesburg that he is "willing and anxious that they should consider the candidates' competing views fully—that they should turn it about and consider the importance of the question, and arrive at a just conclusion." They should "decide, and rightly decide" the fundamental question concerning the extension of slavery before adopting any particular policy (SW 1:721; CW 3:236–37). Yet this appeal to deliberation will only he heeded if it is seen as coming from a friend, from one of their own. By drawing on a common heritage, the heritage of the revolution, and by casting himself as but one of a multitude of beneficiaries in common, Lincoln strives to find the high road to his public's reason. Happily, his need to persuade leads him to the plausible source of the very principles he would espouse. The revolution, as Lincoln conceives or reconceives it, makes him at one with his audience and points them all in common toward the practical policy that conforms to his understanding of justice.

Within the context of the struggle over the expansion of slavery, Lincoln attempts to redirect his contemporaries' thoughts back to the revolution. His immediate aim is that they see afresh who they have been and what they are about. With recollection will come clarity, and with clarity, right action. In all of this Lincoln studiously avoids any suggestion that he is innovating, let alone improving on what earlier generations have wrought. The very language he favors in speaking of the Founders' handiwork—the "legacy bequeathed us" (SW 1:28; CW 1:108), their "inestimable boon" (SW 2:264; CW 4:482)—reinforces the thought that the actions most becoming for latter-day Americans are of preserving and giving thanks. It might appear that with the greater work already accomplished, lesser men could now settle down to tasks better adapted to *their* talents.

Yet in fact Lincoln argues no such thing. For while his praise of the revolution and of the revolutionaries is predictably full, his estimate of that legacy is hardly simple or unmixed. There is, to begin with, no evading the fact that "the noblest of cause drew on some of the unloveliest human traits: the people's "deep rooted principles of hate, and the powerful motive of *revenge*" (SW 1:35; CW 1:114). Further, for all the revolution's "glorious results, past, present, and to come, it had its evils too. It breathed forth famine, swam in blood and rode on fire." It exacted a harsh human price, leaving in its wake orphans, widows, and a suppressed Tory minority (SW 1:89, 167; CW 1:278, 438–39).

Nor is that all. To be sure, the revolution's central proposition—the capability of a people to govern themselves—can no longer be treated as a matter of doubt. Its truth has been demonstrated in practice; the once "undecided experiment" is now understood to be a success (SW 1:33–34; CW 1:113). Yet the work remains strikingly incomplete. Bereft of its "noble ally," a complementary moral revolution, the grander goal of "our political revolution of '76" still lies beyond reach. The envisioned universal liberty of humankind demands not only the release of "every son of earth" from the oppressor's grip but also the breaking of the fiercer bondage of reason to human appetite and passion. No, the revolution can hardly be said to have run its course (SW 1:89–90; CW 1:278–79).

Nowhere is its incompleteness more evident than in the continuing debate over slavery. Lincoln repeatedly urges his countrymen to look back, "away back of the constitution, in the pure fresh, free breath of the revolution" (SW 1:309; CW 2:249). From that vantage point they may come to see both the promise of the revolution and its disappointment. A clue, for Lincoln, lies in Jefferson's having introduced into "a merely revolutionary document, an abstract truth, applicable to all men and all times" (SW 2:19; CW 3:376). Lincoln confesses to having long thought that this revolutionary struggle "must have been something more than common," "something even more than National Independence" (SW 2:209; CW 4:236). The object in view was not that eighteenth century Americans achieve parity with eighteenth century British subjects "in their own oppressed and unequal condition," but rather "the progressive improvement in the condition of all men everywhere" (SW 1:399–400; CW 2:407). It was that expectation which sustained those who endured the miseries of the struggle: "they were cheered by the future" (SW 2:355; CW 5:373). It was that very expectation, now understood as "the principle of the revolution," which gave rise to those systems of gradual emancipation that the states had adopted in the closing decades of the preceding century (SW 1:342; CW 2:278). In the light of that history, and in view of the prosperity that attended the free states' having acted on the principle that "every man can make himself," it is simply absurd to pretend (as Douglas does) that these maxims of free government can be treated as indifferent matters. "No—we have an interest in the maintenance of the principles of the Government, and without this interest, it is worth nothing" (SW 1:379; CW 2:364).

In casting Douglas as the chief villain of the piece, Lincoln is responding particularly to the Democrat's attempt to establish historical credentials for his own policy. By denying or finessing the tension between original intent and current practice, Douglas is in effect erasing the disturbing memory that might impel an erring people to recover and reform. "Judge Douglas is going back to the era of our Revolution, and to the extent of his ability, muzzling the cannon which thunders its annual joyous return. When he invites any people willing to have slavery, to establish it, he is blowing out the moral lights around us" (SW 1:527; CW 3:29).[3] In truth, however, "the spirit of seventy-six and the spirit of Nebraska, are utter antagonisms" (SW 1:339; CW 2:275). Nebraskaism and Dred Scottism are a "burlesque upon judicial decisions, and [a] slander and profanation upon the honored names, and sacred history of republican America" (SW 1:418; CW 2:454).

But how might a deluded people be made to see that? On the evidence of the Know-Nothings' popularity, Lincoln concludes, "Our progress in degeneracy appears to me to be pretty rapid" (SW 1:363; CW 2:323). If a profound change has in fact taken place, then the revolution is indeed incomplete. The union has not only to be saved; it must be so saved, so remade, as "to keep it, forever worthy of the saving." The soiled robe of republican America needs to be washed white "in the spirit, if not the blood, of the Revolution" (SW 1:339–40; CW 2:276). For Lincoln that can only mean a return to the Declaration of Independence.

It belabors the obvious to recall that the Declaration is a great tocsin resounding throughout Lincoln's speeches and writings, evoking memory, alarm, and action. It is his point of departure and his point of return. There simply is no mistaking his regard for "the immortal paper" and its author (SW 1:702; CW 3:220). Lincoln's control and passion vie so impressively in this invocation that one may say that although the subject is hardly original with him, Lincoln emphatically makes it his own.

> All honor to Jefferson—to the man who, in the concrete pressure of a struggle for national independence by a single people, had the coolness, forecast, and capacity to introduce into a merely revolutionary document, an abstract truth, applicable to all men and all times, and so to embalm it there, that to-day, and in all coming days, it shall be a rebuke and a stumbling-block to the very harbingers of reappearing tyranny and oppression (SW 2:19; CW 3:376).

He can in perfect truth declare, "I have never had a feeling politically that did not spring from the sentiments embodied in the Declaration of Independence" (SW 2:213; CW 4:240).

Perhaps the most sublime achievement of Lincoln's *kalam* is the way he reshapes the debate raging over the extension of slavery in the western territories into a debate over the moral foundations of popular government. In that political world of antebellum America, so rife with political theologians and theological politicians, Lincoln succeeds in avoiding the excesses of each. He neither mistakes himself for the appointed agent of the Lord of Hosts nor falls into the idolatry of treating the voice of the majority as the voice of God. By insisting on making the Declaration of Independence the central point of reference, Lincoln is able to occupy a higher but still emphatically political ground. From that ground he can criticize the deniers, sappers, and traducers of its principles. From that high ground, too, he can identify and expose the unthinking forgetfulness that so conveniently encourages people to assume "there is no right principle of action but *self-interest*" (SW 1:315; CW 2:255). By pressing his case as a matter of high political principle—but a principle to which no white man can *afford* to assume or feign indifference—Lincoln leads a reluctant public to a disturbing confrontation with itself.

It is not enough to invoke, with pious tones, the right of self-government or the great principle of popular sovereignty. Where Douglas uses these formulas in an attempt to close off debate, Lincoln insists on using them to reconsider one's assumptions. "[I]f the negro is a man, is it not to that extent, a total destruction of self-government, to say that he too shall not govern himself? When the white man governs *himself* that is self-government; but when he governs himself, and also governs *another* man, that is *more* than self-government—that is despotism." No man, Lincoln insists, is good enough to govern another without that other's consent. That, if anything, is "the leading principle—the sheet anchor of American republicanism" (SW 1:328; CW 2:266). Again, the Declaration's assertion of human equality is not an assertion of equality in all respects but in some: in the right to life, liberty, and the pursuit of happiness, in "the right to put into his mouth the bread that his own hands have earned" (SW 1:477–78, 512; CW 2:520, 3:16). Denial of that principle will not and cannot stop with the black man. The argument that would justify enslaving a race is "the same old serpent" kings have used to bestride the necks of their people. In their fearful preoccupation with anything that might lift black men up, Douglas and those arguing like him are drawing white men down. They threaten to "destroy the principle that is the charter of our liberties" (SW 1:457; CW 2:500–501).

Lincoln takes special pains to so meld the principle and the charter that an attack on the one has to be an attack on the other. His enlarged interpretation of the Declaration's language and intention means that he can present Douglas's interpretation as a diminution, indeed a trivialization, of what even minimally is "the white man's charter of freedom" (SW 1:339; CW 2:276). In fact, Lincoln argues, the Declaration is much more. In its "noble words" lies the origin of popular sovereignty itself, or at least as applied to the Americans (SW 1:443–44, 583; CW 2:489, 3:94). And though it is indeed a charter of freedom, the Declaration embraces a much broader segment of humankind than only those people of British descent who were resident in North America in 1776. Slaves and Englishmen alike fall under its principles (SW 2:135; CW 4:16). Latecomers to America, European immigrants looking at its language, can "feel that that moral sentiment taught in that day evidences their relation to those men, that it is the father of all moral principle in them, and that they have a right to claim it as though they were blood of the blood, and flesh of the flesh of the men who wrote that Declaration, and so they are" (SW 1:456; CW 2:499–500). It is to the Declaration that Lincoln traces the genius of American independence. In it is to be found "the spirit which prizes liberty as the heritage of all men, in all lands, everywhere" (SW 1:585; CW 3:95).

The distinctiveness of America, even its special significance, lies in the stamp of the Declaration's principles upon the hearts and minds of people the world over. In this connection Lincoln has the boldness to speak not simply of his regard for "the opinions and examples of our revolutionary fathers" and of his love for "the sentiments of those old-time men" (SW 1:329; CW 2:267). From Independence Hall's "consecrated" "holy and most sacred walls" one may still hear "breathings rising"; "the teachings coming forth from that sacred hall" are less an episode of the past than a continuing presence. On the eve of his most dreadful new responsibilities, it is to these teachings that Lincoln sees fit to pledge his devotion. In so doing he uses terms that echo the Psalmist's devotion to Jerusalem as he sat weeping by the waters of Babylon (SW 2:212; CW 4:239). It was no mere wordsmith's trope that led him to speak years earlier of "my ancient faith" and of "our ancient faith" (SW 1:328; CW 2:266), and to warn of "giving up the OLD for the NEW faith" (SW 1:339; CW 2:275). But in rendering the ancestral sacred, Lincoln takes care, as we shall see, to keep it within human reach as an object of warm familiarity. It is "that old Declaration of Independence" and the sentiments of "those old men" (SW 1:443, 456–57; CW 2:488, 499), "the good old one, penned by Jefferson" (SW 2:259; CW 4:438), that he keeps before the public eye. To lose these would be to lose the better part of one's self.

Thus the brunt of Lincoln's charge against Douglas's reading of the Declaration is not quite what one might have expected. By maintaining that the black man is not included in its language, Douglas is tending "to take away from him the right of ever striving to be a man" (SW 1:798; CW 3:304); that is bad enough. But this evil is exceeded by the long-term effect of such thinking: "penetrating the human soul and eradicating the light of reason and the love of liberty in this American people," "he is blowing out the moral lights around us" (SW 1:527, 717; CW 3:29, 234).[4] This loss is not conjectural but actual. "When we were the political slaves of King George, and wanted to be free, we called the maxim that 'all men are created equal' a self-evident truth; but now when we have grown fat, and have lost all dread of being slaves ourselves, we have become so greedy to be *masters* that we call the same maxim 'a self-evident lie'" (SW 1:359; CW 2:318). What once had been "held sacred by all, and thought to include all" now is "assailed, and sneered at, and construed, and hawked at, and torn" beyond recognition (SW 1:396; CW 2:404). In calling for a readoption of the Declaration and a return to the practices and policy that harmonized with it, Lincoln is also calling for America to return to its promise.

Lincoln never argues that the fulfillment of that promise is easy or at hand. Yet the overall effect of the Declaration's principle gives cause for hope and for pride: "its constant working has been a steady progress towards the practical equality of all men" (SW 1:386; CW 2:385). In what still remains the outstanding characterization of the Declaration, Lincoln speaks of its authors meaning to set up "a standard maxim for free society, which should be familiar to all, and revered by all; constantly looked to, constantly labored for, and even though never perfectly attained, constantly approximated, and thereby constantly spreading and deepening its influence, and augmenting the happiness and value of life to all people of all colors everywhere" (SW 1:398; CW 2:406).[5] Shorn of its universal intent, of what practical use can that old declaration be? "Mere rubbish—old wadding left to rot on the battlefield" (SW 1:400; CW 2:407). The grandeur of America is inseparable from its Founders' dreams. In daring to give "hope to the world for all future time" (SW 2:21 CW 4:240), they secured an immortal fame for themselves and their successors.

Since Lincoln fixes his eye so firmly on the moral aspect of the American Revolution, he attends as a matter of course to the characters of those who made it. Not surprisingly, he finds those men admirable, although not simply so. Though Lincoln is often eager to present them as figures on a pedestal, he is also able to place them in a somewhat less flattering light. The main thrust of his remarks, however, is to present them as benefactors. Lincoln rings many changes on that theme. He, his contemporaries, and Americans yet unborn all owe gratitude to that race of ancestors, those "iron men" who bequeathed them such fundamental blessings (SW 1:28, 4; CW 1:108, 2:499). Beyond that, the patriots of '76 are models and objects of emulation. Just as they pledged their lives, their fortunes, and their sacred honor in support of the Declaration of Independence, their successors ought to pledge their all in support of the Constitution and the laws (SW 1:32; CW 1:112). Lincoln even goes so far as to urge that his contemporaries adopt the salutary habit of regarding the Constitution as unalterable. "The men who made it, have done their work, and have passed away. Who shall improve, on what *they* did?" (SW 1:196; CW 1:488).

Yet moving in tandem with this vein of filiopiety is a subdued but unmistakable demythologizing. Lincoln's founders are indeed great men—but men, not demigods. Those who ran the risk of failure, derision, and oblivion in order to make the revolution only dared what any might do who "naturally seek the gratification of their ruling passion." Staking "their *all*" upon their success, those men of ambition wagered—and won celebrity, fame, and distinction (SW 1:34; CW 1:113). Whatever the broader reach of their benefaction, its motivating impulse could not be called selfless.

Nonetheless, models they were and models they remain for Lincoln. He does not cease urging his fellows, "degenerated men (if we have degenerated);" to follow the opinions and examples of "those noble fathers—Washington, Jefferson and Madison" (SW 2:76; CW 3:453). It is obvious that this insistent message is not meant to be taken as a commendation of mindless adulation; for beyond the level of prattling babes, Lincoln has not a single good word to say in favor of mindlessness of any sort.

Now and here, let me guard a little against being misunderstood. I do not mean to say we are bound to follow implicitly in whatever our fathers did. To do so, would be to discard all the lights of current experience—to reject all progress—all improvement. What I do say is, that if we would supplant the opinions and policy of our fathers in any case, we should do so upon evidence so conclusive, and argument so clear, that even their great authority, fairly considered and weighed, cannot stand; and most surely not in a case whereof we ourselves declare they understood the question better than we (SW 2:119; CW 3:534–35).

In nothing, perhaps, are the Fathers more to be followed, more to be studied, more to be imitated, than in their opposition to slavery. Here especially, according to Lincoln, they showed their moral clarity and their political prudence. They knew "a vast moral evil" when they saw it (SW 1:450; CW 2:494). When and as they could, they put "the seal of legislation *against its spread*" (SW 1:514; CW 3:18). They assiduously eschewed and rejected anything suggesting that one might have a moral right to enslave another. "The argument of 'Necessity' was the only argument they ever admitted in favor of slavery; and so far, and so far only as it carried them, did they ever go" (SW 1:337, 478, 765, 802; CW 2:274, 520, 3:276, 308). They intended, expected, and encouraged the public to expect, that slavery ultimately would become extinct (SW 1:448, 603, 800, 2:70–71; CW 2:492, 3:117, 306, 448). This, according to Lincoln, was the position of the leading men of the revolution and the position to which they "stuck . . . through thick and thin." "Through their whole course, from first to last, they clung to freedom" (SW 2:48; CW 3:416).

Purer souls, sterner moralists, can and do argue that, far from being models for emulation, the architects of American constitutionalism were temporizers, or whistlers in the dark, or even covenanters with Satan himself. Where such critics may see weakness and confusion, Lincoln unhesitatingly perceives prudence. The premise of his admiration is plain enough: "From the necessities of the case we should be compelled to form just such a government as our blessed fathers gave us" (SW 2:136–37 CW 4:18). Again, what Lincoln has in mind is a defense not of every jot and tittle of earlier policies and provisions but of the general stance the Founders took toward the actual presence of slavery in the new nation. Its presence was a fact, no less a fact than its being a wrong. Neither fact might be ignored or wished away, and the authors of the Declaration responded to both. At one and the same time they both declared the right of all to the equal enjoyment of inalienable rights and took account of the circumstances standing in the way of an immediate universal attainment of these rights (SW 1:398; CW 2:406). A moral imperative was embedded in a far-from-yielding world and then left to work its influence. In surrounding the existing evil with constitutional guards, the forefathers bought peace. But in doing so they did not compromise their understanding of the evil as an evil (SW 1:581–82; CW 3:92–93). "You may have a wen or a cancer upon your person and not be able to cut it out lest you bleed to death; but surely it is no way to cure it, to engraft it and spread it over your whole body." "The peaceful way, the old-fashioned way" of the Fathers is the model for others to follow as well (SW 1:808, 2:38; CW 3:313, 407).

The cancer metaphor also appears in another discussion of the Founders' prudence. Lincoln is struck, as others must be, by the "ambiguous, roundabout, and mystical" language used in the Constitution's provisions respecting slavery (SW 2:142; CW 4:22). "That covert language," he says, "was used with a purpose" and with an eye to the time when, slavery having expired among the Americans, "there should be nothing on the face of the great charter of liberty suggesting that such a thing as Negro slavery bad ever existed among us" (SW 1:801–2; CW 3:307). Without quite saying so, Lincoln implies that the circumlocution was prompted by a sense of shame.

> Thus, the thing is hid away, in the constitution, just as an afflicted man hides away a wen or a cancer, which he dares not cut out at once, lest he bleed to death; with the promise, nevertheless, that the cutting may begin at the end of a given time. Less than this our fathers *could* not do; and *more* they *would* not do. Necessity drove them so far, and farther, they would not go (SW 1:338; CW 2:274).

Principle had made its painful peace with circumstance.

It is to this policy, at once moral and prudential, that Lincoln urges his countrymen to return. In a tireless succession of speeches stretching from 1854 to 1860, he makes the point again and again: by returning to the policy of the fathers, by returning slavery to the position they originally marked out for it, by insisting on treating slavery as an evil (albeit one with constitutional protections), and by restoring the legitimate public expectation that slavery should ultimately become extinct, the country will regain peace and national self-respect (SW 1:340, 458, 470, 514, 803; CW 2:276, 501, 513, 3:18, 308). In this sense it is Douglas himself, not Lincoln and those whom Douglas calls Black Republicans, who is the radical innovator. It is Douglas who cannot let slavery "stand upon the basis upon which our fathers placed it, but removed it and *put it upon the cotton gin basis*" (SW 1:766, 811–12; CW 3:276, 316).

Against the charge that the Republicans are revolutionary and destructive, Lincoln insists upon the ancestral credentials of the new party's program. In seeking to "restore this government to its original tone" as regards slavery, the party's chief and real purpose is "eminently conservative" (SW 2:35, 147; CW 3:404, 4:27). Douglas's version of American history cannot—and, under Lincoln's relentless pressure, will not—conceal the gap between the principles of the contemporary Democratic party and those of its slaveowner-founder, who had confessed that "he trembled for his country when he remembered that God was just" (SW 1:702; CW 3:220). As between the "don't care" policy of the one and the anguished contemplation of the other, Lincoln urges his fellows: "Choose ye between Jefferson and Douglas as to what is the true view of this element among us" (SW 2:42; CW 3:410).

Lincoln's recurrence to the history of the sentiments, policies, and actions of the founders is both a tactical move and a profound necessity. It is both a recollection and a reconception. He believes that his is by far the stronger case, although some later students doubt whether the evidentiary record is as unequivocal as he makes it out to be.[6] Ultimately, Lincoln's historical narrative is a moral tale whose fervor and unmistakable force derive from the centrality he accords the Declaration of Independence. He understands with unrivaled clarity that the Declaration's principle of "Liberty to all" has to be "*the* word, '*fitly spoken*' which has proved an 'apple of gold' to us."[7] The union and the character of the union depend upon the sense that each American has of being historically connected with the nation's astonishing rise to prosperity and might. The recollection of the beginnings, as on the annual Fourth of July celebrations, is a reminder that the bonds are not primarily genetic but moral. The Declaration's principle is "the father of all moral principle" in the Founders' descendants, adoptive as well as biological. But if public sentiment were knowingly or unknowingly corrupted, that principle could no longer serve as "the electric cord" linking together "the hearts of patriotic and liberty-loving men" (SW 1:456; CW 2:499–500). Lincoln's appeals not to break these bonds of affection came too late. In the land of the deaf, the forgetful, and the shrill, the mystic chords of memory would be silenced by guns at Charleston Harbor.

᠕

Abraham Lincoln: Republican in the White House

Stephen B. Oates

THERE IS A POPULAR ARGUMENT in the academies that Abraham Lincoln was "a Whig in the White House" who adhered to some theoretical Whig formula about a restricted presidency beyond what was necessary to save the Union. David Donald, a distinguished Civil War historian and biographer, introduced the "Whig-in-the-White-House" argument in an essay collected in the second edition of his *Lincoln Reconsidered*.[1] There Donald contended that the Lincoln presidency posed "a peculiar paradox." On the one hand, Lincoln was a strong president who expanded and enlarged executive power in unprecedented acts: he entrusted federal funds to private individuals for the public defense, summoned the militia to suppress a giant domestic insurrection, increased the size of the regular army, laid down rules of military conduct, authorized military law in vast areas behind Union lines, sanctioned

This article originally appeared in "Abraham Lincoln and the American Political Tradition," edited by J. L. Thomas (Amherst: University of Mass. Press, 1986). Reprinted with permission from University of Mass. Press.

the arrest of civilians on a scale undreamed of in America, issued an Emancipation Proclamation, and set about building loyal state regimes in Dixie—all without consulting Congress. On the other hand, Donald notes, Lincoln was simultaneously a weak chief executive who abdicated his powers, bowing "not only to the will but to the caprice of the legislators." He seldom initiated legislation on Capitol Hill and used the veto less than any other important American president. Beyond signing his name, he had little connection with the homestead, tariff, railroad, and banking bills that flowed out of the wartime Capitol and altered the role of government in the national economy. What was more, Donald contends, Lincoln had almost no influence on diplomacy and exercised scant control over his own executive departments.

How to account for the passive side of Lincoln's presidency? Here is how Donald's explanation might he summarized. It is not, as many scholars have argued, that Lincoln was too busy with the war to propose legislation or run his cabinet. After all, he found time to deal with an extraordinary amount of minutiae. Nor is it because he was temperamentally unsuited to administration. The explanation. Donald hypothesizes, is that Lincoln had a Whig view of his office: that is, he believed that the president should confine himself largely to executive functions and leave legislation to Congress.

Lincoln supposedly had held this view since his schooling as a Whig legislator and congressman in the 1830s and 1840s. Hating what they regarded as Andrew Jackson's executive usurpations, Whigs of that time advocated a weak president who might advise but would never dictate to Congress. According to Donald, Congressman Lincoln also opposed a strong chief executive—witness his flaying of President James K. Polk for vetoing river and harbor improvements. When the Whig party disintegrated in the 1850s, Lincoln disliked the idea of being "un-Whigged," Donald writes, and was "rather reluctant" to leave his cherished old party for another affiliation. Right here is the crux of Donald's argument. Lincoln grudgingly joined the Republicans, but took with him the Whig creed of a narrowly circumscribed chief executive. And he retained that creed when he became president, which was why he refused to introduce legislation on almost all issues except that of slavery. As Donald sees it, Lincoln's reluctance to control his cabinet was rooted in Whig doctrine, too, which opposed executive tyranny over departmental subordinates.

Yet Lincoln found himself in an unprecedented war in which Whig dogma could not always guide him. Thus, when necessity demanded, as it did in the matter of emancipation, Lincoln flexed his executive muscles and exercised the war power quite as though Congress did not exist. "Necessity," said Lincoln, "knows no law." Yet, Donald maintains, this also was sound Whig doctrine, because the old party bigwigs had defended a vigorous executive use of the war power. Thus, in weakly deferring to Congress and yet strongly asserting his war power when necessity compelled him, Lincoln was following the Whig creed in which he had been schooled. Here, then, is the explanation for "the puzzling ambiguity of his presidency," Donald writes. Paraphrasing one of Lincoln's own memorable statements, Donald concludes that the Civil War president could never "disenthrall" himself from his own Whig education.

Beguiling in its clarity and precision, Donald's essay seduced an entire generation of Civil War and Lincoln scholars. In his own seminal work, *The Era of Reconstruction* (1965), Kenneth M. Stampp argued that Lincoln remained to his dying day a practical, "ever-lasting Whig."[2] In an otherwise superior study, *Lincoln and the Economics of the American Dream* (1978), Gabor S. Boritt carried the Donald thesis to almost absurd lengths, contending that Lincoln was not only "the Whig in the White House," but that his military strategy itself—even his choice of generals—derived from his Whiggish economics.[3] In his prize-winning *Grant: A Biography* (1981). William S. McFeely took the Whig-in-the-White-House theme to its furthest extreme. Since Lincoln was a Whig, McFeely asserts, then it was Grant who became "the first truly Republican president."[4]

With all due respect, is this entire argument not a little preposterous? Lincoln was a *Republican* in the White House, not a Whig. Any attempt to make him into a Whig president, to borrow one of his lines, is "but a specious and fantastic arrangement of words, by which a man can prove a horse chestnut to be a chestnut horse."[5]

From the outset, the Whig thesis is predicated on the assumption that Lincoln left the Whigs reluctantly in 1856 and that ideologically he remained attached to the old party. This does not accord with the evidence. By 1856 he had become convinced that old party labels—even his own Whig label—severely impeded the mobilization of anti-extensionist forces and that a new free-soil party was imperative. The Republicans now loomed as the new major party of the future, and Lincoln readily enlisted in their crusade to contain the spread of slavery. In fact, he gave the keynote address for the formation of the Republican party in Illinois and went on to become its undisputed head. Lincoln never said, in a single surviving document, that he regretted the demise of the Whigs. Indeed, they had become obsolete in the battles over slavery that dominated the 1850s, and he left the old party with scarcely a backward glance.[6]

All his political life, it is true, Lincoln subscribed to the Whig principles of national unity and stability. All his political life, he championed the right of all Americans to rise, to harvest the full fruits of their labors, and to better themselves as their own talent and industry allowed.[7] When the Whig party died, these principles became the economic cornerstone of the Republican party, of former Democrats and Liberty men as well as former Whigs. And Lincoln was a Republican in propounding those principles.

Lincoln marched happily in Republican ranks because they afforded him an ideological home for all his principles, political as well as economic. In Republican ranks, he no longer had to consort with proslavery Southerners, as he had had to with the Whigs. In Republican ranks, he belonged to a party that forthrightly denounced slavery as a moral wrong and that shared Lincoln's views of the American experiment and the inalienable rights of man. He called himself a Republican, thought of himself as a Republican. In 1858 when national party leaders flirted with the idea of endorsing Stephen A. Douglas for the Senate, Lincoln became upset. Douglas is not your man for the Senate, he warned Republican leaders in the East. *I am your man. I, a pure Republican.*[8]

Indeed, nobody upheld Republican dogma more eloquently and unswervingly than Lincoln. No Republican was more determined to block the alleged Slave Power plot to make bondage powerful and permanent on these shores. No Republican was more passionate in his ringing denunciations of slavery as "a vast moral evil" and his equally ringing defenses of America's *"central idea"*—the idea of equality and the right to rise. No Republican was more committed to the principles of free labor, self-help, social mobility, and economic independence, all of which lay at the center of Republican ideology, of Lincoln's ideology. No Republican believed more strongly than he in the Republican vision of a future America, a better America than then existed: an America of thriving farms and bustling villages, an America of self-made agrarians, merchants, and shopkeepers who set examples and provided jobs for self-improving free workers—an America, however, that might never come about should slavery, class rule, and despotism triumph in Lincoln's impassioned time.[9]

When he ran for the presidency in 1860, Lincoln stood emphatically on the Republican platform of free soil, free labor, and free men. In offering him as their candidate, Republicans expected him to be a loyal party man who would defend the Republican cause without letting the standard down. He did not disappoint them. As party standard bearer, he opposed compromising Republican principles, opposed lowering the party platform "a hair's breadth" to let the likes of Douglas on it. Let Republicans resist slavery as a moral wrong regardless of the trials ahead, Lincoln had told his fellow Republicans. "Let us have faith that might makes right. And in that faith, let us, to the end, dare to do our duty as we understand it."[10] Small wonder that even the so-called radical Republicans extolled his addresses, applauded his nomination, and campaigned indefatigably in his behalf.

During the secession crisis, Lincoln remained an unyielding Republican. "Let there be no compromise on the question of *extending* slavery," he exhorted Republican leaders in Congress. "There is no possible compromise upon it, but which puts us under again, and leaves all our work to do over again." "We are not," he declared, going to let the Republican party "become 'a mere sucked egg, all shell and no meat,—the principle all sucked out.'" Directing congressional Republicans to "hold firm, as with a chain of steel," he rallied them to his side and won praise from Republican ranks. Lincoln was all right, said an enthusiastic Massachusetts Republican, because he kept the party firm and steady in its purpose.[11]

Nevertheless, the president-elect endorsed the idea of a limited chief executive when it came to the legislative process. "By the constitution," he said on his way to Washington, "the executive may recommend measures which he may think proper; and he may veto those he thinks improper; and it is supposed he may add to these, certain indirect influences to affect the action of Congress."[12] Lincoln added, however, that "my political education strongly inclines me against a very free use of any of these means, by the Executive, to control the legislation of the country. As a rule, I think it better that Congress should originate, as well as perfect its measures, without external bias."[13]

As a rule, he thought Congress ought to conduct its business without executive interference. What awaited him in Washington, however, was not the rule. What awaited him was a catastrophic civil war, a holocaust for which Lincoln, his party, and his country were totally unprepared, a tornado of blood and wreckage with Lincoln himself whirling in its center. What he did to quell the storm did not conform to sonic Whig theory about executive responsibility. No, he defined and fought the war according to his core of unshakable convictions about America's experiment in popular government and its historic mission in the progress of human liberty. In doing so, he remained a thoroughgoing Republican, deeply principled and yet flexible, willing to adopt new measures and stratagems in order to save the American experiment.

The central issue of the war, he told Congress on Independence Day 1861, was whether a constitutional republic—a system of popular government—could preserve itself. There were Europeans who argued that anarchy and rebellion were inherent weaknesses of a republic and that a monarchy was the more stable form of government. Now, in the Civil War, popular government was going through a fiery trial for its very survival. If it failed in America, if it succumbed to the forces of reaction in the world represented by the slave-based Confederacy, it might indeed perish from the earth. The beacon of hope for oppressed humanity would he destroyed. "This is essentially a People's contest," Lincoln said. "On the side of the Union, it is a struggle for maintaining in the world, that form, and substance of government, whose leading object is, to elevate the condition of men—to lift artificial weights from all shoulders—to clear the paths of laudable pursuit for all—to afford all, an unfettered start, and a fair chance, in the race of life."[14]

Yes, this was the central idea of the war. This was what Lincoln had in mind when he said "I shall do nothing in malice. What I deal with is too vast for malicious dealing." And in various ways he repeated that central idea in the difficult days that followed. They were fighting, he told crowds and visitors at the White House, to preserve something that lay at the heart of the American promise, at the heart of the Republican promise. "I happen temporarily to occupy this big White House," he said to an Ohio regiment. "I am a living witness that one of your children may look to come here as my father's child has. It is in order that each of you may have through this free government which we have enjoyed, an open field and a fair chance for your industry, enterprise and intelligence that you may all have equal privileges in the race of life, with all its desirable human aspirations. It is for this the struggle should he maintained, that we may not lose our birthright."[15]

It was that idea that Lincoln fought for, that he kept uppermost in his mind, as the war dragged endlessly on. The war consumed him, demanding almost all his energy from dawn until late into the night. He had almost no time for his family, for recreation beyond a daily carriage ride, for meals and leisurely jokes and laughter with old friends, for government matters unrelated to the conflict. Every day, whenever he could spare a moment, Lincoln hurried to the telegraph office of the war department to get the latest military news. He was there during almost all the campaigns, pacing back and forth with his hands clasped behind him, sending out anxious telegraph messages to some southern battlefront. *What news now? What from Burnside? From Hooker? What goes?* He even brought documents to the telegraph office and worked on them at a borrowed desk. It was here, as he awaited military developments, that he wrote an early draft of his preliminary Emancipation Proclamation.

As I have argued elsewhere, the war and Lincoln's response to it defined him as a president. As the war grew and changed, so Lincoln grew and changed. At first, he warned that the conflict must not turn into a "remorseless revolutionary struggle," lest that cause vast social and political wreckage.[16] As a consequence, his initial war strategies were cautious and limited. But when the conflict ground on with no end in sight, Lincoln resorted to one harsh war measure after another to subdue the rebellion and save popular government: he embraced martial law, property confiscation, emancipation, Negro troops, conscription, and scorched earth warfare, all of which most of the so-called radical Republicans had urged on him. These turned the war into the very thing he had cautioned against: a remorseless revolutionary struggle whose concussions are still being felt. And it became such a struggle because of Lincoln's unswerving commitment to the war's central idea.[17]

That idea, and the practical demands of the war, dictated Lincoln's dealings with his cabinet and with Congress. In cabinet matters, our Republican president did indeed delegate authority, allowing his secretaries broad discretionary powers in running their departments. But not because Whig theory informed him that this was what William Henry Harrison and Zachary Taylor would have done. Lincoln delegated authority because he simply did not have time to do everything himself. He may have been an extraordinary man, but he was not superman. He also delegated authority because his secretaries, after he got rid of Simon Cameron, were all capable subordinates whose talents he needed.

But if Lincoln allowed his secretaries considerable latitude in handling their affairs, he scarcely let them dominate him. When Secretary of State William H. Seward offered to take over the administration in April 1861, Lincoln put him firmly in his place. "Executive force and vigor are rare qualities," Seward confided to his wife. "The president is the best of us."[18]

Charged with the awesome task of managing the government in the midst of a huge and confusing war, of supervising federal armies of unprecedented size, of searching for generals who knew how to fight, of trying to deal with the crucial slavery problem and the issue of race that underlay it, of coping with a stream of raucous humanity that poured daily through his office, of somehow keeping sight of the historic and global dimensions of the conflict, Lincoln became a tough administrator indeed. "I never knew with what tyrannous authority he runs the Cabinet, till now," John Hay recorded in the summer of 1863. "The most important things he decides & there is no cavil." "He will not be bullied—even by his friends."[19]

As with the cabinet, Lincoln's relationship with Congress depended almost entirely on the pressures and problems of the war, not on Whig voices whispering in his head about what a good president ought to do. True, as Donald says, Lincoln seldom used his veto power and had little connection with the procession of economic legislation coming out of the wartime Capitol. Not that Lincoln lacked interest in such measures. On the contrary, they implemented his own national economic outlook—they promoted the "material growth of the nation" and the rise of the "many," and so were related to the war's central idea. Yet he was too preoccupied with the war and the very survival of popular government to propose economic legislation. As Boritt conceded, economics in wartime—to use a Lincoln saying—seemed "small potatoes and too few in a hill."[20]

Even so, Lincoln maintained close ties with Congress, for he needed its support if the war was to be won and the future of popular government guaranteed. As a consequence, he disregarded what he had once said about how legislators should function without executive bias. It was to Congress, significantly, that Lincoln explained the central idea of the war. It was to Congress that he turned for reform legislation linked to that idea. Shocked by the Sioux war in Minnesota and reports that a corrupt Indian Office was to blame, Lincoln urged Congress to remodel the Indian system so as to avoid fraud and conflicts that only besmirched the American experiment.[21] It was to Congress, moreover, that Lincoln submitted his federal-state emancipation scheme of 1862, to Congress that he recommended a constitutional amendment that would abolish American slavery forever, to Congress that he outlined his ten percent plan of reconstruction.

What was more, it was Lincoln who helped Senator Charles Sumner of Massachusetts guide through Congress a bill that granted widows and orphans of slave soldiers the same benefits as whites; Lincoln who pressed Congress to approve his reconstructed governments in Louisiana and Arkansas; Lincoln who forged with Sumner and other so-called radical Republicans a compromise that would have permitted Negro enfranchisement in other conquered rebel states if Congress would accept his Louisiana regime; Lincoln who employed all the pressure and prestige of his office to get the present Thirteenth Amendment through a recalcitrant House of Representatives. With the outcome much in doubt, Lincoln and congressional Republicans participated in secret negotiations never made public—negotiations that allegedly involved patronage, a New Jersey railroad monopoly, and the release of rebels related to congressional Democrats—to bring wavering opponents into line. "The greatest measure of the nineteenth century," Thaddeus Stevens claimed, "was passed by corruption, aided and abetted by the purest man in America."[22]

Lincoln dealt with Congress in other ways, too. Throughout the war he consulted with numerous individual congressmen, seeking advice on all matter of war problems from military developments to emancipation and diplomacy. As Donald himself has demonstrated, Lincoln made Senator Sumner one of his major foreign-policy advisers, and Sumner in turn became a loyal Lincoln man on Capitol Hill until breaking with the president over reconstruction.[23] In addition to Sumner, Lincoln maintained personal contact with the Joint Committee on the Conduct of the War, composed mainly of hard-line Republicans, whose job it was to ferret out disloyalists and incompetents in both the administration and the military. Lincoln met frequently with the worried patriots who served on the committee, hearing out their complaints about generals and cabinet members and even listening to criticisms of his own war policies. The president and the committeemen often disagreed, sometimes emphatically, but they had a mutual regard for one another and kept the lines of communication open between the White House and Capitol Hill.

In his reconstruction efforts, as I have indicated, Lincoln also sought Congress's approval and cooperation, for he acknowledged that Capitol Hill had a powerful voice in the reconstruction process, since both houses would decide whether to accept representatives from the states he restored. He did clash with Republicans like Sumner, Stevens, and Benjamin Wade, who argued that reconstruction was a congressional and not a presidential responsibility. Sumner also opposed Lincoln's military approach because he did not understand how the army could produce an American state. But, despite their differences, Lincoln and congressional Republicans stood together on most crucial reconstruction issues. They agreed that the South must be remade. They meant to abolish slavery there forever. They were concerned about the welfare of the freedmen. And they intended for southern Unionists to rule in postwar Dixie. Above all, they wanted to prevent ex-Confederate leaders from taking over the postwar South and forming a coalition with northern Democrats that might imperil the gains of the war. Lincoln and his congressional associates often disagreed on how to implement their goals—nearly all congressional Republicans, for example, demanded a tougher loyalty oath than that required by the president's ten percent plan.[24] But even so, the president and congressional Republicans retained a close and mutually respectful relationship, so much so that many contemporaries thought they would remain as united in working out reconstruction problems as they had been in prosecuting the war.[25]

In sum, far from deferring weakly to Congress except in matters of military necessity, Lincoln sought to influence Capitol Hill, to pressure, cajole, consult, and work with his Republican colleagues there, on virtually all issues involving the war and its central idea: the salvation of popular government and the right of all Americans to rise. Clearly this was no latter-day Whig in the White House. It was no Whig who wrote those magnificent state papers about the purpose of the war and the mission of the American experiment. It was no Whig who responded to the entreaties of Republicans like Sumner, defied public opinion, and issued the Emancipation Proclamation—the most revolutionary measure to come from an American president up to that time. It was no Whig who raised Republican ideology to the lofty heights of the Gettysburg Address, giving there the eloquent defense of liberty that critics often find lacking in the proclamation. It was no Whig who delivered the lyrical Second Inaugural, singing out that God perhaps had willed this "mighty scourge of war" on North and South alike, "until all the wealth piled by the bondman's two hundred and fifty years of unrequited toil shall be sunk, and until every drop drawn with the lash, shall he paid by another drawn with the sword."[26]

Nor was it a Whig who in April 1865 was prepared to reconstruct the South with the help of an occupying army. It was no Whig who desired to reform and reshape the South's shattered society in accordance with the ideals of the Republican party: to bring the South into the mainstream of American republicanism, to install a free-labor system there for blacks as well as whites, to establish public schools for both races, to look after the welfare of the former slaves, to grant them access to the ballot and the courts—in short, to build a new South dedicated like Lincoln to the Declaration of Independence and the preservation of popular government. It was no Whig who had fought the war through to a total Union triumph and a larger concept of the inalienable rights of man that now included the American Negro. It was no Whig who had summoned Americans both North and South, Americans both black and white, to dedicate themselves to a new birth of freedom, so that government of, by, and for all the people would not perish from the earth. No, the man who did all that was a principled and dedicated Republican, and he deserves to be remembered that way.

↶

A POLITICAL SOURCE OF GREATNESS:
LINCOLN AND THE REPUBLICAN PARTY

Colleen Shogan and Robert Raffety

AMERICANS ARE FASCINATED by Abraham Lincoln. He is thought of as the emancipator of slaves, a great rhetorician, a political philosopher, a moral exemplar, and a powerful chief executive. Three and a half million people a year visit the Lincoln Memorial. As a nation, we stand in awe of our sixteenth president. Perhaps due to our benign admiration and low opinion of contemporary affairs, Lincoln's skills as a politician are often pushed to the side and perhaps even minimized. However, by neglecting to analyze the sources of Lincoln's political power, we are missing an important part of Lincoln's greatness. In particular, Lincoln's political success would have not been possible without his impressive party leadership.

As a mid-nineteenth century president, political scientists characterize Lincoln's administration as falling within the "Party Era" of the presidency.[1] From Andrew Jackson to Theodore Roosevelt, presidents utilized the resources of their political party to gain power and authority. This was no simple task. The political parties of the nineteenth century bore little organizational similarity to their modern counterparts. In comparison to the programmatic, national parties we have today, premodern parties were locally based organizations that thrived on patronage distribution. In Lincoln's time, presidents were often not considered the political "leaders" of their party, finding themselves subordinate to congressional partisans who wielded more authority within the rank and file.

Unlike the British model, the party system in the United States was not designed to strengthen political ties between the executive and legislature.[2] Instead, James Ceaser argues that the American party system arose in the early nineteenth century to curb presidential ambition.[3] Thus, presidents during the "Party Era" were in the difficult position of trying to lead decentralized, bottom-up organizations whose raison d'être was to subdue executive power. In many administrations during this time period, the party machine effectively circumscribed independent presidential leadership. The faceless "dark horse" presidents of the nineteenth century needed their party's organization to gain election, and once in office, they spent much of their time returning favors with political appointments.

It is curious that our most revered president, Abraham Lincoln, emerged from this difficult leadership situation. After all, British philosopher and politician Edmund Burke argued that one of the main reasons strong political parties are so attractive is that party government could substitute for the lack of great statesmen in democracies.[4] If political parties were conceived as a substitute for eminent statesmanship, how did Lincoln combine party leadership and statesmanship as president?

Given the strength and importance of political parties at mid-century, we are left with two possible explanations for Lincoln's impressive leadership. First, Lincoln may have been a precursor to Franklin Roosevelt, who aimed to "transcend" rather than "reconstruct" the party system in the United States.[5] Perhaps Lincoln's goal was to rise above the party system and establish an independent executive outside of its organizational constraints. The alternative explanation is that Lincoln operated within the party system, but was perhaps the most astute and skilled president to manipulate its apparatus. According to this supposition, the source of Lincoln's greatness was his ability to understand the demands of the Republican machine and suppress its internal divisions.

In this essay, we argue that the latter hypothesis provides the stronger explanation. Lincoln is an anomaly not because he triumphed over his party, but because he mastered the organizational demands of his leadership role. We argue that Lincoln demonstrated impressive party leadership in three ways: his mastery of the nominating convention, the careful distribution of patronage spoils, and his management of the ideological factions within his party. In the following pages, we discuss the origins of Lincoln's Republicanism, outline the strategic elements of Lincoln's party leadership, and explain how his political skill facilitated his eminent statesmanship.

Lincoln the Whig Loyalist

The emergence of Abraham Lincoln as a leader within the Republican party is as interesting and unlikely a story as the birth of the Republican party itself. Indeed, Lincoln spent his early political life as a faithful member of the Whig party, and like many of his Whig contemporaries, he was not eager to change his affiliation. Lincoln did sympathize with the Republicans, a group whose origins were tied heavily to the antislavery, abolitionist movement, but his reluctance to join the Republican cause is a testament to his shrewd preference for affiliating with an established party over a fledging, potentially failed enterprise.

The Whig party formed in opposition to the Jacksonian Democrats. While both the Whigs and Democrats enjoyed remarkable stability through the mid-1830s and 40s, the former remained credible only to the extent that it could offer clear and palatable alternatives to the latter on issues of local, state, and national concern. By the early 1850s, however, a series of political, economic, and social developments led many Americans to view the Whigs and Democrats as more similar than different from each other.[6] This led to significant fracturing within the major parties and ultimately gave rise to a number of third parties, most notably the Free-Soil, Know-Nothing, and Republican parties.

During this time period, pragmatic antislavery advocates, fully aware of the political futility of the existing abolitionist movement, began to advance a more moderate approach to reform. These savvy reformers laid the groundwork for the early Republican party.[7] While they were opposed to slavery, they were more willing than their more radical counterparts to entertain compromise solutions.

As the distinctions between Whigs and Democrats blurred, the Republican party became an increasingly attractive alternative for disgruntled Whigs. But Lincoln was slower than most to consider an outright party switch. As the Illinois Whig nominee for the Senate in 1854, it is clear that Lincoln was well respected among his peers and heavily invested in the state party machine. Even as Lincoln recognized that his party was dying, he was reluctant to abandon it. When questioned by his old friend Joshua F. Speed about his political association, Lincoln replied: "I think I am a Whig; but others say there are no Whigs, and that I am an abolitionist." In his correspondence with Speed, Lincoln went on to denounce the Know-Nothings, and expressed frustration with those who attempted to "unwhig" him.[8] Lincoln's hesitation to leave the Whigs was not due to a lack of ambition, but rather his determination to lead a political life of consequence, and more specifically his uncertainty as to which alternative party he should affiliate.

In January 1856, when it became clear that the future of the Whig party was in great jeopardy, Lincoln finally made his move. He attended a conference of distinguished editors who were meeting in Decatur to draft a new, conservative doctrine designed to attract a broad coalition of moderate abolitionists, foreign-born voters, antislavery Democrats, former Whigs and Know-Nothings, and other politically homeless elements of the time. As the meeting's only non-journalist, Lincoln's presence was conspicuous. At the conclusion of the conference, after playing a significant role in the development of its ideological tenants, Lincoln politely expressed his interest in running as the new party's candidate for Senate.[9]

Lincoln's strategic departure from the Whigs indicates that he understood the importance of the party system during this era. Lincoln knew that he could not ascend to greatness without the backing of a powerful party and its machinery to support him. Only when the Whigs had ceased to function as a palpable alternative to the Democrats did Lincoln seize the opportunity to take part in the formation of a new party. As with other important decisions that Lincoln would make throughout his political life, timing was key. Furthermore, Lincoln's metamorphosis into a Republican demonstrates his knack for opportunity more than the strength of his ideological conviction. It serves as an example of cautious contemplation, and is the first in a series of calculated maneuvers that suggest Lincoln was far more likely to react as events unfolded than to serve as an unabashed catalyst for change.

Securing the Nomination

In 1860, the Republican party was a heterogeneous lot. T. Harry Williams observed, "No polyglot army of an ancient emperor ever exhibited more variety than did the Republican Party in 1860."[10] As Southern states began to threaten secession, the main divisions in the Republicans consisted of converted Whigs and disgruntled former Democrats. In general, the Whigs were more pragmatic and moderate than the Democrats, who switched parties due to their moral beliefs about slavery and their rejection of the Kansas-Nebraska Act.[11] It is fair to say that almost all Republicans shared antislavery tendencies, but disagreed over the timing and implementation of slavery's eradication.

Lincoln's friends and supporters at the second Republican National Convention in Chicago presented their candidate as an unknown quantity and used his obscurity as a political advantage. He firmly resisted any attachments to the various factions of his party, and construed his opinion on slavery as primarily territorial: he recognized the right to own slaves in the states where it now existed, but opposed its expansion. The political circumstances in 1860 made Lincoln, who was not much more than a dark-horse player within the party, a viable alternative to the frontrunner, Senator William H. Seward of New York, who had earned an extremist reputation on the issue of slavery. Lincoln "fitted the exigencies of the moment perfectly."[12] While most of the prominent party leaders divided along predictable ideological factions, Lincoln benefited from the structural rules of the game: two-thirds of the convention vote was needed to secure the nomination. When it became clear that no favorite had emerged, Lincoln's supporters sprung into action.[13] Under Lincoln's direction, they offered their nominee as an acceptable "second choice."

Since Lincoln had not emerged as a major player on the national scene, the disparate factions of the party believed that they could control Lincoln as president. As stated earlier, the party system had been designed with the intention of frustrating executive ambition.

After Lincoln won the Republican nomination, everyone waited to see which side he would join. The more radical faction claimed Lincoln as an antislavery advocate, and the conservatives trusted that Lincoln's pragmatism would bring him to their side. To no avail, the factional leaders waited with baited breath to discern where Lincoln would fall. Lincoln's ingenious response to the eagerness of his new compatriots was silence. During the presidential campaign, Lincoln remained mute. During the nineteenth century, the party apparatus ran the campaign, and nominees rarely made personal appearances. Lincoln adhered to this custom, and did not divulge where he stood with regards to the factional uncertainty of his party. Even after he won the election, Lincoln did not show his cards, despite the urging of some to reveal his position on the issue of slavery and southern secession. An adviser to Lincoln, Joseph Medill, advised him to keep silent in order to "keep his feet out of all such wolfe [sic] traps."[14]

Although Lincoln kept quiet after his election to the presidency, he was not idle. In Springfield, Lincoln studied the nation's finances, and familiarized himself with the most pressing national problems. However, most of his time and ink was spent on figuring out how the national Republican party worked, who the major players were, and how he might handle a very complicated political situation when he arrived in Washington, D.C. During this time, Lincoln corresponded with several members of the Republican congressional delegation, and squelched the possibility of a territorial compromise in response to secession threats. Lincoln's quiet leadership during this interim time period is rarely noted, but these decisions helped established him as the new premier of the Republican party.[15]

Unlike contemporary politics in which the president is unconditionally accepted as the titular head of his party, the task of maintaining partisan leadership was a difficult enterprise for Lincoln. He had inherited a party with a muted ideological identification. Lincoln sought to transform the Republicans into an institution that reflected his own policy preferences and political philosophy. In pursuit of these ends, Lincoln did not operate outside the box. Instead, he pushed the limits of nineteenth century party leadership by mastering two predictable mechanisms: balancing the existing factions of his party and manipulating the spoils system.

Managing the Party

Adopting a lesson from Machiavelli, Lincoln understood the value of keeping his friends close, and his enemies closer. Lincoln's first significant act as president, constructing his cabinet, serves as an excellent example of his obedience to this old adage. To most observers, it may seem more advantageous for a newly elected president to surround himself with like-minded advisors. However, Lincoln knew better. When making his cabinet appointments, Lincoln drew carefully from every major faction of the Republican party.[16] For the premier positions of secretary of state, secretary of treasury, and attorney general, Lincoln named his pre-convention rivals, William H. Seward, Salmon Chase, and Edward Bates, respectively. He not only invited his political enemies to assume these important positions, he insisted upon their acceptance.[17] Lincoln filled other posts with a similar zest for inclusion, even going so far as to appoint several former Democrats to his cabinet. The advantage to this inclusive approach was twofold. First, the ideological diversity of Lincoln's appointees helped satisfy the many elements within his party, thus preventing the Republicans from splintering into a party of irrelevance. Second, and more important from Lincoln's perspective, the appointment of multiple political rivals to his cabinet enabled Lincoln to strategically pit his foes against one another, thus ensuring that no single enemy could gain the strength to challenge his supremacy as president.

Lincoln's use of shrewd political calculus was not reserved for merely his early cabinet appointments. Lincoln strategically distributed patronage jobs to various factions and demographic regions in order to build a broader party apparatus. The portrayal of Lincoln as a statesman above the spoils system is a sanitized, antiseptic depiction that Lincoln himself would despise. As president, Lincoln prided himself on his careful distribution of the spoils, and boasted that he "distributed to his party friends as nearly all the civil patronage as any administration ever did."[18]

For Lincoln, patronage strengthened the party organization in specific regions of the country, such as the border states, where the Republican presence was weak. Lincoln also used patronage as a reward system. Perhaps his most skillful use of patronage occurred in 1864, as Lincoln prepared to fend off a challenge for his party's nomination from Salmon P. Chase, the secretary of the treasury. When Lincoln discovered that Senator Samuel Pomeroy from Kansas supported Chase's candidacy, he withdrew all patronage from his state. After Chase's defeat, Pomeroy politely asked Lincoln to restore the jobs and goodies to his control. Lincoln listened to the plea, and declined Pomeroy's request.[19] Finally, patronage was a source of financial revenue for the party-building activities Lincoln undertook. When Lincoln assumed the leadership of the Republicans, he found the party disorganized and weak. Prior to 1860, it had only existed as an opposition party, and had not developed into a nationally competitive organization with broad appeal. Building and transforming a party requires substantial funds, and Lincoln extracted financial support from those who benefited from the federal patronage. Lincoln demanded a ten percent annual donation from officeholders, and he made sure all cabinet members understood that they were expected to keep track of their departmental contributions. When the secretary of the navy protested the practice of collecting funds from naval shipyard workers, Lincoln summoned him to the White House, where the Republican party chairman informed him that there were no exceptions to the arrangement.[20]

The one area in which Lincoln minimized the importance of patronage was the selection of high-ranking generals for the Union army. Since many Southerners abdicated their military positions after secession, the army that Lincoln inherited was evenly split between Democratic and Whig appointments. It might have been politically scrupulous for Lincoln to fill the army with strategic patronage appointments. However, Lincoln resisted an overtly political approach to the process and instead selected generals based primarily upon military experience and expertise. In fact, evidence suggests that Lincoln preferred nonpartisan professional soldiers. Because they had no political ties and preferences, it was more likely they would follow the administration's orders rather than their own inclinations. Lincoln limited his use of military patronage to appointments in geographic areas that exhibited little likelihood for sensitive action. This careful approach to military appointments placated his fellow partisans in Congress, who controlled the funding and conscription measures of the war.[21]

Lincoln's ambition turned his attention towards a second term in office. Lincoln's ability to secure renomination from his party was a remarkable feat, given the prevalent Whig sentiment of the time that rotation in office was more valuable than stability. The nominating convention of 1864 was not nearly as exciting as 1860. In fact, by the time of the convention, Lincoln's renomination seemed probable, if not certain. But it wasn't for a lack of effort on the behalf of his rivals that Lincoln received his party's nomination again. Republicans in Congress were unenthusiastic about Lincoln's candidacy, and his strongest opposition arose from within his own administration.

Lincoln's strongest challenge for the 1864 nomination came from the secretary of treasury, Samuel P. Chase. From the beginning of Lincoln's first term, Chase had been positioning himself as the alternative to the incumbent.[22] Unable to openly contest the president while serving in his cabinet, Chase convinced other prominent Lincoln critics to promote his name discretely as an alternate candidate for the 1864 nomination. As his presidential ambition became more widely known, to even Lincoln himself, Chase tried to part ways with the administration in which he served. Believing that he could best advance his candidacy from outside Lincoln's cabinet, Chase attempted to resign his post five times, often complaining about some perceived injustice in his department.[23] But, knowing that an unauthorized resignation would be viewed publicly as a cowardly evasion of duty, Lincoln repeatedly denied Chase's requests. Because it would have been unthinkable for Chase to abandon Lincoln's administration during wartime without his express consent, Chase was obligated to serve reluctantly at Lincoln's pleasure. But so long as Chase remained a high-ranking secretary in Lincoln's cabinet, he remained too close to the administration to ever mount a serious, open challenge. Chase's attempt at an "insurgent" candidacy must have given Lincoln a chuckle. Lincoln had broad support amongst the Republican party faithful from the northern states, and even though he did not speak publicly about their machinations, he knew they were working hard to secure the nomination for him.[24]

In June of 1864, after Lincoln had wrapped up the nomination, Chase complained to Lincoln once again and threatened resignation for the sixth time. Since Chase's presence in the cabinet no longer served Lincoln's political purposes, the president graciously accepted the secretary's resignation.

The Limits and Achievements of Party Leadership

Although we have concentrated on how Lincoln utilized his party leadership to strengthen his political authority, Lincoln also understood the ideological purposes of partisanship. As president, Lincoln sought to transform the Republicans from a sectional anti-southern coalition into a national party whose primary goal was to save the Union.[25] In pursuit of this goal, congressional Republicans opposed Lincoln every step of the way. With narrow Republican constituencies, members of Congress saw no need to broaden the base of their party and shed their anti-Southern beliefs. But Lincoln's view as president was much different due to the fact that his constituency was national in scope. Lincoln could not suffer the luxury of a sectional party whose sole purpose was to subjugate an entire demographic region of the country. If Lincoln hoped to reunify the country, he needed to broaden his support throughout the North, the border states, and the readmitted South. Political scientist Stephen Skowronek explains, "Lincoln could not have survived without the support of the Republican party, but neither could he have safely afforded to rest content with it."[26]

Of course, congressional Republicans did not endorse the president's plan, and at the time of Lincoln's death, no consensus had been reached concerning reconstruction. In this light, we must admit that Lincoln's success as a party leader had its limitations. Lincoln was not able to achieve his ultimate goal of reconstructing his party and transforming its narrow purpose. The ideological goals Lincoln pursued as a party leader were not fully realized, and the Republicans remained anti-Southern for decades after the Civil War.

However, Lincoln's inability to forge a wholesale reconstruction of the Republican party does not diminish his notable successes as a party leader. Simply said, no one in the nineteenth century played the game better than Abraham Lincoln. His deft handling of the political machine insured that he controlled the party rather than the party controlling him. Buried in a political era known for producing "no name" presidents, Lincoln exercised executive initiative and refused to be deemed irrelevant and subordinate. His mastery of the Republican machine earned him reelection in 1864, which no president had achieved since Andrew Jackson in 1832.

Unlike many of his predecessors and successors, Lincoln's leadership was not damaged by the demands of political partisanship. Lincoln embraced his role as party leader and pushed the authority of his position to its absolute limits. While Lincoln battled regularly with troublesome factions in the party, such conflict energized, rather than sapped, his strength.[27] After every confrontation, Lincoln emerged victorious and above the fray, which only increased his claims of political independence.

The Constitution demands that the president act as both a politician and a statesman. The chief executive must negotiate the separated power system as a politician, while simultaneously promoting a national ideology as a statesman. During the Civil War, it was imperative that Lincoln fulfilled both of these roles. Lincoln realized that the unifying apparatus that allowed him to excel as both a politician and a statesman was his political party. Lincoln's contributions as a statesman and rhetorician have been analyzed and lauded by scholars; it is now time to appreciate his skill as a political partisan.

༁

Notes to Chapter 4

On Professor Donald's Lincoln

1. Portions of this essay contain material that appeared originally in: Ethan Fishman, *The Prudential Presidency: An Aristotelian Approach to Presidential Leadership* (Westport, CT: Praeger, 2001); and Ethan Fishman, "Under the Circumstances: Abraham Lincoln and Classical Prudence," in *Abraham Lincoln: Sources and Style of Leadership*, eds. Frank J. Williams, William D. Pederson and Vincent Marsala (Westport, CT: Greenwood, 1994), 3–15. Reprinted by permission.

2. David Donald, "A. Lincoln, Politician," in *Lincoln Reconsidered*, ed. David Donald (N.Y.: Vintage Books, 1961), 57.

3. Donald, "A. Lincoln, Politician," 70.

4. Aristotle, *The Ethics*, trans. J. A. K. Thomson (Baltimore: Penguin Books, 1966), 176.

5. Aristotle, *The Ethics*, 177.

6. Aristotle, *The Ethics*, 65.

7. John Hallowell, *Main Currents in Modern Political Thought* (N.Y.: Holt, Rinehart and Winston, 1950), 5–6.

8. Aristotle, *The Ethics*, 28.

9. Walter Lippmann, *The Public Philosophy* (N.Y.: New American Library, 1963), 112–13.

10. Aristotle, *The Ethics*, 61.

11. Aristotle, *The Politics*, trans. Ernest Barker (N.Y.: Oxford University Press, 1962), 231.

12. Aristotle, *The Ethics*, 305.

13. Donald, "A. Lincoln, Politician," 65.

14. Aristotle, *The Ethics*, 4.

15. David Donald, *Lincoln* (N.Y.: Simon and Schuster, 1995), 81.

16. Donald, *Lincoln*, 81.

17. Lincoln quoted in Richard Current, *The Political Thought of Abraham Lincoln* (Indianapolis: Bobbs-Merrill, 1967), 215. All italics in this essay are the author's own.

18. Current, *The Political Thought of Abraham Lincoln*, 298.

19. Current, *The Political Thought of Abraham Lincoln*, 72.

20. Current, *The Political Thought of Abraham Lincoln*, 316.

21. Current, *The Political Thought of Abraham Lincoln*, 298.

22. David Donald, "Abraham Lincoln and the American Pragmatic Tradition," in *Lincoln Reconsidered*, ed. David Donald (N.Y.: Vintage Books, 1961), 128.

23. Donald, *Lincoln*, 15.

24. Donald, *Lincoln*, 332.

25. Donald, *Lincoln*, 452.

26. Lincoln quoted in Donald, *Lincoln*, 222.

27. Current, *The Political Thought of Abraham Lincoln*, 110.

28. Current, *The Political Thought of Abraham Lincoln*, 105.

29. Paul Angle, *Created Equal? The Complete Lincoln-Douglas Debates of 1858* (Chicago: University of Chicago Press, 1958), 111.

30. Harry Jaffa, *Crisis of the House Divided* (Chicago: University of Chicago Press, 1982), 1.

31. William Riordan, *Plunkitt of Tammany Hall* (N.Y.: Dutton, 1963), 3.

32. Riordan, *Plunkitt of Tammany Hall*, 4.

33. Reinhold Niebuhr, *Moral Man and Immoral Society* (N.Y.: Charles Scribner's Sons, 1932), 4.

34. Reinhold Niebuhr, *The Children of Light and the Children of Darkness* (N.Y.: Charles Scribner's Sons, 1944), 40–41.

35. Aristotle, *The Ethics*, 631.

36. Current, *The Political Thought of Abraham Lincoln*, 299.

37. Donald, *Lincoln*, 434.

38. R. G. Mulgan, *Aristotle's Political Theory* (N.Y.: Oxford University Press, 1977), 9.

39. Jaffa, *Crisis of the House Divided*, 1.

40. James G. Randall, *Lincoln the President* (N.Y.: Dodd, Mead, 1945), 1:127.

41. Richard Hofstadter, "Abraham Lincoln and the Self-Made Myth," in *The American Political Tradition*, ed. Richard Hofstadter (N.Y.: Vintage Books, 1961), 100, 116, and 133.

42. Hofstadter, "Abraham Lincoln and the Self-Made Myth," 132.

43. Current, *The Political Thought of Abraham Lincoln*, xxix.

44. Donald, "Abraham Lincoln and the American Pragmatic Tradition," 143.

Lincoln's Revolution

1. The volume and page locations of all quotations in this essay are cited parenthetically in the text. References are to two editions, separated by a semicolon. The first reference is to Abraham Lincoln, *Speeches and Writings*, edited by Don E. Fehrenbacher, 2 vols. (New York: Library of America, 1989); the title is abbreviated SW. The second is to *The Collected Works of Abraham Lincoln*, edited by Roy P. Basler et al., vols. 1–8. (New Brunswick, N.J.: Rutgers University Press, 1953–55); the title is abbreviated CW.

2. That this is at least an overstatement is attested to by the lines that follow and form Lincoln's peroration: a heady, passionate appeal for the use of sober reason.

3. Lincoln's imagery is taken from an 1827 speech by Henry Clay before the American Colonization Society, which he cites in his 1852 eulogy on Clay (SW 1:270; CW 2:131).

4. Ibid.

5. Lincoln uses comparable language in describing the effects of "the just and generous, and prosperous system" of free labor (SW 2:98, 297; CW 3:479, 5:52).

6. The most diverse interpreters assert or concede as much before going on to draw utterly incompatible conclusions. Thus, for example, Harry V. Jaffa (in a seminal study to which I am much in debt) allows that "Lincoln's affirmation of the Founders' and signers' meaning, as distinct from his contradiction of Douglas and Taney, is not itself impeccable on purely historical grounds" and surmises that Lincoln "was not innocent of the nature of his subsequent 'reconstruction'" of their meaning. Jaffa, *Crisis of the House Divided: An Interpretation of the Issues in the Lincoln-Douglas Debates* (New York: Doubleday, 1959), 328 (see also 324, 325). M. E. Bradford charges Lincoln with being "duplicitous" while "appealing to an imaginary history." Bradford, "Against Lincoln," in *The Historian's Lincoln: Pseudohistory, Psychohistory, and History*, edited by Gabor S. Boritt and Norman O. Forness (Urbana: University of Illinois Press, 1988), 111. Garry Wills sees Lincoln's self-conscious artistry as contributing to a romantic, mythic misreading—if not distortion—of Jefferson's principles and intentions. Wills, *Inventing America: Jefferson's Declaration of Independence* (New York: Vintage Books, 1979), xiv–xxiv. More charitable, perhaps, is the assertion by Mark E. Neely, Jr., that "the Jeffersonian legacy was more ambiguous than Lincoln realized." Neely, *The Abraham Lincoln Encyclopedia*, s.v. "Jefferson, Thomas" (New York: McGraw-Hill, 1982), 164.

7. See Lincoln's meditation on Proverbs 25:11 in CW, 4:168–69.

Abraham Lincoln: Republican in the White House

1. David Donald, *Lincoln Reconsidered; Essays on the Civil War Era*, paperback ed. (New York, 1956), 187–208.

2. Kenneth Stampp, *The Era of Reconstruction, 1865–1877* (New York, 1965), 25–49.

3. Gabor S. Boritt, *Lincoln and the Economics of the American Dream* (Memphis. Tenn., 1978), 195–231, 267–74.

4. McFeely, *Grant: A Biography* (New York, 1981), 292. In his review of Grant in the *New Republic* (February 28, 1981), Justin Kaplan, alas, repeats McFeely's assertion as gospel.

5. *The Collected Works of Abraham Lincoln*, ed. Roy P. Basler, Marion Delores Pratt, and Lloyd A. Dunlap, 9 vols. (New Brunswick, N.J., 1953–55), 3:16.

6. Don E. Fehrenbacher, *Prelude to Greatness. Lincoln in the 1850's* (Stanford, Calif., 1962), 44–47, 86. For a history of Lincoln's keynote address at Bloomington, see Elwell Crissey, *Lincoln's Lost Speech* (New York, 1967).

7. See Boritt, *Lincoln and the Economics of the American Dream*, ix and passim: and Stephen B. Oates, *Abraham Lincoln: The Man Behind the Myths* (New York, 1984), 59–60.

8. See Stephen B. Oates, *With Malice Towards None: The Life of Abraham Lincoln* (New York, 1977), 127–40.

9. *Collected Works of Lincoln*, 2:494, 385; 3:462–63, 477–81; and *The Collected Works of Abraham Lincoln—Supplement, 1832–1865*, ed. Roy P. Basler (Westport, Conn., 1974), 43–45. For Republican thought, see Eric Foner, *Free Soil, Free Labor, Free Men: The Ideology of the Republican Party before the Civil War* (New York, 1970).

10. *Collected Works of Lincoln*, 3:547–50.

11. *Collected Works of Lincoln*, 4:149–50, 151–54, 183; *The Letters of Henry Adams*, ed. Worthington Chauncey Ford (Boston and New York, 1930), 68–69; David M. Potter, *Lincoln and His Party in the Secession Crisis* (New Haven and London, 1942), 156–61.

12. *Collected Works of Lincoln*, 4:214. Donald wrongly paraphrases Lincolns remarks,

thereby making it appear that he "did not believe" that the executive should exercise his constitutional prerogatives at all (*Lincoln Reconsidered*, 199).

13. *Collected Works of Lincoln*, 4:214.

14. *Collected Works of Lincoln*, 4:438.

15. *Collected Works of Lincoln*, 5:346; 7:512.

16. *Collected Works of Lincoln*, 5:49.

17. For an elaboration, see Oates, *Lincoln: Man Behind the Myths*, 89–147.

18. Quoted in Benjamin P. Thomas, *Abraham Lincoln* (New York, 1952), 254.

19. Tyler Dennett, ed., *Lincoln and the Civil War in the Diaries and Letters of John Hay* (1939; reprint ed., Westport, Conn., 1972), 76; Helen Nicolay, *Lincoln's Secretary: A Biography of John G. Nicolay* (New York, 1949), 83.

20. David Homer Bates, *Lincoln in the Telegraph Office* (New York, 1907), 266; Boritt, *Lincoln and the Economics of the American Dream*, 231.

21. Lincoln, however, was up against powerful congressional elements with a vested interest in retaining the nefarious Indian system the way it was. In the end, Congress rejected Lincoln's call for reform, and the president turned back to the war. Still, there can be no doubt that he intended to do something about the Indian system when he had the opportunity. As he said (and meant): "If we get through this war, and I live, *this Indian system shall be reformed.*" See David A. Nichols, *Lincoln and the Indians: Civil War Policy and Politics* (Columbia, Mo., and London, 1978), 94–118, 129–46, 148.

22. Quoted in Fawn M. Brodie, *Thaddeus Stevens, Scourge of the South* (New York, 1959), 204.

23. David Donald, *Charles Sumner and the Rights of Man* (New York, 1970), 19ff.

24. For Lincoln's closeness to congressional Republicans, see Peyton McCrary, *Abraham Lincoln and Reconstruction: The Louisiana Experiment* (Princeton, 1978), 3–15; Donald, *Charles Sumner and the Rights of Man*, 207–8; Harold M. Hyman, *A More Perfect Union: The Impact of the Civil War and Reconstruction on the Constitution*, paperback ed. (Boston, 1975), 276–81, and Hyman, *Lincoln's Reconstruction: Neither Failure of Vision nor Vision of Failure*, the third R. Gerald McMurtry Lecture, Fort Wayne, Ind., May 8, 1980; Herman Belz, *Reconstructing the Union: Theory and Policy During the Civil War* (Ithaca, N.Y., 1969), 309–10; Hans L. Trefousse, *The Radical Republicans: Lincoln's Vanguard for Racial Justice* (New York, 1969), 286–304; and Oates, *Lincoln: Man Behind the Myths*, 141–46.

25. George W. Julian, Isaac Arnold, and Hugh McCulloch all thought so. See Belz, *Reconstructing the Union*, 309–10.

26. *Collected Works of Lincoln*, 8:333.

A Political Source of Greatness

1. Stephen Skowronek, *The Politics Presidents Make* (Cambridge, MA: Belknap Press of Harvard University Press, 1997).

2. Sidney Milkis, *The President and the Parties: The Transformation of the American Party System Since the New Deal* (Oxford, Oxford University Press, 1993), 6.

3. James W. Ceaser, *Presidential Selection: Theory and Development* (Princeton, NJ: Princeton University Press, 1979), 123–169.

4. Harvey C. Mansfield, Jr., *Statesmanship and Party Government: A Study of Burke and Bolingbroke* (Chicago: University of Chicago Press, 1965), 17.

5. Milkis, *The President and the Parties*, 5.

6. First, the Whigs and the Democrats both committed in their convention platforms to the Compromise of 1850, thus minimizing partisan distinctions concerning the issue of slavery's expansion. Second, in 1852, the predominantly Protestant Whig party made a bid to recruit Catholic and immigrants to compete with the growing Democratic party. This tactic led to the exodus of the nativist faction of the Whig party. Third, sudden economic prosperity began to minimize differences in financial policy between the two major parties, with the Whigs abdicating their protectionist and interventionist ideology. Michael F. Holt, *Political Parties and American Political Development from the Age of Jackson to the Age of Lincoln* (Baton Rouge, Louisiana State University Press, 1992), 244–45.

7. George Mayer, *The Republican Party: 1854–1966,* 2nd Edition (Oxford, Oxford University Press, 1967), 24.

8. David Herbert Donald, *Lincoln* (New York, Touchstone, 1995), 189.

9. Donald, *Lincoln,* 190.

10. T. Harry Williams, *Lincoln and the Radicals* (Madison, WI: The University of Wisconsin Press, 1941), 4.

11. David M. Potter, *Lincoln and His Party in the Secession Crisis* (New Haven, CT: Yale University Press, 1942), 23.

12. Potter, *Lincoln and his Party,* 34.

13. Two of Lincoln's supporters orchestrated the printing of duplicate convention tickets to ensure that the hall would be packed with "Lincoln men." Donald, 1995: 248.

14. Donald, *Lincoln,* 260.

15. Potter, *Lincoln and His Party,* 170.

16. Mayer, *The Republican Party,* 84.

17. On the eve of Lincoln's inauguration, Seward withdrew his acceptance of the Secretary of State, but Lincoln remained firm and ultimately convinced Seward to reconsider. Mayer, *The Republican Party,* 84.

18. David Donald, *Lincoln Reconsidered* (New York: Vintage Books).

19. Donald, *Lincoln Reconsidered.*

20. Donald, *Lincoln Reconsidered.*

21. Andrew Polsky, "'Mr. Lincoln's Army' Revisited: Partisanship, Institutional Position, and Union Army Command, 1861–1865." *Studies in American Political Development,* 16 (Fall 2002), 176–207.

22. "From his strategic position in the cabinet, Chase had employed the patronage of the Treasury Department to build a personal organization. By arranging for his portrait to appear on the one-dollar national bank notes, Chase placed a 'campaign picture in every man's pocket.'" Mayer, *The Republican Party,* 115, citing Thomas G. Belden, *The Salmon P. Chase Family in the Civil War and Reconstruction: A Study in Ambition and Corruption* (unpublished Ph.D. thesis, University of Chicago, 1952).

23. Eric McKitrick, "Party Politics and the Union and Confederate War Efforts," in *The American Party Systems,* William Nisbet Chambers and Walter Dean Burnham, eds. (New York: Oxford University Press, 1975), 130.

24. Donald, *Lincoln,* 480.

25. Holt, *Political Parties,* 330. To this end, the Republicans even changed their name in 1864, calling themselves the "Union" party in an effort to attract War Democrats to their coalition.

26. Skowronek, *The Politics Presidents Make,* 219.

27. McKitrick, "Party Politics," 145.

Chapter 5

LINCOLN AND EXECUTIVE POWER

Did Lincoln establish a constitutional dictatorship? Does he provide a precedent for the Imperial Presidency?

These measures, whether strictly legal or not, were ventured upon, under what appeared to be a popular demand, and a public necessity; trusting, then as now, that Congress would readily ratify them. It is believed that nothing has been done beyond the constitutional competency of Congress.

Soon after the first call for militia, it was considered a duty to authorize the Commanding General, in proper cases, according to his discretion, to suspend the privilege of the writ of habeas corpus; or, in other words, to arrest, and detain, without resort to the ordinary processes and forms of law, such individuals as he might deem dangerous to the public safety. This authority has purposely been exercised but very sparingly. Nevertheless, the legality and propriety of what has been done under it, are questioned; and the attention of the country has been called to the proposition that one who is sworn to "take care that the laws be faithfully executed," should not himself violate them. Of course some consideration was given to the questions of power, and propriety, before this matter was acted upon. The whole of the laws which were required to be faithfully executed, were being resisted, and failing of execution, in nearly one-third of the States. Must they be allowed to finally fail of execution, even had it been perfectly clear, that by the use of the means necessary to their execution, some single law, made in such extreme tenderness of the citizen's liberty, that practically, it relieves more of the guilty, than of the innocent, should, to a very limited extent, be violated? To state the question more directly, are all the laws, but one, to go unexecuted, and the government itself go to pieces, lest that one be violated?

Abraham Lincoln, Message to Congress in Special Session, July 4, 1861

★ James G. Randall, "Lincoln in the Role of Dictator"
★ Herman Belz, "Lincoln and the Constitution: The Dictatorship Question Reconsidered"
★ Jeffrey Crouch and Mark J. Rozell, "Lincoln and Executive Power: Rebutting the Dictatorship Thesis"
★ Phillip G. Henderson, "Abraham Lincoln and His Cabinet"

ᘓ

LINCOLN IN THE ROLE OF DICTATOR

James G. Randall

"How MANY more thousand books must be written before we learn what sort of man he really was?" This remark was made in a recent brochure by a Lincolnian scholar who was aiming his pointed criticisms at a startling hoax in the form of forged Lincoln documents which had been prominently published in one of the finest and most honorable of the nation's magazines. That such a hoax was possible offers food for reflection both to the historian and to the general public. The forgery, be it noted, was clumsy, not clever. Letters more unlike Lincoln's, in form and substance, could hardly have been fabricated; yet they were for a time accepted as genuine. Though no character in American history is more admired nor more written about than Lincoln, the historian's responsibility of rescuing his personality from the myth and sentimental fiction with which it has become encrusted has not yet been fully met. The burden of the present article is to exhibit a side of Lincoln's presidency which is not fully understood and to show how, as wartime chief in a democracy, the liberal statesman became, by the pressure of events, the wielder of a greatly expanded executive authority—how the advocate of government of, by, and for the people exercised more independent power and approached a dictatorship more closely than has any other president. Presidential authority was enormously increased during the World War; but Wilson's power to deal with disloyal practices and his authority over material factors—over railroads, food, fuel, trade, and shipping—were in the main conferred by Congress; while Lincoln's most striking powers, as in his Emancipation Proclamation and the arbitrary arrests, were independently assumed. As a Constitutional question the subject is of great interest, and in light of present-day dictatorships it has renewed significance; but to many its chief meaning will appear in its commentary on Lincoln himself. It is the reaction of Lincoln's mind to his difficult position, and the manner in which he fitted his personality into an uncongenial role, that specially challenge attention.

Lincoln, the man of peace, author of the Gettysburg Address, wielding a dictator's sceptre, seems a paradox. Yet it was the custom of Lincoln's opponents to denounce him as a despot. Opposition orators spoke of "Dictator Lincoln" and compared the president to Nero or Caligula, while such newspapers as the *New York World* and the *Chicago Times* lashed the administration with severe editorials. Even Lincoln's friends showed distress at his unusual measures. Such a mildly disposed

*This article originally appeared in *South Atlantic Quarterly*, Vol. 28, No. 3, pp. 236–252, 1929, published by Duke University Press. Reprinted with permission from Duke University Press.

conservative as Senator Browning of Illinois, though a close friend, wrote despondently in his diary of the "President's giving himself over to 'the radicals'"; and Senator Fessenden remarked that the suspension of the habeas corpus privilege in the loyal States was "an exercise of despotic power." That the present popular notion should conflict with this contemporary opinion is due in part to the fact that the full story of Lincoln's problems as president is still to be told; for his presidency is that part of his life which is most imperfectly understood and on which the biographers have shed the least light. Yet when all is said one must recognize here a real meeting of opposites—a real uncongeniality between the hard circumstances of Lincoln's day of power and the type of man he was.

I

At the very outset of the Civil War, Lincoln gave the policy of the government a dictatorial turn by assuming far reaching powers independently of Congress. Every other war president has submitted to Congress the question of war or peace; but President Lincoln, taking upon his own shoulders the decision as to how the situation should be met, launched a whole series of war measures and irrevocably committed the country to a definite war policy months before Congress was even called into session. He treated the conflict not as war, but as something like a magnified Whiskey Insurrection, calling forth the militia to suppress "combinations too powerful to be suppressed by the ordinary course of judicial proceedings." And protesting through his secretary of state when the Queen of England quite reasonably recognized Southern belligerency by proclaiming neutrality as between the United States and the Confederate States.

This interpretation of the conflict as insurrection, not war, added to the president's importance. Congress declares war, or the existence of a state of war; but it is the president who determines the existence of insurrection, or rebellion. Suppression of rebellion is an executive function for which special weapons, particularly the summoning of the militia, have been placed in the president's hands. The distinction between insurrection and war was more than a lawyer's quibble; for by the adoption of the insurrectionary theory, the president independently put into play all the enginery without consulting Congress.

It was thus that the "dictatorship" began. A definite course of action was inaugurated while Congress was in recess; and as if to emphasize this presidential monopoly of emergency powers, the date for the assembling of Congress was placed at July 4, though the call was issued on April 1. In the interval between April and July various measures besides the calling of the militia were taken on purely executive authority, The President, for instance, declared a blockade of Southern ports, thus inadvertently bringing the international law of neutrality and the principle of Confederate belligerency (which he had refused to recognize) to bear upon the situation. He expanded the regular army purely on his own authority. Whereas the call of April 15 was a summoning of the militia, which the president has a right to call for the suppression of insurrection, a further call of May 3 was an appeal for recruits to the regular army beyond the total then authorized by law. Increasing the regular army is a Congressional function. "I never met anyone," said John Sherman, "who claimed that the president could, by proclamation, increase the regular army." The rush of patriotic activity, however, left no time for deliberation as to legal authority; and Lincoln did not wait to satisfy himself whether this action was constitutionally authorized. In fact, he even admitted his doubt as to its legality."These measures," he said, in his message of July 4, 1861, "whether strictly legal or not, were ventured upon under what appeared to be a popular demand and a public necessity; trusting . . . that Congress would readily ratify them." There is much more to be said concerning Lincoln's relations with Congress; but this phase of his policy suggests the dictator's typical attitude toward a legislature as a set of men to meet and "ratify" executive measures that have been irrevocably taken.This confronting of Congress with a fait accompli was, in the opinion of four dissenting justices of the Supreme Court, carried too far. They expressed the belief in the *Prize Cases* that the president's power of suppressing an insurrection is not tantamount to the war power, and that even a civil war does not legally begin until recognized by act of Congress. The court as a whole upheld the president in the *Prize Cases*, holding that he had but done his duty in resisting a war that was thrust upon the government, and Congress did ratify his acts; but according to the dissenting justices war did not legally begin in April with proclamations concerning the militia and the blockade, but on July 13, 1861, when Congress passed a resolution recognizing a state of war.

Other examples reveal Lincoln's tendency to expand the executive authority. Early in the war he gave large powers unofficially to certain citizens who were to make arrangements for transporting troops and supplies and otherwise promoting the public defense. Doubting the loyalty of certain persons in the government departments, he directed the secretary of the treasury to advance two million dollars of public money without security to John A. Dix, George Opdyke, and Richard H. Batchford of New York, to pay the expenses of certain "military and naval measures necessary for the defense and support of the Government." Yet the Constitution provides that "No Money shall be drawn from the Treasury, but in Consequence of Appropriations made by Law." Again Lincoln confessed the irregularity of his act, saying he was not aware that a dollar of the public funds "thus confided without authority of law to unofficial persons" was lost or wasted. In Lincoln's mind the honesty of his act seemed to excuse its illegality. But the whole principle of constitutional government supposes that orderly rule depends upon fixed legal guarantees and limitations, not upon the variable factor of a ruler's personality. This is the kernel of truth contained in that misunderstood maxim that we are under "a government of laws, not of men."

That measure of Lincoln's which was most obviously suggestive of dictatorship was his suspension of the habeas corpus privilege. Prior to September 1862, this suspension had been of limited application; but in this month the president issued a proclamation of general scope by which the privilege was denied to "all rebels and insurgents, their aiders and abettors . . . and all persons discouraging . . . enlistments, resisting . . . drafts, or guilty of any disloyal practices." Such persons were, by this proclamation, made "subject to martial law, and liable to trial and punishment by courts martial or military commissions." Thousands were arrested on suspicion by executive order and held for varying periods in military confinement for unspecified offenses, being denied access to the courts for examination of the facts and the judicial merits of their cases. Disloyal activity in the North made these arrests seem to the president necessary; but his action gave color to the charge of dictatorship which his opponents continually urged. By proclamation, they said, he was taking Congressional power; and by denying the habeas corpus privilege he made himself independent of the courts. Old Capitol Prison, Fort Warren, Fort Lafayette, and other military prisons were referred to as "American Bastilles"; and the president's orders for arrest were compared to the *lettres de cachet* of French monarchs. The arrests, though usually made by military officers under the administration of a cabinet secretary, were in law the president's acts; and Lincoln's own order for the arrest of a specified individual is not unknown. The system in force permitted him to do this whenever he wished.

To dwell upon further examples of Lincoln's executive acts would carry us to undue length. By his order or under his authority martial law was at times proclaimed; men were drafted into the army before Congress had enacted the conscription law; newspapers were occasionally suppressed; editors were imprisoned; slaves were declared free in "rebellious" districts; and tribunals hitherto unknown to American law, called "special war courts," were established. As to reconstruction, where Lincoln showed a magnanimity of which Congress was incapable, a most unusual sweep of authority was assumed; for the president took to himself the function of restoring the states of the South to the Union and of directing their governments pending the completion of such restoration. Since in these unusual measures the president often grasped legislative and judicial as well as executive powers, it looked as though one man had largely become, in the words of one of the lawyers of the period, "the impersonation of the country."

II

With all this extraordinary power that Lincoln wielded, we somehow do not think of him as a dictator. May this not be explained in part by the way in which he used his authority? At any rate that is a side of the question which merits close study; for where terrible weapons are held by one man, the disposition of that man is a matter of importance. Had Lincoln's powers been grasped by a typical warlord instead of the prairie lawyer and swapper of stories, the event would have been far different. In this connection it is instructive to study the most prominent of the wartime cases involving the suspension of civil liberties—that of Clement L. Vallandigham, a vigorous antiwar agitator, whose name was a slogan for thousands of Lincoln's opponents and in whose case the whole movement for constitutional guarantees was focused. On May 1, 1863, Vallandigham made a violent speech at Mount Vernon, Ohio, asserting that the war could easily have been concluded by negotiation or by the acceptance of French mediation, but that the administration was needlessly prolonging the bloodshed. The war, he said, was not for the Union but for the liberation of the blacks and the enslavement of the whites; and he spoke with contempt of General Burnside's order threatening punishment for treasonable utterances. Vallandigham was placed under military arrest, which enhanced his importance; was deprived of the habeas corpus privilege; was denied a trial in the regular courts; and was condemned by a military commission to imprisonment during the war.

Lincoln was embarrassed. There were thousands of Vallandighams, and in merely expressing disloyalty (if it amounted to that) they were violating no law; for legally treason is a matter of acts, not words. Severe treatment of such men would but help their cause. The president and all the cabinet regretted Burnside's hasty act in making the arrest; but the administration had to guard against a hasty release that might be interpreted as weakness. In this dilemma Lincoln's sense of humor—a quality no dictator should have—offered a solution; and he commuted Vallandigham's sentence to banishment within the Confederate lines.

From this point, by turning the pages of Vallandigham's voluminous biography (written by his brother), we read of the exile's ride under military escort to the Confederate outposts; his "proposition" to General Rosencrans that he be allowed to address the Union soldiers who would be moved by his words to "tear Lincoln to pieces"; his nomination for the governorship of Ohio on the Democratic ticket; his escape to Canada after a dash through the blockade; his sojourn among admirers at Windsor; his addresses "to the people" in which he rebuked the "weak despots at Washington"; his elaborate reply to visiting students from the University of Michigan (one wonders whether the students did not regard the affair as a lark); and his determination to "recover his liberties, or perish in the attempt." Under a Falstaffian disguise, aided by a thick mustache and a large pillow, he returned to the United States. Then he threw off the disguise and participated prominently in the screaming campaign of 1864. After this return from Elba his speeches were as violent as before; but here again Lincoln's sense of humor allowed Vallandigham to go unmolested, though the terms of the banishment involved reimprisonment in case of return.

The Vallandigham case was a familiar text for those who denounced the Lincoln Government; yet it shows in Lincoln himself a lenient attitude in the face of a set of conditions which offered a plausible justification for much more severe treatment. The case brings into view a menacing opposition laboring to break that morale which alone can sustain armies in the field; and it shows a general and a military commission eager to apply repressive measures; but what is more significant, it reveals a patient president, careful of civil rights, lenient toward political opponents, and aware of the ultimate ineffectiveness of governmental force in dealing with matters of opinion.

III

Lincoln defended his extra-legal measures in his message to Congress and in carefully prepared replies to protesting citizens, particularly in his message of July 4, 1861, his "Birchard letter," and the "Corning letter," for it was Lincoln's manner to treat the opposition with respect. There was no "White House spokesman" and the presidential publicity of that period took the form of occasional letters directed to particular men, but intended for the nation's ear. Lincoln argued the desperateness of the emergency which he thought would justify acts "otherwise illegal"; he invoked the war powers which he conceived to be vested in the president more than in Congress (it was under this power that he freed the slaves); and he pointed to the inability of courts of justice to deal with organized rebellion. When a certain meeting protested against the arrest of an agitator and yet professed loyalty to the government in its prosecution of the war, Lincoln cleverly countered by showing that suppression of the "rebellion" by military force required inflicting the death penalty upon deserters. He then asked: "Must I shoot a simpleminded soldier boy who deserts, while I must not touch a hair of a wily agitator who induces him to desert?"

The government's use of summary process, Lincoln showed, was not for partisan advantage, not even for punishment, but for precautionary purposes. While showing that criminal prosecutions in the courts were meant for quiet times and intended primarily as punishments for deeds already committed, the arrests in cases of rebellion, be said, were made "not so much for what had been done, as for what probably would be done." The purpose, he explained, was "preventive," not "vindictive."

It was in this spirit that Lincoln's "arbitrary" measures were taken. The courts were doing almost nothing in the punishment of disloyalty. Indictments for treason, conspiracy, obstructing the draft, and like offenses, were sometimes brought by zealous grand juries; but the typical procedure in dealing with such indictments was to keep them on the docket from term to term, the offenders meanwhile being free on recognizance, and after a time the indictments were almost invariably dropped. No life was forfeited and no sentence of fine and imprisonment carried out in any judicial prosecution for treason arising out of the "rebellion."

Courts, it must be remembered, do not automatically enforce the law. It is rather the manner in which the courts are used by the executive department that determines the extent of criminal punishment. If the government's prosecutors—the district attorneys acting under the president through the attorney general—are lukewarm in promoting prosecutions, convictions will be few; and this lukewarmness was decidedly manifest in the Lincoln administration. The administration knew very well that success in such a highly technical proceeding as treason would be difficult to obtain, especially in a community sympathetic to the accused; and it also knew that the government's success in such cases, by rendering the victim a martyr, might be even more embarrassing than failure.

The purpose of the Lincoln government was not to punish any individuals for treason or disloyalty. Its purpose was to detain citizens suspected of actively promoting the enemy's cause, to hold them for a time in confinement, and then to release them on promise of good behavior. In his very arbitrariness Lincoln was lenient. Easy release was an essential feature of his system. His releases, in fact, were as arbitrary as the arrests. To have prosecuted cases of disloyalty with vigor in the courts, assuming the existence of adequate laws for such prosecution, would have resulted in fines and prison terms under judicial sentences; whereas by summary methods, the immediate object—protection against the consequences of too flagrant disloyalty—was accomplished at once, and yet the administration was free to release the political prisoners at any time. Summary methods, used by a Lincoln, are less severe than regular judicial process. Though we need not justify arbitrary arrest and military imprisonment on this ground, yet in explaining Lincoln's preference for such measures, this phase of the matter deserves attention.

Lincoln, though a lawyer, was not legalistic. The human element in a situation always appealed to him more than the abstract legal principle. His attitude toward conscientious objectors illustrates this point. In the letter to Mrs. Gurney, wife of a Quaker minister, one sees a fine sympathy for the Quakers; and when a certain Vermont Quaker named Pringle refused military service though drafted, and stood his ground like a martyr, Lincoln directed that the man be sent home. Military discipline would have called for an unbending enforcement of orders in the imprisonment of this serene Quaker, though it could never have made a soldier of him; but Lincoln, though not a weak sentimentalist, was constantly calling for discretion and moderation in the use of military power. Later in the war objectors on religious grounds were given by act of Congress the option of non-combatant service.

IV

In seeking a just historical appraisal of Lincoln's methods of rule it may be instructive to view them first in their American setting, and then to enlarge the perspective by comparing them with executive methods in other countries. One must avoid dogmatizing as to what is, and what is not, "American." It is a common American fault to shut our eyes to the inadequate and inefficient features of our government and to make shallow comparisons which assume a superiority in our system over any other in the world; and it is also a common fault of a democracy to assume a superiority over every monarchy. Matters of politics are not so simple as that, and it is even difficult to define democracy and to indicate where particular countries should be classified as to their democratic or non democratic character. It is, however, possible to show that certain nations have been used to the ways of repressive government, and it requires no unusual discernment to distinguish between the normal reactions of a citizen in such a counry and those of the typical American. There are nations in which force, government by fear, permanent conscription, censorship, suppression of opinion, and martial law, are taken for granted. Constitutional rights, in such a state, are conceived as the gift of the sovereign to his subjects; and government is regarded as master of the people. The individual is thought of as existing only for the state; and to the unthinking citizen the state means the government. In a government of this type the direction of the nation's forces can be so artificially motivated that the nation ceases to "be itself"; and under such circumstances we sometimes speak of a "nation gone mad." Military power, under the type of government we have been describing, is conceived as superior to the civil power. "Necessity knows no law," "inter arma silent leges," are the maxims with which such a government justifies the principle of unrestrained military force.

Before the Great War, von der Goltz wrote thus: "Accustomed as we are to the . . . ruthless employment of force, we might almost believe that war and military institutions had worn these natural features from time immemorial. Yet both were always much dependent upon the state of universal civilization, yes even upon theories, upon the views of right and wrong, and the prejudices of the times. The simple conception of military operations which obtains today, namely, that war, where necessary, revokes all rights incidental to a state of peace, did not obtain in former generations."

There is a real and not merely a seeming contrast between this conception and that which has prevailed in America. The American (if one may generalize roughly on the basis of our whole history) cares more for living safely than for living dangerously. Government, to him, is not master, but servant. Even the government itself is under the "rule of law"; and for illegal acts and unwarranted infringements upon private rights he considers that governmental officers are personally liable. Individual rights, he believes, do not derive from a constitution; much less are they granted from above. Instead, they inherently exist; and the function of a constitution is so to limit the government that these rights will be protected. Military power, in the American view, is subordinate, even in war, to the civil power. The maxim "necessity knows no law" (often a mere excuse for military usurpation) appears as no better than a half-truth; and even amid arms it is maintained that a civilized government will subject its military power to such restraints as are to be found in the laws of warfare, in treaty obligations, and in those civil guarantees which belong to the nation's citizens and to non-combatants under military occupation. Our Supreme Court, in one of its most important decisions held that "the Constitution . . . is law . . . equally in war and in peace," and that in districts where Federal courts are unopposed, the trial by military commission of a citizen unconnected with the military service is illegal.

Martial law, which Sir Matthew Hale referred to as "not a law, but something indulged . . . as a law," has been employed but rarely in this country, its employment by the Federal government being quite unusual. Though one may note a recent tendency to employ martial law in certain labor disputes within the states, as in West Virginia and Colorado, this is at variance with the main trend of American legal tradition. Under Washington judicial process was respected during the Whiskey Insurrection; and the civil courts functioned regularly at the time of the Burr conspiracy when General Wilkinson's prisoners were released on habeas corpus writs. For General Jackson's excess of zeal in suppressing judicial procedure in the War of 1812, a fine of one thousand dollars was imposed; and the authority of regular courts over a military commander was thus vindicated. American precedents were strongly against militaristic measures at the time of Lincoln's presidency; and this may help to explain the vociferous objections to Lincoln's methods of rule.

Holding in mind this American repugnance to irregular executive measures and this preference for constitutional procedures, and recalling the sweeping proclamations and executive orders which Lincoln issued (decreeing martial law, arbitrary arrest, emancipation of slaves, and many other unwonted things), we must admit that he stretched his constitutional powers. Viewed in its American setting, then, and in relation to the preceding seventy-odd years under the Constitution, it appears that the Lincoln administration was departing from established precedents. To say that Lincoln regretted this and that he was solicitous to preserve constitutional restraints, is not to refute the fact. Infraction of the Constitution was one of the many unfortunate concomitants of civil war.

Yet even here we should remember that, amid the war psychology of the 1860s, Lincoln would have found Congressional and popular support in considerable degree for more drastic action than he actually took. Not every one attacked the "dictatorship": there were many who urged the administration to even more severe measures. When Wendell Phillips denounced Lincoln, it was usually for weakness and vacillation; and he even spoke approvingly of "despotic" acts. The government, he said, had neither vigor nor purpose, but drifted with events. Lincoln he characterized as a "first rate second rate man"; yet in referring to the use of large war powers, he said that a democratic government "may safely be trusted, in a great emergency, with despotic power without fear of harm or of wrecking the state." As for Congress, it ratified the president's acts, declared his suspension of the habeas corpus privilege to be "authorized," and showed its own teeth by extreme measures of which Lincoln disapproved, such as the confiscation of "rebel" property. Moreover, Congress, in its attempt to force a reorganization of Lincoln's cabinet in December 1862 (when a senatorial caucus encouraged the Chase faction and demanded Seward's resignation), and in its assumption of military control through its "Committee on the Conduct of the War," seemed in the mood for a dictatorship of its own. And the worst dictatorship our country has ever known was the dictatorship of Congress during reconstruction. Better a dictatorship of a Lincoln than that of a Sumner, a Stevens, or a Wade.

V

When viewed in a larger setting, and in comparison with dictatorships abroad, the irregularities and extralegal procedures of the Lincoln administration bear a milder appearance.

In this day of reactionary and repressive governments the impulse for ruling dangerously, and the strong-man idea, are painfully familiar; and the people of the present generation have suffered disillusionment as to democracy itself. Today the word "dictator" is read with a new connotation. This may be illustrated by putting the question as to how a dictator of the twentieth-century type, if placed in Lincoln's position, would have dealt with Vallandigham. Speaking of extralegal measures, would the agitator not have been extralegally crippled, if not actually murdered? Dictatorships of today are accused of such methods. At least Vallandigham's right to speak and publish his views would have been denied. Furthermore, if present-day styles had been in vogue, his whole party would have been suppressed, its right to representation in Congress withheld, its meetings prohibited, and its newspapers destroyed.

Lincoln's practice, indeed, fell very far short of a thoroughgoing dictatorship. He did not pack his legislature, nor eject his opposition. There was no military "purging" of Congress—nothing analogous to Cromwell's Rump Parliament. Elections were not forced or controlled as under Diaz of Mexico, though military "protection" was in some few cases supplied. There was no Lincoln party constituting a superstate and visiting vengeance upon political opponents. Criminal violence was not employed sub rosa after the fashion of modern dictatorships. There was no juggling of representation so as to give the dominant party an artificial majority as in Fascist Italy; nor was there any parallel to the methods of Bismarck who suppressed parliamentary government in Prussia from 1862 to 1866, forcing through a military program against the opposition of the Reichstag. Lincoln encountered great hostility in Congress, especially in the Senate (what president has not had a Senate "on his hands"?); and he must often have sighed for a legislative recess. Anti-Lincoln Republicans were numerous, not to mention the Democrats; and it was once said that there were only two Lincoln men in the House. Stephenson, in his illuminating biography of Lincoln, writes of the dominant Republicans in Congress as "the Jacobins" and of the Democrats as the "Little Men"; and between them these two elements allowed Lincoln few peaceful moments. Sometimes the opposition of senators reached the point of open defiance, as in connection with the Wade-Davis Reconstruction bill of 1864. Yet one finds in Lincoln's attitude toward the men "on the hill" little of the dictator's manner, and much of tactful conciliation and even at times a yielding to the point of surrendering his own views. Though, as we have noted, Lincoln anticipated congressional action by assuming powers and then seeking a retroactive authorization from Congress (which is a practice that could hardly be justified under our system of government), yet he never thought of coercing Congress into passing a ratifying measure.

Lincoln's attitude toward freedom of thought was not that of a dictator. When the *Chicago Times* was suspended by General Burnside's order, Lincoln promptly revoked that order; and though there were various other instances of repressive action against newspapers, yet repression was not the general policy. When General Schofield brought about the arrest of a Democratic editor in Missouri, Lincoln sent a telegram expressing regret for such action; and to the same general, on another occasion, he sent an order as follows: "You will only arrest individuals and suppress assemblies or newspapers when they may be working palpable injury to the military in your charge, and in no other case will you interfere with the expression of opinion in any form or allow it to be interfered with violently by others, In this you have a discretion to exercise with great caution, calmness and forbearance." There was no Sedition Act during the Civil War; and one needs only to read the abusive out-pourings of Wendell Phillips—to say nothing of more rabid agitators—to realize that the citizen was free to speak his mind against the government, far more so than during the World War.

Unlike the typical dictator, Lincoln submitted to election by the people. The Congressional election of 1862 went so heavily against the administration that it has been called a vote of lack of confidence. The president had formulated the intention, if the people should have chosen McClellan in 1864, to take every measure of coop-eration with the president-elect between the election and the inauguration. The reso-lution which he made on this subject was confided to the cabinet and was thus made a matter of record. Had McClellan been elected, Lincoln intended to call him in and say: "General, the election has demonstrated that you are stronger, have more influence with the American people than I. Now let us together, you with your influence and I with all the executive power of the government, try to save the country."

Very unlike the dictator's tone was this note of submission to popular election, this generous offer of assistance to a rival who had supplanted him.

VI

That democracy should produce dictatorships offers a familiar topic for cynics; yet in going over his writings one finds that Lincoln conceived of his own rule as a saving of democracy. The cause for which he contended he envisaged as the vindica-tion of popular government in the world. He once said to John Hay, "I consider the central idea pervading this struggle is the necessity . . . of proving that popular government is not an absurdity." Again he said, referring to disunion: "And this issue embraces more than the fate of these United States. It presents to the whole family of man the question whether a constitutional republic, or democracy—a gov-ernment of the people by the same people—can or cannot maintain its territorial integrity against its own domestic foes. . . . It forces us to ask: 'Is there in all republics this inherent and fatal weakness?' Must a government of necessity, be too strong for the liberties of its own people, or too weak to maintain its own existence?" The unusual measures he used were to preserve the nation and to preserve democracy in the world. They were like the surgeon's knife, he said, which cuts in order to save. The dictator of today, on the contrary, flouts democracy, and abandons even the pretense of adherence to the democratic faith.

The time to judge the democratic principle is not during war and revolution, nor during the reactionary period that comes in the aftermath of war. If we always have war, perhaps we may despair of democracy, for autocracy shows strongest in abnormal times. Dictatorships are like the quick heartbeat of fever; but democratic rule more resembles the steady pulse of health.

·৵ঀ·

Lincoln and the Constitution:
The Dictatorship Question Reconsidered
Herman Belz

Abstract

Over the past one hundred years historians and political scientists have established the convention that Abraham Lincoln felt justified in exercising dictatorial powers in order to save the union. This understanding distorts American constitutional history and is inaccurate about Lincoln in particular. Lincoln always claimed to be acting within constitutional constraints justifying his actions both with legalistic arguments based on constitutional texts and with more general arguments about the fundamental nature of American constitutional government.

A CONVENTION HAS GAINED acceptance in American historiography which, as 1984, the Orwellian year that has come to symbolize totalitarian rule, recedes, it is fitting to consider. I refer to the convention that regards Abraham Lincoln not simply as a forceful war leader who demonstrated the vast power inherent in the presidency, but as a dictator, albeit in many accounts a benevolent and constitutional dictator. Lincoln, it is said, took the law into his own hands in meeting the attack on Fort Sumter, and subsequently in dealing with the problems of internal security, emancipation, and reconstruction. The author of a well known treatise on emergency government in the Western political tradition states that "it was in the person

*This article originally appeared in *Congress & the Presidency,* Vol. 15, No. 2, Autumn 1988, published by The Lincoln Museum, Fort Wayne, IN. Reprinted with permission from The Lincoln Museum, Fort Wayne, IN, and the author.

of Abraham Lincoln that the constitutional dictatorship was almost completely reposed" (Rossiter, 1948:238). To be sure, some writers use the dictatorship convention in an expressive rather than analytical way to describe the growth of executive power during the Civil War. Moreover, although the characterization derives from contemporary attacks on Lincoln by the Confederate foe and the Democratic political opposition, it has not on the whole been applied with hostility.

Yet it is fair to ask whether any description of Lincoln as a dictator—whether constitutional or otherwise—is accurate. As one who has himself employed the convention, I claim the privilege of reconsidering it. I do so not only with a view toward providing a more historically sound description of Lincoln's exercise of presidential power, but also in order to arrive at a clearer understanding of the conception of constitutionalism that sustained his wartime leadership. The dictatorship charge was directed at Lincoln at the start of the Civil War by both Confederates and northern Democrats who objected to the swift and decisive manner in which he placed the country on a war footing to resist secession. Some of Lincoln's actions, such as his calling up of the militia, were clearly covered by existing law. Other actions, such as his suspending the writ of habeas corpus, ordering an increase in the size of the regular army and navy, and directing that money be paid out of the treasury for war materials, were taken without authority of any existing national statute. Were these actions illegal, unconstitutional, and lawless? This became a bitterly disputed question in the early months of the war, and it aroused even more passionate controversy when Lincoln subsequently, under what he claimed was the war power of the government, imposed martial law in parts of the North, declared military emancipation in rebellious areas, and reorganized loyal state governments in the occupied South. Northern Democrats condemned these measures as the acts of a ruthless military dictator which undermined the Constitution and the rule of law. Southerners joined in the condemnation, and after the war clung to the view of Lincoln as a despot (Davis, 1971: 80, 130–133).

Although in a much modified form, the dictatorship theme appears first to have found serious scholarly expression in the writing of William Archibald Dunning. In his pioneering *Essays on the Civil War and Reconstruction* (1897), Dunning described the emergence in 1861 of a revolutionary brand of constitutionalism that substituted popular demand for express legal mandate as the basis of executive action. Reviewing Lincoln's actions after the attack on Sumter, he wrote: "In the interval between April 12 and July 4, 1861, a new principle thus appeared in the constitutional system of the United States, namely, that of a temporary dictatorship. All the powers of government were virtually concentrated in a single department, and that the department whose energies were directed by the will of a single man" (Dunning, 1904). Dunning interpreted Lincoln's presidential dictatorship, approved by lawmakers and the electorate, as evidence that the idea of a government limited by "the written instructions of a past generation has already begun to grow dim in the smoke of battle." For Dunning and his followers the gravest departures from the old constitutional limits occurred in the name of military necessity and popular demand (Dunning, 1904: 20–21, 56–59).

Dunning's astringent analysis established the dictatorship question as a theme in historical writing on the Civil War. Historians' interest in the question in part represented an attempt to penetrate myths surrounding Lincoln's political career which had prevented it from being studied in a spirit of critical realism. The appeal of the dictatorship thesis also reflected the interest in strong executive leadership evinced by scholars and reformers in the progressive era. Whatever the reasons, scholarly opinion on Lincoln's exercise of power during the Civil War assumed points of view that have persisted to the present.

Three basic positions may be distinguished in the literature. The first, represented in the work of Dunning, adopted a critical if not openly hostile attitude toward the idea of presidential dictatorship. A second point of view, seen in the account of James Ford Rhodes (1893–1900), expressed critical approval of Lincoln's purportedly dictatorial actions. A third position views Lincoln's wartime dictatorship with unqualified approval, and was illustrated in the robust writing of John W. Burgess (1901).

Whereas Dunning drew basically negative conclusions about constitutional dictatorship, James Ford Rhodes described Lincoln's exercise of war powers with qualified approval. In the third volume of his history, Rhodes said executive measures taken at the start of the war were "the acts of a Tudor rather than those of a constitutional ruler." Yet while attributing despotic powers to Lincoln, he observed that "never had the power of dictator fallen into safer and nobler hands" (Rhodes, 1893–1900: III, 441–442). In his fourth volume Rhodes was more critical. Quoting at length from two of Lincoln's keenest critics, former Supreme Court Justice Benjamin R. Curtis and conservative legalist Joel Parker, he expressed disapproval of the arbitrary arrests and interference with freedom of press for which Lincoln was responsible. The respect for the Constitution commonly ascribed to Lincoln, Rhodes suggested, had prevented the post-Civil War generation from appreciating "the enormity of the acts done under his authority." The historian also faulted Lincoln's defense of the government's policy in the famous Valladigham affair as the argument of a clever attorney and politician, not that of a statesman. Nevertheless, Rhodes concluded on a favorable note, declaring that Lincoln was "no Caesar or Napoleon . . . sought no self-aggrandizement, . . . [and] had in his own loyal and unselfish nature a check to the excessive use of absolute power. . . ." (Rhodes, 1893–1900: IV, 169, 171, 234–35, 250).

Arch-nationalist John W. Burgess, not only acknowledging presidential dictatorship during the Civil War but also praising it as both wise and constitutional, represented a third point of view on the dictatorship question. Burgess agreed that certain of Lincoln's actions, such as directing an increase in the size of the army and navy, contradicted express constitutional provisions. Yet may not the president, he asked, "in accordance with the spirit of the constitution, in time of invasion or rebellion

. . . ask his fellow countrymen to come to the armed support of the Government and the country?" Burgess regarded congressional approval of Lincoln's action in 1861 as placing the president "practically in the position of a military dictator." And in his opinion this was "good political science and good public policy." A constitution that did not permit the exercise of extraordinary dictatorial power, he reasoned, invited violation in times of national crisis.[1] Burgess conceded, however, that the question of a president's temporary dictatorial powers was an unresolved constitutional problem (Burgess 1901: I, 228, 232, 236).

World War I stimulated further consideration of the dictatorship problem and reinforced the tendency to examine Lincoln in this light (Ford, 1918; Rogers, 1919; Warren, 1918).[2] For some historians, critical realism demanded acknowledgment of Lincoln's successful exercise of dictatorial powers, tempered by doubts about the wisdom of such a course if attempted by less gifted leaders. Nathaniel W. Stephenson, for example, examining the contradiction during the Civil War between the exercise of war powers and the individual liberty, attributed to Lincoln the belief that in time of emergency the only recourse was to follow the Roman precedent and permit the use of extraordinary power. Lincoln's view, he concluded was that democracy must learn to use the dictator as a necessary war tool. Yet it remained to be seen, Stephenson wrote in 1918, whether Lincoln's approach ought to become the model for democratic governments to follow (Stephenson, 1918: 160–161).[3] In his *Constitutional Problems Under Lincoln* (1926), James G. Randall similarly recounted emergency executive actions far beyond the normal sphere of presidential power. In Randall's view, Lincoln acted with notable restraint and leniency for individual liberty. Reflecting the growing acceptance of the despotism theme, he wrote apologetically: "If Lincoln was a dictator, it must be admitted that he was a benevolent dictator out to be encouraged" (Randall, rev. ed. 1951: 30–47).

Randall explored the dictatorship problem more fully in a subsequent essay. Although accepting the analytical usefulness of the concept, he was concerned to draw distinctions between Lincoln's exercise of power and dictatorship as a phenomenon of twentieth-century politics. Randall conceded that in seeking legislative approval for emergency measures at the start of the war, Lincoln acted in the manner of a dictator, and departed significantly from previous Constitutional practice in the United States. Lincoln's exercise of power was tempered by humane liberal instincts, however, so that compared to contemporary examples his governing methods fell far short of genuine dictatorship. The principal difference between Lincoln and modern dictators, Randall pointed out, was that Lincoln used his extra ordinary powers to save democracy, not to subvert it. Randall's judicious assessment, critical from the standpoint of traditional limited government yet ultimately approving of Lincoln, was echoed in other works of the 1930s and 1940s (Randall, 1929: 236–252. See also William E. Smith's assessment in Fish, 1937: 464; Hockett, 1939: 273–275, 287; Milton, 1944: 109–111).

In 1948 Clinton Rossiter, a political scientist, gave powerful reinforcement to the dictatorship theme in a comparative study of crisis government in England, France, Germany, and the United States. Reflecting the faith in executive power shared by many political scientists in the New Deal era, he argued that temporary conferral of absolute power on a single ruler was an essential feature of constitutional government. Rossiter recognized that federalism, the separation of powers, and civil liberties guarantees were major obstacles to the creation of a constitutional dictatorship in the United States. The existence of a strong executive made it possible, however, and Lincoln's actions during the Civil War first demonstrated this truth. Acting "on no precedent and under no restraint," Lincoln, in Rossiter's view, "was the government of the United States" from the attack on Sumter until the convening of Congress three months later. Therefore the president shared power with the legislature on many issues, but acted unilaterally as necessity demanded. "Lincoln's actions," Rossiter concluded, "form history's most illustrious precedent for Constitutional dictatorship." Although admitting that this precedent could be used for bad as well as good purposes, Rossiter's endorsement of constitutional dictatorship was as enthusiastic and unapologetic as Burgess's fifty years earlier (Rossiter, 1948: 212, 224; see also Rossiter, 1949).

Outside the "lost cause" tradition carried on by unrepentant Confederate sympathizers, few if any writers of serious history in the period 1900 to 1940 applied the dictatorship idea to Lincoln in an outright condemnatory manner (Fehrenbacher, 1982).[4] But this changed in the 1960s as the liberal consensus in American historical writing collapsed, and presidential government—now called the "imperial presidency"—came under attack in the aftermath of the Vietnam War. A harbinger of the overly anti-Lincoln point of view was Edmund Wilson's essay on the Civil War-president in *Patriotic Gore* (1962). Wilson argued that in the Lyceum address of 1838, Lincoln identified with the tyrant against whom his appeal for law and order was ostensibly directed. "In the poem that Lincoln lived," Wilson wrote, "it was morally and dramatically inevitable that this prophet who had crushed opposition and sent thousands of men to their deaths should finally attest his good faith by laying down his own life with theirs" (Wilson, 1962: 130).

In subsequent years several scholars followed the direction pointed by Wilson. Reviving the point of view most clearly expressed earlier by Dunning, political scientist Gottfried Dietze termed Lincoln's constitutional dictatorship a "constitutional tragedy." Though crediting Lincoln with benign motives, Dietze said his wartime actions were nonetheless revolutionary. Lincoln prepared the way for an "omnipotent national executive" who felt entitled to do whatever he considered in the national interest, irrespective of the rights and interests of the states, the coordinate branches of the government, and individual citizens (Dietze, 1968: 17–62). Willmoore Kendall, viewing Lincoln the precursor of liberal activist presidents in the twentieth century, went beyond the dictatorship charge and accused him of derailing the American political tradition. According to Kendall, Lincoln placed the United States on the road to centralized egalitarianism by making equality an all-consuming national purpose, in derogation of the tradition of community self-government under majority rule and legislative supremacy (Kendall and Carey, 1970: 85–94). In an essay comparing Lincoln and Chief Justice Roger B. Taney, Robert M. Spector asserted that Lincoln's example of unilateral executive action formed a dangerous precedent because it could allow a demogogic leader to determine the meaning of the Constitution. Insisting on the law of necessity in contrast to Taney's attempt to maintain the rule of law, Lincoln in Spector's judgment left a destructive constitutional legacy (Spector, 1971).

More recently M. E. Bradford, writing with a passion worthy of preeminent Lincoln hater Lyon Gardiner Tyler, has condemned Lincoln's wartime dictatorship. Bradford sees Lincoln's actions as the start of the imperial presidency and the point in our history where republican government began to degenerate into egalitarian democracy (Bradford, 1980: 355–363).[5] In a breathtaking psychohistorical interpretation that demonstrates the convergence of ideological extremes, radical political scientist Dwight G. Anderson contends that Lincoln "arrogated to himself virtually dictatorial power" and transformed the presidency into an elective kingship. Driven by his desire for fame and distinction, Lincoln is described as having repudiated the constitutional order of the framers and founded a new Union which he made the basis of a political religion. Anderson concludes that Lincoln thus provided a revolutionary model of executive leadership that has driven twentieth-century presidents to project the United States into a world imperialist role (Anderson, 1982: 8, 10–11, 166, 219).[6]

In 1979 Don E. Fehrenbacher stated that more historians have described Lincoln as a dictator or constitutional dictator than any other president (Fehrenbacher, 1979: 127). Fehrenbacher did not do so himself, however, thereby implicitly aligning himself with those historians who have rejected the dictatorship theme in relation to Lincoln.[7] Lord Charnwood, for example with notable simplicity, stated in his biography that Lincoln was neither a dictator nor an English prime minister, but an elected officer whose powers and duties were prescribed by a fixed constitution (Charnwood, 1917: 266). Andrew C. McLaughlin, in a memorable essay of 1936, viewed Lincoln as "an archconstitutionalist" whose "dominating impulse was to protect the very nature of the republic" (McLaughlin, 1936: 4–5). More recently the English scholar K. C. Wheare and the American constitutional historian Harold M. Hyman have criticized the interpretation of Lincoln as a dictator (Wheare, 1949: 165; Hyman, 1973: 75).[8] Nevertheless, the convention persists. Thus Arthur M. Schlesinger, Jr., in his account of the imperial presidency, states that "Lincoln successfully demonstrated that, under indisputable crisis, temporary despotism was compatible with abiding democracy," while political scientist Richard M. Pious in a new study of the presidency describes Lincoln's exercise of power as a constitutional dictatorship (Schlesinger, 1973: 74; Pious, 1979: 57).

In assessing the validity of the dictator theme in the study of Lincoln's presidency the historian may properly turn to the political scientist for analytical assistance. The essence of dictatorship is unlimited absolute power or domination of the state by an individual or a small group. According to the classic work of Alfred Cobban (1939: 26), the political power of the dictator must emanate from his will, it must be exercised frequently in an arbitrary manner, it must not be limited in duration to a specific term of office, and the dictator must not be responsible to any other authority. (See also Stammler, 1968: 161–168). Arbitrary and unpredictable in its effects, dictatorial power has the connotation of transgressing legal limitations and the boundaries of political legitimacy. The concept of constitutional dictatorship is apparently intended to remove the stigma of illegality or nonlegitimacy, and refers to the temporary investing of absolute power in a single ruler (Spencer, 1931: 133).[9]

Notwithstanding the pedigree of this notion, there is merit in the suggestion that the existence of institutions of accountability and responsibility marks the critical and essential difference between dictatorship and constitutional government. Where such institutions exist, the idea of constitutional dictatorship becomes meaningless (Lowenstein, 1949: 1008). Those who have subscribed to the dictatorship thesis in analyzing Lincoln have generally acknowledged that emergency government in the United States bears little resemblance to the methods of crisis government in other countries. Rossiter, the most systematic exponent of the dictatorship idea, even admits that as applied to the United States the term is hyperbole (Rossiter, 1948: 209, 286). How, then, account for the persistence of the convention? For those who are hostile to Lincoln it is of course an effective term of opprobrium. Among those whose historical judgment of Lincoln is favorable, reliance on the dictatorship theme is more puzzling. Perhaps it has dramatic and heuristic appeal as a way of under standing and dealing with situations which require the application of force, without abandoning the idea of limitations on power. It may be that the persistence of the dictatorship convention owes something to the ancient longing for a philosopher-king, especially among intellectuals. More certain it is that the convention reflects the strand of western political thought that emphasizes the necessity of a positive exercise of government power, and specifically in the American context the penchant of twentieth-century liberalism for centralized executive bureaucratic power.

Whatever the reasons may have made the dictatorship idea analytically appealing in the past, it is my contention its use distorts our constitutional history in general, and that it is especially misleading and inaccurate as a description of Lincoln's presidency. Where real and distinct limitations on the exercise of governmental power exist, in the form of counterbalancing authority and institutions of accountability, there dictatorship—be it called constitutional or otherwise—does not exist (Ford, 1918: 632–640; Bracher, 1918: 632–640).[10] The dictatorship theme is particularly inapposite, moreover, with reference to Lincoln's exercise of power during the Civil War, which was constantly subjected to the restraints of congressional initiative and reaction, political party competition, and the correcting pressure of public opinion. But in rejecting the dictatorship convention we have more to rely on than the fact that politics—and the freedom that it necessarily implies—continued during the war. We are afforded unique insight into the problem of wartime government by Lincoln's own analysis of the dictatorship question, and by the constitutional justification that sustained his exercise of power between Sumter and Appomattox.

III

A critic of the Democratic doctrine of broad executive power early in his political career, Lincoln throughout his presidency was conscious of and respected the legal limits which circumscribed the office of chief magistrate. In part seeking to allay Southern apprehension, in part expressing his considered constitutional judgment, he saw fit, upon taking office in 1861, to comment on the generally restricted scope of the federal government's field of action. The Constitution, he said in his First Inaugural address, gave government officials "but little power for mischief." No single administration, he asserted, as long as the people to whom it was accountable remained virtuous and vigilant, could seriously injure the government within a four year term. As chief executive, Lincoln conceived it his duty to administer the government as it came to him and transmit it to his successor unimpaired. Addressing the issue of secession, he emphasized in his Inaugural Address that he had no discretionary authority to fix terms for the separation of the states, a thing that only the people could do if they so desired (Basler, 1953–1955: IV, 270–271).

Lincoln's respect for the legal limits on executive power was evident in his dealing both with pedestrian administrative questions and larger matters of state. In March 1861, for example, he drafted an order establishing a central bureau to supervise the organization, drill, and equipment of the militia. Inquiring as to his legal authority to do so, he was informed by the attorney general that none existed, and the order was not given (Basler, 1953–1955: IV, 291). On numerous other issues Lincoln routinely sought opinions concerning his legal authority to perform executive acts (Basler 1953–1955: IV, 451; V, 270).[11] And consistent with the narrow view of executive power which he had expressed in the 1840s, he denied that he could veto legislation merely on the basis of subjective disagreement with the policy contained in legislation (Basler, 1953–1955: VII, 414).[12]

From time to time Lincoln specifically commented on the dictatorship question, which was a controversial subject throughout the war. He did so for the first time in the Browning letter of September 22, 1861, dealing with his revocation of the emancipation order issued by General John C. Fremont in Missouri. Writing to Republican Senator Orville H. Browning of Illinois, Lincoln expressed the opinion that slaves, like other property, could be seized and temporarily used for military purposes. But their permanent status could not be determined by a military decree, such as Frémont's, that was based on "purely political" reasons "not within the range of military law, or necessity." To do that, said Lincoln, would be "simply 'dictatorship,'" for it would assume that a military commander "may do 'anything' he pleases," such as, in the present instance, confiscating the lands and freeing the slaves of loyal as well as disloyal people. Lincoln believed that Congress might by legislation permanently fix the status of slaves employed for military purposes. "What I object to," he explained, "is that I as President shall expressly or impliedly seize and exercise the permanent legislative functions of the government" (Basler, 1953–1955: IV, 531–532).

The usual view of Lincoln's presidency is that he abandoned this narrow conception of executive power in favor of a more plenary one which allowed him to do what he had prohibited Frémont from doing (Corwin, 1957: 450–451). In May 1862, for example, he revoked another emancipation order, issued by General Davids Hunter in South Carolina. In doing so he announced: ". . . whether it be competent for me, as Commander-in-Chief of the Army and Navy, to declare the Slaves of any state or states, free, and whether at any time, in any case, it shall have become a necessity indispensable to the maintenance of the government, to exercise such supposed power, are questions which, under my responsibility, I reserve to myself. . . ." (Basler, 1953–1955: V, 222). Of apparently similar import is Lincoln's statement of September 1862, that he had no objection to a proclamation of emancipation, since his power as commander in chief gave him "a right to take any measure which may best subdue the enemy" (Basler, 1953–1955: V, 421).[13] It was of course on this military basis that the Emancipation Proclamation rested—a basis succinctly described by Lincoln in the Conkling letter of August 1863 when he wrote: "I think the Constitution invests its commander-in-chief, with the law of war, in time of war" (Basler, 1953–1955; VI, 408).[14]

This apparent progression toward a concept of plenary executive power is cited in support of the constitutional dictatorship thesis (Rossiter, 1948: 233). Yet the position attributed to Lincoln in 1862–1863 does not necessarily contradict the position he assumed in 1861, as expressed in the Browning letter. At that time Lincoln said that military power could not be used for purely political reasons to emancipate slaves and determine their future status. He did not, in the Browning letter, disclaim power as commander-in-chief to free and fix the status of slaves for *military* reasons essential to the preservation of the government. In 1863 he deemed it necessary to exercise such power, which may properly be regarded as having been reserved in the revocation of the Frémont order.

In explaining his view of dictatorship, Lincoln in the Browning letter also disavowed the ability of the executive to exercise "the permanent legislative function of the government," as in determining the permanent status of slaves used for military purposes. This position, too, he maintained later in the war.

Here it is important to note the controversy in 1863 over the validity and legal effect of the Emancipation Proclamation. Democrats called the proclamation an unconstitutional and illegal nullity; conservative Unionists thought it was temporarily effective where military authority might make it so; and the main body of Republicans said it conferred a right of personal liberty (Belz, 1976: 36–40). Lincoln believed the Emancipation Proclamation constitutional, though acknowledging it might be found to be otherwise, and pledged to maintain the freedom of emancipated slaves (Basler, 1953–1955: VI, 411. See also *ibid.* 408).[15] Yet he claimed no authority to fix the legal status of freed slaves, nor to abolish slavery in state laws and constitutions. It soon became clear that a constitutional amendment prohibiting slavery and permanently guaranteeing the freedom of the emancipated blacks was necessary. Lincoln of course lent his political support to this undertaking, but in a constitutional sense the framing and adoption of the Thirteenth Amendment were none of his affair as a chief executive (Basler, 1953–1955: VIII, 253–254).[16] This ultimate exercise of the legislative power, as Lincoln noted in the Browning letter of 1861, belonged to the people and their elected representatives in the lawmaking branch.

Lincoln remained conscious of the restriction on military power which he considered the essential safeguard against dictatorship. Urged by Secretary of the Treasury Salmon P. Chase in 1863 to extend the Emancipation Proclamation to parts of Virginia and Louisiana that had been exempted, he refused on the ground that the order "has no constitutional or legal justification, except as a military measure." To apply it in the absence of military necessity, he told Chase, "without any argument, except the one that I think the measure politically expedient, and morally right," would be to give up "all footing upon the constitution of law. . . ." In the language used in his 1861 comment upon dictatorship, it would be acting for "purely political" reasons. Lincoln asked: "Would I not thus be in the countless field of absolutism?" And would not such a course provoke fears that "without any further stretch I might do the same in Delaware, Maryland, Kentucky, Tennessee, and Missouri; and even change any law in any state?" (Basler, 1953–1955: IV, 428–429).[17]

It is possible of course to dismiss these professions of concern for constitutional limitations and determination to avoid dictatorial solutions as mere rhetoric. It is virtually impossible, however, to deny the most impressive evidence weighing against the dictatorship thesis—the continuation of party competition in the election of 1864.

As Mark E. Neely, Jr. has recently observed, historians have generally failed to appreciate the critical nature of this election in which the Democrats demanded the cessation of hostilities and refrained from opposition to slavery. Although one can not know what should have happened had McClellan won, the possibility of a negotiated settlement recognizing the Confederacy and the greater likelihood of the continuation of slavery ought to be acknowledged (Neely, 1979: 18–21). Historians have also, it should be noted, failed to appreciate the significance for American constitutionalism in the very fact that the election was held. In art this failure stems from the tendency common in stable democratic societies to take for granted institutions and procedures that most other countries must still struggle to achieve. It also reflects the peculiar American attitude towards politics, which at times seems to regard elections as more to be regretted and endured than applauded as a vital part of constitutional government. In any case, in facing the democratic challenge in 1864, Lincoln accepted a risk and permitted his power to he threatened in a way that no dictator, constitutional or not would have tolerated.

Lincoln was aware of the critical nature of the election and of its importance for republican constitutionalism. Although Democratic victory might lead to disunion and the preservation of slavery, he never wavered in his willingness to accept the possibility of a change in administration. In August 1864 he recorded privately his determination, would he lose the election, to cooperate with the Democratic president-elect in a final effort to save the Union. When the election was over, Lincoln told his cabinet of this resolve, explaining that both duty and conscience required it (Basler, 1953–1955: VII, 514).[18] As Charles A. Beard wrote, "This is not the language of a despot, a Caesar or a wrecker. It is the language of a man remarkably loyal to constitutional methods, ready to abide by the decision of the people lawfully made" (Beard, 1944: 68).

During the campaign there were rumors that, if defeated Lincoln would try to "ruin the government," as a dictator might contemplate doing (Basler 1953–1955: VII, 52).[19] In October 1864 Lincoln addressed these rumors. Stating that he was trying to save the government, not destroy it, he publicly pledged that he would serve as president until March 4, 1865, and that whoever was constitutionally elected would at that time be installed as chief magistrate. Lincoln also intended this statement to allay apprehension that if the Democratic party won, it would try to seize the government (Basler, 1953–1955: VIII, 52).[20]

After the election, Lincoln summed up its significance before a public gathering at the White House. If the rebellion tested the people when they were united, he suggested, "must they not fail when *divided*, and partially paralyzed by a political war among themselves?" But the election was a necessity. "We can not have free government without elections," he declared, "and if the rebellion could force us to forego, or postpone, a national election, it might fairly claim to have already conquered and ruined us." Returning to the question that he had posed at the start of the war, namely, whether a democratic government could defend itself, he said the election demonstrated "that a people's government can sustain a national election, in the midst of a great civil war" (Basler, 1953–1955: VIII, 100–101).

Lincoln's well reasoned and persuasive analysis of the dictatorship question ought not to strike us as remarkable. What is remarkable, in view of the evidence that so plainly refutes it, is the persistence of the dictatorship convention. Surely there is a more accurate way to describe the exercise of presidential power during the Civil War and its constitutional justification than by invoking this dubious notion. Nor will the concept of a "constitutional" dictatorship, as I have suggested, answer our needs. In either version the dictatorship argument is flawed because it requires the conclusion that the existing Constitution was inadequate.

An alternative interpretation of Civil War government, noting its substantial continuity with prewar practices, would hold that the Constitution, limitations and all, was adequate to the needs of the Union in this its severest crisis. The nation's organic law was not set aside for an unlimited, dictatorial concentration of power. On the contrary, the Constitution continued to serve both as symbol and source of governmental legitimacy and as a normative standard for the conduct of politics. To assist in understanding this alternative constitutional outlook we can consult no more perceptive or authoritative explanation than the rationale that Lincoln himself offered for wartime executive action.

IV

Lincoln employed a two-track constitutional justification in explaining the legitimacy of controversial measures adopted under executive authority. The first and more familiar track involved legalistic arguments from the text of the Constitution. The second involved more broadly political arguments concerning the relationship between the Union, the Constitution, and nature of republican government.[21]

An able lawyer familiar with constitutional analysis, Lincoln frequently advanced legalistic arguments in which the Constitution was conceived of as a form of positive law (Basler, 1953–1955: IV, 267).[22] Perhaps his best known argument in this mode concerned executive suspension of the privilege of the writ of habeas corpus. In his July 4, 1861 message to Congress, he cited Article I, Section 9 of the Constitution, which confers power to suspend the writ of habeas corpus in cases of rebellion or invasion when the public safety requires it. Since the Constitution does not specify who may exercise this power, Lincoln reasoned that the president could do so, in time of emergency when Congress was not in session (Basler, 1953–1955: IV, 430–431).

Lincoln offered additional constitutional justification of habeas corpus suspension in the Corning letter of June 1863. Democratic critics contended that the government could make no arbitrary arrests nor suspend the habeas corpus privilege outside the area of rebellion and lines of military occupation. Lincoln argued in contrast that since the constitution "makes no such distinction, I am unable to believe that there is any such constitutional distinction." The writ could be suspended and arrests made *whenever* the public safety required it, he insisted, and *whenever* this might occur (Basler, 1953–1955: VI, 265). Lincoln was similarly legalistic in responding to a Democratic argument that rested on the hypothetical assumption that the Constitution be read without the habeas corpus suspension clause. To this Lincoln countered: "Doubtless [*sic*] if this clause of the constitution . . . were expunged, the other guaranties would remain the same; but the question is not how those guaranties would stand with that clause out of the constitution, but how they stand with that clause remaining in it. . . ." (Basler, 1953–1955: VI, 302).

Couched in the usual idiom of constitutional politics, Lincoln's arguments were appropriate expressions of the legalistic side of American constitutionalism.[23] Yet, ironically, it is possible to interpret some of Lincoln's statements in this idiom in a way that supports the dictatorship thesis. In his message to the special session of Congress in 1861, referring to habeas corpus suspension, Lincoln asked: ". . . are all the laws *but one*, to go unexecuted, and the government itself to go to pieces, lest that one be violated?" (Basler 1953–1955: IV, 430).[24] In a message to Congress of May 1862, he described some of the measures taken at the start of the war as "without any authority of law. . . ."(Basler, 1953–1955: V, 242). And in a statement of 1864 he seemed to imply that the Constitution might be broken to save the Union. "By general law life *and* limb must be protected," he observed, "yet often a limb must be amputated to save a life; but a life is never wisely given to save a limb" (Basler, 1953–1955: VII, 281). In this metaphor the nation is the life to be saved, the Constitution the limb that might need amputation. The inference can be drawn that emergency action to save the government is expedient, yet also unconstitutional and lawless.

Lincoln of course denied that emergency measures to save the government were unlawful, adducing the legalistic arguments noted above. In addition, and more persuasively, he offered a political-philosophical defense of executive actions that dwelt on the relationship between the Union and the Constitution.

The perspective from which Lincoln offered this more systemic constitutional justification appears in the fragment on the Constitution and the Union presumably written in January 1861. Reiterating the theme that absorbed him as the struggle over slavery reached its climax, Lincoln stated that beyond the Constitution and Union lay the principle of liberty as expressed in the Declaration of Independence. The assertion of this principle, he wrote, "was the word 'fitly spoken' which has proved an 'apple of gold' to us." "The *Union,* and the *Constitution,*" he continued, "are the *picture of silver,* subsequently framed around it." Observing that the picture was made for the apple and not the other way around, he urged actions to ensure "that neither *picture,* or *apple* shall ever be blurred, or bruised or broken" (Basler, 1953–1955: IV, 168–169).

In this passage Lincoln was primarily concerned to define republican liberty as the fundamental purpose of national existence. For our purposes what is of interest is the equivalence of identity assumed to exist between the nation (the Union) and the Constitution. Destroy liberty—or allow this sacred principle to be eroded by the spread of slavery—and both the nation and the Constitution would be lost.

Justifying emergency actions taken at the start of the war, Lincoln in his message to Congress of July 4, 1861 reaffirmed liberty as the purpose of national existence. The war, he declared, was "a People's contest . . . a struggle for maintaining in the world, that form, and substance of government, whose leading object is to elevate the condition of men" (Basler, 1953–1955: IV, 438). But an equally important issue was also involved: "whether a constitutional republic, or a democracy . . . can, or cannot, maintain its territorial integrity, against its own domestic foes." "Is there in all republics," Lincoln asked, "this inherent, and fatal weakness?" "Must a government, of necessity, be too *strong* for the liberties of its own people, or too *weak* to maintain its own existence?" Seeking to avoid both extremes, Lincoln announced: ". . . no choice was left but to call out the power of the Government; and so to resist force, employed for its own destruction, by force, for its preservation" (Basler, 1953–1955: IV, 426).

Was it, then, lawful and constitutional to defend the Union and the Constitution? And was it possible to do so without resort to dictatorial power? Plainly Lincoln believed it was, and this not mainly in consequence of any construction of positive law or constitutional text, but rather on the self-evident truth that the Constitution justifies extraordinary action to preserve the substance of political liberty that constitutes both its own end and the purpose of the nation. In the Hodges letter of April 1864, Lincoln expressly equated Union and Constitution in justifying executive actions. He wrote: "I felt that measures, otherwise unconstitutional, might become lawful, by becoming indispensable to the preservation of the Constitution, "I could not feel that to the best of my ability, I had even tried to preserve the constitution," he added, "if, to save slavery, or any minor matter, I should permit the wreck of government, country, and Constitution all together" (Basler, 1953–1955: VII, 281).

In this sentence Lincoln twice uses the word "constitution," spelling it with a lower-case and then an upper-case "C." Does this mean he has in mind two different conceptions of the term? One may perhaps draw that inference, considering the two-track constitutional justification he employed to explain the lawfulness of emergency war measures. The Constitution was not only the written instrument of government adopted at the nation's founding and intended to function as a supreme legal code. It was also the principles, ideals, institutions, laws and procedures tending toward the maintenance, of republican liberty by which the American people agreed to order their political existence. The Constitution, in other words, was not merely positive law, derivative or reflective of national life, as in the life-and-limb metaphor noted above that is typically used to illustrate Lincoln's approach to constitutional justification. Rather, the Constitution *was* the nation, or—to put it the other way around in a way that is perhaps more meaningful and revealing—the nation *was* the Constitution: America was the system of political liberty created by the founders and now defended against an internal enemy.[25] In the Hodges letter Lincoln asked whether it was "possible to lose the nation, and yet preserve the constitution" (Basler, 1953–1955: VII, 281). If the Constitution was simply a legal code, the possibility existed. But under Lincoln's political-philosophical view of the Constitution it was not possible to lose the nation while preserving the Constitution. To lose one was to lose the other.

This nonlegalistic, nonjudicial conception of the Constitution was not nearly so uncommon in the nineteenth century as it has become today. Indeed, it was vigorously expressed in an influential treatise by Lincoln's legal advisor in the War Department, William Whiting, in his widely circulated *War Powers Under the Con-*

stitution of the United States (1871). Strict constructionists, Whiting noted, insisted on the letter of the Constitution and were unable to see that the Constitution was "only a frame of government, a plan in outline for regulating" national life. Strict constructionists saw the Constitution as "incapable of adaptation to our changing conditions, as if it were . . . an iron chain, girdling a living tree, which could have no further growth unless by bursting its rigid ligature." Whiting rejected this narrow legalism. The Constitution, he wrote, "more resembles the tree itself, native to the soil that bore it, waxing strong in sunshine and in storm, putting forth branches, leaves, and roots, according to the laws of its own growth. . . ." Foregoing metaphor, Whiting then offered an historical analogy: "Our Constitution, like that of England, contains all that is required to adapt itself to the present and future changes and wants a free and advancing people" (Whiting, 1871: 8–9). To be sure, these are Whiting's words, not Lincoln's. Yet they seem aptly to express the tendency of Lincoln's constitutionalism.

It is of course the nature of Lincoln's constitutionalism that is placed in dispute by the dictatorship convention. Advocates of that interpretation ultimately see Lincoln as disregarding or transcending constitutional limitation. Their position is implicitly reinforced by those who describe Lincoln as a pragmatic instrumentalist who subscribed to the theory of the "living constitution" and regarded it as a social document capable of organic growth (see Dowd, 1962). This is perhaps a plausible conclusion which the quotation from Whiting and Lincoln's own equating of the Constitution and the nation, might appear to support. The trouble with the pragmatic-instrumentalist approach to the Constitution, however, is that it tends to negate the idea of constitutional limitations. It encourages an "anything goes" mentality that justifies purposes and objects remote from those envisioned by the framers of the Constitution, and presumably excluded by them except through the process of constitutional amendment. It rejects original intention as a guide to constitutional interpretation. And, I believe, it gravely misunderstands Lincoln and the Civil War generation, who were closer in outlook to the fixed constitutionalism of the Founding Fathers than to pragmatic liberalism of the twentieth century.

We may take Chief Justice John Marshall as illustrative of the constitutional outlook of the founding generation and the early national period, which informed Lincoln's statesmanship. In his most famous admonition, in *McCulloch v. Maryland*, Marshall declared: "We must never forget that it is a *constitution* we are expounding . . . intended to endure for ages to come, and consequently, to be adapted to the various *crises* of human affairs" (McCulloch v. Maryland, 407). Marshall did not mean that the constitution was infinitely flexible or that new powers and purposes of government could be fashioned out of whole cloth, as advocates of the "living constitution" seem to assume. He meant that the purposes and objects set forth by the Framers in the fundamental law must always be the touchstone and test of constitutional legitimacy, the criterion to be employed in constitutional adaptation and adjudication. May we not consider defense of the Union and the Constitution a legitimate object assigned to the federal government by the Framers? And may we not conclude that Lincoln's exercise of power to this end was compatible with the concept of a fixed Constitution?

Ultimately Lincoln appealed to a kind of constitutional common sense that while respecting the requirements of procedural regularity and formal legality, was concerned above all with preserving the substance of republican liberty—the purpose both of American nationality and the constitutional order. One sees this in Lincoln's opinion on the admission of West Virginia to the Union in December 1862.

In accordance with constitutional requirement, the Unionist movement in Virginia, sustained by the Lincoln administration and recognized as the loyal government of the state, had given its approval to the creation of West Virginia. Opponents of partition condemned it as unconstitutional on the ground that the loyal Pierpont government was not the legitimate government of the state, because chosen at an election in which the majority of Virginia voters (living in rebellious areas) had not participated. Lincoln rejected this argument. "Can this government stand," he asked, "if it indulges constitutional constructions by which men in open rebellion against it, are to be counted . . . the equals of those who maintain their loyalty to it?" Only by entertaining "these absurd conclusions," he reasoned, could it be denied that the body that consented to the creation of West Virginia was the legislature of Virginia. Lincoln continued: "It is said, the devil takes care of his own. Much more should a good spirit—the spirit of the Constitution and the Union—take care of its own. I think it can not do less, and live" (Basler, 1953–1955: VI, 27). This was not the urging of a dictator, whether benevolent or otherwise, but of a constitutionalist faithful to the purpose for which the Union and the Constitution were created and ordained.

⁂

LINCOLN AND EXECUTIVE POWER: REBUTTING THE DICTATORSHIP THESIS

Jeffrey Crouch and Mark J. Rozell

DURING THE FIRST twelve weeks of the Civil War, President Abraham Lincoln broke new ground in the field of presidential power. Elected with an electoral college majority but under forty percent of the popular vote, Lincoln assumed office at a time when the Union was beginning to break apart over the question of slavery. To preserve the Union, Lincoln assumed powers that were absent from the plain text of the Constitution.

Specifically, Lincoln summoned the militia to put down a rebellion by seven

Southern states. Then, he ordered that the ports of seceded states should be blocked. He added 22,714 to the army and 18,000 to the navy, and ordered the Treasury to appropriate emergency funding. Finally, and perhaps most significantly, Lincoln suspended the writ of habeas corpus.[1]

In taking these actions, Lincoln adopted a view of presidential power that would become known as the "stewardship" theory, the understanding that a president could use all of the executive powers that were not expressly forbidden by the Constitution. This interpretation stands in stark contrast to the view espoused by President William Howard Taft, who believed that a president, like Congress, has only those powers specifically mentioned in the Constitution.[2]

Over time, presidents responding to crises have acted outside the Constitution, but not without criticism of their actions or the precedents they set. Lincoln remains a target for criticism. Some political observers have argued that Lincoln was a "constitutional dictator." This view may explain why the topic has been little debated over the years by scholars who instead of defending Lincoln are "more or less embarrassed by Lincoln's record on the Constitution," so much so that scarce literature exists defending him.[3]

A "constitutional dictatorship" is, according to Clinton Rossiter, a term used to describe the prerogative and other powers assumed by a leader during a crisis. Rossiter outlines the extent of power a leader can justifiably assume in a constitutional dictatorship by identifying its three characteristics. "First, the complex system of government of the democratic, constitutional state is essentially designed to function under normal, peaceful conditions, and is often unequal to the exigencies of a great national crisis."[4] The Civil War unquestionably fits into this framework: it was not a "normal, peaceful condition": in fact, it was not only "a great national crisis," it was 'The most severe and dangerous crisis in American history."[5]

Second, because the normal state of government is inadequate to respond to a desperate emergency, "in time of crisis a democratic, constitutional government must be temporarily altered to whatever degree is necessary to overcome the peril and restore normal conditions. This alteration invariably involves government of a stronger character; that is, the government will have more power and the people fewer rights."[6] "Finally," Rossiter warns, "this strong government, which in some instances might become an outright dictatorship, can have no other purposes than the preservation of the independence of the state, the maintenance of the existing constitutional order, and the defense of the political and social liberties of the people."[7]

The government in place at the beginning of the Civil War was plainly inadequate to deal with the new demands placed upon it by this unprecedented threat to the Union. The second and third characteristics of a constitutional dictatorship are less than straightforward. But the point here is not to criticize Rossiter for using vague language. Indeed, a constitutional dictatorship is by definition an unclear concept describing the nebulous office of the president, whose powers are described only briefly in Article I of the Constitution. The purpose of beginning with Rossiter is to provide a loose framework by which to judge the actions of Lincoln during the Civil War, which were appropriate under the circumstances.

Indeed, Lincoln's use of prerogative powers was part of a measured, necessary response to the unprecedented threat to the Union presented by the Civil War. Criticism of Lincoln for being a "dictator" is wrong-headed because, to use Rossiter's terms, Lincoln "temporarily altered" the government no more than was necessary, as shown by subsequent approval for his actions given by Congress and the Supreme Court. Although he may have "changed the existing constitutional order" to save the Union, he had "no other purpose," such as personal gain or gratification, for his actions. Thus, the stigma attached to constitutional dictatorship is misguided. Lincoln's only goal was to preserve the United States, and his success in doing so preserves his legacy.

Lincoln walked a lonely path to greatness, however. During approximately twelve weeks in 1861—from the beginning of the Civil War when the first shots were fired on Fort Sumter on April 12 until his address to Congress on July 4—he exercised broad, extra-constitutional prerogative powers to combat the national emergency.[8] During this period, only "one man was the government of the United States."[9] And while modern presidents can look to precedents established by Lincoln and others, as well as complicated frameworks of statutory authority from which to draw power, Lincoln was blazing a new trail others would follow.

Lincoln believed in expansive presidential power, and to guarantee himself an opportunity to act without interference, he issued his orders while Congress was out of session and he did not seek approval until July 4, when he finally summoned Congress back to Washington, D.C. for a special session.[10] Once reassembled, however, Congress enacted a statute that stated "all the acts, proclamations, and orders of the President respecting the army and navy of the United States . . . are hereby approved and in all respects made valid . . . as if they had been issued and done under the previous express authority and direction of the Congress of the United States."[11] Congress continued to ratify Lincoln's measures. For example, in 1862 Congress retroactively approved Lincoln's censoring of telegraph lines and passed the Militia Act to allow the president to draft more troops. In 1883, Congress passed a law approving Lincoln's action to suspend the writ of habeas corpus and approved a draft law that merely legitimized the president's earlier unilateral issuance of the draft.[12]

With the vast arsenal of constitutional weapons at their disposal, including outright disapproval, the ability to end appropriations for future war-related activities, even the power to impeach and remove the president from office, the fact that Congress approved Lincoln's actions says much about the circumstances Lincoln faced. Congress accepted the fact that Lincoln must be given considerable leeway to preserve the Union. The Supreme Court was also sympathetic to the president's plight When Lincoln's power to block the ports of Southern states was challenged in the

Prize Cases, the blockade was upheld, and the court even endorsed Lincoln's prerogative powers to some degree, declaring that the president fulfilled his duty to put down the rebellion by using whatever force was necessary to do so, even if he acted before Congress could approve.[13] The *Prize* majority ruled that Lincoln's actions before July 13, 1861, the date all of the Justices agreed was the official beginning of the "state of war," were not beyond his authority; and even if they were, Congress's subsequent approval was sufficient to vindicate Lincoln.[14] The *Prize Cases* ruling approved extensive executive war powers even in a domestic emergency by recognizing that the president has the constitutional power to treat domestic belligerents as if they were enemies of the United States.

Even though the president's powers appeared nearly unlimited, they were not completely unchecked. The *Prize* decision may seem to have approved vast executive power in general, but was really meant to give Lincoln special leeway because he "had not initiated a war, but had taken measures to resist a war that was thrust upon the Government."[15] Had Lincoln initiated war or had there been precedent established for him to follow, the Court may have been less deferential. Furthermore, after Lincoln's death, the Court checked Lincoln's use of prerogative powers. In *Ex parte Milligan*, the Court ruled that Lincoln exceeded his authority in subjecting non-military prisoners to military commissions if the civil courts in the area were operating.[16]

Overall, the other two branches of government agreed to give Lincoln the benefit of the doubt and support his extraordinary actions. He only "temporary altered" the government long enough to save it, to use Rossiter's analysis, if the actions of Congress and the Supreme Court approving Lincoln's actions are accorded proper deference. In this sense, Lincoln did not exceed the limits of the power he needed to ensure the survival of the Union during the relevant twelve week period, but did only what he viewed to be necessary at the time under the unique circumstances he confronted.

Turning to Rossiter's last criterion, Lincoln draws perhaps the most criticism for altering "the existing constitutional order." While Lincoln himself may have been able to control his newfound power, one notable scholar in particular feared the consequences for the country if Lincoln's actions were used as precedent by future presidents, who would award themselves power by ignoring Congress and reinterpreting vague constitutional language to expand executive branch prerogatives. Edward S. Corwin grumbled in 1940 that Lincoln's boldness following the *Prize* decision and his disinclination to work with Congress "led him to break over constitutional bonds and become a dictator even exceeding the Roman model."[17] Corwin suggests that the "sudden emergence" of the commander in chief clause used by Lincoln to justify his actions "occurred almost overnight" as a result of Lincoln's fusing it with another clause charging the president "to take care that the laws be faithfully executed" and thereby "deriv[ing]" from the now-united clauses "what he termed the 'war power' to justify the series of extraordinary measures that he took in the interval between the fall of Fort Sumter and the convening of Congress in special session on July 4, 1861."[18] As if there were any doubt about Corwin's implication, he makes his view crystal-clear later, when he singles out actions by Lincoln during his constitutional dictatorship as *"assert[ing] for the President, for the first time in our history, an initiative of indefinite scope in meeting the domestic aspects of a war emergency."*[19] To Corwin, Lincoln's constitutional dictatorship, no matter how necessary or brief, was an extreme deviation from "conventional constitutional law, [which] even as late as 1866 still described the President's power as Commander-in-Chief in Hamilton's terms in *The Federalist*, as the power simply to direct the operation of the national forces . . ." and not "an indefinite power . . . attributed to the President to take emergency measures."[20]

Other observers are more forgiving. Rossiter recognized the magnitude of the crisis faced by Lincoln and the necessity of the steps he took to preserve the Union. Rossiter wrote that under the circumstances, "[i]t is remarkable how little change in the structure of government and how little abridgement of civil liberty accompanied the prosecution of this bitter war."[21] It made sense for Lincoln to take these unprecedented actions, Rossiter contended, because "[c]onstitutionally, historically, and logically the office of the president is the focus of crisis government in the United States."[22] This is an important point. Aside from the ambiguity of constitutional language delineating war-making powers in general, a domestic crisis brings into sharp focus the necessity for the president, an individual with the ability to respond quickly to emergencies, to be able to do so. In contrast, Congress as a body must deliberate and arrive at some consensus, a process that takes time and invites disagreement among its members.

Without history as a guide, the widespread acceptance of his powers depended not only on Lincoln's leadership, but also on his capacity for self-restraint. Lincoln proved it was possible for the government to be powerful and yet still protect the rights and liberties of the people. Indeed, "it was not what Lincoln did, but what he failed to do and did not attempt to do, which constitutes the center of his greatness as a democratic leader." Instead of using his new power for selfish reasons, Lincoln "did not ignore legal forms and prohibitions or sweep them aside with an impatient gesture; he was forced to go beyond them. . . . [He] sought not to magnify the office or disregard the Constitution but to save it. In days that threatened the very existence of the nation and the Constitution, he battled to save both."[23]

Lincoln was justified in "going beyond" the written text of the Constitution because he had the approval of the people to do so, and because "a nation must have a constitution [but] . . . a real constitution is more than ink on paper."[24] Andrew McLaughlin observed that:

> "A constitution need not be looked upon as only a piece of parchment stored away in a safe, free from the prying eyes of the multitude, consigned to the clever exposition of politicians and subjected to the astute arguments of jurists. In a very real sense the

actual structure of a nation, even if we are thinking only of its habitual political activities and its customary political reactions, is something more than a document and all
the incrustations of statutes and judicial interpretations; it includes the common and
conventional attitudes of the citizens, the principles which animate them, their substantial concepts of justice, liberty, and safety, their readiness to be ruled by others or
their determination to compel their rulers to serve them. To the extent that a formal
written constitutional system or any other kind of constitution is at variance with the
character of a people, it is wanting in substantial reality."[25]

Thus, the interest of the public and its commonly held values and beliefs must be
considered a part of the Constitution. Lincoln never lost sight of his mandate from
the people and how far it extended. As Schlesinger wrote, Lincoln "successfully demonstrated that, under indisputable crisis, temporary despotism was compatible with
abiding democracy."[26] What is more, he "exercised his war powers under a profound
conviction of human frailty. He never pretended to the nation that these were
merely the routine powers of the Presidency."[27] Instead, "as Lincoln repeatedly
emphasized, these were temporary powers, defined by the duration as well as by the
size of the emergency."[28]

So Lincoln appears to fit Rossiter's notion of an acceptable "constitutional dictator," but whether the term should apply at all is debatable. No one would deny that
"constitutional dictator" has a negative implication, but drawing a line between
what Lincoln did and what a "dictator" would do has been a tricky proposition.
One can see a distinct difference between a true dictatorship, in which the dictator
is unchecked by popular opinion, and Lincoln's situation because when a president
is limited by the other branches of government and "institutions of accountability,"
he is arguably not a "constitutional" or any other kind of dictator.[29]

Specifically, "[t]he dictatorship theme is particularly inapposite, moreover, with
reference to Lincoln's exercise of power during the Civil War, which was constantly
subjected to the restraints of congressional initiative and reaction, political party
competition, and the correcting pressures of public opinion."[30] In fact, as Belz
observed, it is difficult to suggest a state of constitutional dictatorship exists when
there is still political party competition, as was the case in the election of 1864.[31]
This is because "in facing the Democratic challenge in 1864, Lincoln accepted a risk
and permitted his power to he threatened in a way that no dictator, constitutional
or not, would have tolerated."[32] Lincoln had even privately resigned himself to work
with his possible Democratic successor to save the Union, as shown by a memorandum written on August 23, 1864, shortly before the Democratic Convention.[33] He
later communicated his intentions publicly that October.[34]

These moves were key to understanding Lincoln and how he viewed his role
under the circumstances: "Ultimately, Lincoln appealed to a kind of constitutional
common sense that, while respecting the requirements of procedural regularity and
formal legality, was concerned above all with preserving the substance of republican
liberty—the purpose both of American nationality and of the constitutional

order."[35] An argument can he made that instead of a "constitutional dictator," Lincoln was actually a "constitutionalist who used the executive power to preserve and extend the liberty of the American Founding."[36]

Conclusion

In assessing Lincoln's actions a number of matters should be kept in mind. First, the president adopted many of his measures when Congress was out of session and unable to convene. A major defense of presidential prerogative is the practical issue of Congress not always being in session and the president more easily being able to act swiftly. Second, Congress approved Lincoln's measures. Congress instead could have chosen to challenge those measures, or even impeach and remove the president. Third, by seeking congressional approval for his measures, Lincoln exercised extraordinary powers under the republican notion of the consent of the governed. Fourth, Lincoln's measures were directed to the purposes of the war. His "constitutional dictatorship" pertained specifically to the war powers. Congress carried on its normal legislative responsibilities in other areas. In no sense was Lincoln acting as an absolute dictator. Congress, too, even established for itself a part of the war power. A Joint Committee on the Conduct of the War went beyond normal investigative powers as its members visited the military front, interrogated generals, and tried to advise Lincoln's officers on wartime measures.

Although Lincoln's actions speak loudly about his view of the prerogative power, the president best articulated that view in his famous letter to A. G. Hodges on 4 April 1864:

"My oath to preserve the Constitution to the best of my ability, imposed on me the duty of preserving, by every indispensable means, that government—that nation, of which that Constitution was the organic law. Was it possible to lose the nation and yet preserve the Constitution? By general law, life and limb must be protected, yet often a limb must be amputated to save a life; but a life is never wisely given to save a limb. I felt that measures otherwise unconstitutional might become lawful by becoming indispensable to the preservation of the Constitution through the preservation of the nation. Right or wrong, I assumed this ground. And now avow it. I could not feel that, to the best of my ability, I had even tried to preserve the Constitution, if, to save slavery or any minor matter, I should permit the wreck of government, country, and Constitution together."[37]

Jeffrey Crouch is a Ph.D. candidate in American Politics and **Mark J. Rozell** is professor and chair at The Catholic University of America in Washington, D.C.

∼

Abraham Lincoln and His Cabinet

Phillip G. Henderson

*"To those who knew Abraham Lincoln, or who were at all intimate with his
Administration, the representation that he was subordinate to any member
of his Cabinet, or that he was deficient in executive or administrative ability,
is absurd."*
Gideon Welles, 1874

Abraham Lincoln's use of the cabinet as an advisory body says much about his
political skill and executive style. In the modern sense, Lincoln was not a disciplined
administrator or highly organized executive. His administrative predilections would
have been more in keeping with the freewheeling approach to governance of Franklin Roosevelt or John F. Kennedy, than with the highly systematic and formalistic
style of Dwight Eisenhower or Richard Nixon. As John Hay noted in a letter to
William Herndon, Lincoln "was extremely unmethodical: it was a four years' struggle on Nicolay's part and mine to get him to adopt some systematic rules. He would
break through every regulation as fast as it was made."[1]

Like Roosevelt during his crises-dominated presidency, Lincoln operated largely
on the basis of astute political instinct in managing the affairs of state. It followed
that Lincoln's use of the cabinet was more ad hoc than systematic. Yet, Lincoln
accorded his cabinet an important role in his administration, not just as an administrative arm of the executive, but as a useful sounding board for important policies.
Though Lincoln was confident enough in his own judgment to ignore his cabinet's
advice altogether in some instances, on more than one occasion, his cabinet secretaries served as an effective forum for helping the president to formulate, revise, or
moderate his policy decisions. Individually, particularly in Secretary of State William
Seward's case, or collectively as a formal advisory and administrative arm of the presidency, Lincoln utilized his cabinet with great skill and acumen.

Assembling the Cabinet

Lincoln's cabinet was composed of seven individuals who represented virtually every
faction within the Republican party of 1860. The president-elect sought leaders of
stature to serve as his top advisors. William H. Seward and Salmon P. Chase were
not only distinguished United States Senators, but leaders in the antislavery movement. Edward Bates and Simon Cameron also possessed reputations within the

Republican party that made them seem more likely to win the Republican nomination for president in 1860 than Lincoln. Yet, it was Lincoln who reigned victorious at the Republican National Convention in Chicago in May of 1860. Of the seven men named by Lincoln to serve in the cabinet, "there was probably not one who did not regard himself, in experience, intellect, and capacity to lead, superior to the nominal chieftain."[2] Lincoln's appointment of individuals who considered themselves better suited for the presidency indicates that the president-elect was not only self-confident but that he possessed "a conscious sense of leadership."[3] As Burton Hendrick writes: "He deliberately sought the most commanding associates he could find, not at all fearful that they would gain the upper hand, entirely confident of his own ability to control and direct and to retain complete authority in his own hands."[4]

Lincoln admired Seward and Chase. Their opposition to slavery and their two term governorships in New York and Ohio, respectively, made them distinguished figures in the Republican party. "What's the use of talking of me for President," Lincoln told Jesse W. Fell, "when we have such men as Seward, Chase, and others, who are so much better known and whose names are so intimately associated with the principles of the Republican party?"[5] Yet, Lincoln was supremely confident in his own ability to lead his distinguished assemblage of experienced statesmen. A brief sketch of the appointees named to the four principal departments represented in Lincoln's cabinet indicates the breadth of experience represented:

William Seward (Secretary of State 1861–1869) was unquestionably the most impressive of Lincoln's associates in the cabinet. Seward was a highly personable and ambitious individual. Like Lincoln, he was a skilled storyteller, which made him sympathetic to Lincoln's yarns, though some members of the cabinet found them "undignified."[6] A New Yorker, educated at Union College, Seward was a student of Burke, Bacon, Bolingbroke, and Cicero. His circle of friends and acquaintances was impressive ranging from Charles Sumner, who enjoyed conversing with Seward, to Jefferson Davis, who remained one of his closest friends up to the time he became President of the Confederate States.

Seward played an active role in New York state politics, becoming aligned with Thurlow Weed, a major political operative in the state. Seward was the frontrunner for the nomination in 1860, but his reputation as an antislavery advocate made him appear radical to the West. Seward pondered Lincoln's offer of the secretary of state position for more than two weeks, sending Thurlow Weed to Springfield to discuss Seward's "unsettled views" before finally accepting the appointment. Seward's towering ambition and his reputation led him to erroneously conclude that Lincoln would defer to him in the selection of the cabinet and in its operation. Many observers "took it for granted that Seward would be the brains and engine" of the Lincoln administration.[7] Lincoln had no such illusion. "The election of 1860, he believed, had marked a turning point in American history. A national crisis had called into existence a new party, made him its head, and elected him President; he intended to accept the mandate and the responsibility thus conferred."[8] Lincoln, in a conversation with Gideon Wells, said that it was fitting to name Seward secretary of state "in view of his admitted talents and great public services." But, he "did not think it came within the scope of his duty or courtesy" to turn over to Seward "the selection of the men with whom he was to be associated as advisers."[9] In summarizing Lincoln's views, historian Burton Hendrick writes:

> He had no intention of abdicating the Presidency and transferring it to a political clique dominated by Seward and Thurlow Weed. He sincerely desired to give Seward first place in the Cabinet; that formed an indispensable part of his plan of a composite administration. . . . But Lincoln intended to have Seward on his own terms, not on Seward's.[10]

Salmon P. Chase, Secretary of the Treasury (1861–1864) was born in a "particularly puritanical" section of New Hampshire in 1808. Even as a boy, Chase was noted for his "good behavior, scholarly tastes, and sobriety in conduct and religious observation."[11] Upon his father's untimely death he was raised by his uncle, Philander Chase, a distinguished Bishop in the Episcopal Church in Worthington, Ohio. A devout Episcopalian and graduate of Dartmouth College, Chase moved to Cincinnati to practice law in 1830. Chase became active in the antislavery movement and argued that the Framers of the Constitution had intended to abolish slavery soon after the Constitution was ratified.[12]

Chase was elected Governor of Ohio in 1857 as a Republican after serving one term as a Democrat. Lincoln wrote Chase that the Ohio Republican party's plank urging repeal of the Fugitive Slave Law was "damaging" the Republican party in Illinois and could "explode" the national party if introduced for discussion in 1860. Chase held firm, saying that a declaration in favor of the repeal of the Fugitive Slave Act of 1850 was indispensable. Nonetheless, Lincoln was grateful for Chase's support in the 1858 Senate race. Though a leading candidate for the Republican presidential nomination in 1860, Chase was "too austere and too humorless . . . too theological and too ostentatiously moral," to become a commanding leader.[13] After a dismal showing on the first ballot, Chase switched his forty-five delegates to Lincoln.

Chase was an influential member of Lincoln's cabinet, but was not as close to the president as Secretary Seward. Chase did not get along well with Seward and in 1862 launched a behind-the-scenes campaign to weaken Seward's influence. In 1863 Chase improved the national banking system in order to increase the sale of government bonds and solidify the national currency. Chase used his organizational ability and financial sophistication to enable the Treasury Department to meet the pressing financing needs of war. After a series of disagreements with the president over appointment and policy issues, Lincoln accepted Chase's resignation from the cabinet in June 1864. Earlier that year, Chase allowed his supporters to begin efforts to oppose Lincoln for the Republican presidential nomination in 1864. Despite their differences, Lincoln appointed Chase as Chief Justice of the Supreme Court in December of 1864, realizing that his first choice, Montgomery Blair, would never be confirmed by the Senate. The last time that the two men met face to face was on March 4, 1865, on the porch of the Capitol, where Chief Justice Chase administered the oath of office to Lincoln on his inauguration to a second term.[14]

Edward Bates, Attorney General (1861–1864), was born in Virginia in 1793, and despite Quaker roots, fought in the War of 1812. After the war, he moved to St. Louis where he became a lawyer and took part in framing the Missouri constitution. By 1820, Bates and Thomas Hart Benton had become Missouri's two most famous politicians. Bates, a Hamiltonian in philosophy, had broken away from the Democratic Party to join the Whig Party in the late 1820s. President Fillmore offered Bates appointment as secretary of war in 1850 but Bates declined. Lincoln was favorably impressed with Bates when he heard him deliver a highly regarded speech in Chicago in 1844 in his capacity as president of the Rivers and Harbors Convention.

Bates supported repeal of the Missouri Compromise in 1854, but unlike Seward and Chase, he was not a passionate follower of the antislavery movement. At the Republican convention of 1860, Bates had the support of Horace Greely, Montgomery Blair, and Schuyler Colfax as an alternative to the presumed frontrunner, William Seward. Bates assumed that most of the anti-Seward delegates would support him, but like Chase, he underestimated Lincoln's organization and strength at the 1860 convention.

As attorney general, Bates defended Lincoln's suspension of habeas corpus and the Emancipation Proclamation. Although Bates was a loyal supporter of the president, he thought that Lincoln's "amiable weakness" led to vacillation and indecisiveness on such matters as whether to dismiss General George McClellan as general-in-chief of the army. On December 31, 1861, Bates wrote: "The President is an excellent man, and in the main wise, but he lacks *will* and *purpose*."[15] Bates was unaware of the fact that Seward had made similar aspersions concerning Lincoln's ability to decide policy earlier that year, and that the president had made abundantly clear that he was fully in charge of his administration.

Simon Cameron of Pennsylvania served as Secretary of War (1861–1862). Cameron was a native of Pennsylvania and had been a newspaper editor before amassing a fortune as an entrepreneur in the construction of canals and railroads. He served in the United States Senate from 1845 until his appointment in the cabinet. Cameron was a highly influential figure in Pennsylvania politics, first as a Whig, then in the Know-Nothing party, and finally as a Republican. He came in third behind Seward and Lincoln in the first round of balloting for the Republican presidential nomination in 1860. Cameron campaigned vigorously for Lincoln in 1860 and in 1864.

Lincoln received numerous endorsements for placing Cameron in the cabinet, but he also received many letters against his appointment, some of them charged Cameron with corruption. Lincoln hesitated, and even attempted to rescind his offer of appointment to Cameron until he was convinced that there was no conclusive evidence of corruption, even if there may have been some ethical lapses.

Cameron presciently advised Lincoln to call up more than the initial seventy-five thousand men that had been requested after the fall of Fort Sumter.[16] He was released from the cabinet when he leaked a report calling for freeing and arming slaves as soldiers. Lincoln ordered the report's distribution halted and its contents altered, but the story made its way into the newspapers.[17]

Charges of corruption in the administration of contracts were leveled at Cameron, but his chief fault may have been more squarely that he was not a skilled administrator in the department of government that most needed effective administration. When Congress tried to censure Cameron, however, Lincoln defended him saying that the War Department's careless practices resulted from the dire emergency that the nation faced, and that the president and the other department heads "were at least equally responsible . . . for whatever error, wrong, or fault was committed."[18]

Edwin M. Stanton replaced Cameron as Secretary of War in 1862 and served as head of the department until 1868. Stanton, like Chase was raised in Ohio, but moved to Pittsburgh to practice law. He was one of the top lawyers in America and practiced frequently before the United States Supreme Court.[19] Stanton was critical of the new president in 1861, finding "no token of any intelligent understanding by Lincoln, or the crew that govern him."[20]

Stanton served as a legal advisor to Secretary of War Cameron at the time Lincoln removed Cameron from the cabinet. Ironically, Lincoln asked Stanton to take Cameron's place, even though Stanton had supported Cameron's controversial report calling for the freeing and arming of slaves. Secretary of State Seward and Treasury Secretary Chase both urged Lincoln to appoint Stanton to head the War Department. Stanton was much more proficient organizationally than Cameron had been. He soon turned the War Department into an efficient organization while doubling its size. He regularized the procedures for administration of contracts and ridded the department of the stigma of shoddiness and corruption that had surrounded it under Cameron's lax management.[21]

Stanton refused to alter state quotas for conscription or delay the draft, as some members of Congress had requested. He "was stern and pragmatic in all things having to do with achieving Union victory."[22] Stanton was an early fan of the talents of Ulysses S. Grant, and shared with Lincoln a desire to promote generals who were decisive and victorious. Stanton was one of only two members of the cabinet to urge Lincoln to issue his proclamation of emancipation when the president first presented the idea to the cabinet on July 22, 1862.

Beyond the four principal departments of the federal government, Lincoln named Gideon Welles of Connecticut as his secretary of the navy, Caleb B. Smith of Indiana as his secretary of the interior, and Montgomery Blair of Maryland as his postmaster-general.

In composing the cabinet, Lincoln had many purposes in mind. The result was an adept blending and balancing of geography, political background, experience, and talent. As Lincoln's trusted White House aides, John Nicolay and John Hay would later write:

> He needed advisers, helpers, executive eyes and hands, not alone in department routine, but in the higher qualities of leadership and influence; above all, his principal motive seems to have been representative character. . . . He wished to combine the experience of Seward, the integrity of Chase, the popularity of Cameron; to hold the West with Bates, attract New England with Welles; please the Whigs through Smith, and convince the Democrats through Blair.[23]

In assembling his cabinet, Lincoln displayed the qualities that were to distinguish his administration: "Independence of opinion, absolute reliance on his own judgment," a willingness to listen to the advice of others, even when that advice ran against his own position, "a readiness to compromise, so long as the main object was achieved, and a logically thought out scheme of action."[24]

William Seward as First Secretary of the Cabinet

Lincoln first met William Seward while campaigning for Zachary Taylor in Boston in 1848. Lincoln had been impressed with a speech given by Seward in which he emphasized the need to contain slavery. The two me did not meet again until 1860 when they both sought the Republican presidential nomination. Seward was the clear front-runner for the nomination and Lincoln was a dark horse candidate. Lincoln's ultimate victory in securing the nomination stunned and "mortified" Seward.[25] Seward had a sense of entitlement concerning the nomination which made his defeat by Lincoln all the more humiliating. Even after his appointment as secretary of state, Seward referred to Lincoln disparagingly as the "little Illinois lawyer," who had handed him an unexpected defeat.[26]

David Donald describes Seward's endorsement of Lincoln as "patently insincere." Nonetheless, Lincoln felt obligated to offer the popular Republican the top post in the cabinet—secretary of state. The perception of Seward's stature as an eminence grise in the Lincoln administration was widely held. Even the commissioners sent to Washington by the newly formed Confederate States of America to negotiate the surrender of Fort Sumter turned to Seward as the presumptive spokesman for the incoming administration.[27] As Donald notes: "Nearly everybody assumed that Seward would become the 'premier' of the new administration, really running the government while Lincoln simply followed his advice."[28] Seward did nothing to quell such notions, writing to his wife some six months into Lincoln's presidency: "I look back, and see that there has not been a day since last January, that I could, safely for the Government, have been absent."[29]

Lincoln was well aware of Seward's huge ego and his pretentious behavior. But it still must have come as a shock to the new president when a month into the administration Seward wrote a terse, egotistical, and remarkably candid memorandum to Lincoln in which he critiqued the president's performance during his first month in office. Seward criticized Lincoln for spending too much time on minor patronage matters and for not taking direct "energetic" action in some instances, including removal of federal troops from Fort Sumter. Seward kept his memo strictly confidential and Lincoln showed remarkable restraint in the face of Seward's "impertinence" and near insubordination.[30] Lincoln wrote a response to Seward which apparently was never sent, but which likely was conveyed in the form of a private face-to-face rebuke. Lincoln undoubtedly made it clear to Seward that he intended to run his own administration and that he intended to have no trumped-up wars with European nations of the type that Seward had advocated to "unify" the nation.[31]

Lincoln was particularly disturbed to find that Seward had been engaged in discussions with Southerners close to Jefferson Davis, providing assurances that Fort Sumter in South Carolina would not be reinforced, on the presumption that Lincoln would submit to Seward's wisdom.[32] The cabinet had been sharply divided on the issue with some urging reinforcement and others, especially Seward, urging abandonment of the fort as a means of averting war. On March 29, 1861, Lincoln informed his cabinet of his decision to send a resupply party (but no troop reinforcements) to Fort Sumter, thus making it crystal clear who was in charge, and leaving it to the South to decide on whether they wished to commence a civil war.[33]

Lincoln viewed Seward as an indispensable member of his cabinet notwithstanding Seward's bouts with megalomania. As David Donald notes:

> Lincoln knew that he needed Seward and began a systematic campaign to win his loyalty and even his affection. When Lincoln tried to be charming, he was irresistible, and he knew how to court Seward. Aware of the Secretary's self-importance and vanity, he encouraged Seward to drop in at the White House nearly every day. . . .[34]

Though Seward was given broad latitude by Lincoln, the president had the final say on all administration policy. When the secretary of state drafted a strong admonition to the British government against extending diplomatic recognition to the Confederacy, Lincoln took steps to ensure that a more tactful approach was utilized. Seward's draft communique, Despatch No. 10, posed a stern warning to the British that recognition of the Confederacy would have grave consequences: "We from that hour shall cease to be friends and become once more, as we have twice before been forced to be, enemies of Great Britain."[35] Lincoln circled the strident passage in Seward's despatch and marked it: "Leave Out."[36] Lincoln was also troubled by Secretary Seward's instruction to the American Minister to Great Britain, Charles Francis Adams, to take the message to the Foreign Office and read it directly to Lord John. Lincoln believed that such directness was dangerously provocative.[37] Lincoln excised this directive and instructed Adams merely to summarize the Despatch. More important, Lincoln made specific changes in the wording of the document so as to tone down Seward's more strident language.

Whereas Seward had written that intercourse of any kind with the Confederate mission in London would be "wrongful," Lincoln deleted this word and substituted "hurtful."[38] And while Seward's draft threatened reprisals if Southern cruisers found refuge in British harbors, Lincoln instructed Seward to delete any mention of this. In so doing, Lincoln "adroitly changed Despatch No. 10 from what was virtually a threat," to a secret, and considerably less confrontational paper to guide Adams in his sensitive discussions with the British.[39] Historian Burton Hendrick suggests that "Lincoln's shrewd modification of Despatch No. 10, and the determination he had displayed," gave Secretary of State Seward "a new conception of his chief." Seward now understood "that Lincoln was indeed President, and intended to remain President."[40] Indeed, on June 5, Seward wrote his wife in terms very different from his earlier, more disparaging letters. "Executive skill and vigor," he wrote, "are rare qualities. The President is the best of us, but he needs constant and assiduous co-operation."[41]

Prior to the finalizing of Despatch No. 10, Seward may have been impervious to the degree to which Lincoln was really in control of his own administration. For as David Donald suggests, Lincoln's delegation of authority to Seward was so masterful, that Seward himself may not have realized the fine line at which his authority blended with that of the president. As Donald puts it:

> In routine diplomatic affairs, Lincoln was usually willing to follow Seward's advice, but on important foreign policy questions, the President made the decisions. In so doing, he handled the Secretary with great finesse, allowing Seward to appear to shape policy—and perhaps to believe that he did so.[42]

According to Donald, Lincoln's ability to maneuver Seward in the direction that he favored is perhaps best illustrated in the *Trent* affair of 1861. The affair began on November 8 when the USS *San Jacinto* boarded the *Trent*, a British mail-packet and captured two Confederate envoys, James Mason and John Slidell. The envoys were headed to England in an attempt to secure formal diplomatic recognition of the South. The capture of Mason and Slidell "outraged British public opinion," and, in the view of the British government was a clear violation of international law.[43] The British government "demanded that the envoys be surrendered," and backed their demand with preparations for war. When the British issued an ultimatum demanding an answer by December 30, 1861, Lincoln convened the cabinet to discuss the matter. Fully aware of the gravity of the situation, Lincoln warned of the danger of having two wars at one time. At the meeting, Seward conceded that the government might be obligated under international law to release the envoys. With the cabinet divided on the issue, Lincoln adjourned the meeting until the next day. The president then asked Seward to stay after the meeting when he said: "Governor Seward, you will go on . . . preparing your answer, which . . . will state the reasons why they [the Confederate envoys] ought to be given up. Now I have a mind to try my hand at stating the reasons why they ought not to be given up. We will compare the points on each side."[44]

When the cabinet reconvened the next day Seward, Donald notes, had "studied up all the works ever written on international law, and came . . . loaded to the muzzle with the subject."[45] He then proceeded to make a strong argument for release of the envoys. Seward noted that by siding with Britain in this affair, he was actually defending traditional American doctrines of the freedom of the seas that had been set forth in protest against British violations of neutrality at sea during Madison's administration. Although Secretary Chase and other members of the cabinet were unhappy with the prospect of heeding Seward's advice to release the envoys, they conceded that Seward had made such a powerful argument in favor of such action that they were in agreement that it should be carried out.

David Donald, drawing on Seward's *Reminiscences*, notes that after the meeting, the secretary of state asked Lincoln about his comment the day before that he would frame an argument for the other side. Seward recalled that Lincoln smiled and shook his head, saying: "I found I could not make an argument that would satisfy my own mind, . . . and that proved to me that your ground was the right one."[46] Donald speculates that Lincoln was "unwilling to reveal that he had maneuvered the Secretary of State into adopting the position that he had favored all along."[47]

As the *Trent* affair makes clear, while Lincoln was clearly in charge of his cabinet, he was willing, indeed eager, to draw upon the talents and good ideas of those who served in the cabinet, often refining and improving upon their contributions. There is no question that Lincoln profited from the counsel of Secretary Seward and other members of his cabinet. John Nicolay and John Hay, in their meticulous documentation of the crafting of Lincoln's First Inaugural Address of March 4, 1861, reveal the important role that Seward played in developing this landmark speech. One of the most profound changes suggested by Seward called for the addition of a paragraph at the end of the Inaugural speech. Lincoln's original draft closed with the following sentence: "In your hands, my dissatisfied fellow-countrymen, and not in mine, is the momentous issue of civil war. The Government will not assail you, *unless you first assail it . . . You can forbear the assault upon it, I cannot shrink from the defense of it. With you, and not with me, is the solemn question of "Shall it be peace or a sword?"*[48]

Nicolay and Hay note that "Mr. Seward did not like this termination." Seward suggested in his letter to Lincoln that "something besides or in addition to argument is needful—to meet and remove prejudice and passion in the South, and despondency and fear in the East. Some words of affection—some of calm and cheerful confidence."[49] Seward then volunteered two separate drafts for a closing paragraph to substitute for the "Shall it be peace or a sword?" closing in Lincoln's draft. Seward's second draft appealed to Lincoln. In it, Seward wrote:

I close. We are not, we must not be, aliens or enemies, but fellow-countrymen and brethren. Although passion has strained our bonds of affection too hardly, they must not, I am sure they will not, be broken. The mystic chords which, proceeding from so many battlefields and so many patriot graves, pass through all the hearts and all hearths in this broad continent of ours, will yet again harmonize in their ancient music when breathed upon by the guardian angel of the nation.[50]

Praising Seward's draft for "containing the germ of a fine poetic thought," Nicolay and Hay record that "Mr. Lincoln took, and, in a new development and perfect form, gave it the life and spirit and beauty which have made it celebrated in the text."[51] In one of the most eloquent and memorable passages in American history, Lincoln thus transformed Seward's idea into the following words:

I am loth to close. We are not enemies, but friends. We must not be enemies. Though passion may have strained, it must not break our bonds of affection. The mystic chords of memory, stretching from every battlefield, and patriot grave, to every living heart and hearthstone, all over this broad land, will yet swell the chorus of the Union, when again touched, as surely they will be, by the better angles of our nature.[52]

Cabinet Deliberations

Although Secretary Seward dominated discussion in some of the meetings of the cabinet, Lincoln was attentive to the arguments and comments of all members of the cabinet. At the end of cabinet discussions, Lincoln would often sum up the pros and cons of the policies under consideration and announce his decisions. According to Gideon Wells, who served as secretary of the navy throughout Lincoln's presidency, the president's positions frequently ran counter to those of Seward.[53] Yet, despite Lincoln's ability to take stands quite different from Seward's, some members of the cabinet were resentful of the special role that Lincoln had accorded to Seward as an advisor and confidant.

Lincoln was conversant in the activities of all of the departments in the federal government and discussed them freely and frequently with Seward. Other members of the cabinet, particularly Treasury Secretary Salmon P. Chase, were concerned that they were not privy to the affairs of the State Department, much less what was going on in the rest of the government. Chase and others were not happy with the appearance that Seward exercised disproportionate influence. In frustration, Chase argued in favor of more frequent and regularized meetings of the cabinet. Citing custom, Chase suggested that the cabinet meet on a routine schedule with its members acting as a general council to address affairs of state. Not surprisingly, all of Chase's colleagues supported the proposal except Seward, who could see no value in periodical gatherings. Despite Chase's objections, Lincoln "approved the suggestion and directed that the time-honored 'cabinet days' be restored."[54] The regular schedule of meetings, however, did not persist, in part because of Seward's continued opposition. Routine was replaced by the earlier "easygoing" state of affairs.

Seward's persistent meddling in the affairs of the other departments aggravated others besides Chase. Attorney General Bates, "not easily moved to anger, was outraged when he learned that Seward was sending instructions—without the attorney general's knowledge—to district attorneys' and marshals' offices which were exclusively under the jurisdiction of the Department of Justice."[55] Seward's intrusion into Justice Department activities rekindled the demand for regular meetings of the full cabinet as a council to the president. Now it was Bates, not Chase, who "brought up the whole question of 'cabinet unity' and a more regular procedure in full cabinet meetings."[56] Bates protested to the president against the lack of methodical and dignified arrangements in the conduct of public business by the cabinet. Again, all members of the cabinet, except Seward, supported Bates's demand. And once again, Lincoln overruled the secretary of state and ordered that regular meetings of the cabinet be held on Tuesdays and Fridays. According to Burton Hendricks, the secretary of navy intimated that Lincoln himself probably instigated Bates in bringing the matter before the whole cabinet.[57] This time, the new routine was adhered to, and Tuesdays and Fridays, for the rest of the administrations were regular "cabinet days."

The internal rivalry with Seward, however, persisted, and would ultimately precipitate the Cabinet Crisis of 1862. Part of the problem stemmed from the cabinet overestimating Seward's overall influence with the president. As great as Seward's influence over Lincoln was, Hendricks writes, he in no way exercised the type of control that his colleagues suspected.

> In the great early issues of the conflict, it was the will of Lincoln, not that of Seward, which prevailed. He had utterly disregarded Seward's policy of avoiding conflict by compromising with the South. The decision to preserve the Union, even at the cost of civil war, was Lincoln's not Seward's. He overruled Seward's policy on the relief of Sumter.[58]

The loss of the Battle of Fredericksburg on December 13, 1862 and the political loss of Republican majorities in New York, Pennsylvania, Ohio, Illinois, and Indiana in the midterm elections of November 1862 combined to precipitate what is known as the "Cabinet Crisis of 1862." Many disgruntled Republicans in Congress argued for a change in the cabinet to facilitate more vigorous prosecution of the war.[59] Treasury Secretary Chase had indiscreetly remarked to members of Congress that the cabinet in general, and Secretary Seward in particular, had been indecisive in the war effort. Congress drafted a protest that suggested a reorganization of the cabinet and denounced Seward by name. Upon hearing of the backlash in the Republican ranks, Seward submitted his resignation to the President. Lincoln was not inclined to accept Seward's resignation. Instead, he adroitly invited a committee of disgrun-

tled senators to the White House to present their grievances and to make their case
against Seward.

Lincoln convened his cabinet the next morning, (December 19, 1862) to say that
he was surprised to hear that members of the senate were under the impression that
the cabinet was divided. He invited the entire cabinet, except Seward, to meet with
the senate delegation that very evening to register their concerns. Secretary Chase
was now placed in the position of either repeating his accusations about the cabinet
in front of its members or withholding his criticism. Chase chose the latter course,
but ended up offering his own resignation to the president the following day. "Lincoln refused both resignations and the crisis was over."[60]

David Donald suggests that the friction between members of the cabinet was
based on conflicts of personality more than of ideology. For that reason, the rifts
were not as pronounced, in Lincoln's view, as they may have seemed on the surface.
As Donald puts it:

> Welles and Chase distrusted Seward because they suspected his bland amiability and
> his perpetual optimism and believed that he failed to understand the seriousness of the
> nation's crisis. Stanton's irascible, secretive manner prevented other cabinet members
> from becoming his friends, though he generally managed to work amicably with
> Chase. . . .
>
> . . . Lincoln was not only aware of this dissonance; he was prepared to tolerate, and
> perhaps even to encourage, creative friction among his advisers. He understood that
> the conflicts among his cabinet members were not so fundamental as they seemed.
> The irritable clashes among the cabinet officers reflected differences in personality, not
> ideology; unconsciously they were rivals for the esteem and affection of the President.
> It was a problem that Lincoln, like other men of enormous personal magnetism, had
> to live with throughout his life; and he understood that the rivalry between Seward
> and Chase, or between Stanton and Welles, was much like that between Herndon and
> Mary Lincoln back in Springfield, or between Mrs. Lincoln and Nicolay and Hay dur-
> ing the White House years.[61]

To the extent that Lincoln tolerated this creative tension among his cabinet officers, his style of leadership had many of the ingredients that political scientists have
come to associate with the successful leadership of a distant successor: Franklin Roosevelt. Stephen Hess describes Roosevelt's "cold blooded practice" of managing the
cabinet as "management by combat."[62] FDR's approach to management, tolerated,
indeed encouraged a degree of competition among cabinet members and agency
directors for the president's ear, and approval. This competitive style sometimes
resulted in bruised egos and threats of resignation from various members of the cabinet. In a memorandum to Sam Rosenman, Roosevelt wrote: "Get [Budget Director]
Harold Smith, usually known as 'Battling Smith,' into a room with the Secretary of
the Treasury, usually known as 'Sailor Morgenthau,' lock them in and let the survi-
vor out."[63] In a revealing comment to Frances Perkins, Roosevelt once said: "A little
rivalry is stimulating you know. It keeps everybody going to prove he is a better
fellow than the next man."[64]

Lincoln, like Roosevelt in a later crisis-dominated era, apparently realized that the tension of competition for the boss's approval helped stimulate creative thinking and good performance. And, just as Lincoln turned frequently to subordinates outside the cabinet for information, Roosevelt was fond of digging deep into the bureaucracy for information. He had mid-level informants in several of the key departments of government as well as in the army and navy to keep him apprised of situations independent of departmental bias.

The Cabinet as a Moderating Influence

Initially, at least, Lincoln attempted to micromanage many of the details of the executive branch, particularly military operations. As Donald notes, "he thought he could issue orders directly to officers in the navy, without even informing Secretary Welles, and he attempted, without congressional authorization, to create a new Bureau of Militia in the War Department."[65] But Lincoln, even in his capacity as commander in chief, was not a one-man show. His confidence allowed him to listen carefully to the advice of his cabinet officers and to heed their advice when it seemed prudent to do so. Early in his administration, as Fort Sumter became the focus of attention, Lincoln asked each member of his cabinet to respond in writing to the question: "Assuming it to be possible to now provision Fort Sumter, under all the circumstances, is it wise to attempt it?"[66] Though the entire cabinet except for Secretary Chase opposed resupplying Sumter, Lincoln followed his own instinct on the matter. By engaging in open discussion of the issue, however, the president had given the cabinet a stake in the deliberations and decisions of the administration.

On other occasions the cabinet's influence was more decisive. In September 1863, for example, the cabinet played an important role in cooling the passions of the president regarding a developing judicial crisis in Pennsylvania. On September 14, the president informed his cabinet "that military officers in Pennsylvania were complaining that judges were issuing writs of habeas corpus to free recruits and draftees. The officers were compelled to appear in court to explain why certain men were held in the army."[67] The practice had become so widespread that it threatened mobilization of the army in Pennsylvania. Lincoln's proposed response to the crisis was to instruct officers to respond to writs of habeas corpus with force, if necessary, indicating to judges that the prisoners were being held by presidential authority. The president was prepared to instruct officers in the army that "if said court or judge [shall attempt] to take such officer, or to arrest such officer, he resist such attempt, calling to his aid any force that may be necessary to make such resistance effectual."[68] In discussion, the cabinet convinced Lincoln to tone-down his toughly worded order.

Treasury Secretary Chase told the president that he feared that the potential defiance of judicial authority implicit in the commander in chief's explicit order might bring about civil war in the free Northern states. Chase and others believed that Lincoln's strongly worded order would challenge established precedent in the United States that civilian authority reigned supreme over the military.[69] Lincoln stated his strong objection to the practice used by some judges in Pennsylvania to employ writs of habeas corpus "to frustrate the conscription system enacted by Congress in 1863."[70] Lincoln was angered that judges would work to obstruct a federal law to raise an army "in a case when the power is given by the Constitution in express terms."[71] After hearing the arguments of his cabinet, however, Lincoln accepted their advice to issue a less confrontational proclamation suspending the writ of habeas corpus in which he merely admonished judges not to follow the obstructionist tactics of the judges in Pennsylvania. As Mark E. Neely, Jr. notes, Lincoln issued his more drastic enforcement orders discreetly, behind the scenes, rather than issuing an edict that appeared to confront judicial authority. "By preparing public opinion first, the policy worked."[72]

The cabinet had moderated the president's impulses on other occasions, most notably when he read his early draft of the Emancipation Proclamation to the entire cabinet on July 22, 1862. The proposed proclamation seemed to catch the cabinet off-guard. As Donald notes: "The curious structure and awkward framing of the document showed that Lincoln was still trying to blend his earlier policy of gradual, compensated emancipation with his new program of immediate abolition."[73] Lincoln told his cabinet from the outset that he had "resolved upon this step, and had not called them together to ask their advice, but to lay out the subject-matter of a proclamation before them."[74] Whereas Stanton and Bates urged "immediate promulgation" of the proclamation, Chase, Seward, Welles, and Postmaster General Blair expressed reservations. Blair was concerned that the proclamation would have adverse impact on the fall elections. Seward argued that the timing was poor. Issuing the proclamation after a series of serious military reverses by the Union army would "be viewed as the last measure of an exhausted government, a cry for help."[75] Seward suggested, according to Lincoln's own recollection, that the proclamation "would be considered our last shriek, on the retreat."[76] As eager as Lincoln had been to issue the proclamation, the cabinet debate forced him to consider the possibility that the order for emancipation would be viewed as a desperate act unless it was accompanied by a major Union victory. Lincoln waited three months, until McClellan's victory at Antietam, to issue the proclamation. The timing would never be ideal for such a profound edict, but now the president could act from a position of strength rather than weakness.

Conclusion

In the *Trent* affair of 1861, as in the timing of the issuance of the Emancipation Proclamation, and in the crisis over habeas corpus in 1863, Lincoln allowed the collective wisdom of his cabinet to help refine and modify his decisions. From his early days as a lawyer Lincoln had developed good listening skills which paid off in his ability to discern the merits of arguments made by the members of the cabinet. Lincoln's folksy and unassuming style of leadership appears to have led even members of his own cabinet to underestimate his ability and accomplishments. The president's untimely death and the successful end of the war for Union would make many who had served Lincoln realize more fully the extent of his greatness. Seward's close confidant, Thurlow Weed, in compiling his autobiography twenty-five years after the fact, would write of his first meeting with Lincoln with the advantage of hindsight. Recalling his first impression of Lincoln when the two met in Springfield to discuss the formation of the cabinet Weed wrote: "I found Mr. Lincoln sagacious and practical. He displayed throughout the conversation so much good sense, such intuitive knowledge of human nature, and such familiarity with the virtues and infirmities of politicians that I became impressed very favorably with his fitness for the duties which he was not unlikely to be called upon to perform."[77] Even allowing that Weed's recollection may have been influenced by the course of events after his meeting with the president-elect in Springfield, there is no doubt that his words accurately capture the true essence of Lincoln's leadership.

ℒ

Notes to Chapter 5

Lincoln and the Constitution

From time to time, *Congress and the Presidency* will publish articles of interest to its readers, which have been published in formats with limited distribution and unlikely to be reported in reference works. This address, the seventh annual R. Gerald McMurtry Lecture, sponsored by the Louis A. Warren Lincoln Library and Museum, received such limited publication in 1984. It is with the permission of the Lincoln Library and Museum that it is republished here (copyright 1984, Louis A. Warren Lincoln Library and Museum).

1. The same point was made by Sydney George Fisher in "The Suspension of Habeas Corpus During the War of the Rebellion" (1988). Fisher, thoroughly approving of Lincoln's actions, did not describe them as in any way dictatorial.

2. In 1923 John W. Burgess wrote a bitter lamentation condemning the growth of democratic Caesarism and the demise of limited government. Not surprisingly, considering his Unionist background, yet perhaps significantly, he attributed none of this development to Lincoln, but rather saw Theodore Roosevelt as its source. See Burgess, 1923.

3. Reflecting the anti-Radical outlook of most historians at this time, Stephenson believes that the Radical Republicans in Congress presented a far more serious threat of dictatorship than Lincoln. See Stephenson, 1922.

4. Edgar Lee Masters attacked Lincoln as a tyrant in *Lincoln the Man* (1931), but while his work was not in the neo-Confederate tradition, neither ought it to be regarded as a serious scholarly contribution.

5. A little-noticed irony occurred in 1981 when Bradford, author of notorious anti-Lincoln

diatribes, was considered for the position of director of the National Endowment for the Humanities by the newly elected Republican administration of President Ronald Reagan. More than any president in recent memory, Reagan has invoked the principles and rhetoric of Lincoln. Fortunately the appointment was not made, evidence that the Southernization of the Republican party has not proceeded so far as to place a passionate critic of Lincoln in a position of scholarly and intellectual leadership.

6. Anderson's critique, written from a leftist point of view, strikingly resembles the Kendall-Bradford conservative attack. What both points of view have in common of course is hostility toward bourgeois capitalism and liberal democracy, with which Lincoln identified himself.

7. In describing the dictatorship convention I do not imply that virtually every book on Lincoln presents him in this light. Most works in the Lincoln field, general biographical accounts and specialized studies, are not concerned with governmental problems and do not take up the dictatorship question. In referring to historians who have rejected the dictatorship thesis, I refer to those few who have expressly considered it and found it unpersuasive.

8. Also to be noted are two accounts of the civil liberties question during the Civil War which refute the dictatorship argument: Cole, 1926–1927 and Bernard, 1951. Richard N. Current aptly observes that political scientists and politicians invoking Lincoln's example have exaggerated his usurpations as president. "Neither by work nor by deed," Current concludes, "did Lincoln give any real justification for the idea of 'executive privilege' or of an 'imperial presidency'" (Current, 1979: 32).

9. The concept of constitutional dictatorship appears to have been an attempt to retain the original meaning of dictatorship as the voluntary adoption of one-man rule by a republic or democracy, in the face of the establishment in the twentieth century of permanent dictatorships by totalitarian states. In earlier time the idea of a permanent dictatorship would have been regarded as a contradiction in terms, and would have been described as despotism. Cf. Brooks, 1935: 22.

10. Henry Jones Ford, a prominent advocate of executive power in the early twentieth century, provides a good example of the scholarly attraction to the dictatorship idea despite its apparent incompatibility with basic democratic values. Ford emphasized the distinction between responsible and irresponsible government, rather than limitations on executive power, as the essential difference between constitutional government and despotism. Strangely, however, Ford did not regard the enforcing or accountability as a limitation on power. It is difficult to see in Ford's analysis, and the writings of other proponents of the constitutional dictatorship thesis, the existence in the United States of the absolute and unlimited power which in their view characterized this institutional condition.

Pertinent in this connection is the assertion of Karl Dietrich Bracher that crisis government results when "the system of limitation and balance of power typical of a constitutional government" is abandoned in favor of enlarged executive or military power. Bracher does not cite the United States as an example of crisis government in this sense. He states that in the United States constitutional theory agrees on implied or inherent powers for the president as a way of dealing with emergencies. He notes, however, that controls by courts and the legislature are not curtailed in emergencies by the exercise of executive power (Bracher, 1968: 514).

11. For example, to appoint an officer whose assignment would be temperance work among the troops, or to remit a fine imposed on a restaurateur for selling spirits to a soldier (Basler, 1953–1955: V, 270).

12. This was with regard to a veto concerning a bill reducing the fees paid to the marshal of the District of Columbia.

13. This statement was made in reply to a memorial supporting emancipation adopted by a public meeting of Christians of all denominations in Chicago in September 1862.

14. Lincoln described the Emancipation Proclamation "as a fit and necessary war measure" for suppressing the rebellion, authorized under the power vested in him as commander-in-chief of the army and navy "in time of actual armed rebellion against authority and government of the United States. . . ."

15. Lincoln wrote in August 1863: "During my continuance here, the government will return no person to slavery who is free according to the proclamation or to any of the acts of Congress, unless such return shall be held to be a legal duty, by the proper court of final resort, in which case I will promptly act as may then appear to be my personal duty" (Basler, 1953–1955: VI, 411).

16. For obvious political reasons, Lincoln signed the resolution submitting the Thirteenth Amendment to the states. This action, however, was constitutionally anomalous, as the Senate pointed out in a resolution of February 7, 1865, stating that presidential approval of resolutions proposing constitutional amendments was unnecessary.

17. See also Lincoln's letter to Albert G. Hodges, April 4, 1864, in which he stated his belief that the presidency did not confer "an unrestricted right to act officially" upon the basis of his antislavery feelings, or "in ordinary civil administration . . . to practically indulge my primary abstract judgment on the moral question of slavery" (Basler, 1953–1955: VII, 281).

18. Lincoln wrote this memorandum on August 23, a few days before the Democratic convention. He believed that should the Democratic candidate win, "he will have secured his election on such ground that he cannot possibly save (the Union) afterwards." The final effort to save the Union must therefore come between the election and the inauguration of the next president in March 1865, Lincoln evidently anticipated a "peace plank" such as the Democrats included in their platform. The platform called for "a cessation of hostilities, with a view to an ultimate convention of the States, or other peaceable means, to the end that, at the earliest practical moment, peace may be restored on the basis of the federal Union of the States."

19. Lincoln acknowledged the rumors in response to a serenade, October 19, 1864.

20. Lincoln noted that the Democratic convention did not adjourn "sine die," but to meet again if called to do so. This fact, he said, had led to speculation that, if elected, the Democratic candidate would try to seize the government immediately.

21. In positing this concept of constitutional reasoning and justification I follow the views expressed in Black, 1969.

22. Lincoln's effective use of the conceptual outlook can be seen in the First Inaugural Address, in the contention that no right "plainly written in the Constitution" had ever been denied. In lawyer-like fashion, he cleverly sought to disarm the secessionists by arguing that only if a "plainly written" constitutional right were denied by an electoral majority, would revolutionary action by a minority (in this instance, secession) be morally justified. Happily, he continued, "All the vital rights of minorities and of individuals are so plainly assured to them by affirmations and negations, guaranties and prohibitions, in the constitution, that controversies never arise concerning them." In fact, he explained, controversies arise over rights and powers that are not "plainly written," such as the fugitive slave law and slavery in the territories.

23. I refer to the fact that while the American constitution in the broadest sense is the

complex of principles, institutions, laws, practices, and traditions by which political life is carried on, its minimal and irreducible basis is a form of positive law—the written documentary Constitution, This circumstance gives American constitutionalism a highly legalistic character.

24. See Corwin's interpretation of this statement in Corwin, 1957: 450–51.

25. Compare the recent analysis of Lincoln's constitutional theory by political scientist Gary Jacobsohn: "Lincoln saw the constitution as both a legal code and a statement of the ideal which we as a people chose 'in the end to live by'" (Jacobsohn, 1983: 66).

Lincoln and Executive Power

1. Clinton L. Rossiter, *Constitutional Dictatorship: Crisis Government in the Modern Democracies* (Princeton, NJ: Princeton University Press, 1948), 225–227.

2. Howard Taft, *Our Chief Magistrate and His Powers* (New York, 1916), 138. Theodore Roosevelt articulated the "stewardship" theory. See Wayne Andrews, S., *The Autobiography of Theodore Roosevelt* (New York, 1958), 197–200.

3. Mark E. Neely. Jr., *The Fate of Liberty: Abraham Lincoln and Civil Liberties* (New York, NY: Oxford University Press, 1991), 231–232.

4. Rossiter, 5.

5. Andrew C. McLaughlin, "Lincoln, the Constitution and Democracy," *The International Journal of Ethics* Vol. 47. No. I (1936), 1.

6. Rossiter, 5.

7. Rossiter, 7.

8. James G. Randall, *Constitutional Problems Under Lincoln* (New York, NY: D. Appleton and Co., 1926), 51; John P. Roche, "Executive Power and Domestic Emergency: The Quest for Prerogative," *The Western Political Quarterly* Vol. 5, No. 4 (1952), 598.

9. Rossiter, 224.

10. Roche, 598.

11. Roche, 599.

12. Richard Pious, *The American Presidency* (New York: Basic Books, 1979), 58.

13. *The Prize Cases* 67 U.S. 635 (1863).

14. Randall, 56.

15. Randall, 57.

16. Roche, 600.

17. Edward S. Corwin, *The President: Office and Powers 1787–1984,* 5th rev. ed., (New York, NY: New York University Press, 1984), 356.

18. Edward S. Corwin, *Total War and the Constitution* (New York, NY: Alfred A. Knopf, Inc., 1947), 16.

19. Corwin *TWC*, 19 (emphasis original).

20. Corwin *POP*, 268–269.

21. Rossiter, 223.

22. Rossiter, 218.

23. McLaughlin, 1, 12.

24. McLaughlin, 4.

25. McLaughlin, 2.

26. Arthur M. Schlesinger Jr., *The Imperial Presidency* (Boston, MA: Houghton Mifflin Co., 1973), 65.

27. Schlesinger, 66.

28. Schlesinger, 66.

29. Herman Belz, *Abraham Lincoln, Constitutionalism, and Equal Rights in the Civil War Era* (New York, NY: Fordham University Press, 1998), 28.

30. Belz, 28.

31. Belz, 33.

32. Belz, 33.

33. Belz, 33.

34. Belz, 34.

35. Belz, 41.

36. Belz, 43.

37. "Letter to A. G. Hodges," in Carl Van Doren, ed., *The Literary Works of Abraham Lincoln.* Norwalk, CT: Easton Press, 261.

Abraham Lincoln and His Cabinet

1. Emanuel Hertz, *The Hidden Lincoln: From the Letters and Papers of William H. Herndon* (New York: The Viking Press, 1938), 307.

2. Burton J. Hendrick, *Lincoln's War Cabinet* (Boston: Little, Brown and Company, 1946), 6.

3. Hendrick, *Lincoln's War Cabinet*, 6.

4. Hendrick, *Lincoln's War Cabinet*, 6.

5. Hendrick, *Lincoln's War Cabinet*, 6.

6. Hendrick, *Lincoln's War Cabinet*, 9.

7. Hendrick, *Lincoln's War Cabinet*, 81.

8. Hendrick, *Lincoln's War Cabinet*, 81.

9. Hendrick, *Lincoln's War Cabinet*, 82.

10. Hendrick, *Lincoln's War Cabinet*, 81.

11. Hendrick, *Lincoln's War Cabinet*, 32.

12. Mark E. Neely, Jr., *The Abraham Lincoln Encyclopedia* (New York: DaCapo Press/ McGraw Hill, 1982), 53.

13. Hendrick, *Lincoln's War Cabinet*, 41.

14. Hendrick, *Lincoln's War Cabinet*, 463.

15. Hendrick, *Lincoln's War Cabinet*, 310.

16. Neely, Jr., *The Abraham Lincoln Encyclopedia*, 46.

17. Neely, Jr., *Encyclopedia*, 46.

18. Neely, Jr., *Encyclopedia*, 46.

19. Neely, Jr., *Encyclopedia*, 287.

20. Neely, Jr., *Encyclopedia*, 287.

21. Neely, Jr., *Encyclopedia*, 287.

22. Neely, Jr., *Encyclopedia*, 287.

23. John G. Nicolay and John Hay, *Abraham Lincoln A History, Vol. 3* (New York: The Century Co., 1890), 373.

24. Hendrick, *Lincoln's War Cabinet*, 3.

25. David Herbert Donald, *"We Are Lincoln Men:" Abraham Lincoln and his Friends* (New York: Simon & Schuster, 2003), 147.

26. Donald, *Lincoln Men*, (Donald draws on Glyndon G. Van Deusen's *William Henry Seward* in forming this assessment.

27. Donald, *Lincoln Men*, 148–149.

28. Donald, *Lincoln Men*, 149.

29. Donald, *Lincoln Men*, 159.

30. Donald, *Lincoln Men*, 152.

31. Hendrick, *Lincoln's War Cabinet*, 192.

32. Andrew Delbanco, editor, *The Portable Abraham Lincoln* (New York: Penguin Books, 1992), 192.

33. Delbanco, *Portable AL*, 192.

34. Donald, *We Are Lincoln Men*, 155.

35. Donald, *Lincoln Men*, 154.

36. Donald, *Lincoln Men*, 154.

37. Hendrick, *Lincoln's War Cabinet*, 196.

38. Hendrick, *Lincoln's War Cabinet*, 196.

39. Hendrick, *Lincoln's War Cabinet*, 196.

40. Hendrick, *Lincoln's War Cabinet*, 198.

41. Hendrick, *Lincoln's War Cabinet*, 198.

42. Donald, *We Are Lincoln Men*, 160.

43. Neely, Jr., *The Abraham Lincoln Encyclopedia*, 310.

44. Donald, *Lincoln Men*, 162.

45. Donald, *Lincoln Men*, 162.

46. Donald, *Lincoln Men*, 162.

47. Donald, *Lincoln Men*. Lincoln's shrewd manipulation of Seward and his instigation of Attorney General Bates to propose regularized meetings of the cabinet (discussed later in this chapter) so as to avoid personally offending Seward, suggest a subtle form of behind the scenes leadership which brings to mind Princeton professor Fred Greenstein's analysis of President Eisenhower's "hidden-hand" leadership. (See Greenstein, *The Hidden-Hand Presidency: Eisenhower as Leader* (New York: Basic Books, 1982). Indeed, Lincoln's image as a country-lawyer led many a supporter and opponent to underestimate the cunning beneath the shell. With regard to Eisenhower, presidential aide Robert Murphy had this to say: "He had that ability to dissimulate that I've seen on so many occasions, putting on that bland exterior and saying, 'Well, I'm just a simple soldier, I don't know anything about politics.' If he said that once, I've heard it a dozen times. . . . Lots of people believed that he was a nice simple man. But Eisenhower had a very definite shrewdness and purpose in it all." Quoted in Phillip G. Henderson, *Managing the Presidency: The Eisenhower Legacy* (Boulder, Colorado: Westview Press, 1988), 22.

48. Nicolay and Hay, *Abraham Lincoln: A History, Vol. 3*, 342–343.

49. Nicolay and Hay, *History*, 343.

50. Nicolay and Hay, *History*.

51. Nicolay and Hay, *History*.

52. Nicolay and Hay, *History*, 343–344.

53. Hendrick, *Lincoln's War Cabinet*, 191.

54. Hendrick, *Lincoln's War Cabinet*.

55. Hendrick, *Lincoln's War Cabinet*.

56. Hendrick, *Lincoln's War Cabinet*.

57. Hendrick, *Lincoln's War Cabinet*, 192.

58. Hendrick, *Lincoln's War Cabinet*.

59. Mark E. Neely, Jr., *The Last Best Hope of Earth: Abraham Lincoln and the Promise of America* (Cambridge, MA, Harvard University Press, 1993), 168–169.

60. Neely, Jr., *Last Best Hope*, 169–170.

61. David Herbert Donald, *Lincoln* (New York: Simon & Schuster, 1995), 400–401.

62. Stephen Hess, *Organizing the Presidency, Second Edition* (Washington, D.C.: The Brookings Institution, 1988), 32.

63. Hess, *Organizing the Presidency*.

64. Hess, *Organizing the Presidency*, 26.

65. David Herbert Donald, *Lincoln*, 285.

66. Donald, *Lincoln*, 286.

67. Neely, Jr., *Last Best Hope*, 164.

68. Neely, Jr., *Last Best Hope*.

69. After Lincoln's death, the Supreme Court reinforced the cardinal principle of civilian judicial authority prevailing over the military in *Ex Parte Milligan*.

70. Neely, Jr., *Last Best Hope*, 165.

71. Neely, Jr., *Last Best Hope*.

72. Neely, Jr., *Last Best Hope*.

73. Donald, *Lincoln*, 365.

74. Donald, *Lincoln*.

75. Donald, *Lincoln*, 366.

76. Donald, *Lincoln*.

77. Quoted in Hendrick, *Lincoln's War Cabinet*, 87.

Chapter 6

LINCOLN'S RELIGION AND POLITICS

What was Lincoln's "political religion"? Was his combination of religion and politics destructive or constructive?

Both read the same Bible, and pray to the same God; and each invokes His aid against the other. It may seem strange that any men should dare to ask a just God's assistance in wringing their bread from the sweat of other men's faces; but let us judge not that we be not judged. The prayers of both could not be answered; that of neither has been answered fully. The Almighty has His own purposes. "Woe unto the world because of offences! for it must needs be that offences come; but woe to that man by whom the offence cometh!" If we shall suppose that American Slavery is one of those offences which, in the providence of God, must needs come, but which, having continued through His appointed time, He now wills to remove, and that He gives to both North and South, this terrible war, as the woe due to those by whom the offence came, shall we discern therein any departure from those divine attributes which the believers in a Living God always ascribe to Him? Fondly do we hope—fervently do we pray—that this mighty scourge of war may speedily pass away. Yet, if God wills that it continue, until all the wealth piled by the bondsman's two hundred and fifty years of unrequited toil shall be sunk, and until every drop of blood drawn with the lash, shall be paid by another drawn with the sword, as was said three thousand years ago, so still it must be said "the judgments of the Lord are true and righteous altogether."

Abraham Lincoln, Second Inaugural Address, March 4, 1865

★ William Lee Miller, "Lincoln's Second Inaugural: The Zenith of Statecraft"
★ Michael P. Zuckert, "Lincoln and the Problem of Civil Religion"
★ Bruce P. Frohnen, "Lincoln and the Problem of Political Religion"
★ Reinhold Niebuhr, "The Religion of Abraham Lincoln"

ॐ

LINCOLN'S SECOND INAUGURAL: THE ZENITH OF STATECRAFT
William Lee Miller

THE LAST PARAGRAPH of Lincoln's Second Inaugural—almost as well known as the Gettysburg Address—is carved there behind him in his memorial in Washington. But the speech as a whole has not often received the full portal-to-portal examination accorded that more famous address by Lincoln, or the Declaration of Independence, or the Preamble to the Constitution (not to mention, at the hands of lawyers, the Constitution itself). Perhaps the Second Inaugural does not have the unity of the ten sentences that make up the Gettysburg Address, and it does not contain the capsule statement of American purposes represented by these other entries in the national scriptures. Nevertheless, I believe that the Second Inaugural ought to be included in any gathering up of central documents from the two hundred years of American history and that it is worthy, for different reasons, of the close attention these others have received.

It supplies a contrast, and perhaps a corrective, to the thread of national self-congratulation that is woven into American history, and that can be found here and there in these other famous American pieces of paper. It holds an unusual place in the field of political ethics, which if it is not a field ought to be one. Politics and statecraft pose distinct problems for human conduct, because power and violence are built into their makeup, and because the visions that guide them are shaped not merely by the individual but by the collective egotism. If the student of power and morals can learn something from—for example—Thucydides, Machiavelli, Weber, and Thoreau, then he ought also to examine this famous short speech by Abraham Lincoln. And the speech represents an unusual joining of religious belief and statecraft.

I propose to examine the Second Inaugural for the reasons just given, going through it in the more or less exegetical or new-critical way in which other short classics have been examined, using it for ruminations on the large topics I have named. To adapt a remark by an American literary critic, this composition is more worthy of close reading than a minor poem of John Donne or a bloodthirsty tale from the Book of Judges.

It is as instructive as the Declaration of Independence that Lincoln himself so much revered. In the years just past I have sat through several seminars devoted to scraping, peeling, and slicing fundamental American documents, to the accompani-

*This article originally appeared in *The Center Magazine*, Vol. 13, no. 4, July/August 1980, pp. 53–64. Reprinted with permission from the author.

ment of bicentennial music. It has seemed to me each time that Lincoln's Second Inaugural might have been included.

The last paragraph, with the familiar clauses about malice toward none and charity for all, gains power from what goes before.

Lincoln gave the address on Saturday, March 4, 1865, six weeks before his death, less than five weeks before the end of the war, on the east portico of the Capitol. He began not with the sweeping historical vista of the Gettysburg Address, but in a diminished mode, quietly contrasting this occasion to the first inauguration four years earlier. He observed that, this time, he did not need to say much.

> "Fellow Countrymen:
>   At this second appearing to take the oath of the Presidential office, there is less occasion for an extended address than there was at the first. Then a statement, somewhat in detail, of a course to be pursued, seemed fitting and proper. Now, at the expiration of four years, during which public declarations have been constantly called forth on every point and phase of the great contest which still absorbs the attention; and engrosses the energies, of the nation, little that is new could be presented. The progress of our arms, upon which all else chiefly depends, is as well known to the public as to myself; and it is, I trust, reasonably satisfactory and encouraging to all. With high hope for the future, no prediction in regard to it is ventured."

His short speech—701 words, 505 of one syllable—did not include any sounding of the trumpets of anticipated triumph in battle. Victories by the Union armies had helped him win re-election the previous November, and now he makes no stirring prediction, but only this brief reference (certainly understated, for a commander in chief in a civil war that is still going on) to the "progress of our arms, upon which all else chiefly depends."

The speech is to be set in contrast not only—as he does in the first two paragraphs—to his own longer and more argumentative First Inaugural, but also to most such speeches before or since. There is virtually nothing in it about public policy or specific issues of the day, nor anything hortatory, celebrational, or self-congratulatory.

One of its distinctive features—the evenhanded treatment of both sides—appears in the second paragraph.

> On the occasion corresponding to this four years ago, all thoughts were anxiously directed to an impending civil war. All dreaded it—all sought to avert it. While the inaugural address was being delivered from this place, devoted altogether to saving the Union without war, insurgent agents were in the city seeking to destroy it without war—seeking to dissolve the Union, and divide effects, by negotiation. Both parties deprecated war; but one of them would make war rather than let the nation survive; and the other would accept war rather than let it perish. And the war came.

"*All* dreaded it; *all* sought to avert it"; "*both* parties deprecated war." An involved leader of one side usually does not present the origin of the conflict so bothsidedly.

Lincoln himself in fact had stated the point rather differently on the earlier occasion to which he refers. In his First Inaugural, trying to avert war, he said to the secessionists: "In *your* hands, my dissatisfied countrymen, and not in *mine*, is the momentous issue of civil war." But he was then trying to prevent war; he was engaged in argument, not blame. Now, after four years of the "terrible scourge of war" he does not blame the secessionists for it. He does say they would *make* war, whereas the Union side would simply *accept* war, but the South dreaded it, sought to avoid it, deprecated it, too. And the paragraph ends with that extraordinary sentence: "And the war came."

We are instructed by rhetoricians ordinarily to prefer sentences with an active agent, but here Lincoln—whose literary powers were central to his achievement—avoids, for deliberate effect, such a subject: the war *came*, the outcome of clashing purposes and contending actions that neither side intended.

To make a contrast to Lincoln's attitude we may quote a paragraph about the man who would succeed him six weeks after this speech, Andrew Johnson, as described in General Grant's remarkable *Memoirs*: "Mr. Johnson's course towards the South did engender bitterness of feeling. His ever-ready remark, 'Treason is a crime and must be made odious,' was repeated to all those men of the South who came to him to get some assurances of safety. . . . Many Southerners were driven to a point almost beyond endurance."

Or for another contrast we may refer to another wartime president, another major figure in the White House, Woodrow Wilson. To be sure, he dealt with a different war, a different enemy, and a different situation, but for all that one may believe that Lincoln would not have spoken as Wilson did—for an example—to Congress in his war speech on December 4, 1917, of the "overcoming of evil, by the defeat once for all of the sinister forces that interrupt peace and render it impossible." Wilson pinned the full blame for the coming of the war, and a monopoly of "evil" also, on those "sinister forces" located exclusively on the German side.

Nearer the end of a conflict the apparent victor is by no means to be expected to demonstrate the magnanimity and evenhandedness of Lincoln's Address. Max Weber, in "Politics as a Vocation," introduces his discussion of ethics and politics by dismissing the "quite trivial falsification" in which "ethics" is exploited as a means of "being in the right." (It is a rich subject on which he could have written more.) He gives as one instance the way that "after a victorious war the victor in undignified self-righteousness claims, 'I have won because I was right.'" With Lincoln it is otherwise: "And the war came."

He did have an interpretation of the cause of the war. It did not, however, work out to a self-vindicating result.

> One-eighth of the whole population were colored slaves, not distributed generally over the Union, but localized in the Southern part of it. These slaves constituted a peculiar and powerful interest. All knew that this interest was, somehow, the cause of the war.

> To strengthen, perpetuate, and extend this interest was the object for which the insurgents would rend the Union, even by war; while the government claimed no right to do more than to restrict the territorial enlargement of it.

He thus states explicitly that slavery caused the war. There is no hint of those later interpretations that would question or complicate that point. But his statement of the point does not have the bane of self-righteousness. It has the generous imprecision represented by that marvelous "somehow" in the sentence in the middle of this paragraph: all knew that this interest (slavery) was "somehow" the cause of the war.

"Rend the Union" would not be the secessionist way of speaking; as, in the earlier paragraphs, the phrases "civil war," "insurgent agents," and "would make war rather than let the nation survive" would not be. These and the phrase "the government claimed no right to do more than to restrict the territorial enlargement" may be faintly argumentative; at least they honestly preserve Lincoln's interpretation of what had happened . . . but without moralizing it or making it absolute. That the "somehow" is the governing attitude of the speech is made explicit in the sentences that follow.

> Neither party expected for the war, the magnitude, or the duration, which it has already attained. Neither anticipated that the cause of the conflict might cease with, or even before, the conflict itself should cease. Each looked for an easier triumph, and a result less fundamental and astounding.

He did not blame the South for the war, or for its size or destructiveness: neither party expected this "terrible" destruction; neither party wanted it, or is to bear exclusive blame for it. He does not reach back and claim retroactively a sweeping moral objective to vindicate the outcome now known, a "result" so "fundamental and astounding." (He does not try to claim that the North was fighting from the start for emancipation and equality, which it wasn't.)

Again one may refer by contrast to Woodrow Wilson, because he represents the more common American, and human, response. Against the background of the complicated issues about submarine warfare and the British blockade of Germany, Wilson was quite explicit that *Germany* had caused the war and was morally obnoxious for that and for additional reasons. In the speech quoted above he referred to "this intolerable Thing of which the masters of Germany have shown us the ugly face, this menace of combined intrigue and force which we now see so clearly as the German power, a Thing without conscience or honor or capacity for covenanted peace." The use of the word "Thing" with its capital letter, occurred yet another time in that speech. Although later in that speech he did speak about a peace under universal rules with no vindictiveness, and in other speeches about "peace without victory," Wilson's sharply righteous definition of the terms upon which such a non-punitive peace should be arrived at had drained much of the generosity or understanding from those attitudes. The "evil" Thing, "without conscience or honor," was to capitulate to the forces of righteousness. Thereafter, out of their goodness, the latter would construct a nobler world.

There are widely differing ways that any virtue or value can function, and that is true even of forgiveness and charity. If they are predicated upon a melodrama in which the forgiver is wholly righteous by definition, prior to his forgiving, and his forgiving is known by himself to pile upon him further righteousness, and if his opposite number is wholly in the wrong and must admit it, and in addition is required to be grateful for being forgiven for his manifest sins—then the apparent virtue of magnanimity is no virtue at all.

Lincoln's address differs from that. It explicitly sets aside an emphasis now upon who was right and wrong in the first place, and explicitly refers to larger forces than those of the contending parties. Now he puts those points in religious terms:

> Both read the same Bible, and pray to the same God; and each invokes His aid against the other.

The outlook in these sentences is a long way from that of, say, the Battle Hymn of the Republic, in which God is enlisted unequivocally on the Northern side. He has loosed the fateful lightening of His terrible swift sword, by means of the Union armies. His truth is marching on, strictly on that side of the war.

Lincoln's sentences, by contrast, represent one of those thoughtful moments when there is no drumbeat of a battle hymn and no serpents to be crushed by anyone's heel. In such a moment the observer of the complex life of humankind, and the role of religious belief in it, notices the irony of the two sets of believers killing each other, each praying to the same God for victory over the other. In this unusual case the reflective observer is himself a central participant.

Now comes a sentence, almost an aside, about the "interest" that "somehow" caused the war:

> It may seem strange that any men should dare to ask a just God's assistance in wringing their bread from the sweat of other men's faces; but let us judge not that we be not judged.

Reinhold Niebuhr wrote that this passage "puts the relation of our moral commitments in history to our religious reservations about the partiality of our moral judgments mores precisely than, I think, any statesman or theologian has put them." The moral commitment against slavery is expressed in the remark that it may seem strange that any men should dare to ask a just God's assistance in wringing their bread from the sweat of other men's faces. But that remark is quickly followed by the religious reservation: "but let us judge not that we be not judged."

Lincoln had often before used the figure of speech about toil and sweat and bread—it seemed to be one he particularly favored, with its echo of the sentences in

Genesis when Adam and Eve are sent out of Eden—as a way to express the moral wrong of slavery (you work, you sweat, I'll eat the bread). And he had linked it to a universal and perennial moral struggle. Thus he had said, condemning slavery, in the 1858 debates with Stephen A. Douglas: "It is the eternal struggle between these two principles—right and wrong—throughout the world. They are the two principles that have stood face to face from the beginning of time . . . one is the common right of humanity and the other the divine right of kings. It is the same principle in whatever shape it develops itself. It is the same spirit that says, 'You work and toil and earn bread, and I'll eat it.'"

It is important for an understanding of the Second Inaugural to underline Lincoln's moral condemnation of slavery, which stood alongside his devotion to the Union. It is the fully appropriated moral complexity that gives that speech its greatness. Lincoln was a conservative among the antislavery forces, but he was clearly and deeply—"morally"—antislavery. That fact was a key to his rapid rise in national politics. He was the first successful presidential candidate of a party which had its first identity as an antislavery party.

Lincoln was of course a man of the nineteenth century, not of the late twentieth; he had been an "ultimate extinctionist," not an abolitionist, he was a politician, not a social prophet. In his ascent he articulated the opposition to slavery at the point that it became politically realistic: reluctantly to tolerate slavery in the states where it already existed, but only there. He proposed to *contain* it, as we might now say, and not to allow it to expand, by "popular sovereignty" or otherwise; and to put it "on the road to ultimate extinction." Of course as politician he could as an occasion demanded put the emphasis on the noninterference with existing slavery in the slave states as well as on the opposition to any expansion into the territories. But the very clearly articulated premise of the position was that slavery was a moral evil, and it was as the spokesman for a politically realistic version of that position that Lincoln emerged as a national politician. In the speech Lincoln came east to deliver at Cooper's Institute in February 1860, he put the explicit moral judgment against slavery—casting the issue in terms of the eternal warfare between right and wrong in this way: "if slavery is *right* all words, acts, laws, and constitutions against it are *wrong*, and should be silenced, and swept away. If it is *right*, we cannot justly object to its nationality—its universality; if it is *wrong*, they cannot justly insist upon its extension—its enlargement. All they ask, we could readily grant, if we thought slavery right; all we ask, they could as readily grant, if they thought it wrong. Their thinking it right, and our thinking it wrong, is the precise fact upon which depends the whole controversy." In that Cooper's Union speech Lincoln rejected, just as moralists of our own time do, any "groping for some middle ground between the right and the wrong."

Lincoln sought, on the moral issue itself, no such middle ground. But even with forceful conviction he was able to add, in this different situation five years later, the "religious reservation":

. . . but let us judge not that we be not judged.

This paraphrase of the sentence from Matthew, from the collection of sayings that is called the Sermon on the Mount, had appeared in a different way in the Lincoln-Douglas debates. When Lincoln had insisted on the moral difference between the two sides, Stephen A. Douglas had responded with a reference to this familiar sentence. But Douglas in 1858 was saying (judgmentally) to Lincoln and his partisans—to his opponents—that *they* should not judge, lest they be judged. Here seven years later Lincoln as wartime president is saying the same thing to his own followers—and to himself as well—that they "judge not."

This sentence, one would think, should never be used as defense, attack, or riposte but only as confession or self-criticism; otherwise the speaker himself is tripped by its meaning, and one has an instance of the "comic" self-contradiction that Kierkegaard wrote about: to use this sentence against "judging" as a means of doing so:

The prayers of both could not be answered; that of neither has been answered fully.

Lincoln completes the paragraph of compassionate evenhandedness by his observation about these two sets of believers in the same God: not only does he now say that they could not both have their prayers answered but that neither in fact has been answered fully . . . not those of the South, that wanted its victory, with secession and slavery, nor those of the North that wanted the Union preserved painlessly.

With the first sentence of the next paragraph—the key sentence perhaps of the address—Lincoln sets the frame of the larger drama within which these human actors play their limited roles:

The Almighty has His own purposes. . . .

These purposes, plainly, are not identical with the purposes of either party to the conflict, or of any man. Lincoln himself, commenting afterward on the speech in a letter to Thurlow Weed, remarked that "men are not flattered to be told there has been a difference of purpose between the Almighty and them." "To deny [i.e., this difference of purpose] however in this case," Lincoln went on to say in the short letter to Weed, "is deny that there is a God governing the world."

Belief in a God governing the world can do much damage in politics, and the modern nonbelieving world has often listed the ways. One kind of damage is fanaticism, self-righteousness, uncompromising zeal for cruelty to infidels masquerading as devotion to God. When the belief in an Absolute—in "the mighty"—is put forward in the mingled relativities of human social conflict, the result can often be confusion and inhumanity. (The cultured among the despisers of religion, who are quick enough to spot these perils of religious belief in politics, sometimes imply that being free of the belief they are also free of the perils, but of course it does not work that way.) Lincoln's speech, an unusual degree for a political document drenched in Biblical outlook, avoids these perils, and in the way that is appropriate to the source: by turning its affirmations critically against his own side and himself rather than using them self-defensively against opponents. In his letter to Weed about this speech he went on to say: "It is a truth [i.e., the truth that the Almighty has purposes different from those of human actors] which I thought needed to be told, and as whatever of humiliation there is in it falls most directly on myself I thought others might afford for me to tell it."

Now he breaks suddenly into a fierce biblical quotation that he applies to slavery and the war.

> Woe unto the world because of offenses! for it must needs be that offenses come; but woe to that man by whom the offense cometh!

Lincoln quoted this (Matthew 18:7), of course, from the King James Version. He had no modern Biblical scholar standing by to tell him that he would do better to use a different translation; that this passage, in the middle of the "woes," right after a well-known sentence condemning those who tempt little children, and right before a sentence about cutting off your hand if it "offends," probably does not mean what he took it to mean. The word "offense," which he took to mean a gross moral evil, is later translated "temptations" or "stumbling blocks." That gives the sentence a different twist and may link it back to the "little ones" not to be tempted, woe to you if you do.

But Lincoln did not know all that. He found the sentence he wanted in the King James Version, and made—as has happened before and since—his own use of it. In his case it was very much in keeping with the spirit of a profound version of biblical religion. Indeed, this whole paragraph is a sudden bursting out of "prophetic" utterance, darker, deeper, less "rational" perhaps, than what goes before or follows (also more difficult and less often quoted):

> If we shall suppose that American slavery is one of those offenses which, in the providence of God, must needs come, but which, having continued through His appointed time, He now wills to remove, and that He gives to both North and South, this terrible war, as the woe due to those by whom the offense came, shall we discern therein any departure from those divine attributes which the believers in a Living God always ascribe to Him?

Niebuhr said that Lincoln retained in this most biblically religious of presidential addresses still a trace of his youthful skepticism when he referred to "those divine attributes which believers in a Living God always ascribe to Him" without specifically numbering himself among those believers. But the youthful skepticism certainly is not present in the rest of the paragraph, nor in the one that follows, which reverberates with the outlook of "believers in a Living God" in one of its most teeth-rattling forms. Perhaps something like Lincoln's youthful fatalism or determinism is contained in these sentences—but it has now taken on the shape of the Calvinistic providential history—arranging God. It does make quite a difference even if one believes that historical events are determined, and beyond the control of any human actor, whether or not one sees that determination done with a purpose by an agent with an active will, and with the "attributes," to which Lincoln refers, which "believers in a Living God" assign to Him. Human history certainly is seen in that providentially ordered way in this speech by Lincoln: "in the providence of God"; "*His* appointed time"; "*He* now wills to remove"; "*He* gives to both North and South, this terrible war." To many modern minds it may not be very appealing, may even be repugnant: this picture of a God by whose providence slavery "came," who allows it for an "appointed time," and who then removes it with terrible war as a "woe" to the human participants. But though Lincoln had read skeptics in his youth he has now come to speak a different language, embracing life's mystery in these religious terms.

The "offense" that is sent, and now to be removed, is slavery. Whose "fault" is it? Where does it come from? Neither in malt, nor in Milton, nor in Lincoln's Address, nor in the world as we know it, is there a satisfactory accounting for the origins and cause of such gross moral evils. As Lincoln said earlier the war *came*, so slavery *came*. By whose agency? The point at least is this, that it did not "come" by the will of the Southerners, secessionists, or slaveholders alone. In some sense it "came" by "the providence of God." In another sense, it is the responsibility of *both* sides in the terrible war. "*Woe* to that man," said the King James Version of Matthew, "by whom the offense cometh!" "That man" is not only the slave power, or the South. "Woe" has been sent to North as well as South, the "woe" of the war.

"Fondly do we hope—fervently do we pray—that this mighty scourge of war may speedily pass away."

The moral commitments of this political leader were, as is usual in difficult situations, not simple, single, and unitary but complicated and multiple. It is necessary to prefer one good to others; it is necessary to do destructive acts in order to avoid other evils; it is necessary to sacrifice some goods in order to protect or attain others. All serious political action is interwoven with tragedy. The human temptation in such a many-sided tragic moment is to repress, slight, or pass over the evils done or goods neglected in one or another direction, in order to make the choice easier. As the *practical* will driving toward decision is inclined to simplify the field of action, and make 51–49 (or 50–50) into 80–20, or 100–0, to make choice easier, so the *moral* will is inclined to underestimate the evils done, or goods neglected, in order to make the chosen course of action seem more worthy. As the practical will simplifies to stave off hesitation and regret, so the moral will simplifies to stave off guilt and uneasy conscience. Lincoln does not do that. He holds the moral pieces together.

His overriding moral and political commitment, and as president his sworn duty, was the preservation of the Union. In *Patriotic Gore* Edmund Wilson expands on the statement of Alexander Stephens that "for Lincoln the Union had risen to the sublimity of religious mysticism." This devotion was not to the Union for its own sake but rather to the Union as the bearer of universal values. The preservation of that Union had to be his overriding commitment. But he did not therefore slight or obscure either the evil of slavery, the dispute over which brought the Union to a moral logjam, or the destructiveness that the war to defend that Union entailed. The elements of the moral drama, the tragedy, remained alive within him, as here, in this sentence and those that follow, with their deep sense of the horror of the "scourge" of war.

Suddenly there comes a dark and powerful passage that is more like Dostoyevsky or the Book of Job than a straight-thinking American boy from Illinois:

> "Fondly do we hope—fervently do we pray—that this mighty scourge of war may speedily pass away. Yet, if God wills that it continue, until all the wealth piled by the bondsman's two hundred and fifty years of unrequited toil shall be sunk, and until every drop of blood drawn with the lash, shall be paid by another drawn with the sword, as was said three thousand years ago, so still it must be said 'the judgments of the Lord are true and righteous altogether.'"

Imagine the fierce passion and anguish in which this wartime president wrote that terrible paragraph, with its grim imagining of a retribution in which the long two-hundred-fifty-year-old evil of American slavery is compensated by the destruction of every bit of wealth that slavery created, and further by all the killing in the war: a retribution, of course, against *both* sides, against the whole country, matching slavery's drops of blood on the one side with warfare's drops of blood on the other. It is a horrendous vision.

The passage implies, at the same time, not only a deep and simultaneous abomination of slavery and revulsion against the war, but also the most somber determination to finish that war. The dramatic picture—drop of blood for drop of blood—sets up the affirmation at the end, the severe piety, some might say the perverse piety, of an acceptance of the whole terrible mixture, no matter what. Even if there should be so dreadful a bloodletting, *still* it must be said: the judgments of the Lord are true and righteous altogether.

Lincoln found this sentence in the King James Version of the Nineteenth Psalm, the familiar Psalm that begins "The heavens are telling the glory of God, and the firmament showeth His handiwork," and that ends with the stanza that is often used as a benediction: "Let the words of my mouth, and the meditations of my heart be acceptable in Thy sight." We are told that this is one of the oldest of the Psalms; Lincoln may even have underestimated its age when he said "three thousand years ago." Ironically, it is rather a serene poem, praising the creator of the sky and the stars, who is (as in Kant's famous sentence) the maker of the *moral* law within as well as of the physical law that governs the heavens. From this tranquil ancient poem of wonder and of praise an American president more than three thousand years later took this one sentence to make a ringing statement in quite a different religious context: the mood of "no matter what," "nevertheless," and "even so," like that of Job. When his wife said to him after his multiple afflictions that he should "curse God and die," Job, instead, answered, "the Lord giveth and the Lord taketh away, blessed be the name of the Lord." But in that famous exchange the adversity in the face of which the unshaken affirmation is made is a *personal* adversity; in Lincoln's great speech the adversity is collective and in part prospective: even though such terrible historical offenses and woes have come, even though something still worse might come, nevertheless—God is just.

In the overly complicated earlier sentence there was a rhetorical question—"shall we discern therein [i.e., in the sending of the terrible war as a "woe" to offensegivers] any departure from those divine attributes which the believers in a Living God always ascribe to Him?" The implied answer, of course, was "No." One may be permitted to discern the struggle of the man writing this speech to give that answer, in the face of the terrors of history—human slavery and a civil war with which his life had made him intimately acquainted. Perhaps there is in this paragraph the element of an act of will that marks religious faith, in this case the act of will of a strong person: *nevertheless*, despite all this "offense" and "woe" there is no "departure" from the "divine attributes." What are the "divine attributes"? The sentence at the end of the paragraph, appropriated from the Psalm, gives the answer: "the judgments of the Lord, are true and righteous altogether."

Then with an appropriate abruptness the mood shifts, from that terrible, powerful affirmation, to the still more powerful consequence of it. In one of the finest sentences ever written by an American president—not to take in any larger territory—Lincoln sets forth the motives and purposes of strong persons who have been through the woes and offenses and held nevertheless to the affirmation he has made:

> With malice toward none; with charity for all; with firmness in the right, as God gives us to see the right, let us strive on to finish the work we are in; to bind up the nation's wounds, to care for him who shall have borne the battle, and for his widow, and his orphan—to do all which may achieve and cherish a just, and a lasting peace, among ourselves, and with all nations.

"Malice" is the name of the deepest human evil. Human action to serve our values—and our interests—spills over into a desire to harm those who stand in our way. We project our anger at the frustrations of the world onto other people. There is some part of Iago or Claggart in all of us. We wish others harm; we take (usually secret) satisfaction in their defeat; we nurse grudges and cultivate envy and hatred. And this human sea of envy and malice—so evident, for one example, to Samuel Johnson—is multiplied in collective life. Sometimes it becomes institutionalized.

Grangerfords spend their lives hating, hunting, and hurting the Shepherdsons—and vice versa. "Enlightened self-interest" isn't going to be a sufficiently powerful motive to overcome the deep undertow of malice, envy, and self-love. "Charity" (as in the King James Version of I Corinthians 13) is the corrective for that human inclination. It is the central theme of the religion of which this address is, whatever its author's true state of belief may have been, so remarkable an expression.

The habit of charity—not achieved by human beings for often or for long or ever purely, even without the passions of warfare—depends upon what has gone before: the cleansing away of self-righteousness, with its secret links to cruelty, to ill will, and to malice; the avoidance of "judging" others (that is, setting oneself categorically in the place of superior righteousness); the recognition of the working of a purpose—"the Almighty has his purposes"—beyond one's own; the affirmation even after the most terrible events that "the judgments of the Lord are true and righteous altogether." As the religion this speech reflects has seen it, these are the humbling preconditions for whatever humankind may achieve in the emptying out of malice, the affirmation of charity.

But now, in Lincoln's speech, we do not get to the widows and orphans right away, or to the binding up of wounds and the taking care of veterans. There is first:

firmness in the right, as God gives us to see the right . . .

Here is the moral affirmation again, with the important qualifying apposition ("as God gives us to see the right") that was characteristic of Lincoln. He had ended his Cooper's Union speech, to great applause (it is reported) from the gathering of New York leaders, "Let us have faith that right makes might, and in that faith, let us, to the end, dare to do our duty as we understand it." Perhaps it crippled his peroration a little to end with the qualifying phrase "as we understand it," but it is to Lincoln's moral if not his rhetorical credit that he did it. It is characteristic and desirable that even in the very moment of a ringing affirmation of "right" he adds the grace note that implies that our own understanding of what is right is not the whole story.

And still we don't come to the widows and orphans:

let us strive on to finish the work we are in . . .

Charity, yes, malice, no, but—finish the work. We continue the war, bring it to a successful conclusion, preserve the Union, follow the Emancipation Proclamation with the beginning of what would become the Thirteenth and Fourteenth Amendments. The whole larger, deeper vision does not obliterate but itself gives meaning to a central merely human but still "firm" purpose, done without fanaticism or self-congratulation or vindictiveness, but finished all the same:

To bind up the nation's wounds; to care for him who shall have borne the battle, and for his widow, and his orphan—to do all which may achieve and cherish a just, and a lasting peace, among ourselves, and with all nations.

This address does not have the tight structure of the Gettysburg, but after the furious paragraphs about the drops of blood and the righteous God it has this coda of healing: no malice; act from charity, bind up the wounds, care for the bereaved and injured; achieve and "cherish" peace among ourselves, and with all our fellow human beings on this troubled earth.

Whoever deals in politics, wrote Max Weber, traffics with the devil, and treads in a realm in which one should not seek salvation of the soul. Politics is defined by the search for and the use of power. The ultimate resort is violence: the march of the Northern armies. "Power" means the imposition of will on other wills; against other wills: South Carolina may not secede from the Union. The supreme political institution, the state, has the "monopoly of legitimate violence"; for Weber that was its definition. Weber's definition of state and of politics is one-sided or selective; the achievement of common purposes and of a shared order—a common life—which the individual self needs and wants is as much a part of the essence of the state as the resort to force which it requires. We do want and need a shaped, shared common life under law, an order of life with our fellow beings, a United States, or a South Carolina, or a Confederate States—a juridical unit for our shared life with our fellow beings.

To make such a unit, small or large, there must be *power*. Woven through all our social life there is the thread of power—of the fitting together of disparate and conflicting wills, values, and interests by subordination and compliance. There must be subordination even in a government of the people, by the people, and for the people which, partly because of Lincoln's leadership, has not perished from the earth. Some part of the mixture must tell another part this shall be done, that, shall not be done, thus shall it be: you may not secede; this is no gathering of still "sovereign" states but rather a Union which South Carolina may not leave, even though a majority of South Carolinians want to; this man and that one must risk obtaining or not obtaining his red badge of courage in battle—he is drafted, riots in New York City against the draft notwithstanding, to fight in the Union armies, whether he wants to or not. In other words, compulsion is a necessity.

The power that is necessary and constitutive to social life is also a temptation and a moral danger. The individual ego has the defensive-aggressive self-love described by, among others and in their different ways, St. Paul, St. Augustine, Thomas Hobbes, Samuel Johnson, Sigmund Freud, and Reinhold Niebuhr. And the individual in politics is not characteristically one whose egotism expresses itself in passive, modest, self-critical ways; the world of power does not ordinarily attract or elevate those who are by nature self-restraining. Lincoln, himself, turned into a legend and a gentle hero, almost a saint, in American mythology, was said by his law partner

William Herndon to have had an *ambition* that was like an engine working cease-lessly for his advancement.

But the egotism of the political realm is not that of ambitious power-seeking individuals only; it is also that of the social unit. The individual power-holder has his ego; the collective has its cruder ego. To say to others it shall be so, to interpret to others how it is, in the great clash of social life, holds out the temptation to over-reach. Stamp out the infamous thing. Crush the serpent with His heel. Treason is a crime and must be made odious. Four legs good; two legs bad. *Delenda Est Carthago*. Secessionists overreach and Radical Republicans overreach. There stands behind the politician and statesman the flag-waving, slogan-making, overreaching impulse of the collective. Therefore there are intrinsic and peculiar moral dangers of politics; therefore there's an intrinsic (not merely additive) importance of the combination represented by Lincoln's Second Inaugural: clarity and firmness of purpose; an awareness of purposes larger than one's own, therefore criticism and restraint toward oneself, and magnanimity—and absence of vindictiveness at least—toward oppo-nents. Lincoln wrote in another connection, "I shall do nothing in malice. What I deal with is too vast for malicious dealings."

The Englishman Lord Charnwood in his older (1915), one-volume biography of Lincoln remarks that Lincoln's great speeches are, uniquely, of a kind that a great dramatist might have composed for a character in such a situation in a tragedy. This remark applies particularly to the Second Inaugural. The character is himself the dramatist composing the speech, and the drama is real.

Edmund Wilson, who wrote about the "tautness and distinction" in Lincoln's writing (in contrast to the "coarse-meshed" Carl Sandburg), said that "alone among American presidents, it is possible to imagine Lincoln, grown up in a different milieu, becoming a distinguished writer." In addition to his evident knowledge of the devices of classical rhetoric, Lincoln had also the persistent striving for clarity of thought and for getting at the heart of the matter shown in the steady working out of his thought and his style in the years from his reentry into politics in 1854 through to his death. He became a forceful writer, using the cadence, and balance of classical rhetoric, choosing strong; hard, solid, economical, and dignified language, and lift-ing the whole to a solemn eloquence with a powerful intellectual drive. I think this last should be underscored: it was not *style* alone, or literary talent alone, that make Lincoln's speeches distinctive; it was also his analytical power. He was a thinker as well as writer. But he was such a thinker and writer exactly in his role as statesman. When someone shaped by a more recent outlook says—this is very common—that a speech like this is "words" (sometimes "mere" words) and therefore not *real* as bayonets and budgets are real, as *policies* are real, as *actions* are real, one has to respond that this speech was *in itself* a political act of the highest importance. It expressed, and helped to shape, the *interpretation* on the basis of which policies are formed and actions taken. Two-thirds of politics, as a notable political thinker has said, consists of words—that is, the communicating back and forth of our interpre-tations, intentions, and purposes. Lincoln's Address is a great political *act*.

Some say that the speech was *politics* ("mere" politics perhaps) and that we should look at, and judge it by, the *political* calculations it might be fulfilling (e.g., that Lincoln knew the Southern leaders would hear him and was sending them a signal to encourage ending the war). To be sure there must have been, and should have been in a responsible leader, a *political* awareness that the Southerners, the Radical Republicans, and many others would hear the speech. But that is neither reprehensible nor the total meaning of the address. Other political men in the same situation made a different "political" choice. The man writing this address took the national occasion and the political claims of the moment and made of it all a lasting human achievement: an achievement at once political, historical, literary. He wrote in the letter to Weed that he expected it "to wear as well as—perhaps better than—anything I have produced" even though it would not be immediately popular, and he was right on both counts.

It takes on its extraordinary significance, of course, because the man who delivered it was no more poet or essayist "composing for the anthologies" (as the late Justice Robert Jackson once wrote, disdainfully one supposes, in an opinion from the bench), nor even your ordinary president, but rather the nation's leader in a war which would "rend the Union." Lincoln had not only his exalted, mystical devotion to that Union but also a sworn obligation to uphold it. He had said to the secessionists, in his First Inaugural: "You have no oath registered in Heaven to destroy the government, while I shall have the most solemn one to 'preserve, protect, and defend' it." Nevertheless, despite all the accumulated reasons for Lincoln to be righteous, angry, argumentative, and partisan, his speech resounds with a quiet acceptance of purposes beyond his own, and an absence of vindictiveness that would be remarkable even if written by that solitary essayist in his chambers.

The address, as given by that man in that circumstance, combined active moral "engagement" (to use a word that would come to prominence in a later war) with an explicit awareness of the larger drama within which that engagement played its role. That awareness, then, led to the rare humility and evenhandedness about the conflict, and the magnanimous attitude toward opponents, for which the address is remembered. It is a supreme example—better perhaps than bullfighters of "grace under pressure." The observation about the larger purposes together with the even-handed references to "both sides," "neither side," and especially then the repudiation of malice at the speech's end, give it its stature. Or rather—that stature comes from the *combination* of these sentences and the moral engagements already described.

It is the entire combination, in its setting, that makes the speech remarkable. To turn the combination around, the generosity, self-criticism, and perspective for which the address is justly renowned did not cloud the speaker's moral perception or diminish the executive force with which he pursued his purposes. The address, therefore, is a model, not simply of charity and largeness of spirit; it is a model of these qualities held by an engaged, active, "committed," embattled, and political human being.

Either part without the other would not be so significant. Many a statesman and political leader has stood forth with fierce and simple "moral" statements of the sort I have quoted from Lincoln in the debates with Douglas and the Cooper's Union speech. And Lincoln's other commitments also are by no means unique: most war leaders believe the victory has a larger significance than the protection of the interests of their country, often a universal significance. Winston Churchill on the eve of World War II said that we were fighting against the Nazis for no less than "Christian civilization," and Wilson's sentences about the eternal and universal significance of World War I are well known. An implacable determination of leaders in the midst of war to pursue it to the end, no matter what, is common. One thinks of Winston Churchill when Britain stood alone: ". . . we shall defend our island, whatever the cost may be, we shall fight on the beaches, we shall fight on the landing grounds, we shall fight in the fields and in the streets, we shall fight in the hills; we shall never surrender." Very well. Lincoln had such resolution, too. What is distinct in the Second Inaugural is no one part of the complex moral engagement nor perhaps even the complexity of the mixture, but the depth that is added by the perspective within which they are set: let us judge not that we be not judged; the Almighty has His own purposes.

It must also be said, then, that this larger awareness and self-criticism would not be so impressive were it not joined to the moral engagement that it qualifies. Other persons, reflecting on the drama of history in tranquility, have had no trouble seeing both sides in a battle inclined to fanaticism. Observers on the sidelines have repeatedly noticed the irony that a couple of sets of believers in the same God each pray to Him for victory over the other. Historians looking back regularly notice that neither party to a conflict expected or wanted war; the causes and dynamics are more complicated than the will of either combatant. And any of us finds it easy enough to discern, in some far-off struggle between strangers, that neither side has a monopoly on justice. There is more than enough detachment and relativism and shoulder-shrugging by observers of somebody else's struggle. And in the older believing days one heard often enough a pro forma acknowledgement that the purposes of God are larger than those of any side, person, or party. What is distinctive in Lincoln's case is that this acknowledgement is not pro forma, that there is no shrug of the shoulders; the serious recognition of the limitation of his own side and party is joined to his equally serious engagement in the moral issue: his determination, as a leader in battle and in moral struggle, to "finish the work we are in."

An American cannot avoid—and should not wish to avoid—the claim to a moral "truth" about human society that is built into the now so widely advertised founding of his country—"self-evident" truths, universal in application: men are created equal, "endowed" with rights; just governments founded to "secure" those rights, resting upon the "consent of the governed." At the same time an American cannot and should not avoid the mischievous result that can follow upon an unguarded claim to such universal moral truth. The United States not only has a collective egotism, like other countries, and not only has, like other "great powers," thrown its weight around; it has rationalized these activities to an unusual degree, by reference to the universal ideals of which it saw itself as bearer: "Manifest Destiny," "American Century," "Leader of the Free World." Lincoln was himself not only a thoroughgoing believer in the founding universal moral truths but their most eloquent spokesman. He had referred to this nation as "the last, best hope of earth," and to us Americans as "an almost chosen people." (The "almost" is interesting, and certainly saves that phrase: the greatness of Lincoln is in the "almost" and the "somehow.') If we were listing the deep moral engagement of Lincoln, we would put first of all "the Union." But it was not "the Union" for its own sake that he loved, but the Union because this unified nation was the bearer and the test of a form of government with universal significance; we were testing "whether this nation *or any nation so conceived and so dedicated can long endure*"; the favorable result of the war would assure mankind that government of, by, and for the people shall survive.

But there certainly is the danger of pretension in all that. An Englishman, for example, might have objected to the idea that the continuation of the United States was the *sole* test for the whole history of liberty, not for this nation or this continent but for the entire earth and for any nation "so conceived." Citizens of many other countries might find it overreaching for an American to claim that his country is the last best hope of earth. The proud claim that we are the bearers of a universally valid form of government, and even that we are the sole and unique bearers, has had its unfortunate effects upon this country's behavior before and after Lincoln.

The corrective, for that time and for one hundred years later, is found in Lincoln's Second Inaugural: although there is moral truth about human beings living together, no "side"—no nation or ideology—has full possession of it. We do not need to believe that we hold that truth in a pure and undiluted form, or that we have a monopoly on it, or that those whom we must oppose are excluded absolutely from it and purely evil, in order to be resolute, active, and persistent in defense of it. His countrymen a century later should have had, in the "Cold War," more of the chastened firmness that Lincoln exhibited in the Civil War, and particularly in this address near its close.

This is by no means to undercut the seriousness of one's moral understanding. The spirit of Lincoln's address is not relativistic or shoulder-shrugging or "conservative." Its attitude is not "live and let live," or "there is no accounting for tastes," or "deliberate social action does more harm than good." He certainly did not say, with a modern reductionist, that some people "prefer" slavery, some people don't "prefer" it: Who is to choose? He did not say that being for or against the Union was a matter of "preference" merely, determined by geography or taste, with no rational or objective foundation. In his Cooper's Union speech he had explicitly repudiated a "policy of 'don't care' on a question about which all true men do care." He did not say: leave things alone and they will work out better, in the long run. Instead he had solemn convictions about these matters, upon which he acted: only when a person has such convictions, and takes such action, does one appropriately add with Lincoln, the qualifying, chastening, deepening themes of this address.

Why add those themes? Because the absolutism even of men whose cause is just, can itself be the cause of a new injustice. The commendable abhorrence of human slavery gathers up a great many less commendable motives as it flows on into Reconstruction after Lincoln's death. The just repugnance at racial discrimination spills over into an epithetical contempt for "racists," "rednecks," and "ethnics" ironically not unlike the stereotypical prepossession it started out repudiating.

Self-righteousness is an invitation to cruelty, malice, and blindness, even in men (or women) who are indeed generally "right" about the issue at stake. Fanaticism is a menace even on the part of those whose cause is just. The egotism and irrationality to which we are all tempted are by no means obliterated when we fight for a righteous purpose. (Of course in our own self estimation we rarely fight for any other purpose; our own cause is almost always "right" and "just.") The field of "battle" is never as simple as in our crusading right/wrong picture of it (in the metaphors of battle, fight, crusade).

There are other issues, too, besides the ones that occupy us; the people we oppose are human and complex, not simple instruments of the evil we oppose. There are other human beings affected by our outlook and action whom self-righteous blindness may prevent us from seeing. And the cause today is not the same as it was yesterday. Tomorrow's injustice is created or fed by the vindictive spirit in which today's injustice is combated.

The historical drama is never so simple that actors in it need pay attention only to one cause, one issue, one purpose without regard to the mystery and freedom of the historical drama in which they play only a single part. Therefore, politics requires, if possible, charity for all, and, if not that, at least malice toward none.

⁂

LINCOLN AND THE PROBLEM OF CIVIL RELIGION

Michael P. Zuckert

By GENERAL CONSENSUS, Abraham Lincoln is the greatest statesman to have arisen in America, and Lincoln called, in no uncertain terms, for a civil or political religion.[1] Moreover, he did not leave that a merely theoretical call: of the components

*From *Law and Philosophy: The Practice of Theory: Essays in Honor of George Anastaplo*, Vol. II. Ed. John Murley, Robert L. Stone, and William Braithwaite (Athens, Ohio: Ohio University Press, 1992). Reprinted with permission of Ohio University Press, Athens, Ohio.

of his greatness none was greater than his rhetoric, and what was that rhetoric but a more or less sustained preaching of the civil religion he had called for?[2] As Lincoln's great biographer Lord Charnwood put it, referring to the Second Inaugural Address, "Probably no other speech of a modern statesman uses so unreservedly the language of intense religious feeling."[3] John Diggins went further and insisted that Lincoln saw as his highest task—a task higher even than the one that faced Washington—the articulation of "a new political theology."[4] If the great speeches of his maturity, the Gettysburg Address and the Second Inaugural, are, as most observers of Lincoln cannot help but suspect, the greatest of Lincoln's accomplishments, then the civil religion that he preached there, as the highest thing in the greatest American statesman, stands somehow as the peak of American political practice.

Yet, the very idea of civil or political religion—a set of beliefs that finds sacred meaning in civil life and lends the support of the divine to earthly politics[5]—whether in the mouth of a Lincoln or of a lesser politician, makes many very uneasy.[6] The kind of union of religion and politics implicit in the idea of civil religion seems to be dangerous to either or both partners. To focus on the civic functions of religion seems to some degrade or trivialize religion.[7] Others react strongly to the intermingling of religious with political concerns as politically dangerous.[8] The historical experience of the West shows how divisive and dangerous a force religion can be in politics. Politics works best, it seems, when matters of ultimate concern and commitments of ultimate depth are kept out of the public sphere. Such at least was the rationale for classical liberalism.[9] And twentieth-century experiences of political fanaticism seem to corroborate traditional liberal suspicions of religion and religion-like political commitments. Driven by a sense of divinely certified righteousness, political leaders can come to engage in "pious cruelty" in the service of unjust or unattainable political ends.[10] Despite misgivings, however, the issue of civil religion fails to retreat. Issues from abortion to defense policy, to say nothing of obvious First Amendment problems, continue to puzzle us with their insistent posing of the question, What is the proper relation between politics and religion? Within that context we turn to Lincoln for his wisdom on the problem of civil religion.

The theme of civil religion came early to Lincoln. In 1838, when he was only twenty-nine, he delivered an "Address on the Perpetuation of Our Political Institutions," in which he called for a "political religion." This speech, and a companion statement made five years later,[11] reveals more about Lincoln's thinking on civil religion than the later speeches in which he actually preached it, because in the earlier speeches he focused far more explicitly on the reasons for, and the nature of, civil religion.[12]

His earliest statement was presented in an address of distinctly odd structure. The speech opens with an analysis of a certain political evil and moves from there to the prescription of a cure for that evil—a political religion of obedience to the laws. Having apparently finished his talk—having brought out the threat to the survival of American institutions and having outlined a solution to that threat—Lincoln, instead of closing his speech, started anew with a return to the theme of the threats to American political survival, and moved once again to a prescription for a solution. The speech has two main parts, then, that echo but do not simply repeat each other. The task of understanding the Perpetuation Address, one could say with only a little exaggeration, is to understand this structural oddity. That task has never been undertaken heretofore.[13]

I can state the result of that reconsideration at the outset: the dualistic structure of the Perpetuation Address reflects the dualistic character of the problem of civil religion as Lincoln saw it. He first brought out the problems that point to the need for a civil religion; he then brought out the reasons why that civil religion is itself a problem, why the religion he had called for could not succeed. The speech concluded with a transformed call for civil religion, but a transformation so severe and a version of civil religion so new and so paradoxical as to pose the question whether the intervening discussion has not left Lincoln less with a solution to his problem than with a desideratum that he has shown cannot be realized.

The unsatisfactory situation in which he left the issue in the Perpetuation Address no doubt accounts for Lincoln's return to the theme in his even more important, more complex, and literarily more mature Address to the Washingtonian Temperance Society delivered in 1842. There Lincoln presented his definitive answer to the problem apparently settled in the negative in the earlier speech: Is civil religion possible? How?

I. The Problem for Civil Religion

At the literal center of his Perpetuation Address, the young Lincoln called for a political religion (P.A., 80–81).[14] He proposed it as a solution to the political problem he had described in the earlier part of his speech: "the increasing disregard for law," the "outrages committed by mobs," which Lincoln saw as "the everyday news of the times" (P.A., 77). No region or section of the United States was innocent of mob violence, both slave and free territories alike.

Lincoln was not concerned about violence as such, but about mob violence that substitutes for legal processes. Speaking in 1838, he was especially concerned about a problem that arose in the era of Andrew Jackson: if, as the General and his Democratic Party preached, the basis of all legitimate political power in the American democracy is popular sovereignty, then why should mobs, direct embodiments of the people's original power, not replace the slow and imperfect forces of the law? Lincoln answered that mobs commit injustices, for they "substitute the wild and furious passions, in lieu of the sober judgment of Courts." But injustices are not the worst danger that mob rule poses. The "indirect consequences" overshadow the direct, for mob violence weans every element of the community from its obedience and attachment to law. Some men, the "lawless in spirit," having never rendered obedience except through "dread of punishment," become "lawless in practice": "Having ever regarded Government as their deadliest bane, they make a jubilee of the suspension of its operations; and pray for nothing so much as its total annihilation" (P.A., 79). Others, "the good men," who love tranquility, who desire to abide by the laws and enjoy their benefits, become disgusted with a government that proves unable to protect their persons, families, and property. Their "feelings . . . become more or less alienated" from government. Without "the attachment of the people" free government cannot stand. Thus, Lincoln concluded, all favorable signs to the contrary notwithstanding, there really was reason to worry about the "perpetuation of our political institutions" (P.A., 79–80). The intoxication induced by popular sovereignty could be the undoing of the regime based on popular sovereignty.

In response to this danger he proposed his political religion of "reverence for the laws"—not only of strict obedience to the law, but also total intolerance of disobedience by others (P.A., 80–81). The connection to the danger of lawlessness is clear. But why a political religion? Harry V. Jaffa has supplied the answer: "Lincoln's call to make reverence for the Constitition and laws the political religion of the nation is recognition that a merely utilitarian view of the value of freedom and free institutions can never induce the sacrifices necessary for their preservation."[15] Lincoln's own argument was a rational argument, but he called for an adherence to the rational principle on non-rational grounds—habituation from earliest youth, frequent repetition, association of the appeal for obedience with the most emotion-charged attachments the American people possessed: Christianity and the Revolution. A calculating reason can discover the political good of obedience, but the achievement of that good is a task for reverence, not for calculation. In the people, feeling and passion outstrip reason and calculation, even a reason that put itself in the service of passion.

II. The Problem of Civil Religion

By the midpoint of his Address, Lincoln had thus presented his diagnosis of the problem and his prescription for a cure. He did not conclude here, however, but made a fresh start, beginning with almost a paraphrase of the question with which he had launched his initial inquiry: "But, it may be asked, why suppose danger to our political institutions? Have we not preserved them for more than fifty years?" (P.A., 82; cf., 77). In this reprise of the theme of the dangers facing American democracy, Lincoln identified other and deeper dangers that, on reflection, prove to undermine the political religion he had first posed as a solution.

His reference to the fifty years during which American institutions have been preserved set the theme for the second presentation of the dangers to American institutions. Their preservation required special conditions that the passage of time and the great success of America were inexorably unsettling. The burden of the argument shifted entirely—the forces of dissolution are not adventitious novelties like mob violence but inherent features of human nature that special American circumstances had thus far masked.[16] Lincoln's analysis betrays an almost Hobbesian pessimism regarding the conditions of political stability (P.A., 82).

Like Machiavelli, Lincoln seemed to think that political societies consist essentially of two types of human beings, princes (leaders, elites) and the people. And, according to Lincoln, the dangers to the future of American institutions derived from both. Even more than Machiavelli, Lincoln believed that the natures of neither princes nor of peoples conduce readily to stable and free political life. Like their Machiavellian counterparts, Lincolnian princes seek "celebrity, and fame, and distinction" (P.A., 82). They wish to be "immortalized." Lesser princes are content with lesser fame, the kind of fame that can be won in holding ordinary political office in an ongoing polity. But others, princes who "belong to the family of the lion, or the tribe of the eagle" seek more—they seek the special fame that comes to great founders, to those who make a way for others to follow (P.A., 83).[17] Such great princes potentially threaten all established political orders, but so far, the great experiment of America, the "practical demonstration" of "the capability of a people to govern themselves," has successfully enlisted the ambitions of even the greatest princes. By 1838, however, two and a half generations after the Founding, the experiment seemed a proven success; as Lincoln said, "the game is caught and with the catching end the pleasures of the chase" (P.A., 82). Future great princes will turn against the experiment, even though justified by nothing more than their own ambitions.

Lincoln cannot have understood the political religion he had just called for as a guard against such men. They "disdain a beaten path," but Lincoln's political religion demands that the people swear by "the blood of the Revolution" and show total devotion to the cause of law-abidingness—that is, to the cause of maintaining the legal-political order the Founders established. He demanded from the people the same dedication to the established order as the Founders showed to the cause of overturning the established order and founding an altogether unprecedented one. Needless to say, Lincoln's sketch of the great princes demonstrated that they cannot be expected to devote themselves to upholding the work—and the fame—of others.

The only safeguard against the great prince then seems to lie with the people. When such a prince rises in America, Lincoln said, "it will require the people to be united with each other, attached to the government and laws, and generally intelligent, to successfully frustrate his designs" (P.A., 33). Thus, the right kind of people is the simply indispensable precondition for "the perpetuation of our political institutions," not a special kind of anti-prince political savior. Thus, it should be here with the people, if anywhere, that Lincoln's political religion can play its part.

But Lincoln's presentation of the people in the second part of his address was notably more negative, more despairing than that in the first part, or even than in Machiavelli's account. According to Machiavelli, the people are the "home of morality," their goals are fundamentally decent;[18] according to Lincoln, the people by nature are marked by "jealousy, envy and avarice." They are moved by "the deep-rooted principle of hate, and the powerful motive of revenge" (P.A., 83). According to Lincoln, princes and peoples are distinguished from each other by their dominant or driving passion—ambition for princes, the pettier drives of envy and avarice for peoples. On the whole, not a pretty picture on either side. That picture of leaders and peoples in the second part of Lincoln's speech surely counters the impression the reader took away from the first part where the older generation, princes and peoples both, were presented by Lincoln as "hardy, brave and patriotic" (P.A., 77).

Just as the political problem posed by great princes has so far been masked in America by the "great experiment," Lincoln suggested, the problem posed by the people has been masked by the special circumstances of the times. Those unflattering passions "incident to our nature, and so common to a state of peace, prosperity, and conscious strength, were for the time rendered inactive; while the deep-rooted principle of *hate* and the powerful motive of *revenge*, instead of being turned against each other, were directed exclusively against the British nation" (P.A., 83). Lincoln's pervasive sense of the ironies of politics lends a special poignancy to his analysis: the success of America inevitably breeds the conditions for its failure. When the normal passions emerge with their natural force, the people will no longer be "united with each other, [and] attached to the government and laws" (P.A., 83). In their envy, hatred, and avarice the people are likely to encourage and foster designs of great (and lesser) princes, rather than resist them.

The people's commitment to the American experiment depended not on the positive lure of the great task to be achieved, but rather on the more reactive forces of threats posed and injuries suffered. Every family knew at firsthand of the Revolutionary War, every family bore in some of its members "the inevitable testimonies of [the] authenticity" of that history, "in the limbs mangled, in the scars of wounds received" (P.A., 84). In the people, the war left a legacy of "mutilated limbs," and from that history of injury came internal unity and a projection of hatred outward. The threat and the experience of injury have a wonderful way of focusing the passions. Yet time erases such memories. Books may supply knowledge of the events of history, but they cannot produce the same effects on the passions. "Their influence *cannot be* what it heretofore has been" (P.A., 84; emphasis in original).

The political religion was needed to supply the place of the special channeling of passion through memory and experience on which the preservation of American institutions had theretofore depended. But just as Lincoln cannot have expected the political religion to work for princes, so he cannot have expected it to work for the people either. The feelings prompted by the Revolution depended on the living experiences he recited; he gave no reason to expect that his political religion would be exempt from the fate of all dead history. "In history, we hope, they will be read of, and recounted, so long as the bible shall be read;—but even granting that they will, their influence *cannot be* what it heretofore has been" (P.A., 84; emphasis in original). The political religion was to be enforced by oaths taken "on the blood of the Revolution"; every American was to "remember that to violate the law, is to trample on the blood of his father" (P.A., 80–81). But these ties can bind only so long as the living memory to which they appeal survives in the community. But then they were not really needed. If possible, then unnecessary—that is the problem of political religion as Lincoln has presented it in the Perpetuation Address.

The political religion was to be a passion-aided means to the reason-discerned end of civil peace through law. But following the analysis just presented, it can come as no great surprise that Lincoln now concluded that "passion had helped us; but can do so no more. It will in future be our enemy." Not passion but "reason, cold calculating, unimpassioned reason, must furnish all the materials for our future support and defence" (P.A., 84). From "these materials" can grow "reverence for the laws," said Lincoln. But he did not say how, and the analysis of human nature as passionate and irrational that preceded this appeal to reason provided no grounds to expect "cold, calculating, unimpassioned reason" to prove able to rule hot passion. Thus neither natural passion, nor civil religion, nor pure reason would seem capable of providing for the "perpetuation of our political institutions." Beneath Lincoln's rhetoric of optimism and hope lay a teaching of despair. Or, alternatively, if Lincoln retained hope for cure, the grounds for hope did not appear in his Perpetuation Address.[19]

III. The Possibility of Civil Religion

The quandary to which the Perpetuation Address leads stemmed from Lincoln's thoroughgoing analysis of the problem posed for free politics by the passions. As Jaffa and others have observed, Lincoln implicitly challenged the political science of the Founders by showing that the solution to the problem posed by the passions cannot be supplied merely by the passions, not even the passions as guided and channeled by the constitutional reason of the Founders.[20] Rather, Lincoln insisted, moral reform of some sort is required, but his analysis did no more than show the necessity for such reform without showing its possibility. The significance of the second major address of the young Lincoln's career, the so-called Temperance Address, lies precisely in the fact that it returned to the theme of moral reform and gave an answer to the problems uncovered, but not resolved, in the earlier speech.

This second speech, delivered four years after the first, evoked an almost altogether different moral universe. Rather than depicting moral decline represented by the spread of mob violence, Lincoln spoke instead of the powerful moral movement for temperance reform. And temperance reform was but one of a bevy of such reform movements visible in America in the second third of the nineteenth century. It was a time when, in Jaffa's words, "the numerous communist societies . . . flourished, along with the numerous radical reform movements—to abolish slavery, to abolish strong drink, to reform prison systems, to bring about full equality of rights for women, to abolish war, and many others."[21] Rather than leading up to despair over the possibility of moral reform, the Temperance Address took its point of departure in the actuality of moral reform movements. If actual, then possible—the main burden of the Temperance Address was to explore the conditions for the possibility of moral reform in the modern world.

Far more than in the Perpetuation Address, the audience for this speech obtruded itself into it.[22] Lincoln spoke to the Springfield branch of the Washingtonian Temperance Society, and the overt topic of the speech was the great success of the Washingtonian Temperance Society itself. The Washingtonians were at once the addressees and chief subject of the speech. The rhetoric and the structure of the speech reflect the centrality of the Washingtonians, for it contains three main sections, each relating the Washingtonians and their movement to another group or movement: first, to the previous generation of temperance reformers; then, to "ordinary people;" and finally, to the revolutionaries of 1776.

Lincoln thus identified four distinct groups of reformers (or potential reformers)—the political revolutionaries of the generation of 1776, the Old (temperance) Reformers of the 1820s, the New (Washingtonian) Reformers of the 1840s, and the ordinary people to some degree onlookers and potential adherents of the 1840s. Lincoln did not, however, cast his eye equally on all four groups. He attended above all to the contrast between the Old Reformers and the New Reformers, but almost equally he concerned himself with the emergence of the Old Reformers themselves, for the appearance of a reform movement dedicated to the eradication of alcohol was perhaps an even more extraordinary event than the great success now enjoyed by the New Reformers

The use of alcohol, Lincoln pointed out, was no recent innovation, no newborn practice, but was for all practical purposes, "just as old as the world itself." Even in the recent past, alcohol was "recognized by everybody, used by everybody, and repudiated by nobody." Its use was limited to no single stratum of society—parsons drank, as well as politicians, the rich and respectable as much as the ragged and rowdy. And so it was "everywhere a respectable article of manufacture and merchandize" (T.A., 134–35). In sum, Lincoln concluded, "universal public opinion not only tolerated but recognized and adopted its use." And universal public opinion plays no small role in human affairs. "The universal *sense* of mankind, on any subject, is an argument, or at least an *influence* not easily overcome" (T.A., 135).

If universal public opinion is not easily overcome, then the question arises, How did the opinions favoring, or at least tolerating, alcohol come to be reversed to so marked a degree by 1842? Lincoln conceded that the evils of alcohol had been recognized in earlier days: "Even then it was known and acknowledged, that many were greatly injured by it, but none seemed to think the injury arose from the *use* of a *bad thing* but from the *abuse* of a *very good thing*" (T.A., 135). What, he forces us to ask, can be responsible for a shift of such magnitude?

What Lincoln said of the Old Reformers does not at first sight help with that question for there is an unmistakable odor of Christianity about the Old Reformers as Lincoln described them. Of the three classes of "champions" he identified with the earlier temperance movement, preachers are given pride of place, and the tactics of the Old Reformers—use of the thundering tones of anathema and denunciation—surely put one in mind of the preacher. Christianity had been a power in the world almost as long as alcohol had been used, but, as Lincoln presented it at least, the temperance movement emerged only in the 1820s nearly two thousand years after the emergence of Christianity. If temperance reform derived directly from Christianity or even from Protestantism, it took a long while to do so.

Lincoln did point to one recent event of a magnitude and power to shake such long-standing and universal opinions: "our political revolution of '76" (T.A., 140). Lincoln carefully noted that that revolution was merely a political revolution that supplied Americans with "a degree of political freedom far exceeding that of any other of the nations of the earth" (T.A., 140). It solved the question "as to the capability of man to govern himself." But beyond that, it also contained "the germ which has vegetated, and still is to grow and expand into the universal liberty of mankind" (T.A., 140).

The temperance movement was in turn, part of the "march" toward "universal" or "perfect liberty," of which the revolution has served as germ (T.A., 140). "And what a noble ally this [temperance revolution is], to the cause of political freedom. With such an aid, its march cannot fail to be on and on, till every son of earth shall drink in rich fruition, the sorrow quenching draughts of perfect liberty" (T.A., 140). We should not allow our distaste for the rhetoric, or better, our deep suspicion of irony in this passage to conceal from us Lincoln's truly serious point. He was speaking of a "contagion of liberty," (to use Bernard Bailyn's phrase), from the political sphere to the moral sphere.[23] Temperance reform, and the whole variety of other reform movements of that and later times—abolitionism, feminism, communitarianism, communism, and so on—were the fruits of that contagion.

The Old Reformers, Lincoln implied, represented a combination or synthesis of two pre-existing forces—Christianity and the Revolution of '76—that transformed both. Originally restricted to the political realm and seeking no more than political freedom, the revolutionary impetus became "liberty-intoxicated" and was broadened into a movement for "perfect liberty," for moral liberty and moral reform in addition to political liberty.

Although it had always had the breadth of concern and the moral center of the Old Reformers, Christianity had not made that moral concern the focus of crusading political action, as the Old Reformers—and now the New Reformers—did. In the fallen world, Christianity recognized limits to the possibilities of human reform. Those limits were expressed in a variety of ways, of which Lincoln reminded his listeners. For example, at one point in his speech he used the phrase "that the grace of temperance might abound," an obvious reference to the Christian doctrine of grace (T.A., 136). To the extent that salvation, conversion, or moral regeneration depended on divine grace, they cannot reasonably become the object of a political movement. Likewise, Lincoln reminded his listeners more than once that the Christian hope lay not in this world, but in the next. The Christian could hope to be worthy of heaven but would be under no illusion that unaided human effort could win heaven, nor, even more, that heaven could be "a place on earth." But the temperance revolution, or the broader movement for moral reform of which it was a part, went far beyond. As Lincoln, ironically speaking on behalf of the movement, put it: It sought the "happy day, when, all appetites controlled, all passions subdued, all matters subjected, *mind*, all conquering *mind*, shall live and move the monarch of the world" (T.A., 140; emphasis in original). The synthesis thus represented a broadening of the this-worldly spirit of the American revolution from the political to the moral and social sphere, and an immanentization of the other-worldly spirit of Christianity.

Before the Old Reformers appeared, before the unprecedented combination of Christian moral concern and revolutionary fervor, the victims of alcohol "were pitied, and compassionated, just as now are, the heirs of consumption, and other hereditary diseases" (T.A., 135). Human beings lacked confidence in their ability to control alcohol abuse and other abuses brought about by other passions. Their passionate nature, resistant to the rule of "mind, all conquering mind," was the result of fallen nature—in the formula of orthodox Christianity, the "hereditary disease" of original sin. When human beings began to imagine new possibilities for countering the rule of passion, they began to react differently to those who suffered from their passions. One such response was that of the Old Reformers, another that of the New Reformers. Both had in common, however, the view that something could, in principle, be done about the evils of human existence, that such matters were within the disposal of human effort because within the sphere of "the universal liberty of mankind."

Temperence reform emerged then as the synthesis of Christian moral concerns with the this-worldly political revolution of 1776. Such a synthesis occurred because the two elements of which it was composed supplemented each other in a peculiarly potent way. Old and pervasive as it is, Christianity was shown by Lincoln in the Temperance Address to be of limited effectiveness:

> There is something so ludicrous in the *promises* of good, or *threats* of evil, a great way off, as to render the whole subject with which they are connected, easily turned into ridicule. "Better lay down that spade you're stealing, Paddy,—if you don't you'll pay for it at the day of judgment." "By the powers, if you'll credit me so long, I'll take another, just." [T.A., 136–37]

Christian moral concerns produced little by way of practical results, because the sanctions, the payoffs—for good or evil—were so distant. Like Machiavelli, Lincoln sought "the effective truth."[24] The Italian, moreover, could well have endorsed Lincoln's claim, "Pleasures to be enjoyed, or pains to be endured, *after* we shall be dead and gone, are but little regarded" (T.A., 136; emphasis in original).

But as Lincoln emphasized so strongly in the Perpetuation Address, the American Revolution, the great American political "experiment" had proven effective—on *this* earth, not merely as an ideal or a hope. The fact of its success, here and now, had established, here and now, the truth of human liberty and had opened out hopes for other, more thoroughgoing applications of the principle of liberty. The success of the revolution had brought human hopes to earth. America, said Lincoln, became "the birthplace and cradle" for political and temperance reform, as well as a large number of other movements that would have been considered merely utopian in aspiration, had it not been for the example of the revolution. Christianity promised a redeemed world but pushed that redemption back to another place—and thereby cut off much of its own influence. The Revolution showed, or seemed to, the real possibility of redemption here and now. Thus emerged the peculiar fusion of moral concern and moral energy with the this-worldly political orientation of modern politics. Lincoln was perhaps the first to see that far from "demoralizing" politics as some of the fathers of the Revolution had anticipated, modernity had instead made available for politics forces that had for the most part stayed outside the political realm. Or when they had entered it, had done so with often disastrous effects— religious warfare, intolerance, and oppression.[25]

IV. The Possibilities and Limits of Civil Religion

The new politics of "perfect liberty" contains at least part of an answer to the problem of "the perpetuation of our political institutions" posed in Lincoln's earlier speech. American institutions were threatened, Lincoln had argued, because neither the princes nor the people retained a stake in maintaining them once their success had been demonstrated and the living memories of the revolutionary struggle had faded. Lincoln's later analysis reveals that he had drawn the alternatives facing men of great ambition too narrowly when he said they could either follow in paths made by others or, like Caesar, make new paths of their own by obliterating those made by others. According to the new politics of liberty, there are many new and great tasks to appeal to ambitious men who neither simply follow in already trodden ways nor simply turn away from them. The extension of the principle of liberty from the political to the moral and social spheres, as in temperance reform or the labor movement, is a task derivative from, and therefore in principle compatible with, established American institutions.[26] To be a great innovator does not require being a Caesar.

The new civil religion of liberty can engage the people as well as the princes. The people, Lincoln argued, are more reflexive, less able to imagine "new modes and orders" than the princes; the negative passions of envy, resentment, and avarice are especially powerful among them. Despite that fact, the people have been enlisted in the experiment of American democracy because those passions were masked, or, perhaps more accurately, channeled into that experiment by the circumstances of the break with England. The new politics of liberty provides similar opportunities, it would seem, to channel the people's negative passions. Every movement for liberation always uncovers an oppressor against whom feelings of hatred can be directed. Every movement for liberation promises gain, material gain for the people, and thus appeals to their avarice. More than that: Lincoln's new analysis shows he had also drawn the character of the people too narrowly. They may depend on the princes to generate the ideas for new projects, but they can join in such projects out of "intoxication with liberty" as well. Thus, under certain conditions at least, the new politics of liberty can hold the people in their attachment to free institutions and prevent American public life from decaying into the war of all against all that the passions might otherwise produce.

As should be clear to the thoughtful reader, however, the civil religion of liberty is far from perfect as a response to the problem of perpetuation. The new oppressors who come to light may not be foreigners, like the British, or relatively neutral forces, like the wilderness or like disease, but may be one's fellow citizens, like Southern slaveholders, or husbands, or employers. The new civil religion of liberty can exacerbate rather than deflect the problems posed by the negative passions.

In the Temperance Address Lincoln showed a lively awareness of the limits of the new civil religion; the failure of the Old Reformers revealed one such limit, and Lincoln's (thinly) veiled prophecy of the failure of the New Reformers revealed another. Even though the Old Reformers emerged in reply to the example of the effectiveness of the revolution of '76, Lincoln found them extremely ineffective. He harshly criticized the tactics of the Old Reformers as responsible for their ill-success. One way to restate the basis for the transformation of the pre-revolutionary moral concern into the post-revolutionary moral reform movement is to say that the example of the success of the Revolution gave hope that far more was humanly possible than had ever been thought before. A new birth of hope was responsible in the first instance for the birth of the new freedom. Inspired by that new hope, the Old Reformers nonetheless took an approach to reform which failed to keep hold of the hope-inspiring element of reform. Instead, they denounced "dram sellers and dram drinkers" and blamed them mightily for "all the vice and misery and crime in the land" (T.A., 133). Ineffective as it was, denunciation did cohere with the intellectual impetus that produced the reform movements in the first place: the recognition or postulation of moral freedom. If human beings were free to do otherwise, then it made eminent sense to blame them for following evil—and unfree—ways.

But denunciation failed quite miserably. "It is not much in the nature of man to be driven to anything; still less to be driven about that which is exclusively his own business; and least of all, where such driving is to be submitted to, at the expense of pecuniary interest, or burning appetite" (T.A., 133). The Old Reformers failed because moral freedom is not the only or whole truth of human nature. Not merely freedom, but "appetite" and "interest" built on appetite, contribute to the makeup of men. By making men proud of their power of self-determination, freedom itself makes human beings resist the denunciation of others attempting to induce a change in their way of life. So both freedom-inspired pride and freedom-qualifying appetite conspire to doom the Old Reformers' denunciatory tactics.

When they failed to reach the reprobate through denunciation (i.e., through the appeal to moral freedom in itself), the Old Reformers turned in an almost opposite direction. They decreed the drinkers "incorrigible" and called for them to be "turned adrift" from the community (T.A., 136). That move made good psychological sense: if the vicious did not heed the call for reform, that meant either that they actually lacked the moral freedom they had been thought to possess, or that they chose to exercise their freedom in a perverse way. Either way, the Old Reformers could conclude, they were beyond the reach of reform. The possibilities of reform thus came to depend on rooting out the vicious, not on changing them. The initial enthusiasm and hope for change produced frustration, and this frustration produced purges. This new approach, in effect, gave up the initial hope that had inspired the reform movement. And, Lincoln emphasized, it led to yet further enervation of the principle of hope. The limits of reform here and now meant that the "benefits of the reformation to be effected" were pushed back into an indefinite future. The Old Reformers thus returned full circle to the distant or utopian hopes of Christianity, and suffered the same loss of effectiveness. The expected benefits "were too remote in time, to warmly engage many on [the movement's] behalf. Few can be induced to labor exclusively for posterity; and none will do it enthusiastically" (T.A., 136).

The New Reformers improved on the Old precisely in their greater ability to keep hold of the hope that initially generated the reform movement. "By the Washingtonians, this system of consigning the habitual drunkard to hopeless ruin, is repudiated. . . . *They* go for the present as well as the future good. . . . They teach *hope* to all—*despair* to none" (T.A., 137; emphasis in original). The New Reformers did not deny the principle of moral freedom, but they embodied it in a form that also had room for those other forces in human nature to which Lincoln called attention. Appetite, self-interest, moral weakness in general were all given play in the New Reformers' reliance on the reformed drunkard as chief agent and example.

Because of the delicacy of his rhetorical situation, Lincoln muted his reservations against the New Reformers, but they were nearly as strong as those against the Old Reformers. Many readers of the speech—and apparently some of its auditors who came to suspect Lincoln of having fun at their expense—have noted the heavily ironic closing.[27] "Every son of earth," he said, "shall drink in rich fruition the sorrow quenching draughts of perfect liberty" (T.A., 140). Staggering from one form of inebriation to another, the New Reformers' new enthusiasm is no more viable than their old.

The Washingtonians may have set a better model than the Old Reformers, but the prospects for moral reform were far more limited than either group recognized. Moral freedom is only part of the story of human nature, a valuable, perhaps even the most valuable part, but part nonetheless. Lincoln also spoke of "human nature, which is God's decree, and never can be reversed" (T.A., 132); Lincoln presented an almost Kantian dualism between freedom and determinism. A just estimate of human possibility must recognize how passions and pride limit the scope of "universal liberty" and prevent the total rule of "mind, all conquering mind." The New Reformers in their more extravagant moments forgot what they knew in their more sober moments—the knowledge that, according to Lincoln at least, produced what success they had—the knowledge of human limits and human frailty.[28] Like the Old Reformers, they too were prone to extravagant hopes. Both groups require moderation.

Thus, for Lincoln civil religion was at once an integral part of the modern post-revolutionary world, an opportunity, and a problem. Yet, Lincoln was not struck by quite the same problematic aspects as many of the modern critics of the phenomenon. Lincoln would not agree with those who fear that civil religion trivializes religion. The new civil religion of freedom was far from trivial—it dealt with the most fundamental human aspirations, possibilities, and hopes. It was a vehicle for bolstering political life and for infusing a truly moral character into that political life. Only a religiosity that insisted on the "ineffective truth" of another world could condemn the new politics of liberty as trivial, and Lincoln indicated his own impatience with that religion.

Lincoln would have greater sympathy for those critics who see political dangers in civil religion, as we have already seen. His perspective is broader than that of many of those critics, however, in that he saw this fervor as dangerous, yes, but at the same time as potentially extraordinarily beneficial, and in any case, as probably unavoidable in the context of modern, post-revolutionary politics. Civil religion may be playing with fire, but such play, Lincoln implied while still a young man, was the most serious undertaking imaginable for statesmen in a revolutionary regime. The new political world ushered in by the success of the American Revolution is marked by a new political force of great power, but of great danger as well.

The new civil religion of liberty thus is a fact, but more than that, according to Lincoln, it is a task for the statesman-prophet who sees into its nature. It is the statesman-prophet's task to set the civil religion of liberty onto the correct paths—a formidable task, for the example of both Old and New Reformers showed how easy it was to stray. Lincoln's entire career ought to be seen in light of this task, but we have not the space for that effort here; instead, we can attempt only to collect some of Lincoln's indications of that path's general direction.

Lincoln's two speeches pointed to the specific tasks facing the statesman-prophet. First, the initial call for civil religion came as a means to "the perpetuation of our political institution"—that is, to the preservation of the political achievements of the past through the inculcation of reverence for those achievements. Without that civil religion, Lincoln argued, those achievements were unlikely to survive, but, as he indicated in the Perpetuation Address and even more in the Temperance Address, the new religion of liberty supplies no guarantee of that preservation, for it supplies no sure foundation for reverence. The intoxication with liberty that produced the new politics endangers the accomplishments of the past and can contribute to loosening the bonds of law; it encourages love of innovation and impatience of all restraint. It encourages, in other words, attitudes far removed from reverence.

The new religion of liberty, at the same time, threatens to exacerbate the natural tendencies for the passions of envy and hatred to find harmful outlets exemplified in the ultimate fate of the Old Reformers. New possibilities of liberation turn up new enemies and oppressors, and immoderate hopes for reform can lend special edge to the hatred focused against those enemies. The new religion of liberty can therefore threaten the very integrity of the community, as one group turns against another, seeing in the religion of liberty the vicious obstruction to its own aspirations for liberation or reform. And in so doing, like the Old Reformers, one group breaks the ties of community with the others. The New Reformers, as Lincoln presented them, embodied the needed response to this threat of excessive denunciation: charity. Civil religion has to exist in such a form that charity tempers hatred and creates bonds between those who seek reform and those against whom they act.

And finally there is the task posed by the problem of hope. The Old Reformers and the New both failed because they both hoped for too much. As a result the Old Reformers had already fallen into despair, and the New were likely to do so sometime in the future. One must find a mean, Lincoln suggested, between the otherworldly hopes of the Christians and over-apocalyptic hopes of the reformers. Liberty in the here and now, yes, but not all of it right away. The civil religion, then, must both hold on to hope, for it is this that inspires men to exercise their liberty, and at the same time must moderate the natural tendency to excessive hope.

These three then—reverence, charity, and hope—are the qualities that the statesman-prophet must attempt to instill in the people through civil religion. Those three correspond in turn to the three dimensions of time: a people needs to be properly oriented toward the past through reverence, in the present with charity, and toward the future with hope.[29] The Temperence Address presents the outlines of the solution to the problem of time, a solution Lincoln was to present in much greater detail in the great preaching of his maturity.

Lincoln's analysis in the Temperance Address points to the solution to the problem of the past, the problem of reverence: the new civil religion of liberty originated in the Revolution and the hope that feeds it depends on the continued success of the political idea of liberty here and now. The statesman-prophet must above all remind his audience of the link between their strivings for liberation and reform and their heritage from the past. To "their fathers" they owe the original "conception in liberty" from which they now strive to bring forth yet "new births of freedom." Moreover, the success of the first experiment in liberty reveals the mutual connection of liberty and restraint, for political liberty is the product of sound laws soundly enforced and soundly obeyed. A liberty-intoxicated people may be inclined to forget this, but the statesman-prophet must call them back to the law as the source and mainstay of their liberty. Thus, Lincoln opposed those who sought liberty at the expense of law, like the abolitionists, with as much zeal as he opposed those who denied liberty altogether, like the slaveowners.

The failure of the Old Reformers revealed the need for a charitable orientation of the new civil religion in the present. Focusing entirely on hope-inspiring moral freedom, paradoxically they abandoned all hope for the unregenerate and fell into the tactic of denunciation and threat. They absolutized the gap between themselves and the unreformed and therein lost all purchase on those who were not already with them. The Washingtonians were better in practice, and in principle better yet. They appealed to moral freedom, but knew also of its limits; they urged reform, but never broke the ties with the unreformed. As Lincoln presented them, they knew that all human beings are frail. Who is not touched by moral weakness? Who has the right to feel smug or to reject others? Who can rightly expect to achieve the whole good and thus fall prey to bitter frustration when only able to achieve a partial good? The spirit Lincoln distilled from the New Reformers at their best was captured, I think, in the ever-moving words of his Second Inaugural Address, especially the closing: "With malice toward none, with charity for all, with firmness in the right as God gives us to see the right. . . ." And earlier in the same speech he had quoted the biblical injunction: "Judge not that you be not judged." From the perception of universal failure to achieve the whole good, and thus the universal sharing in the guilt of falling short, emerges the spirit of charity that tempers hatred and refuses to cast any entirely outside the moral community.

For the future, a people must hold fast to a moderate hope. Since liberty derives from the exercise of moral liberty and not from some miraculous intervention of grace, nor from some magical transformation of the externals of human existence, one can never expect an eschaton, a moment when human beings cross the divide into the realm of freedom. For the future, Americans must see themselves as caught up in a continuing action aimed at, but never fully achieving, the realm of freedom. Only thus will hope not die in frustration and be reborn as despair. Thus, it was in these terms that Lincoln taught his countrymen the meaning of the Declaration of Independence:

> They [the Founders] meant to set up a standard maxim for a free society, which should be familiar to all, and revered by all; constantly looked to, constantly labored for, and even though never perfectly attained, constantly approximated, and thereby constantly spreading and deepening its influence, and augmenting the happiness and value of life to all peoples everywhere.[30]

That is, he taught Americans to conceive their common life as a recurrent testimony and effortful dedication to the further spread of the liberty of their origin. That spread would never be complete, and thus would never give ground for the immoderate hopes of utopianism.[31]

V. Lincoln and the Problem of Civil Religion

Despite his endorsement and practice of civil religion, Lincoln saw civil religion as a problem. He did not see it, however, as the same sort of problem that such earlier modern thinkers as John Locke had. The problem of civil religion as ultimately visible in the thought of Locke derives from Locke's conviction on the one hand that healthy civil society requires civil religion and thus the (continued) presence of a religious attitude; at the same time, healthy political life requires the cultivation of the spirit of liberty, which Locke believed required the undermining of the spirit of religion.[32]

Lincoln's treatment was both more and less optimistic. Most significantly, Lincoln saw the deep compatibility in the post-revolutionary age of the spirit of religion and the spirit of liberty. In this he was closer to Alexis de Tocqueville than to Locke. At the same time he saw dangers in the combination of politics and religion that Tocqueville did not and that even Locke, with his horror of religion-inspired warfare, seemed not to have fully appreciated. The task of politics for Lincoln thus came to light quite differently from the way it did for Locke or even for Tocqueville. For Lincoln the greatest political role was the statesman-prophet he became; surely no one would confuse him with the political economist, or "godly prince," whose chief task, Locke thought, was the right managing of property (i.e., of economic growth).

A full-scale assessment of Lincoln's version of the problem of civil religion is certainly not feasible here, but George Anastaplo pointed in the direction such an assessment ought to take when he wondered whether Lincoln's practice of civil religion—and, by extension, his theory of civil religion—did not reflect the peculiarities of a certain moment in American history when the resonances of inherited Christianity were powerful enough to mobilize for public purposes, but not so powerful as to resist such adaptation. Anastaplo's musings are relevant, for, it is clear, Lincoln depended not only in a general way on residual Christianity for his civil religion, but in quite specific ways as well, as in his commitment to the "judge not" theme. But what does one make of Lincoln's practice or analysis next to Locke's or Tocqueville's in the light of the very different public presence of Christianity at other times?

ॐ

LINCOLN AND THE PROBLEM OF POLITICAL RELIGION

Bruce P. Frohnen

IN FACING THE CRISIS of the Civil War, Lincoln the president had to reassure the union's supporters of the justness of their cause. Slavery and its arguable antithesis, equality, clearly played a role in this reassurance. The Civil War was bound up with

issues relating to slavery,[1] and chattel slavery as practiced in the United States constituted a denial of fundamental rights, most especially those related to the formation
and maintenance of families and family life.[2] Thus it is understandable and perhaps
inevitable that Lincoln would call union supporters to arms in the name of a natural
equality that by nature condemned chattel slavery.

My purpose in this essay is not to criticize Lincoln for fulfilling the presidential
role of civic educator, question his political or military conduct, or even question
the sincerity of his political motivations. Rather, I want to examine Lincoln's chosen
response to the crisis of the Civil War and analyze its inherent nature and sociopolit-
ical effects. That response was a political religion with its roots deep in Lincoln's
pre-Civil War thought. In what follows I argue that Lincoln's political religion, like
all political religions, focuses the people's attentions and affections directly on the
state and its purpose. And this focus on the political state and its collectivized goal
is inimical to ordered liberty.

From an Augustinian perspective in particular, the state's proper purpose is to
foster associations and institutions in which individuals and groups can lead good
lives, devoted to virtue and the service of God. Political religion replaces all such
constitutive associations and purposes with one, central association—the state—and
the political goals that state serves. However understandable the crisis ushering in
the political religion at issue, it by nature turns the people into isolated individuals,
dependent on the state, or rather on democratic political action aimed at using the
state to further some particular end or ends.

Political Religion

There can be little doubt that Lincoln propounded a political religion. The famous
passage from his "Address to the Young Men's Lyceum of Springfield, Illinois"
would seem conclusive:

> Let every American, every lover of liberty, every well wisher to his posterity, swear by
> the blood of the Revolution, never to violate in the least particular, the laws of the
> country; and never to tolerate their violation by others. As the patriots of seventy-six
> did to the support of the Declaration of Independence, so to the support of the consti-
> tution and Laws, let every American pledge his life, his property, and his sacred
> honor;—let every man remember that to violate the law, is to trample on the blood of
> his father, and to tear the character of his own, and his children's liberty. Let reverence
> for the laws, be breathed by every American mother, to the lisping babe, that prattles
> on her lap;—let it be taught in schools, in seminaries, and in colleges;—let it be writ-
> ten in Primmers, spelling books, and in Almanacs;—let it be preached from the pulpit,
> proclaimed in legislative halls, and enforced in courts of justice. And, in short, let it
> become the *political religion* of the nation; and let the old and the young, the rich and
> the poor, the grave and the gay, of all sexes and tongues, and colors and conditions,
> sacrifice unceasingly upon its altars.[3]

Here we have no mere assertion that one should follow the laws. Rather, we have a full-fledged profession of political faith. Lincoln's is a political (or "civil" as the term is often used)[4] religion. It meets, for example, the criteria conveniently laid out by W. Lance Bennett, who argues that

> a civil religion can be thought of as the collection of myths and rituals that explain and dramatize the origins, guiding principles, rules of order, and destiny of a political culture. The most powerful accomplishment of a civil religion, then, is the creation of an unquestionable pattern of social relations and civic obligations."[5]

Lincoln wants Americans to use means encompassing all of life—from legislative halls to churches, schools, and nurseries—to inculcate devotion to the nation and its laws. He would have all Americans join together to propagate a definite set of beliefs concerning the nature and purpose of the nation (as embodied in the Declaration of Independence) and the duty to follow the laws and precepts established by a fabled set of heroic, self-sacrificing Fathers. The religious language is unmistakable—sacrifices are to be made upon altars and blood is to be sworn by. The object of veneration seems clear as well: the laws of the nation as sanctified by the Revolution and given meaning by the Declaration the Fathers swore to protect. When we add to the Lyceum Address Lincoln's later assertion in his Gettysburg Address that the American nation is "dedicated to the proposition that all men are created equal" and that the people must be devoted to the "cause" for which the union dead fell, "that government of the people, by the people, for the people, shall not perish from the earth,"[6] we see a complete dogma regarding the purpose and destiny as well as the duty of the American people.

To preach obedience to the laws may seem an obvious good. But I will argue that Lincoln's political religion, like all political religions, is detrimental to human liberty. Such criticism may begin with Saint Augustine, who asked "Remove justice, and what are kingdoms but gangs of criminals on a large scale?"[7] Of course, justice for Augustine was not mere law-abidingness, but pursuit of the ultimate good, communion with God. True justice being impossible on earth, laws must seek merely to restrain vice and foster virtue as prudence allows.[8]

From an Augustinian viewpoint, the elevation of human law to divine status is both impious and dangerous because it chains human awe to fallible, earthly rulers and focuses the people's attentions on the realm of politics rather than that of more fundamental areas of human life, in which virtue and vice become habit and character. Moreover, Lincoln's use of political religion makes use of this awe for the government in order to undermine law and the true function of the state, which is to protect the more fundamental associations of social life. Like all political religions—and this essay concerns political religion as a category—Lincoln's revolutionizes society, undermining the associations of social life along with stable, prudent government in the attempt to fulfill an abstract proposition, in Lincoln's case that all men are created equal.

Lincoln's political religion undermined the American tradition of ordered liberty, and did so by necessity. Some observers argue that some kind of political religion is necessary for liberty, and that only political religions promoting bad policies are dangerous; they see danger specifically in the concentration of the people's efforts on achieving improper ends. But the very concentration of affections, loyalty, and conduct in the state that is promoted by any political religion undermines those other centers of loyalty and affection that limit the state so as to prevent tyranny and provide the opportunity for personal and social fulfillment.

Varieties of Political Religion?

The extensive literature on political religion includes significant worries, particularly over the possibility that it might lead to "national self-worship,"[9] the use of sacred symbols to hoodwink the masses into accepting civic corruption[10] or a divisive split among groups adhering to competing visions.[11] Yet defenders of political religion claim it is necessary for maintenance of "collective and binding moral order" in political life.[12] For example, Robert Bellah argues that political religion is needed to spur the people to do great national deeds through conversion experiences rooted in the principle of equality.[13] Harry Jaffa argues that Lincoln's particular political religion served to protect the people from would-be Caesars as it bound them to their own more-than-human leader, Lincoln, and to the principle of equality he found in the Declaration of Independence.[14]

Political religion, then, is good or bad, according to commentators of varying political viewpoints, depending on what cause it is used to serve. If it is used to serve the powers that be as they pursue selfish ends inconsistent with the principle of equality, as defined quite differently by Bellah and Jaffa, for example, it is harmful. But if it is used to bind people to the right principles and conduct, it is a force for good.

Whatever the goal it serves, political religion is exactly what the name would imply: a religion of politics, binding the people through religious awe to a particular nation and set of political precepts. Indeed, on this interpretation, government itself is "a direct evolution of primitive religion." As A. M. Hocart argued, "the functions now discharged by king, prime minister, treasury, public works . . . were originally part . . . of an organization to promote life, fertility, prosperity by transferring life from objects abounding in it to objects deficient in it."[15] Today the state gives meaning and energy to our lives in the same way that religion once did for more primitive man.

Political religion replaces God with the state or political community in explaining life and giving it purpose and meaning. This is not to say that political religions must promise otherworldly rewards for their adherents, or even that they must be based on a set of principles claiming an objective truth rooted in religion. Indeed,

William Corlett defends Lincoln's political religion precisely on the grounds that it eschews such "transcendental virtue" in favor of purely political ends and means.[16] And Lincoln's thought gives some credence to such a view, rejecting as it does the conviction that the creator's will can be known with any precision.[17] Bellah, however, defends the clerical element in political religion to the extent that it serves egalitarian principles.[18] Garry Wills illustrates the impulse central to political religion, arguing that Americans must "complete the effort of . . . removing religion from state ceremony and proclamations" while retaining "religious leadership" in the form of a "conscience politics" necessary for the promotion of political and economic equality.[19]

The central point seems to be one of concern lest religious standards promote an improper, apolitical moral code on the people, lest it bind them too closely to a moral vision that would interfere with their attachment to correct principles and political action based in these principles. Thus political religion is seen as a tool necessary for binding potentially selfish individuals to a greater whole and to the good which commentators believe should be served by that whole.

The Religious, the Social, and the Political

In an article on "Rousseau and Totalitarianism," Robert Nisbet argues that Rousseau's insistence on toleration for "all religions that tolerate others, so long as their dogmas contain nothing contrary to the duties of citizenship" should be read in light of the fact "that the criteria of good citizenship are far reaching." And according to Nisbet these criteria are extremely far reaching. Rousseau's political religion has as its central tenets "respect for the Sovereign, allegiance to the state alone, and subordination of all interests to the law of the realm."[20] Rousseau's Sovereign is to replace Christianity, with its focus on living for the next life, with a political religion that will eliminate the injustices and oppressions he found inherent in social life. And this would entail, for example, taking away from families the role of educating children so that the people would be "early accustomed to conceive their individuality only in its connection with the body of the state, and to be aware, of their own existence merely as parts of the state." The authority of the father would be subsumed in that of the citizen as all become parts of a greater, political whole.[21]

Nisbet terms Rousseau totalitarian on account of the demands of his political religion. His Rousseau would eliminate social institutions, including the family, which get in the way of total identification of the individual with the state. Freedom, for Nisbet's Rousseau, consists in the breaking of social bonds in favor of an all-encompassing political bond.[22] In effect, Nisbet's Rousseau would eliminate intermediary institutions and loyalties in favor of the central state. This would destroy liberty and even individuality because, as Nisbet elsewhere points out, individual liberty "is only possible within the context of a plurality of social authorities, moral codes, and historical traditions, all of which, in organic articulation, serve at one and the same time as 'the inns and resting places' of the human spirit and intermediary barriers to the power of the state over the individual."[23]

Nisbet thus presents a strong argument for liberty as the product of social pluralism, with excessive political identification as a threat to that pluralism, and to its product. But is this relevant to Lincoln? Merely because Nisbet sees Rousseau's political religion as subjugating all individuals and social institutions to the state, does that mean that a different political religion, that of Lincoln, would do the same thing? I am convinced that it does, not because Lincoln shares Rousseau's particular political vision, but because the mechanism of political religion, whatever its substantive goals, focuses all passions, interests, and even self-identification on the state. Lincoln focused all attention on the nation, conceived as a teleological unity, gathering the people to itself in pursuit of a common, political goal more important than the local loyalties, customs, and traditions constituting ordered liberty. Lincoln dedicated the American people to a proposition, that all men are created equal. He bound the nation to the project of making an abstract political principle the guiding rule of their lives. In this way Lincoln transformed American politics. He rendered American politics a centralized realm of political religion, where once it had been a collection of local communities and states, each pursuing their own customs and ways of life while joining together for limited instrumental purposes.

Political Religion and Constitutional Government

In a frequently cited "Meditation on Proverbs 25:11," Lincoln refers to the Declaration of Independence and, in particular, the principle "Liberty to all" as an "apple of gold," continuing, "The *Union,* and the *constitution,* are the *picture* of *silver,* subsequently framed around it. The picture was made, not to *conceal,* or *destroy* the apple; but to *adorn* and *preserve* it. The picture was made for the apple—not the apple for the picture."[24] Here as in the Lyceum address Lincoln appropriates religious language and imagery in arguing for the special status that should be accorded the Declaration of Independence. More than this, he uses religious imagery to literally subjugate the American Constitution to the Declaration of Independence and, in particular, to one core concept in that Declaration, that calling for "Liberty to all."

What does Lincoln's "liberty to all" mean? That specific phrase is not found in the Declaration. But the phrase "all men are created equal" is found there, and fits not only with the notion of "liberty for all" (that is, equal freedom, equal rights and/or equality of opportunity) but also with Lincoln's later declaration in the Gettysburg Address that the Declaration bound the American people to the "proposition" that "all men are created equal." Moreover, interpreters as varied as Bellah, Jaffa, and Wills maintain that the proposition of universal human equality is at the core of Lincoln's political religion.[25]

In discussing equality and Lincoln's political religion, the Gettysburg Address is of central importance. Wills argues that the speech constituted a "verbal coup."[26] That may be an overstatement. But the Gettysburg Address and in particular Lincoln's dedication of Americans as a nation to a single, abstract principle, instituted a political religion that transformed the United States and still wields great power today.

To restate a well-known analysis, the Gettysburg Address "refounded" America by emphasizing the role of the Declaration over that of the Constitution, and of the American people over pre-existing local loyalties and social and political structures. Beginning with the phrase "Four score and seven years ago" Lincoln sets the beginnings of the United States at independence in 1776 rather than at adoption of the Constitution as the American form of government. Moreover, he speaks of bringing forth "a new nation," as later he speaks repeatedly of "the people" as a unity—as one, single nation joining one people, radically disjointed from any formative past, cultural history, or separate existence as independent colonies or sovereign states. And what bound this nation? Dedication "to the proposition that all men are created equal."

Interpreters have differed over the precise meaning of the phrase "all men are created equal" as used in the Declaration. John C. Calhoun simply dismissed the phrase as erroneous.[27] George Carey has argued that it means that the American people are equally entitled to the status of a sovereign nation as other peoples, such as the British or French.[28] But the principle debate in the literature on Lincoln's political religion seems to be that between those who share Jaffa's interpretation of Lincoln's meaning and those who share Bellah's. Jaffa argues that this phrase, as used by both Lincoln and Jefferson, refers to the equal right of every individual to be ruled only with his consent.[29] Bellah argues that Lincoln's statement (and in the sense that it is open to further development, Jefferson's also) must be interpreted as a call for the state to provide for equal treatment and financial means for all.[30]

Lincoln's specific call on the American people was to dedicate themselves to the unfinished work of those who died at Gettysburg—to see that "government of the people, by the people, for the people, shall not perish from the earth." In its most narrow sense, this would mean assuring the Union's survival by achieving victory in the Civil War. In a wider sense, however, Lincoln's call has been taken to mean making the proposition that all men are created equal into a concrete reality. Jaffa on the one hand and Bellah and Wills on the other have taken the achievement of this goal to mean very different things in terms of specific political policies.[31] But all agree that it entails the reformation or elimination of local institutions, beliefs, and practices that violate the principle of universal equality.

I do not seek to defend particular customs, many of which may indeed be unjust. Moreover Wills, for example, criticizes Lincoln for dedicating Americans to a single proposition rather than to popular consensus.[32] But dedication to any abstract principle, including consensus, when imposed upon a community through political institutions and rhetoric, and when played out in a single, national forum that encompasses all of public life, makes politics the sole source of public meaning. It undermines the actual laws of the people, along with their constitutional structure, in pursuit of an abstract principle. Because all existing laws, customs, and institutions must be modified so as to achieve the proposition, the government must be the focus of all power and action, even as it itself is transformed in pursuit of the one true goal.

The Constitution and Lincoln's Political Religion

Carey notes that Lincoln succeeded in "derailing" the American political tradition. As a result of Lincoln's rhetoric and actions, "the Constitution is increasingly viewed from a *teleocratic* perspective, as an instrument designed the fulfill the ends, commitments, or promises of the Declaration." So much seems clearly to have been Lincoln's intention. But what have been the results? According to Carey, the constitutional structure of separated powers and checks and balances, "designed to preserve and promote deliberative self-government" has been destroyed. The Supreme Court in particular has assumed the powers of the other political branches, including even the power of taxation, as it has pursued equality in all spheres of life. Thus today's government meets the Founders' definition of tyranny: it combines in one branch of government the powers of all three. And the people accept this rule as legitimate on account of the end pursued—equality.[33]

Carey is criticizing Lincoln for setting in motion an ideological campaign to achieve an ideological goal—equality—at the expense of the Constitution. By an ideological goal I mean an all-encompassing end, to achieve which the ideologue would revolutionize all of society—political, moral, and social.[34] No pre-existing institution, belief, or practice can be allowed to stand if it fails to serve the ideologue's end because each is justified only by its service to the greater good. Local governments, private associations, and even the family are being redefined, particularly by the courts, to make them fit a predetermined vision of equality that bars forms of discrimination from the purely private (e.g., standards for membership in a group) to the deeply rooted and legal (e.g., the forms of relationship eligible for the status of marriage).

The first victim of the courts' campaign has been the Constitution. This Constitution consisted of rules of political conduct intended to promote the very limited goal of protecting more local and social institutions and, more fundamentally, the inherent good of self-government. From a group of semi-autonomous communities seeking to protect their practices of self-rule Lincoln turned America into a single entity, uniting individuals in pursuit of the single goal of equality. Carey, criticizing Lincoln from a conservative perspective, clearly regrets Lincoln's influence. More important than Carey's moral judgment, for my purposes, is the fact that a writer like Bellah shares his analysis in large measure.

At first it may seem curious that critics on the other side of the political spectrum share Carey's view of Lincoln's impact on the United States. But Bellah's assertion, that Lincoln's speech ushered in a conversion experience that transformed the nation, is in keeping with Carey's own. According to Bellah, Lincoln helped produce the Civil War Amendments and strengthened an underground version of the American political religion dedicated to instituting equality. And this equality has been, as it must be, read in opposition to mere constitutional barriers that too often protect elites and various forms of substantive inequality.[35]

Bellah praises the pursuit of equality as one belonging to an "underground" political religion. He argues that the pursuit of equality actually undermines existing power structures, thus, it would seem, legitimating not only the end pursued by the political religion, but also the means. One might argue that this makes Lincoln's political religion a friend to the oppressed and enemy to established power. But, while Bellah's egalitarians may be undermining pre-existing constitutional structures, along with pre-existing centers of economic, social, and in some sense political power, their result is the concentration of all power in the central state, acting (however erratically) in the name of the people. Laws and administrative actions may change in character and tone, but the competence and legitimacy of the central political authority is all encompassing.

Bertrand de Jouvenel has argued that precisely this understanding of power, demanding popular control at the expense of political institutions intended to limit the reach of government, leads to power's concentration, and to the stifling of human liberty. French intellectuals and political leaders in the nineteenth century made the mistake of believing that no power is bad if it is identified with the people. The result was an omnicompetent state, ruling without limit or check on account of its claim to represent the people.[36]

Jouvenel points out that the French state increasingly during the modern era has gained unlimited power, "at the expense of all other authorities. Not only has it subdued them to its overlordship, but in addition, thanks to the dismemberment of the Church, the temporal monarch has claimed to be in direct communion with the divine suzerain." Thus during the modern era "Power, which had till then been on a footing with the other authorities and the prisoner of right, tended to absorb within itself the various social authorities and even right itself."[37] Democracy, taken to the extreme of a political ideology devoted to the (equal) will of the people, has reduced transcendent faith, which once gave effect to natural law principles *above* politics, to mere justifications for ever-growing power in the hands of the state. As Eric Voegelin might say, the people have "immanentized the eschaton;" they have sought to make real in this world, through the state, the experience of perfection destined only for the next, and in the process handed over all legitimacy to the political powers.[38]

By making the state the repository of the good, or more precisely by making politics the sole realm in which the good can be realized, political religion concentrates all attention on the political arena, delegitimizing intermediary institutions and empowering the state to gather all power to itself. Jouvenel points to the importance of "makeweights"—interests representing sections of the nation—in limiting the potentially absolute power of the state. These makeweights might be based in class, region, or profession.[39] In the American context they can be likened to the intermediary institutions of family, church, and local association, including townships, so important to Tocqueville.

Unfortunately, as Tocqueville feared might happen in America, in France, according to Jouvenel, the people, as a mass, gave to the state powers no tyrant would dare exercise in his own name.

> How did omnipotence rise to the top? By destroying in the name of *the mass,* which it claimed to represent, though its existence was only a fiction, the various *groups,* whose life was a reality. By making a handmaid of the law to which in former times the public authority had itself been subject.[40]

The ideology of equality, the demand that everything make way for the power and interests of the people, empowered the state to sweep away the makeweights standing in its way. As a result, the state came to be seen as the repository of all power and all goodness. Thus it was inevitable that the people "would lose in the end the instinct of association and the tendency to form societies within society, which had in other days been the precious bulwarks of liberty."[41]

And in what way is this phenomenon politically religious? Because the pursuit of equality has taken on the character of a religious crusade. As Jouvenel points out, everywhere "the handling of public affairs gets entrusted to a class which stands in physical need of certitudes and takes dubious truths to its bosom with the same fanaticism as did in other times the Hussites and the Anabaptists." In the name of reason, "Faith has been pitchforked out of the political scene, but to no purpose. Religious aspiration is natural to man" such that "he even invests interests and opinions with the haloes of idolatrous cults." And so "Power, on passing into the hands of a victorious sect, takes on the character of a theocracy, a character without which it could not hope to win the degree of obedience necessary to the accomplishment of its tasks as protector of all."[42] Through the use of "certain master words" the power Jouvenel likens to the man-beast Minotaur

> unites in his own person the spiritual and temporal powers, joining together what Western civilization had always until then kept separate . . . [and] men feel in their bones that there is now no longer room for what used to be called "private life."
>
> Such is the Minotaur's success in moulding the lives of individuals that escape from him is impossible; there is, therefore, no salvation but in seizing him. The words "I will live in a certain way" are now pointless; what must be said is, "To live in a certain way myself, I must seize the controls of the great machine and employ them in such manner as suits me."[43]

Lincoln and Tocqueville

At this point the reader may be asking (indeed, may have asked many times) "but what about Tocqueville? He espoused a civil religion, much like Lincoln's, yet you are attempting to use Tocqueville's argument against Lincoln." This is an important question because it points to the distinction between appreciation for the political benefits of religion and subsuming religion to a political project.

Cushing Strout, for example, takes Tocqueville's observation that America included great denominational pluralism combined with consensus regarding the need for religious morality to support liberty as the basis of a "civil" religion. Here Strout uses Max Lerner's distinction between a political religion, which points in the direction of totalitarianism, from merely "civil" religion, constituted by a "respect for institutions, 'flowing out of self-respect and self-restraint.'"[44] Unfortunately, however, Lerner's definition of civil religion demands the excising of transcendent religious elements while leaving intact the central aspect of political religion: concentration of moral legitimacy in the national political forum. That is, Strout is correct to see in Tocqueville the recognition that religion in America provided a moral ethos, buttressed by religious certainty and conviction as to the dignity of the human person, necessary for ordered liberty,[45] but improperly minimizes the extent to which religion *qua* religion is necessary as a counterweight to political power.

Peter Dennis Bathory points out that Tocqueville saw Americans' attachment to the union as one of individuals' combined self-interest, even "cupidity," rather than one of religious zeal, and believed that it should be so.[46] Sanford Kessler argues that the civil religion debates of the 1970s illustrated the need for religion as a support for ordered liberty. He further argues that the tradition of such thought includes Washington's Farewell Address, which alludes to the necessity of religion and morality as "indispensable supports" of the "dispositions and habits which lead to political prosperity" and Jefferson's statement that the "liberties of a nation" have their only security in "a conviction in the minds of the people that these liberties are of the gift of God."[47]

Tocqueville belonged to an established tradition that recognized the beneficial effects of religion in building stable, virtuous characters, and the necessity for such characters if political liberty is to last. He saw the importance of the separate spirits of religion and of liberty in America—two separate spirits acting on the people and their institutions to produce an ordered democratic republic. This is not the tradition of political religion. That tradition, with its roots in Machiavelli and in the early pagan republic, sought to use religion in a direct, concrete political manner. Practitioners and theoreticians in this tradition used household gods and mythic heroes to elicit religious awe, binding the people to the nation and its purpose or purposes.[48] Serving the nation in its pursuit of its own ends, political religion of this kind undermines any meaningful self-rule on the part of individuals or social groups.

Tocqueville saw mass politics in the age of democracy as a great danger to liberty. The tyranny of the majority could take on religious dimensions as it sapped the ability of religion and other intermediary institutions to protect individuals and their communities. "By whatever political laws men are governed in the ages of equality, it may be foreseen that faith in public opinion will become for them a species of religion, and the majority its ministering prophet." If the people were not careful, "after having broken all the bondage once imposed on it by ranks or by men, the human mind would be closely fettered to the general will of the greatest number."[49] Lincoln's political religion was more powerful than the ancients because he was able to call upon commitment to a higher law tradition, according to which the state properly is subject to a moral law more authoritative than itself—in linking the people's awe, first to the laws, and then to a proposition that actually undermined those laws in pursuit of his ideological end.

Conclusion

I would not want to be interpreted as claiming that Lincoln was, throughout his career, a messianic egalitarian, seeking to revolutionize the nation in pursuit of an abstract ideal. Lincoln repeatedly and persuasively denied any such charge. For example, in the fifth Lincoln-Douglas debate Lincoln stated that he would not seek to establish racial equality, or even question the existence of slavery where it already existed. Rather, Lincoln sought only to limit the institution of slavery to those areas where it had become a part of the people's way of life; where its importance to the local culture dictated prudent treatment that would preserve continuity and peace. Only "in legislating for new countries where" slavery had not yet been established was it the case that "there is no just rule other than that of moral and abstract right!"[50]

It is possible to interpret Lincoln as having had a significant respect for convention, the importance of pre-existing institutions and the danger of removing even clearly abusive practices given the fragile nature of political society. Such a reading would lead to the conclusion that Lincoln developed his political religion largely in response to the tragedy of the Civil War. But times of great upheaval are dangerous precisely because of their tendency to bring out the messianic streak in the people and their leaders.[51] Moreover, one cannot deny the existence in Lincoln's thought of a profound religious attachment to a particular ideology rooted in his reading of the Declaration of Independence; a reading found not only in the Gettysburg but also in the Lyceum Address.[52]

It may even be the case, given trends in economic, political, and military developments, that centralization was inevitable in the United States, as the Civil War itself may have been inevitable. But Lincoln had the choice whether to interpret events as demanding concentration of all moral legitimacy in the nation, and of focusing the nation on achievement of a single proposition. That choice, of political religious zeal, had significant consequences, and the job of students of politics is to discern events and their causes where possible. The results of political religion, I have argued, always and everywhere will be the concentration of power in the central arena of politics, to the detriment of intermediary institutions and loyalties, and ultimately of human liberty.

⨍

The Religion of Abraham Lincoln

Reinhold Niebuhr

AN ANALYSIS OF Abraham Lincoln's religion in the context of the prevailing religion of his time and place and in the light of the polemical use of the slavery issue, which corrupted religious life in the days before and during the Civil War, must lead to the conclusion that Lincoln's religious convictions were superior in depth and purity to those held by the religious as well as by the political leaders of his day.

This judgment may seem extravagant, and the casual reader may suspect that it has been influenced by the hagiography which envelops the heroes of a nation, substituting symbolic myths for sober reality. It is true of course that Lincoln, the savior and therefore the second father of his nation, is enveloped in historical myth. But only poetic symbol adequately describes the status of Lincoln as a more authentic embodiment of American democracy than was the eighteenth century aristocrat George Washington, who holds first place in the national pantheon as the "father" of his country.

It is nevertheless easy to validate the judgment as derived from sober history; Lincoln's superior religious convictions are attested to in part by the fact that, though he was of deeply religious temperament, he joined none of the religious sects of the frontier. His abstention has led some historians to number him among the religious skeptics. Lincoln was not a sophisticated modern, but he was a thoughtful and well-read man; one must suppose that this was why he did not share the orthodox beliefs of the frontier or make common cause with the frontier evangelist Peter Cartwright (who, incidentally, was one of his political opponents).

Lincoln's religious faith was informed primarily by a sense of providence, as is indeed the case with most of the world's statesmen past and present. In his eloquent Second Inaugural Address he voiced his belief thus:

The Almighty has His own purposes. "Woe unto the world because of offenses! for it must needs be that offenses come; but woe to that man by whom the offense cometh." If we shall suppose that American slavery is one of those offenses which, in the providence of God, must needs come, but which, having continued through His appointed time, He now wills to remove, and that He gives to both North and South this terrible war as the woe due to those by whom offense came, shall we discern therein any departure from those divine attributes which the believers in a living God always ascribe to Him?

It is to be noted that both the pious and the skeptical veins in Lincoln's faith are expressed in these words. When he speaks of the "divine attributes which the believers in a living God always ascribe to Him," he does not explicitly number himself among the believers. As he goes on to spell out the workings of providence one can sense why there were in him, as in all men except the most conventional believers, both faith and skepticism concerning the concept of providence. For while the drama of history is shot through with moral meaning, the meaning is never exact. Sin and punishment, virtue and reward are never precisely proportioned.

Lincoln spells out the dilemma of faith as he applies the idea of providence to the issue of slavery; in the words of Scripture, his concept involves the "sins of the fathers" being visited on the children of another generation. The Second Inaugural continues:

Fondly do we hope—fervently do we pray—that this mighty scourge of war may speedily pass away. Yet, if God wills that it continue until all the wealth piled by the bondsman's two-hundred and fifty years of unrequited toil shall be sunk, and until every drop of blood drawn with the lash shall be paid by another drawn with the sword, as was said three thousand years ago, so still it must be said, "The judgments of the Lord, are true and righteous altogether."

Lincoln's faith is closely akin to that of the Hebrew prophets, who first conceived the idea of a meaningful history. If there was an element of skepticism in his grand concept, one can only observe that Scripture itself, particularly the Book of Job, expresses some doubts about giving the providential aspects of history exact meanings in neat moral terms. Incidentally, this eloquent passage surely expresses Lincoln's moral abhorrence of slavery. The point is important because the abolitionists had expressed some doubt on this issue.

As a responsible statesman, Lincoln was not primarily an abolitionist; rather he confessed that his primary purpose was to save the union. But the chief evidence of the purity and profundity of Lincoln's sense of providence is the fact that he was able to resist the natural temptation to do what all political leaders, indeed all men, have done through the ages: identify providence with the cause to which he was committed. Alone among statesmen of the ancient and modern periods, Lincoln had a sense of historical meaning so high as to cast doubt on the intentions of both sides, to put the enemy into the same category of ambiguity as the nation to which his life was committed. In his Second Inaugural Address Lincoln put the whole tragic drama of the Civil War in a religio-dramatic setting:

> Neither party expected for the war the magnitude or the duration which it has already attained. Neither anticipated that the cause of the conflict might cease with, or even before, the conflict itself should cease. Each looked for an easier triumph, and a result less fundamental and astounding. Both read the same Bible, and pray to the same God; and each invokes His aid against the other.

There follows a thoughtful passage which shows—more precisely, I think, than has any other statesman or any theologian—the relation of our moral commitments in history to our religious reservations about the partiality of our moral judgments. First, the moral judgment: "It may seem strange that any men should dare to ask a just God's assistance in wringing their bread from the sweat of other men's faces." Then, the religious reservation: "But let us judge not, that we be not judged. The prayers of both could not be answered. That of neither has been answered fully."

Surely such a nice balance of moral commitment and religious reservation in regard to the partiality of all historic commitments of biased men is a unique achievement. It is particularly remarkable for a responsible political leader; for it is the very nature of political commitments that those who make them claim more ultimate virtues for their cause than either a transcendent providence or a neutral posterity will validate. It was Lincoln's achievement to embrace a paradox which lies at the center of the spirituality of all Western culture: affirmation of a meaningful history along with religious reservation about the partiality and bias which human actors and agents betray in their definition of that meaning.

To embrace this paradox was an important achievement. For the evil by-product of the historical dynamism of Western culture was a fanaticism which confused partial meanings and contingent purposes with the ultimate meaning of life itself. Lincoln's lack of fanaticism, his spirit of magnanimity, was revealed in many of his policies but most of all in his attitude toward the defeated secessionists, a spirit beautifully expressed in his Second Inaugural: "With malice toward none; with charity for all; with firmness in the right, as God gives us to see the right, let us strive on to finish the work we are in. . . ." Unfortunately his untimely death at the hands of an assassin prevented him from carrying out his design of pacification and launched the nation into a terrible period characterized by vindictive crushing of a vanquished foe—a disaster from which we have not yet recovered. The stubbornness of the South's resistance to the present integration movement is part of the price we pay for the vindictiveness which Lincoln would have avoided.

But since the spirit of magnanimity grew from his apprehension of the biased character of all historic judgments and did not annul those judgments, we must turn to Lincoln's scheme of moral principles, his hierarchy of values, to ascertain the complexity of his compound of moral preferences, political and personal. His abhorrence of slavery was variously expressed but most vividly in the Second Inaugural. Yet Lincoln was not an abolitionist. The secessionist, he said in his First Inaugural, had "no oath registered in Heaven to destroy the government," but he himself had a "most solemn one to 'defend, preserve and protect' it." One might regard this preference as that of a patriot expressing a nation's primal impulse for collective survival. But his preference represented more than mere national patriotism. He had a Jeffersonian belief in the mission of the new nation to initiate, extend, and preserve democratic self-government. Thus for him not only national survival but the survival of democracy itself was involved in the fortunes of the Civil War.

In his brief but eloquent Gettysburg address, Lincoln defined the mission of the new nation in Jeffersonian terms: ". . . our fathers brought forth on this continent a new nation conceived in liberty and dedicated to the proposition that all men are created equal. Now we are engaged in a great civil war testing whether that nation, or any nation so conceived and so dedicated, can long endure." Lincoln evidently believed that the whole democratic cause was being tested in the destiny of our own nation—a belief which was natural in the middle of the nineteenth century when many European critics were prophesying the failure of our system of government and when the trends of history which would make democracy a universal pattern of government in western Europe were not yet apparent. The peroration of the Gettysburg address returned to the same theme: "that we here highly resolve that these dead shall not have died in vain, that this nation under God shall have a new birth of freedom, and that government of the people, by the people, for the people, shall not perish from the earth."

Lincoln's passion for saving the union was viewed by some critics as a personal concept of the irrevocable character of the covenant of the Constitution. A very high-minded leader of the secessionist states, Robert E. Lee, had a different conception: though he detested slavery, he felt himself bound in loyalty to his state of Virginia rather than to the nation. Since the Civil War itself, not to speak of the many unifying forces which made the nation one, subsequently altered the loyalties of our citizens, making state loyalty subordinate to national loyalty, it is safe to say that if Lincoln's conception of the irrevocable character of the national covenant was a personal conviction, it was eventually transmuted into a national one. In his First Inaugural Lincoln argued in favor of the irrevocability of the covenant in words which many of his contemporaries did not accept but which we take for granted:

> I hold that, in contemplation of universal law and of the Constitution, the Union of these states is perpetual. Perpetuity is implied, if not expressed, in the fundamental law of all national governments. It is safe to assert that no government proper ever had a provision in its organic law for its own termination. To the extent of my ability I shall take care, as the Constitution expressly enjoins me, that all the laws shall be faithfully executed in all the states.

There was of course a residue of moral ambiguity in Lincoln's devotion to national union. Sometimes that devotion involved his abhorrence of slavery. Thus:

> When he [Stephen A. Douglas] invites any people, willing to have slavery, to establish it, he is blowing out the moral lights around us. When he says he "cares not whether slavery is voted down or voted up—that it is a sacred right of self-government"—he is, in my judgment, penetrating the human soul and eradicating the light of reason and the love of liberty in this American people.

This absolute rejection of slavery seems at variance with the sentiment Lincoln expressed in a letter to Horace Greeley, assuring him that his "paramount object" was to save the union, and that if he could save it half slave and half free, he would do it. The contradiction in the two attitudes may be explained by the fact that the point at issue in the Douglas debates was the extension of slavery into free territories, as provided in the Kansas-Nebraska act. Lincoln was violently opposed to this policy, the more so since he believed that if the institution could be restricted to the original slave states, it would gradually die. In holding to this position he felt himself in firm accord with the Founding Fathers:

> The framers of the Constitution found the institution of slavery amongst their other institutions at the time. They found that by an effort to eradicate it, they might lose much of what they had already gained. They were, obliged to bow to this necessity. They gave power to Congress to abolish the slave trade at the end of twenty years. They also prohibited slavery in the territories where it did not exist. They did what they could and yielded to necessity for the rest. I also yield to all which follows from that necessity.

Lincoln's opposition to slavery cannot be questioned. If there is moral ambiguity in his position, it is an ambiguity which he shared with the Founding Fathers, the author of the Declaration of Independence, and with all responsible statesmen who pursue their ideals within the framework of the harmony and survival of the community. In short, he exhibited not his own moral ambiguity but the moral ambiguity of the political order itself.

Lincoln's attitude toward the principle of the Declaration of Independence "that all men are created equal" was, of course, informed by the ethos of his day. It was not the same as our present ethos, when we are charged with eliminating the last vestiges of slavery from our national life. Lincoln's attitude toward racial equality exhibited that compromise between the ideal of equality and the customary inequality which the institution of slavery had introduced into the ethos of the nation, which presumably was exhibited in the attitude of Thomas Jefferson, author of the Declaration.

In one of his debates with Douglas, Lincoln said:

I do not understand the Declaration to mean that all men are created equal in all respects. They are not our equal in color; but I suppose that it does mean to declare that all men are equal in some respects: they are equal in their right to "life, liberty, and the pursuit of happiness." Certainly, the Negro is not our equal in color—perhaps not in many other respects; still, in the right to put into his mouth the bread that his own hands have earned, he is the equal of every other man.

That affirmation of basic human equality is beyond reproach. One might argue that the assumption of a difference in color implies inequality; Lincoln either shared the color prejudices of his and our day or he was politically astute enough not to challenge popular prejudices too radically.

The chief source of tension between Lincoln and the abolitionists was his hesitancy to free the slaves. That hesitancy was not personal; it was the political calculation of a responsible statesman concerned to retain the loyalty of the border states (Lincoln reprimanded the commanders who freed the slaves in those states). And when he finally issued the Emancipation Proclamation (postponed for a year until victory would ensure that it was not regarded as a final desperate effort of a defeated nation), it was made applicable only to the Negroes in territories under Union arms. And in the words of a distinguished historian, "it had the eloquence of a bill of lading."

Not only our own abolitionists but also the critical British liberals failed to be moved by the proclamation. But both its timing and its immediate scope were the fruits of statesmanlike calculations; they revealed that Lincoln was primarily not a moral prophet but a responsible statesman. All his actions and attitudes can be explained and justified by his hierarchy of values, succinctly expressed in his statement to Greeley, "My paramount object in this struggle is to save the Union."

A conscientious politician is compelled to relate all the moral aspirations and all the moral hesitancies of the social forces of a free society to the primary goal, the survival of the community. In the political order, the value of justice takes an uneasy second place behind that of internal order. In reviewing Lincoln's catalogue of values one must come to the conclusion that his sense of justice was strong enough to give that value a position immediately beneath survival, not only of the nation's physical life but also of its system of democratic self-government, which he identified— perhaps too simply, as did all our fathers—with the survival of democracy throughout the world.

It may be significant that the moral ambiguities in the idealism of this man proved themselves religiously superior to the pure moral idealism of the abolitionists—the Horace Greeleys, the William Lloyd Garrisons, the Wendell Phillipses. This fact does not prove that responsible statesmen are morally superior to pure idealists; the idealists' opposition to slavery was an indispensable contribution to the dramatic struggle which saved the nation and purged it of the hated institution of human bondage. In his message to Congress in 1862 Lincoln, with caution prompted

by diverse sentiments on the issue within the union, revealed both the moral imperatives which prompted emancipation and the political considerations which made
him more cautious than the abolitionists wished:

> Among the friends of the Union there is great diversity of sentiment and of policy in
> regard to slavery and the African race amongst us. Some would perpetuate slavery;
> some would abolish it suddenly and without compensation; some would abolish it
> gradually and with compensation: some would remove the freed people from us, and
> some would retain them with us; and there are yet other minor diversities. Because
> of these diversities we waste much strength in struggles among ourselves. By mutual
> concession we should harmonize and act together.

As president, however, Lincoln acted for the nation, and the moral imperative of
the emancipation was eloquently expressed in these words from the same message:

> In giving freedom to the slave we assure freedom to the free—honorable alike in what
> we give and what we preserve. We shall nobly save or meanly lose the last best hope of
> earth. Other means may succeed; this could not fail. The way is plain, peaceful, gener-
> ous, just—a way which if followed the world will forever applaud and God must for-
> ever bless.

Lincoln's sense of the indivisibility of freedom and his conviction that emancipation of the slaves implied the opportunity to "nobly save . . . the last, best hope of
earth"—the cause of democratic government—is particularly significant for a generation called upon to remove the last remnants of human bondage from our national
life. It reminds us that as we give freedom we preserve our freedom and the prestige
of free institutions. It is clear that Lincoln believed that in a nation "conceived in
liberty and dedicated to the proposition that all men are created equal," moral ambiguity is limited to the field of tactics; in his case it was prompted by the diversity of
opinion on the issue of slavery. But the ambiguity ends in the strategy. The emancipation of the slaves gave and preserved liberty, gave it to the slave and preserved it
for all free men. Lincoln's 1862 message to Congress throws light not only on the
moral problems of politics in general but on our current integration problems.

Lincoln's moral superiority over the idealists stemmed primarily not from his
conscientiousness as a statesman but from the depth and height of his religious sense
of the meaning of the drama of history; from his consequent sensitivity to the problem posed by the taint of self-interest in the definitions of meaning; by the way
human agents corrupt the meaning in which they are involved; and from the magnanimity which was the natural fruit of this sensitivity.

The idealists were—as are most if not all idealists—self-righteous and consequently vindictive. Garrison may have made the southern response to the abolitionist movement the more stubborn because he interpreted social attitudes and evils as
the fruits of criminal tendencies. He did not understand that good men may inherit

social attitudes and become the bearers of social evil, even though their own consciences may be not perverse but merely conventional.

Failure to understand the complex causes of historical and societal evil made for the vindictiveness exhibited by the victors in the Civil War and for the consequent horrors of Reconstruction. As we try, now, a century later, to eliminate the last vestiges of slavery, we frequently encounter resentments in the South which are the fruits not so much of the terrible conflict as of the vengeance displayed in Reconstruction, when the actions of men from the North revealed that without humility idealism can be easily transmuted into cruelty.

If we analyze the whole import of the relation of moral idealism to fanaticism and of religious humility and contrition to magnanimity, and if we set the tension between Lincoln and the abolitionists in the context of this problem, the conclusion is inevitable: Abraham Lincoln was not only a statesman who saved the nation in the hour of its greatest peril but also a rare and unique human being who could be responsible in the discharge of historic tasks without equating his interpretation of the task with divine wisdom.

It is not too much to claim that, more adequately than any other statesman of modern history, Lincoln demonstrated the paradox of all human spirituality, and of Western historical dynamism in particular. The measure of his spiritual achievement becomes apparent when we compare him with the religiously inspired idealists among statesmen of the modern period—from Oliver Cromwell to Woodrow Wilson.

⌘

Notes to Chapter 6

Lincoln and the Problem of Civil Religion

1. Abraham Lincoln, "On the Perpetuation of Our Political Institutions: An Address before the Young Men's Lyceum of Springfield, Ill., Jan. 27, 1838," in *Abraham Lincoln: His Speeches and Writings,* ed. Roy P. Basler (Cleveland and New York, 1946), 76–85. Hereafter this address will be referred to in the text as "P.A."

2. As Dwight Anderson put it, the establishment of a political religion was one of two items on Lincoln's agenda for his presidency. *Abraham Lincoln and the Quest for Immortality,* (New York, 1982), 16.

3. Lord Charnwood, *Abraham Lincoln* (Garden City, N.Y., 1917), 439, as quoted by Glen Thurow, *Abraham Lincoln and American Political Religion* (Albany, N.Y., 1976), 11. Cf. also Robert Bellah, "Religion and the Legitimation of the American Republic," in *Varieties of Civil Religion,* ed. Robert Bellah and Phillip Hammond (San Francisco, 1980), 15: Abraham Lincoln was "our greatest, perhaps our only civil theologian."

4. John P. Diggins, *The Lost Soul of American Politics* (New York, 1984), 305.

5. Cf. the recent effort to generate a satisfactory definition of civil religion by Ellis M. West, "A Proposed Neutral Definition of Civil Religion," *Journal of Church and State* (Winter 1980), 23–40.

6. Consider the debate over Robert Bellah's recent discussion of civil religion. Robert Bellah, "Civil Religion in America," *Daedalus* (Winter 1967), 1–21; Bellah, *Beyond Belief* (New York, 1970); Bellah, *The Broken Covenant* (New York, 1975); Bellah and Hammond, *Varieties of Civil Religion*. Some typical critical reactions are assembled in Donald J. Jones and Russell E. Richey, *American Civil Religion* (New York, 1974); also cf. Phillip Hammond, "Pluralism and Law in the Formation of American Civil Religion," in Bellah and Hammond, eds., Varieties, 138; Bellah, "Religion and Legitimation," 3, 12.

7. Consider Richard Fenn, *Toward a Theory of Secularization*, (Norwich, CT, 1978), xviii; Bellah, "Religion and Legitimation," 4; Herbert U. Richardson, "What Makes a Society Political?" and Jurgen Moltmann, "The Cross and Civil Religion" in *Religion and Political Society* (New York, 1974), 9–49, 95–120.

8. Cf. Walter Berns, "Religion and the Founding Principle" in *The Moral Foundations of the American Republic*, ed. Robert Horwitz (Charlottesville, VA, 1986), 204–29.

9. John Locke, *The Letter Concerning Toleration*; Michael P. Zuckert, "Locke and the Problem of Civil Religion" in Horwitz, *Moral Foundations*, 180–203.

10. Cf. Edgar Lee Masters, *Lincoln the Man* (New York, 1931), 471–72, as quoted in Thurow, *American Political Religion*, 15–16; Anderson, *Quest for Immortality*, 99, sees Lincoln as the very tyrant he had warned against in the Perpetuation Address; his "political religion" had much to do, Anderson believes, with the genesis of that tyranny. A classic statement of the general point is J. L. Talmon, *The Origins of Totalitarian Democracy* (London, 1952).

11. Abraham Lincoln, Address delivered before the Springfield Washingtonian Temperance Society, 22 Feb. 1842, in Basler, ed., *Abraham Lincoln: His Speeches and Writings*, 131–41. Hereafter references to this address will be referred to in the text as "T.A."

12. Cf. Thurow, *American Political Religion*, 21.

Neither the Perpetuation Address nor the later Temperance Address have gone unnoticed before, of course, but I believe a new analysis is warranted. As George Anastaplo pointed out, the most serious previous reading of the speeches, that by Harry Jaffa, slighted the theme of civil religion in favor of themes like the political savior less visibly (if at all) present. Harry V. Jaffa, *Crisis of the House Divided* (Garden City, NY, 1959), chap. 9; George Anastaplo, "American Constitutionalism and the Virtue of Prudence: Philadelphia, Paris, Washington, Gettysburg," in *Abraham Lincoln, the Gettysburg Address, and American Constitutionalism*, ed. Leo Paul de Alverez (Irving, TX, 1976), 128, 165–67.

Glen Thurow does place the theme of civil religion at the center of his discussion of the Perpetuation Address. He thus remains closer than Jaffa to Lincoln's ostensible line of argument. Yet his interpretation culminates in a paradox he never satisfactorily resolved. He argues that the civil religion of reverence for the laws is the solution to which Lincoln appeals, but in making that appeal, Thurow also sees, "Lincoln invokes an authority whose power is fading" to guard against the results of the very fading of that power (Thurow, *American Political Religion*, 31, 33, 35–36). In other words, were the solution to which Lincoln appealed available, the solution would be unneccessary.

Thurow approaches Lincoln with the thought that Lincoln endorsed political religion "because of its relevance to political problems," and thus in terms of Lincoln's more or less explicit understanding of the political problems facing modern democracies (ibid., 14). Other, more recent studies used a psycho-historical approach in their attempts to fathom Lincoln's civil religion. According to George Forgie, the Perpetuation Address is testimony to Lincoln's deeply ambivalent relationship to "the fathers." On the one hand, he had a deep streak of "filio-piety": he wished to be a good son, a follower in their path and a preserver of their work. On the other hand, he sought the very highest kind of political fame, in the way of which stood the work of the fathers. Lincoln was thus drawn into patricidal and patriloyal attitudes at once, a situation psychically unsatisfactory and unstable. His "solution" was the tyrant he warned against in his Address. He created the tyrant out of "the undesireable wishes he could not recognize in himself." The tyrant was an externalized or "reified" version of his own "antagonistic feelings" toward the fathers. The tyrant was "the image of the bad son" he himself was but could not face. George Forgie, *Patricide in the House Divided* (New York, 1979), 56–87.

Like many such examples of psychological interpretation, Forgie's speculations are interesting, but also they distort the phenomenon they are attempting to explain. Even though the Perpetuation Address clearly looked to political religion as the solution to the problem described, Forgie arbitrarily dismisses this as "banal"; instead, he says, "it is indeed the prophecy of the tyrant rather than the plea for reason that represents Lincoln's solution to the problem of the post-heroic age. He looked less to preventing the emergence of this figure than to combatting and vanquishing him once he appeared." (ibid., 83) That interpretation may fit well with Forgie's psychological theory about Lincoln and his age, but it does not fit well with the speech it supposedly explicates.

Similar to Forgie's psychological interpretation—but not as clear—is Dwight Anderson's. In addition to psychological speculation of most uncertain relation to Lincoln's text, Anderson writes with a strong animus against Lincoln's project of a civil religion, which he sees as the source of "the ideological rationale for America to be the lawgiver to the world." Moreover, it threatens "religious absolutism and fanaticism," and provides a vehicle for later presidents to indulge their "imperial ambitions." (Anderson, *Quest for Immortality*, 8–10.) Such strong political prejudices, combined with the looseness of the psychological analysis, do not instill confidence in the analysis they produce.

13. The most careful textual study of the Perpetuation Address, Thurow's, provides the best example of the effects of missing this structural oddity. He treats the speech as though the call for a political religion is the climax of the talk, rather than its midpoint. *American Political Religion*, 20–37, esp. 23.

14. The call came in the twelfth paragraph of a twenty-four-paragraph speech.

15. Harry V. Jaffa, "Reflections on Thoreau and Lincoln: Civil Disobedience and the American Tradition," in *On Civil Disobedience*, ed. Robert Goldwin (Chicago, 1969), 59.

16. Many contemporary scholars now accept Lincoln's analysis. Cf. Bellah, "Religion and Legitimation," 14.

17. Forgie, (*Patricide*, 56–57,) claims that Lincoln presents the Founders as "impervious to personal ambition"!

18. Niccolò Machiavelli, *The Prince*, chap. 9.

19. Even Jaffa, in a place less well known than his famous *Crisis*, expresses doubts about the "solution" Lincoln propounds in the Perpetuation Address. Cf. "Reflections," 58.

20. Jaffa, *Crisis*, chap. 9; Thurow, *American Political Religion*, 65; Anderson, *Quest for immortality*, 68–72; Diggins, *Lost Soul*, 306–19.

21. Jaffa, "Reflections," 48–49.

22. But cf. Thurow's observations on the Perpetuation Address: "Mob violence was not only the subject, but the setting of Lincoln's address" (*American Political Religion*, 22).

23. Bernard Bailyn, *The Ideological Origins of the American Revolution* (Cambridge, Mass., 1967), chap. 6.

24. Machiavelli, *The Prince*, chap. 15.

25. Cf. Michael P. Zuckert, "Locke and the Problem of Civil Religion," in Horwitz, *Moral Foundations*, 183–89.

26. A presentation of a moral-political reform movement that shares much with Lincoln's account is Nathaniel Hawthorne's *Blithedale Romance*. See Catherine H. Zuckert, *Natural Right and the American Imagination* (Savage, Md., 1989), chap. 4. The founding of the Blithedale community is a task that appeals to a man of great talent and ambition like Hollingsworth. Hawthorne shared Lincoln's suspicion of the utopian character of the new moral impetus.

27. Cf. Anderson, *Quest for Immortality*, 105.

28. Cf. Thurow, *American Political Religion*, 118–19.

29. The role of time in Lincoln's thought has been frequently noticed before. Cf. Eva Brann, "A Reading of the Gettysburg Address," in de Alvarez, *The Gettysburg Address*, 20–21; Thurow, *American Political Religion*, 70–71, 91.

30. Speech at Springfield, Ill., 23 June 1857, in Basler, ed., *Abraham Lincoln: His Speeches and Writings*, 361.

31. I have sketched some of the chief features of the Lincolnian theory of a healthy civil religion and demonstrated echoes of these in his later speeches. Yet I have not mentioned the central but difficult issue—God. The practice of Lincoln's civil preaching showed clearly enough that God was to play a role at times, as in the Second Inaugural Address, but hardly in the Gettysburg Address. Interestingly enough, Lincoln indicated scarcely anything of what that role was to be in the two early speeches of chief concern here. A full-scale analysis of Lincoln's civil religion would require sustained meditation on Lincoln's appeals to God, but I cannot engage in that task here. The best treatment in the literature is in Thurow's discussions of the Gettysburg and Second Inaugural Addresses.

32. Cf. Zuckert, "Locke," 201–03.

Lincoln and the Problem of Political Religion

1. The reader will note that I am not making the claim that slavery itself was the sole or even primary cause of the Civil War. Rather, it seems clear that issues related to slavery, including duties imposed on the north by the Fugitive Slave Act, fears in the south regarding potential federal action against slaveholders' interests and issues related to the value of free labor and the role of the courts, combined to produce animosity and war.

2. Several states allowed for the practice of "studding" male slaves, and many positively excluded the formation and obligatory maintenance of families by masters. For a discussion of this phenomenon and its limits see Herbert George Gutman, *The Black Family in Slavery and Freedom, 1750–1925* (New York: Random House, 1977).

3. Abraham Lincoln, "Address to the Young Men's Lyceum of Springfield, Illinois," in *Lincoln: Speeches, Letters, Miscellaneous Writings, The Lincoln-Douglas Debates,"* (New York: Library of America, 1989), 32–33. Emphasis in original.

4. While, as Cushing Strout points out, discussion of civil religion in America goes back at least as far as Carl Becker's 1914 treatment of the Great Awakening revivals ("Tocqueville and Republican Religion," *Political Theory*, 8 [February 1980] 9, 11), Robert N. Bellah gener-

ally is credited with having popularized the notion of an "American Civil Religion." See his *Beyond Belief: Essays on Religion in a Post-Traditional World* (New York: Harper & Row, 1970). That the extensive literature on civil religion makes frequent reference to Lincoln's "political religion" shows that the two terms are intended to convey the same meaning. Here I use the phrase "political religion" for the simple reason that it was Lincoln's.

5. W. Lance Bennett, "Imitation, Ambiguity, and Drama in Political Life: Civil Religion and the Dilemmas of Public Morality," 41 *Journal of Politics* 1 (February, 1979), 106–133, 109. (Citations omitted). Sanford Kessler's working definition is succinct and indicative: "Civil religion refers to religion which serves secular as opposed to transcendent or otherworldly ends." That is, "civil" religion is political in its purpose. Sanford Kessler, "Tocqueville on Civil Religion and Liberal Democracy," *Journal of Politics*, vol. 39, 1977, 120.

6. "Address at Gettysburg, Pennsylvania" in *Lincoln*, vol. 1, 536.

7. St. Augustine, trans. Henry Bettenson (New York: Penguin, 1972) Book IV, chap. 4, 139.

8. Augustine states, for example, that "true justice is found only in that commonwealth whose founder and ruler is Christ." *City of God*, Book II, chap. 21, 75.

9. *Beyond Belief*, 168. See also Garry Wills, *Under God: Religion and American Politics* (New York: Simon & Schuster, 1990), 116–17.

10. Bennett, "Imitation," 106.

11. Thus the need for political religion to "transcend the symbolism of divided social experience and create a semblance of political solidarity." Bennett, "Imitation," 111.

12. Bennett, "Imitation," 107.

13. Robert N. Bellah, *The Broken Covenant: American Civil Religion in Time of Trial* (New York: Seabury Press, 1975) 62.

14. Harry V. Jaffa, *The Conditions of Freedom* (Baltimore: Johns Hopkins University Press, 1975) 189. See also the discussion in William S. Corlett, Jr., "The Availability of Lincoln's Political Religion," *Political Theory*, 8 (November 1982), 520, 527–28.

15. See Bennett, "Imitation," 110.

16. Corlett, "Availability," 537.

17. This point, rooted particularly in Lincoln's Second Inaugural Address, is easily overstated. There Lincoln notes that both sides in the Civil War read the same Bible and prayed to the same God, that God's providence may be supposed to have willed both the coming and the going of slavery, as well as the payment for its inherent abuses through the blood spilled in war. Yet the language is ambiguous ("If we shall suppose that" slavery was willed by God, "with firmness in the right, as God gives us to see the right.") Thus the speech could be seen as merely urging humility in assessing mankind's limited but real ability to read the will of God. Still, it can be argued that Lincoln saw Providence, not as the means by which God influences this world, but as the work of laws instituted by God, placing God at two removes from human action. See my "The Intellectuals and Abraham Lincoln," *University Bookman*, 41 (Fall/Winter 2001), 38.

18. See especially *Beyond Belief: Essays on Religion in a Post-Traditional World* (New York: Harper & Row, 1970), 181–82, where Bellah praises the biblical/republican strain within the American civil religion for supplying the millennial expectations necessary for great national projects like Lyndon Johnson's Great Society.

19. Garry Wills, *Under God*, 382–82; 379–80.

20. Nisbet, "Rousseau and Totalitarianism," *The Journal of Politics*, 5 (May 1943), 106.

21. Nisbet, "Rousseau and Totalitarianism," 107–108.

22. For a contemporary Rousseauean argument for the elimination of the "private" sphere see Wills, *Under God,* 302, where he praises the fact that, with the elimination of a private sphere, "women and priests can participate in public life *only* as citizens, with no special preserve of their own to make people fall silent." (Emphasis in original).

23. Robert A. Nisbet, "Uneasy Cousins" in George W. Carey, ed., *Freedom and Virtue: The Conservative/Libertarian Debate* (Wilmington, DE: ISI Books, 1998), 38–39. Nisbet attributes the argument, here, to Edmund Burke, noting its continuing applicability.

24. Lincoln, "A Meditation on Proverbs 15:11," in Roy P. Basler, ed., *The Collected Works of Abraham Lincoln* (New Brunswick: Rutgers University Press, 1953), vol. iv, 168 (emphasis in original).

25. On Bellah see especially "The Revolution and the Civil Religion," in Jerald C. Grauer, ed., *Religion and the American Revolution* (Philadelphia: Fortress Press, 1976). Jaffa's work centers on this theme. See for example *A New Birth of Freedom: Abraham Lincoln and the Coming of the Civil War* (Lanham, MD: Rowman & Littlefield, 2000). I take up Wills's interpretation below.

26. Garry Wills, *Lincoln at Gettysburg: The Words that Remade America* (New York: Simon & Schuster, 1992), 40.

27. Calhoun, *Union and Liberty: The Political Philosophy of John C. Calhoun,* ed. Ross Lence (Liberty Fund, 1992), 565–70.

28. Willmoore Kendall and George W. Carey, *The Basic Symbols of the American Political Tradition* (Washington, D.C.: Catholic University Press, 1995), 155.

29. Harry V. Jaffa, *A New Birth of Freedom.*

30. See for example "The Moral Crisis in American Public Life," (October 17, 1995 Address at Southwest Missouri State University, viewed online at http://publicaffairs.smsu.edu/why/articles/bellah.html, June 2, 2003).

31. Jaffa interprets Lincoln's equality as one of opportunity, Bellah and Wills demand a more substantive equality that will assure full participation in public life. All agree that equality entails equal rights, but wish to establish rights to different things.

32. Garry Wills, *Inventing America: Jefferson's Declaration of Independence* (Garden City, NY: Doubleday, 1978), xxii–xxiv.

33. Introduction to *Basic Symbols,* xxii–xxiii. Emphasis in original.

34. See for example Russell Kirk "The Errors of Ideology" in *The Politics of Prudence* (Bryn Mawr, PA: Intercollegiate Studies Institute, 1993).

35. One recent formulation of Bellah's program for reorganizing the world is "global localism," whereby the democratic process will be used to eliminate current institutions, beliefs, and practices in favor of ethnic variety and "openness." See Robert N. Bellah, Richard Madsen, William M. Sullivan, Ann Swidler, and Steven M. Tipton, *The Good Society* (New York: Knopf, 1991), 275.

36. Bertrand de Jouvenel, *On Power* (Indianapolis: Liberty Fund, 1993), 329.

37. Jouvenel, *On Power,* 15.

38. Eric Voegelin, *The New Science of Politics: An Introduction* (Chicago: University of Chicago Press, 1952), 188.

39. Voegelin, *New Science of Politics,* 317–18. Jouvenel specifically mentions the British aristocracy as well as workmen's guilds, employers, and the French parliamentary class.

40. Voegelin, *New Science of Politics,* 326.

41. Voegelin, *New Science of Politics*, 320–21.

42. Voegelin, *New Science of Politics*, 394.

43. Voegelin, *New Science of Politics*, 395.

44. Cushing Strout, "Tocqueville and Republican Religion: Revisiting the Visitor" *Political Theory,* Vol. 8, No. 1, February 1980, 14–15. Here Strout quotes Lerner's introduction to Tocqueville's *Democracy in America* (New York: Harper & Row, 1966), iii.

45. This much should be non-controversial. See for example vol. 1, 316: "The law permits Americans to do what they please, religion prevents them from conceiving, and forbids them to commit, what is rash or unjust." See also vol. 1, 303–307 for Tocqueville's discussion of religion's indirect influence on political society, emphasizing its provision of steady morals, support for the marriage tie and bounds within which to confine the restless imagination.

46. Peter Dennis Bathory, "Tocqueville on Citizenship and Faith: A Response to Cushing Strout," *Political Theory,* Vol. 8, No. 1, February 1980, 33–34.

47. See Kessler, "Tocqueville on Civil Religion," 120–21 and citations therein.

48. Kessler, "Tocqueville on Civil Religion," 120.

49. Tocqueville, *Democracy,* vol. 2, 11.

50. In Frohnen, ed., *The American Republic: Primary Sources* (Indianapolis: Liberty Fund, 2003), 710.

51. See for example Tocqueville, *Democracy,* v. 2, 7, where he discusses the tendency of all revolutions to break down accepted ideas and institutions, throwing individuals back on their own reason and interest while at the same time calling accepted general ideas into question.

52. That, as Allen Guelzo points out, Lincoln's use of the Declaration for political-religious purposes had roots in Whig Party rhetoric is a point of historical interest, but has little bearing on Lincoln's responsibility for the faith he propagated. See Guelzo, *Abraham Lincoln: Redeemer President* (Grand Rapids, MI: Eerdmans, 1999), 194–7.

Chapter 7

LINCOLN, THE UNION, AND THE ROLE OF THE STATE

What did the Union mean to Lincoln? Did his preservation of the Union upset the federal division of power between the national and state governments?

I hold, that in contemplation of universal law, and of the Constitution, the Union of these States is perpetual. Perpetuity is implied, if not expressed, in the fundamental law of all national governments. It is safe to assert that no government proper, ever had a provision in its organic law for its own termination. Continue to execute all the express provisions of our national Constitution, and the Union will endure forever—it being impossible to destroy it, except by some action not provided for in the instrument itself.

Again, if the United States be not a government proper, but an association of States in the nature of contract merely, can it, as a contract, be peaceably unmade, by less than all the parties who made it? One party to a contract may violate it—break it, so to speak; but does it not require all to lawfully rescind it?

Descending from these general principles, we find the proposition that, in legal contemplation, the Union is perpetual, confirmed by the history of the Union itself. The Union is much older than the Constitution. It was formed in fact, by the Articles of Association in 1774. It was matured and continued by the Declaration of Independence in 1776. It was further matured and the faith of all the then thirteen States expressly plighted and engaged that it should be perpetual, by the Articles of Confederation in 1778. And finally, in 1787, one of the declared objects for ordaining and establishing the Constitution, was *"to form a more perfect union."*

Abraham Lincoln, First Inaugural, March 4, 1861

★ Frank J. Williams and William D. Pederson, "Lincoln as an Advocate of Positive Government"
★ Thomas J. DiLorenzo, "The Great Centralizer: Abraham Lincoln and the War between the States"
★ Rogan Kersh, "Forever Worthy of the Saving: Lincoln and a More Moral Union"
★ George Anastaplo, "Walt Whitman's Abraham Lincoln"

రం

LINCOLN AS AN ADVOCATE OF POSITIVE GOVERNMENT

Frank J. Williams and William D. Pederson

TRADITIONALLY, conservatives and liberals are considered political polar opposites. Conservatives favor less government. They advocate laissez-faire economics and preservation of property rights. Liberals embrace governmental involvement. They champion government regulation of the economy and expansion of human rights. Because conservatives tend to want to preserve the status quo they resist change; liberals challenge the status quo to accomplish change.

Partisan parties have emerged and vanished from the American political landscape throughout U.S. history, but tensions between conservative and liberal philosophies of government continue unabated. Presidents representing both philosophies can be identified, but not all presidents fit entirely under the umbrella of conservatism or liberalism.

In particular, the sixteenth president, Abraham Lincoln, cannot be categorized simplistically as liberal or conservative. Both can be detected in his presidential behavior, but he cannot be defined as one or the other. He blended characteristics of conservatism and liberalism in his touchstone presidency to become the enduring model of democratic leadership.

Lincoln's appeal to both camps is reflected in his diverse admirers. For instance, in contemporary America, Harry Jaffa, a former speechwriter for conservative Republican Barry Goldwater, admires Lincoln. But so does Mario Cuomo, the former liberal governor of New York.[1]

It is telling that Lincoln's most serious critics today are neither conservatives nor liberals. Despite their disparate philosophies, both conservatives and liberals understand that democratic politics requires that they engage in an ongoing dialogue over what is and what ought to be.

Lincoln's most serious critics today are "libertarians," who would overlay privatization of all government services—except a domestic police force and military for national self-defense—with laissez-faire economics. In this respect they take conservatism to the extreme. Similar to liberals in the arena of human rights but more extreme, libertarians are absolutists about personal rights. They reject any type of governmental intrusion into their personal lives—especially conduct in the privacy of one's home—as abhorrent.

Like other extremists, especially abolitionists in the years leading up to the Civil War, they would have ignored the plight of the slaves and permitted the South to secede from the Union in the name of a right to self-determination. As a result of Lincoln's pro-Union stance, contemporary libertarians view him as the equivalent of a dictator rather than as the greatest democrat in world history. They argue that not only did Lincoln deny the South its right to secede but also that he committed massive habeas corpus violations against some thirteen thousand Southern sympathizers. It is noteworthy that modern day Lincoln detractors have little to say about the institution of slavery or the Union perspective about why the Civil War was fought.

The purpose of this essay is to determine Lincoln's view of the role of government in society. To accomplish its purpose, this essay is divided into four parts: (1) Lincoln's overall philosophy of government (2) his view of the presidency and "positive government" (3) his domestic policies, and (4) some conclusions about Lincoln's practice of the proper role of government in a democratic polity.

Because there has never been a libertarian polity in history, the argument of this essay contends that libertarians are idealists who do not really understand the nature of democratic politics and, therefore, have never succeeded in developing a practical application from their concepts. Instead, they cloak their elitism with self-righteousness and foist themselves on the back of society's less gifted and less talented without using their platform to address the needs of their supporters. They are not their brothers' keepers. In fact, they seem to think that the Bible had it wrong—the self-anointed elite are owed a better life that should be maintained in perpetuity by their less fortunate brethren.

Lincoln's Philosophy of Government

As a lawyer-politician for virtually his entire adult life, Abraham Lincoln had the time to contemplate the proper role of government in society, the types of government throughout history and in particular how America's experiment in self-government fit into the historical evaluation of law and democratic politics. In fact, some scholars credit Lincoln as one of the top ten lawyers in American history, largely because he understood the significance of the Civil War in the evolution of democratic government.[2]

In his 1838 "Address before the Young Men's Lyceum," one of Lincoln's first public speeches, he clearly positioned himself against anarchy and lawlessness. Government was a necessity and so were reason and the rule of law, which he contrasted with mob violence.[3] From his early life experiences tied to the border state where he was born and Indiana and Illinois where he later lived, Lincoln developed an appreciation of the need for economic development and how national government could assist in that process. By 1854, he articulated an explanation for the purpose of government:

> The legitimate object of government, is to do for a community of people, whatever they need to have done, but cannot do, *at all*, or cannot, *so well do*, for themselves—in their separate, and individual capacities.[4]

That philosophy defines "positive government"—government that has a duty to step in and help people when they cannot help themselves. Dwight David Eisenhower repeatedly quoted Lincoln's standard of positive government during his administration. Rather than try to dismantle the New Deal which FDR had created to deal with the Great Depression and World War II, to the surprise of many he tried to build on it. In fact, the greatest public works project in world history was the building of the interstate highway system which Eisenhower signed into law. Rather than pure laissez-faire economics, Lincoln and Eisenhower believed in a mixed governmental intervention. Jefferson's notion of "negative government," that the best government is the least amount of government might sound attractive, but when tempted with one of the greatest land deals in modern history, Jefferson went against his stated position to make the 1803 Louisiana Purchase. When philosophy collided with practicality, Jefferson suddenly became a Hamiltonian.

In the clash between free labor and slavery, there was no question that the Great Emancipator would favor free enterprise. He displayed a photograph of the English liberal John Bright (1811–1889) in the outer office of the presidential mansion.[5] In his December 1861 message to Congress, Lincoln wrote

> Labor is prior to and independent of capital. Capital is only the fruit of labor, and could never have existed if labor had not first existed. Labor is the superior of capital, and deserves much the higher consideration. Capital has its rights, which are as worthy of protection as any other rights.[6]

The reason that Lincoln found the Union worth preserving was that it was founded on the notion of natural rights, which he believed governments were obligated to observe. This suggested that governments also should observe "the right to rise" in society, just as Lincoln himself had done.[7] A Whig until he finally joined the new Republican Party, Lincoln was a strong advocate of Henry Clay's "America System" that encouraged internal development. Lincoln was the only president to hold a patent, which was related to the use of canals, and he was a railroad lawyer during his attorney days. Both gave Lincoln perspective about economic development and persuaded him that economic development was essential not only to building the West but also as a tool for improving the lives of individual Americans.

The Presidency and Positive Government

Lincoln wore the mantle of presidential power comfortably and his use of it surprised many during his time as well as later. Rather than a restrained use of presidential power, as one might expect from a one-time Whig since the Whigs criticized Andrew Jackson's exercise of it with the derisive moniker "King Andrew," Lincoln actively exercised more extra-constitutional power than any other president prior to Franklin Roosevelt. In direct contrast to James Buchanan, his predecessor who refused to deal with the threat of secession, Lincoln acted like a Hamiltonian in regard to presidential power. In the *Federalist Papers*, No. 70, Hamilton wrote "Energy in the executive is a leading character of good government."

Compared to Buchanan's inertia, Lincoln's actions were breathtaking. He instituted a blockade of Southern ports, closed U.S. mail to "disloyal politicians," expanded the regular military, pledged the federal government's credit to private parties, required army officers to renew their loyalty oaths, suspended the writ of habeas corpus and issued the Emancipation Proclamation.[8] What separates Lincoln from a dictator is that he fully understood that the Congress had the right to pass judgment on his unilateral actions.

Not only did the Republican Congress back up Lincoln's actions, its members came to power with a legislative agenda that set precedent for FDR's historical "First Hundred Days" in dealing with the Great Depression. Based on both the South's secession and his own broad interpretation of the Constitution, Lincoln signed into law three pieces of legislation in 1862 which are ranked by some among the top ten pieces of Congressional legislation in history.[9] They were legislative landmarks crafted to broaden the emerging middle class and assist it in its collective effort to rise in society.

Perhaps the most important piece of the three is the Land Grant College Act of 1862, in many ways the first significant social legislation ever enacted by the Congress. It opened higher education to the working and middle class—including women—by creating "institutions of agricultural and mechanical instruction" that often evolved into general universities on federal lands. It was a giant governmental step that nudged the middle class along the ladder of upward social and economic mobility. Ultimately some sixty-eight land grant colleges and universities were established in the United States, many of them becoming major research institutions. The result was transformation of higher education into one of America's great success stories and the envy of the world.

The second piece of legislation was the Homestead Act, signed into law by Lincoln on May 20, 1862. It made the dream of land ownership a reality for the immigrant masses. The Homestead Act opened large tracts of land, divided into 160-acre farms, to those who were willing to become citizens, pay a ten dollar registration fee, and work the land for five years. Thousands of immigrants to the United States seized the opportunity to realize their American dreams.

The third major piece of legislation was also a plank of the Republican Party platform in 1860 and 1864. It made possible the building of a railroad to California, which would become the backbone for development of the nation's heartland. On July 1, 1862, Lincoln signed legislation which led to the eventual building of the first transcontinental railroad and telegraph line.

Both the Homestead Act and the Pacific Railroad Act were viewed as military necessities, but they achieved a broader goal of tying together the emerging geographic giant that was emerging as a world industrial force.

Lincoln also backed Salmon P. Chase's national banking system in February 1863. It created a new office of the Comptroller of the Currency, a federal income tax with a progressive rate. He also signed into law the legislation which created the first paper currency issued by the federal government.

His lifelong interest in science and technology inspired Lincoln to create the National Academy of Science, the Armed Forces Institute of Pathology, and the Department of Agriculture. He also created the Bureau of Veterans Affairs.

Conclusion

Whereas his Democratic predecessors in the presidency acted as if they were constitutionally constipated in addressing the new needs of an expanding middle class, Lincoln actively supported the Republican platform to tackle those needs. Moreover, he was willing to use his presidential war powers to prevent secession. He transformed the nation with his Emancipation Proclamation. The Republican legislative agenda similarly wrought profound national change by aiding America's burgeoning middle class and starting the economic modernization of the nation. Lincoln used government as a tool to dignify human beings regardless of race, class, or gender.

Critics, primarily libertarians, who point to America's sixteenth president as the instigator of "big government" misread American and world history. As the United States developed as a nation, Lincoln was willing to use the national government to facilitate that development. He was willing to fight to preserve the Union's embodiment of self-government which gave all people a "right to rise" in society. Secession would not only have sacrificed black Americans but would also likely have allowed the Old World powers to balkanize "the last best hope" of mankind. It was Lincoln's willingness "to think anew" and guide the democratic progress using the powers of positive government that makes his views of government relevant, even in the age of the global economy.[10] If the United States is reluctant to assert itself in the world both domestically and internationally, governments abroad—both past and present—have shown and continue to show an eagerness to step in to promote their own self-interests above American interests. They are not hampered by libertarian tenets. Today's idealists need to take a history lesson from Thomas Jefferson who was able to divorce himself from ideological constraints in order to acquire an expanded geographic republic. It was a lesson that Abraham Lincoln understood in his determination to preserve the Union.

ॐ

THE GREAT CENTRALIZER: ABRAHAM LINCOLN
AND THE WAR BETWEEN THE STATES

Thomas J. DiLorenzo

> By the 1850s the authority of all government in America was at a low
> point; government to the American was, at most, merely an institution
> with a negative role, a guardian of fair play.
>
> David Donald, *Lincoln Reconsidered*

> The war . . . has tended, more than any other event in the history of the
> country to militate against the Jeffersonian idea, that "the best govern-
> ment is that which governs least."
>
> Illinois Governor Richard Yates, January 2, 1865

MANY HISTORIANS CONSIDER President Franklin D. Roosevelt's New Deal a
point of demarcation with respect to the role of government in America, whereby
the political economy was transformed from a limited, constitutional government
to a highly centralized welfare-warfare state. Others go farther back to the so-called
Progressive Era of the early twentieth century. But a clearer breaking point in the
relationship between American citizens and the state was the South's defeat in its
war for independence.

Lincoln's election in 1860 effectively signaled the long-fought-for victory of the
(by then defunct) Whig Party, the political descendants of the Federalists. Lincoln
considered himself the political heir of Henry Clay, the leader of the Whigs, who
for forty years championed the building of an American empire through protectionist tariffs, corporate welfare (euphemistically called "internal improvements"), a central bank, and a highly centralized state. Clay called that policy combination the
"American System." Commenting on Lincoln's July 16, 1852, eulogy for Clay, Roy
Basler, the editor of Lincoln's collected works, observed that "one could hardly read
any paragraph in [the eulogy] without feeling that Lincoln was, consciously or
unconsciously, inviting comparison and contrast of himself with [Clay]" (1946, 18).

Before his election as president, Lincoln spent virtually his entire twenty-eight-
year political career promoting the so-called American System. Basler writes that as

*This article is reprinted with permission of the publisher from The Independent Review: A
Journal of Political Economy (Fall 1998, vol. III, no. 2, pp. 243–271). Copyright 1998, The Independent Institute, 100 Swan Way, Oakland, California 94621–1428 USA; info@independent.org; www
.independent.org.

of 1857 Lincoln "had no solution to the problem of slavery except the colonization idea which he had inherited from Henry Clay . . . when he spoke . . . of respecting the Negro as a human being, his words lacked effectiveness" (23). The American System, not slavery, preoccupied Lincoln's political mind.

Lincoln will forever be remembered as the Great Emancipator. But he was also the Great Centralizer, whose policies did much to undermine the decentralized, federal system established by the Founders.

Slavery's Role in Precipitating and Sustaining the War

Historical research on the causes of the War between the States ranges from claims that slavery was the predominant cause (Foner 1974) to the view of James Ford Rhodes that "of the American Civil War it may safely be asserted that there was a single cause, slavery" (Stampp 1974, 118). Slavery was certainly an important element, but its importance seems to have been exaggerated as much as other causes—particularly economic motivations—have been overlooked or ignored.

For well over a century, objective analyses of Lincoln have been all but censored by the history profession through the tactic of insinuating that anyone who criticizes Lincoln must secretly approve of antebellum slavery. So, for the record, I affirm that slavery is an evil institution—as are all government-enforced racial policies, including forced segregation, coerced integration, and mandatory racial quotas. Such policies have no place in a free society because they rest on the collectivist idea that people should be judged as members of racial or ethnic groups, not as individuals. But a free society must be based on the idea of the equality of *individual* rights under the law, with the role of government restricted to protecting those individual rights and removing barriers to their enjoyment. In this sense the abolition of slavery was a giant step forward for the cause of human freedom everywhere.

In that light, open-minded Americans should consider that many of Lincoln's personal views on race relations can be described only as the views of a white supremacist. Indeed, he even used the words "superior and inferior" to define the "proper" places of the two races in American society. In the September 18, 1858, debate with Senator Stephen Douglas, he stated:

> I will say then that I am not, nor ever have been in favor of bringing about in any way the social and political equality of the white and black races—that I am not nor ever have been in favor of making voters or jurors of Negroes, nor of qualifying them to hold office, nor to intermarry with white people; and I will say in addition to this that there is a physical difference between the white and black races which I believe will for ever forbid the two races from living together on terms of social and political equality. And inasmuch as they cannot so live, while they do remain together there must be the position of superior and inferior, and I as much as any other man am in favor of having the superior position assigned to the white race. (Basler 1953, 145–46)

When asked what should be done if the slaves were ever freed, Lincoln's initial response was to suggest sending them all back to Africa: "Send them to Liberia, to their own native land. But free them and make them politically and socially our equals? My own feelings will not admit this" (Basler 1953, 255–56). As president, Lincoln held a meeting in the White House with freed black leaders, whom he encouraged to lead a colonization effort back to Africa by example. He developed plans to send freed blacks to Haiti and Central America—anywhere but the United States (370–75).

Lincoln's idol, Henry Clay, was a lifelong member of the American Colonization Society and was its president when he died. In his 1852 eulogy, Lincoln approvingly quoted Clay's statement that "there is a moral fitness in the idea of returning to Africa her children" (Basler 1946, 266). Clay's colonization proposal "was made twenty-five years ago," Lincoln observed, but "every succeeding year has added strength to the hope of its realization—May it indeed be realized!" (277).

Some ten years later, in his December 1, 1862, message to Congress, Lincoln reiterated that "I cannot make it better known than it already is, that I strongly favor colonization" (685).

Lincoln frequently castigated the abolitionists as zealots who "would shiver into fragments the Union of these States; tear to tatters its now venerated constitution; and even burn the last copy of the Bible, rather than slavery should continue a single hour" (Basler 1946, 274). But being the master politician, he adopted the position of his political role model, slave owner Henry Clay. As described by Robert Johannsen, that position was "opposition to slavery in principle, toleration of it in practice, and a vigorous hostility toward the abolition movement" (1991, 22).

Lincoln had no intention to disturb Southern slavery in 1860. In his First Inaugural Address he announced that "I have no purpose, directly or indirectly, to interfere with the institution of slavery in the States where it exists. I believe I have no lawful right to do so, and I have no inclination to do so" (Basler 1946, 580). He also promised in the same address to uphold and strengthen the fugitive slave clause of the Constitution, even though lax or nonenforcement of that clause would have quickened slavery's demise.

Interestingly, none of the four political parties that fielded candidates in the 1860 election even mentioned the abolition of Southern slavery in its platform (Louisiana State University Civil War Institute 1998). When the issue of slavery was brought up, it was in the context of its prohibition in the territories, not in the South. Even then, the reason for objecting to the extension of slavery was not always a moral one. Although undoubtedly some sincere abolitionists believed that disallowing slavery in the territories would contribute to its eventual demise everywhere, a prominent concern was that freed slaves would then compete with white laborers in the territories. As William Seward explained, "the motive of those who protested against the extension of slavery had always really been concern for the welfare of the white man, and not an unnatural sympathy for the Negro" (McPherson 1966, 24).

Horace Greeley explained the Republican Party's position on the extension of slavery in the new territories: "All the unoccupied territory . . . shall be reserved for the benefit of the white Caucasian race—a thing which cannot be except by the exclusion of slavery" (Berwanger 1967, 130). Illinois senator and Lincoln confidant Lyman Trumball announced in 1859 that "we, the Republican party, are the white man's party. We are for the free white man, and for making white labor acceptable and honorable, which it can never be when Negro slave labor is brought into competition with it" (133).

When Representative David Wilmot of Pennsylvania introduced his historic proviso to exclude slavery from the territories acquired after the Mexican War, he carefully explained that he had "no morbid sympathy for the slave," but "plead the cause and the rights of white freemen. I would preserve to free white labor a fair country, a rich inheritance, where the sons of toil, of my own race and color, can live without the disgrace which association with Negro slavery brings upon free labor" (Litwack 1961, 47).

Lincoln's actions were consistent with his words with regard to the slavery issue. In the summer of 1861 he was presented with an opportunity to liberate thousands of slaves, but he refused to do so. General John Frémont, the Republican candidate for president in 1856, was the Union army's military commander in Missouri. Frémont drew a line across the state from east to west separating the pro-Confederacy side from the pro-Union side and issued an order stating that any individual on the Confederate side caught carrying a firearm would be shot and that anyone aiding the secessionists would have his slaves emancipated. Slave-owning Unionists would be left undisturbed (Nevins 1959, 337; Foote 1986, vol. 1, 95–97; Randall and Donald 1961, 371–72).

When Frémont sent his order to Lincoln for approval, Lincoln not only disapproved it; he stripped Frémont of his command. For Lincoln's stated objective was to "save the Union" and to preserve federal power, not to free the slaves. As he stated in his famous August 22, 1862, public letter to *New York Daily Tribune* editor Horace Greeley:

> My paramount object in this struggle is to save the Union, and is *not* either to save or to destroy slavery. If I could save the Union without freeing *any* slave I would do it; and if I could save it by freeing some and leaving others alone I would also do that. What I do about slavery, and the colored race, I do because I believe it helps to save the Union. (Basler 1946, 652)

Some Northern opinion makers and politicians excoriated Lincoln for his treatment of Frémont. Senator Ben Wade of Ohio wrote "in bitter execration" that "the President don't object to General Frémont's taking the life of the owners of slaves, when found in rebellion, but to confiscate their property and emancipate their slaves he thinks monstrous" (Nevins 1959, 340).

Unlike Frémont's order, which would have liberated some slaves, Lincoln's Emancipation Proclamation did not free a single slave. The proclamation applied only to rebel territory, even though at the time the North controlled large parts of the South, including much of Tennessee and Virginia, where it would have been possible to emancipate thousands of slaves.

Indeed, many slaves who ended up in the hands of the Union army were not set free but were put to work doing some of the most unpleasant tasks in and around army encampments. Others were sent back to their owners by federal troops.

Congress passed several "confiscation acts," which permitted Union soldiers to confiscate the slaves (and other property) in conquered rebel territory. The slaves were then enslaved by the Union army. As one Illinois lieutenant reported, "I have eleven Negroes in my company now. They do every particle of the dirty work. Two women among them do the washing for the company" (McPherson 1997, 119).

Specifically exempted from the Emancipation Proclamation were the Louisiana parishes of "St. Bernard, Plaquemines, Jefferson, St. John, St. Charles, St. James, Ascension, Assumption, Terrebonne, Lafourche, St. Mary, St. Martin, and Orleans" (Eliot 1910, 324). Also exempted by name were the federally controlled areas of West Virginia, large parts of Virginia, and all the Union-controlled border states, such as Maryland and Kentucky.

The *New York World* newspaper sharply criticized Lincoln's action by editorializing, "The President has purposely made the proclamation inoperative in all places where we have gained a military footing which makes the slaves accessible. He has proclaimed emancipation only where he has notoriously no power to execute it" (Foote 1986, vol. I, 708). The *London Spectator* (October 11, 1862) agreed completely, writing that "the principle is not that a human being cannot justly own another, but that he cannot own him unless he is loyal to the United States government" (Foote 1986, 707–8).

A case can be made that the Emancipation Proclamation was primarily a public relations strategy employed out of desperation because of the utter failure of the federal armies to subdue the rebels during the first eighteen months of the war. Most likely it was designed to encourage the European powers—especially England—to cease trading with the South.

After the Confederates scored smashing victories over Union armies in the battles of First Manassas (July 1861), Seven Days (June 1862), Second Manassas (August 1862), and Fredericksburg (December 1862), "the nadir of Northern depression seems to have been reached" (Randall and Donald 1966, 225). In this military context, Lincoln decided on the Emancipation Proclamation, which he considered to be more or less a last-ditch effort after the Union had reached "the end of our rope on the [military] plan of operation" (Angle 1947, 407).

But if the objective of the Emancipation Proclamation was to encourage England to stop assisting the secessionists by trading with them, it was a failure. Most British opinion makers criticized the proclamation as a transparent ruse. In his survey of

British attitudes toward the war, the historian Sheldon Vanauken observed that by January of 1863,

> The Confederate States were winning the war. Only a few days before, Lee had smashed Burnside at Fredericksburg. The Proclamation freed all the slaves *within* the Confederate lines, that is, the slaves which the Federal armies were manifestly unable to reach. These slaves were grouped on the isolated plantations, controlled for the most part by women since their gentlemen were off to the wars. The only possible effect of the Proclamation would be the dreaded servile insurrection. . . . Either a slave rising or nothing. So Englishmen saw it. Lincoln's insincerity was regarded as proven by two things: his earlier denial of any lawful right or wish to free the slaves; and, especially, his not freeing the slaves in "loyal" Kentucky and other United States areas or even in Confederate areas occupied by the United States troops, such as New Orleans. (1989, 302)

Most Northerners in 1863 were shocked and surprised by the Emancipation Proclamation because they had not previously been told by their government that the reason they were fighting and dying by the tens of thousands was to emancipate black strangers in faraway states where most Northerners had never been. In July 1863, draft riots occurred in New York City, where between three hundred and one thousand civilians were shot dead (there are no hard data on the number of deaths) by federal troops called in from the recently concluded Battle of Gettysburg.

The draft was the main object of the protest, but there was also seething resentment at the idea of being drafted for the ostensible purpose of emancipating the slaves—and over the application of the draft to whites only (Bernstein 1990). Consequently, the rioters went on a racist rampage, hunting down and murdering dozens of innocent black people. An eyewitness account of the riots was given by Colonel Arthur Fremantle, the British emissary to the Confederacy during the spring and summer of 1863, who happened to be departing the country from the Port of New York at the time. In his widely read diary, first published in 1864 under the title *Three Months in the Southern States: April–June 1863,* Fremantle wrote:

> The reports of outrages, hangings, and murder [of blacks] were now most alarming, the terror and anxiety were universal. All shops were shut: all carriages and omnibuses had ceased running. No colored man or woman was visible or safe in the streets, or even in his own dwelling. Telegraphs were cut, and railroad tracks were torn up. The draft was suspended, and the mob evidently had the upper hand. (Fremantle 1991, 302)

When Fremantle "inquired of a bystander what the Negroes had done that they should want to kill them," the bystander replied, "Oh sir, they hate them here; they are the innocent cause of all these troubles" (300).

The Emancipation Proclamation caused a desertion crisis in the United States Army. At least two hundred thousand Northern soldiers deserted; another one hundred twenty thousand evaded conscription; and at least ninety thousand Northern men fled to Canada to evade the draft, while thousands more hid in the mountains of central Pennsylvania "where they lay beyond the easy reach of enrolling officers" (Gallagher 1998, 31). Enlistment rates plummeted, as did subscriptions to Union war bonds. In the words of the historian James McPherson, "Plenty of soldiers believed that the proclamation had changed the purpose of the war. They professed to feel betrayed. They were willing to risk their lives for the Union, they said, but not for black freedom. . . . Desertion rates rose alarmingly. Many soldiers blamed the Emancipation Proclamation" (1994, 63).

McPherson writes of a "backlash of anti-emancipation sentiment" and quotes various Union officers expressing sentiments such as this: "If emancipation is to be the policy of this war . . . I do not care how quick the country goes to pot" (1997, 120). Many Northern soldiers felt the way a Massachusetts sergeant from the famed Irish Brigade did, according to McPherson. In July 1862 the sergeant wrote in a letter that "if anyone thinks that this army is fighting to free the Negro . . . they are terribly mistaken" (1997, 121). Among the other statements McPherson reports being made by Union officers: "I don't want to fire another shot for the negroes and I wish that all the abolitionists were in hell"; "I don't want the negro freed . . . I say the Democrats ougt [sic] to go in with the south and kill all the Abolitionists of the north and that will end this war"; and "I am sick of the war. . . . I do not fight or want to fight for Lincoln's Negro proclamation one day longer" (1997, 122–24).

The historian Iver Bernstein makes the case that the New York City draft riots occurred when they did—in July 1863, six months after the Emancipation Proclamation was formally issued and some three months after the federal conscription act was passed by Congress—because not until then "did New Yorkers fully realize that Democratic officials [who dominated New York politics] would fail to shelter them from the draft" (1990, 13).

There were virtually no federal troops in the city on July 1—they had all been sent to Gettysburg—and hence federal authorities had no means of enforcing the draft, which was just then being implemented for the first time. The rioters clearly made a connection between the hated draft and the Emancipation Proclamation in venting their violent anger on hapless blacks and white abolitionists. At one point a mob led by men on horseback waving swords approached the home of prominent abolitionist James Sloan Gibbons, where Horace Greeley was also said to be residing at the time. Shouting "Greeley! Gibbons! Greeley! Gibbons!" the mob ransacked the house, whose residents fortunately escaped (Bernstein 1990, 25).

White Northerners' Attitudes toward Blacks

Northerners discriminated against blacks in cruel and inhumane ways during the 1850s and 1860s. As Alexis de Tocqueville remarked in *Democracy in America,* "The prejudice of race appears to be stronger in the states that have abolished slavery than in those where it still exists" (1945, 359).

The *Revised Code of Indiana,* for example, stated in 1862 that "Negroes and mulattos are not allowed to come into the state"; "all contracts with such Negroes and mulattos are declared to be void"; "any person encouraging them to come, or giving them employment, is to be fined from $10 to $500"; "Negroes and mulattos are not to be allowed to vote"; "No Negro, or mulatto having even one-eighth part of Negro blood, shall marry a white person" [with punishment of up to ten years in prison]; and "Negroes and mulattos are not allowed to testify against white persons" (Bensel 1990, 62). This last regulation was an open invitation to the criminal abuse of blacks. Illinois and Oregon added similar provisions to their state constitutions in 1848 and 1857, respectively (Litwack 1961, 70). The referendum to amend the Illinois constitution to prohibit the immigration of blacks passed by a margin of more than two to one; the margin was eight to one in Oregon (71).

Most Northern states that did permit immigration by blacks required them to post a bond of up to one thousand dollars that would be confiscated by the state if they acted "improperly." To the extent that this provision was enforced, it served as a deterrent to black immigration.

Although New York state helped to elect Lincoln, it overwhelmingly rejected a proposal to allow Negro suffrage. As late as 1869, New York voters defeated equal suffrage referenda (Litwack 1961, 91). Between 1849 and 1857, Michigan, Iowa, and Wisconsin overwhelmingly rejected equal-suffrage referenda.

Four Northern states—Illinois, Ohio, Indiana, and Iowa—prohibited Negro testimony in cases where a white person was a party, and Oregon forbade Negroes to own real estate, enter into contracts, or maintain lawsuits (Litwack 1961, 93).

Restaurants, hotels, libraries, and theaters excluded blacks in the North; black children were excluded from public schools or placed in inferior ones, even though their parents were taxpayers; and most Northern states had established their own state colonization societies for blacks. The public schools in Washington, D.C., were not desegregated until the 1950s—nearly a century after the end of the war.

Lyman Trumball, a U.S. Senator from Illinois and a close friend of Lincoln's, announced that "there is a very great aversion in the West—I know it to be so in my State—against having free Negroes come among us. Our people want nothing to do with the Negro" (Curry 1968, 79).

In 1861 Illinois was considered to be part of "the west." Similar anti-black attitudes were apparently pervasive in the "far west"—Iowa, California, Oregon, and Kansas—as well. In *The Frontier against Slavery* (1967), Eugene H. Berwanger documents how "state legislatures, overwhelmed by the fear of being inundated by manumitted slaves or free Negroes from the South, were enacting laws to deprive the Negro immigrants of any semblance of citizenship, to exclude them from the states, and to encourage them to colonize in Africa." "Prejudice against the Negro found special acceptance" in these Northern states (1).

Racist attitudes toward blacks were pervasive among Northern opinion makers as well as politicians. The *Philadelphia Daily News* editorialized on November 22, 1860, that "it is neither for the good of the colored race nor of our own that they should continue to dwell among us to any considerable extent. The two races can never exist in conjunction except as superior and inferior. . . . The African is naturally the inferior race" (Perkins 1964, 425). The *Niles (Mich.) Republican* wrote on March 30, 1861, that "this government was made for the benefit of the white race . . . and not for Negroes" (499). The *Daily Chicago Times* remarked on December 7, 1860, that "evil, and nothing but evil, has ever followed in the track of this hideous monster, Abolition. . . . Let [the slave] alone—send him back to his master where he belongs" (431).

On January 22, 1861, the *New York Times* announced that it opposed the abolition of slavery. Instead, it proposed that slaves should be allowed to legally marry, to be taught to read, and to invest their money in savings accounts. Those actions should be taken "to ameliorate, rather than to abolish, the Slavery of the Southern States" and would permit slavery to become "a very tolerable system" (Perkins 1964, 438). "We have no more right to meddle with slavery in Georgia, than we have to meddle with monarchy in Europe," declared the *Providence Daily Post* on February 2, 1861 (441). The *Columbus (Ohio) Crisis* added five days later that "we are not Abolitionists nor in favor of Negro equality" (44). The *New York Herald,* the newspaper with the largest circulation in the country at the time, actually sang the praises of slavery on March 7, 1861, when it wrote of how "the immense increase of numbers [of slaves] within so short a time speaks for the good treatment and happy, contented lot of the slaves. They are comfortably fed, housed and clothed, and seldom or never overworked" (455).

The *Philadelphia Inquirer* endorsed Lincoln's colonization ideas on March 11, 1861, when it pointed out that "Hayti lies in the torrid zone, the proper residence of the Negro" (456). "The proposition that the Negro is equal by nature, physically and mentally, to the white man, seems to be so absurd and preposterous, that we cannot conceive how it can be entertained by any intelligent and rational white man," the *Concord (N.H.) Democratic Standard* declared on September 8, 1860 (469). The *Boston Daily Courier* added on September 24, 1860, that "we believe the mulatto to be inferior in capacity, character, and organization to the full-blooded black, and still farther below the standard of the white races" (472).

The foregoing discussion demonstrates that the idea that racially enlightened Northerners marched south and died by the hundreds of thousands for the benefit of black strangers in Alabama and Mississippi, and then marched happily back singing the Battle Hymn of the Republic—as has been taught in the public schools and portrayed in books, films, and the popular culture in general for more than a century—is simply not credible.

It is conceivable that many white racists in the North nevertheless abhorred the institution of slavery. However, given the attitudes of most Northerners regarding blacks, it is doubtful that their abhorrence of slavery was sufficient motivation for most (not all) of them *to give their lives* on bloody battlefields. It is one thing to proclaim one's opposition to slavery, but quite another to die for it.

I do not deny that slavery was *a* cause of the war, but I maintain that it was one cause among many and that its importance may have been exaggerated.

Why Not Peaceful Emancipation?

By 1861 there was a long history of *peaceful* abolition of slavery throughout the world, including the northern United States. That abolition usually involved "the freeing, not of adults, but of children born on some date after the emancipation was enacted. Moreover, the freeing of slave children was delayed until their eighteenth, twenty-first, or in some cases, twenty-eighth birthday" (Fogel and Engerman 1974, 35). That method served as a means of "compensated emancipation," whereby slave owners were partially "compensated" for losing their slaves by being able to keep—and exploit—the slaves' children until they reached adulthood.

England had ended slavery in the West Indies a mere twenty years earlier; and gradual emancipation had occurred since the turn of the century in the countries listed in the table. During and after the War between the States, peaceful emancipation was also accomplished in the Dutch colonies (1863), Brazil (1871–88), Puerto Rico (1873), and Cuba (1886) (Fogel and Engerman 1974, 33–34). Thus, from the turn of the century to 1860, slavery had been eliminated peacefully in dozens of countries, and not a single country had resorted to warfare in the process (earlier, the 1794 revolution in Haiti led to a violent overthrow of the slavocracy there).

TABLE 1
Peaceful Emancipation, 1813–1854

Country/Region	Year of Peaceful Emancipation
Argentina	1813
Colombia	1814
Chile	1823
Central America	1824
Mexico	1829
Bolivia	1831
Uruguay	1842
French and Danish colonies	1848
Ecuador	1851
Peru	1854
Venezuela	1854

Source: Fogel and Engerman 1974, 33–34.

Given the enormous costs of the War between the States (including more than six hundred twenty thousand deaths, many thousands more crippled for life, the near destruction of some 40 percent of the nation's economy), many Americans, North and South, in retrospect might have chosen compensated emancipation—the route much of the rest of the world had previously taken.

Lincoln did propose a compensated emancipation bill in 1862, albeit one combined with his colonization plan (Basler 1946, 676). But the man whom historians would later consider to be perhaps the nation's preeminent "master politician" of all time apparently failed to utilize his legendary political skills to persuade Congress to pass the bill. Nor did he simply spend the funds to do so on a trial basis in just a few states. He did not hesitate to spend money without congressional approval for other purposes, such as sending 75,000 troops to invade South Carolina.

Nor did Lincoln demonstrate much concern for the plight of the freedmen near the end of the war. When asked by Confederate Vice President Alexander Stephens at the 1865 Hampton Roads, Virginia, "peace" conference what would become of the freedmen without property or education, Lincoln sarcastically recited the words to a popular minstrel song, "root, hog or die" (Stephens 1870, 615).

In an April 16, 1863, letter to the War Department regarding the fate of ex-slaves should emancipation become a reality, Lincoln wrote: "They had better be set to digging their subsistence out of the ground" (Berlin 1987, 306). And although the Homestead Act was passed during the war, very little land was later offered to the freedmen: 80 percent of the land went to railroad and mining companies, and much of the remainder went to new European immigrants, many of whom were recruited into the Union army with the promise of free land (Johnson 1978, 110–20).

What They Fought For

Very few of the men who fought in the War between the States believed they were fighting for or against slavery. In his book *What They Fought For, 1861–1865* (1994), James McPherson reported on his reading of hundreds of letters and diaries written by soldiers on both sides of the war on the question of what they believed they were fighting for. These men belonged to the most literate armies in history up to that point, writes McPherson; they came from the world's most politicized and democratic society; they were "preeminent" newspaper readers.

McPherson concluded that nearly all Confederate soldiers—only a small fraction of whom were slave owners—believed they "fought for liberty and independence from what they regarded as a tyrannical government." Most Unionists "fought to preserve the nation created by the founders" (McPherson 1994, 7). As one Illinois officer explained, "We are fighting for the Union . . . a high and noble sentiment, but after all a sentiment. They are fighting for independence, and are animated by passion and hatred against invaders" (19).

Fighting for the same principles the American revolutionaries of 1776 fought for was a recurring theme in almost all the letters and diaries of the Confederates in McPherson's sample. "The letters and diaries of many Confederate soldiers bristled with the rhetoric of liberty and self-government and with expressions of a willingness to die for the cause" (9).

Some Union soldiers believed they were fighting to end slavery, especially during the final two years of the war. Many of these men were sincere abolitionists, but according to McPherson, others simply understood that taking slaves away from Southern slave owners would harm the Southern economy and therefore likely shorten the war (121–24).

Lincoln's Real Agenda: The "American System"

Lincoln had been a politician for some twenty-eight years when he was elected president in 1860 (with 34 percent of the popular vote). As previously noted, he scarcely even mentioned the topic of slavery until 1854. The political topic that *did* draw most of his attention was the economic policy platform of the Whig Party, which from 1820 until the early 1850s was literally defined by Lincoln's political idol, Henry Clay. As Johannsen (1991) has written, "From the moment Lincoln first entered political life as a candidate for the state legislature during the decisive 1832 presidential election, he had demonstrated an unswerving fidelity to the party of Henry Clay and to Clay's American System, the program of internal improvements, protective tariff, and centralized banking" (14).

During the Lincoln-Douglas debates, notes Johannsen, "the two men reflected the divergent points of view in the political culture of nineteenth-century America—Lincoln the latitudinarian concepts of national centralization and authority, Douglas the strict constructionist emphasis on local self government and states' rights" (9).

Lincoln took his political cues from Clay, whom he eulogized on July 16, 1852, as "the beau ideal of a statesman," the "great parent of Whig Principles" (Basler 1946, 264), and the "fount from which [Lincoln's] own political views flowed" (Johannsen 1991, 20). "During my whole political life," Lincoln said, "I have loved and revered [Clay] as a teacher and leader" (Basler 1946, 264).

As soon as the Whig Party began to crumble, however, Lincoln quickly abandoned it and joined the new Republican Party, all the while assuring Illinoisans that there was no difference between the principles of the Whig Party as expounded by its great leader Clay and those of the Republican Party. For "Lincoln had labored for twenty-five years in behalf of Henry Clay's American System, the program that tied economic development to strong centralized national authority, and he was not prepared to give up that investment" (Johannsen 1991, 45).

When Lincoln was warned by a political adviser that the new Republican Party included a small number of abolitionists from whom he should dissociate himself, he responded by saying, "What care we how many may feel disposed to labor for our cause?" He "would accept support from wherever he could get it, so long as he himself was not tarred with the abolitionist brush" (Basler 1946, 344).

Stephen Douglas characterized Lincoln's political intentions as wanting to "impose on the nation a uniformity of local laws and institutions and a moral homogeneity dictated by the central government," which "placed at defiance the intentions of the republic's founders" (Johannsen 1991, 81). The rhetorical contest between Lincoln and Douglas, writes Johannsen, "was the contest all over again between the 'one consolidated empire' of the Federalists and Whigs, and the 'confederacy of sovereign and equal states' of Jefferson and Jackson" (81). "Lincoln goes for consolidation and uniformity in our government," Douglas charged, "while I go for maintaining the confederation of the sovereign states" (92).

"During the Civil War," writes Clay biographer Maurice Baxter, "Lincoln and the Republican party implemented much of the American System" that Clay had fought for during his entire career (1995, 209). The three main elements of Clay's American System were federally funded "internal improvements," considered by many to be nothing but corporate welfare for steamship, canal, and railroad businesses; high protective tariffs, leading to economic autarky; and central banking and fiat money. In short, the Clay-Lincoln American System consisted of mercantilism, protectionism, the centralization of governmental power, and inflationism.

A brief overview of some of the high points of Clay's political career reveals just what attracted Lincoln to the Whig Party from the time he was a young man.

When Clay entered national politics in 1811 as a member of Congress, one of his first actions was to help convince his colleagues to invade Canada, which they did, three times. He waged a thirty-year political battle with James Madison, James Monroe, John C. Calhoun, John Randolph, Andrew Jackson, and other defenders of the Jeffersonian philosophy of limited, decentralized, and constitutional government. Presidents Madison and Monroe both vetoed "internal improvements" bills sponsored by Clay, judging them unconstitutional (Remini 1991, 226).

Clay was unequivocally the fiercest proponent of protectionism in Congress from 1811 until his death in 1852. That advocacy brought him into lifelong conflict with Southern politicians. The majority of U.S. exports came out of the South. Because the South's economy was almost exclusively an agrarian one, high tariffs meant that Southerners would have to pay higher prices for manufactured goods, whether they purchased them from Europe or from Northern manufacturers. Since the 1820s, Southern politicians such as John C. Calhoun had ritually condemned the tariff as an unconstitutional tool of political plunder whereby Southerners were burdened by the lion's share of the cost of the tariff while most of the expenditures financed by tariff revenue took place in the North.

Thus, when Clay proposed a sharp tariff increase in 1824 (which became law), Southern members of Congress attacked it. Undeterred by the attacks, Clay then became the chief proponent of the 1828 "Tariff of Abominations," which raised tariffs even higher. The higher rates were necessary, Clay explained, because the lower 1824 tariff rates "fell short of what many of my friends wished" (Remini 1991, 232).

The Tariff of Abominations almost precipitated a secession crisis as a South Carolina political convention voted to nullify the tariff. That resistance eventually forced the federal government to compromise, reducing the rates in 1833. Clay was apparently infuriated by the compromise and promised on the floor of the House of Representatives that he would someday "defy the South, the President, and the devil" himself, if necessary, to raise tariff rates once again (Baxter 1995, 75).

Clay was also a lifelong proponent of central banking. He fought a pitched political battle with Andrew Jackson (which Jackson won) over the rechartering of the Bank of the United States. Neither Clay nor any of the other Whigs ever made much of a principled argument in favor of a central bank. They merely saw it as an essential tool for the financing of all the political patronage they hoped to ladle out if the "American System" were ever realized.

As Speaker of the House of Representatives, Clay personally demonstrated the usefulness of the Bank of the United States to ambitious politicians such as himself. He used his political position to place his political cronies on the bank's board of directors, enabling them to reward their political supporters with cheap credit. Having incurred $40,000 in personal debt, Clay left Congress for two years in 1822 to earn money as general counsel of the Bank of the United States. As Clay biographer Maurice Baxter explains,

> His income from this business apparently amounted to what he needed [to pay off the $40,000 debt]: three thousand dollars a year from the bank as chief counsel; more for appearing in specific cases; and a sizable amount of real estate in Ohio and Kentucky in addition to the cash. . . . When he resigned to become Secretary of State in 1825, he was pleased with his compensation. (1995, 75)

One of the first things Clay did as secretary of state was to effectively endorse a policy of ethnic genocide toward the American Indians. At a cabinet meeting he announced: "There never was a full-blooded Indian who took to civilization," for "it was not in their nature." He "did not think them, as a race, worth preserving"; they were "inferior" to Anglo-Saxons; and their "breed could not be improved." "Their disappearance from the human family will be no great loss to the world" (Remini 1991, 314).

Lincoln in Office: Mercantilism, Protectionism, Inflation, Dictatorship, and Total War

Upon taking office, Lincoln bent over backward to assure everyone that he had no intention to disturb Southern slavery and that, even if he wished to, it would be unconstitutional to do so. He favored strengthening the fugitive slave clause and was always willing to compromise on the issue, something which earned him the wrath of Northern abolitionists.

Not so when it came to the tariff. With respect to the tariff, Lincoln was completely unwilling to compromise. He even promised in his First Inaugural Address to launch a military invasion of any state that failed to collect its share of tariffs. "The power confided in me will be used to hold, occupy, and possess the property, and places belonging to the government, and to collect the duties and imposts; but beyond what may be necessary for these objects, there will be no invasion—no using force against, or among the people anywhere" (Basler 1946, 583). To Lincoln, Southern slavery was tolerable; failure to collect tariff revenues was not.

The Morrill tariff of 1861 was passed by the House of Representatives in the congressional session preceding the election of Lincoln; the Senate passed the bill in early 1861, after Lincoln had been elected. Thus, Lincoln had little to do *formally* with the Morrill tariff in any *official* capacity. But as the Republican Party's presidential nominee in 1860, he was the leader of the party. Given that one of the party's top policy priorities was the Morrill tariff, it is most unlikely that Lincoln the master politician had little (or nothing) to do with it.

By 1857, wrote Frank Taussig, the maximum duty on imports had been reduced to 24 percent; many raw materials were duty free; and "the level of duties on the whole line of manufactured articles was brought down to the lowest point which has been reached in this country since 1815. It is not likely we shall see, for a great many years to come, a nearer approach to the free-trade ideal" (1931, 157).

Once the Southern Democrats had left Congress, however, the Republicans did what they (and before them the Whigs) had dreamed of doing all along: they flew into a protectionist frenzy that lasted for decades beyond the war. As Taussig explained: "In the next regular [congressional] session, in December 1861, a still further increase of duties was made. From that time until 1865 no session, indeed, hardly a month of any session, passed in which some increase of duties on imports was not made" (1931, 160). By 1862 the average tariff rate had crept up to 47.06 percent, which "established protective duties more extreme than had been ventured on in any previous tariff act in our country's history" (167). Lincoln and the Republicans explained that the sharp tariff increases would serve to compensate Northern manufacturers, who had been heavily taxed to support the war, for their sacrifices.

Great sacrifices were being made throughout the North during the war, but not by the Northern manufacturers who bankrolled the Republican Party. For them, "great fortunes were made by changes in legislation urged and brought about by those who were benefited by them." Congress enacted tariff legislation "whose chief effect was to bring money into the pockets of private individuals" (Taussig 1931, 167). Long after the war, "almost any increase of duties demanded by domestic producers was readily made" (166).

Most scholars either ignore or denigrate the idea that economic aims were an important cause of the War between the States, even though throughout history many wars have been fought over economic aims. But even a casual reading of the history of the period shows that the tariff was indeed a paramount issue. Southerners, who had been protesting, nullifying acts of Congress, and threatening secession over the tariff issue since 1824, were such ardent proponents of free trade that the Confederate Constitution outlawed protectionist tariffs altogether (it did permit a revenue tariff).

The Confederate Constitution was essentially a carbon copy of the U.S. Constitution, except for the following provisions, all of which dilute the power of the central government (DeRosa 1992): protectionist tariffs were unconstitutional; government subsidies to private businesses were outlawed; no government funds could be spent on "internal improvements" except for dredging rivers and harbors; all congressional appropriations required a two-thirds majority vote, although a majority vote could be held if requested by the president; the president was given a line-item veto and limited to one six-year term; states could initiate constitutional amendments but Congress could not; central government officials could be impeached by the state legislatures as well as by the House of Representatives; and the general welfare clause of the U.S. Constitution was eliminated.

Elimination of the general welfare clause was a momentous change. For years the Whigs had attempted to manipulate the clause to justify various corporate-welfare schemes, some of which were vetoed by President Madison, the acknowledged "father" of the U.S. Constitution.

The constitutional outlawing of protective tariffs by the Southern states was regarded by Northerners as potentially devastating to their economy, especially inasmuch as England had abolished all tariffs in 1850 and France was sharply reducing its tariff rates as well. Lincoln and the Republicans simply could not tolerate a reduction in tariff rates, for as Richard Bensel observed, "The tariff was the centerpiece of the Republican program" (1995, 73). Free trade in the South would have brought about a substitution of shipping from New York, Boston, and Baltimore to Charleston, Savannah, and New Orleans. This fear was widely expressed in Northern newspapers just prior to the war.

It is important to recall that in the nineteenth century most newspapers were openly associated with a political party. Therefore, newspaper editorials often expressed a party line.

The *Daily Chicago Times* candidly admitted on December 10, 1860, that the tariff was indeed a tool used by Northern manufacturers for the purpose of plundering the South, and the editor warned that that valuable mechanism for political plunder was threatened by the existence of free-trade ports in the Southern states:

> The South has furnished near three-fourths of the entire exports of the country. Last year she furnished seventy-two percent of the whole . . . we have a tariff that protects our manufacturers from thirty to fifty percent, and enables us to consume large quantities of Southern cotton, and to compete in our whole home market with the skilled

labor of Europe. This operates to compel the South to pay an indirect bounty to our skilled labor, of millions annually. (Perkins 1964, 573)

"Let the South adopt the free-trade system," the Chicago paper ominously warned, and the North's "commerce must be reduced to less than half what it now is." "Our labor could not compete . . . with the labor of Europe," a "large portion of our shipping interest would pass into the hands of the South," and "these revulsions will bring in their train very general bankruptcy and ruin" (574).

On March 12, 1861, the *New York Evening Post,* another Republican paper, advocated that the U.S. Navy "abolish all ports of entry" into the Southern states, because sending hordes of customs inspectors there to enforce the Morrill tariff would be too expensive. After all, protectionism requires "a collector, with his army of appraisers, clerks, examiners, inspectors, weighers, gaugers, measurers, and so forth" (Perkins 1964, 600).

Another Republican Party mouthpiece, the *Newark (N.J.) Daily Advertiser,* was clearly aware that the free-trade economics of Adam Smith had taken a strong hold in Britain, France, and the Southern states. The paper warned on April 2, 1861, that Southerners had apparently "taken to their bosoms the liberal and popular doctrine of free trade" and that they "might be willing to go . . . toward free trade with the European Powers," which "must operate to the serious disadvantage of the North," as "commerce will be largely diverted to the Southern Cities" (Perkins 1964, 601). "We apprehend," the Republican editorial writers announced, that "the chief instigator of the present troubles—South Carolina—have all along for years been preparing the way for the adoption of free trade" and must be stopped by "the closing of the ports" in the South by military force (602).

These editors understood an economic doctrine that would be "discovered" some ninety years later by economist Jacob Viner (1950) as the trade-diversion effect of customs unions or free-trade blocks. Free trade among England, France, other European countries, and the Confederate States of America would have diverted a great deal of commerce away from the (remaining) United States unless the Union, too, reduced its tariff rates. That reduction, however, was unacceptable to Lincoln and the Republicans, who considered the tariff the "centerpiece" of their ambitious program for a greatly expanded central government.

Some Northern newspapers dissented from the protectionist zealotry of the Republican Party propaganda organs. The *New Haven Daily Register,* which supported Stephen Douglas in 1860, editorialized on February 11, 1861, that "there was never a more ill-timed, injudicious and destructive measure proposed, than the Morrill tariff bill," because "while Congress is raising the duties for the Northern ports, the Southern [Constitutional] Convention is doing away with all import duties for the Southern ports, leaving more than three-fifths of the seafront of the Atlantic States . . . beyond the reach of our . . . tariff" (Perkins 1964, 589–90). The Southern ports would then "invite the free trade of the world," which would be economically damaging to the North. Leave the South alone, the Connecticut paper advised, and repeal the Morrill tariff.

That advice was not to be taken, of course, for as Bensel has astutely observed, Lincoln's decision to wage war was just what was needed to break the logjam behind which the Whig agenda had languished for decades. The war would provide the ideal occasion for "the implementation of the political economic agenda of the groups allied within the Republican party that had been proposed and debated in the prewar period" (Bensel 1995, 2).

The Demolition of Civil Liberties

Although Lincoln is credited with "saving" the Union, he saved it only in a geographic sense. What was really saved, if not invented out of whole cloth, was the notion of federal supremacy over the states and the citizens. The existence of the Union as a *voluntary* association of states was destroyed when the South was compelled at gunpoint to remain a part of it.

Scholars may argue forever over the legality of secession, but the fact is that before the war the vast majority of Americans believed in the dictum set forth in the Declaration of Independence, that governments derive their just powers from the consent of the governed, and that forcing the South to remain in the Union was therefore tyrannical and immoral.

Jefferson himself, the principal author of the Declaration, stated in his First Inaugural Address, "If there be any among us who would wish to dissolve this Union or to change its republican form, let them stand undisturbed as monuments of the safety with which error of opinion may be tolerated where reason is left free to combat it" (Peterson 1993, 140). Jefferson believed strongly in a state's right of secession, although he did not necessarily think that exercising the right would be wise. If a state (or states) wanted to secede, "God bless them both and keep them in the union if it be for their good, but separate them if it be better," he said while president (610).

The Revolution of 1776 was, after all, a war of secession. The Founding Fathers could hardly have been opposed to the principle of secession after creating their new government by that very means.

Such was the understanding of the New England Federalists who, from the time Jefferson took office in 1801 until 1814, plotted to secede. The attempted secession failed at the Hartford Secession Convention of 1814 (Banner 1970), but none of the Federalist Party leaders ever questioned the *right* of secession—only its practical wisdom.

The leader of that failed secessionist movement was the Massachusetts senator Timothy Pickering, who had previously served as adjutant general of the Revolutionary army, as a member of Congress, and as secretary of war and secretary of state in the Washington administrations. Pickering was so upset with Jefferson that he concluded in 1803 that "the principles of our Revolution [of 1776] point to a remedy—a separation" (Adams 1877, 338). "I will rather anticipate a new confederacy, exempt from the corrupt and corrupting influence and oppression of the aristocratic Democrats of the South," Pickering said (Adams 1877, 338).

Before the war, most American opinion makers still believed in a state's inherent right of secession. Evidence of this belief is that the overwhelming majority of *Northern* newspaper editors favored peaceful secession prior to the onset of the war. On February 21, 1861, Horace Greeley, the abolitionist editor of the *New York Daily Tribune,* began an editorial by saying,

> The great principle embodied by Jefferson in the Declaration of American independence, that governments derive their just powers from the consent of the governed, is sound and just; and that, if the Slave States, the Cotton States, or the Gulf States only, choose to form an independent nation, they have a clear moral right to do so. (Perkins 1964, 359)

The *New York Times* added on March 21, 1861, that "it cannot be denied that there is a growing sentiment throughout the North in favor of *letting the Gulf States go*" (Perkins 1964, 365). "Shall we, by such a policy [of invading the South], change our government from a voluntary one, in which the people are sovereigns," the *New York Journal of Commerce* asked on January 12, 1861, "to a despotism where one part of the people are slaves? Such is the logical deduction from the policy of the advocates of force" (342).

Those sentiments were expressed far and wide throughout the North, and were perhaps best stated by the Kenosha, Wisconsin, *Democrat* on January 11, 1861:

> The very freedom claimed by every individual citizen, precludes the idea of compulsory association, as individuals, as communities, or as States. The very germ of liberty is the right of forming our own governments, enacting our own laws, and choosing our own political associates. . . . The right of secession inheres to the people of every sovereign state. (335)

So widely held was the belief that the right of secession was a prerequisite to a free country that Mayor Fernando Woods of New York City proposed having the city secede from both the state and federal governments. Serious attempts were made to create a Central Confederacy in the Middle Atlantic states (Wright 1973). Secessionist sentiment was especially strong in New Jersey. The one thing all these secessionist movements seemed to have in common was a desire to form a government that did not include the New England Yankees.

The right of secession was destroyed by Lincoln's execution of the war. Moreover, so many other civil liberties were crushed that the historians Samuel Morison and Henry Steele Commager described Lincoln as "a dictator from the standpoint of American Constitutional law and practice" (1942, 699–700). Likewise, the political scientist Clinton Rossiter made the "Lincoln dictatorship" a major case study in his book *Constitutional Dictatorship* (1948, 223–39). As long ago as 1897 the historian William Archibald Dunning (1897) referred to the Lincoln administration as a "temporary dictatorship."

Even Lincoln's early defenders and idolaters, such as James Ford Rhodes (1900, 441), called him a dictator, but added that "never had the power of dictator fallen into safer and nobler hands." "If Lincoln was a dictator, it must be admitted that he was a benevolent dictator," claimed James G. Randall (1951, 30). The civilian victims of Lincoln's tyrannical behavior undoubtedly would have disagreed.

Among the unconstitutional and dictatorial acts performed by Lincoln were initiating and conducting a war by decree for months without the consent or advice of Congress; declaring martial law; confiscating private property; suspending habeas corpus; conscripting the railroads and censoring telegraph lines; imprisoning as many as thirty thousand *Northern* citizens without trial; deporting a member of Congress, Clement L. Vallandigham of Ohio, after Vallandigham—a fierce opponent of the Morrill tariff—protested the imposition of an income tax at a Democratic Party meeting in Ohio; and shutting down hundreds of Northern newspapers (Randall 1951). Lincoln's Republican Party associates in Congress created three new states—Kansas, West Virginia, and Nevada—which helped them rig the 1864 election (Donald 1956, 79).

Voters were routinely intimidated and compelled to vote Republican by federal soldiers. "Under the protection of Federal bayonets, New York went Republican by seven thousand votes" in 1864 (Donald 1961, 81).

In Maryland, federal troops arrested and imprisoned without trial thirty-one state legislators, the mayor of Baltimore, a congressman, and dozens of newspaper editors who opposed the war. Even the grandson of Francis Scott Key was thrown into prison at Fort McHenry (Talbert 1995; Hummel 1996). All these actions were taken in the name of *preserving* constitutional government.

Centralization through Taxation

The federal government was greatly enlarged and centralized during the war. Tariff rates were raised and excise taxes were imposed on virtually all manufactured goods. Occupational licensing taxes, stamp taxes, and inheritance taxes were imposed. The first income tax in U.S. history was adopted with a top rate of 10 percent on incomes over $10,000 (Randall and Donald 1966, 344). The income tax was eliminated in 1872, but other wartime taxes, such as the excises on tobacco products and liquor, were retained, providing a new, permanent revenue source for the federal government. A federal internal revenue bureaucracy was created for the first time, and it has grown steadily since then.

In 1860 the only contact the average citizen had with the federal government was through mailing a letter at the post office. But by 1865 "every citizen now had direct contact with, and felt the direct influence of, the federal government. A great centralizing force had been set into motion. . . . The needs of the government had resulted in a drastic redrawing of the federal tax base. Never again would it be contracted to its prewar scope" (Curry 1968, 179).

The government went deep into debt to finance the war (thereby disguising part of its cost to the public). That enormous borrowing gave the Republicans a further excuse to enact another plank of Clay's vaunted American System, central banking.

The National Currency Acts of 1863 and 1864 created a network of nationally chartered banks that issued national bank notes supplied to them by the comptroller of the currency. The national banks were required to hold federal government bonds as backing for their note issues—thus did the Treasury artificially increase the demand for its bonds. State banks were driven out of the business of making loans via note issue by a prohibitive 10 percent federal tax on the issuance of their bank notes. The historian Heather Cox Richardson writes approvingly of how Lincoln and fellow Republicans' "willingness to introduce government control of the nation's money" led inevitably to expanding "permanently the national government's economic role in the nation" (1997, 90).

Congressman Lazarus Powell of Kentucky was not quite as enthusiastic at the time. The establishment of central banking, he ominously forecast, "would enable the national Congress to destroy every institution of the States and cause all power to be consolidated and concentrated here [in Washington, D.C.]" (Richardson 1997, 87).

But that outcome was exactly what the sponsor of the bank legislation, Senator John Sherman of Ohio, wanted. Sherman favored "the permanently increased government power embodied in the bill," claiming it would foster "a sentiment of nationality" (87).

Opening the Floodgates of Corporate Welfare

The American military-industrial-congressional complex was born during the war as hundreds of Northern businesses developed "partnerships" with the government. Corruption became rampant and continued for decades, especially during the notorious Grant administrations (1869–1877).

With the Southern Democrats no longer a political factor, the Republicans were able to distort the general welfare clause to justify funding for pork-barrel programs that benefited narrow special interests—especially the banks and railroads that bankrolled the Republican Party—not the general public. The fifty-year constitutional debate over the permissibility of using tax dollars for corporate welfare was ended once and for all by force of arms.

The rent-seeking corporate lobbyists were so influential that even during the dark days of 1862, when the Confederates were scoring shocking victories and Lincoln was admittedly at the end of his rope regarding the military plan, Lincoln and the Congress diverted millions of dollars from the war effort to the building of railroad tracks in Utah, Colorado, and other western areas of the country far removed from the hostilities in the east. Government subsidies were said to be necessary for such railroads to be built. James J. Hill, however, built his own transcontinental railroad, the Great Northern Railroad, without a dime in government subsidies (Folsom 1988).

As the historian Leonard Curry has observed, "Throughout the remainder of the nineteenth century (and beyond), corporate interests—apparently insatiable—returned again and again to demand direct and indirect federal subsidies . . . national legislative and executive officers were corrupted and representative government made a mockery" (1968, 247). In 1862 the U.S. Department of Agriculture was created and quickly began dispensing farm welfare, as it has done ever since. The Clay-Lincoln American System was in full bloom.

War Crimes

Over the centuries, the rules of warfare had evolved to the point that only combatants were considered legitimate targets. The Union army disregarded that rule when it intentionally targeted civilians in an organized campaign of terror and conquest, establishing a precedent that would be followed all too commonly in the twentieth century.

Lincoln is famously known as a micromanager of the war effort. It is therefore inconceivable that he did not know of the atrocities perpetrated against unarmed civilians by federal armies. As the commander in chief, he had the power to stop the atrocities, but he did not do so. His insouciance is all the more remarkable when one considers that the victims of the atrocities were not invading armies but fellow citizens—unarmed women, children, and old men for the most part.

The Confederates were finally forced to evacuate the Shenandoah Valley by the autumn of 1864. All that remained there were small, ragged farms and towns occupied mostly by women, children, and old men. With no army to oppose him, General Ulysses S. Grant told cavalry officer Phillip Sheridan that "we want the Shenandoah Valley to remain a barren waste" and famously ordered him to make sure that even a crow flying over the valley would have to pack its own lunch (Foote 1986, vol. 1, 563). Sheridan and the Union cavalry went on a rampage of pillaging, plundering, burning, and the murdering of civilians that came to be known as "the Burning." As one Union soldier described the scene, "The atmosphere, from horizon to horizon, has been black with the smoke of a hundred conflagrations and at night a gleam brighter and more lurid than sunset has shot from every verge. . . .

The completeness of the devastation is awful. Hundreds of nearly starving people are going north" (Morris 1992, 209).

General William Tecumseh Sherman was the most notorious Union general with respect to targeting innocent civilians. In the fall of 1862 Sherman was annoyed by Confederate sharpshooters who had been targeting Union gunboats on the Mississippi River near Memphis. He responded by burning to the ground the small town of Randolph, Tennessee. "Small Union units under his command expelled families from river towns and killed others who refused to be evacuated" (Fellman 1995, 141). Declaring that America—especially the South—was "too free and too ungoverned" (Fellman 1995, 147), Sherman waged war on civilians with a vengeance. This action included occasionally ordering his men to pick a civilian at random and kill him. In one notable instance "a Union company attacked the nearest house, that of the White family, beat to death the twenty-three-year-old boy living there, and burned down the home" (141). After the incident Sherman wrote to Grant requesting that Grant "act with magnanimity" toward the White family, who turned out to be Unionists. The following summer Sherman had his troops set fire to Jackson, Mississippi, *after the Confederate army had evacuated,* and boasted to Grant that "the [civilian] inhabitants are subjugated. They cry aloud for mercy. The land is devastated for 30 miles around . . . we have annihilated the city" (145).

Sherman's chief engineer, O. M. Poe, was deeply disturbed by the killing of women and children during the shelling of Atlanta and expressed concerns to Sherman on several occasions. But Sherman responded only that such deaths were "a beautiful sight" because they would quicken a Union victory (184). At that time it was also Sherman's policy to require male civilians to either take a loyalty oath or be shot (Vetter 1992, 223).

Sherman boasted of having destroyed at least $100 million in private property during his march to the sea, and his troops carried off another $20 million worth. One Illinois private wrote home and told of how the army would run women, children, and old men from their homes, "sometimes kill them at their own doors," and then "take everything of value and burn the rest" (Fellman 1995, 184). "Never in modern times did soldiers have such fun," observed a plundering Union officer (Davis 1980, 167).

When Sherman's army finally arrived in Colombia, South Carolina, the heart of secessionism,

> Ladies were hustled from their chambers, their ornaments plucked from their persons. . . . Men and women bearing off their trunks were seized . . . and in a moment the trunk burst asunder with the stroke of an axe or gun butt, the contents laid bare, rifled, and the residue sacrificed to the fire. . . . The soldiers plundered and drank. There were no reports of raped white women, but the black women of the city suffered terribly. (Davis 1980, 167)

Conclusion

All these cries of having "abolished slavery," of having "saved the country," of having "preserved the union," of establishing a "government of consent," and of "maintaining the national honor" are all gross, shameless, transparent cheats—so transparent that they ought to deceive no one. Lincoln should be remembered as the Great Centralizer as much as the Great Emancipator. He spent nearly his entire political career prior to becoming president working in the trenches of the Whig and Republican parties, promoting centralized governmental power through protectionist tariffs, central banking, and mercantilist corporate-welfare schemes. After taking office, that long-sought centralization is exactly what he (and the Republican Party) accomplished. Lincoln's actions supported his repeated statements that he considered the emancipation policy to be only a means to an end, the end being to "save" the Union or, more accurately, to establish, once and for all, federal supremacy over the states.

Famed Northern abolitionists Charles Sumner, Wendell Phillips, and Ben Wade, who were all prominent and influential Republicans, openly admitted that the abolition of slavery was not so much a humanitarian imperative as a prerequisite to the success of their mercantilist schemes. As long as slavery existed, the three-fifths clause of the Constitution inflated Southern (and Democratic) representation in Congress, which hindered the Republicans' plans. But once freed, the ex-slaves could be easily manipulated into voting Republican—which they were. "The freedmen, loyal to the party that set them free, must have the ballot," Phillips announced (Donald 1961, 106).

By destroying the right of secession, Lincoln and the Republican Party opened the door to the unrestrained, centralized, despotic state the U.S. government has become. The great principle of the Declaration of Independence, that governments derive their just powers from the consent of the governed, was effectively overturned. Lincoln the master politician replaced it with the myth of the "perpetual union," a phrase found not in the Constitution or in the Declaration of Independence but in the "Articles of Confederation of Perpetual Union." In replacing the Articles of Confederation, however, the ratifiers of the Constitution had rendered the notion of "perpetual union" null and void.

Lord Acton, the great historian of liberty and a dominant intellectual force in Victorian England, viewed the South's defeat, conquest, and subsequent military occupation as a severe blow to the cause of liberty throughout the world. Like other British intellectuals and opinion makers, he did not believe that the primary cause of the war was slavery. In a November 4, 1866, letter to Robert E. Lee he wrote:

> I saw in States Rights the only availing check upon the absolutism of the sovereign will, and secession filled me with hope, not as the destruction but as the redemption of Democracy. The institutions of your Republic have not exercized on the old world

the salutary and liberating influence which ought to have belonged to them, by reason of those defects and abuses of principle which the Confederate Constitution was expressly and wisely calculated to remedy. I believed that the example of that great Reform would have blessed all the races of mankind by establishing true freedom purged of the native dangers and disorders of Republics. Therefore I deemed that you were fighting the battles of our liberty, our progress, and our civilization; and I mourn for the stake which was lost at Richmond more deeply than I rejoice over that which was saved at Waterloo. (Fears 1985, 363)

Lee responded presciently on December 15, 1866:

While I have considered the preservation of the constitutional power of the General Government to be the foundation of our peace and safety at home and abroad, I yet believe that the maintenance of the rights and authority reserved to the states and to the people, not only are essential to the adjustment and balance of the general system, but the safeguard to the continuance of a free government. I consider it as the chief source of stability to our political system, whereas the consolidation of the states into one vast republic, sure to be aggressive abroad and despotic at home, will be the certain precursor of that ruin which has overwhelmed all those that have preceded it. (Fears 1985, 365)

The South's defeat and subjugation radically changed the very nature of American government from a decentralized, federal system to a consolidated national system and effectively destroyed local sovereignty as an effective check on the centralizing powers of the state.

The only unequivocal good that came of the war was the abolition of slavery. We are left to wonder why peaceful, compensated emancipation—which occurred throughout the Western Hemisphere in the nineteenth century—was never seriously attempted as the means of abolishing slavery in the South.

Lincoln was arguably the most successful president in U.S. history, in that he accomplished exactly what he set out to do—something that American politicians in the Federalist/Whig tradition had failed to achieve during the preceding seventy-five years, namely, turning the United States into one consolidated empire. As the Republican senator John Sherman of Ohio, a powerful figure in the Republican Party, said of Lincoln upon his election as president:

Those who elected Mr. Lincoln expect him . . . to secure to free labor its just right to the Territories of the United States; to protect . . . by wise revenue laws, the labor of our people; to secure the public lands to actual settlers . . . ; to develop the internal resources of the country by opening new means of communication between the Atlantic and Pacific. (Donald 1961, 105–6)

Translated from the politician's idiom into plain English, writes David Donald, this statement meant that Lincoln and the Republicans "intended to enact a high protective tariff that mothered monopoly, to pass a homestead law that invited spec-ulators to loot the public domain, and to subsidize a transcontinental railroad that afforded infinite opportunities for jobbery" (106). In those endeavors, Lincoln suc-ceeded beyond anything he might have imagined in his wildest dreams.

༄

FOREVER WORTHY OF THE SAVING: LINCOLN AND A MORE MORAL UNION

Rogan Kersh

AMONG THE MOST potent political terms over the first century and a quarter of U.S. history was "union," and few public figures were more closely identified with the concept than Abraham Lincoln. From his early career, Lincoln saw "a unified America" as highly desirable both "practically and . . . intellectually." His struggle to reconceive political union in a morally progressive fashion, while remaining gen-erally faithful to the Framers' original conception of a "more perfect union," was criticized by both impatient abolitionists and accomodationist centrists (not to men-tion proslavery Southerners). During the Civil War, however, Lincoln's moral-unionist outlook came to epitomize what Frederick Douglass called "something incomparably better than the old Union."[1] Lincoln's efforts at conceptual revision evolved gradually: only during the war did he directly associate a more moral union with the status of black Americans. But his principled vision of national unity pointed the way to a desirable postwar consensus.

I. Lincoln, Unionist

Like George Washington, Daniel Webster, and a few other figures before him, Lin-coln came to be considered the personal incarnation of national union in America. One such idealization was drawn by Ralph Waldo Emerson, who portrayed Lincoln as a new "Representative Man" in an 1862 *Atlantic* essay. Two years later Emerson described renewed possibilities of "fraternity in this land," naming Lincoln as the inspiration. Such treatments continue into the present. As historian David Donald describes, Lincoln continues to "live in memory as the nation's martyred President who freed the slaves and saved the Union."[2] Thus a mass of secondary opinion must be sifted in addressing the question: what was national union to Lincoln?

According to one strand of commentary, Lincoln viewed union in intensely per-sonal terms. Some describe his vision of unity as a sort of "sublim[e] . . . religious mysticism," as Confederate Vice President Alexander Stephens recalled. Historian

Gabor Boritt likewise sees union as "carry[ing] a certain aura" in Lincoln's thought, a theme that Charles Strozier pursues at book length, suggesting that Lincoln's inability to resolve his "ambivalent quest for union—with his dead mother, his bride, his alienated father—gave meaning to the nation's turbulence as it hurtled towards civil war." To bridge this divide, Lincoln "turned outward and attempted . . . to solve for all what he could not solve for himself alone," aiming to "purposely shape his heroic image to fit a nation longing for unity and greatness."[3]

Other scholars find union less central in Lincoln's political purview, portraying Lincoln's defenses of "the white Union" as "a technical point," a "shibboleth," a convenient rhetorical cover for his feeble antislavery or reconstruction policies. Self-interest is also alleged as a factor, as when Lincoln's proposed "Union Party" retitling of the Republican Party is depicted as a cynical stratagem to ensure his re-election.[4] Most common among historians is a view of Lincoln's unionist pronouncements as a weak version of the nationalism that overtook the United States during and after the war. The dean of Civil War historians, James McPherson, provides one oft-quoted example in his observation that Lincoln frequently used the term "Union" during his First Inaugural Address, but switched decisively to "nation" during his famous speech at Gettysburg, signalling a new nationalist commitment that swiftly spread among Americans.[5]

This interpretative range, while insightful in particulars, fails to explain Lincoln's understanding of political unity. In each example "union" becomes a marker for other concerns—Lincoln's psychological state, or his antipathy to black rights, or the growth of American nationalism—and remains unexamined in its own right, as a distinctive source of political meaning. Without taking up each interpretative strain at length, recall that, as McPherson elsewhere notes, "Lincoln had *arguments* for Union, not just a kind of mystical attachment to it." Moreover, Lincoln's frequent repetition of the term over time (including in his *Second* Inaugural, more than a year after Gettysburg) indicates that the concept held far more than instrumental interest. With little help from main scholarly currents in evaluating his union ideas, let Lincoln himself be our guide: "I only ask all who are eager for the truth, that . . . they will turn to my own words and examine for themselves."[6]

Such an inspection suggests, first of all, that Lincoln was not forced into a hasty consideration of national unity by imminent civil war. His public observations on the subject date from the 1830s, and were refined over the subsequent quarter-century. As he testified before the war: "I have often inquired of myself what great principle or idea it was that kept this Confederacy so long together."[7] His own efforts would help to reshape the answer.

II. Towards a More Moral Union

In certain respects Lincoln's unionist vision recalled that of his predecessors, most notably Daniel Webster. As a major Whig spokesman in the 1856 presidential campaign, Lincoln quoted Webster so often that one newspaper accused him of plagiarism. Lincoln's ardent arguments for perpetuating the Union were principally drawn from Webster, as was his strongest union metaphor, a "house divided," with which he first won national attention in 1854. Lincoln's "Lost Speech," delivered two years later at the Illinois Republican Convention, concludes with Webster's most famous words, the "Liberty *and* Union, now and forever" peroration from his Senate response to early threats of secession. Paul Erickson affirms that Lincoln's unionist "faith" derived from "the works of Daniel Webster, [from] his . . . prophetic vision of disunion."[8]

Yet the influence of Webster, and other union-minded Framers, went only so far—as Lincoln plainly stated. "I do not mean to say we are bound to follow implicitly in whatever our fathers did. To do so, would be to discard all the lights of current experience—to reject all progress—all improvement," the new president declared in 1860. Lincoln wrestled throughout his career with the burden of "supporting and maintaining an edifice that has been erected by others." One field of improvement on Jacksonian-era luminaries, and even what he called the "deathless names" of the founding, was unionist ideas and related policies.[9] Lincoln treated Webster and others' unconditional-union claims ("now and forever") as excessive, given his own insistence on precise language. In speeches and letters drafted with such care that Lincoln warned editors "I do not wish the sense changed, or modified, to a hair's breadth," he expressed union in simple figures: marriage, family, divided houses. Lincoln painstakingly shaped his public statements to draw on the tremendous potency union had attained in Americans' political talk, but he did so with a subtlety uncommon during the heat of the antebellum and wartime crisis.[10]

Not only in linguistic usage did Lincoln depart from previous generations. Where Webster and other antebellum unionists were content to rest on established doctrine, Lincoln systematically revalued the concept. Beginning with the territory comprising the American nation and insisting on its profound integrity as *united*, he proceeded to declare that "citizens of the United States" were "united by a purpose to perpetuate the Union."[11] Girding this source of mutuality, in Lincoln's view, was citizens' expanded political participation, guided by enlightened self-interest; and by an association of union with strong moral values, particularly equality. The Union of states would be perpetuated not through idle worship of the nation, but a careful balance of territorial integrity, popular sovereignty, and legal precedent.

Lincoln's Territorial Union

Lincoln's account of national union began with American territory. "A nation may be said to consist of its territory, its people, and its laws. The territory is the only part which is of certain durability. . . . It is of the first importance to duly consider, and estimate, this ever-enduring part," the new president told Congress in 1861. The American land, he concluded, was "advantageous [only] for one united people."[12]

Extolling united U.S. territory was a familiar note in period oratory, but Lincoln's emphasis was dramatically different. Previous generations had been occupied with separation and expansion, first breaking with Britain then variously obtaining territory from British, French, Spanish, Mexican, and Native American Indian holders. The founders and their early-nineteenth-century legatees freely played on fear of outside (especially British) aggression to bolster their geostrategic arguments, defending territorial acquisitions on the grounds of enhanced national security.

In contrast, freshman Congressman Lincoln's first notable act was to oppose Polk's Mexican policy. With some other Whigs, his "fear [was] that expansion and war with Mexico, like slavery, would destroy the moral core of national identity." And long after his fellow Whigs rejoined the expansionist fold—long after the Whig party's demise, indeed—Lincoln's continued attention to territorial union revolved around *maintaining* existing territory, and thereby keeping the United States one. "The question," Lincoln told Congress in his first public statement on the war, was "whether a constitutional republic, or democracy—a Government of the people by the same people—can or cannot maintain its territorial integrity against its own domestic foes."[13] This was not a matter of protection from external danger, Lincoln made clear: "All the armies of Europe, Asia and Africa combined, with all the treasures of the earth, with a Buonaparte for a commander, could not by force, take a drink from the Ohio." His account instead marshalled commercial rationales ("[S]eparate our common country into two nations . . . and every man of this great interior region is cut off from sea-ports"), arguments from propinquity ("Physically speaking, we cannot separate"), and principle.[14] The last drew on a robust conception of "territorial integrity."

Integrity, in Lincoln's carefully specified terms, connoted both 'integrated'—joined as a single whole—and the moral rectitude also commonly associated with the idea. "The Union must be preserved in the purity of its principles," Lincoln told campaign crowds in 1856. Only then could Americans claim "integrity of its territorial parts." He first related principle and territory two years earlier during the Kansas-Nebraska debates, with a crescendo of rhetorical questions opposing slavery in the territories: "[I]s not Nebraska, while a territory, a part of us? Do we not own the country? And if we surrender the control of it, do we not surrender the right of self-government? It is part of ourselves . . . when all the parts are gone, what has become of the whole? What is there left of us? What use for the General Government, when there is nothing left of us?"[15]

Investing territory with "integrity" drew on the sacral authority conferred by tradition. This notion was not new among U.S. politicians; Lincoln's departure was to insist that unified territory could only remain a legitimate source of "one national family" when it was *free* land, upholding the "purity" of the Union's "principles." Free-soil ideology dated to the colonial era, but it was Lincoln and fellow Republicans who popularized the idea of principled territorial union, ensuring that "the goals of Union and free soil were intertwined, and neither could be sacrificed without endangering the other." Similarly transfigured in Lincoln's account was union among the people, whose status as bearers of mutual affection was exchanged for that of active citizens, most notably those "who gave their lives that [the] nation might live."[16]

Equality and Union

Lincoln's First Inaugural Address culminated by moving from territorial-union arguments to invoking "bonds of affection" among Americans. "We are not ene-mies, but friends. We must not be enemies," Lincoln implored, offering the vision of a renewed "chorus of the Union." This affective-unionist theme in fact marks an exception in Lincoln's public statements, and undoubtedly owed much to the con-text surrounding its delivery, on the threshold of national division. Elsewhere Lin-coln rarely appealed to personal bonds among Americans of different regions, despite such appeals' fervent use by antebellum speakers from Daniel Webster to Jefferson Davis. Lincoln's occasional references to mutual affection were universal rather than national in scope. Deploring lynchings of black workers during the July 1863 New York draft riots, he said, "The strongest bond of human sympathy, out-side of the family relation, should be one uniting all working people, of all nations, and tongues, and kindreds."[17]

Rather than rote praise for mutual affection among Americans—a declaration that increasingly rang hollow as war approached—Lincoln proposed another basis for unifying the people, one in keeping with a more moral understanding of national union. If at first cautiously, Lincoln insisted on a union dedicated to a particular proposition: equality. The "central idea in our political public opinion" was, Lin-coln said over and over, "the equality of all men."[18] Commentators from Karl Marx forward have credited Lincoln with redefining ideas of equality, but this was not in fact the thrust of his "second American revolution."[19] Lincoln deliberately reasserted doctrines sounded by Jefferson and others during the founding era. As he testified: "Little by little . . . we have been giving up the *old* for the *new* faith. Near eighty years ago we began by declaring that all men are created equal: but now from that beginning we have run down."[20]

Instead Lincoln's innovation lay in his nuanced association of equality and union—a connection that appeared unlikely on its face. "Union" denoted stability, compromise, even stasis; equality retained a strong revolutionary flavor, especially in the supercharged ideological environment before and during the war. In the antebel-lum period, indeed, advocates of equality routinely were portrayed as agents of *dis*-union, given Southerners' (reasonably accurate) view of egalitarian doctrines as "abolitionism, pure and simple." Accordingly an either/or relationship between equality and union was frequently posited during Lincoln's time. Said Stephen Douglas: "we should unite to save the Union before we should quarrel as to the mode in which it was to be governed." Similar judgments are reached today: constitutional historian Paul Kahn writes that "to Lincoln, union is more important than truth," given that "It would not be enough, for example, for the seceding states to affirm the same true principles at their foundation. Full vindication of the moral truths of equality and liberty would not justify a failure to maintain the community."[21]

Yet without the commitment to inequality inherent in slaveholders' ideology, "the community" would not have been in danger to begin with. Lincoln by the mid-1850s consistently cast union as a dependent virtue, no longer defensible in its own right alone. The thrust of his "House Divided" speech, for example, was that "under the guise of allaying controversy and establishing national unity, the Democratic party had constantly pushed slavery into new territory and had thwarted all efforts aimed at control and ultimate extinction of the evil." Two months before the war began, Lincoln declared that he "would rather be assassinated" than preserve a Union open to expanded slavery.[22]

Lincoln thus treated the ostensibly divergent values of equality and union as mutually reinforcing. In one debate with Douglas, Lincoln insisted that honoring the moral principles ("the practices, and policy") of the Declaration would mean "we shall not only have saved the union, but we shall have so saved it as to make, and to keep it, forever worthy of the saving." He opposed the "Crittenden Compromise" in 1860, which conceded certain territories to the slaveholding South in exchange for continued national unity. As the president-elect wrote William Seward, who supported the legislation, "[It] acknowledges that slavery has equal rights with liberty, and surrenders all we have contended for. . . . A year will not pass, till we shall have to take Cuba as a condition upon which [the southern states] will stay in the Union."[23]

Lincoln's idea of equality was closely connected with property and free labor, as historian Daniel Walker Howe notes: "Equality meant, in the first instance, an equal opportunity to work for one's living and an equal right to retain the fruits of one's labor." A nation of affectively joined friends was a dim prospect; Lincoln instead hoped that Americans would respond to a vision of shared entitlement to the political goods of civic participation and economic growth. The desire to advance free of artificial obstacles was, Lincoln insisted, a universal one. Hence he viewed Southern society as also reflecting devotion to equal opportunity—at least for white men. In one summary: "Especially in the South, the republican 'ideal of equal opportunity' . . . was of great significance for social mobility and social self-understanding of whites on all social levels."[24]

In Lincoln's reworking of a biblical proverb, in which "the Union, and the Constitution, are the picture of silver" and "the assertion of that [equality] principle . . . has proved an 'apple of gold' to us," he set out the relation between union and equal liberty. "The picture was made for the apple, not the apple for the picture. So let us act, that neither picture, or apple, shall ever be blurred, or broken."[25] Presenting Union and Constitution as foundations of equality invested national unity with a moral standing it had never so explicitly been granted. Linking this achievement with Lincoln's attempt to realize political union on a wider scale than ever before, the thrust of his conceptual revision becomes clear. If the people were to be more closely bound together, it would be as moral equals.

Institutional Union: Rule of Law and Popular Sovereignty

Lincoln's predecessors, especially James Madison, offered cautious defenses of "virtuous leaders" as custodians of national union. Lincoln instead abandoned the expectation. "Politicians," the latter declared in his Lyceum Address, were "a set of men who have interests aside from the interests of the people, and who, to say the most of them, are, taken as a mass, at least one long step removed from honest men." The few outstanding exceptions were likely to prove even more dangerous. From early in his career Lincoln warned against the political "genius" turned tyrant, who "thirsts and burns for distinction; and, if possible . . . will have it, whether at the expense of emancipating slavery, or enslaving freemen." Simultaneously, he denounced "that lawless and mobocratic spirit . . . which is already abroad in the land; and is spreading with rapid and fearful impetuosity, to the ultimate overthrow of every institution, or even moral principle, in which persons and property have hitherto found security."[26] With leaders and followers alike tending to venality, severely limiting the possibility of the Founders' "special understanding" between governors and governed, where to turn?

REVERENCE FOR THE LAWS

Rule of law was Lincoln's substitute for enlightened leaders as the institutional agent of political union. Recognizing that "the strongest bulwark of any Government, and particularly those constituted like ours" was "the *attachment* of the People," he urged "every American" to "swear by the blood of the Revolution, never to violate in the least particular, the laws of the country." Such "reverence for the laws" would enhance citizens' sense of mutual connectedness, Lincoln argued consistently. Legal securities ensured both protection of equality and of private property. In 1862, Lincoln described even the Civil War as a "struggle to preserve the rule of law, the constitutional Union."[27]

Lincoln's calls for "reverence" likely rang oddly in mid-nineteenth century America, where rule of law was not a widely hallowed ideal and laissez-faire was a guiding principle in federal and state lawmaking alike. Daniel Webster, the period's best-known constitutional lawyer, rarely extolled law as such apart from sentimental salutes to the Constitution in public addresses; and it is difficult to imagine Andrew Jackson or any of his immediate successors delivering a speech like Lincoln's first wartime message to Congress, fully a third of which was devoted to justifying the legality of his presidential actions.[28]

Lincoln considered legal securities far more reliable restraints on popular excess than he did political leaders' tutelage. Yet reducing the importance of politicians and the people alike while proclaiming reverence for law bordered on the disingenuous, considering the roles of the former as lawmakers and latter as law's guarantors. With higher-law securities in place, Lincoln advanced an ideal closer to unfettered popular rule than had any other American political figure, Thomas Jefferson's asides on the ward system notwithstanding. Discarding the complex mechanism which linked a people united in friendship to a set of representatives, in 1858 Lincoln asked rhetorically "What does Popular Sovereignty mean?" "Strictly and literally it means the sovereignty of the people over their own affairs—in other words, the right of the people . . . to govern themselves."[29]

POPULAR SOVEREIGNTY AND REPRESENTATION

Lincoln's early comments on popular rule were vague and sonorous. The essence of the American "experiment," he said in 1838, was "the capability of a people to govern themselves." A decade later, his views had become more specific. Speaking in the House on "the will of the people," he professed "the one great living principle of all Democratic republican government" to be "the principle that the representative is bound to carry out the known will of his constituents." Lincoln viewed legislators not as independent paragons of political wisdom, but as delegates requiring instruction. His advice to constituents:

> Send up members of Congress from the various districts, with opinions according to your own, and if they are for [my preferred measures], I shall have nothing to oppose; if they are not for them, I shall not . . . attempt to dragoon them into their adoption. Now, then, can there be any difficulty in understanding this? . . . [I am] in favor of making Presidential elections and the legislation of the country distinct matters; so that the people can elect whom they please, and afterwards, legislate just as they please. . . . In leaving the people's business in their hands, we cannot be wrong.[30]

This speech came amid the debate over war with Mexico, an event which galvanized Lincoln's thinking on popular sovereignty. As in the later "people's contest" over which he presided, reports of dead and suffering soldiers powerfully illustrated the extent of central government claims on American citizens.[31] Recognizing that those claims at times required the ultimate personal sacrifice, Lincoln constructed a blueprint for a deliberative collectivity of competent self-governors.

In an antebellum polity featuring huge turnouts for political speeches and torchlight parades, passionate partisanship, and record voting levels, it could appear that political activity was integral to human existence.[32] Lincoln's views of popular sovereignty approached such a characterization, although he offered no civic-humanist encomiums about political activity as the best life. Rather, his commitment to popular rule connected individual and national identity. Building on the idea of territorial integrity, Lincoln rooted participation in the nation's temporal continuity. People living on—inheriting—the ground consecrated by their forebears were obliged to engage in government to preserve both private and public achievements.[33] Lincoln made this point most powerfully in wartime addresses like that at Gettysburg, striking chords among listeners whose commitment to the public order starkly required blood, but the seeds were present as early as the 1830s.

How did conceiving personal identity in civic terms translate into commitment to national union? For one, participation in governing would inspire a sense of shared purpose. Political activity was, Lincoln insisted, "an important principle to rally and unite the people . . . [this is] a fundamental idea, going about as deep as anything."[34] Establishing common laws and otherwise exercising sovereignty aroused individuals' spirit of mutuality. Rather than a subject of everyday politics, the citizen in Lincoln's vision became an architect of the political order, which in turn was seen as constitutive of his or her[35] individual identity.

By Lincoln's presidency he clearly believed, as evidenced in his informal talks to audiences ranging from inaugural well-wishers to Union regiments, that political participation promised considerable benefits to the citizen and republic alike. The contrary idea, that government was a difficult business best carried on by those with great foresight and fortitude, had a long pedigree in America. (As did the view that it was the province of incompetent knaves.) But Lincoln suggested that political activity could be personally meaningful for most people. Where the founders had filtered and blocked mass governance in various ways, Lincoln came to see relatively unmediated participation in politics as a necessary source of national unity. In an 1854 aside, Lincoln compared American ideals to those of "most [other] governments"; he might have been contrasting his own view with that of the Founders. "*They* said, some men are too ignorant, and vicious to share in government. Possibly so, said we; and, by your system, you would always keep them ignorant, and vicious. We proposed to give all a chance; and we expected the weak to grow stronger, the ignorant, wiser; and all better, and happier *together*."[36]

In this way Lincoln remained faithful to a basic tenet guiding unionist philosophy since the early republic: that citizens had actively to express an ethic of mutuality for the Union to remain viable. His doubts about interpersonal affection as the basis for this ethic led Lincoln to emphasize popular participation in governance instead. His aim was to inspire a sense of common purpose and also a consensus about the value of higher principles, most notably equality. Lincoln related popular sovereignty and equal rights on occasion, as when he asked in 1858 "If the Negro is a man, is it not to that extent a total destruction of self-government to say that he too shall not govern himself?"[37] His views on black equality—and African Americans' inclusion in a union of sovereign citizens—would become much more publicly apparent during the Civil War. Though the war was not an immediate inspiration for Lincoln's unionism, it was a spur to realizing changes long present in theory.

III. African Americans, Equality, and Union

Issuing the *Dred Scott* majority opinion in 1857, Chief Justice Taney stated what Lincoln later called the "amended" view of the Declaration.[38] "The general words," admitted Taney, "would seem to embrace the whole human family, and if they were used in a similar instrument at this day would be so understood. But it is too clear for dispute, that the enslaved African race were not intended to be included." Lincoln was outspoken in response: his opposition to the decision formed the heart of his "House Divided" speech.[39] Lincoln's very different interpretation of the Founders' views on equality and union is evident in a campaign address from shortly before his famous debates with Douglas:

> When they look back . . . they find that those old men say that 'We hold these truths to be self-evident, that all men are created equal,' and then they feel that that moral sentiment taught in that day evidences their relation to those men, that it is the father of all moral principle in them, and that they have a right to claim it as though they were blood of the blood, and flesh of the flesh of the men who wrote that Declaration, and so they are. That is the electric cord in that Declaration. That links the hearts of patriotic and liberty-loving men together. . . . [L]et us discard all this quibbling about this man and the other man—this race and that race and the other race being inferior, and therefore they must be placed in an inferior position—discarding our standard that we have left us. Let us discard all these things, and unite as one people throughout the land, until we shall stand up once more declaring that all men are created equal.

Lincoln spoke primarily of European immigrants, but evidently referred to African Americans as well: "If one man says it [the Declaration] does not mean the Negro, why not another say it does not mean another man?" Extending the Declaration's familiar passage to include different races, and emphasizing that *all* Americans should "unite as one people"—these were novel positions for a national public figure, both practically and theoretically.[40]

Though a body of scholarship dismisses Lincoln's emancipatory intent,[41] he is sometimes read today as exhibiting a "growing radicalism" on issues of black rights.[42] Specific to our purposes is whether his outlook extended to including African Americans in a reformulated union. In numerous speeches shortly before and during the war, Lincoln made clear that the Declaration's "all men" clause encompassed blacks. Moreover, union membership, in Lincoln's understanding, entailed more than vague references to "shared humanity," particularly given his stress on the benefits of political participation.

In 1858 Lincoln said "There is a physical difference between the white and black races, which I suppose, will forever forbid the two races living together upon terms of social and political equality." These words came in the heat of a senatorial race in which Lincoln was repeatedly badgered on racial-purity issues, a tactic which probably lost him the election.[43] LaWanda Cox holds, plausibly, that Lincoln's rhetoric during the Douglas debates "was a formulation that accepted rather than championed white dominance," and that there is "a larger consistency between the presidential and pre-presidential Lincoln" than most scholars admit.[44] But was long-standing white opposition to integration so enduring that Lincoln dared not proceed beyond private musings on black equality?

Lincoln's evolving position indicates otherwise. While in 1855 he could still write that he along with "the great body of the Northern people do crucify their [anti-slavery] feelings, in order to maintain their loyalty to the constitution and the Union," his views were already changing. In 1857 he repeated before several audiences his powerful affirmation of free labor and equality. Responding to Douglas's race-baiting, Lincoln defended the "natural right" of any "black woman [to] eat the bread she earns with her own hands," and concluded "in this . . . she is my equal and the equal of all others." At the 1859 Wisconsin Agricultural Fair the not-yet-declared presidential candidate avowed:

> From the first appearances of man upon the earth, down to very recent times, the words 'stranger' and 'enemy' were quite and almost synonymous. . . . To correct the evils, great and small, which spring from want of sympathy and from positive enmity, among *strangers*, as nations or as individuals, is one of the highest functions of civilization. [Such corrections] make more pleasant, and more strong, and more durable, the bond of social and political union among us.

Lincoln's statement nowhere identifies free or slave blacks as the "strangers" to be embraced. Yet it is no great speculative leap to read this meaning into his words, given the prominence of slavery issues in 1859. His annual message to Congress in 1862 addressed blacks' inclusion even more clearly, concluding "It is not 'can *any* of us *imagine* better?' but 'can we *all* do better'? Object whatsoever is possible, still the question recurs 'can we do better?' "[45] Lincoln's subsequent statements, especially after he dropped support for colonization in 1863, suggest his further movement towards the conviction that African Americans should be full-fledged constituents of a reconstructed union.

Lincoln's last public address, delivered to a White House crowd serenading his return from Appomattox, leads one historian to "suspect that many were disappointed in that audience . . . for Lincoln spoke not in the vein of celebration but of heavy conviction." Midway through, Lincoln warned against saying "To the blacks . . . 'This cup of liberty which these, your old masters, hold to your lips, we will dash from you, and leave you to the chances of gathering the spilled and scattered contents in some vague and undefined when, where, and how.' " Instead, Lincoln urged, "recognize, and sustain the new government of Louisiana." Thus "the colored man, too, in *seeing all united for him*, is inspired."[46]

Lincoln by 1857 was declaring African Americans within the Declaration's guarantee of equality—and hinting, especially after the war began, at their membership in a reformulated national union. Notable in this regard was Lincoln's controversial decision to enlist blacks in the Union Army—assuring them an especially deep form of community membership, the right to die for it. Frederick Douglass heralded the decision: African American soldiers would, he wrote, "rise in one bound from social degradation to the plane of common equality with all other varieties of men."[47] Black suffrage, as Lincoln privately endorsed in 1865, was a similarly strong guarantee.

Lincoln's "advoca[cy] of the more and more immediate realization of the promise of [black] equality" fell short in practice. The limits of his leadership are evident in the postwar situation W. E. B. DuBois later described: "the races . . . liv[ing] for many years side by side, united in economic effort, obeying a common government, sensitive to mutual thought & feeling, yet subtly and silently separate in many matters of deeper human intimacy."[48] Recall, however, that Lincoln viewed affective exchange even between whites as an unpromising source of unity; political union, not "deeper human intimacy," was his aim in 1865. During the last two years of the war (and of his life), Lincoln's commitment to enhancing African Americans' status was far deeper than would be any nationally prominent white political leader's over the rest of the century, save perhaps Charles Sumner. No less an astute analyst than Douglass concluded in 1876, with Reconstruction's reversal well underway, that "measuring [Lincoln] by the sentiment of his country—a sentiment he was bound as a statesman to consult—he was swift, zealous, radical, and determined." Dorothy Wickenden affirms that "In strikingly similar terms, Abraham Lincoln and Frederick Douglass described a more perfect union, one they together helped to construct."[49]

Lincoln's insistence on *principled* union, and his simultaneous drawing back from the unconditional usage most other politicians favored, was immensely influential. As the war proceeded, moral unionism was more widely voiced among Northerners, and ethnocultural ("union for whites only") claims were far less common, especially after black soldiers joined Union ranks.[50] Unconditional-union claims retained currency, of course; Lincoln's own secretary of state, William Seward, regularly asserted that "No one of us ought to object when called upon to reaffirm his devotion to the Union, however unconditionally." The phrase resonated beyond the North: "unconditional unionist" became loyalist Southerners' self-description during the war, among those "who opposed secession and who never voluntarily aided the Confederacy."[51] But Lincoln's effort to relate union to equality and other moral values won a degree of acceptance, thanks to his great prominence in public life and subsequent martyrdom. In one telling example, the formerly disunionist abolitionist J. W. Bliss proposed to Sumner "in Lincoln's vein" the doctrine "We mean both *Emancipation* and *Union* . . . the one for the sake of the other and both for the sake of the country." McPherson cites numerous examples of Union soldiers affirming "Lincoln's great evocation of Union war aims," particularly liberty and equality, as well as "the perception that the abolition of slavery was inseparably linked to the goal of preserving the Union."[52]

Abraham Lincoln did much to place union on a coherent and principled foundation, during antebellum and wartime circumstances that propelled the term to the
center of American political talk. By insisting, even if only cautiously, on blacks'
inclusion in a more moral union, he staked much of his own prestige on the revised
understanding. That prestige soared to uncharted heights after Lincoln's death,
cementing national union's identification as a morally-informed instrument. As it
turned out, the achievement was all too temporary.

Rogan Kersh is Associate Professor of Political Science and Public Administration at the Maxwell School, Syracuse University. His recent publications include
Dreams of a More Perfect Union (Cornell, 2001); "New Horizons in American Political Development," *Perspectives on Politics* (2003); "How the Personal Becomes Political," *Studies in American Political Development* (2002); "Influencing the State:
Campaign Finance and Its Discontents," *Critical Review* (2003); and "The Politics
of Obesity," *Health Affairs* (2002).

~

WALT WHITMAN'S ABRAHAM LINCOLN[1]

George Anastaplo

My God! My God! What will the country say?

—Abraham Lincoln[2]

I.

WALT WHITMAN'S DIRGE for Abraham Lincoln, "When Lilacs Last in the Door-
yard Bloom'd," has been called his masterpiece by various scholars, including Mark
Van Doren, one of the most distinguished American literary critics of the twentieth
century.[3] Mr. Van Doren, himself a serious poet, concluded his article on Whitman
in the *Dictionary of American Biography* seven decades ago with these observations:

> His death in Camden on March 26, 1892, was the occasion for many attempts to sum
> up his excellence and his importance. For the most part these were failures, since the
> shadow of the disciples and the executors still obscured him. During [the] forty years
> [since his death] this shadow has gradually been dissipated under the influence of bio-
> graphical research, a saner criticism, and the passage of time. The claims originally
> made for him as a man and moralist are made less often, and promise to disappear.
> . . . It is now difficult if not impossible to believe that [Whitman] came into the world
> to save it, or that he will save it. The world in general pays little attention to his name;
> he has never been a popular poet, accepted of democracies as he hoped, nor has he

been often imitated by other poets, as he also hoped. But as his isolation grows more apparent it grows more impressive, so that his rank among the poets of his country and his century, and indeed of the world, is higher than it has ever been before. His work manages to survive the attacks made either upon its author as a man or upon what George Santayana called before 1900 the "barbarism" of his mind. It survives as certainly the most original work yet done [this Van Doren appraisal was published in 1936] by any American poet, and perhaps as the most passionate and best. It is easier now to comprehend Whitman as the artist that he was, though it is not easy and it never will be. As a maker of phrases, as a master of rhythms, as a weaver of images, as an architect of poems he is often beyond the last reach of analysis. His diaries of the [Civil War], his prefaces to *Leaves of Grass*, his *Democratic Vistas*, and his notes on the landscapes at Timber Creek are a permanent part of American prose. He himself, looked back at purely as a writer, will always loom a gigantic and beautiful figure in nineteenth-century letters.[4]

Two decades later, Mark Van Doren, in a talk at the Library of Congress, offered this appraisal of Whitman's "Lilacs" dirge:

The Civil War, just ended with Lincoln's life, had been not so much the making as the remaking of the great poet who slept in Whitman's bones. Death now had become tragic and particular: the deaths of soldiers, the death of America as Whitman had known it in the days of Eden, the days of the Children of Adam; and now the death of "the sweetest, wisest soul of all my days and lands." The greatest man in Whitman's world had died, a man not himself, a man quite outside himself; and that was an advantage too for the poet who was to begin his crowning piece, for the subject matter of poetry should be outside, must be outside, if one is to go and put oneself in it.[5]

Such Van Doren comments reflect an awareness of the concern, expressed by many critics, that Whitman was too self-centered in his poetry, that he made too much of himself.[6] Mr. Van Doren continues his assessment of "Lilacs" thus:

Whitman went to the subject of Lincoln with good and evil defined in his imagination, with each of those great things limited and made lifelike by the other. And he bore with him a set of symbols which to the accomplishment of magnificent music he could weave and intertwine as plastic artists do their visible, their tangible materials. The lilac, the star, the bird are concrete, irreducible images; the poem organizes itself around them as if by a natural process, though it is of course the artistic process at its best. Whitman is there too; "Lilac and star and bird" are "twined with the chant of my soul." The importance of the subject is finally in the understanding Whitman has of it. But it is something to be understood; and once more the song of a bird assists the musician of the spirit to find his voice: once more [as in Whitman's "Calamus" poems] there is a great hymn to death:

>   Come lovely and soothing death,
>   Undulate round the world, serenely arriving, arriving,

> In the day, in the night, to all, to each,
> Sooner or later delicate death.
>
> Prais'd be the fathomless universe,
> For life and joy, and for objects and knowledge curious,
> And for love, sweet love—but praise! praise! praise!
> For the sure-enwinding arms of cool-enfolding death.[7]

Mark Van Doren's praise of "Lilacs" has been endorsed for me in a letter from his talented son, John Van Doren: "'Lilacs' seems to me a hauntingly beautiful poem that combines love and veneration in striking ways—not easy to do."[8] If "Lilacs" *is* Whitman's masterpiece, then any reservations one has about it would probably apply at least as much to the rest of his poetry.

But before proceeding further along the line of inquiry that I have indicated thus far, attention should be called to Mark Van Doren's reading of the remarkable Whitman poem, "A Noiseless Patient Spider."[9] That careful reading provides us guidance to the study of those Whitman poems that do reward careful inspection. Here is the "Spider" poem:

> A noiseless patient spider,
> I mark'd where on a little promontory it stood isolated,
> Mark'd how to explore the vacant vast surrounding,
> It launch'd forth filament, filament, filament, out of itself;
> Ever unreeling them, ever tirelessly speeding them.
>
> And you, O my soul, where you stand,
> Surrounded, detached, in measureless oceans of space,
> Ceaselessly musing, venturing, throwing, seeking the
>   spheres to connect them;
> Till the bridge you will need be form'd, till the ductile
>   anchor hold,
> Till the gossamer thread you fling catch somewhere, O
>   my soul.[10]

Among the Van Doren observations on this poem is one that holds Whitman's long-troubled soul up to view:

> It is an ancient idea, this of man's mind or soul that in its little sphere of flesh can achieve a correspondence with the great sphere of creation around it. And there have been times when this correspondence was spoken of as easy to bring about—indeed, it almost happened by itself. Not so with Whitman, whose modern soul was haunted by the difficulties of the task. Whitman studied loneliness like a scholar, and made his various music out of solitude, his great subject.[11]

These and like observations in Mark Van Doren's assessments of Whitman should be kept in mind as we proceed with our study of the poet's career, especially during the Civil War.

Permit me, before returning to my own inquiry into the work and the effect of Whitman, to make a suggestion in response to a question that has been posed as to why the Vietnamese should now be as interested in American studies (including Whitman) as we have been told that they are, despite their decade-long war with the United States. It is not generally remembered in this country that the Vietnamese, when they began their revolution against French colonialists during the Second World War, modeled much of their rhetoric, if not also some of their thinking, upon the American Declaration of Independence. It seems to have been political folly on our part, for which both we and the Vietnamese paid dearly, that we allowed ourselves to appear to take up in Indochina where the French left off.

Even so, any intelligent people in the modern world today must sense that the political principles that can provide an emerging nation reliable guidance toward a prosperous and otherwise decent life are principles which have at least some of their roots in the Spirit of 1776. It makes sense then for the Vietnamese to take American studies seriously, adapting the lessons found there to their circumstances. Comments of this kind, I presume to add, should be kept in mind as we consider what to do, in the months and years ahead, in the Middle East and elsewhere.[12]

II.

Highlights of Whitman's career are provided in the 1911 edition of the *Encyclopedia Britannica*. Its entry on the poet is written by John Burroughs, a Whitman biographer of note who may even have first interested the poet in the hermit thrush featured in the "Lilacs" dirge.[13] Burroughs writes,

> The book [*Leaves of Grass*, first published on July 4, 1855] did not attract the attention of the critics and the reading public till a letter from [Ralph Waldo] Emerson to the poet, in which the volume was characterized as "the most extraordinary piece of wit and wisdom that America has yet contributed," was published [evidently without Emerson's permission] in the *New York Tribune*. This created a demand for the book, and started it upon a career that has probably had more vicissitudes and called forth more adverse as well as more eulogistic criticism than any other contemporary literary work.[14]

This Burroughs entry says the sort of thing that respectable critics could say about Whitman during the generation following his death. This *Britannica* entry (most of a page in the 1911 edition of the encyclopedia) includes this description of the man:

> Whitman never married, never left America [he did visit Canada?], never laid up, or aimed to lay up, riches; he gave his time and his substance freely to others, belonged

to no club nor coterie, associated habitually with the common people—mechanics, coach-drivers, working men of all kinds—was always cheerful and optimistic. He was large and picturesque of figure, slow of movement, tolerant, receptive, democratic and full of charity and goodwill towards all. His life was a poet's life from first to last—free, unworldly, unhurried, unconventional, unselfish, and was contentedly and joyously lived.[15]

A curious feature of this 1911 *Britannica* entry, which recognizes Whitman's Civil War activities (especially his service as a quite helpful visitor to military hospitals in Washington, D.C.), is that there is no reference in that entry either to Abraham Lincoln or to Whitman's writings about him.

Whitman spent most of the war in New York (especially Brooklyn) and in Washington. He was forty years old when the war started, a little too old for military service unless he was determined to join the fight in person. Still, he *has* been criticized as "a man who bragged of consummate health and called on all others to fight [while remaining] at the comparatively remote distance of the hospital."[16]

Whitman, who began his writing career as a newspaperman, recorded his impression of the war and of the many soldiers he ministered to, quite conscientiously, and from whom he learned much. He was particularly moved throughout the war by the threats to the country represented by the Southern Secessionist movement. And, of course, he recorded his glimpses of Lincoln, first in New York City and later (quite frequently, he says) in Washington.[17]

A half-dozen of Whitman's poems about Lincoln have survived. The most popular is "O Captain, My Captain," an effusion of twenty lines that Whitman is said to have almost lamented that he had ever written. He evidently did not like the way it was exploited by others. Even so, he could regard Lincoln as the Man of the Century, saying so, one way or another, in both poetry and prose.

His anguish, upon the murder of Lincoln, is testified to again and again, including in an oration he gave annually, beginning in 1879, on the anniversary of *his* president's death.[18] Indeed, it can be suspected that Lincoln was regarded by Whitman as a spiritual father, someone to be joined in veneration with his mother whom he evidently adored. One may detect here (as well as in his sometimes shameless self-promotion) the charm and perhaps the related immaturity (if not the vulnerability) of Whitman, traits which helped shape his political positions as well as his personal relations.

III.

The "Lilacs" poem, originally published in 1865, comes to us in sixteen numbered sections. It had first been divided into twenty-one sections (with the central one then being the section which is still numbered as 11, a more or less bucolic scene celebrating everyday pursuits).[19] But perhaps more instructive is that the poem had, in its 1865 publication, its stanzas numbered (as a few other Whitman poems were once numbered), with forty-three stanzas thus marked in this poem (with very small numbers). The central stanza, in the original arrangement, is that found in our Section 13, which begins, "Sing on, sing on you gray-brown bird." That twenty-second stanza reads (in its entirety),

> O liquid and free and tender!
> O wild and loose to my soul—O wonderous singer!
> You only I hear—yet the star holds me, (but will soon depart,)
> Yet the lilac with mastering odor holds me.[20]

At this point in the poem are the central lines (103 and 104) of this 206-line dirge, lines which include a recognition of the "voice of uttermost woe" that can be heard in "human song," even when it is "liquid and free and tender."[21]

It is the song of the hermit thrush that the poem builds up to. That song, designated in one edition as the "Death Carol," was eventually put in italics by Whitman. This Death Carol, from which Mark Van Doren quoted in a passage I have taken from him, speaks lovingly of "delicate death," of "cool-enfolding death."[22]

It has been noticed, by Mr. Van Doren and others, that Whitman, in the "Lilacs" poem, avoids the self-centeredness evident in so much of his poetry. But, it might be said, he does not so much avoid it as conceal it. Even in "Lilacs," however, he (or an alter ego) is very much there, with almost one hundred uses of "I," "my," and "me." Still more revealing is the considerable praise he lavishes upon the carol of the bird, for in doing this he praises of course the music that he himself has provided for the bird.

Much of what Whitman does even in "Lilacs" seems to be mannered, at times excessive, bordering upon the sentimental. Particularly challenging is what he says about death. We, too, can be enraptured by death, or at least by its consequences, without realizing it. This may be seen in our enthusiasm about splendid autumn leaves, which are, after all, "corpses" of once living things. Even so, light (that is, the illumination provided by some "living" body) is needed if such colors of leaves are truly to be seen.

Whitman himself is at his best, and indeed quite good, in "Lilacs" when he describes the cross-country funeral procession for Lincoln, with the coffin moving by train for a month or so on its way to Springfield for burial. He does not mention, perhaps because of the effect he wants to create, that the coffin of one of Lincoln's children, who had died in Washington, was also on the train for reburial with his father in Illinois.[23] The talented journalist in Whitman may be seen in his account, even though he himself evidently missed seeing that melancholy pageant anywhere along its cross-country route. (But, then, Homer was probably never at Troy.)

The self-centeredness of the poet—something far less evident both in the Homer and the Shakespeare whom Whitman did admire—that self-centeredness may be seen in the eighth section, when he addresses the planet Venus:

> O western orb sailing the heaven,
> Now I know what you must have meant as a month since I walk'd,
> As I walk'd in silence the transparent shadowy night,
> As I saw you had something to tell as you bent to me night after night,
> As you droop'd from the sky low down as if to my side,
>   (while the other stars all look'd on,)
> As we wander'd together the solemn night, (for something I know
>   not what kept me from sleep,)
> As the night advanced, and I saw on the rim of the west
>   how full you were of woe,
> As I stood on the rising ground in the breeze in the cool
>   transparent night,
> As I watch'd where you pass'd and was lost in the
>   netherward black of the night,
> As my soul in its trouble dissatisfied sank, as where you
>   sad orb,
> Concluded, dropt in the night, and was gone.[24]

That is, he reports here a "visitation" of sorts whereby the planet Venus had antici- pated for him (and only for him?) the assassination of Lincoln. Why he (Whitman the man, not only Whitman the poet) was so privileged (on this as on other occa- sions) is not explained.

But, then, Whitman always made much of heavenly phenomena, including the weather, as if they were somehow in harmony with human events, or at least with those events that mattered to him. And here he makes much of the fact, if fact it was, that the lilacs had bloomed early the spring that Lincoln was struck down.

IV.

"Lilacs," we have been told on good authority, is Whitman's masterpiece. But it does seem, at least to me, to be deeply flawed, exhibiting the limitations evident again and again in Whitman's poetry, some of which I have already indicated.

I even venture to suggest that there is something else prepared by him about Lincoln that is superior to "Lilacs"—and that is the talk, "Death of Abraham Lin- coln," first delivered by him in New York on the fourteenth anniversary of Lincoln's shooting and repeated almost a dozen times thereafter on the anniversary of that fateful weekend.[25]

The 1879 "Death of Abraham Lincoln" talk is more attractive, more solid, than any of the half-dozen Lincoln poems by Whitman. That talk is, in effect, a prose poem, which is less mannered, as well as less "personal," than Whitman was inclined to be when he pressed for effect.

Lincoln, too, tried his hand at conventional poetry—but in this he was markedly inferior to Whitman.[26] However, Lincoln's best prose poems (particularly his Get-

tysburg Address and his Second Inaugural Address) soar above anything that Whitman ever did.[27] Frederick Douglass called the Second Inaugural Address a sacred
effort.[28] It is doubtful that Whitman ever plumbed the depths of Lincoln's thought,
at least to the extent of recognizing that there were treasures there beyond anything
he was personally capable of unearthing.

Whitman did consider himself superior in political judgment when compared to
the typical politician of his day. He could speak in disdain about one president after
another, aside from Lincoln. But it can be wondered how well he understood the
fundamental political, and perhaps social, issues of his day, issues that his democratic
doctrines, as well as his grasp of the natural in erotic relations, may not have been
deep enough for. One can compare his wartime poetry with, for instance, the robust
Battle Hymn of the Republic.[29]

With these questions, to which I will return, we can be reminded of that tension
between poetry and philosophy which Plato's Socrates spoke of.[30] Who is more
apt—the poet or the philosopher—to recognize the merits as well as the limitations
of statesmanship? Mark Van Doren indicated something critical about Whitman
here when he observed, "The art of oratory as he understood it was the art of saying
very little with vast force."[31]

V.

It does seem that Whitman himself was disturbed by the disillusionment that is said
to have afflicted the country after the great conflict. Perhaps this disillusionment was
inevitable, considering how keyed-up everyone, both North and South, had long
been by the mighty challenge and its unanticipated massive sacrifices.

Twenty years after the war Whitman could look back upon the epic struggle that
had, by then, begun to assume a mythic status. Here, for example, is his 1885 poem
when Ulysses S. Grant died:

Death of General Grant

As one by one withdraw the lofty actors,
From that great play on history's stage eterne,
That lurid, partial act of war and peace—of old and new contending,
Fought out through wrath, fears, dark dismays, and many a long suspense;
All past—and since, in countless graves receding, mellowing,
Victor's and vanquish'd—Lincoln's and Lee's—now thou with them,
Man of the mighty days—and equal to the days!
Thou from the prairies!—tangled and many-vein'd and hard has been thy part,
To admiration has it been enacted![32]

The use of "enacted" here may reflect the extent to which the war had been transformed, at least for Whitman, into something staged for the edification of the
human race.

Did Whitman, now in the last decade of his life, find himself in less intimate contact with the great men of his day, however much he had come to be visited by notables of this country and from across the Atlantic? He *had* once spoken familiarly of Lincoln, whom he had observed passing again and again in Washington. Whitman was able, as a journalist, to speak about momentous events as if he had been personally present. Consider, for example, how effectively (how accurately, I do not happen to know) he described "the murder of Abraham Lincoln" (this comes from his 1879 "Death" talk). The action described here follows upon a routine pause in the play being staged that night at Ford Theatre:

> At this period came the murder of Abraham Lincoln. Great as all its manifold train, circling round it, and stretching into the future for many a century, in the politics, history, art, &c., of the New World, in point of fact the main thing, the actual murder, transpired with the quiet and simplicity of any commonest occurrence—the bursting of a bud or pod in the growth of vegetation, for instance. Through the general hum following the stage pause, with the [actors'] change of positions, came the muffled sound of a pistol-shot, which not one-hundredth part of the audience heard at the time—and yet a moment's hush,—somehow, surely, a vague startled thrill—and then, through the ornamented, draperied, starr'd and striped spaceway of the President's box, a sudden figure, a man, raises himself with hands and feet, stands a moment on the railing, leaps below to the stage, (a distance of perhaps fourteen or fifteen feet,) falls out of position, catching his boot-heel in the copious drapery, (the American flag,) falls on one knee, quickly recovers himself, rises as if nothing had happen'd, (he really sprains his ankle, but unfelt then)—and so the figure, Booth, the murderer, dress'd in plain black broadcloth, bare-headed, with full, glossy, raven hair, and his eyes like some mad animal's flashing with light and resolution, yet with a certain strange calmness, holds aloft in one hand a large knife—walks along not much back from the foot-lights—turns fully toward the audience his face of statuesque beauty, lit by those basilisk eyes, flashing with desperation, perhaps insanity—launches out in a firm and steady voice the words *Sic semper tyrannis*—and then walks with neither slow nor very rapid pace diagonally across to the back of the stage, and disappears. (Had not all this terrible scene—making the mimic ones preposterous—had it not all been rehears'd, in blank, by Booth, beforehand?)

> A moment's hush—a scream—the cry of *murder*—Mrs. Lincoln leaning out of the box, with ashy cheeks and lips, with involuntary cry, pointing to the retreating figure, *He has kill'd the President*. And still a moment's strange, incredulous suspense—and then the deluge!—then that mixture of horror, noises, uncertainty—(the sound, somewhere back, of a horse's hoofs clattering with speed)— . . . [33]

What, precisely, "the deluge" eventually consisted of can be debated. It may even be wondered, many years later, whether Lincoln was done a personal favor of sorts by his assassin, especially if (as has been suggested) he was himself (because of genetic defects) not destined to live much longer. His murderer had seen himself striking down, in the name of ancient republicanism, a modern Caesar, but without appreciating, it seems, how the original Caesar was immortalized and hence grandly empowered by being struck down in his hour of triumph, having been saved thereby from the "reaction" that could be expected when the widely-acclaimed victor settled into the messy business of humdrum postwar governance.

VI.

How had Whitman understood the great civil strife in America? The terrible thing for him, throughout the war, was the prospect of the dismemberment of the Union, that sacred Union to which his family had been dedicated since the beginning of the Republic (and, it can be said, long before). That dedication may be seen in the name of his soldier-brother, George Washington Whitman.

The Secessionists, about whom Whitman wrote an instructive essay, had to be repelled, for their good as well as for the good of the Unionists. But they were not the only ones responsible for the war. Here is how Whitman recalls, in 1879, the prewar days:

> For twenty years, and especially during the four or five before the war actually began, the aspect of affairs in the United States, though without the flash of military excitement, presents more than the survey of a battle, or any extended campaign, or series, even of Nature's convulsions. The hot passions of the South—the strange mixture at the North of inertia, incredulity, and conscious power—the incendiarism of the abolitionists—the rascality and *grip* of the politicians, unparallel'd in any land, any age.[34]

Thus, the country was so much a natural whole for Whitman that its afflictions could be traced to malignant causes both North and South. (Whether any country can be truly a natural whole may ultimately be questioned, but not irresponsibly.) Lincoln's great accomplishment was, for Whitman, his insistence upon keeping the nation together, being able to rally the best in the country even in the worst circumstances. Whitman speaks of "the stunning cast-down, shock, and dismay of the North" after the early disaster at Bull Run.[35]

The challenges faced by Lincoln are implicit in various opinions held by Whitman himself, a devoted Loyalist. Thus, Whitman remains very much in favor of State Sovereignty, a sometimes crippling sentiment (both North and South) that Lincoln often had to defer to in the way that the war was prosecuted.

VII.

A critical difference between Lincoln and Whitman may be seen in what each thought about slavery and the causes of the war. Lincoln, like Whitman, could have reservations about the influence of abolitionists—but for somewhat different reasons: Lincoln, more than Whitman (even though Whitman was at times also a Free Soiler), always saw slavery as an evil, to be tolerated perhaps (for the sake of national unity) but nevertheless an evil, and an affliction for both South and North that the Founders had deliberately placed in the course of ultimate extinction.[36]

We can see in Whitman's somewhat erratic approach to these matters why Lincoln had to be careful, in the opening years of his presidency (as well as in his earlier decade-long campaign for the presidency), not to permit his official policy to be transformed prematurely into an antislavery crusade. He believed that there were in the North, as well as in the slaveholding Middle States, far more people prepared to make great sacrifices to save the Union than there were to emancipate the slaves. Consider here the testimony of James Garfield in the House of Representatives on April 15, 1879:

> Do gentlemen know that (leaving out all the border States) there were fifty regiments and seven companies of white men in our army fighting for the Union from the States that went into rebellion? Do they know that from the single State of Kentucky more Union soldiers fought under our flag than Napoleon took into the battle of Waterloo? more than Wellington took with all the allied armies again Napoleon? Do they remember that 186,000 color'd men fought under our flag against the rebellion and for the Union, and that of that number 90,000 were from the States which went into rebellion?[37]

Fundamental to Lincoln's oratory was his constant awareness of, and prudential accommodation to, the passions, the aspirations, and the tribulations of the people at large. He sensed as well that the conventional view of things, especially if long established, usually has much to be said for it.[38]

The limitations of Whitman as thinker, especially as a political thinker, are suggested by his failure to understand where Lincoln really stood here and why. Whitman, in his "Lilacs" dirge, does not make much, if anything, of the challenge of slavery, however much the poet can sympathize elsewhere (but certainly not always) with the bondsman's plight (but rarely with that of the native Indians). Again and again in Whitman's writings the preservation of the Union is emphasized, not the eventual abolishment of slavery. I do not recall, for example, any record of a Whitman comment, in 1862 or 1863, about the Emancipation Proclamation.[39] Nor do I recall any instance of Whitman's forming the kind of relation with anyone of African descent that Lincoln formed with Frederick Douglass.[40]

And yet, consider what Lincoln had to say, in the month before he was gunned down, about the significance of slavery for the onset of the Civil War. This is in his Second Inaugural Address:

> One-eighth of the whole population were colored slaves, not distributed generally over the Union, but localized in the Southern part of it. These slaves constituted a peculiar and powerful interest. All knew that this interest was, somehow, the cause of the war.

To strengthen, perpetuate, and extend this interest was the object for which the insurgents would rend the Union, even by war; while the government claimed no right to
do more than to restrict the territorial enlargement of it.[41]

Whitman reports, in diary entries, on the 1865 Inauguration and the Inauguration
Ball. But the slavery-related aspect of the Lincoln policy, referred to in this passage
from the Second Inaugural Address, does not, at that time, register with him. He
stresses, instead, the "human" side of the president as in this description of Lincoln
after the Inauguration:

> [He] look'd very much worn and tired; the lines, indeed, of vast responsibilities, intri-
> cate questions, and demands of life and death, cut deeper than ever upon his dark
> brown face; yet all the old goodness, tenderness, sadness, and canny shrewdness,
> underneath the furrows. (I never see that man without feeling that he is one to become
> personally attach'd to, for his combination of purest, heartiest tenderness, and native
> western form of manliness.)[42]

By the time of Whitman's "Death of Abraham Lincoln" talk, the Lincolnian
understanding of the war had evidently had time (more than a decade) to shape the
thought of the country at large. And the effect of that understanding, which was not
limited of course to how Lincoln was regarded, may be seen in Whitman's 1879 talk.
He could speak, then and thereafter, of how Lincoln's death was to be seen:

> For not in all great deaths, nor far or near . . . outvies that terminus of the secession
> war, in one man's life, here in our midst, in our own time—that seal of the emancipa-
> tion of three million slaves—that parturition and delivery of our at last really free
> Republic, born again, henceforth to commence its career of genuine homogeneous
> Union, compact, consistent with itself.[43]

It was almost as if the Lincoln policy with respect to slavery could not be properly
seen until some years after it had been baptized in his own blood. Even so, Whitman, in one of his shorter poems (an 1871 epitaph for Lincoln, summing up his
career) said nothing explicitly about the slavery issue:

This Dust Was Once the Man

> This dust was once the man,
> Gentle, plain, just and resolute, under whose cautious hand,
> Against the foulest crime in history known in any land or age,
> Was saved the Union of these States.[44]

Does, then, our assessment of Whitman's best poetry (as published in 1865)
depend, in part, upon our grasp of what it was that he did and did not understand
about Lincoln? To what extent, or in what way, did Whitman's instinctively self-

centered approach (an approach which "personalized" even great matters of state before they could be securely grasped by him) limit what this poet could truly see?[45] True, it can be properly said of Whitman that he "never laid up, or aimed to lay up, riches"—but he did have a way of appropriating to himself, and transforming in his own image, whatever he really cared for. He did care deeply for the Union, and that may have made him (as a fundamentally *gentle* man) more inclined toward reconciliation with the South than most victorious Northerners at war's end were apt to be.

Whitman can speak of Lincoln, in the closing lines of his "Lilacs" poem, as "the sweetest, wisest soul of all my days and lands."[46] The "sweetest" talk may well be what psychiatrists call "projection," insofar as it is the attribution to the toughminded Lincoln of a trait that Whitman likes, or at least wants, in himself.

As for the appellation "wisest": the meaning and soundness of that attribution may depend upon how well Walt Whitman truly understood Abraham Lincoln, a statesman with a self-discipline, an intellectual rigor, and perhaps a respect for the truly natural that the self-celebrating poet might not have been either equipped or inclined to grasp in what he extols, in effect, as his own "wondrous chant."[47]

We may well wonder whether any poet with an almost compulsive reliance upon lists in one poem after another,[48] as if quantity could substitute for quality (a temptation to which we Americans often succumb?)—we may well wonder whether the poet both sensed and admired (even if he could not often imitate) that rigor and that most expressive terseness repeatedly exhibited by the dedicated statesman who truly knows what he is doing.[49]

ॐ

Notes to Chapter 7

Lincoln as an Advocate of Positive Government

1. For example, Harry V. Jaffa, *A New Birth of Freedom. Abraham Lincoln and the Coming of the Civil War* (Lanham, Md.: Rowman and Littlefield, 2000) and Mario Cuomo and Harold Holzer, *Lincoln on Democracy* (New York: HarperCollins, 1990).

2. Bernard Schwartz, *A Book of Legal Lists* (New York: Oxford University Press, 1997), 210–236.

3. Abraham Lincoln, "The Perpetuation of Our Political Institutions," *Collected Works*, 1:108–112.

4. Abraham Lincoln, "To Do for the People What Needs to be Done," July 1, 1854, in *Lincoln Democracy*, 64–65.

5. William W. Haggard, "Was Lincoln a Conservative or a Liberal," in Eugene Fairbanks, compiler, *Abraham Lincoln Sculpture* (Bellingham, Washington: Fairbanks Art and Books, 2002), 84.

6. Abraham Lincoln, "Annual Message to Congress, December 3, 1861," in *Lincoln on Democracy*, 232.

7. Gabor S. Boritt, *Lincoln and the Economics of the American Dream* (Memphis: Memphis State University Press, 1978).

8. Daniel Farber, *Lincoln's Constitution* (Chicago: University of Chicago Press, 2003).

9. Steven M. Gillon, "Top 10 Legislative Landmarks in U.S. History," *George*, January 1998, 48–50.

10. Robert D. Hormats, "Abraham Lincoln and the Global Economy," *Harvard Business Review*, (August 2003), 59–67.

The Great Centralizer

REFERENCES

Adams, Henry. 1877. *Documents Relating to New-England Federalism.* Boston: Little, Brown.

Angle, Paul. 1947. *The American Reader.* New Brunswick, N.J.: Rutgers University Press.

Banner, James M. 1970. *To the Hartford Convention: The Death Struggle of the Federalists.* New York: Knopf.

Basler, Roy, ed. 1946. *Abraham Lincoln: His Speeches and Writings.* New York: Da Capo.

———, ed. 1953. *The Collected Works of Abraham Lincoln.* New Brunswick, N.J.: Rutgers University Press.

Baxter, Maurice. 1995. *Henry Clay and the American System.* Lexington: University Press of Kentucky.

Bensel, Richard. 1990. *Yankee Leviathan.* Cambridge: Cambridge University Press.

Berlin, Ira. 1987. *Freedom: A Documentary History of Emancipation.* Cambridge: Cambridge University Press.

Bernstein, Iver. 1990. *The New York City Draft Riots.* New York: Oxford University Press.

Berwanger, Eugene H. 1967. *The Frontier Against Slavery.* Urbana, Ill.: University of Illinois Press.

Curry, Leonard P. 1968. *Blueprint for Modern America: Nonmilitary Legislation of the First Civil War Congress.* Nashville, Tenn.: Vanderbilt University Press.

Davis, Burke. 1980. *Sherman's March.* New York: Vintage.

DeRosa, Marshall. 1992. *The Confederate Constitution of 1861: An Inquiry into American Constitutionalism.* Columbia: University of Missouri Press.

Donald, David. 1961. *Lincoln Reconsidered.* New York: Vintage.

Dunning, William Archibald. 1897. *Essays on the Civil War and Reconstruction.* New York: Macmillan.

Eliot, Charles W. 1910. *The Harvard Classics.* Vol. 43, *American Historical Documents.* New York: P. F. Collier.

Fears, J. Rufus, ed. 1985. *Selected Writings of Lord Acton.* Vol. 1, *Essays in the History of Liberty.* Indianapolis, Ind.: Liberty Classics.

Fellman, Michael. 1995. *Citizen Sherman.* Lawrence: University Press of Kansas.

Fogel, Robert, and Stanley Engerman. 1974. *Time on the Cross: The Economics of American Negro Slavery.* New York: Norton.

Folsom, Burton. 1988. *Entrepreneurs versus the State.* Herndon, Va.: Young America's Foundation.

Foner, Eric. 1970. *Free Soil, Free Labor, Free Men: The Ideology of the Republican Party before the Civil War.* New York: Oxford University Press.

Foote, Shelby. 1986. *The Civil War: A Narrative,* 3 vols. New York: Random House.

Fremantle, Arthur J. L. 1991. *Three Months in the Southern States: April–June 1863.* Lincoln: University of Nebraska Press.

Gallagher, Gary. 1998. *The Confederate War.* Cambridge, Mass.: Harvard University Press.

Hummel, Jeffrey Rogers. 1996. *Emancipating Slaves, Enslaving Free Men.* Chicago: Open Court.

Johannsen, Robert. 1991. *Lincoln, the South, and Slavery: The Political Dimension.* Baton Rouge: Louisiana State University Press.

Johnson, Ludwell. 1978. *Division and Reunion: America, 1848–1877.* New York: Wiley.

Litwack, Leon F. 1961. *North of Slavery: The Negro in the Free States, 1790–1860.* Chicago: University of Chicago Press.

Louisiana State University Civil War Institute. 1998. Online database available at http://www .cwc.lsu.edu.

McPherson, James. 1966. *The Struggle for Equality: Abolitionists and the Negro in the Civil War and Reconstruction.* Princeton, N.J.: Princeton University Press.

———. 1994. *What They Fought For, 1861–1865.* Baton Rouge: Louisiana State University Press.

———. 1997. *For Cause and Comrades: Why Men Fought the Civil War.* New York: Oxford University Press.

Morison, Samuel E., and Henry Steele Commager. 1942. *The Growth of the American Republic.* New York: Oxford University Press.

Morris, Roy. 1992. *Sheridan.* New York: Vintage.

Nevins, Allan, 1959. *Ordeal of the Union.* Vol. 3, *The Improvised War.* New York: Macmillan.

Perkins, Howard Cecil, ed. 1964. *Northern Editorials on Secession.* Gloucester, Mass.: Peter Smith.

Peterson, Merrill D. 1970. *Thomas Jefferson and the New Nation: A Biography.* New York: Macmillan.

———, ed. 1993. *The Political Writings of Thomas Jefferson.* Monticello, Va.: Thomas Jefferson Memorial Foundation.

Randall, James G. 1951. *Constitutional Problems under Lincoln.* Urbana: University of Illinois Press.

———, and David Donald. 1966. *The Civil War and Reconstruction.* Boston: D.C. Heath.

Remini, Robert V. 1991. *Henry Clay: Statesman for the Union.* New York: Norton.

Rhodes, James Ford. 1900. *History of the United States from the Compromise of 1850 to the Final Restoration of Home Rule at the South in 1877.* New York: Macmillan.

Richardson, Heather Cox. 1997. *The Greatest Nation of the Earth: Republican Economic Policies during the Civil War.* Cambridge, Mass.: Harvard University Press.

Rossiter, Clinton. 1948. *Constitutional Dictatorship: Crisis Government in the Modern Democracies.* Princeton, N.J.: Princeton University Press.

Stampp, Kenneth M. 1974. *The Causes of the Civil War.* Englewood Cliffs, N.J.: Spectrum.

———. 1980. *The Imperiled Union: Essays on the Background of the Civil War.* New York: Oxford University Press.

Stephens, Alexander. 1870. *A Constitutional View of the Late War between the States.* Philadelphia: National Publishing Co.

Talbert, Bart. 1995. *Maryland: The South's First Casualty.* Berryville, Va.: Rockbridge.

Taussig, Frank. 1931. *The Tariff History of the United States.* 8th ed. New York: Putnam.

Tocqueville, Alexis de. [1835/1840] 1945. *Democracy in America.* New York: Macmillan.

LINCOLN'S AMERICAN DREAM

Vanauken, Sheldon. 1989. *The Glittering Illusion: English Sympathy for the Southern Confederacy.* Washington, D.C.: Regnery/Gateway.
Vetter, Charles Edmond. 1992. *Sherman: Merchant of Terror, Advocate of Peace.* Gretna, La.: Pelican Publishing.
Viner, Jacob. 1950. *The Customs Union Issue.* Chicago: University of Chicago Press.
Wright, William C. 1973. *The Secession Movement in the Middle Atlantic States.* Rutherford, N.J.: Farleigh Dickinson University Press.

Acknowledgment: This article is based on a paper presented at the Mises Institute's fifteenth anniversary conference in Atlanta, September 25, 1997.

Forever Worthy of the Saving

1. Blassingame, ed., *Frederick Douglass Papers*, 4: 91. On American ideas of union more generally, see Kersh, 2001, from which parts of this essay are drawn.

2. *Atlantic Monthly* 10 (Nov. 1862), 639; Edman, ed., *Emerson's Essays*, 332; Donald, 1978: 160.

3. On religious mysticism: Stephens in Howe, 1979: 296; Boritt, 1988: 99. Cf. Wilson, 1962: ch. 3 ("The Union as Religious Mysticism"). On psychological union: Strozier, 1982: 233, 1988: 230; cf. Forgie, 1979: 6–8, passim.

4. On union as excuse: quotes from Harding, 1981: 223 (see generally 215–36); DuBois, 1989: 13. Cf. Fredrickson, 1975. On union as disingenuous/pragmatic: see the summary in Holt, 1992: 331–33.

5. McPherson, 1991: viii, 31–2 (a similar point is made by Donald, 1978: 215). See also McCoy, 2002.

6. McPherson, 1992: 4; Basler, ed., *Collected Works of Lincoln* (hereafter *CW*), 1: 315; 2: 525. Wayne Fields (1996, 141) notes that "The Second Inaugural vindicated no other American ideal or virtue save Union."

7. Basler, ed., *Lincoln: His Speeches and Writings* (hereafter *SW*): 577.

8. *CW*, 2: 341; Erickson, 1986: 114. On Lincoln's reliance on Webster, see Howe, 1979: 284 (on plagiarism charge); Donald, 1995: 163, 270; Wills, 1992: 122–33, who finds that "Lincoln used [Webster's] style and arguments . . . as models all through his political life." On Webster's unionism, see Kersh, 2001: 110–15.

9. *SW*, 575, 82–3. On the founders' appeal for Lincoln, see Jaffa, 2000: 11–26 and passim.

10. *SW*, 545; Forgie, 1979: 39. On "union" images, see inter alia *SW*, 571, 748; on Lincoln's rhetorical style, see Wills, 1992: 52–62; Black, 2000.

11. *SW*, 575.

12. *SW*, 676.

13. Thelen, 1998: 382; *SW*, 598. On Lincoln and constitutional maintenance, cf. Kahn, 1992; Jaffa, 1982.

14. *CW*, 1: 108; *SW*, 678, 586. Cf. ibid.: 617.

15. *CW*, 2: 341; *SW*, 305.

16. Foner, 1970: 225 (cf. 11–40); *CW*, 7: 23.

17. *SW*, 588; cf. *SW*, 310, where Lincoln refers to a "national feeling of brotherhood" but in the context of "concession and compromise."

18. *CW*, 4: 267–8; 2, 385. Cf. *SW*, 335–36, 361, 577.

19. Marx in Padover, 1972: 264; Boritt, 1988: 94–5; Jaffa, 1982: 221–8; Wills, 1992: 120–4; Fletcher, 2001.

20. *CW*, 2: 275–76.

21. Holzer, ed., 1993: 140; Kahn, 1992: 142 (cf. Donald, 1995: 170).

22. Basler, intro. to *SW*, 24; *CW*, 4: 75.

23. *CW*, 3: 9; ibid., 4: 155, 172.

24. Howe, 1979: 297 (on Lincoln and free labor, see also Foner, 1970: 38, 296; idem., 1998: 67–8, 91–2).

25. *SW*, 513.

26. *SW*, 68, 71. On virtuous leaders as a source of national unity, see Kersh, 2001: 81–85.

27. *SW*, 80–83; Paludan, 1988: 27. Cf. *SW*, 354–59, 396–98, 417–20, 585–86.

28. *SW*, 594; cf. ibid.: 629–30; 699–708; 720–23. Friedman, 1973: 165–6, 295–9. Madison's *Federalist* No. 49 is the principal founding-era account of "reverence for the laws."

29. *SW*, 472.

30. *SW*, 235–39. Cf. ibid.: 587–88, 602. Debates over whether elected representatives should be "delegates," as Lincoln suggests, or "trustees" in the Burkean tradition, continue today.

31. Lincoln's "people's contest" line is at *SW*, 607.

32. See Gienapp, 1982: esp. 15, 32–45, 62–66; Formisano, 1999.

33. In 1838 Lincoln described political activity as a "task of gratitude to our fathers, justice to ourselves, duty to posterity," a responsibility facing "every young man . . . to the last generation." *SW*, 77. On this topic see also Kahn, 1992: esp. 54.

34. *CW*, 6: 424.

35. In Lincoln's first (1836) campaign, he said: "I go for all sharing the privileges of the government, who assist in bearing its burthens. Consequently I go for admitting all whites to the right of suffrage, who pay taxes or bear arms (by no means excluding females)." *SW*, 58.

36. *SW*, 279.

37. *CW*, 3: 19 (cf. ibid., 94–95, 446–47).

38. "If Judge Douglas and his friends are not willing to stand by [the Declaration], let them come up and amend it. Let them make it read that all men are created equal, except Negroes." *SW*, 422.

39. 19 How. 393, 419 (1857). Lincoln's views of *Dred Scott* are in *CW*, 2: 494; 3: 255.

40. *SW*, 401–03.

41. E.g., Fredrickson, 1971: 149–51; Harding, 1981; DiLorenzo, 1998: 244–48; Donald, 1995: 269–70 (though cf. ibid., 373–7, 526–7, 541–2, 583–5); Guelzo, 2000; see also sources cited in Cox, 1981: ch. 1, note 30.

42. Quote from Current, 1988: 383. Lincoln's views on black inclusion are assessed in Cox, 1981, chs. 1–3; see also Howe, 1979: 292–3; McPherson, 1991: 51–6, 134–52; Smith, 1997: 249–51, 272–73, 279–82.

43. Holzer, ed., 1993: 189. Douglas's words which inspired the remark: "I believe this Government was made on the white basis. . . . I am in favor of confining citizenship to white men, instead of . . . inferior races."

44. Cox, 1981: 20–21. For similar views about Lincoln's consistently principled support for black rights, see Bromwich, 2001; Smith, 1999: 35–41; Tullai, 2001: 86–92; Jaffa, 2000: esp. 159–62.

45. *CW*, 2: 320; *SW*, 444, 493, 688.

46. Basler in *SW*, 801; *SW*, 800 (emphasis added).

47. *Douglass' Monthly*, Feb. 1863: 225. Compare Justice Taney in *Dred Scott*, explicitly banning "the African race" from this right by noting their exclusion from state militias. 19 How. 393, 410, 415–16.

48. Current, 1988: 383; DuBois, 1989: 86–7.

49. *Douglass Papers*, 5: 277; Wickenden, 1990: 112.

50. On "ethnocultural" unionist views, see Kersh, 2001: 89–90, 115–22, 154.

51. Seward in Smith, 1997: 275; Abbott, 1997: 39 n5.

52. Quoted in Stampp, 1992: 136; McPherson, 1997: 104–30 (quotes at 104, 117).

Walt Whitman's Abraham Lincoln

1. This essay was originally prepared for a Weekend Conference of the Basic Program of Liberal Education for Adults, The University of Chicago, November 3, 2002. The quotations from Walt Whitman in this essay are taken from the versions of his work found in the 1982 Library of America edition, *Complete Poems and Collected Prose*.

2. This was said by President Lincoln when General Joseph Hooker lost seventeen thousand dead at Chancellorsville (the 1863 battle in which General Thomas "Stonewall" Jackson was killed). It was after this battle that Walt Whitman went looking for his soldier brother—and this led to the dramatic shift in his wartime activities, enriching immeasurably his experience of the world as he conscientiously served wounded soldiers of both the North and the South.

3. See *Dictionary of American Biography* (New York: Charles Scribner's Sons, 1936), XX, 149.

4. *Dictionary of American Biography*, XX, 151–52. See note 48, below.

5. Mark Van Doren, *The Happy Critic and Other Essays* (New York: Hill and Wang, 1961), 48.

6. Even so, some critics nominate "Song of Myself" as Whitman's masterpiece. See, on Whitman's self-centeredness, note 45, below.

7. Van Doren, *The Happy Critic*, 48–49.

8. See, for samples of John Van Doren's own poetry, John A. Murley, William T. Braithwaite and Robert L. Stone, eds., *Law and Philosophy* (Athens, Ohio: Ohio University Press, 1992), II, 1054.

9. See Mark Van Doren's *Introduction to Poetry* (New York: William Sloane Associates, 1951), 42–45.

10. Van Doren, *Introduction to Poetry*, 42–43.

11. Van Doren, *Introduction to Poetry*, 45.

12. See, on our Vietnam War, Anastaplo, *Human Being and Citizen: Essays on Virtue, Freedom and the Common Good* (Chicago: Swallow Press, 1975), 151; Anastaplo, *The American Moralist: On Law, Ethics, and Government* (Athens, Ohio: Ohio University Press, 1992), 225, 245. See, on the Middle East and elsewhere, Anastaplo, "September Eleventh: The ABCs of a Citizen's Responses," 29; *Oklahoma City University Law Review* 165 (2004).

13. See M. Wyn Thomas, "Weathering the Storm: Whitman and the Civil War," *Walt Whitman Quarterly Review*, 15: 87, 105 (1998).

14. John Burroughs, "Walt Whitman," *Encyclopedia Britannica* (11th Edition, 1911), XXVIII, 610.

15. Ibid.

16. Walt Whitman, *Drum-Taps*, ed., F. DeWolfe Miller (Gainesville, Fl.: Scholars Facsimiles & Reprints, 1959), xii. See, also, ibid., xv (on the career of James Russell Lowell). The problem in leaders "call[ing] on all others to fight" is touched on here and there in Anastaplo, "September Eleventh."

17. The relations between Presidents and Citizens seemed remarkably more relaxed, if not even more natural, in those days. During his 2003 visit to England, our President could sometimes be addressed by journalists as "Mr. Bush."

18. See Whitman, *Complete Poetry and Collected Prose*, 1036. This oration was given first in New York City, April 14, 1879.

19. That eleventh section begins with these questions (Whitman, *Complete Poetry and Collected Prose*, 462):

> O what shall I hang on the chamber walls?
> And what shall the pictures be that I hang on the walls,
> To adorn the burial-house of him I love?

The answer to these questions begins, "Pictures of growing spring and farms and homes . . ."

20. Whitman, *Complete Poetry and Collected Prose*, 463.

21. Lines 102–105 of the "Lilacs" poem are these:

> Sing on, dearest brother, warble your reedy song,
> Loud human song, with voice of uttermost woe.
>
> O liquid and free and tender!
> O wild and loose in my soul—O wondrous singer.

Whitman, *Complete Poetry and Collected Prose*, 463.

22. See the text at note 7, above.

23. I was told many years ago, as something noteworthy, that the Lincoln funeral train passed along the embankment behind our house in what would become the South Side of Chicago. It was thus that millions could "participate in" the great national drama.

24. Whitman, *Complete Poetry and Collected Prose*, 461.

25. It happened to be the Easter weekend. Nothing is said explicitly about *that* by Whitman either in the "Lilacs" poem or in his "Death of Abraham Lincoln," however much it may be implicit, especially for us in the West, in his talk about martyrs and the like. See, for different presuppositions about the enduring nature of things, Anastaplo, *But Not Philosophy: Seven Introductions to Non-Western Thought* (Lanham, Md.: Lexington Books, 2002).

26. See, e.g., Anastaplo, *Abraham Lincoln: A Constitutional Biography* (preferred title: *Thoughts on Abraham Lincoln*) (Lanham, Md.: Rowman and Littlefield, 1999), 135.

27. See, on these two addresses, Anastaplo, *Abraham Lincoln*, 229, 243. See, also, Anastaplo, "Abraham Lincoln and the American Regime," 35 *Valparaiso University Law Review* 39, 137 (2000).

28. See, also, "Abraham Lincoln and the American Regime," 141.

29. See, on the songs of the Civil War, Anastaplo, "Abraham Lincoln and the American Regime," 172.

30. See, e.g., Plato, *Republic* 607B. Compare Anastaplo, *The Constitutionalist: Notes on the First Amendment* (Dallas: Southern Methodist University Press, 1971), 278–81.

31. Van Doren, *The Happy Critic*, 36.

32. Whitman, *Complete Poetry and Collected Prose*, 622. It is, of course, Grant as military leader, not as president, who is celebrated here.

33. Whitman, *Complete Poetry and Collected Prose*, 1042–43.

34. Whitman, *Complete Poetry and Collected Prose*, 1037.

35. Whitman, *Complete Poetry and Collected Prose*, 1040. This was the first Battle of Bull Run, July 21, 1861.

36. See, e.g., Anastaplo, *Abraham Lincoln*, 157.

37. Whitman, *Complete Poetry and Collected Prose*, 735n. Garfield used "border states" where Lincoln would usually have used "middle states."

38. See Anastaplo, *But Not Philosophy*, 300.

39. See, on the Emancipation Proclamation, Anastaplo, *Abraham Lincoln*, 197.

40. See Anastaplo, *Abraham Lincoln*, 168.

41. *The Collected Works of Abraham Lincoln*, ed. Roy P. Basler (New Brunswick, N.J.: Rutgers University Press, 1953), VIII, 332.

42. Whitman, *Complete Poetry and Collected Prose*, 758.

43. Whitman, *Complete Poetry and Collected Prose*, 1045.

44. Whitman, *Complete Poetry and Collected Prose*, 468.

45. Whitman's instructive self-centeredness may even be seen in changes made in his "Lilacs" poem over the years. In Section 12, for example, "Mighty Manhattan" in the original draft becomes (by the final version), "My own Manhattan."

46. Whitman, *Complete Poetry and Collected Prose*, 467.

47. Whitman, *Complete Poetry and Collected Prose*, 467.

48. See Van Doren, *The Happy Critic*, 34 ("his famous catalogues which no one can read through"). Other such catalogues may be found in the *Bhagavad Gita* and in the writings of Henry Thoreau. See, for an assessment of the criticisms of Whitman by George Santayana and others, Christopher Benfey, "The Art of Consolation," *New York Review of Books*, April 28, 2005, 38–40 (reviewing Helen Vendler's *Poets Thinking* [Harvard University Press]).

49. See, for a debate about the limitations of President Lincoln, Anastaplo, *Abraham Lincoln*, 344–49.

Chapter 8

LINCOLN FOR OUR TIME

What was Lincoln's vision of America? What did America promise?

It is not merely for to-day, but for all time to come that we should perpetuate for our children's children this great and free government, which we have enjoyed all our lives. I beg you to remember this, not merely for my sake, but for yours. I happen temporarily to occupy this big White House. I am a living witness that any one of your children may look to come here as my father's child has. It is in order that each of you may have through this free government which we have enjoyed, an open field and a fair chance for your industry, enterprise and intelligence; that you may all have equal privileges in the race of life, with all its desirable human aspirations. It is for this the struggle should be maintained, that we may not lose our birthright—not only for one, but for two or three years. The nation is worth fighting for, to secure such an inestimable jewel.

Abraham Lincoln, Speech to One Hundred Sixty-sixth Ohio Regiment, August 22, 1864

★ Richard N. Current, "What Is an American? Abraham Lincoln and 'Multiculturalism'"
★ George McKenna, "On Abortion: A Lincolnian Position"

WHAT IS AN AMERICAN? ABRAHAM LINCOLN AND "MULTICULTURALISM"

Richard N. Current

ABRAHAM LINCOLN is a dead white male. He was a honkey. He was a WASP. His world was quite different from the world we inhabit today. You might wonder, then, what relevance his memory could possibly have for the question of the validity and

*This article originally appeared in *What Is an American? Abraham Lincoln and "Multiculturalism,"* published by Marquette University Press, 1993. Reprinted with permission from Marquette University Press.

desirability of multiculturalism. The question is a very serious one. It amounts to this: What is—and what should be—an American?

The current buzzword "multiculturalism" means different things to different people; the issue is, in part, semantic.[1] As some use the word it refers to efforts to enhance recognition and respect for ethnic and racial minorities, as well as for women, homosexuals, and others who may feel marginalized or oppressed. To achieve these goals, schools and colleges are undertaking to broaden the curriculum, provide counseling in regard to "diversity," and prevent offensive speech. Advocates of such programs differ among themselves as to specifics, but they generally agree that multiculturalism is a good thing—even when others use the word to justify far more drastic measures.[2]

These others do not see multiculturalism as a means of enriching a culture that everyone shares or aspires to share. Instead, they question whether any such common culture is either possible or desirable. "Unlike earlier periods in the history of this country," says one multicultural pronouncement, the 1991 New York curriculum report, "the various peoples who make up our nation seem determined to maintain and publicly celebrate much of that which is peculiar to the culture with which they identify." These various ethnic and racial groups "now insist . . . that their knowledge and perspective be treated with parity."[3] This New York multicultural manifesto continues as follows:

> Before this time [the 1960s] the dominant model of the typical American has been conditioned primarily by the need to shape a unified nation out of a variety of contrasting and often conflicting European immigrant communities. But following the struggle for civil rights, the unprecedented increase in non-European Immigration over the last two decades and the increasing recognition of our nation's indigenous heritage, there has been a fundamental change in the image of what a resident of the United States is. With this change . . . previous ideals of assimilation to an Anglo-American model have been put in question and are being set aside.[4]

According to this multiculturalist view, there is no longer a single, homogeneous American culture, if indeed there ever was one. Rather, there are now five distinct and separate cultures in the United States: Indian or Native American, African American, Asian American, Hispanic or Latino American, and European American. These, it is argued, are all of exactly the same intrinsic worth, have contributed equally to American life, and must be "treated with parity." The traditionally predominant European American culture, the argument goes, has actually been Anglo-American, and to allow it to continue to predominate is to be guilty of "Anglocentrism," which is the worst form of "Eurocentrism."

As proof of "the Anglocentrism of American culture so far," Professor Ali A. Mazrui of SUNY Binghamton points with alarm to the fairly obvious fact that American "political culture" is similar to British, Canadian, Australian, and New

Zealand political culture.[5] An even more obvious sign of Anglocentrism is the prevalence of the English language in the United States. All languages must be declared equal, it appears, and "language rights" must be protected as if they were civil rights. Opponents of "parallel language rights in government"—proponents of making English the official language of the country—are condemned as "mean-spirited" characters who favor legislation that is "discriminatory and divisive." "The movement to repress undocumented people [illegal aliens] and the movement to repress our language rights are the same movement," said a Hispanic member of the Massachusetts legislature, who recently filed a resolution to declare Massachusetts a multicultural and multilingual state.[6]

When it comes to the school and college curricula, not all the reformers are satisfied with such modest changes as broadening the Western Civilization course into a World Civilizations course.[7] Some demand that American history be taught strictly as ethnic history. New textbooks take this approach. One of them bears the title *A Different Mirror: A History of Multicultural America,* and its author is Ronald Takaki, a Japanese American professor at the University of California, Berkeley. Takaki focuses on blacks, Indians, Chinese, Japanese, Mexicans, Irish, and Jews and their struggles for status in this country. "What we need," he says, "is a new conceptualization [of American history], where there is no center. . . ." His book mentions Thomas Jefferson only as a slave holder, not as an author of the Declaration of Independence. "There is little here," a reviewer points out, "about the drafting of the Constitution or the evolution of the Republic's democratic ideals."[8]

Multiculturalists aim to bring about a "radical rethinking of what being an American means," as Chinese American Professor Sau-Ling Wong of Berkeley puts it.[9] Already (to repeat the words of the New York curriculum report) "there has been a Fundamental change in the image of what a resident of the United States is." Interestingly, the state's curricular experts speak of a "resident," not a citizen, of the United States. They and other multiculturalists see each resident as belonging not to American society but only to one of the groups into which they divide that society. According to this view, there are no longer any Americans as such. There are only Native, African, Asian, Hispanic, and European Americans. Residents derive their identity from their ancestors; it is their inheritance; it is in their blood. Even though they may be third-generation residents—they and their parents born in this country—they cannot become culturally naturalized. Assimilation has never really worked; it has been nothing more than the imposition of "Anglo-conformity" on all the groups. Such is the conclusion that follows from a "radical rethinking of what being an American means."

There is no place for Abraham Lincoln in that kind of radical rethinking. He had a very different conception of what it means to be an American. With him, it was a matter of commitment to certain principles, not a matter of racial or cultural inheritance. The principles were those of "a new nation, conceived in Liberty, and dedicated to the proposition that all men are created equal."[10] Lincoln made the most explicit statement of this idea at an Independence Day celebration in Chicago in July 1858:

> We find a race of men living in that day [1776] whom we claim as our fathers and grandfathers. . . . We have besides these men—descended by blood from our ancestors—among us perhaps half our people who are not descendants at all of these men, they are men who have come from Europe—German, Irish, French and Scandinavian—men who have come from Europe themselves, or whose ancestors have come hither and settled here, finding themselves our equals in all things. If they look back through this history to trace their connection with those days by blood, they find they have none, they cannot carry themselves back into that glorious epoch and make themselves feel that they are part of us, but when they look through that old Declaration of Independence they find that these old men say that "We hold these truths to be self-evident, that all men are created equal," and then they feel that the moral sentiment taught in that day evidences their relation to those men, that it is the father of all moral principle in them, and that they have a right to claim it as though they were blood of the blood and flesh of the flesh of the men who wrote that Declaration, and so they are.[11]

To become an American—to become a citizen of the United States—an immigrant "should be put to some reasonable test of his [or her] fidelity to our country and its institutions," and he or she "should first dwell among us a reasonable time to become generally acquainted with the nature of those institutions." So Lincoln believed. And the "naturalization laws should be so framed as to render citizenship under them as convenient, cheap, and expeditious as possible."[12] Thus, in Lincoln's view, it should be fairly easy to become an American, regardless of the immigrant's inherited nationality or culture.

Lincoln therefore condemned the discriminatory immigration and naturalization policies that the Know-Nothings advocated. "As a nation, we began by declaring that '*all men are created equal*,'" he wrote. "We now practically read it 'all men are created equal, *except* negroes.' When the Know-Nothings get control, it will read, 'all men are created equal, except negroes *and foreigners and catholics.*' When it comes to this I should prefer emigrating to some country where they make no pretence of loving liberty—to Russia, for instance, where despotism can be taken pure, and without the base alloy of hypocrisy. . . ."[13]

Disagreeing with Lincoln on this as on other matters was Stephen A. Douglas, who insisted in the 1858 debates that Negroes were not included in the Declaration of Independence. Lincoln replied:

> I think the authors of that notable instrument intended to include *all* men, but they did not mean to declare all men equal *in all respects*. They did not mean to say all men were equal in color, size, intellect, moral development or social capacity. They defined with tolerable distinctness in what they did consider all men created equal—equal in certain inalienable rights, among which are life, liberty and the pursuit of happiness.

This they said, and this they meant. They did not mean to assert the obvious untruth, that all men were then actually enjoying that equality, nor yet that they were about to confer it immediately upon them. In fact they had no power to confer such a boon. They meant simply to declare the *right* so that the *enforcement* of it might follow as fast as circumstances should permit.

They meant to set up a standard maxim for free society which should be familiar to all: constantly looked to, constantly labored for, and even though never perfectly attained, constantly approximated and thereby constantly spreading and deepening its influence and augmenting the happiness and value of life to all people, of all colors, everywhere.[14]

The United States, based as it was on these principles, was unique in the history of the world. Here was a "system of political institutions conducing more essentially to the ends of civil and religious liberty than any of which the history of former times tells us."[15] In his very first political statement, as a young man of twenty-three, Lincoln proposed that everyone "receive at least a moderate education and thereby be enabled to read the histories of his own and other countries, by which he may duly appreciate the value of our free institutions."[16]

That kind of comparative history might well be recommended to the multicultural curriculum makers of today. Such a history would be especially appropriate for the education of those who pontificated: "African-Americans, Asian Americans, Puerto Rican/Latinos and Native Americans have all been the victims of an intellectual and educational oppression that has characterized the culture and institutions of the United States and the European American world for centuries."[17] As a comparison of the United States with other countries would have shown, none of the others has welcomed so many and such diverse newcomers, none has enabled the various peoples to live together in as great a degree of harmony, and none has succeeded so well in merging them into a single nationality.

With the passage of the immigration act of 1965, the gates were opened wider than they had been for generations. No longer were Northern and Western Europeans—or any Europeans—favored. Some five million people entered the country in the five years from 1985 to 1990. They constituted nearly 8 percent, or approximately one in twelve, of the entire population. The largest number—even if illegal immigrants are not counted—came from Mexico and the next largest number from the Philippines. A majority of all the newcomers, 60 percent of them, had not yet become citizens.[18]

It remains to be seen how many of these people will eventually look upon themselves as Americans rather than Hispanic Americans, Asian Americans, and so on. Multiculturalists would expect to see—and would prefer to see—that very few ever did so.

But there is persuasive evidence that self-appointed spokesmen sometimes exaggerate and misrepresent the ethnic consciousness of their respective groups. A recent survey shows, for example, that a majority of the Hispanics in this country do not consider themselves members of a single Hispanic community, with shared cultural, political, and economic interests. Instead, they think of themselves as Mexican, Cuban, or Puerto Rican in heritage, and the three groups have little interaction with one another. Most members speak English as their main or only language. Most do not favor increased immigration (their attitude is a sure sign of assimilation). "We have a population here," the survey concludes, "that is in fact very American, very pro-American and wanting to make it in the mainstream."[19]

To make it in the mainstream would be much more difficult, if not impossible, in most other countries. Take Germany as an extreme example. A German is a German by virtue of his German blood. A foreigner—even a foreigner's child born in Germany—has to go through a long, expensive, and discouraging process to become a citizen. Hence the nearly two million Turks, along with more than four million other foreigners, remain non-citizens despite their eagerness to be naturalized. As it is, they have the burdens but not the benefits of citizenship; they must pay taxes but they cannot vote.[20]

The prime minister of Turkey has called upon the German government to agree to dual citizenship for the Turks living in Germany. For them, this might be an improvement, though it would seem to mean that they would be only half-German and half-Turkish, with divided loyalties. The president of the Gabon Republic has proposed that his own country and other countries in Africa do much the same thing for blacks in the United States. "We should offer dual citizenship to our African-American brothers and sisters," the Gabon president has said. This would, no doubt, give new significance to the term "African American," which would come to mean African *and* American.[21]

Africa, as we know, remains divided by tribal loyalties and enmities. Japan has never welcomed immigrants, and the Koreans residing there constitute an extremely disadvantaged minority. China, traditionally xenophobic and recently the scene of the Tiananmen Square massacre, is hardly a haven for the oppressed. Communists used to brag that the Soviet Union was a model of multiculturalism, a country where a great variety of ethnic groups lived in complete harmony under Communism. We all know what has happened to the Soviet Union and to the formerly multicultural states of Czechoslovakia and Yugoslavia. France has its Algerian minority and Great Britain its Scottish and its Welsh nationalists, not to mention its dark-skinned minorities and its problems in Northern Ireland. Indeed, there are today few if any important nations that are immune to ethnic and other internal strains.

"As a nation of immigrants, Australia is becoming like the United States," an Australian writes. "Yet so far Australia is still more self-conscious about race and immigration than America," this Australian goes on to say. "Americans take a melting-pot society for granted. Australians do not." Perhaps the writer should have said that Americans used to take a melting-pot society for granted. Anyhow, he concludes that "it will be important to maintain a continuity of established Australian values and institutions, and a clear-eyed commitment to individual liberty—as distinct from the rights of ethnic blocs."[22] It is likewise important for the United States to maintain a continuity of established American values and institutions, and a clear-eyed commitment to individual liberty—as distinct from the rights of ethnic blocs.

Canada is the country that most closely resembles the United States as a nation of immigrants. But in Quebec's demand for a separate culture and identity, if not for a separate existence, Canada faces a problem of ethnic divisiveness more threatening to national unity than any that has yet arisen in the United States—if we except secession and the Civil War.

This, of course, is not to say we have had no problems of ethnic divisiveness in this country. Ethnic and racial conflict is a well-known and recognized part of our history and has been from the beginning. We have always needed to temper prejudice and mitigate conflict—as Lincoln himself tried to do.

Like a great many other Americans, Lincoln was shocked by the 1863 New York draft riot, in which Irish Americans attacked African Americans. When, several months later, he was elected an honorary member of the New York Workingmen's Association, he responded with some advice for his fellow members: "Let them beware of prejudice, working division and hostility among themselves. The most notable feature of a disturbance in your city last summer was the hanging of some working people by other working people. It should never be so. The strongest bonds of human sympathy, outside the family relation, should be one uniting all working people, of all nations, and tongues, and kindreds."[23]

The question for us today is not whether some groups have been—and are—prejudiced and hostile toward other groups. The question is this: Will an emphasis on group separateness and ethnic distinctiveness tend to moderate—or to exacerbate—such prejudice and hostility? Will it contribute to national unity? or to disunity?

National unity does not require the members of any group to give up their whole ethnic heritage. In this country, families have always been allowed to show pride in their ancestral homeland, to maintain a sentimental attachment to it, to speak its language, to fly its flag, even to boast of the connection on a bumper sticker. Americans have always been free to worship in the way their forebears did. To criticize multiculturalism is not to object in the slightest to the preservation of cultural vestiges of these kinds. (I personally could not very well object, since I have been spending a good deal of time lately teaching myself to read what was my mother's first language—Norwegian.)

A great many Americans, however, can no longer trace their roots to one particular group, but have ancestors of two or more nationalities (and again I am a personal example). American culture, like the American people, is a blend of elements that come from a variety of ethnic sources—including the aboriginal, African, Hispanic, and Asian as well as the European. This does not mean that all groups have contributed equally to the prevailing mix. So far, English remains the national language, and the political system is primarily English in origin.

This is due to the fact that the English were much the most numerous among the early immigrants. It is not because their language or their institutions were, or are, necessarily any better than others. It would be hard to demonstrate, though, that English is any worse for our purposes than, say, Nahuatl or Swahili. It would also be hard to demonstrate that ethnic minorities in this country would be better off if our system of law and government had derived from Uganda or China or Japan—despite the multiculturalist complaint that all the non-European minorities have been victims of an "oppression that has characterized the culture and institutions of the United States and the European American world for centuries." It would seem, rather, that this culture and these institutions have helped to attract so many and such diverse people to this country. Certain it is that this culture and these institutions make it possible for multiculturalists freely to denounce this very culture and these very institutions.

Lincoln, as we have seen, did not pretend that American democracy was perfect or anywhere near perfect. He looked upon it as an experiment, and he invited people of all countries, cultures, and creeds to share in the great political experiment as well as the economic opportunities of the United States. Only time, he believed, would tell whether the principles of the Declaration of Independence and the Constitution would permanently work. The Founders of the republic—in declaring that "all men are created equal" and are endowed with the rights of life, liberty, and the pursuit of happiness—intended to set up a "standard maxim for free society," as he said, to be "constantly labored for" and thereby to be constantly "augmenting the happiness and value of life to all people of all colors everywhere."[24]

Nowadays all people of all colors everywhere are not necessarily interested in human rights as Thomas Jefferson described them in the Declaration of Independence and Abraham Lincoln advocated them in his many references to the Declaration.

At the UN Conference on Human Rights, which met in Vienna in June 1993, some of the delegates appealed to multiculturalism in denouncing the Western democratic—that is, the Euro-American—conception of individual liberties. The Chinese delegate Liu Huaqiu declared: "One should not and cannot think of the human rights standards and models of certain countries as the only proper ones and demand all other countries comply with them." A spokesman for Singapore, Lee Kuan Yew, said that many Asian countries, whose culture was Confucian, place a higher value on group consensus than on individual freedom. Representatives of other Third World governments similarly argued that there is no universal standard of human rights—that standards must vary according to economic development and cultural inheritance.[25]

This is precisely the kind of cultural relativism that multiculturalists apply to the United States when they assert, or imply, that the inherited culture of each ethnic group is of exactly the same value as the Euro-American for standards of life, including political life, in this country. In that view, every resident of the country derives his or her own standards from his or her ethnic background. It follows that there can be no such thing as an American except as a permanent member of one or another ethnic or tribal group.

Lincoln saw it quite differently. In his view, an American is a citizen who, regardless of his or her ancestry, believes in the democratic principles on which the republic was founded. Lincoln was as well aware as any of us that the promise of the Declaration of Independence has not been and never will be completely realized. Still, as he once asked, "Is there any better, or equal, hope in the world?" This is a good question for those of us who today would sit by, with indifference or even with approval, while others reject the democratic ideal with its unifying power and call, instead, for a miscellany of tribalistic values and loyalties. The more diverse the people become, the greater the need for common and cohesive principles—rather than a cacophony of cultures such as the multiculturalists advocate. We would all do well to remember and give heed to Lincoln's warning: "A house divided against itself cannot stand."[26]

や

ON ABORTION: A LINCOLNIAN POSITION

George McKenna

Principled yet pragmatic, Lincoln's stand on slavery offers a basis for a new politics of civility that is at once anti-abortion and pro-choice.

TWENTY-TWO YEARS AGO abortion was made an individual right by the Supreme Court. Today it is a public institution—one of the most carefully cultivated institutions in America. It is protected by courts, subsidized by legislatures, performed in government-run hospitals and clinics, and promoted as a "fundamental right" by our State Department. As Supreme Court Justice Sandra Day O'Connor observed in the 1992 *Casey* decision, which reaffirmed *Roe v. Wade*, a whole generation has grown up since 1973 in the expectation that legal abortion will be available for them if they want it.

Today our nation's most prestigious civic groups, from the League of Women Voters to the American Civil Liberties Union, are committed to its protection and subsidization. The Accreditation Council for Graduate Medical Education now requires that abortion techniques be taught in all obstetrics and gynecology residency training programs. Influential voices in politics and the media are now demanding the assignment of U.S. marshals to protect abortion clinics against vio-

*This article originally appeared in *The Atlantic Monthly*, December 1995. Reprinted with permission from the author.

lence, and a federal law passed last year prescribes harsh criminal penalties for even nonviolent acts of civil disobedience if they are committed by demonstrators at abortion clinics. Some private organizations that administer birth-control programs and provide abortions, notably Planned Parenthood, are closely tied to government bureaucracies: Planned Parenthood receives one third of its income from the federal government. Abortion today is as American as free speech, freedom of religion, or any other practice protected by our courts.

With this difference: unlike other American rights, abortion cannot be discussed in plain English. Its warmest supporters do not like to call it by its name.

Abortion is a "reproductive health procedure" or a "termination of pregnancy." Abortion clinics are "reproductive health clinics" (more recently, "women's clinics"), and the right to obtain an abortion is "reproductive freedom." Sometimes the word abortion is unavoidable, as in media accounts of the abortion controversy, but then it is almost invariably preceded by a line of nicer-sounding words: "the right of a women to choose" abortion. This is still not enough to satisfy some in the abortion movement. In an op-ed piece that appeared in the *New York Times* shortly after a gunman killed some employees and wounded others at two Brookline, Massachusetts, abortion clinics, a counselor at one of the clinics complained that the media kept referring to her workplace as an abortion clinic. "I hate that term," she declared. At the end of the piece she suggested that her abortion clinic ought to be called "a place of healing and care."

The Clinton administration, the first administration clearly committed to abortion, seems to be trying hard to promote it without mentioning it. President Bill Clinton's 1993 health care bill would have nationalized the funding of abortion, forcing everyone to buy a "standard package" that included it. Yet nowhere in the bill's 1,342 pages was the word abortion ever used. In various interviews both Clintons acknowledged that it was their intention to include abortion under the category of "services for pregnant women." Another initiative in which the Clinton Administration participated, the draft report for last year's United Nations International Conference on Population and Development, used similar language. Abortion, called "pregnancy termination," was subsumed under the general category of "reproductive health care," a term used frequently in the report.

Why, in a decade when public discourse about sex has become determinedly forthright, is abortion so hard to say? No one hesitates to say abortion in other contexts—in referring, for example, to aborting a plane's takeoff. Why not say "abortion of a fetus"? Why substitute a spongy expression like "termination of pregnancy"? And why do abortion clinics get called "reproductive health clinics" when their manifest purpose is to stop reproduction? Why all this strange language? What is going on here?

The answer, it seems to me, is unavoidable. Even defenders and promoters of abortion sense that there is something not quite right about the procedure. "I abhor abortions," Henry Foster, President Clinton's unconfirmed nominee for surgeon general, has said. Clinton himself, who made no secret of his support for abortion during his 1992 campaign, still repeats the mantra of "safe, legal, and rare" abortion. Why "rare"? If abortion is a constitutional right, on a par with freedom of speech and freedom of religion, why does it have to be "rare"? The reason Clinton uses this language should be obvious. He knows he is talking to a national electorate that is deeply troubled about abortion. Shortly before last year's congressional elections his wife went even further in appealing to this audience by characterizing abortion as "wrong" (though she added, "I don't think it should be criminalized").

Sometimes even abortion lobbyists show a degree of uneasiness about what it is they are lobbying for. At the end of 1993 Kate Michelman, the head of the National Abortion and Reproductive Rights Action League, was interviewed by the *Philadelphia Inquirer* about NARAL's new emphasis on the prevention of teen pregnancies. The reporter quoted Michelman as saying, "We think abortion is a bad thing." Michelman complained that she had been misquoted, whereupon she was reminded that the interview had been taped. Nevertheless, NARAL issued a statement a few days later declaring that Michelman "has never said—and would never say—that 'abortion is a bad thing.'" Michelman, who had reason to know better, sought only to "clarify" her remark in a letter to the *Inquirer*. "It is not abortion itself that is a bad thing," she wrote. "Rather, our nation's high rate of abortion represents a failure" of our system of sex education, contraception, and health care. But a month later Michelman herself, testifying before a House subcommittee on energy and commerce, insisted that "the reporter absolutely quoted me incorrectly," and she later told a *Washington Post* reporter, "I would never, never, never, never, never mean to say such a thing." Not until the Post reporter showed her the transcript did Michelman finally acknowledge—somewhat evasively—that she had said it: "I'm obviously guilty of saying something that led her to put that comment in there."

Whatever else Michelman's bobbing and weaving reveals, it shows how nervous abortion advocates can get when the discussion approaches the question of what abortion is. Even if we accept Michelman's amended version of her remark, which is that it is not abortion but the "high rate" of abortion that is a bad thing, the meaning is hardly changed. If one abortion is not a bad thing, why are many abortions bad? What is it about abortion that is so troubling?

The obvious answer is that abortion is troubling because it is a killing process. Abortion clinics may indeed be places of "healing and care," as the Planned Parenthood counselor maintains, but their primary purpose is to kill human fetuses. Whether those fetuses are truly "persons" will continue to be debated by modern scholastics, but people keep blurting out fragments of what was long a moral consensus in this country. Once in a while even a newscaster, carefully schooled in Sprachregelungen, will slip up by reporting the murder of "a woman and her unborn baby," thus implying that something more than a single homicide has taken place. But that "something" must not be probed or examined; the newscaster must not speak its name. Abortion has thus come to occupy an absurd, surrealistic place in the national dialogue: It cannot be ignored and it cannot be openly stated. It is the corpse at the dinner party.

Douglas and the Democrats

Only one other institution in this country has been treated so evasively, and that is the institution that was nurtured and protected by the government during the first eighty-seven years of our nation's existence: the institution of slavery.

The men who drafted the Constitution included representatives from slave states who were determined to protect their states' interests. Yet they were all highly vocal proponents of human liberty. How does one reconcile liberty with slavery? They did it by producing a document that referred to slavery in three different places without once mentioning it. Slaves were "persons"—or, sometimes, "other persons"—in contrast to "free persons." The slave trade (which the Constitution prohibited Congress from banning until 1808) was referred to as "the Migration or Importation of such Persons as any of the States now existing shall think proper to admit." Free states were required to return fugitive slaves to their masters in the slave states, but in that clause a slave was a "person held to Service or Labour" and a master was "the party to whom such Service or Labour may be due."

At least the Founders recognized the humanity of slaves by calling them "persons"; but in the next generation the status of slaves, and of blacks in general, steadily declined. By the end of the 1820s slaves were reduced to a species of property to be bought and sold like other property. Thomas Jefferson, who in 1776 had tried to insert into the Declaration of Independence a denunciation of the King for keeping open "a market where MEN should be bought & sold," now agonized only in private. Publicly all he could say on the fiftieth anniversary of the Declaration (the last year of his life) was that the progress of enlightenment had vindicated the "palpable truth, that the mass of mankind has not been born with saddles on their backs, nor a favored few booted and spurred, ready to ride them legitimately, by the grace of God," adding vaguely, "these are grounds of hope for others."

Jefferson often shied away from public controversy, but even the most flamboyant political leaders of the early nineteenth century could become suddenly circumspect when the talk turned to slavery. Andrew Jackson left office in 1837 blaming the South's secession threats on those Northerners who insisted on talking about "the most delicate and exciting topics, topics upon which it is impossible that a large portion of the Union can ever speak without strong emotion." Such talk, he said, assaulted "the feelings and rights" of Southerners and "their institutions." Jackson, usually a plainspoken man, would not mar the occasion of his last presidential address by saying the words "abolitionist" and "slavery." When slavery was discussed during the antebellum period, it was usually in the language of "rights"—the property rights of slaveholders and the sovereign rights of states. In 1850 the famous

Whig senator Daniel Webster defended his support for a tough fugitive-slave law on such grounds. What right, he asked, did his fellow Northerners have "to endeavor to get round this Constitution, or to embarrass the free exercise of the rights secured by the Constitution to the persons whose slaves escape from them? None at all, none at all."

Webster supported the Compromise of 1850, which attempted to settle the question of slavery in the territories acquired from Mexico by admitting California as a free state and Utah and New Mexico "with or without slavery as their constitution may provide at the time of their admission." This last principle was seized upon by Stephen A. Douglas, the "little giant" of the Democratic Party, and made the basis of the Kansas-Nebraska Act, which Douglas pushed through Congress in 1854. Nullifying the Missouri Compromise of 1820, it opened the remaining territories to slavery if the people in them voted for it. Douglas's rationale was "popular sovereignty," a logical extension of states' rights. The premise of states' rights was that any institution a state wanted to have, it should have, so long as that didn't conflict with the Constitution. Since slavery not only did not conflict with the Constitution but was protected by it, Douglas said, it followed that each state had "a right to do as it pleases on the subject of slavery," and the same principle should apply to the territories. Douglas's appeal was not to the fiery proslavery minorities in the South, who insisted that slavery was morally right, but to the vast majority in the North, who simply felt uncomfortable talking about the subject. He assured them that they didn't have to—that they could avoid the subject altogether by leaving it to the democratic process. Let the people decide: if they "want slavery, they shall have it; if they prohibit slavery, it shall be prohibited." But what about the rights of slaves? That, Douglas said, was one of those issues that should be left to moralists and theologians. It did not belong in the political or legal realm. In speaking of the right to own slaves, he said,

> I am now speaking of rights under the Constitution, and not of moral or religious rights. I do not discuss the morals of the people of Missouri, but let them settle that matter for themselves. I hold that the people of the slaveholding States are civilized men as well as ourselves, that they bear consciences as well as we, and that they are accountable to God and their posterity and not to us. It is for them to decide therefore the moral and religious right of the slavery question for themselves within their own limits.

Looking back today on Douglas's words, now one hundred thirty-seven years old, one is struck by how sophisticated and "modern" they seem. He ruled out of order any debate on the morality of slavery. That was a "religious" question. It had no place in a constitutional debate, and we had no right to judge other people in such terms. In one of his debates with Lincoln in 1858, Douglas scolded his opponent for telling the people in the slave states that their institution violated the law of God. "Better for him," he said, to cheers and applause, "to adopt the doctrine of 'judge not lest ye be judged.'"

The same notions and even some of the same language have found their way into the abortion debate. In *Roe v. Wade,* in 1973, Justice Harry Blackmun observed that philosophers and theologians have been arguing about abortion for centuries without reaching any firm conclusions about its morality. All "seemingly absolute convictions" about it are primarily the products of subjective factors such as one's philosophy, religious training, and "attitudes toward life and family and their values." As justices, he said, he and his colleagues were required to put aside all such subjective considerations and "resolve the issue by constitutional measurement free of emotion and of predilection." As the abortion debate intensified, particularly after Catholic bishops and Christian evangelicals entered the fray in the 1970s, the word "religious" was increasingly used by abortion defenders to characterize their opponents. They used it in exactly the same sense that Douglas used it in the slavery debate, as a synonym for "subjective," "personal," and thus, finally, "arbitrary." In this view, religion is largely a matter of taste, and to impose one's taste upon another is not only repressive but also irrational. This seems to be the view of the philosopher Ronald Dworkin in his book *Life's Dominion* (1993) and in some of his subsequent writings. What the opposition to abortion boils down to, Dworkin says, is an attempt "to impose a controversial view on an essentially religious issue on people who reject it."

The approach has served as useful cover for Democratic politicians seeking to reconcile their religious convictions with their party's platform and ideology. The most highly publicized use of the "religious" model was the famous speech given by Mario Cuomo, then the governor of New York, at the University of Notre Dame during the 1984 presidential campaign. Characterizing himself as an "old-fashioned" Catholic, Cuomo said that he accepted his Church's position on abortion, just as he accepted its position on birth control and divorce. But, he asked rhetorically, "must I insist you do?" By linking abortion with divorce and birth control, Cuomo put it in the category of Church doctrines that are meant to apply only to Catholics. Everyone agrees that it would be highly presumptuous for a Catholic politician to seek to prevent non-Catholics from practicing birth control or getting a divorce. But the pro-life argument has always been that abortion is different from birth control and divorce, because it involves a nonconsenting party—the unborn child. At one point in his speech Cuomo seemed to acknowledge that distinction. "As Catholics," he said, "my wife and I were enjoined never to use abortion to destroy the life we created, and we never have," and he added that "a fetus is different from an appendix or a set of tonsils." But then, as if suddenly recognizing where this line of reasoning might lead, he said, "But not everyone in our society agrees with me and Matilda." In other words, it was just a thought—don't bother with it if you don't agree. *De gustibus non est disputandum.*

Cuomo's speech received considerable press coverage, because it was perceived as a kind of thumb in the eye of New York's Cardinal John O'Connor, who had been stressing the Church's unequivocal moral condemnation of abortion. The argument, then, was newsworthy but not at all original. New York Senator Daniel Patrick Moynihan, another pro-choice Catholic, had been saying much the same thing since the mid-1970s, and by the 1980s it had become the standard argument. One hears today from the Clintons, from spokespeople for the American Civil Liberties Union, and from the philosopher Ronald Dworkin, the journalist Roger Rosenblatt, and the celebrity lawyer Alan Dershowitz, and from legions of others that opposition to abortion is essentially religious, or private, and as such has no place in the political realm. There is a patient philosophical response to this argument, which others have spelled out at some length, but it finds no purchase in a mass media that thrives on sound bites. There is also a primal scream—"Murder!"—that is always welcomed by the media as evidence of pro-life fanaticism. But is there a proper rhetorical response, a response suited to civil dialogue that combines reason with anger and urgency? I believe there is, and the model for it is Abraham Lincoln's response to Stephen Douglas.

Lincoln and the Republicans

Lincoln had virtually retired from politics by 1854, having failed to obtain a much-coveted position in the administration of Zachary Taylor. Then came the passage of the Kansas-Nebraska Act, Stephen Douglas's masterwork, which permitted the extension of slavery into the territories. Lincoln was horrified. In his view, slavery was like a cancer—or a "wen," as he called it. It could be eliminated only if it was first contained. If it ever metastasized, spreading into the new territories, it could never be stopped. He viewed the Kansas-Nebraska Act as a stimulant to the growth of the cancer because it invited slave-owning "squatters" to settle in the new territories, create electoral majorities, and establish new slave states. One of the longest and most passionate of Lincoln's speeches was his 1854 address on the act, which rehearsed many of the themes that would reappear in his debates with Douglas.

Douglas had boasted that the Kansas-Nebraska Act furthered democracy by leaving the question of whether or not to adopt slavery up to the people in the territories. Lincoln quickly homed in on the critical weakness in this "self-government" argument: "When the white man governs himself, that is self-government; but when he governs himself and also governs another man, that is more than self-government—that is despotism." It would not be despotism, of course, if slaves were not human: "That is to say, inasmuch as you do not object to my taking my hog to Nebraska, therefore I must not object to you taking your slave." This, Lincoln said, "is perfectly logical, if there is no difference between hogs and negroes." Lincoln kept returning to the question of the humanity of slaves, the question that Douglas ruled out of bounds as essentially "religious." Everywhere, Lincoln said, even in the

South, people knew that slaves were human beings. If Southerners really believed that slaves were not human, why did they join in banning the international slave trade, making it a capital offense? And if dealing in human flesh was no different from dealing in hogs or cattle, why was the slave-dealer regarded with revulsion throughout the South?

You despise him utterly. You do not recognize him as a friend, or even as an honest man. Your children must not play with his; they may rollick freely with the little negroes, but not with the "slave-dealers" children. If you are obliged to deal with him, you try to get through the job without so much as touching him.

People's moral intuitions could not be repressed; they would surface in all kinds of unexpected ways: in winces and unguarded expressions, in labored euphemisms, in slips of the tongue. Lincoln was on the lookout for these, and he forced his opponents to acknowledge their significance: "Repeal the Missouri Compromise—repeal all compromises—repeal the Declaration of Independence—repeal all past history, you still can not repeal human nature. It will still be the abundance of man's heart, that slavery extension is wrong; and out of the abundance of his heart, his mouth will continue to speak."

Douglas tried to evade the force of these observations by insisting that he didn't care what was chosen; all he cared about was the freedom to choose. At one point Douglas even tried to put his own theological spin on this, suggesting that God placed good and evil before man in the Garden of Eden in order to give him the right to choose. Lincoln indignantly rejected this interpretation. "God did not place good and evil before man, telling him to make his choice. On the contrary, he did tell him there was one tree, of the fruit of which, he should not eat, upon pain of certain death. I should scarcely wish so strong a prohibition against slavery in Nebraska."

Lincoln's depiction of slavery as a moral cancer became the central theme of his speeches during the rest of the 1850s. It was the warning he meant to convey in his "House Divided" speech, in his seven debates with Douglas in 1858, and in the series of speeches that culminated in the 1860 presidential campaign. In all these he continually reminded his audience that the theme of choice without reference to the object of choice was morally empty. He would readily agree that each state ought to choose the kind of laws it wanted when it came to the protection and regulation of its commerce. Indiana might need cranberry laws; Virginia might need oyster laws. But "I ask if there is any parallel between these things and this institution of slavery." Oysters and cranberries were matters of moral indifference; slavery was not.

The real issue in this controversy—the one pressing upon every mind—is the sentiment on the part of one class that looks upon the institution of slavery as a wrong, and of another class that does not look upon it as a wrong. The sentiment that contemplates the institution of slavery in this country as a wrong is the sentiment of the Republican party.

Lincoln has been portrayed as a moral compromiser, even an opportunist, and in some respects he was. Though he hoped that slavery would eventually be abolished within its existing borders, he had no intention of abolishing it. Although he said, in his "House Divided"speech of 1858, that "this government cannot endure, permanently half slave and half free," Lincoln made it clear in that speech, and in subsequent speeches and writings, that his intention was not to abolish slavery but to "arrest the further spread of it, and place it where the public mind shall rest in the belief that it is in course of ultimate extinction. . . ." In his First Inaugural Address, desperate to keep the South in the Union, he even hinted that he might support a constitutional amendment to protect slavery in the existing slave states against abolition by the federal government—a kind of reverse Thirteenth Amendment. The following year he countermanded an order by one of his own generals that would have emancipated slaves in South Carolina, Georgia, and Florida. In that same year he wrote the much-quoted letter to Horace Greeley stating that his "paramount object" was not to free slaves but to save the Union, and that if he could save the Union without freeing a single slave, he would do it. But when it came down to the commitment he had made in the 1850s, Lincoln was as stern as a New England minister. Slavery, he insisted, was an evil that must not be allowed to expand—and he would not allow it to expand. He struggled with a variety of strategies for realizing that principle, from gradual, compensated emancipation to outright abolition, but he never for a moment swerved from the principle. A month after his election Lincoln replied in this way to a correspondent who urged him to temper his opposition to slavery in the territories: "On the territorial question, I am inflexible. . . . You think slavery is right and ought to be extended; we think it is wrong and ought to be restricted."

A Lincolnian Position on Abortion

I suggested that we can find in Lincoln's antislavery rhetoric a coherent position that could serve as a model for pro-life politicians today. How would this rhetoric sound? Perhaps the best way to answer this is to provide a sample of what might be said by a politician devoted to a cause but no less devoted to building broad support for it. With the reader's indulgence, then, I will play that politician, making the following campaign statement:

"According to the Supreme Court, the right to choose abortion is legally protected. That does not change the fact that abortion is morally wrong. It violates the very first of the inalienable rights guaranteed in the Declaration of Independence—the right to life. Even many who would protect and extend the right to choose abortion admit that abortion is wrong, and that killing 1.5 million unborn children a year is, in the understated words of one, 'a bad thing.' Yet, illogically, they denounce all attempts to restrain it or even to speak out against it. In this campaign I will speak out against it. I will say what is in all our hearts: that abortion is an evil that needs to be restricted and discouraged. If elected, I will not try to abolish an institution that the Supreme Court has ruled to be constitutionally protected, but I will do everything in my power to arrest its further spread and place it where the public can rest in the belief that it is becoming increasingly rare. I take very seriously the imperative, often expressed by abortion supporters, that abortion should be rare. Therefore, if I am elected, I will seek to end all public subsidies for abortion, for abortion advocacy, and for experiments on aborted children. I will support all reasonable abortion restrictions that pass muster with the Supreme Court, and I will encourage those who provide alternatives to abortion. Above all, I mean to treat it as a wrong. I will use the forum provided by my office to speak out against abortion and related practices, such as euthanasia, that violate or undermine the most fundamental of the rights enshrined in this nation's founding charter."

The position on abortion I have sketched—permit, restrict, discourage—is unequivocally pro-life even as it is effectively pro-choice. It does not say "I am personally opposed to abortion"; it says abortion is evil. Yet in its own way it is pro-choice. First, it does not demand an immediate end to abortion. To extend Lincoln's oncological trope: it concludes that all those who oppose abortion can do right now is to contain the cancer, keep it from metastasizing. It thus acknowledges the present legal status of "choice" even as it urges Americans to choose life. Second, by supporting the quest for alternatives to abortion, it widens the range of choices available to women in crisis pregnancies. Studies of women who have had abortions show that many did not really make an informed "choice" but were confused and ill-informed at the time, and regretful later. If even some of those reports are true, they make a case for re-examining the range of choices actually available to women.

Would a candidate adopting this position be obliged to support only pro-life nominees to the Supreme Court? To answer this, let's consider Lincoln's reaction to *Dred Scott v. Sanford*, the 1857 Supreme Court ruling that Congress had no right to outlaw slavery in the territories. Lincoln condemned the decision but did not promise to reverse it by putting differently minded justices on the Court. Instead his approach was to accept the ruling as it affected the immediate parties to the suit but to deny its authority as a binding precedent for policymaking by the other branches of the federal government. If he were in Congress, he said in a speech delivered in July of 1858, shortly before his debates with Douglas, he would support legislation outlawing slavery in the territories—despite the *Dred Scott* decision. In our analogy we need not follow Lincoln that far to see the valid core of his position. Yes, he was saying, the Supreme Court has the job of deciding cases arising under the Constitution and laws of the United States. But if its decisions are to serve as durable precedents, they must be free of obvious bias, based on accurate information, and consistent with "legal public expectation" and established practice, or at least with long-standing precedent. Since *Dred Scott* failed all these tests, Lincoln believed that it should be reversed, and he intended to do what he could to get it reversed. But he would not try to fill the Court with new, "catechized" justices (a process to which he thought Douglas had been party regarding the Illinois state bench). Instead he would seek to persuade the Court of its error, hoping that it would reverse itself. Lest this seem naive, we must remember that he intended to conduct his argument before the American people. Lincoln knew that in the final analysis durable judicial rulings on major issues must be rooted in the soil of American opinion. "Public sentiment," he said, "is everything" in this country.

With it, nothing can fail; against it, nothing can succeed. Whoever moulds public sentiment, goes deeper than he who enacts statutes, or pronounces judicial decisions. He makes possible the inforcement [*sic*] of these, else impossible.

The lesson for pro-life leaders today is that instead of trying to fill the Supreme Court with "catechized" justices, a strategy almost certain to backfire, they should content themselves with modest, competent justices who are free of ideological bias, and all the while keep their eyes on the real prize: "public sentiment." *Dred Scott* was overturned within a decade by the Civil War, but *Plessy v. Ferguson*—the 1896 ruling validating state-imposed racial segregation—darkened the nation for fifty-eight years before it was overturned in *Brown v. Board of Education*. Yet during that long night civil-rights advocates were not silent. In thousands of forums, from university classrooms and law-school journals to churches and political conventions, they argued their case against American-style apartheid. In the end they not only won their legal case but also forged a new moral consensus.

It took time—time and patience. The lesson for pro-life advocates is that they need to take the time to lay out their case. They may hope for an immediate end to abortion, and they certainly have a First Amendment right to ask for it, but their emphasis, I believe, should be on making it clear to others why they have reached the conclusions that they have reached. They need to reason with skeptics and listen more carefully to critics. They need to demand less and explain more. Whatever the outcome, that would surely contribute to the process of reasonable public discourse.

The "campaign statement" I presented above is my own modest contribution to that process. It seeks common ground for a civil debate on abortion. It does not aim at a quick fix; it is based on the Lincolnian premise that nothing is possible without consensus. At the same time, it suggests that some measures can be taken here and now, and with broad public support, to contain the spread of abortion.

Would either party, today, endorse such an approach? Probably not.

It is easy to see why Democrats would run from it. Since 1972 pro-choice feminists have become increasingly important players in Democratic Party councils. In 1976 abortion lobbies got the Democratic platform committee to insert a plank in the party platform opposing a constitutional amendment banning abortion, and since then they have escalated their demands to include public funding of abortion and special federal protection of abortion clinics. No Democrat with serious national ambitions would ever risk offending them. A long list of Democrats who were once pro-life—Edward Kennedy, Jesse Jackson, even Al Gore and Bill Clinton—turned around in the seventies and eighties as the lobbies tightened their grip on the party.

In 1992 Robert Casey, the pro-life governor of Pennsylvania, a liberal on every issue except abortion, was not even permitted to speak at the Democratic National Convention.

What is more puzzling—at first glance, anyway—is the tepid reception the pro-life position has received over the years from centrist Republican leaders. In the present, heated atmosphere of Republican presidential politics, most Republican candidates have been wooing pro-life voters, obviously anticipating their clout in next spring's primaries. But in the day-to-day management of party affairs few Republican leaders have shown much enthusiasm for the cause. Among the ten items in Newt Gingrich's Contract With America there is no reference to abortion (in fact, there is no reference to any of the social-cultural issues that the Republicans once showcased, beyond demands for tougher child-pornography laws and "strengthening rights of parents"). The Republican national chairman, Haley Barbour, is at odds with pro-life Republicans who accuse him of trying to scuttle the party's pro-life position. The party's leading spokespeople include vocal abortion supporters like Christine Todd Whitman, the governor of New Jersey, and William Weld, the governor of Massachusetts, and its most prominent candidates in last year's elections—Mitt Romney in Massachusetts, Michael Huffington in California, George Pataki in New York—all declared themselves pro-choice.

It would be hard to find any Republican seriously seeking national office today who would say of abortion what Lincoln said of slavery: "The Republican Party think it wrong—we think it is a moral, a social, and a political wrong." Why? Wasn't it the Republicans who first promised to support a "human-life amendment" outlawing abortion? Didn't Ronald Reagan often use his bully pulpit to speak out in behalf of the unborn? Yes—but that was then. In 1980 the Republicans set out to woo those who were later called Reagan Democrats, and one of the means was a pro-life plank, designed to counter the plank the Democrats had put in their platform four years earlier. The wooing worked all too well. Many of the conservative Catholics and evangelical Protestants who streamed into the Republican Party in 1980 were ex-New Dealers, and they retained elements of the old faith. They may have cooled toward the welfare state, but they were not opposed to the use of government to promote social goals. Their primary goal, the outlawing of abortion, would itself involve the use of government; but even beyond that, these new "social conservatives" never really shared the Republicans' distrust of an activist government. Republican leaders thus greeted them warily. These Democrats-turned-Republican were seen to be useful during elections but a nuisance afterward. During the Reagan years they were given considerable verbal support, which at times greatly helped the pro-life cause (as, for example, at the UN International Conference on Population in Mexico City in 1984, when Reagan officials helped push through a final report stating that "abortion in no way should be promoted as a method of family planning"), though it never got beyond lip service. During the Bush Administration even lip service faltered as Republican officials decided that their party's "big tent" needed to accommodate the pro-choice view. "Read my lips," Bush said, but he was talking about "no new taxes." Bush's failure to keep his tax promise was seen as a major cause of his defeat in 1992, but in the ashes of this defeat lay what Republican leaders took to be a new sign of hope: they figured they could win elections on tax-and-spend issues as long as they kept their promises; they didn't need the "social issues" people anymore.

The Republicans have thus returned to where they feel most comfortable. Back in the 1880s William Graham Sumner used to say that the purpose of government is "to protect the property of men and the honor of women." Modern Republicans would hasten to add "the property of women" to this meager agenda, but the philosophy is the same. It sees the common good as the sum of individual private satisfactions. Its touchstone is the autonomous individual celebrated by John Locke in *Of Civil Government* (1690): "free, equal, and independent" in the state of nature, the solitary savage enters society only to protect what is his—or hers. Here is a philosophy radically at odds with pro-life premises. If a woman has an absolute, unqualified right to her property, and if her body is part of her property, it follows that she has a right to evict her tenant whenever she wants and for whatever reason she pleases. This "despotic" concept of individual ownership is Republican, not Democratic. If Democrats are pro-choice for political reasons, Republicans are pro-choice in their hearts. Talk radio's greatest Republican cheerleader, Rush Limbaugh, has also been an outspoken pro-lifer, but even Limbaugh has been softening that part of his message lately—and small wonder. Here is Limbaugh castigating the environmental movement: "You know why these environmentalist wackos want you to give up your car? I'll tell you the real reason. They don't want you to have freedom of choice." There it is. Freedom of choice: the philosophical center of modern-day Republicanism.

Well, the reader asks impatiently, if Democrats are pro-choice politically and Republicans are pro-choice philosophically, what's the point of that pro-life "campaign statement"? Who is going to adopt it? Perhaps the good folks in some little splinter party, but who else? I answer as follows: American party politics is very tricky, at times seemingly unpredictable. Who, in the early sixties, would have dared to predict that the Democrats would become the abortion party? But there was a subtle logic at work. By 1964 it was clear that the Democrats were about to become the civil-rights party. The feminism of the sixties rode into the reform agenda on the back of civil rights (by the end of the decade "sexism" had entered most dictionaries as a counterpart to "racism"), and high on its agenda was not just the legalization but the moral legitimization of abortion. Nevertheless, it took a dozen years for the full shift to occur. I think that within the next dozen years the shift could be reversed. To explain why, I must take a long look backward, to the parties' respective positions in Lincoln's time.

Pro-life Democrats

In the 1850s it was not the Republicans but the Democrats who were the champions of unbridled individualism. As heirs of Andrew Jackson's entrepreneurialism—and ultimately of Jefferson's distrust of "energetic government"—the Democrats were wary not only of national action but also of any concept of the common good that threatened individual or local autonomy. It was the Republicans, heirs of Whig nationalism and New England transcendentalism, who succeeded—under Abraham Lincoln's tutelage—in constructing a coherent philosophy of national reform. In *The Lincoln Persuasion* (1993), a brilliant, posthumously published study of Lincoln's political thought, the political scientist J. David Greenstone traced the roots of that thought to the communitarian "covenant theology" of seventeenth-century Puritanism. Lincoln combined this theology, with its emphasis on public duty and public purpose, with the nationalism and institutionalism of Henry Clay and other leading Whigs, arriving at a position of "political humanitarianism." Lincoln's synthesis, Greenstone noted, did not deny the importance of individual development, but it did assert that "the improvement of individual and society were almost inseparably joined." Combining moral commitment with political realism, Lincoln arrived at a concept of the public good that resonated deeply among northerners, especially those large segments steeped in the culture of New England. At the time of the Civil War, then, the Democratic and Republican parties were divided not only on the slavery question but also on the larger philosophical question of national responsibility. The Democrats adopted a position of economic and moral laissez-faire, while the Republicans insisted that on certain questions the nation had to do more than formulate procedural rules; it had to make moral judgments and act on them.

This philosophical alignment, persisting through the Civil War and Reconstruction, was blurred during the Gilded Age. Then, over the course of the next forty years, something surprising happened: the parties reversed positions. Populist Democrats in the 1890s weakened their party's attachment to laissez-faire, and after "progressive" Republicans (whose model was Lincoln) failed to take over their party in 1912, many started moving toward the Democrats. Woodrow Wilson welcomed them—and so, twenty years later, did Franklin Roosevelt. By 1936 it was the Democrats who were sounding the Lincolnian themes of national purpose and government responsibility, while the Republicans had become the champions of the autonomous individual. Since then both parties have veered and tacked, sometimes partly embracing each other's doctrines, but today the congressional parties stand as far apart as they were at the height of the New Deal. President Clinton may have muddied the waters with his "me, too, but more moderately" response to Republican retrenchment, but in Congress the programmatic differences between the parties are spelled out almost daily in party-line votes reminiscent of the late 1930s. Now as then, Republicans emphasize the role of government as a neutral rule maker that encourages private initiative and protects its fruits. Now as then, Democrats emphasize the role of government as a moral leader that seeks to realize public goals unrealizable in the private sphere.

If this analysis is correct, it follows that the proper philosophical home for pro-lifers right now is the liberal wing of the Democratic Party. To test this, go back to that "campaign statement" I sketched earlier and make one simple change: substitute the word "racism" for abortion. Without much editing the statement would be instantly recognizable as the speech of a liberal Democrat. Democrats know that racism, like abortion, cannot be abolished by governmental fiat. But they also know that it is wrong to subsidize racist teachings publicly or to tolerate racist speech in public institutions or to permit racist practices in large-scale "private" enterprises. Democrats also insist that government has a duty to take the lead in condemning racism and educating our youth about its dangers. In other words, the same formula—grudgingly tolerate, restrict, discourage—that I have applied to abortion is what liberal Democrats have been using to combat racism over the past generation. With abortion, as with racism, we are targeting a practice that is recognized as "wrong" (Hillary Clinton) and "a bad thing" (Kate Michelman). With abortion, as with racism, we are conceding the practical impossibility of outlawing the evil itself but pledging the government's best efforts to make it "rare" (Bill Clinton et al.). When it comes to philosophical coherence, therefore, nothing prevents Democrats from adopting my abortion position. Indeed, there is very good reason to adopt it.

It is, however, politically incorrect. Any liberal Democrat taking this stance would incur the wrath of the abortion lobbies. Protests within the party would mount, funding would dry up, connections with the party leadership would be severed, and there might be a primary challenge. Because politicians do not court martyrdom, the intimidatory power of these lobbies is formidable.

But no power lasts forever, and power grounded more in bullying than in reason is particularly vulnerable in our country. Within the liberal left, from which the Democrats draw their intellectual sustenance, there is increasing dissatisfaction with the absolutist dogma of "abortion rights." Nat Hentoff, a columnist in the left-liberal *Village Voice*, wonders why those who dwell so much on "rights" refuse to consider the bare possibility that unborn human beings may also have a few rights. Hentoff, who is a sort of libertarian liberal, sees a contradiction between abortion and individual rights, but the socialist writer Christopher Hitchens may actually be more in tune with the communitarian bent of post-New Deal liberalism in his critique of pro-choice philosophy. Hitchens caused an uproar among readers and staffers of *The Nation* in 1989 when he published an article in which he observed with approval that more and more of his colleagues were questioning whether "a fetus is 'only' a growth in, or appendage to, the female body." While supporting abortion in some cases, he insisted that society has a vital interest in restricting it. What struck him as ironic, and totally indefensible, was the tendency of many leftists suddenly to become selfish individualists whenever the topic turned to abortion.

It is a pity that . . . the majority of feminists and their allies have stuck to the dead ground of "Me Decade" possessive individualism, an ideology that has more in common than it admits with the prehistoric right, which it claims to oppose but has in fact encouraged.

Hitchens's critique of the pro-choice position comes from his socialist premises, but even some liberal critics closer to the center have adopted a similar view. *The Good Society* (1991), by the sociologist Robert Bellah and his associates, reads like the campaign book of a decidedly liberal Democratic politician, someone who might challenge Bill Clinton from the left in 1996. The root of what is wrong in America, it says, is our "Lockean political culture," which emphasizes "the pursuit of individual affluence (the American dream) in a society with a most un-Lockean economy and government." When the authors get to the topic of abortion, they again see Lockeanism as the culprit: it has turned abortion into an "absolute right." In place of this kind of extreme individualism they suggest we consider the practices of twenty other Western democracies.

There is respect for the value of a woman's being able to choose parenthood rather than having it forced upon her, but society also has an interest in a woman's abortion decision. It is often required that she participate in counseling; she is encouraged to consider the significance of her decision, and she must offer substantial reasons why the potential life of the fetus must be sacrificed and why bearing a child would do her real harm.

Despite its use of the strange term "potential life" (a usage favored by Justice Blackmun) for a living fetus, Bellah's formulation expresses coherently what modern liberalism points toward but usually resists at the last minute: a responsible communitarian position on abortion. It is not the same as my campaign statement, but it is within debating distance, and setting the two statements side by side might bring together in civil debate reasonable people from both sides.

Of course, neither position would pass muster with NARAL, NOW, the ACLU, and other pro-choice absolutists. But at some point, I think, sooner rather than later, the grip of these lobbies will have to loosen. One lesson of last year's congressional elections is that the Democratic Party will suffer at the polls if it is perceived by the public as the voice of entrenched minority factions. For better or worse, the Republicans articulated a philosophy in 1994, while the Democrats, by and large, believed that all they had to do was appeal to "their" people. The party needs to rediscover the idea of a common good, and the abortion issue may be as suitable a place as any to start. But the Democrats will first have to break free of the abortion lobbies. That will be a formidable challenge, though not an impossible one. As the political scientist Jeffrey Berry has observed, one of the most startling features of modern American politics is how quickly political alliances can shift. National politics, Berry writes, no longer works by means of "subgovernments"—cozy two-way relationships between particular lobbyists and politicians. Today we live in a world of "issue networks," in which many lobbies vie for attention. Something like this, I believe, is starting to happen on women's issues. One of the fast-growing feminist groups in the country right now is Feminists for Life (FFL), which has offices nationwide and has recently moved its headquarters to Washington, D.C. Founded in the 1970s by former NOW members who had been expelled for their pro-life views, FFL supports almost the entire agenda of feminism—except "abortion rights." Citing the pro-life stands of the founders of American feminism, including Susan B. Anthony and Elizabeth Cady Stanton, they view themselves as reclaiming authentic feminism. Gay-rights groups, usually allied with the abortion lobbies, now include PLAGAL, the Pro-Life Alliance of Gays and Lesbians. In issue networks, Jeffrey Berry observes, alliances can be composed "of both old friends and strange bedfellows"; there are "no permanent allies and no permanent enemies." The new pragmatic alliances of gays and straights, religious believers and secularists, feminists and traditionalists, may soon be demanding seats at the Democratic table. It would not be surprising if they were welcomed as liberators by many Democrats who have been forced to endorse a Me Decade ideology at odds with the spirit of their party.

Pro-choice Republicans

What about the Republicans? Where are they headed? It is hard to say. As already noted, on a range of domestic issues the party seems to have embraced a philosophy of possessive individualism that has a distinctly pro-choice ring to it, and in this respect is no longer the party of Lincoln. Lincoln's Republicanism, as Greenstone pointed out in *The Lincoln Persuasion*, combined a Whiggish sense of national responsibility with a New England ethic of moral perfection. Then as now, Republicans believed in capitalist enterprise and fiscal prudence—but in those days they put them in the service of broader humanitarian goals. "Republicans," Lincoln said, "are for both the man and the dollar; but in cases of conflict, the man before the dollar." This was true for a long time in the Republican Party. Theodore Roosevelt's notion of "stewardship" had traces of the Lincolnian synthesis of humanitarianism and institutional responsibility; early in this century many of the Progressives came from Republican backgrounds. Even in the 1950s Eisenhower's brand of "modern Republicanism" faintly echoed the old tradition of active government and moral leadership. Someday, I think, it will be rediscovered. It is a noble tradition.

Right now, though, it is out of season. The Republicans are on a laissez-faire roll. The strategy of their leaders is to marginalize right-to-lifers, get their plank out of the platform, and avoid any more messy debates over social issues. They see a golden opportunity to win more recruits by appealing to yuppies and other libertarians who hate taxes and welfare but like "abortion rights." What can be said to these shrewd Republican leaders? In shrewdness and wiliness it would be hard to match Abraham Lincoln. Let us, then, listen to Lincoln as he warned against weakening his party's antislavery plank in order to win the votes of "moderates." "In my judgement," he wrote to an Illinois Republican official in 1859, "such a step would be a serious mistake—would open a gap through which more would pass out than pass in." And so today. Many Reagan Democrats came to the Republicans in the 1980s because their own party deserted them on social issues. If the Republicans do the same, many will either drift back to the Democratic Party (many of these, remember, are former New Deal Democrats, rather liberal on economic issues) or join a third party or simply drop out (many evangelicals were apolitical before Reagan came along). For every pro-choice yuppie voter the Republicans won, they might lose two from the "religious right."

In truth, however, no one can be sure about the gains and losses resulting from one position or another on abortion, and such considerations are beside my main point, which is this: It is time at last in America for the abortion issue to be addressed with candor and clarity by politicians of both major parties. There needs to be engagement on the topic. Right now, as the philosopher Alasdair MacIntyre puts it, the arguments pro and con on this issue are "incommensurable"—they sail past each other; the two sides are talking about different things. Part of the blame for the mindless "emotivism," as MacIntyre calls it, can be attributed to the more extreme elements in the pro-life movement, who have stifled reasoned argument with their cries of "Murder!" But much of it results from the squeamishness of pro-choicers, who simply refuse to face up to what abortion is. Nervousness, guilt, even anguish, are all hidden behind abstract, Latinate phrases. Only rarely does reality intrude. That is why Christopher Hitchens caused such a howl of pain when he published his *Nation* article on abortion. His crack about the "possessive individualism" of pro-choicers undoubtedly caused discomfort, but what must have touched a raw nerve was his description of abortion itself. After sympathizing with the emotions of rank-and-file members of the pro-life movement—with their "genuine, impressive, unforced revulsion at the idea of a disposable fetus"—Hitchens added,

> But anyone who has ever seen a sonogram or has spent even an hour with a textbook on embryology knows that emotions are not the deciding factor. In order to terminate a pregnancy, you have to still a heartbeat, switch off a developing brain and, whatever the method, break some bones and rupture some organs.

Here, then, is the center of it all. If abortion had nothing to do with the stilling of heartbeats and brains, there would be no abortion controversy.

Suppose, now, I were to define the controversy in this manner: It is a fight between those who are horrified by the above-mentioned acts, considering them immoral, and those who are not horrified and do not consider them immoral. "Unfair," most pro-choicers would say. "We are also horrified. Have we not said that we abhor abortion? Have we not called it wrong? Have we not said it should be rare?" All right, then, let the debate begin: How rare should it be? How can we make it rare? In what ways, if any, can public institutions be used to discourage abortion? If abortion means stilled hearts and ruptured organs, how much of that can we decently permit?

In this debate I have made my own position clear. It is a pro-life position (though it may not please all pro-lifers), and its model is Lincoln's position on slavery from 1854 until well into the Civil War: tolerate, restrict, discourage. Like Lincoln's, its touchstone is the common good of the nation, not the sovereign self. Like Lincoln's position, it accepts the legality but not the moral legitimacy of the institution that it seeks to contain. It invites argument and negotiation; it is a gambit, not a gauntlet.

The one thing certain right now is that the abortion controversy is not going to wither away, because the anguish that fuels it keeps regenerating. Some Americans may succeed in desensitizing themselves to what is going on, as many did with slavery, but most Americans feel decidedly uncomfortable about the stilled heartbeats and brains of 1.5 million human fetuses every year. The discomfort will drive some portion of that majority to organize and protest. Some will grow old or weary, and will falter, but others will take their place. (I have seen it already: there are more and more young faces in the annual "march for life.") Pro-life protests will continue, in season and out of season, with political support or without it. Abortion, a tragedy in everyone's estimation, will continue to darken our prospect until we find practicable ways of dealing with it in order to make it rare. But before we can even hope to do that, we have to start talking with one another honestly, in honest language.

⟳

Notes to Chapter 8

What Is an American?

1. An excellent discussion of the semantic and other aspects of the issue is to be found in Philip Gleason, *Speaking of Diversity: Language and Ethnicity in Twentieth-Century America* (Baltimore: Johns Hopkins University Press, 1992), containing essays on such topics as "The Melting Pot," "Pluralism and Assimilation," "Minorities (Almost) All," "Identifying Identity," and "Americans All."

Before "multiculturalism," the catchword was "cultural pluralism." I have discussed Lincoln's position on cultural pluralism in *Unity, Ethnicity, and Abraham Lincoln* (Fort Wayne, Ind.: Warren Lincoln Library and Museum, 1978), which is reprinted in my *Speaking of Abraham Lincoln: The Man and His Meaning for Our Times* (Urbana and Chicago: University of Illinois Press, 1983), 105–25. I have also criticized the idea in "The 'New Ethnicity' and American History," *The History Teacher* 15 (November 1981), 43–53, which is reprinted in my *Arguing with Historians: Essays on the Historical and the Unhistorical* (Middletown, CT: Wesleyan University Press, 1987), 162–73.

2. Diane Ravitch, "Multiculturalism: E Pluribus Plures," *The Key Reporter* 50 (Autumn 1990), 2, draws a distinction between "pluralistic" and "particularistic" multiculturalism. "The pluralists seek a richer common culture; the particularists insist that no common culture is possible or desirable," Ravitch writes. "Advocates of particularism propose an ethnocentric curriculum to raise the self-esteem and academic achievement of children from racial and ethnic minority backgrounds." (Ravitch's essay appeared at somewhat greater length in the *American Scholar*, Summer 1990.)

Many people use the term "multiculturalism" indiscriminately, with no apparent aware-ness of the difference in connotations that Ravitch points out. In criticizing the idea, I have in mind the particularist version of it.

3. *Report of the New York State Social Studies Review and Development Committee* (Albany: The State Education Department, June 1991), "Executive Summary," unpaged.

4. *Report . . . Committee*, 1.

5. *Report . . . Committee*, "annex" by Ali A. Mazrui, 86. Two members of the committee dissented from the report. Arthur Schlesinger, Jr., pointed out, 91 "A basic question is involved: should public education seek to make our young boys and girls contributors to a common American culture? or should it strengthen and perpetuate separate eth[n]ic and social subcultures?" Kenneth T. Jackson argued, 80, that "it is politically and intellectually unwise for us to attack the traditions, customs, and values which attracted immigrants to these shores in the first place."

6. After bomb threats and explosive rhetoric, the Dade County, Florida, commissioners repealed a law making English the county's official language. "There are those for whom the language issue provides opportunity to act out their prejudices in ways that are both mean-spirited and destructive of the whole notion of living in harmony in a multicultural commu-nity," commented Arthur N. Teitelbaum, Southern director of the Anti-Defamation League of B'Nai B'Rith. *Boston Globe*, May 19, 1993, 5.

In Massachusetts, State Representative Nelson Merced proposed a "multicultural state" in opposition to a movement to declare English the official state language. Yale Newman, a spokesman for US English, objected: "We see efforts being made to demand parallel language rights, and we feel that that would convert the US into a tower of Babel." *Boston Globe*, Nov. 22, 1989.

7. The Tufts University faculty, for example, approved a year course in World Civiliza-tions to be taught by professors from several departments and to be required of all freshmen. The Association of American Colleges was encouraging its members to introduce similar "required survey courses with a strong multicultural content." *Boston Globe*, Sept. 16, 1991, 1.

8. See the article on Takaki and his book in the Chronicle of Higher Education, May 26, 1993, A9, from which the quotation is taken. Takaki sees the book as describing a "multicul-tural America" that celebrates "our wholeness as members of humanity as well as one nation." But he provides no unifying theme—such as the progressive realization of the Declaration of Independence—which would contribute to such national wholeness. The reviewer in the *Bos-ton Globe*, June 7, 1993, 31, thinks the book "especially valuable in the effort to develop multi-cultural curricula." The book does seem interesting as the text for a course in ethnic conflict and adjustment in American history, but hardly suitable for a comprehensive survey course.

9. Professor Wong was one of more than two hundred educators who gathered in Boston to discuss diversity in America. At the conference, according to a reporter. "Multiculturalism was discovered, rediscovered and passionately embraced [as] the antidote for racism, sexism, classism, [and] homophobia," but was "as yet ill-defined." *Boston Globe*, June 30, 1991, 25.

10. Gettysburg Address, Nov. 19, 1863, Roy P. Basler et al., eds., *The Collected Works of Abraham Lincoln* (8 vols. and an index vol.; New Brunswick, N.J.: Rutgers University Press, 1953–1955), 7: 93.

11. Speech at Chicago, Illinois, July 10, 1858, *Collected Works*, 2:499–500.

12. Resolutions on Anti-Catholic Riots, June 21, 1844, *Collected Works*, 1: 337–38.

13. Letter to Joshua Speed, Aug. 24, 1885, *Collected Works*, 2: 323.

14. Seventh Debate with Douglas, Alton, Illinois, Oct. 15, 1858, *Collected Works*, 3: 301.

15. Address before the Springfield Young Men's Lyceum, Jan. 27, 1838, *Collected Works*, 1: 108.

16. Appeal to the Voters of Sangamo County; Mar. 9, 1832, *Collected Works*, 1: 8.

17. These words, from the report of a New York task force on minorities that preceded the 1991 curriculum report, are quoted in *Time*, July 8, 1991, 13.

18. US Census Bureau report summarized in the *Boston Globe*, Apr. 20, 1993, 70. The long census form, which went to one household in six in 1990, asked people about their ancestry. One family in four said German; one in six, Irish; one in eight, English; one in ten, African; and one in seventeen, Italian. But the largest number described their ancestry simply as American. *Boston Globe*, Dec. 17, 1992.

19. The findings of the Latino National Political Survey are summarized in an Associated Press dispatch in the *Boston Globe*, Dec. 16, 1992. A much fuller account is given by the principal investigator for the survey, Rodolfo O. de la Garza, in the *Chronicle of Higher Education*, June 2, 1993, B 1–3.

Other investigations have arrived at similar conclusions. "A 1988 study by the Educational Testing Service found that the overwhelming majority of Hispanic parents—78% of Mexican-Americans and 82% of Cubans, for example—are opposed to teaching in Spanish if it meant less English instruction, and most said that the family was primarily responsible for teaching about the native culture," Linda Chavez reported in the *Wall Street Journal*, Oct. 22, 1991. She added: "A Houston Chronicle poll last year revealed that 87% of Hispanics—native-born and immigrant—believe it 'their duty to learn English,' and a majority favored making English the official language of the country."

20. *Boston Globe*, May 31, 1993, 1, 8. Ethnic Germans coming to Germany are entitled to automatic citizenship.

21. *Boston Globe*, May 27, 1993.

22. Ross Terrill, "The Asianization of Australia," *Boston Globe*, Jan. 1, 1989, 75. "Multiculturalism is at its best a principle of tolerance," Terrill observes, and he favors that kind of multiculturalism for Australia.

But multiculturalism at its worst seems to be gaining ground. In 1992 the UN Commission on Human Rights put out a report saying that "the source of racism at the present time lies in a new ideology" which "emphasizes allegedly insurmountable differences between cultures." "By asserting a radical cultural pluralism, the new racism based on cultural differences tries, paradoxically, to look like genuine antiracism and to show respect for all group identities."

According to a monograph issued by the University of Virginia's Center for the Study of the Mind and Human Interaction, an "ideological commitment to the virtues of difference" can lead to the "dark side of enlightened multiculturalism." This happens when the encouragement of minorities to "take pride in their distinct heritage and culture" implies that "different cultures are, in the end, profoundly incapable of assimilating or even communicating with one another."

The two paragraphs above are derived from H. D. S. Greenway, "Racism That Wears a Multicultural Cloak" *Boston Globe*, June 10, 1993, 19.

23. Reply to a committee of the New York Workingmen's Democratic Republican Association, Mar. 21, 1864, *Collected Works*, 7: 259.

24. This point is well put by Everett Carll Ladd in a wonderfully perceptive article origi-

nally published in the *Christian Science Monitor* and republished in the *Boston Globe*, Jan. 18, 1993, 15. Ladd quotes G.K. Chesterton's observation that "America is the only nation in the world that is founded on a creed," and he cites Lincoln's view of the Declaration of Independence as the basis of the creed. "Whatever my ethnic roots and culture, my political culture must be American," Ladd wisely affirms.

25. On the UN conference, see the articles by Ellen Goodman, Jonathan Kaufman, and Curt Goering and Joshua Rubenstein in the *Boston Globe*, 1993: June 17, 23; June 20, 2; June 22, 15.

26. The quotations are from the First Inaugural Address, Mar. 4, 1861, and the speech accepting the Republican senatorial nomination, June 16, 1858, in the Collected Works, 2: 461 and 4: 270.

AFTERWORD

Lincoln and the Preservation of Liberal Democracy

"HEREWITH IS A LITTLE SKETCH," as you requested, wrote Abraham Lincoln to one of his political backers, Jesse Fell, a year before he was elected sixteenth president of the United States. The "sketch" was a capsule autobiography, which Fell had had to pry out of a reluctant Lincoln for campaign purposes. "There is not much of it, for the reason, I suppose, that there is not much of me." Lincoln warned another backer who also wanted some biographical material from him, "It is a great piece of folly to attempt to make anything out of my early life. It can all be condensed into a single sentence, and that sentence you will find Gray's *Elegy*: 'The short and simple annals of the poor.' That's my life, and that's all you or anyone else can make of it."[1]

None of this, of course, was true, although Lincoln believed it was. To be sure, Abraham Lincoln was neither a philosopher nor an 'intellectual,' in the usual sense of the word. But he had intellectual gifts far in excess of what people expected from a man of his extremely rough-hewn origins and lack of formal education. His closest friend, Joshua Speed, remembered that "He read law, History, [Thomas] Browns Philosophy or [William] Paley—Burns, Byron, Milton or Shakespeare."[2] John Todd Stuart, his mentor and first law partner, thought Lincoln had a "mind of a metaphysical and philosophical order" and was "always Studying into the nature of things." He was not the sort of professional thinker and essayist that Emerson was; he read widely, but he did not discuss, analyze, and argue with the books he was reading. What he did was visit them, look for direction in them, and especially in the cases of his favorite poets—Burns and Shakespeare in particular—he let them speak for him when he was anxious or depressed, as he did for Jesse Fell by citing Thomas Gray's *Elegy in a Country Churchyard* as an answer to Fell's request. Those who met Lincoln for the first time found that "he had the appearance of a rough intelligent farmer"; but anyone who for that reason "took Lincoln for a simple minded man would very soon wake [up] with his back in a ditch."[3]

If he had a favorite among strictly "metaphysical" problems, it was free will. "I have all my life been a fatalist,"Lincoln informed his Illinois Congressional ally,

Isaac Arnold, and he meant that in the most literal and deterministic sense. As Herndon discovered, Lincoln believed that "there was no freedom of the will," that "men had no free choice." Since Lincoln"believed that what was to be would be, and no prayers of ours could arrest or reverse the decree," then "men were but simple tools of fate, of conditions, and of laws," and no one "was responsible for what he was, thought, or did, because he was a child of conditions." This, Herndon believed, was the real spring of Lincoln's "patience" and "his charity for men and his want of malice for them everywhere." So, even in his greatest and most well-known judgment—"with malice toward none, with charity for all"—Lincoln was, according to Herndon, "moved and controlled by his philosophy."[4]

But more than "metaphysics," Lincoln loved political economy, and especially the classical liberal versions of political economy created by the Enlightenment. Liberalism's sense of mobility, of unfettered social and economic opportunity to define yourself after your own preferences, underlay Alexander Hamilton's embrace of liberal republicanism in the 1790s, and it did very much the same thing for Abraham Lincoln half a century later. "Lincoln, I think, liked political economy, the study of it," remembered Herndon. "Theoretically, Mr. Lincoln was strong on financial questions," recalled Shelby Cullom, "On political economy he was great." Central to that strength was Lincoln's reading of the English political philosopher John Stuart Mill's two-volume *Principles of Political Economy* (1848), whose formulations of liberal capitalism dovetailed perfectly with Lincoln's devoted attachment to the Whig party, and Henry Clay's neo-Hamiltonian "American System" of government-sponsored market development. Mill spoke for a generation of restless middle-class English intellectuals who sensed the power that capitalism had placed in their hands and resented the deadening restraints the English-landed aristocracy tried to place on that power through its lopsided dominance of Parliament and restrictive agricultural legislation like the Corn Laws. It was Mill, and American redactions of Mill like Francis Wayland's *Elements of Political Economy* (1837), which Lincoln "ate up, digested, and assimilated."[5]

The key virtue of liberal capitalism for Lincoln was mobility. "We stand at once the wonder and admiration of the whole world," Lincoln said in 1856, and the "cause is that every man can make himself." This was partly due to the genius of American government, which limited the reach of government over the people to the performance of "whatever they need to have done, but can not do, at all, or can not, so well do, for themselves—in their separate, and individual capacities"—a formula which neatly restrained government from suffocating American liberty, without forbidding it from serving the American economy. But it was also partly due to the opportunities offered by liberal capitalism and free wage labor. The equality promised by the Declaration of Independence was not a negative equality, in which all were held to a certain limit in order to prevent the rest from falling below a lower limit, but a positive equality in which everyone had equal access to self-improvement, whether they used it or not.

I take it that it is best for all to leave each man free to acquire property as fast as he can. Some will get wealthy. I don't believe in a law to prevent a man from getting rich; it would do more harm than good. So while we do not propose any war upon capital, we do wish to allow the humblest man an equal chance to get rich with everybody else. When one starts poor, as most do in the race of life, free society is such that he knows he can better his condition; he knows that there is no fixed condition of labor, for his whole life. I am not ashamed to confess that twenty-five years ago I was a hired laborer, mauling rails, at work on a flat-boat—just what might happen to any poor man's son! I want every man to have the chance . . . in which he can better his condition—-when he may look forward and hope to be a hired laborer this year and the next, work for himself afterward, and finally to hire men to work for him! That is the true system.[6]

It was by no means the true system in the South, however. Slavery presented Lincoln with the ugliest possible contradiction of the principles of liberal capitalism, and it made Lincoln a lifelong enemy and critic of slavery.[7] But unlike the Garrisonian abolitionists, Lincoln was restrained by his regard for the Constitution, and the firewall the Constitution had erected between state and federal jurisdictions. Slavery was not a federal matter; slavery existed because of individual state enactments and statutes, and so long as it remained a matter of individual state enactment, the federal government had no grounds for interference. Lincoln did not share the abolitionists' confidence that "doing justice though the heavens fall" was a particularly prudent formula. But that did not mean that there was nothing that could be done at all about the blot of slavery. For one thing, Congress could forbid the expansion of slavery into any of the United States' unorganized territories in the West; without room to expand, slavery would asphyxiate on its own, and it was on the platform that he ran for the Senate in 1858, no longer as a Whig, but as a champion of the new antislavery party, the Republicans. Likewise, the federal government might not be able to interfere with slavery directly; but indirectly, it could offer federally-funded buy-outs to those Southern states where slavery had the weakest hold, and set up a domino effect that would result in the gradual eradication of slavery before the end of the century. With a plan for federal compensation, a gradual timetable, and some form of referendum, either through Congress or the state legislatures, he was "quite sure" slavery "would not outlive the century. . . . Gradual emancipation and governmental compensation, would bring it to an end."[8]

The Garrisonians have always enjoyed the moral high ground in American memory, but they were never much of a serious threat to the reality of slavery. By contrast, it is a mark of how much real political punch Lincoln's unglamorous strategy of non-expansion and gradual buy-outs packed that, as soon as Lincoln was elected as the first Republican president in November 1860, the slave states immediately began seceding from the Union to form an independent slave-holding Confederacy. Lincoln adamantly refused to recognize the legitimacy of secession, and when Confederate forces attempted forcibly to eject the federal garrison at Fort Sumter, in the harbor of Charleston, South Carolina, Lincoln put the Union on a war footing.

What followed was a bloodbath of four years' duration, a carnage-strewn Civil War that cost six hundred thousand lives, wrought $6 billion in destruction through the South, forced the surrender of the Confederacy, and provided Lincoln with the legal justification to emancipate the slaves by proclamation on January 1, 1863, as a use of the presidential "war powers." None of this conformed to any pattern of liberal progress he had known, and it drove over the course of his presidency to look for explanations in theology—not the smiling theology of the Emersonians, but something close to the somber Calvinism of Charles Hodge. A month before the end of the war, and six weeks before an assassin's bullet cut him down, Lincoln used his Second Inaugural Address to speculate on God's hidden purposes in bringing this war upon the country, and the conclusion was eerily reminiscent of a Puritan preacher, analyzing the universal effects of total depravity:

> If we shall suppose that American Slavery is one of those offences which, in the providence of God, must needs come . . . and that He gives to both North and South, this terrible war, as the woe due to those by whom the offence came, shall we discern therein any departure from those divine attributes which the believers in a Living God always ascribe to Him? . . . If God wills that it continue, until all the wealth piled by the bondsman's two hundred and fifty years of unrequited toil shall be sunk, and until every drop of blood drawn with the lash, shall be paid by another drawn with the sword, as was said three thousand years ago, so still it must be said "the judgments of the Lord, are true and righteous altogether."[9]

What had begun as a struggle to secure the triumph of liberal democracy had become, in the end, a demonstration of theological mystery. And in that, Lincoln stumbled onto a fundamental bipolarity in American thinking. We are, as a people, one body; but we are historically equipped with two souls, one of them the inheritance of our Puritan and Pietist forebears, the other the creation of the eighteenth-century Enlightenment. Our private life has been shaped by the demands of the first; our public life by the demands of the second. But the demands of the private and the public have not always been content with their separate spheres. In the case of slavery, the moral demand "to let the captive go free" clashed with the Enlightenment demand to respect the boundaries of "property" (which is what a slave, in the view of the law, was). In the end, Lincoln could not keep the imperatives of morality from spilling over into the secular sphere of the public. In fact, his greatest moment of intellectual frustration was to discover that his instinctive moral loathing for slavery had to find some way of penetrating the secularism of the public sphere, in order to have any sort of theoretical basis on which to challenge slavery's existence. There was a point at which Lincoln's Enlightenment liberalism failed him, and he had to call in the assistance of the moral and theological. He began this process tentatively in the 1850s; by 1865, his appeal to heaven for explanations and justifications had acquired a sophistication which mounted to the metaphysical levels he had so long admired in others.

Lincoln's example remains a powerful one for Americans on a number of political levels, starting with his fundamental convictions about liberty and union and rising to his embrace of the mobility, equality, and prudence promised by a liberal political economy. But he is also a powerful example for the way in which he realized the limitations of Enlightenment liberalism. Liberal democracy, for Lincoln, described the ideal public polity. But our public lives as citizens do not describe us fully as people. There always remains the metaphysical, the moral, and the theological, and those aspects of our lives will not always be content to dwell in the realm of the private. Nor should they. Lincoln's greatest gift to our political self-understanding may, in the end, be found in the peroration of the Gettysburg Address: that this is a nation under God, that it must undergo a new birth—a religious conversion—of freedom, and that only then will the liberal dream of government of the people, by the people, and for the people bloom and thrive in the desert of our days.

ALLEN C. GUELZO
Gettysburg College

꒳

Notes to Afterword

1. Lincoln, "To Jesse Fell, Enclosing Autobiography," in *Collected Works of Abraham Lincoln*, ed. R.P. Basler (New Brunswick, NJ, 1953), volume three, 511; Don and Virginia Fehrenbacher, eds., *Recollected Words of Abraham Lincoln* (Stanford, CA, 1996), 395–396.

2. Matilda Johnston Moore (Herndon interview), September 8, 1865; Caleb Carman to Herndon, November 30, 1866; Joshua F. Speed to Herndon, December 6, 1866; Robert B. Rutledge to Herndon, November 30, 1866; John T. Stuart (Herndon interview), December 20, 1866, in *Herndon's Informants: Letters, Interviews and Statements about Abraham Lincoln*, Douglas L. Wilson and Rodney O. Davis, eds., (Urbana, IL, 1998), 109, 499, 519.

3. David L. Mearns, ed., *The Lincoln Papers: The Story of the Collection with Selections to July 4, 1861* (Garden City, NY, 1948), volume one, 159; *Recollected Words*, 648; Herndon to Jesse Weik, January 5, 1886, in Herndon-Weik Papers Library of Congress; Herndon, "Analysis of the Character of Abraham Lincoln," in *The Abraham Lincoln Quarterly* 1 (September 1941), 373–375; Emmanuel Hertz, ed., *The Hidden Lincoln: From the Letters and Papers of William H. Herndon* (New York, 1937), 243, 251, 418; *Herndon's Informants*, 251, 350, 576, 636.

4. Isaac Arnold, *The Life of Abraham Lincoln* (1884; Lincoln, NE, 1994), 81; Herndon to Jesse Weik, February 25, 1887, in Herndon-Weik Papers, Library of Congress; Herndon, "Analysis of the Character of Abraham Lincoln," 364.

5. "Shelby M. Cullom," in Walter B. Stevens, *A Reporter's Lincoln*, ed. Michael Burlingame (Lincoln, NE, 1998), 154–155; Herndon to Jesse Weik, January 1, 1886, in *The Hidden Lincoln*, 117.

6. Lincoln, "Speech at Kalamazoo, Michigan," "Fragment on Free Labor," and "Speech at New Haven," in *C.W.*, volume two, 364, volume three, 462, and volume four, 24.

7. Lincoln, "To Albert G. Hodges," in *C.W.*, volume seven, 281.

8. *Recollected Words*, 183.

9. Lincoln, "Second Inaugural Address," in *C.W.*, volume eight, 332.

Contributors

George Anastaplo teaches at the Loyola University of Chicago. Among his many publications is *Abraham Lincoln: A Constitutional Biography*.

Herman Belz teaches at the University of Maryland. Among his many publications is *Abraham Lincoln, Constitutionalism, and Equal Rights in the Civil War Era*.

M. E. Bradford taught for many years at the University of Dallas. Among his many publications is *A Better Guide to Reason*.

Jeffrey Crouch is a Ph.D. candidate at the Catholic University of America.

Richard N. Current taught for many years at the University of Wisconsin. Among his many publications is *The Lincoln Nobody Knows*.

Richard O. Curry teaches at the University of Connecticut-Storrs. Among his many publications is *Slavery in America: Theodore Weld's American Slavery as It Is*.

Thomas J. DiLorenzo teaches at Loyola University in Maryland. Among his many publications is *The Real Lincoln: A New Look at Abraham Lincoln, His Agenda, and an Unnecessary War*.

Kenneth L. Deutsch teaches at State University of New York at Geneseo. Among his many publications is *Leo Strauss, the Straussians, and the American Regime*.

Jean Bethke Elshtain is the Laura Spelman Rockefeller Professor of Social and Political Ethics in Divinity School at the University of Chicago. Among her many publications, her most recent is *Just War against Terror: The Burden of American Power in a Violent World*, 2003.

Don E. Fehrenbacher taught for many years at Stanford University. Among his many books is *Prelude to Greatness: Lincoln in the 1850's*.

Ethan Fishman teaches at the University of South Alabama. Among his many publications is the *Presidential Presidency*.

Joseph R. Fornieri teaches at The Rochester Institute of Technology. He is the author of *Abraham Lincoln's Political Faith*.

Bruce P. Frohnen teaches at Ave Maria Law School. Among his many publications is *The Promise of Conservatism*.

Allen C. Guelzo is the Director of the Civil War Institute at Gettysburg College. Among his many publications is *Lincoln's Emancipation*.

Phillip G. Henderson teaches political science at the Catholic University of America. He is the author of *Managing the Presidency: The Eisenhower Legacy*.

Harry V. Jaffa taught at Claremont Graduate School. Among his many publications is *Crisis of the House Divided: An Interpretation of the Lincoln-Douglas Debates.*

Willmoore Kendall taught for many years at the University of Dallas. Among his many publications is *John Locke and the Doctrine of Majority Rule.*

Rogan Kersh teaches at Syracuse University. He is the author of *Dreams of a More Perfect Union.*

Ralph Lerner teaches at the University of Chicago. Among his many publications is *The Thinking Revolutionary.*

George McKenna is Professor Emeritus at City College of New York. Among his many publications is *The Drama of Democracy.*

William Lee Miller is Professor Emeritus at the University of Virginia. Among his many publications is *Lincoln's Virtues: An Ethical Biography.*

Lucas E. Morel teaches at William and Lee University. He is the author of *Lincoln's Sacred Effort.*

Mark E. Neely, Jr., teaches at Pennsylvania State University. Among his many publications is *The Last Best Hope of Earth: Abraham Lincoln and the Promise of America.*

Reinhold Niebuhr taught at Union Theological Seminary. Among his many publications is *The Irony of American History.*

Stephen B. Oates teaches at University of Massachusetts at Amherst. Among his many publications is *With Malice Towards None: A Biography of Abraham Lincoln.*

William D. Pederson teaches at Louisiana State University in Shreveport where he is the Director of American Studies. Among his many publications is *Franklin D. Roosevelt and Abraham Lincoln: Competing Perspectives on Two Great Presidencies.*

Robert Raffety is a Program Director for the Capitol Hill Campus branch of the Mercatus Center at George Mason University and an adjunct professor of public administration in GMU's Department of Public and International Affairs.

James G. Randall taught for many years at the University of Illinois. Among his many publications is *Lincoln the Liberal Statesman.*

Mark J. Rozell teaches at George Mason University. Among his many publications is *Executive Privilege: Presidential Power, Secrecy, and Accountability.*

Colleen Shogan teaches at George Mason University. She has published articles in *Polity, Women & Politics, Studies in American Political Development,* and *White House Studies.*

Jason H. Silverman teaches at Winthrop University. Among his many publications is *America Before 1877: A Synoptic History.*

Frank J. Williams is Chief Justice of the Rhode Island Supreme Court and President of the Lincoln Forum. Among his many publications is *Judging Lincoln.*

T. Harry Williams taught for many years at the Louisiana State University at Baton Rouge. Among his many publications is *Lincoln and his Generals.*

Michael P. Zuckert teaches at the University of Notre Dame. Among his many publications is *Natural Rights and the New Republicanism.*

INDEX